MACMILLAN ANTHOLOGIES
OF ENGLISH LITERATURE

General Editors:
A. Norman Jeffares, formerly Professor of English,
University of Stirling
Michael Alexander, Berry Professor of English Literature,
University of St Andrews

MACMILLAN ANTHOLOGIES
OF ENGLISH LITERATURE

Volume 1 THE MIDDLE AGES (700–1550)
Michael Alexander and Felicity Riddy

Volume 2 THE RENAISSANCE (1550–1660)
Gordon Campbell

Volume 3 THE RESTORATION AND
EIGHTEENTH CENTURY (1660–1798)
Ian McGowan

Volume 4 THE NINETEENTH CENTURY (1798–1900)
Brian Martin

Volume 5 THE TWENTIETH CENTURY (1900–present)
Neil McEwan

MACMILLAN ANTHOLOGIES
OF ENGLISH LITERATURE

THE
MIDDLE AGES
(700–1550)

Edited by
Michael Alexander
and
Felicity Riddy

Selection and editorial matter © Michael Alexander and Felicity Riddy, 1989

All rights reserved. No reproduction, copy or transmission of this publication may be made without written permission.

No paragraph of this publication may be reproduced, copied or transmitted save with written permission or in accordance with the provisions of the Copyright Act 1956 (as amended), or under the terms of any licence permitting limited copying issued by the Copyright Licensing Agency, 33–4 Alfred Place, London WC1E 7DP.

Any person who does any unauthorised act in relation to this publication may be liable to criminal prosecution and civil claims for damages.

First published 1989

Published by
MACMILLAN EDUCATION LTD
Houndmills, Basingstoke, Hampshire RG21 2XS
and London
Companies and representatives
throughout the world

Typeset by Wessex Typesetters
(Division of The Eastern Press Ltd)
Frome, Somerset

Printed in Hong Kong

British Library Cataloguing in Publication Data
The Middle Ages: (700–1550)
1. English literature, 1066–1558
— Anthologies
I. Alexander, Michael, *1941–*
II. Riddy, Felicity, *1940–*
820.8'001
ISBN 0–333–39264–7
ISBN 0–333–46476–1 Pbk

Contents

Acknowledgements	xi
General Introduction	xiii
Introduction: The Middle Ages	xv
Note on Annotation and Glossing	xxiv
A Note on the Texts	xxiv

OLD ENGLISH LITERATURE

BEDE	3
From *Ecclesiastical History*	
[The Conversion of Edwin]	3
[The Poet Caedmon]	4
Caedmon's Hymn	6
Bede's Death and *Death Song*	7
RIDDLES	9
The Dream of the Rood	13
Deor	19
***From* Beowulf**	21
ELEGIES	
The Ruin	69
The Wife's Complaint	71
The Husband's Message	73
Wulf and Eadwacer	75
The Wanderer	75
The Seafarer	79
KING ALFRED	83
From *Preface* to *The Pastoral Care*	84
From *Preface* to St Augustine's *Soliloquies*	86
Brunanburh	88
Maldon	91
CYNEWULF	100
From *Elene*	
[From the conclusion]	101

From *Advent Lyrics* VII
 [Joseph's Reproach] 102
From The Phoenix 103
AELFRIC 104
 From *Sermon on Easter Day*
  Easter Sunday 104
WULFSTAN 108
 From *Sermo Lupi Ad Anglos* 108

MIDDLE ENGLISH LITERATURE

From **The Peterborough Chronicle** 115
 [The reign of Stephen] 117
LAYAMON 121
 From *Brut*
  [The Death of Arthur] 123
From **The Owl and the Nightingale** 131
 [Summer and Winter] 133
From **Ancrene Wisse** 141
 [On Love] 143
LYRICS BY UNKNOWN POETS
 I Cannot Come to My Love 148
 Merry it is While Summer Lasts 148
 When I See on Rood 149
 From Where Beth They Before Us
  Weren? 149
 Alas How Should I Sing? 151
 I Am of Ireland 151
From **Harley Lyrics**
 Between March and April 152
 When the Nightingale Sings 154
 Now Shrink Rose and Lily Flower 155
 Winter Wakens All My Care 157
Sir Orfeo 158
LAURENCE MINOT 177
 Scots out of Berwick 177
RICHARD ROLLE 179
 From *Form of Living*
  [Active and Contemplative Lives] 180

Jesu, God's Son	183
Mercy is Most in My Mind	185
JOHN BARBOUR	187
From *The Bruce*	
[The Eve of Bannockburn]	188
WILLIAM LANGLAND	194
From *Piers Plowman*	
Prologue	197
Passus 18	209
Robert of Sicily	232
SIR JOHN MANDEVILLE	246
From *Travels*	
[The Earthly Paradise]	247
JOHN GOWER	250
From *Confessio Amantis*	
[Ceix and Alceone]	251
JULIAN OF NORWICH	262
From *Revelations of Divine Love*	
[The First Showing]	262
***GAWAIN*-POET**	268
From *Sir Gawain and the Green Knight*	
[Gawain's Journey]	271
Patience	287
GEOFFREY CHAUCER	322
The Parliament of Fowls	324
From *The Canterbury Tales*	
The Pardoner's Prologue and Tale	349
The Shipman's Tale	369
The Nun's Priest's Tale	383
From Morte Arthure	402
[The Death of Gawain]	405
In a Valley of this Restless Mind	416
In a Tabernacle of a Tower	421
JOHN LYDGATE	426
As a Midsummer Rose	427
MARGERY KEMPE	432
From *The Book of Margery Kempe*	
[The Vow of Chastity]	433

Corpus Christi Plays	437
Wakefield *Second Shepherds' Play*	438
York Butchers' *Play of the Death of Christ*	469
SIR THOMAS MALORY	487
From *Le Morte Darthur*	
[The Fair Maid of Ascolat]	488
ROBERT HENRYSON	519
From *The Fables*	
The Preaching of the Swallow	520
WILLIAM CAXTON	532
From *The Book of the Order of Chivalry*	
Epilogue	533
From **Paston Letters**	536
Richard Calle Writes to Margery Paston	537
Margery Brews Writes to John Paston III	541
WILLIAM DUNBAR	544
I that in Heill Was	545
Done is a Battle	549
My Head Did Ache	551
Sweet Rose of Virtue	552
In to these Dark and Drublie Days	553
Lucina Shining in Silence of the Night	555
JOHN SKELTON	558
Womanhood, Wanton, Ye Want	559
The Ancient Acquaintance, Madam	560
Merry Margaret	562
My Darling Dear	563
Gup, Scot	564
GAVIN DOUGLAS	567
From *Eneados*	
Book 6 [Aeneas Meets Dido in the Underworld]	568
Prologue to Book 13	570
THOMAS MORE	573
From *The History of Richard III*	
[The Character of Richard III]	574

[The Murder of the Princes in the Tower]	577
Bibliography	583
Index of First Lines	591
Index of Authors	594

Acknowledgements

The editors wish to thank Ray Barron, Priscilla Bawcutt, Kenneth Maidment and Neil Rhodes for their advice on specific points, and Patricia Richardson for invaluable help in preparing the typescript.

The editors and publishers wish to thank the following for permission to use copyright material: Anvil Press Poetry Ltd for Riddles Nos 27 and 60 from Michael Alexander, *Old English Riddles* (1983); The Council of the Early English Text Society for extracts from *The Book of Margery Kempe*, eds S. B. Meech and H. E. Allen, OS 212 (1940), *The Prologues and Epilogues of William Caxton*, ed. W. J. B. Crotch, OS 176 (1928); *The English Works of John Gower*, ed. G. C. Macaulay, ES 81 (1900), and *Ancrene Wisse*, ed. J. R. R. Tolkien, OS 249 (1962); J. M. Dent & Sons Ltd for extracts from M. J. Swanton's *Anglo Saxon Prose* (1975); Faber & Faber Ltd for 'The Wanderer', 'The Battle of Maldon' and 'The Seafarer' from *A Choice of Anglo Saxon Verse*, translated by Richard Hamer (1970); Manchester University Press for extracts from *Sir Gawain and the Green Knight*, ed. and translated by W. R. J. Barron (1974), and *The Wakefield Pageants*, ed. A. C. Cawley (1958); Thomas Nelson and Sons Ltd for Wrenn's translation of Bede in *A Study of Old English Literature* (1967); Oxford University Press for extracts from *The Peterborough Chronicle*, ed. Cecily Clark (OUP, 1958), *Selections from Layamon's Brut*, ed. G. L. Brook (Clarendon Press, 1963), *The Poems of Laurence Minot*, ed. J. Hall (Clarendon Press, 1887), *English Writings of Richard Rolle, Hermit of Hampole*, ed. Hope Emily Allan (Clarendon Press, 1931), *The Vision of William Concerning Piers the Plowman by William Langland*, ed. W. W. Skeat (OUP, 1886), *Mandeville, Travels*, ed. M. C. Seymour (Clarendon Press, 1967), *The Parliament of Fowls* from *The Complete Works of Geoffrey Chaucer*, Vol. I, ed. W. W. Skeat (Clarendon Press, 1899, repr. 1963), 'As a Midsummer Rose' from *John Lydgate: Poems*, ed. J. Norton-Smith (1966), *Selections from Gavin Douglas*, ed. D. F. C. Coldwell (Clarendon Press, 1964), and *Paston Letters and Papers of the Fifteenth Century*, Vol. I, ed. Norman Davis (Clarendon Press, 1976); Penguin Books Ltd for extracts from *Beowulf*, translated by Michael Alexander (Penguin Classics, 1973), copyright © Michael Alexander, 1973, and Riddles

7, 25, 26 and 30 and five major poems from *The Earliest English Poems*, translated by Michael Alexander (Penguin Classics, 1966, 1977), copyright © Michael Alexander, 1966, 1973; Pontifical Institute of Mediaeval Studies for an extract from *A Book of Showings to the Anchoress Julian of Norwich*, eds Edmund College and James Walsh, pp. 289–303, copyright © 1978 by the Pontifical Institute of Mediaeval Studies, Toronto.

Every effort has been made to trace all the copyright holders but if any have been inadvertently overlooked the publishers will be pleased to make the necessary arrangements at the first opportunity.

General Introduction

There can often be a gulf between the restricted reading required by a school, college or university syllabus and the great expanse of English literature which is there to be explored and enjoyed. There are two effective ways of bridging that gulf. One is to be aware of how authors relate or have related to their contemporary situations and their contemporaries, how they accept, develop or react against what has been written by their predecessors or older contemporaries, how, in short, they fit into the long history of English literature. Good histories of literature – and there is a welcome increase of interest in them – serve to place authors in their context, as well as giving a panoptic view of their careers.

The second way is to sample their work, to discover the kind or kinds of writing they have produced. Here is where the anthology contributes to an enjoyment of reading. It conveys the flavour of an author as nothing but reading that author can. And when an author is compared to his or her fellow writers – a thing a good anthology facilitates – the reader gains several extra dimensions, not least an insight into what thoughts, what fears, what delights have occupied writers at different times. To gain such insights is to see, among other things, the relevance of past authors to the present, to the reader. Reading an anthology shows something of the vast range of our literature, its variety of form and outlook, of mood and expression, from black despair to ecstatic happiness; it is an expansive experience widening our horizons, enhancing specialised study, but also conveying its own particular pleasures, the joy of finding familiar pieces among unfamiliar, of reacting to fresh stimuli, of reaching new conclusions about authors, in short, of making literature a part of oneself.

Anthologies also play a part in the life of a literature. If we are the beneficiaries of our literary inheritance, we are also trustees for it, and the maintenance of the inheritance for future generations requires new selections of properly edited texts. The Macmillan Literary Anthologies, which have followed on from the Macmillan Histories of Literature, are designed to present these texts with the essential pertinent information. The selection made of poetry, prose and plays has been wide and inclusive, authors appear in the order of their dates of birth, texts – with the exception of the Middle English section – are modernised and footnotes are kept to a minimum. A broadly representative policy has been the aim of the general editors, who have maintained a similar format and proportion in each volume, though the medieval volume has required more annotation.

ANJ
MJA

Introduction: The Middle Ages

The thousand-year interval between the end of the Roman Empire and the Renaissance, known as the Middle Ages, largely coincides in Britain with the period between the coming of the Angles and Saxons in the fifth century and the establishment of the Tudor dynasty on the throne of England at the end of the fifteenth. The Norman Conquest of 1066, which marked the end of Anglo-Saxon England, divides this period in two. The language of the pre-Conquest era is known as Old English or Anglo-Saxon; it is so remote from modern English that it requires to be learned or translated if it is to be understood. For this reason the Old English texts in this anthology, apart from a few specimens, are given in translation. The form of the language as it is recorded from the twelfth century to the mid-fifteenth is known as Middle English. It is distinguished from Old English by, among other things, the gradual loss of inflections (so that the grammatical relations between words come to be conveyed, as in modern English, by their order in a sentence rather than by their endings) and by the disappearance of grammatical gender. Middle English is easier for the modern reader to understand than Old English, and so post-Conquest texts are given here in their original language, accompanied by very full glossing or translation where necessary. By the late fifteenth century the changes which distinguish Old from Middle English are complete; the language of Skelton and More, at the end of this anthology, is recognisably early modern.

Old English

In popular opinion, English literature 'begins' with Chaucer in the fourteenth century. In fact, as this anthology shows, English literature predates Chaucer by many hundreds of years. The Angles and Saxons produced a vernacular literature in verse and prose which is recorded in manuscripts earlier than those containing the literatures of other Western European countries. The four chief manuscript collections of Old English poetry, the Vercelli Book, the Junius Book, the Exeter Book and the *Beowulf* manuscript, date from about the year 1000.

The Venerable Bede tells us how an unlettered cowherd named Caedmon was inspired to compose a song about the Creation in Old English verse, the text of which is preserved; that had been in the 680s when Bede was a boy. By the time of Bede's death in 735 a carved stone cross had been erected at Ruthwell in southwest Scotland, bearing upon it Old English verses which form part of the remarkable poem known as *The Dream of the Rood*. Bede himself composed verse in his mother tongue, and leading clerics of his day composed and exchanged Latin riddles. Some of the many extant Old English riddles may date from the eighth century, as may heroic poems such as *Deor* and *Beowulf* itself. The striking poetic elegies such as *The Ruin*, *The Wanderer*, *The Seafarer* and *The Wife's Complaint* are probably of almost equal antiquity.

The authorship, place and circumstances of origin of these poems are unknown, though they must come from the fusion between the Mediterranean literacy of the clergy and native traditions of composition at the courts of the kingdoms of the Angles and Saxons. The intense literacy of the Roman missionaries to Britain and their successors in the seventh century, particularly Theodore of Tarsus, Archbishop of Canterbury (669–90) and of natives such as Bede, faded. King Alfred later wrote that when he had come to the throne of Wessex in 871 there were hardly any priests who could understand Latin. But the decay of Latin created a need for a more widespread literacy in English, and Alfred inaugurated a series of translations from Latin which established a tradition of general writing in English. Apart from his own translations, Alfred's reign saw the inception of *The Anglo-Saxon Chronicle*, which was to be continued until the twelfth century. Towards the end of the tenth century there was a widespread renewal of culture, known as the Benedictine Revival, involving all the arts. From this period come most of the Anglo-Saxon literary manuscripts, and such late poems as *Brunanburh*, *The Phoenix*, *The Battle of Maldon* and *Judith*. This last is not represented in this selection, and nor are the many paraphrases of scriptural narratives and lives of the saints which form the bulk of extant Old English verse. Religious verse is here represented by Caedmon's *Hymn*, *The Dream of the Rood* and short extracts from *The Phoenix* and the poet Cynewulf. Pride of place is given to the epic *Beowulf*, much the largest as well as the greatest poem to survive, and to the Elegies, but room has been made for representative passages from Alfred and from the homilies of Aelfric and Wulfstan. The literature of the Anglo-

Saxons, religious or secular, is united by its ethical orientation and the value it places on the collected wisdom of common experience.

Most, though not all, of the verse translations included are by the editor of the Old English section of the volume. They are designed to be read aloud and to recreate some of the characteristics of Old English versification, which was based upon stress-count rather than syllable-count. There are two main stresses in each half of an Old English line. One or other of the stressed syllables in the first half of the line must begin with the same sound as the first stress in the second half of the line; the fourth stress should not alliterate. Each verse is thus braced across a marked pause in the middle of the line in a symmetrical pattern, and many half-lines are somewhat traditional, even formulaic in diction. Movement and phrasing are often grave, ceremonious and considered, as in the line and a half of *Beowulf* summarising the effect of the visit of the monster Grendel to the banqueting-hall of Hrothgar the Dane:

> Night's table-laughter turned to morning's
> Lamentation.

The art of the Germanic poet was already ancient before it was committed to writing; although archaic, it was very far from primitive. Indeed the history of Old English poetry, so far as it can be reconstructed from its patchy survival and conjectural chronology, seems to show a qualitative decline in the last century of Anglo-Saxon England. Old English prose writing was brought to an end by the Norman Conquest, but by that time Old English verse was already virtually dead.

Middle English

After 1066 William the Conqueror established a French-speaking administration in England; as a result, French replaced English as the medium of official communication and the imported language of the ruling class became the language of literature. The mass of the people still spoke English, of course, and must have continued to sing songs and tell stories in their own tongue. Because they were not literate, however, their voices were only rarely recorded. This anthology presents a very partial picture indeed of the literature and culture of England in the centuries immediately after the Conquest. Not only are the non-literate majority excluded by definition, but so are their compatriots who wrote in Latin or in Anglo-Norman (as the form of French used in England is called). Nevertheless Thomas's *Tristan* (*c.* 1160), the *Lais* of Marie de France (*c.* 1170) and Hugh de Roteland's *Ipomedon* (*c.* 1185) are as much part of the culture of England as is *The Owl and the Nightingale* and, indeed, appear to have had a greater influence on later writers in English than that work.

The imposition of French helped to change English culture by providing contact with new themes and forms. France was the fountainhead of the new currents of thought which flowed through the literature, learning, art and spirituality of Europe in the twelfth century, and which have led historians to describe this period as a renaissance. French-speaking England, united politically with Normandy until 1204, was closely in touch with the new ideas, both in Latin and in the vernacular, and these influenced writings in English as profoundly as those in Anglo-Norman. The nightingale of *The Owl and the Nightingale*, written around 1200, speaks of love and springtime in the accents of the twelfth-century French troubadours; moreover, having arrived in English poetry, she is here to stay. And when the unknown author of *Ancrene Wisse* writes in the early thirteenth century of the nature of spiritual love, he does so in a way which is deeply affected by the mysticism of Bernard of Clairvaux (1090–1150) and Hugh of St Victor (1096–1141). Fourteenth-century English writers – Richard Rolle, Julian of Norwich, the author of 'In a Valley of this Restless Mind' – still carry the indelible impress of the twelfth-century transformation of religious feeling.

Nevertheless English writers were not only influenced by new ways of feeling and modes of thought; they also seized the opportunities for technical experimentation offered by French and Provençal-derived lyric and narrative forms. The four-stress rhyming couplets used by the poet of *The Owl and the Nightingale* break with the traditions of Old English verse. Even in Layamon's *Brut*, composed around 1200, which can be seen as the final flowering of the native heroic mode before the Alliterative Revival of the mid-fourteenth century, alliteration has been reinforced by assonance and internal rhyme picked up, no doubt, from the couplets of Layamon's Anglo-Norman source. The interplay of alliteration and rhyme was to be a continuing source of poetic vitality for several centuries to come.

For almost three hundred years after the Conquest – that is, until the middle of the fourteenth century – literature in English tended to be popular in character. It was above all accessible, occupying the ground left on the one hand by intellectual and courtly writings in Latin and French, and on the other by oral compositions such as folksong and folktale. Most of the authors in the Middle English section of this anthology are educated men, the majority of them clerics, often writing for audiences less literate than themselves. It would be a mistake to assume too readily, however, that the readers of English works in the twelfth, thirteenth and early fourteenth centuries are all from the lower classes, or that people who read English did not also read French in a society in which many homes must have been bilingual. *Sir Orfeo*, composed around or soon after 1300 and perhaps translated from French, is neither sophisticated nor learned and yet the earliest text survives in a manuscript which was assembled around 1330 for a very well-to-do Londoner. The 'Harley lyrics' are included in a roughly contemporary manuscript which contains works in English, French and Latin, proving that the readership of the three languages could sometimes overlap.

Very few of the authors in this anthology are women: female illiteracy seems to have extended higher up the social scale than did that of males. The fifteenth-century townswoman, Margery Kempe, could not write out her own memoirs, and later in that century the women of the Paston family were mostly illiterate; Margery Brews had to dictate her love letters to John Paston III to her father's secretary. And yet the practice of listening to works of literature read aloud – widespread throughout the period – meant that women could hear books read even though they could not write. Although there are few women authors here, several works are addressed to women, including *Ancrene Wisse* and Rolle's discussion of Active and Contemplative Lives in his *Form of Living*. The fact that the author of *Ancrene Wisse* translates most of his Latin quotations from the Bible suggests, not surprisingly, that the women for whom he wrote were literate in English but not in Latin; William Langland, whose earliest readers at the end of the fourteenth century were probably mostly male clerics, does not feel under the same obligation to translate the Latin quotations in *Piers Plowman*.

Langland was one of a generation of great poets born in the 1330s and 1340s, including Geoffrey Chaucer, John Gower and the *Gawain*-poet (whose dates are uncertain), who grew up at a time when French was losing ground to English, even at court. The beginning of the Hundred Years' War with France in 1337 fostered chauvinistic feelings which may have hastened an inevitable resurgence of English. In 1362

English was used as a language of record in the law courts, and in the same year the proceedings of Parliament were conducted in English for the first time. John Trevisa tells us in his translation of Ranulph Higden's *Polychronicon*, or world history, that by 1385 English had taken the place of French as the medium of instruction in all the grammar-schools in England, with the result that children 'know no more French than their left heel does'. In the reign of Richard II (1377–99) English poetry flowered. Gower, slightly older than Chaucer, wrote in French, Latin and English; the fact that Chaucer's works, read by members of the court, are all in English is striking evidence of the status and capacities of his native tongue.

An aspect of this new status, though one which is still not fully understood, is the revival of alliterative poetry which takes place from the mid-fourteenth century, and which includes Langland's *Piers Plowman*, *Sir Gawain and the Green Knight*, *Patience* and *Morte Arthure*. The York Butchers' *Play of the Death of Christ*, though stanzaic, is also a product of this fashion. It is in *Piers Plowman*, the first versions of which were written before any of Chaucer's major works, that Middle English poetry can be said to come of age.

How or why alliteration should be revived from about 1350 as the basis of versification after disappearing for over a century is not clear. The movement seems to have started in the west midlands, where unbroken traditions of literacy went back to pre-Conquest days and where knowledge of the old alliterative mode must have been preserved, though whether in oral or written form is still debated. Middle English alliterative verse is freer than its 'classical' Old English progenitor: the lines are longer; there are often more than three alliterating syllables; alliteration commonly occurs in the final stressed syllable of the second half-line (which should not alliterate in Old English verse); and alliteration can be combined with other modes: for example, with a rhyming bob-and-wheel in *Sir Gawain and the Green Knight* or, in *Piers Plowman*, with non-alliterating lines of Latin. The fashion for alliterative verse lasted for about a hundred years in England and was then taken up in Scotland, where the earliest surviving alliterative verse was written in the 1440s and where it did not die out for another century and a half.

Alliterative verse was mostly composed in the west midlands and the north, though Langland may have written in London and *Morte Arthure* is from the north-east. Although this verse is provincial it is not unsophisticated: the *Gawain*-poet, represented here by an extract from *Sir Gawain and the Green Knight*, the greatest of Middle English romances, and the unlikely comedy, *Patience*, is one of the most conscious artists of the whole period. The metropolitan writers Chaucer and Gower presumably knew alliterative poetry, since Chaucer refers to it in the Parson's prologue and imitates it briefly in two battle-passages. Nevertheless they preferred French models for their versification: Gower perfected English octosyllabics, while Chaucer introduced a variety of new forms, including the five-stress couplet that was to remain a staple for centuries. He also turned to Italy for his matter, to the recent writings of Dante (1265–1321) and Boccaccio (?1313–75), hitherto virtually unknown, it seems, to poets writing in English. Chaucer was, in comparison with the *Gawain*-poet and Langland, an experimental and *avant garde* writer; during the thirty years or so between the composition of *The Book of the Duchess* and his death in 1400 which left *The Canterbury Tales* unfinished, he kept exploring new possibilities for the English language and for English poetry.

The regionalism of these different literary traditions is related to the dialectal diversity which is a characteristic of Middle English. There had been a variety of dialects spoken in pre-Conquest England too, but a standard written form of the language had been provided by the dialect of Wessex, which emerged in the late Old English period as the most powerful kingdom and under which England was finally unified. Scribes from all over the country were trained to write in West Saxon, so that no matter what their spoken dialects were, they were mutually intelligible when they wrote. After the Norman Conquest French, and in some contexts Latin, fulfilled this function; it is not until the fifteenth century, when French had receded, that a new standard form of written English developed to fill the gap, a standard now based however on London, the new centre of government, rather than Winchester. For most of the Middle English period there was no standard form of the language; writers composed in their own local dialects, and then their works were copied by scribes who frequently translated them into their own, different dialects. John Trevisa, who was a Cornishman, says that the way in which the men of Yorkshire speak is so harsh, grating and irregular that 'we southern men can scarcely understand that tongue'. Printing, which aided the process of standardisation, because a universally intelligible form of language was essential if printed books were to reach a national audience, was not introduced into England until 1476. In the Middle

English section of this anthology the texts have not been normalised (though obsolete letters have been replaced, as explained below in the Note on the Texts). The editors' intention is to show how diverse the literary language of the later middle ages is, not only chronologically but also geographically. No other period of English literature is comparable in this respect.

The introduction of printing in the late fifteenth century also assisted the development of prose which, in Britain at least, seems to have been particularly fostered by reading in private. Printing made relatively inexpensive texts widely available, creating the possibility that reading could become for many people a solitary rather than a shared activity. In the epilogue to *The Book of the Order of Chivalry* (1484) Caxton asks that it be 'read unto other yong lordes', envisaging the old mode of dissemination which in fact his own technology was already rendering obsolete. Prose fiction belongs to the era of the press; Malory's *Le Morte Darthur*, one of the earliest works of imaginative prose in English, was completed in 1469/70 and printed by Caxton in 1485.

Earlier English prose had been practical, personal and overwhelmingly religious. An exception is the first Middle English passage in this anthology, from the twelfth-century *Peterborough Chronicle*, continuing a historiographical tradition, unbroken from the days of King Alfred, which was to be superseded after 1157 by Latin and French. For the next century and a half, vernacular history, if it was written at all, was in verse and was thus assimilated to epic and romance, as both Layamon's *Brut* and Barbour's *Bruce* are in their different ways. Secular prose re-emerges in the lifetime of Chaucer, especially in translations from French and Latin: by Trevisa, for example, or by Chaucer himself in his rendering of Boethius' *Consolation of Philosophy*, or in the anonymous translations of Mandeville's *Travels*. Devotional prose throughout the period is much richer; it is the vehicle not only of religious instruction but also of intensely personal meditation as in the works of the fourteenth-century mystics, including Julian of Norwich, or the spiritual autobiography of Margery Kempe.

Drama is illustrated in this anthology by two mystery plays drawn from northern Corpus Christi cycles which present the birth and death of Christ, though using markedly different dramatic techniques. The Corpus Christi plays are peculiar to the late middle ages: they had their origins in religious rite, but in their fifteenth-century heyday they expressed secular and civic values as well as religious ones. Another late-medieval dramatic tradition, not illustrated here, and more obviously the precursor of the theatre of Marlowe, Shakespeare and Jonson, is that of the morality play, in which the characters represent moral abstractions and in which the action takes the form of a conflict between virtue and vice.

In Scotland, which was an independent kingdom until 1603, no prose to speak of has survived from before the late fifteenth century, and no drama from before the mid-sixteenth. Scots poetry – in a form of language distinct from that of northern England, that is – starts comparatively late, with Barbour's *Bruce*, written in the 1370s. Nevertheless at the end of the medieval period, England has noone, with the possible exception of Skelton, to compare with Henryson, Dunbar or Douglas for poetic maturity, self-confidence and range. These three were all university men and therefore had access to a learned culture; at the same time they were widely read in vernacular poetry, both of the Chaucer–Lydgate tradition and that of northern England and Scotland. Standing outside English regionalism, they could afford to be eclectic; writing in the aftermath of a great and diverse period of creativity in England, they were able to exploit and extend its riches in a way their English contemporaries could not.

Douglas's translation of Virgil's *Aeneid* into Scots is a sign of confidence in his native tongue comparable, perhaps, to Chaucer's transformations of Dante and Boccaccio. Both are also auguries of the new orientation of culture. The matrix of the sixteenth-century renaissance is not France but Italy, and not contemporary Italy only but ancient Rome and, beyond it, Greece as well. The last extract in this anthology is from *The History of Richard III* by the humanist Thomas More, writing in a style modelled on that of classical historians about the disastrous reign that brought the Wars of the Roses to an end. Here, if anywhere, is the close of the middle ages.

MJA
FR

Note on Annotation and Glossing

An asterisk * at the end of a word indicates that such words are glossed in the margin.

A dagger † at the end of a word or phrase indicates that the word or phrase is annotated, or given a longer gloss, at the foot of the page.

In the Middle English section, a dagger at the beginning of a line of verse indicates that the whole line is glossed or annotated. Where notes and glosses occur together, notes are set in square brackets.

In *Piers Plowman* and *Morte Arthure* a dagger at the beginning of a line indicates a note and/or gloss on the facing page.

A Note on the Texts

The Middle English texts presented in the second part of this volume are not modernised or normalised except in the following details of spelling.

Obsolete letter-forms have been modernised as follows: *yogh* is represented as *gh*, *w* or *y*; *wynn* as *w*; *eth* and *thorn* as *th*. Capital and lower case *i* have been distinguished from *j*, and *u* from *v*; *u* and *v* have been normalised where necessary for clarity to *f* (*uele* > *fele*; *vor* > *for*); *w* has been normalised where necessary to *u* (*wnto* > *unto*); conversely, *u* has been occasionally normalised to *w* (*ansuare* > *answare*). The digraph *ff* appears as *F*; *&* has been expanded to *and*; other contraction marks have been silently expanded. Punctuation and layout are editorial. For reasons of space emendations have not been signalled.

OLD ENGLISH LITERATURE
Edited by
Michael Alexander

Bede
673–735

The Venerable Bede, a Benedictine monk and scholar, completed his *Historia Ecclesiastica Gentis Anglorum* (*Ecclesiastical History of the English People*) in 731, four years before he died. A learned student of chronology, it was his reckoning of Easter that was used by his successors, and is recognised as having been chiefly responsible for introducing to Europe, and so to the world, the method of reckoning by the years of the Christian era devised in Syria two centuries earlier but never used. His many Latin works survive, the *Ecclesiastical History* in over 160 complete manuscript copies, but of his Old English verse we have only his 'Death Song'. The *Ecclesiastical History* is a work of great human and artistic as well as historical value, and, since Englishmen wrote Latin before they wrote English, extracts given here are translated from Latin rather than from the Alfredian Old English version. The final extract is from a Latin account of Bede's own death by his disciple Cuthbert.

From ECCLESIASTICAL HISTORY
[The Conversion of Edwin†]

[II.xiii, trans. J. Stevens]

Another of the king's chief men, approving of his words and exhortations, presently added: 'The present life of man, O king, seems to me, in comparison of that time which is unknown to us, like to the swift flight of a sparrow through the room wherein you sit at supper in winter, with your commanders and ministers, and a good fire in the midst, whilst the storms of rain and snow prevail abroad; the sparrow,

---

Conversion of Edwin this is the speech Bede gives to an anonymous counsellor of King Edwin of Northumbria. Having heard the preaching of Paulinus, Edwin called a council of his wise men at York in 627 in order to decide whether they should accept Christianity, the religion of his wife. The chief priest of the old heathen religion urged acceptance. Then follows this speech which led to the baptism of Edwin.

I say, flying in at one door, and immediately out at another, whilst he is within, is safe from the wintry storm; but after a short space of fair weather, he immediately vanishes out of your sight, into the dark winter from which he had emerged. So this life of man appears for a short space, but of what went before, or what is to follow, we are utterly ignorant. If, therefore, this new doctrine contains something more certain, it seems justly to deserve to be followed.'

[The poet Caedmon]

[IV.xxiv, trans. C. L. Wrenn]

In the monastery of this abbess† there was a certain brother specially distinguished by divine grace because he was accustomed to making poems fitting to religion and piety. This he did in such wise that, whatsoever he had learned from divine Scriptures through interpreters, this he himself after a short time would bring forth in his own tongue – that is, the language of the Angles – composed in poetic words with the greatest sweetness and moving quality. By these poems of his the minds of many were often enkindled to the despising of the world and to the longing for the heavenly life. Yet indeed there were others after him among the people of the Angles who strove to make religious poems: but none was ever able to match him. For himself had learned the art of poesy not through men nor taught by a man: but he had received the gift of song freely by divine aid. Wherefore he could never make anything of frivolous or vain poetry, but only those verses which belong to piety, which were becoming to that religious tongue of his. In fact he had been settled in the secular way of life until he was of advanced age: and he had not at any time learned anything of poems. Hence it was that sometimes when at a party, when it had been decided for joyful entertainment that all in turn must recite verses to the harp's accompaniment, he when he saw the harp getting near to himself would arise from the midst of the feast and go out and walk back to his house. When on a certain occasion he had done this, and leaving the house where the party was held had gone out to the cattle-pens, as their care had been assigned to him for that night, and when there he had at the normal time given his limbs to sleep, a certain man was standing by him in a dream and, greeting him and calling him by his name, said: 'Caedmon, sing me something.' But he in answering said: 'I do not know how to sing: for it was just for this reason that I came away

---

abbess St Hilda, abbess of Whitby, who died in 680. Caedmon is both the first Old English poet and the only one about whom we have any details

from the feast and departed hither, because I could not sing.' Again he who was talking with him said: 'Yet you *can* sing to me.' 'What', said Caedmon, 'must I sing?' Then the other said: 'Sing of the beginning of created things.' Now when Caedmon had received this answer, immediately he began to sing verses in praise of God the creator which he had never heard, of which this is the sense: 'Now we must praise the Author of the Kingdom of Heaven, the might of the Creator and the thoughts of His mind – the deeds of the Father of glory. [We must sing] how he who is eternal God, the Author of all marvellous things, was manifest: he who first created heaven as a roof-covering for the sons of men, and then as almighty guardian of mankind made the earth.' This is the sense but not the actual order of the words of what Caedmon had sung while sleeping. For poems, however excellently composed, cannot be translated word for word from one language into another without damage to elegance and dignity. Now when he had risen from his sleep, he retained in his memory everything which he had sung while sleeping. And to these verses he quickly added more in the same rhythm and metre in words of a poem worthy of God.

When morning had come, he went to the steward who was his chief and showed him what sort of gift he had received. He was then conducted to the Abbess and commanded to show what he had dreamed in the presence of many learned men and to recite the poem: so that by the judgment of everyone it might be tested of what kind or from whence had come what he had related. And it seemed to them all that it was a grace from heaven and granted by God. Then they expounded to him a discourse of sacred history or doctrine, and commanded him, if he could, to render this into the melody of poetry. So he, when he had finished these matters, went away: and in the morning he came back and produced it composed as had been ordered in the most excellent poetry. Wherefore the Abbess, immediately embracing the grace of God in the man, instructed him with a proposal that he should abandon the secular habit and take that of a monk. So she added him, with his goods, after receiving him into the monastery, to the company of the brethren: and she commanded that he should be taught the whole sequence of sacred Scripture. Now he, taking all that he could learn by hearing, retaining it in his mind, and turning it over like a clean beast ruminating, converted it into the sweetest poetry. Indeed by the sweetness of its melody he made his teachers in their turn become his listeners. Now he sang of the creation of the world and of the origin of the human race and the whole narrative of Genesis, concerning the going out from Egypt of the Israelites and their entry into the land of promise. He sang about very many other historical parts of sacred Scripture, about the Incarnation of the Lord, His Passion, Resurrection, and Ascension into heaven, about the coming of the Holy Ghost and

the teaching of the Apostles. Likewise he made many songs of the terror
of Judgment to come and the horror of the punishment of hell and the
sweetness of the heavenly kingdom. But furthermore he made very
many other compositions concerning divine blessings and judgments,
by all of which he sought to turn men's minds from delight in
wickednesses, and indeed to stir them to the love and skilful practice
of good deeds. For he was a most religious man who subjected himself
with humility to the disciplines of monastic rule. But against others
who wished to act otherwise he was aflame with fervid zeal. Hence it
was that he closed his life with a beautiful ending.

Caedmon's Hymn†

Nu scylun hergan   hefaenricaes uard,
metudæs maecti   end his modgidanc,
uerc uuldurfadur,   sue he uundra gihuaes,
eci dryctin,   or astelidæ.
5 He aerist scop   aelda barnum
heben til hrofe,   haleg scepen;
tha middungeard   moncynnæs uard,
eci dryctin,   æfter tiadæ,
firum foldu,   frea allmectig.

Nu we sculan herian   heofonrices Weard,
Metodes mihte   and his modgeþonc,
weorc Wuldorfæder;   swa he wundra gehwæs,
ece Dryhten,   ord onstealde.
5 He ærest gesceop   eorðan bearnum
heofon to hrofe,   halig Scyppend:
ða middongeard   moncynnes Weard,
ece Dryhten,   æfter teode
firum foldan,   Frea ælmihtig.

Caedmon's Hymn   several Old English
versions of *Caedmon's Hymn* exist in the
manuscripts of the *Ecclesiastical History*. The
first version is in Early Northumbrian in an
MS of 747, the second in a late West Saxon
MS of the early eleventh century. The
translation which follows is a word-for-word,
line-for-line gloss

Now (we) must praise the Keeper of Heaven's Kingdom,
The Maker's might, and His conception,
The deed of the Father of Glory; as He of all wonders
– The Eternal Lord – established the beginning.
5   He first created for the children of men
Heaven as a roof, the Holy Shaper;
Then Middle Earth (did) Mankind's Keeper,
The Eternal Lord, afterward ordain,
The earth of men, the Almighty Lord.

[The disciple Cuthbert's account of Bede's death]

... he was translating the gospel of St John into our language, for the use of the Church. And one of those who were with him said 'Dear Master, there is still one chapter missing. Does it seem to you too difficult to be asked to finish it?' But he said
5   'It is easy; take your pen, make ready, and write swiftly.' And he did so. And about the ninth hour he said to me: 'Run quickly and call the priests of our monastery to me once more, that I may give them little presents, such as God has given to me. Rich people in the world are careful to give gold and silver as precious things; and with much charity
10 and joy will I give to my brothers what God has given.' And speaking to each one he begged them to say Mass for him and to pray earnestly; and they willingly promised. And all mourned and wept, because he said that they should see his face no more in this world. They rejoiced when he said 'It is time that I go to Him who sent me, who made me,
15 who formed me from nothing. I have lived a long time; it is well; my loving Judge foresaw my life; the time of my dissolution is at hand; I long to be dissolved and to be with Christ.' These and many other things he said with joy. The day wore on till evening, and the same boy said: 'Dear Master, there is yet one sentence unwritten,' and he said
20 'Write quickly.' And after a moment the boy said 'Now the sentence is written.' And he said 'Good. In truth I can say, it is finished. Take my head in thy hands, for I would like much to sit facing the holy place where I was accustomed to pray, that, thus sitting, I may call upon my Father.' And so, upon the pavement of his cell, singing 'Gloria Patri, et
25 Filio et Spiritui Sancto,' he breathed the last breath from his body and thus went away to the Kingdom of Heaven.

Bede's Death Song

Fore thaem neidfaerae   naenig uuirthit
thoncsnotturra,   than him tharf sie
to ymbhycggannae   aer his hiniongae
hwaet his gastae   godaes aeththae yflaes
aefter deothdaege   doemid uueorthae.

[Before that sudden journey no one is wiser in thought than he needs to be, in considering, before his departure, what will be adjudged to his soul, of good or evil, after his death-day.]

Riddles
? 8th century

Riddling was a popular form taken up by the educated clergy of Bede's day; abbots and archbishops and saints composed and exchanged Latin riddles, some of them on topics which go back to a third-century collection by one Symphosius, otherwise unknown. More than ninety Old English riddles are found, without solutions, in the manuscript collection of Anglo-Saxon poetry known as the Exeter Book (along with the Elegies and other poems), of which six are included here. A familiar thing is described in an unfamilar way, or speaks and asks us to guess its name. Playful animism, both primitive and literary, is near to the heart of the Anglo-Saxons' attitude to language in their poetry, which is full of allusion, disguise, euphemism and understatement. The riddles show the world of the Anglo-Saxons in a less official way which is quite fascinating. Though some of them are trivial or clever, many have charm or beauty, and most display a true poetic awareness of otherness and identity. Solutions to the riddles are given on p. 12.

A

    When it is earth I tread, make tracks upon water
    Or keep the houses, hushed is my clothing,
    Clothing that can hoist me above house-ridges,
    At times toss me into the tall heaven
5   Where the strong cloud-wind carries me on
    Over cities and countries; accoutrements that
    Throb out sound, thrilling strokes
    Deep-soughing song, as I sail alone
    Over field and flood, faring on,
10 Resting nowhere. My name is ——.

B†

I'm the world's wonder, for I make women happy
— A boon to the neighbourhood, a bane to no one,
Though I may perhaps prick the one who picks me.

I am set well up, stand in a bed,
5   Have a roughish root. Rarely (though it happens)
A churl's daughter more daring than the rest
— And lovelier! — lays hold of me,
Rushes my red top, wrenches at my head,
And lays me in the larder.
10   She learns soon enough,
The curly-haired creature who clamps me so,
Of my meeting with her: moist is her eye!

C†

I am the scalp of myself, skinned by my foeman:
Robbed of my strength, he steeped and soaked me,
Dipped me in water, whipped me out again,
Set me in the sun. I soon lost there
5   The hairs I had had.
                         The hard edge
Of a keen-ground knife cuts me now,
Fingers fold me, and a fowl's pride
Drives its treasure trail across me,
10 Bounds again over the brown rim,
Sucks the wood-dye, steps again on me,
Makes his black marks.
                         A man then hides me
Between stout shield-boards stretched with hide,
15 Fits me with gold. There glows on me
The jewelsmith's handiwork held with wires.

Let these royal enrichments and this red dye
And splendid settings spread the glory
Of the Protector of peoples — and not plague the fool . . . .

B it is a learned opinion that *double-entendre* riddles are of popular origin
C this riddle contains miniature riddles on calf-skin, quill and ink. The concluding devotional application is omitted

D

    Men are fond of me. I am found everywhere,
    Brought in from the woods and the beetling cliffs,
    From down and from dale. In the daylight wings†
    Raised me aloft, then into a roof's shade
5   Swung me in sweetly. Sweltered then
    By men in a bath, I am a binder now,
    Soon a thrasher, a thrower next:
    I'll put an old fellow flat on the ground.
    A man who tries to take me on,
10 Tests my strength, soon finds out,
    If his silly plan doesn't pall on him,
    That it is his back that will hit the dust.
    Loud in words, he has lost control
    Of his hands and feet, and his head doesn't work:
15 His strength has gone. Guess my name
    Who have such mastery of men of earth
    That I knock them about in broad daylight.

E†

    I am fire-fretted and I flirt with Wind
    And my limbs are light-freighted and I am lapped in flame
    And I am storm-stacked and I strain to fly
    And I am a grove leaf-bearing and a glowing ember.

5   From hand to friend's hand about the hall I go,
    So much do lords and ladies love to kiss me.
    When I hold myself high, and the whole company
    Bow quiet before me, their blessedness
    Shall flourish skyward beneath my fostering shade.

---

wings   bees bring in pollen to make honey
E   compare *The Dream of the Rood* and the
    last line of *Piers Plowman*, Passus 18

F†

I was by the sand at the sea-wall once:
Where the tide comes I kept my dwelling,
Fast in my first seat. There were few indeed
Of human kind who cared to behold
5 My homeland in that lonely place,
But in every dawning the dark wave
Lapped about me. Little did I think
That early or late I ever should
Speak across the meadbench, mouthless as I am,
10 Compose a message. It is a mysterious thing,
Dark to the mind that does not know
How a knife's point and a clever hand,
A man's purpose and a point also,
Have pressed upon me to the purpose that
15 I might fearlessly announce, for none but us two,
A message to you, so that no man beside
Might spread abroad what is spoken between us.

F a variation upon the *Arundo* (*Reed*) of Symphosius, itself based upon the history of Syrinx in the *Metamorphoses* of the Roman poet Ovid. Compare *The Husband's Message*

SOLUTIONS: A. Swan B. Onion C. Gospel-book D. Mead E. Wood F. Reed-pen. (These are the riddles numbered 7, 25, 26, 27, 30 and 60 in *The Anglo-Saxon Poetic Records*, vol. 3.)

The Dream of the Rood
700–1000

The Dream of the Rood is the most remarkable of all Old English poems. At its heart is a speech spoken by the Cross upon which Christ was crucified, in a striking development of the riddle-tradition exemplified in riddle E (Wood in various forms, ending with a Cross). The Tree tells how it obeyed its Lord like an unwilling thane. Fifteen lines from this speech are carved in Old English in runic characters upon the sides of the Ruthwell Cross, a cross standing six metres high at Ruthwell near Dumfries in Scotland. This great rood was erected in the early 700s: it is covered in handsome panels, mostly from the New Testament, in deep relief, each surrounded by a text.

The poem survives in a 156-line form in the Vercelli Book of the late tenth century, and in this expanded form it opens with the speech of the dreamer who then reports the words of the cross. In the latter part of the poem, the Cross exhorts the dreamer to save himself through the difficult understanding of the Crucifixion. The first part of the poem is a tour-de-force of visionary intensity, where the creature suffers the passion of its creator, and is covered with blood and at the same time with gold representing Christ's glorious victory over death. There is an emphasis, as in the hymns of Venantius Fortunatus (*c.* 530– *c.* 603), upon the victory of the Atonement. The Saviour, a 'young' Germanic 'hero', is said to be weary after the great struggle; his suffering and death are understated rather than, as in later Gothic art, emphasised; see, for example, 'In a Valley of this Restless Mind'. The suffering Christ felt in his human nature is expressed indirectly through the words of his creature. The later devotional application of the vision is less striking and is here represented in prose.

THE DREAM OF THE ROOD

>   *Hwaet!*†
> A dream came to me
>   at deep midnight
>   when humankind
> 5   kept their beds
>   – the dream of dreams!
>   I shall declare it.
>
>   It seemed I saw the Tree itself
>   borne on the air, light wound about it,
> 10 – a beam of brightest wood, a beacon clad
>   in overlapping gold, glancing gems†
>   fair at its foot, and five stones
>   set in a crux flashed from the crosstree.
>
>   Around angels of God
> 15   all gazed upon it,
>   since first fashioning fair.
>   It was not a felon's gallows,
>   for holy ghosts beheld it there,
>   and men on mould, and the whole Making shone for it
> 20 – *signum*† of victory!
>   Stained and marred,
>   stricken with shame, I saw the glory-tree
>   shine out gaily, sheathed in yellow
>   decorous gold; and gemstones made
> 25 for their Maker's Tree a right mail-coat.
>
>   Yet through the masking gold I might perceive
>   what terrible sufferings were once sustained thereon:
>   it bled from the right side.
>   Ruth in the heart.

Hwaet a call for attention
gems jewelled crosses were common expressions of the cult
signum Old English *segen*, from Latin *signum*, a standard. The Emperor Constantine used the sign of the Cross on his standards in his victory of the Milvian Bridge in 312

30 Afraid I saw that unstill brightness
    change raiment† and colour
           – again clad in gold
    or again slicked with sweat,
           spangled with spilling blood.

35 Yet lying there a long while
    I beheld, sorrowing, the Healer's Tree
    till it seemed that I heard how it broke silence,
    best of wood, and began to speak:

    'Over that long remove my mind ranges
40 back to the holt where I was hewn down;
    from my own stem I was struck away,
           dragged off by strong enemies,
    wrought into a roadside scaffold.
           They made me a hoist for wrongdoers.

45 The soldiers on their shoulders bore me,
           until on a hill-top they set me up;
    many enemies made me fast there.
           Then I saw, marching toward me,
    mankind's brave King;
50   He came to climb upon me.

    I dared not break or bend aside
    against God's will, though the ground itself
    shook at my feet. Fast I stood,
    who falling could have felled them all.

55 Almighty God ungirded Him,
           eager to mount the gallows,
    unafraid in the sight of many:
           He would set free mankind.
    I shook when His arms embraced me
60   but I durst not bow to ground,
    stoop to Earth's surface.
           Stand fast I must.

---

raiment a possible allusion to the changes in
  the cross's liturgical vestments in Holy Week

I was reared up, a rood.
　　I raised the great King,
65　liege lord of the heavens,
　　　　dared not lean from the true.
　　They drove me through with dark nails:
　　　　on me are the deep wounds manifest,
　　wide-mouthed hate-dents.
70　　　　I durst not harm any of them.
　　How they mocked at us both!
　　　　I was all moist with blood
　　sprung from the Man's side
　　　　after He sent forth His soul.

75　Wry weirds a-many I underwent
　　up on that hill-top; saw the Lord of Hosts
　　stretched out stark. Darkness shrouded
　　the King's corse. Clouds wrapped
　　its clear shining. A shade went out
80　wan under cloud-pall. All creation wept,
　　keened the King's death. Christ was on the Cross.

　　But there quickly came from far
　　earls to the One there. All that I beheld;
　　had grown weak with grief,
85　　　　yet with glad will bent then
　　meek to those men's hands,
　　　　yielded Almighty God.

　　They lifted Him down from the leaden pain,
　　　　left me, the commanders,
90　standing in a sweat of blood.
　　　　I was all wounded with shafts.

　　They straightened out His strained limbs,
　　　　stood at His body's head,
　　looked down on the Lord of Heaven
95　　　　– for a while He lay there resting –
　　set to contrive Him a tomb
　　　　in the sight of the Tree of Death,
　　carved it of bright stone,
　　　　laid in it the Bringer of victory,
100　spent from the great struggle.
　　　　They began to speak the grief-song,

            sad in the sinking light,
                    then thought to set out homeward;
            their hearts were sick to death,
105   their most high Prince
            they left to rest there with scant retinue.†

            Yet we three, weeping, a good while
            stood in that place after the song had gone up
            from the captains' throats. Cold grew the corse,
110   fair soul-house.
                            They felled us all.
            We crashed to ground, cruel Weird,
            and they delved for us a deep pit.

            The Lord's men learnt of it,
115   His friends† found me . . .
            it was they who girt me with gold and silver . . .

            [78–156 *of the Vercelli text*]

   'Now, my dear man, you may understand that I have suffered to the
end the pain of grievous sorrows at the hands of dwellers in misery.
The time is now come that men on earth, and all this marvellous
creation, shall honour me far and wide and address themselves in prayer
5 to this sign. On me the Son of God spent a time of suffering. Therefore
do I now tower up glorious beneath the heavens, and I have the power
to save every man who fears me. Formerly I was made the worst of
punishments, the most hateful to the peoples – before I opened to men,
the speech-bearers, the right way to life.
10   Behold, the Prince of Glory then exalted me above the trees of the
forest, the Keeper of the Kingdom of Heaven; just as He also, Almighty
God, for the sake of all mankind, exalted His mother, Mary herself,
above all womankind.
    I now command you, my dear man, to tell men about this sight,
15 reveal in words that this is the tree of glory on which Almighty God
suffered for the many sins of mankind and Adam's deeds of old. He
tasted death thereupon; yet afterwards the Lord rose up, to help men
with His great might. Then He went up to the heavens. Hither He shall
come again to seek out mankind on the day of doom, the Lord Himself,
20 Almighty God, and with Him His angels, when He then will adjudge –

---

scant retinue an overstatement meaning with no retinue
friends the True Cross was discovered by Helena, the Emperor Constantine's mother, in Jerusalem (as recorded in the Old English poem *Elene*)

Who has the power of judgement – to each and every one according to how he shall formerly have deserved for himself here in this transitory life. Nor can anyone there be unconcerned about the word that the Ruler shall utter. He shall ask before the multitude, Where is the man who is willing to taste bitter death for the Lord's name's sake? – as He had formerly done on the tree. But they shall then be afraid, and few shall think what they shall begin to answer to Christ. Yet no one there shall need to be afraid who has borne in his bosom the best of signs. But every soul on earth who intends to dwell with the Lord shall come to the Kingdom through the Rood.'

Then I prayed to the tree with cheerful heart and high zeal, alone as I was and with small retinue. My spirit was drawn forth on its way hence; in all it had endured many times of longing. The hope of my life is now that I should seek out that tree of victory, alone and more frequently than all men, to worship it fully. The desire to do this is strong in my mind, and my hope of protection is all bent on the rood. I have not many powerful friends on earth. On the contrary, they have departed hence out of the world's joys, have sought out the King of Glory and live now in the heavens with the Almighty Father, dwelling in glory; and every day I look for the time when the Lord's rood, which once I gazed on here on earth, shall fetch me forth from this fleeting life and then shall bring me where there is great rejoicing, happiness in the heavens, where the Lord's people is seated at the feast, where there is bliss everlasting; and then He shall appoint me to a place where after I may dwell in glory, and fully share in joy among the blest.

May the Lord be my friend, who here on earth once suffered on the gallows tree for the sins of man. He ransomed us and gave us life, a heavenly home. Hope was made new, with glory and with bliss, for those who had suffered burning there. The Son was victorious on that expedition,† mighty and triumphant, when He came, the Almighty Sovereign, with a multitude, a host of spirits, into God's Kingdom, to the bliss of the angels and all of the saints who had previously dwelt in glory, when their Ruler came, Almighty God, into His own Kingdom.

---

expedition The Harrowing of Hell

Deor
? 8th century

Deor is a heroic-elegiac poem in the late-tenth-century collection known as the Exeter Book, and is unique in its strophic form. The refrain *Thaes ofereode; thisses swa maeg* means literally 'it passed over in respect of that; it may do so in respect of this'. Each strophe is a compressed allusion to a tragedy from the remote Germanic past, cast in a knowing dramatic form very like that of poems in the Old Norse *Edda*, which were probably composed after 800, somewhat later than *Deor*.

Deor is an imagined singer of tales who recalls from his repertory of legend these examples of misfortunes endured in order to cheer himself up now that he has been supplanted as the *scop* at the court of King Heoden by the new poet, Heorrenda.

DEOR

    Wayland† knew the wanderer's fate:
    that single-willed earl suffered agonies,
    sorrow and longing the sole companions
    of his ice-cold exile. Anxieties bit
5   when Nithhad put a knife to his hamstrings,
    laid clever bonds on the better man.

        That went by; this may too.

    Beadohild† mourned her murdered brothers:
    but her own plight pained her more
10 – her womb grew great with child.
    When she knew that, she could never hold
    steady before her wit what was to happen.

        That went by; this may too.

Wayland   Wayland, the smith of the gods, was captured by Nithhad and hamstrung. But he killed Nithhad's sons, ravished his daughter Beadohild, and escaped

Beadohild   Wildia, the offspring of her unwilling union with Wayland, grew up to become a famous hero

All have heard of Hild's† ravishing:
15 the Geat's lust was ungovernable,
their bitter love banished sleep.

    That went by; this may too.

Thirty winters Theodric† ruled
the Maering city: and many knew it.

20   That went by; this may too.

We all know that Eormanric†
had a wolf's wit. Wide Gothland
lay in the grasp of that grim king,
and through it many sat, by sorrows environed,
25 forseeing only sorrow; sighed for the downfall
and thorough overthrow of the thrall-maker.

    That went by; this may too.

When each gladness has gone, gathering sorrow
may cloud the brain; and in his breast a man
30 can not then see how his sorrows shall end.
But he may think how throughout this world
it is the way of God, who is wise, to deal
to the most part of men much favour
and a flourishing fame; to a few the sorrow-share.

35 Of myself in this regard I shall say this only:
that in the hall of the Heodenings I held long the makarship,
lived dear to my prince, Deor my name;
many winters I held this happy place
and my lord was kind. Then came Heorrenda,
40 whose lays were skilful; the lord of fighting-men
settled on him the estate bestowed once on me.

    That went by; this may too.

Hild   Not identified, but another victim whose grief seems to have passed. *Geat* also is unidentified
Theodric   Probably Theodoric the Ostrogoth who ruled Merano for 30 years before Eormanric exiled him
Eormanric   King of the Goths who died in 375; in legend a tyrant

Beowulf
?mid-8th–mid-9th centuries

Beowulf probably existed in nearly its present form of 3182 verses by the early 800s. After 793, when the Danes had sacked Lindisfarne, *Beowulf*'s setting in the southern Scandinavia of the sixth century, largely at the Danish court, might have seemed unwelcome. *Beowulf* is a good story and a great epic poem but the nature of its greatness has not always been recognised. Both historical, legendary and mythical, it is concerned with and meditates constantly upon human destiny, on the fate of heroes, kings and empires, on human glory and human vanity, on heroic worth and its outcome: 'What the unsearchable dispose/ Of Highest Wisdom brings about', as Milton called it in *Samson Agonistes*. Though *Beowulf* is unmistakably of the North, it is not a grisly folk or fairy tale in the manner of Grimm, nor is its true interest antiquarian, philological or fantastic. It is what Aristotle called *philosophoteron*, more interested in wisdom, an epic poem like the *Aeneid* of Virgil in its tragic morality.

A strange feature of *Beowulf* is its unaccountable and early superiority. Epics are often anonymous, but their cultural origin is usually evident enough. *Beowulf* is composed for a milieu which we cannot identify beyond saying that it seems aristocratic, Anglian, and clearly after the seventh-century conversion of England. It would have been of ancestral interest to leading families in most of the Anglian courts of England, conscious of their old links with northern Europe. The unique manuscript, in the West Saxon dialect, is usually dated about the year 1000, much later than the period of original composition. It contains other tales about monsters.

In ages of liberal enlightenment, monsters can be dismissed, but in our illiberal century one of *Beowulf*'s most telling recommendations is its unforgiving grasp on how deeply human is the desire for vengeance and how unavailing are our efforts to contain it. Early in *Beowulf* we are reminded that the first man born of woman was a fratricide: Cain and the Giants of Genesis are repeatedly named as the ancestors of the man-eating monster Grendel, who terrorises the court of the Danish King Hrothgar. Beowulf kills Grendel and his mother, and, much later, a dragon, yet he is not a Herculean monster-slayer but rather a guardian against monsters. He kills only in defence, and is a markedly restrained Northern hero, deeply loyal to his lord and reluctant to take the throne of his native land. He begins as a good young hero and becomes a good mature king.

Beowulf when he dies boasts that he has sworn 'no unrightful oaths' and has taken on no unnecessary feuds. But 'the primal strife' set off by Cain is to continue after Beowulf's death against the dragon; his people are to be crushed by their enemies. The greatness of *Beowulf* lies in the human and historical part of the story; the monsters embody extreme forms of human tendencies to pride and possessiveness. *Beowulf* is full of the history of the tribes of Southern Scandinavia over two or three generations in the fifth and sixth centuries, often glancingly or riddlingly told in the circumlocutory style of Old English verse, here at its richest. These digressive episodes give the poem a quality of temporal depth, but the allusive methods employed are at first somewhat baffling, and several of the most condensed passages of allusion have been cut in the version here presented, as has the whole central episode, the fight with Grendel's grotesque mother. The excisions, made largely for reasons of space, reduce the length of the poem by half: they simplify the narrative, which is far from chronologically straightforward, and leave the sombre end of the poem, the dragon fight, balanced clearly against the excitement of its beginning, the fight against Grendel.

From BEOWULF

Attend!
We have heard of the thriving of the throne of Denmark,†
how the folk-kings flourished in former days,
how those royal athelings* earned that glory.   *princes*

5   Was it not Scyld Shefing† that shook the halls,
took mead-benches,† taught encroaching
foes to fear him – who, found in childhood,
lacked clothing? Yet he lived and prospered,

---

throne of Denmark   the Danish empire was ruled by the Scylding dynasty, founded by Scyld

Shefing   name meaning either son of Sceaf or with a sheaf
took mead-benches   the mead-bench was the focus of loyalty

  grew in strength and stature under the heavens
10 until the clans settled in the sea-coasts neighbouring
  over the whale-road* all must obey him   sea
  and give tribute. He was a good king!

  A boy child was afterwards born to Scyld,
  a young child in hall-yard, a hope for the people,
15 sent them by God; the griefs long endured
  were not unknown to Him, the harshness of years
  without a lord. Therefore the Life-bestowing
  Wielder of Glory† granted them this blessing.
  Through the northern lands the name of Beow,†
20 the son of Scyld, sprang widely,
  For in youth an atheling should so use his virtue,
  give with a free hand while in his father's house,
  that in old age, when enemies gather,
  established friends shall stand by him
25 and serve him gladly. It is by glorious action
  that a man comes by honour in any people.

  At the hour shaped for him Scyld departed,
  the hero crossed into the keeping of his Lord.
  They carried him out to the edge of the sea,
30 his sworn arms-fellows, as he had himself desired them
  while he wielded his words, Warden of the Scyldings,
  beloved folk-founder; long had he ruled.

  A boat with a ringed neck rode in the haven,
  icy, out-eager, the atheling's vessel,
35 and there they laid out their lord and master,
  dealer of wound gold, in the waist of the ship,
  in majesty by the mast. A mound of treasures
  from far countries was fetched aboard her,
  and it is said that no boat was ever more bravely fitted out
40 with the weapons of a warrior, war accoutrement,
  swords and body-armour; on his breast were set
  treasures and trappings to travel with him
  on his far faring into the flood's sway.

Wielder of Glory   one of the many titles given to God in the poem

Beow   Beowulf the Dane, not the hero of the poem

This hoard was not less great† than the gifts he had had
45 from those who at the outset had adventured him
over seas, alone, a small child.
High over head they hoisted and fixed
a gold *signum*;† gave him to the flood,
let the seas take him, with sour hearts
50 and mourning mood. Men under heaven's
shifting skies, though skilled in counsel,
cannot say surely who unshipped that cargo.

[Here lines 53–63 of the original are omitted. Scyld's successor Beowulf the Dane (not the hero of the poem) was succeeded by his son Healfdene, who had three sons, Heorogar, Hrothgar and Halga, and also a daughter who married the Swede Onela.]

Then to Hrothgar was granted glory in battle,
mastery of the field; so friends and kinsmen
55 gladly obeyed him, and his band increased
to a great company. It came into his mind
that he would command the construction
of a huge mead-hall, a house greater
than men on earth ever had heard of,
60 and share the gifts God had bestowed on him
upon its floor with folk young and old –
apart from public land and the persons of slaves.
Far and wide (as I heard) the work was given out
in many a tribe over middle earth,†
65 the making of the mead-hall.† And, as men reckon,
the day of readiness dawned very soon
for this greatest of houses. Heorot† he named it
whose word ruled a wide empire.
He made good his boast, gave out rings,
70 arm-bands at the banquet. Boldly the hall reared
its arched gables; unkindled the torch-flame
that turned it to ashes. The time was not yet
when the blood-feud should bring out again
sword-hatred in sworn kindred.†

---

not less great a characteristic understatement: Scyld had had nothing on arrival
signum OE *segen*, from the Latin for standard
middle earth *middanyeard*, the enclosure in the middle (between heaven and hell, and surrounded by Ocean)
mead-hall hall where heroes drank mead (and also beer and wine) and feasted with their lord
Heorot the hall's name means 'Hart'
sword ... kindred alludes to the eventual burning-down of Heorot at the wedding-feast of the Heathobard prince Ingeld and Hrothgar's daughter Freawaru

75 It was with pain that the powerful spirit
    dwelling in darkness endured that time,
    hearing daily the hall filled
    with loud amusement; there was the music of the harp,
    the clear song of the poet, perfect in his telling
80 of the remote first making† of man's race.
    He told how, long ago, the Lord formed Earth,
    a plain bright to look on, locked in ocean,
    exulting established the sun and the moon
    as lights to illumine the land-dwellers
85 and furnished forth the face of Earth
    with limbs and leaves. Life He then granted
    to each kind of creature that creeps and moves.

    So the company of men led a careless life,
    all was well with them: until One began
90 to encompass evil, an enemy from hell.
    Grendel† they called this cruel spirit,
    the fell and fen his fastness was,
    the march his haunt. This unhappy being
    had long lived in the land of monsters
95 since the Creator cast them out
    as kindred of Cain.† For that killing of Abel
    the eternal Lord took vengeance.
    There was no joy of that feud: far from mankind
    God drove him out for his deed of shame!
100 From Cain came down all kinds misbegotten
    – ogres and elves and evil shades –
    as also the Giants,† who joined in long
    wars with God. He gave them their reward.

    With the coming of night came Grendel also,
105 sought the great house and how the Ring-Danes†
    held their hall when the horn had gone round.
    He found in Heorot the force of nobles
    slept after supper, sorrow forgotten,
    the condition of men. Maddening with rage,

---

first making see *Caedmon's Hymn* (page 6) and Genesis 1

Grendel the name of Beowulf's antagonist, who is both a man, a monster and a demon, suggests grinding

Cain outcast from Eden in Genesis 4 for the murder of his brother Abel

Giants the Giants of Genesis 6 were seen as the descendants of Cain

Ring-Danes the Danes are also called East-Danes, West-Danes and North-Danes

110   he struck quickly, creature of evil:
      grim and greedy, he grasped on their pallets
      thirty warriors, and away he was out of there,
      thrilled with his catch: he carried off homeward
      his glut of slaughter, sought his own halls.

115   As the day broke, with the dawn's light
      Grendel's outrage was openly to be seen:
      night's table-laughter turned to morning's
      lamentation. Lord Hrothgar
      sat silent then, the strong man mourned,
120   glorious king, he grieved for his thanes
      as they read the traces of a terrible foe,
      a cursed fiend. That was too cruel a feud,
      too long, too hard!
                          Nor did he let them rest
      but the next night brought new horrors,
125   did more murder, manslaughter and outrage
      and shrank not from it: he was too set on these things.

      It was not remarked then if a man looked
      for sleeping-quarters quieter, less central,
      among the outer buildings; now openly shown,
130   the new hall-thane's† hatred was manifest
      and unmistakable. Each survivor
      then kept himself at safer distance.

      So Grendel became ruler; against right he fought,
      one against all. Empty then stood
135   the best of houses, and for no brief space;
      for twelve long winters torment sat
      on the Friend of the Scyldings, fierce sorrows
      and woes of every kind; which was not hidden
      from the sons of men, but was made known
140   in grieving songs, how Grendel warred
      long on Hrothgar, the harms he did him
      through wretched years of wrong, outrage
      and persecution. Peace was not in his mind
      towards any companion of the court of Hrothgar,
145   the feud was not abated, the blood-price† was unpaid.

---

hall-thane Grendel. A thane is a valued retainer

blood-price in Germanic law a feud might be settled (and vengeance avoided) by paying compensation: *wergild* (man-price)

Nor did any counsellor have cause to look for
a bright man-price at the murderer's hand:
the dark death-shadow drove always against them,
old and young; abominable
150 he watched and waited for them, walked nightlong
the misty moorland. Men know not
where hell's familiars fleet on their errands!

Again and again the enemy of man
stalking unseen, struck terrible
155 and bitter blows. In the black nights
he camped in the hall, under Heorot's gold roof;
yet he could not touch the treasure-throne†
against the Lord's will, whose love was unknown to him.
A great grief was it for the Guardian of the Scyldings,
160 crushing to his spirit. The council lords
sat there daily to devise some plan,
what might be best for brave-hearted
Danes to contrive against these terror-raids.
They prayed aloud, promising sometimes
165 on the altars of their idols† unholy sacrifices
if the Slayer of souls would send relief
to the suffering people.
                      Such was their practice,
a heathen hope; Hell possessed
their hearts and minds: the Maker was unknown to them,
170 the Judge of all actions, the Almighty was unheard of,
they knew not how to praise the Prince of Heaven,
the Wielder of Glory.
                      Woe to him who must
in terrible trial entrust his soul
to the embrace of the burning, banished from thought
175 of change or comfort! Cheerful the man
able to look to the Lord at his death-day,
to find peace in the Father's embrace!

This season rocked the son of Healfdene*   Hrothgar
with swingeing sorrows; nor could the splendid man
180 put his cares from him. Too cruel the feud,
too strong and long-lasting, that struck that people,
a wicked affliction, the worst of nightmares!

---

treasure-throne Hrothgar's throne or, in an alternative translation, God's throne
idols here the Danes, unlike the audience of *Beowulf*, are heathen. But their king uses Christian language in his speech of thanks after Beowulf has killed Grendel's mother

This was heard of at his home by one of Hygelac's[†] followers,
a good man among the Geats, Grendel's raidings;
185 he was for main strength of all men foremost
that trod the earth at that time of day;
build and blood matched.

                              He bade a seaworthy
wave-cutter be fitted out for him; the warrior king
he would seek, he said, over swan's riding,
190 that lord of great name, needing men.
The wiser sought to dissuade him from voyaging
hardly or not at all,[†] though they held him dear;
they whetted his quest-thirst, watched omens.
The prince had already picked his men
195 from the folk's flower, the fiercest among them
that might be found, with fourteen men
he sought sound-wood; sea-wise Beowulf[†]
led them right down to the land's edge.

Time running on, she rode the waves now,
200 hard in by headland. Harnessed warriors
stepped on her stem; setting tide churned
sea with sand, soldiers carried
bright mail-coats to the mast's foot,
war-gear well-wrought; willingly they shoved her out,
205 thorough-braced craft, on the craved voyage.

Away she went over a wavy ocean,
boat like a bird, breaking seas,
wind-whetted, white-throated,
till the curved prow had ploughed so far
210 – the sun standing right on the second day –
that they might see land loom on the skyline,
then the shimmer of cliffs, sheer fells behind,
reaching capes.

Hygelac Beowulf's lord, King of the Geats in Southern Sweden, killed in 521
hardly . . . all understatement: they encouraged Beowulf

Beowulf the hero of the poem; son of Edgetheow the Waymunding; nephew of Hygelac

                    The crossing was at an end;
           closed the wake. Weather-Geats†
215   stood on strand, stepped briskly up;
           a rope going ashore, ring-mail clashed,
           battle-girdings. God they thanked
           for the smooth going over the salt-trails.

           The watchman saw them. From the wall where he stood,
220   posted by the Scyldings to patrol the cliffs,
           he saw the polished lindens pass along the gangway
           and the clean equipment. Curiosity
           moved him to know who these men might be.

           Hrothgar's thane, when his horse had picked
225   its way down to the shore, shook his spear
           fiercely at arm's length, framed the challenge:
           'Strangers, you have steered this steep craft
           through the sea-ways, sought our coast.
           I see you are warriors; you wear that dress now.
230   I must ask who you are.

                              In all the years
           I have lived as look-out at land's end here
           – so that no foreigners with a fleet-army
           might land in Denmark and do us harm –
           shield-carriers have never come ashore
235   more openly. You had no assurance
           of welcome here, word of leave
           from Hrothgar and Hrothulf†

                              I have not in my life
           set eyes on a man with more might in his frame
           than this helmed lord. He's no hall-fellow
240   dressed in fine armour, or his face belies him;
           he has the head of a hero.
                              I'll have your names now
           and the names of your fathers; or further you shall not go
           as undeclared spies in the Danish land.

Weather-Geats or Storm-Geats, a name for Beowulf's seafaring people

Hrothulf son of Hrothgar's brother Halga; the uncle and nephew are sometimes presented as joint rulers of the Danes

Stay where you are, strangers, hear
245 what I have to say! Seas crossed,
it is best and simplest straightaway to acknowledge
where you are from, why you have come.'

The captain gave him a clear answer,
leader of the troop, unlocked his word-hoard:
250 'We here are come from the country of the Geats
and are King Hygelac's hearth-companions.
My noble father was known as Edgetheow,†
a front-fighter famous among nations,
who had seen many seasons when he set out at last
255 an old man from the halls; all the wiser men
in the world readily remember him.

It is with loyal and true intention that we come
to seek your lord the son of Healfdene,
guardian of the people: guide us well therefore!
260 We have a great errand to the glorious hero,
the Shepherd of the Danes;* the drift of it   Hrothgar
shall not be kept from you. You must know if indeed
there is truth in what is told in Geatland,
that among the Scyldings some enemy,
265 an obscure assailant in the opaque night-times,
makes spectacles of spoil and slaughter
in hideous feud. To Hrothgar I would
openheartedly unfold a plan
how the old commander may overcome his foe;
270 if indeed an easing is ever to slacken
these besetting sorrows, a settlement
when chafing cares shall cool at last.
Otherwise he must miserably live out
this lamentable time, for as long as Heorot,
275 best of houses, bulks to the sky.'

The mounted coastguard made reply,
unshrinking officer: 'A sharp-witted man,
clear in his mind, must be skilled
to discriminate deeds and words.

Edgetheow a Waymunding who married the
  only daughter of the Geat King Hrethel;
  slayer of Heatholaf

280 I accept what I am told, that this troop is loyal
to the Scyldings' Protector. Pass forward with your
weapons and war-dress! I am willing to guide you,
commanding meanwhile the men under me
to guard with care this craft of yours,
285 this new-tarred boat at its berth by our strand
against every enemy until again it bear
its beloved captain over the current sea,
curve-necked keel, to the coasts of the Geat;
such a warrior shall be accorded
290 unscathed passage through the shocks of battle.'

The vessel was still as they set forward,
the deep-chested ship, stayed at its mooring,
fast at its anchor. Over the cheek-pieces
boar-shapes† shone out, bristling with gold,
295 blazing and fire-hard, fierce guards
of their bearers' lives. Briskly the men went
marching together, making out at last
the ample eaves adorned with gold:
to earth's men the most glorious
300 of houses under heaven, the home of the king;
its radiance lighted the lands of the world.

The coastguard showed them the shining palace,
the resort of heroes, and how they might
rightly come to it; this captain in the wars
305 then brought his horse about, and broke silence:
'Here I must leave you. May the Lord Almighty
afford His grace in your undertakings
and bring you to safety. Back at the sea-shore
I resume the watch against sea-raiders.'

310 There was stone paving on the path that brought
the war-band on its way. The war-coats shone
and the links of hard hand-locked iron
sang in their harness as they stepped along
in their gear of grim aspect, going to the hall.

---

boar-shapes animals depicted on the helmets

315 Sea-wearied, they then set against the wall
     their broad shields of special temper,
     and bowed to bench, battle-shirts clinking,
     the war-dress of warriors. The weapons of the seamen
     stood in the spear-rack, stacked together,
320 an ash-wood grey-tipped. These iron-shirted men
     were handsomely armed.

                              A high-mannered chieftain
     then enquired after the ancestry of the warriors.
     'From whence do you bring these embellished shields,
     grey mail-shirts, masked helmets,
325 this stack of spears? I am spokesman here,
     herald to Hrothgar; I have not seen
     a body of strangers bear themselves more proudly.
     It is not exile but adventure, I am thinking,
     boldness of spirit, that brings you to Hrothgar.'

330 The gallant Geat gave answer then,
     valour-renowned, and vaunting spoke,
     hard under helmet: 'At Hygelac's table
     we are sharers in the banquet; Beowulf is my name.
     I shall gladly set out to the son of Healfdene,
335 most famous of kings, the cause of my journey,
     lay it before your lord, if he will allow us kindly
     to greet in person his most gracious self.'

     Then Wulfgar spoke; the warlike spirit
     of this Wendel* prince, his wisdom in judgement,   Vandal
340 were known to many. 'The Master of the Danes,
     Lord of the Scyldings, shall learn of your request.
     I shall gladly ask my honoured chief,
     giver of arm-bands, about your undertaking,
     and soon bear the answer back again to you
345 that my gracious lord shall think good to make.'

     He strode rapidly to the seat of Hrothgar,
     old and grey-haired among the guard of earls,
     stepped forward briskly, stood before the shoulders
     of the King of the Danes; a court's ways were known to him.

350　Then Wulfgar addressed his dear master:
'Men have come here from the country of the Geats,
borne from afar over the back of the sea;
these battle-companions call the man
who leads them, Beowulf. The boon they ask
355　is, my lord, that they may hold
converse with you. Do not, kind Hrothgar,
refuse them audience in the answer you vouchsafe;
accoutrement would clearly bespeak them
of earls' rank. Indeed the leader
360　who guided them here seems of great account.'

　　The Guardian of the Scyldings gave his answer:
'I knew him when he was a child!
It was to his old father, Edgetheow, that
Hrethel† the Geat gave in marriage
365　his one daughter. Well does the son
now pay this call on a proven ally!

　　The seafarers used to say, I remember,
who took our gifts to the Geat people
in token of friendship – that this fighting man
370　in his hand's grasp had the strength
of thirty other men. I am thinking that
the Holy God, as a grace to us
Danes in the West, has directed him here
against Grendel's oppression. This good man shall be
375　offered treasures in return for his courage.

　　Waste no time now but tell them to come in
that they may see this company seated together;
make sure to say that they are most welcome
to the people of the Danes.'
　　　　　　　　　　　　　Promptly Wulfgar
380　turned to the doors and told his message:
'The Master of Battles bids me announce,
the Lord of the North Danes, that he knows your ancestry;
I am to tell you all, determined venturers
over the seas, that you are sure of welcome.
385　You may go in now in your gear of battle,
set eyes on Hrothgar, helmed as you are.

Hrethel father of Herebeald, Hathkin,
　Hygelac and an unnamed daughter

> But battle-shafts and shields of linden wood
> may here await your words' outcome.'

The prince arose, around him warriors
in dense escort; detailed by the chief,
a group remained to guard the weapons.
The Geats swung in behind their stout leader
over Heorot's floor. The hero led on,
hard under helmet, to the hearth, where he stopped.

Then Beowulf spoke; bent by smith's skill
the meshed rings of his mailshirt glittered.
'Health to Hrothgar! I am Hygelac's kinsman
and serve in his fellowship. Fame-winning deeds
have come early to my hands. The affair of Grendel
has been made known to me on my native turf.
The sailors speak of this splendid hall,
this most stately building, standing idle
and silent of voices, as soon as the evening light
has hidden below the heaven's bright edge.
Whereupon it was urged by the ablest men
among our people, men proved in counsel,
that I should seek you out, most sovereign Hrothgar.
These men knew well the weight of my hands.
Had they not seen me come home from fights
where I had bound five Giants – their blood was upon me –
cleaned out a nest of them? Had I not crushed on the wave
sea-serpents by night in narrow struggle,
broken the beasts? (The bane of the Geats,
they had asked for their trouble.) And shall *I* not try
a single match with this monster Grendel,
a trial against this troll?

                    To you I will now
put one request, Royal Scylding,
Shield of the South Danes, one sole favour
that you'll not deny me, dear lord of your people,
now that I have come thus far, Fastness of Warriors;
that I alone may be allowed, with my loyal and determined
crew of companions, to cleanse your hall Heorot.

As I am informed that this unlovely one
is careless enough to carry no weapon,
425 so that my lord Hygelac, my leader in war,
may take joy in me, I abjure utterly
the bearing of sword† or shielding yellow
board in this battle! With bare hands shall I
grapple with the fiend, fight to the death here,
430 hater and hated! He who is chosen
shall deliver himself to the Lord's judgement.

If he can contrive it, we may count upon Grendel
to eat quite fearlessly the flesh of Geats
here in this war-hall; has he not chewed
435 on the strength of this nation? There will be no need, Sir,
for you to bury my head; he will have me gladly,
if death should take me, though darkened with blood.
He will bear my bloody corpse away, bent on eating it,
make his meal alone, without misgiving,
440 bespatter his moor-lair. The disposing of my body
need occupy you no further then.
But if the fight should take me, you would forward to Hygelac
this best of battle-shirts, that my breast now wears.
The queen of war-coats, it is the bequest of Hrethel
445 and from the forge of Wayland.† Fate will take its course!'

Then Hrothgar spoke, the Helmet of the Scyldings:
'So it is to fight in our defence, my friend Beowulf,
and as an office of kindness that you have come to us here!
Great was the feud that your father set off
450 when his hand struck down Heatholaf† in death
among the Wylfings. The Weather-Geats
did not dare to keep him then, for dread of war,
and he left them to seek out the South-Danish folk,
the glorious Scyldings, across the shock of waters.
455 I had assumed sway over the Scylding nation
and in my youth ruled this rich kingdom,
storehouse of heroes. Heorogar was then dead,
the son of Healfdene had hastened from us,
my elder brother; a better man than I!

---

sword Beowulf nobly gives up the advantage conferred by arms
Wayland the smith of the gods
Heatholaf a Wylfing prince slain by Edgetheow. Hrothgar averted the revenge of the Wylfings by paying a *wergild* which would have been beyond the means of the Geats

460 I then settled the feud with fitting payment,
sent to the Wylfings over the water's back
old things of beauty; against which I'd the oath of your father. . . .

Yet sit now to the banquet, where you may soon attend,
should the mood so take you, some tale of victory.'

465 A bench was then cleared for the company of Geats
there in the beer-hall, for the whole band together.
The stout-hearted warriors went to their places,
bore their strength proudly. Prompt in his office,
the man who held the horn of bright mead
470 poured out its sweetness. The song of the poet
again rang in Heorot. The heroes laughed loud
in the great gathering of the Geats and the Danes.

[Here lines 499–641 of the original are omitted. Hrothgar's counsellor, Unferth, scoffs at Beowulf's vaunted victories over men and monsters at sea. Beowulf spiritedly vindicates his reputation as a swimmer and monster-slayer, and brands Unferth as a killer of kindred. Hrothgar's queen, Wealhtheow, brings the cup of hospitality to Beowulf, who again vows to kill Grendel or die in the attempt.]

Then at last Heorot heard once more
words of courage, the carousing of a people
475 singing their victories; till the son of Healfdene
desired at length to leave the feast,
be away to his night's rest; aware of the monster
brooding his attack on the tall-gabled hall
from the time they had seen the sun's lightness
480 to the time when darkness drowns everything
and under its shadow-cover shapes do glide
dark beneath the clouds. The company came to its feet.

Then did the heroes, Hrothgar and Beowulf,
salute each other; success he wished him,
485 control of the wine-hall, and with this word left him:
'Never since I took up targe and sword
have I at any instance to any man beside,
thus handed over Heorot, as I here do to you.
Have and hold now the House of the Danes!
490 Bend your mind and your body to this task
and wake against the foe! There'll be no want of liberality
if you come out alive from this ordeal of courage.'

Then Hrothgar departed, the Protector of the Danes
passed from the hall at the head of his troop.
495 The war-leader sought Wealhtheow his queen,
the companion of his bed.
                    Thus did the King of Glory,
to oppose this Grendel, appoint a hall-guard
– so the tale went abroad – who took on a special
task at the court – to cope with the monster.
500 The Geat prince placed all his trust
in his mighty strength, his Maker's favour.
He now uncased himself of his coat of mail,
unhelmed his head, handed his attendant
his embellished sword, best of weapons,
505 and bade him take care of these trappings of war.

Beowulf then made a boasting speech,
the Geat man, before mounting his bed:
'I fancy my fighting-strength, my performance in combat,
at least as greatly as Grendel does his;
510 and therefore I shall not cut short his life
with a slashing sword – too simple a business.
He has not the art to answer me in kind,
hew at my shield, shrewd though he be
at his nasty catches. No, we'll at night play
515 without any weapons – if unweaponed he dare
to face me in fight. The Father in His wisdom
shall apportion the honours then, the All-holy Lord,
to whichever side shall seem to Him fit.'

Then the hero lay down, leant his head
520 on the bolster there; about him many
brave sea-warriors bowed to their hall-rest.
Not one of them thought he would thence be departing
ever to set eyes on his own country,
the home that nourished him, or its noble people;
525 for they had heard how many men of the Danes
death had dragged from that drinking-hall.
But God was to grant to the Geat people
the clue to war-success in the web of fate –
His help and support; so that they all did
530 overcome the foe – through the force of one
unweaponed man. The Almighty Lord
has ruled the affairs of the race of men
thus from the beginning.

                    Gliding through the shadows came
            the walker in the night; the warriors slept
535   whose task was to hold the horned building,
            all except one. It was well-known to men
            that the demon could not drag them to the shades
            without God's willing it; yet the one man kept
            unblinking watch. He awaited, heart swelling
540   with anger against his foe, the ordeal of battle.
            Down off the moorlands' misting fells came
            Grendel stalking; God's brand was on him.
            The spoiler meant to snatch away
            from the high hall some of human race.
545   He came on under the clouds, clearly saw at last
            the gold-hall of men, the mead-drinking place
            nailed with gold plates. This was not the first visit
            he had paid to the hall of Hrothgar the Dane:
            he never before and never after
550   harder luck nor hall-guards found.

            Walking to the hall came this warlike creature
            condemned to agony. The door gave way,
            toughened with iron, at the touch of those hands.
            Rage-inflamed, wreckage-bent, he ripped open
555   the jaws of the hall. Hastening on,
            the foe then stepped onto the unstained floor,
            angrily advanced: out of his eyes stood
            an unlovely light like that of fire.
            He saw then in the hall a host of young soldiers,
560   a company of kinsmen caught away in sleep,
            a whole warrior-band. In his heart he laughed then,
            horrible monster, his hopes swelling
            to a gluttonous meal. He meant to wrench
            the life from each body that lay in the place
565   before night was done. It was not to be;
            he was no longer to feast on the flesh of mankind
            after that night.
                            Narrowly the powerful
            kinsman of Hygelac† kept watch how the ravager
            set to work with his sudden catches;
570   nor did the monster mean to hang back.

---

kinsman   Beowulf is Hygelac's nephew

         As a first step he set his hands on
         a sleeping soldier, savagely tore at him,
         gnashed at his bone-joints, bolted huge gobbets,
         sucked at his veins, and had soon eaten
575   all of the dead man, even down to his
         hands and feet.
                          Forward he stepped,
         stretched out his hands to seize the warrior
         calmly at rest there, reached out for him with his
         unfriendly fingers: but the faster man
580   forestalling, sat up, sent back his arm.
         The upholder of evils at once knew
         he had not met, on middle earth's
         extremest acres, with any man
         of harder hand-grip: his heart panicked.
585   He was quit of the place no more quickly for that.

         Eager to be away, he ailed for his darkness
         and the company of devils; the dealings he had there
         were like nothing he had come across in his lifetime.
         Then Hygelac's brave kinsman called to mind
590   that evening's utterance, upright he stood,
         fastened his hold till fingers were bursting.
         The monster strained away: the man stepped closer.
         The monster's desire was for darkness between them,
         direction regardless, to get out and run
595   for his fen-bordered lair; he felt his grip's strength
         crushed by his enemy. It was an ill journey
         the rough marauder had made to Heorot.

         The crash in the banqueting-hall came to the Danes,
         the men of the guard that remained in the building,
600   with the taste of death. The deepening rage
         of the claimants to Heorot caused it to resound.
         It was indeed wonderful that the wine-supper-hall
         withstood the wrestling pair, that the world's palace
         fell not to the ground. But it was girt firmly,
605   both inside and out, by iron braces
         of skilled manufacture. Many a figured
         gold-worked wine-bench, as we heard it,
         started from the floor at the struggles of that pair.

The men of the Danes had not imagined that
610 any of mankind by what method soever
might undo that intricate, antlered hall,
sunder it by strength – unless it were swallowed up in
the embraces of fire.†
                              Fear entered into
the listening North Danes, as that noise rose up again
615 strange and strident. It shrilled terror
to the ears that heard it through the hall's side-wall,
the grisly plaint of God's enemy,
his song of ill-success, the sobs of the damned one
bewailing his pain. He was pinioned there
620 by the man of all mankind living
in this world's estate the strongest of his hands.

Not for anything would the earls' guardian
let his deadly guest go living:
he did not count his continued existence
625 of the least use† to anyone. The earls ran
to defend the person of their famous prince;
they drew their ancestral swords to bring
what aid they could to their captain, Beowulf.
They were ignorant of this, when they entered the fight,
630 boldly-intentioned battle-friends,
to hew at Grendel, hunt his life
on every side – that no sword on earth,
not the truest steel, could touch their assailant;
for by a spell he had dispossessed all
635 blades of their bite on him.
                              A bitter parting
from life was that day destined for him;
the eldritch spirit was sent off on his
far faring into the fiends' domain.

It was then that this monster, who, moved by spite
640 against human kind, had caused so much harm
– so feuding with God – found at last
that flesh and bone were to fail him in the end;
for Hygelac's great-hearted kinsman
had him by the hand; and hateful to each
645 was the breath of the other.

---

fire   see note to line 74   *least use*   understatement: 'of any use'

                         A breach in the giant
flesh-frame showed then, shoulder-muscles
sprang apart, there was a snapping of tendons,
bone-locks burst. To Beowulf the glory
of this fight was granted; Grendel's lot
650 to flee the slopes fen-ward with flagging heart,
to a den where he knew there could be no relief,
no refuge for a life at its very last stage,
whose surrender-day had dawned. The Danish hopes
in this fatal fight had found their answer.

655 He had cleansed Heorot. He who had come from afar,
deep-minded, strong-hearted, had saved the hall
from persecution. He was pleased with his night's work,
the deed he had done. Before the Danish people
the Geat captain had made good his boast,
660 had taken away all their unhappiness,
the evil menace under which they had lived,
enduring it by dire constraint,
no slight affliction. As a signal to all
the hero hung up the hand, the arm
665 and torn-off shoulder, the entire limb,
Grendel's whole grip, below the gable of the roof.

There was, as I heard it, at hall next morning
a great gathering in the gift-hall yard
to see the wonder. Along the wide highroads
670 the chiefs of the clans came from near and far
to see the foe's footprints. It may fairly be said
that his parting from life aroused no pity in any
who tracked the spoor-blood of his blind flight
for the monster's mere-pool;† with mood flagging
675 and strength crushed, he had staggered onwards;
each step evidenced his ebbing life's-blood.

The tarn was troubled; a terrible wave-thrash
brimmed it, bubbling; black-mingled,
the warm wound-blood welled upwards.
680 He had dived to his doom, he had died miserably;
here in his fen-lair he had laid aside
his heathen soul. Hell welcomed it.

---

mere-pool   Grendel (and his mother) live at the
bottom of a mere, a deep pool on the moors

Then the older retainers turned back on the way
journeyed with much joy; joined by the young men,
685   the warriors on white horses wheeled away from the mere
in bold mood. Beowulf's feat
was much spoken of, and many said,
that between the seas, south or north,
over earth's stretch no other man
690   beneath the sky's shifting excelled Beowulf,
of all who wielded the sword he was worthiest to rule.
In saying this they did not slight in the least
the gracious Hrothgar, for he was a good king.

Where, as they went, their way broadened
695   they would match their mounts, making them leap
along the best stretches, the strife-eager
on their fallow horses. Or a fellow of the king's,
whose head was a storehouse of the storied verse,
whose tongue gave gold to the language
700   of the treasured repertory, wrought a new lay
made in the measure. The man struck up,
found the phrase, framed rightly
the deed of Beowulf, drove the tale,
rang word-changes.

[Here lines 874–915 of the original are omitted. The Danish poet now tells of the greatest of dragon-slayers, Sigemund, who took away the dragon's gold (and later died from the curse placed upon it). Beowulf is then compared favourably with a previous Danish King, Heremod, who went mad with arrogance and greed.]

705   The riders returning came racing their horses
along dusty-pale roads. The dawn had grown
into broadest day, and, drawn by their eagerness
to see the strange sight, there had assembled at the hall
many keen warriors. The king himself,
710   esteemed for excellence, stepped glorious
from his wife's chambers, the warden of ring-hoards,
with much company; and his queen walked
the mead-path by him, her maidens following.

            Taking his stand on the steps of the hall,
715   Hrothgar beheld the hand of Grendel
            below the gold gable-end; and gave speech:
            'Let swift thanks be given to the Governor of All,
            seeing this sight! I have suffered a thousand
            spites from Grendel: but God works ever
720   miracle upon miracle, the Master of Heaven.
            Until yesterday I doubted whether
            our afflictions would find a remedy
            in my lifetime, since this loveliest of halls
            stood slaughter-painted, spattered with blood.
725   For all my counsellors this was a cruel sorrow,
            for none of them imagined they could mount a defence
            of the Scylding stronghold against such enemies,
            warlocks, demons!
                                            But one man has,
            by the Lord's power, performed the thing
730   that all our thought and arts to this day
            had failed to do. She may indeed say,
            whoever she be that brought into the world
            this young man here – if yet she lives –
            that the God of Old was gracious to her
735   in her child-bearing. Beowulf, I now take you
            to my bosom as a son, O best of men,
            and cherish you in my heart. Hold yourself well
            in this new relation! You will lack for nothing
            that lies in my gift of the goods of this world:
740   lesser offices have elicited reward,
            we have honoured from our hoard less heroic men,
            far weaker in war. But you have well ensured
            by the deeds of your hands an undying honour
            for your name for ever. May the Almighty Father
745   yield you always the success that you yesternight enjoyed!'

            Beowulf spoke, son of Edgetheow:
            'We willingly undertook this test of courage,
            risked a match with the might of the stranger,
            and performed it all. I would prefer, though,
750   that you had rather seen the rest of him here,
            the whole length of him, lying here dead.

I had meant to catch him, clamp him down
with a cruel lock to his last resting-place;
with my hands upon him, I would have him soon
755 in the throes of death – unless he disappeared!
But I had not a good enough grip to prevent
his getting away, when God did not wish it;
the fiend in his flight was far too violent,
my life's enemy. But he left his hand
760 behind him here, so as to have his life,
and his arm and shoulder. And all for nothing:
it brought him no respite, wretched creature.
He lives no longer, laden with sins,
to plague mankind: pain has set
765 heavy hands on him, and hasped about him
fatal fetters. He is forced to await now,
like a guilty criminal, a greater judgement,
where the Lord in His splendour shall pass sentence upon him.'

The son of Edgelaf† was more silent then
770 in boasting of his own battle-deeds:
the athelings gazed at what the earl's strength
had hung there – the hand, high up under the roof,
and the fingers of their foe. From the front, each one
of the nail-sockets seemed steel to the eye,
775 each spur on the hand of that heathen warrior
was a terrible talon. They told each other
nothing could be hard enough to harm it at all,
not the most ancient of iron swords
would bite on that bloody battle-hand.

780 Other hands were then pressed to prepare the inside
of the banqueting-hall, and briskly too.
Many were ready, both men and women,
to adorn the guest-hall. Gold-embroidered tapestries
glowed from the walls, with wonderful sights
785 for every creature that cared to look at them.

---

son of Edgelaf Unferth (see the editorial note
following line 472)

The bright building had badly started
in all its inner parts, despite its iron bands,
and the hinges were ripped off. Only the roof survived
unmarred and in one piece when the monstrous one,
flecked with his crimes, had fled the place
in despair of his life.
                    But to elude death
is not easy: attempt it who will,
he shall go to the place prepared for each
of the sons of men, the soul-bearers
dwelling on earth, ordained them by fate:
laid fast in that bed, the body shall sleep
when the feast is done.
                    In due season
the king himself came to the hall;
Healfdene's son would sit at the banquet.
No people has gathered in greater retinue,
borne themselves better about their ring-giver.

Men known for their courage came to the benches,
rejoiced in the feast; they refreshed themselves kindly
with many a mead-cup; in their midst the brave kinsmen,
father's brother and brother's son,
Hrothgar and Hrothulf. Heorot's floor was
filled with friends: falsity in those days†
had no place in the dealings of the Danish people.

[Here lines 1020–1159a of the original are omitted. Hrothgar gives Beowulf arms and horses, and compensates and rewards the Geats. Hrothgar's bard then tells how the marriage of a Danish princess to Finn, the Frisian, failed to heal an ancient feud between the peoples. Finn treacherously attacked Danish guests in Finnsburgh. The Danish hero Hengest avenged the murder of the princess's brother and her son (this is probably Hengest the Jute who conquered Kent in the mid-fifth century).]

---

in those days a hint that Hrothulf will usurp
the throne after Hrothgar's death

                              Thus the story was sung,
810   the gleeman's lay. Gladness mounted,
      bench-mirth rang out, the bearers gave
      wine from wonderful vessels. Then came Wealhtheow forward,
      going with golden crown to where the great heroes
      were sitting, uncle and nephew;† their bond was sound at that time,
815   each was true to the other. Likewise Unferth the spokesman
      sat at the footstool of Hrothgar. All had faith in his spirit,
      accounted his courage great – though to his kinsmen he had not been
      kind at the clash of swords.
                          The Scylding queen then spoke:
      'Accept this cup, my king and lord,
820   giver of treasure. Let your gaiety be shown,
      gold-friend of warriors, and to the Geats speak
      in words of friendship, for this well becomes a man.
      Be gracious to these Geats, and let the gifts you have had
      from near and far, not be forgotten now.

825   I hear it is your wish to hold this warrior
      henceforward as your son. Heorot is cleansed,
      the ring-hall bright again: therefore bestow while you may
      these blessings liberally, and leave to your kinsmen
      the land and its people when your passing is decreed,
830   your meeting with fate. For may I not count
      on my gracious Hrothulf to guard honourably
      our young ones here, if you, my lord,
      should give over this world earlier than he?
      I am sure that he will show to our children
835   answerable kindness, if he keeps in remembrance
      all that we have done to indulge and advance him,
      the honours we bestowed on him when he was still a child.'

      Then she turned to the bench where her boys were sitting,
      Hrethric and Hrothmund,† among the heroes' sons,
840   young men together; where the good man sat also
      between the two brothers, Beowulf the Geat.

---

uncle and nephew literally, father's brother and brother's son – a sacred relationship in Germanic heroic society. Hrothgar and his nephew Hrothulf sit with Unferth, who has slain his own kin

Hrethric and Hrothmund Hrothgar's sons. Though Beowulf, adopted as their brother, sits with them, they are later to be slain (according to tradition) by Hrothulf. Wealhtheow's hopes are to be disappointed

Then the cup was taken to him and he was entreated kindly
to honour their feast; ornate gold
was presented in trophy; two arm-wreaths,
845 with robes and rings also, and the richest collar
I have ever heard of in all the world.

[Here lines 1197–1214a of the original are omitted. The golden collar
is compared to one made by the Brising fire-dwarves and later stolen
by Eormanric. Beowulf's prize is to be presented to his lord Hygelac
and to be lost at Hygelac's death in battle.]

                        Applause filled the hall;
then Wealhtheow spoke, and her words were attended.

'Take pride in this jewel, have joy of this mantle
850 drawn from our treasuries, most dear Beowulf!
May fortune come with them and may you flourish in your youth!
Proclaim your strength; but in counsel to these boys
be a gentle guardian, and my gratitude will be seen.
Already you have so managed that men everywhere
855 will hold you in honour for all time,
even to the cliffs at the world's end, washed by Ocean,
the wind's range. All the rest of your life
must be happy, prince; and prosperity I wish you too,
abundance of treasure! But be to my son
860 a friend in deed, most favoured of men.
You see how open is each earl here with his neighbour,
temperate of heart, and true to his lord.
The nobles are loyal, the lesser people dutiful;
wine mellows the men to move to my bidding.'

865 She walked back to her place. What a banquet that was!
The men drank their wine: the weird they did not know,
destined from of old, the doom that was to fall
on many of the earls there. When evening came
Hrothgar departed to his private bower,
870 the king to his couch; countless were the men
who watched over the hall, as they had often done before.
They cleared away the benches, and covered the floor
with beds and bolsters: the best at the feast
bent to his hall-rest, hurried to his doom.

875   Each by his head placed his polished shield,
        the lindens of battle. On the benches aloft,
        above each atheling, easily to be seen,
        were the ring-stitched mail-coat, the mighty helmet
        steepling above the fray, and the stout spear-shaft.
880   It was their habit always, at home or on campaign,
        to be ready for war, in whichever case,
        whatsoever the hour might be
        that the need came on their lord: what a nation they were!

[Here lines 1231–2208a of the original are omitted. Grendel's mother avenges Grendel's death by carrying off Hrothgar's friend Ashhere to the Mere. Beowulf is led by the Danes to the Mere, where he kills the ogress in an underwater fight. He takes the head of Grendel back to Heorot, where the Danes are feasting. Hrothgar makes a speech of thanks, warning Beowulf against pride and complacency. The hero returns with his prizes to the court of Hygelac the Geat in southern Sweden and recounts his adventures. After the deaths of Hygelac and his son Heardred, the guardianship of the kingdom of the Geats comes to Beowulf.]

                      Half a century
885   he ruled it, well: until One began
        – the king had grown grey in the guardianship of the land –
        to put forth his power in the pitch-black night-times
        – the hoard-guarding Dragon† of a high barrow
        raised above the moor.
                      Men did not know
890   of the way underground to it; but one man did enter,
        went right inside, reached the treasure,
        the heathen hoard, and his hand fell
        on a golden goblet. The guardian, however,
        if he had been caught sleeping by the cunning of the thief,
895   did not conceal this loss. It was not long till the near-
        dwelling people discovered that the dragon was angry.

---

hoard-guarding Dragon   dragons are traditionally the jealous guardians of gold.   For the next 20 lines the MS is damaged and some readings are conjectural

The causer of his pain had not purposed this;
it was without relish that he had robbed the hoard;
necessity drove him. The nameless slave
900 of one of the warriors, wanting shelter,
on the run from a flogging, had felt his way inside,
a sin-tormented soul. When he saw what was there
the intruder was seized with sudden terror;
but for all his fear, the unfortunate wretch
905 still took the golden treasure-cup . . . .
There were heaps of hoard-things in this hall underground
which once in gone days gleamed and rang;
the treasure of a race rusting derelict.

In another age an unknown man,
910 brows bent, had brought and hid here
the beloved hoard. The whole race
death-rapt, and of the ring of earls
one left alive; living on in that place
heavy with friend-loss, the hoard-guard
915 waited the same weird. His wit acknowledged
that the treasures gathered and guarded over the years
were his for the briefest while.
                              The barrow stood ready
on flat ground where breakers beat at the headland,
new, near at hand, made narrow of access.
920 The keeper of rings carried into it
the earls' holdings, the hoard-worthy part
fraught with gold, and few words he spoke:

'Hold, ground,† the gold of the earls!
Men could not. Cowards they were not
925 who took it from thee once, but war-death took them,
that stops life, struck them, spared not one
man of my people, passed on now.
They have had their hall-joys. I have not with me
a man able to unsheathe this. . . .
930 Who shall polish this plated vessel,
this treasured cup? The company is elsewhere.

Hold, ground Compare the views of treasure in *The Ruin* and the final speech in *The Wanderer*. The last survivor of this heroic race is a 'hoard-guard'; his successor is the 'hoard-guarding' dragon

        This hardened helmet healed with gold
shall lose its shell. They sleep now
whose work was to burnish the battle-masks;
935   so with the cuirass that in the crash took
bite of iron among breaking shields:
it moulders with the man. This mail-shirt travelled far,
hung from a shoulder shouldered warriors:
it shall not jingle again.
                        There's no joy from harp-play,
940   glee-wood's gladness, no good hawk
swings through hall now, no swift horse
tramps at the threshold. Terrible slaughter
has carried into darkness many kindreds of mankind.'

        So the sole survivor, in sorrowful mood,
945   bewailed his grief; he wandered cheerless
through days and nights until death's flood
reached to his heart.
                     The Ravager of the night,
the burner who has sought out barrows from of old,
then found this hoard of undefended joy.
950   The smooth evil dragon swims through the gloom
enfolded in flame; the folk of that country
hold him in dread. He is doomed to seek out
hoards in the ground, and guard for an age there
the heathen gold: much good does it do him!

955   Thus for three hundred winters this waster of peoples
guarded underground the great hoard-hall
with his enormous might; until a man awoke
the anger in his breast by bearing to his master
the plated goblet as a peace-offering,
960   a token of new fealty. Thus the treasure was lightened
and the treasure-house was breached; the boon was granted
to the luckless slave, and his lord beheld
for the first time that work of a former race of men.

        The waking of the worm awoke the feud:
965   he glided along the rock, glared at the sight
of a foeman's footprint: far too near his head
the intruder had stepped as he stole by him!

(An undoomed man may endure affliction
and even exile lightly, for as long as the Ruler
continues to protect him.) The treasure-guard eagerly
quartered the ground to discover the man
who had done him wrong during his sleep.
Seething with rage, he circled the barrow's
whole outer wall, but no hint of a man
showed in the wilderness. Yet war's prospect pleased him,
the thought of battle-action! He went back into the mound
to search for the goblet, and soon saw that one
of the tribe of men had tampered with the gold
of the glorious hoard.
                         The hoard's guardian
waited until evening only with difficulty.
The barrow-keeper was bursting with rage:
his fire would cruelly requite the loss
of the dear drinking-vessel.
                         At last day was gone,
to the worm's delight; he delayed no further
inside his walls, but issued forth flaming,
armed with fire.
                 That was a fearful beginning
for the people of that country; uncomfortable and swift
was the end to be likewise for their lord and treasure-giver!

So the visitant began to vomit flames
and burn the bright dwellings; the blazing rose skyward
and men were afraid: the flying scourge
did not mean to leave one living thing.
On every side the serpent's ravages,
the spite of the foe, sprang to the eye —
how this hostile assailant hated and injured
the men of the Geats. Before morning's light
he flew back to the hoard in his hidden chamber.
He had poured out fire and flame on the people,
he had put them to the torch; he trusted now to the barrow's walls
and to his fighting strength; his faith misled him.

Beowulf was acquainted quickly enough
with the truth of the horror, for his own hall had itself
been swallowed in flame, the finest of buildings,
and the gift-stool of the Geats. Grief then struck
into his ample heart with anguished keenness.

The chieftain supposed he had sorely angered
the Ruler of all, the eternal Lord,
by breach of ancient law. His breast was thronged
with dark unaccustomed care-filled thoughts.
1010 The fiery dragon's flames had blasted
all the land by the sea, and its safe stronghold,
the fortress of the people. The formidable king
of the Geats now planned to punish him for this.

The champion of the fighting-men, chief of the earls,
1015 gave commands for the making of a marvellous shield
worked all in iron; well he knew
that a linden shield would be of little service
– wood against fire. For the foremost of athelings
the term of his days in this transitory world
1020 was soon to be endured; it was the end, too, for the dragon's
long watch over the wealth of the hoard.

The distributor of rings disdained to go
with a troop of men or a mighty host
to seek the far-flier. He had no fear for himself
1025 and discounted the worm's courage and strength,
its prowess in battle. Battles in plenty
he had survived; valiant in all dangers,
he had come through many clashes since his cleansing of Heorot
and his extirpation of the tribe of Grendel,
1030 hated race.

[Here lines 2354b–96 of the original are omitted. Beowulf had survived the fateful raid on Friesland in which Hygelac was killed (a historical event which occurred in 521 AD). He had swum away with thirty men's mailcoats on his arm. But he refused the throne of the Geats, preferring to serve Heardred, Hygelac's son, succeeding him when he was killed by Onela, who had usurped the Swedish throne. Beowulf later upheld the rightful claims of Onela's nephews.]

So the son of Edgetheow survived unscathed
each of these combats, calamitous onslaughts,
works of prowess: until this one day
when he must wage war on the serpent.
1035 The Lord of the Geats went with eleven companions
to set eyes on the dragon; his anger rose in him.

He had by then discovered the cause of the attack
that had ravaged his people; the precious drinking-cup
had passed into his hands from the hands of the finder.
1040 He who had brought about the beginning of the feud
now made the thirteenth man in their company;
a miserable captive; cowed, he must show them
the way to the place, an unwilling guide.
For he alone knew the knoll and its earth-hall,
1045 hard by the strand and the strife of the waves,
the underground hollow heaped to the roof
with intricate treasures. Attendant on the gold
was that underground ancient, eager as a wolf,
an awesome guardian; it was no easy bargain
1050 for any mortal man to make himself its owner.

The stern war-king sat on the headland,
spoke encouragement to the companions of his hearth,
the gold-friend of the Geats. Gloomy was his spirit though,
death-eager, wandering; the weird was at hand
1055 that was to overcome the old man there,
seek his soul's hoard, and separate
the life from the body; not for long now
would the atheling's life be lapped in flesh.

Beowulf spoke, son of Edgetheow:
1060 'Many were the struggles I survived in youth
in times of danger; I do not forget them.
When that open-handed lord beloved by the people
received me from my father I was seven years old:
King Hrethel† kept and fostered me,
1065 gave me treasure and table-room, true to our kinship.
All his life he had as little hatred† for me,
a warrior in hall, as he had for a son,
Herebeald, or Hathkin, or Hygelac my own lord. . . .'

[Here lines 2435–2510 of the original are omitted. Beowulf recalls how Herebeald was accidentally killed by an arrow shot by his brother Hathkin. The father Hrethel died of grief, unable either to avenge his son or to exact *wergild* (legal compensation). On Hrethel's death the Swedes attacked the Geats from the north, killing Hathkin but losing their own king Ongentheow. Beowulf had served as Hygelac's champion and had slain Dryraven, the champion of the Franks.]

Hrethel   the patriarch of the Geats, Beowulf's maternal grandfather

as little hatred   as much love

Beowulf made speech, spoke a last time
1070 a word of boasting: 'Battles in plenty
I ventured in youth; and I shall venture this feud
and again achieve glory, the guardian of my people,
old though I am, if this evil destroyer
dares to come out of his earthen hall.'

1075 Then he addressed each of the men there
on this last occasion, courageous helm-bearers,
cherished companions: 'I would choose not to take
any weapon to this worm, if I well knew
of some other fashion fitting to my boast
1080 of grappling with this monster, as with Grendel before.
But as I must expect here the hot war-breath
of venom and fire, for this reason I have
my board and corselet. From the keeper of the barrow
I shall not flee one foot; but further than that
1085 shall be worked out at the wall as Weird shall decide for us,
every man's master. My mood is strong;
I forgo further words against the winged fighter.

    Men in armour! Your mail-shirts protect you:
await on the barrow the one of us two
1090 who shall be better able to bear his wounds
after this onslaught. This affair is not for you,
nor is it measured to any man but myself alone
to match strength with this monstrous being,
attempt this deed. By daring will I
1095 win this gold; war otherwise
shall take your king, terrible life's-bane!'

The strong champion stood up beside his shield,
brave beneath helmet, he bore his mail-shirt
to the rocky cliff's foot, confident in his strength,
1100 a single man; such is not the coward's way!
Then did the survivor of a score of conflicts,
the battle-clashes of encountering armies,
excelling in manhood, see in the wall
a stone archway,† and out of the barrow broke
1105 a stream surging through it, a stream of fire
with waves of deadly flame; the dragon's breath
meant he could not venture into the vault near the hoard
for any time at all without being burnt.

---

stone archway   the barrow is a stone structure
    covered by earth

Passion filled the prince of the Geats:
1110 he allowed a cry to utter from his breast,
roared from his stout heart: as the horn clear in battle
his voice re-echoed through the vault of grey stone.
The hoard-guard recognised a human voice,
and there was no more time for talk of friendship:
1115 hatred stirred. Straightaway
the breath of the dragon billowed from the rock
in a hissing gust; the ground boomed.

He swung up his shield, overshadowed by the mound,
the lord of the Geats against this grisly stranger.
1120 The temper of the twisted tangle-thing was fired
to close now in battle. The brave warrior-king
shook out his sword so sharp of edge,
an ancient heirloom. Each of the pair,
intended destruction, felt terror at the other:
1125 intransigent beside his towering shield
the lord of friends, while the fleetness of the serpent
wound itself together; he waited in his armour.
It came flowing forward, flaming and coiling,
rushing on its fate.
                  For the famous prince
1130 the protection lent to his life and person
by the shield was shorter than he had shaped it to be.
He must now dispute this space of time,
the first in his life when fate had not assigned him
the glory of the battle. The Geat chieftain
1135 raised his hand, and reached down such a stroke
with his huge ancestral sword on the horribly-patterned snake
that, meeting the bone, its bright edge turned
and it bit less strongly than its sorely-straitened lord
required of it then. The keeper of the barrow
1140 after this stroke grew savage in mood,
spat death-fire; the sparks of their battle
blazed into the distance.
                       He boasted of no triumphs then,
the gold-friend of the Geats, for his good old sword
bared in the battle, his blade, had failed him,
1145 as such iron should not do.

                            That was no easy adventure,
when the celebrated son of Edgetheow
had to pass from that place on earth
and against his will take up his dwelling
in another place; as every man must give up
1150 the days that are lent him.
                            It was not long again
to the next meeting of those merciless ones.
The barrow-guard took heart: his breast heaved
with fresh out-breath: fire enclosed
the former folk-king; he felt bitter pain.

1155 The band of picked companions did not come
to stand about him, as battle-usage asks,
offspring of athelings; they escaped to the wood,
saved their lives.†
                            Sorrow filled
the breast of one man. The bonds of kinship
1160 nothing may remove for a man who thinks rightly.
This was Wiglaf,† Weoxstan's son,
well-loved shieldsman, a Scylfing prince
of the stock of Alfhere; he could see his lord
tormented by the heat through his mask of battle.
1165 He remembered then the favours he had formerly bestowed on him,
the wealthy dwelling-place of the Waymundings,†
confirming him in the landrights his father had held.
He could not then hold back: hand gripped the yellow
linden-wood shield, shook out that ancient
1170 sword that Eanmund,† Ohthere's son,
had left among men.

[Here lines 2612b–25a of the original are omitted. Eanmund's sword came to his killer, Weoxstan; and descended to Wiglaf.]

---

saved their lives   see *Maldon*, line 185

Wiglaf   a prince of the Scylfing dynasty of Sweden, Wiglaf acts as a kinsman of Beowulf

Waymundings   Wiglaf's family, to which Beowulf is also connected

Eanmund   son of Ohthere, the son of Ongentheow the Swede. Eanmund had taken refuge with the Geats after his uncle Onela had seized the throne. Eanmund was killed by Weoxstan, Wiglaf's father, who was fighting for Onela, from whom he received Eanmund's sword as a prize. The history of the sword which first wounds the dragon is complex, involving the divided loyalties of a family on the border between warring peoples

                        For the youthful warrior
        this was the first occasion when he was called on to stand
        at his dear lord's shoulder in the shock of battle.
1175   His courage did not crumble, nor did his kinsman's heirloom
        weaken at the war-play; as the worm found out
        when they had got to grips with one another.

        Wiglaf then spoke many words that were fitting,
        addressed his companions; dark was his mood.
1180   'I remember the time, as we were taking mead
        in the banqueting hall, when we bound ourselves
        to the gracious lord who granted us arms,
        that we would make return for these trappings of war,
        these helms and hard swords, if an hour such as this
1185   should ever chance for him. He chose us himself
        out of all his host for this adventure here,
        expecting action; he armed me with you
        because he accounted us keen under helmet,
        men able with the spear – even though our lord
1190   intended to take on this task of courage
        as his own share, as shepherd of the people,
        and champion of mankind in the achieving of glory
        and deeds of daring.
                        That day has now come
        when he stands in need of the strength of good fighters,
1195   our lord and liege. Let us go to him,
        help our leader for as long as it requires,
        the fearsome fire-blast. I had far rather
        that the flame should enfold my flesh-frame there
        alongside my gold-giver – as God knows of me.
1200   To bear our shields back to our homes
        would seem unfitting to me, unless first we have been able
        to kill the foe and defend the life
        of the prince of the Weather-Geats. I well know
        that former deeds deserve not that, alone
1205   of the flower of the Geats, he should feel the pain,
        sink in the struggle; sword and helmet,
        corselet and mail-shirt, shall be our common gear.'

        He strode through the blood-smoke, bore his war-helmet
        to the aid of his lord, uttered few words:
1210   'Beloved Beowulf, bear all things well!

You gave it out long ago in your youth
that, living, you would not allow your glory
ever to abate. Bold-tempered chieftain,
famed for your deeds, you must defend your life now
1215 with all your strength. I shall help you.'

When these words had been spoken, the worm came on wrathful,
attacked a second time, terrible visitant,
sought out his foes in a surge of flame,
the hated men.
          Mail-shirt did not serve
1220 the young spear-man; and shield was withered
back to the boss by the billow of fire;
but when the blazing had burnt up his own,
the youngster stepped smartly to take
the cover of his kinsman's. Then did that kingly warrior
1225 remember his deeds again and dealt out a sword-blow
with his full strength: it struck into the head
with annihilating weight. But Nailing† snapped,
failed in the battle, Beowulf's sword
of ancient grey steel. It was not granted to him
1230 that an iron edge could ever lend him
help in a battle; his hand was too strong.
I have heard that any sword, however hardened by wounds,
that he bore into battle, his blow would overtax
– any weapon whatever; it was the worse for him.

1235 A third time the terrible fire-drake
remembered the feud. The foe of the people
rushed in on the champion when a chance offered:
seething with warspite, he seized his whole neck
between bitter fangs: blood covered him,
1240 Beowulf's life-blood, let in streams.
Then I heard how the earl alongside the king
in the hour of need made known the valour,
boldness and strength that were bred in him.
His hand burned as he helped his kinsman,
1245 but the brave soldier in his splendid armour
ignored the head and hit the attacker
somewhat below it, so that the sword went in,
flashing-hilted; and the fire began
to slacken in consequence.

Nailing this is the second sword to fail Beowulf in fighting a monster: Hrunting, Unferth's sword, had been useless against Grendel's mother

                    The king once more
1250 took command of his wits, caught up a stabbing-knife
      of the keenest battle-sharpness, that he carried in his harness:
      and the Geats' Helm struck through the serpent's body.

      So daring drove out life: they had downed their foe
      by common action, the atheling pair,
1255 and had made an end of him. So in the hour of need
      a warrior must live. For the lord this was
      the last victory in the list of his deeds
      and works in the world. The wound that the earth-drake
      had first succeeded in inflicting on him
1260 began to burn and swell; he swiftly felt
      the bane beginning to boil in his chest,
      the poison within him. The prince walked across
      to the side of the barrow, considering deeply;
      he sat down on a ledge, looked at the giant-work,†
1265 saw how the age-old earth-hall contained
      stone arches anchored on pillars.
      Then that excellent thane with his own hands washed
      his battle-bloodied prince, bathed with water
      the famous leader, his friend and lord,
1270 sated with fighting; he unfastened his helmet.

      Beowulf spoke; he spoke through the pain
      of his fatal wound. He well knew
      that he had come to the end of his allotted days,
      his earthly happiness; all the number
1275 of his days had disappeared: death was very near.
      'I would now wish to give my garments in battle
      to my own son, if any such
      after-inheritor, an heir of my body,
      had been granted to me. I have guarded this people
1280 for half a century; not a single ruler
      of all the nations neighbouring about
      has dared to affront me with his friends in war,
      or threaten terrors. What the times had in store for me
      I awaited in my homeland; I held my own,
1285 sought no secret feud, swore very rarely†
      a wrongful oath. In all of these things,
      sick with my life's wound, I may still rejoice:

---

giant-work anything of seemingly superhuman manufacture, especially building in stone, was attributed to giants

very rarely that is, never

    for when my life shall leave my body
    the Ruler of Men may not charge me
1290 with the slaughter of kinsmen.
          Quickly go now,
    beloved Wiglaf, and look upon the hoard
    under the grey stone, now the serpent lies dead,
    sleeps rawly wounded, bereft of his treasure.
    Make haste, that I may gaze upon that golden inheritance,
1295 that ancient wealth; that my eyes may behold
    the clear skilful jewels: more calmly then may I
    on the treasure's account take my departure
    of life and of the lordship I have long held.'

    Straightaway, as I have heard, the son of Weoxstan
1300 obeyed his wounded lord, weak from the struggle.
    Following these words, he went in his ring-coat,
    his broidered battle-tunic, under the barrow's roof.
    Traversing the ledge to the treasure-house of jewels
    the brave young thane was thrilled by the sight
1305 of the gold gleaming on the ground where it lay,
    the devices by the wall and the den of the serpent,
    winger of the darkness. Drinking-cups stood there,
    the unburnished vessels of a vanished race,
    their ornaments awry. Old and tarnished
1310 were the rows of helmets and the heaps of arm-rings,
    twisted with cunning. Treasure can easily,
    gold in the ground, get the better of
    one of human race, hide it who will!
    High above the hoard there hung, as he also saw,
1315 a standard all woven wonderfully in gold,
    the finest of finger-linkages: the effulgence it gave
    allowed him to see the surface of the ground
    and examine the treasures. No trace of the worm
    was to be seen there, for the sword had finished him.

1320 I heard of the plundering of the hoard in the knoll,
    that ancient Giant-work, by that one man;
    he filled his bosom with such flagons and vessels
    as he himself chose; he took the standard also,
    best of banners.

                    Old Beowulf's sword,
1325 iron of edge, had already struck
the creature who had been keeper of the treasures
for so long an age, employing his fire-blast
in the hoard's defence, flinging out its heat
in the depth of the nights; he died at last, violently.

1330 The envoy made haste in his eagerness to return,
urged on by his prizes. He was pressed by anxiety
as to whether he would find his fearless man,
the lord of the Geats, alive in the open
where he had left him, lacking in strength.
1335 Carrying the treasures, he came upon his prince,
the famous king, covered in blood
and at his life's end: again he began
to sprinkle him with water, until this word's point
broke through the breast-hoard.
                                    The battle-king spoke,
1340 an aged man in sorrow; he eyed the gold.
'I wish to put in words my thanks
to the King of Glory, the Giver of All,
the Lord of Eternity, for these treasures that I see,
that I should have been able to acquire for my people
1345 before my death-day an endowment such as this.
My life's full portion I have paid out now
for this hoard of treasure; you must attend to the people's
needs henceforward; no further may I stay.
Bid men of battle build me a tomb
1350 fair after fire, on the foreland by the sea
that shall stand as a reminder of me to my people,
towering high above Hronesness†
so that ocean travellers shall afterwards name it
Beowulf's barrow, bending in the distance
1355 their masted ships through the mists upon the sea.'

He unclasped the golden collar from his neck,
staunch-hearted prince, and passed it to the thane,
with the gold-plated helmet, harness and arm-ring;
he bade the young spear-man use them well:

Hronesness a headland in Geatland
  (*hron* whale)

1360 'You are the last man left of our kindred,
the house of the Waymundings! Weird has lured
each of my family to his fated end,
each earl through his valour; I must follow them.'

This was the aged man's uttermost word
1365 from the thoughts of his breast; he embraced the pyre's
seething surges; soul left its case,
going its way to the glory of the righteous.

[Here lines 2821–959 of the original are omitted. The hero and the dragon are dead. Wiglaf vainly tries to awaken his lord with water as the ten Geats approach.]

There was a rough and a ready answer
on the young man's lips for those who had lost their nerve;
1370 Wiglaf spoke, Weoxstan's offspring,
looked at them unlovingly, and with little joy at heart:
'A man who would speak the truth may say with justice
that a lord of men who allowed you those treasures,
who bestowed on you the trappings that you stand there in
1375 – as, at the ale-bench, he would often give
to those who sat in hall both helmet and mail-shirt
as a lord to his thanes, and things of the most worth
that he was able to find anywhere in the world
– that he had quite thrown away and wasted cruelly
1380 all that battle-harness when the battle came upon him.
The king of our people had no cause to boast
of his companions of the guard. Yet God vouchsafed him,
The Master of Victories, that he should avenge himself
when courage was wanted, by his weapon single-handed.
1385 I was little equipped to act as body-guard
for him in the battle, but, above my own strength,
I began all the same to support my kinsman.
Our deadly enemy grew ever the weaker –
when I had struck him with my sword – less strongly welled
1390 the fire from his head. Too few supporters
flocked to our prince when affliction came.

Now there shall cease for your race the receiving of treasure,
the bestowal of swords, all satisfaction of ownership,
all comfort of home. Your kinsmen every one,
1395 shall become wanderers without land-rights
as soon as athelings over the world
shall hear the report of how you fled,
a deed of ill fame. Death is better
for any earl than an existence of disgrace!'

1400 He bade that the combat's result be proclaimed in the city
over the brow of the headland: there the band of earls
had sat all morning beside their shields
in heavy spirits, half expecting
that it would be the last day of their beloved man,
1405 half hoping for his return. The rider from the headland
in no way held back the news he had to tell;
as his commission was, he called out over all:
'The Lord of the Geats lies now on his slaughter-bed,
the leader of the Weathers, our loving provider,
1410 dwells in his death-rest through the dragon's power.
Stretched out beside him, stricken with the knife,
lies his deadly adversary. With the edge of the sword
he could not contrive, try as he might,
to wound the monster. Weoxstan's son
1415 Wiglaf abides with Beowulf there,
one earl waits on the other one lifeless;
in weariness of heart he watches by the heads
of friend and foe.
                The fall of the king,
when it spreads abroad and is spoken of
1420 among the Frisians and the Franks,† forebodes a time
of wars for our people. The war against the Hugas
had a hard beginning when Hygelac sailed
into the land of the Frisians with his fleet-army:
there it was that the Hetware hurled themselves upon him
1425 and with their greater strength stoutly compelled
that battle-clad warrior to bow before them;

Frisians and the Franks the Frisians, as part of the Merovingian Frankish empire, will avenge the attack Hygelac made on them. The messenger then recalls vividly the bitter First Swedish War, in which Ongentheow killed Hathkin but was himself slain by Hygelac's thanes. The Hugas (1421) is a name for the Franks; the Hetware (1424) are associates of the Frisians

he fell among the troop, distributed no arms
as lord to the guard. It has not been granted to us since
to receive mercy from the Merovingian king.

[Here lines 2921–98 of the original are omitted. The messenger recalls the killing of Hathkin by Ongentheow the Swede, and how Ongentheow was killed in turn by the thanes of Hygelac.]

1430 It is this feud, this fierce hostility,
this murder-lust between men, I am moved to think,
that the Swedish people will prosecute against us
when once they learn that life has fled
from the lords of the Geats, guardian for so long
1435 of hoard and kingdom, of keen shield-warriors
against every foe. Since the fall of the princes†
he has taken care of our welfare, and accomplished yet more
heroic deeds.
      Haste is best now,
that we should go to look on the lord of the people,
1440 then bring our ring-bestower on his road,
escort him to the pyre. More than one portion of wealth
shall melt with the hero, for there's a hoard of treasure
and gold uncounted; a grim purchase,
for in the end it was with his own life
1445 that he bought these rings: which the burning shall devour,
the fire enfold. No fellow shall wear
an arm-ring in his memory; no maiden's neck
shall be enhanced in beauty by the bearing of these rings.
Bereft of gold, rather, and in wretchedness of mind
1450 she shall tread continually the tracks of exile
now that the leader of armies has laid aside his mirth,
his sport and glad laughter. Many spears shall therefore
feel cold in the mornings to the clasping fingers
and the hands that raise them. Nor shall the harper's melody
1455 arouse them for battle; and yet the black raven,†
quick on the marked men, shall have much to speak of
when he tells the eagle of his takings at the feast
where he and the wolf bared the bodies of the slain.'

---

princes Herebeald, Hathkin, Hygelac and Heardred

raven the triumph of the beasts of battle: the raven and the wolf shall boast to the eagle

Such was the rehearsal of the hateful tidings
1460 by that bold messenger; amiss in neither
words nor facts. The war-band arose;
they went unhappily under Earna-ness†
to look on the wonder with welling tears.
They found him on the sand, his soul fled,
1465 keeping his resting-place: rings he had given them
in former times! But the final day
had come for the champion; and the chief of the Geats,
the warrior-king, had met his wondrous death.

[Here lines 3038–75 of the original are omitted. The dragon lies dead beside the hoard which had been hidden in vain.]

Wiglaf spoke, Weoxstan's son:
1470 'Many must often endure distress
for the sake of one; so it is now with us.
We could not urge any reason
on our beloved king, the keeper of the land,
why he should not approach the protector of the gold
1475 but let him lie where he had long been already
and abide in his den until the end of the world.
He held to his high destiny.
      The hoard has been seen
that was acquired at such a cost; too cruel the fate
that impelled the king of the people towards it!
1480 I myself was inside there, and saw all
the wealth of the chamber once my way was open
– little courtesy was shown in allowing me to pass
beneath the earth-wall. I urgently filled
my hands with a huge heap of the treasures
1485 stored in the cave, carried them out
to my lord here. He was alive still
and commanded his wits. Much did he say
in his grief, the old man; he asked me to speak to you,
ordered that on the place of the pyre you should raise
1490 a barrow fitting your friend's achievements;
conspicuous, magnificent, as among men he was
while he could wield the wealth of his stronghold
the most honoured of warriors on the wide earth.

Earna-ness   a headland in Geatland
(*earn*   eagle)

Let us now hasten to behold again,
1495 and approach once more that mass of treasures,
awesome under the walls; I shall guide you
so that from near at hand you may behold sufficiently
the thick gold and the bracelets. Let a bier be made ready,
contrive it quickly, so that when we come out again
1500 we may take up our king, carry the man
beloved by us to his long abode
where he must rest in the Ruler's keeping.'

Then the son of Weoxstan, worthy in battle,
had orders given to owners of homesteads
1505 and a great many warriors, that the governors of the people
from far and wide should fetch in wood
for the hero's funeral pyre.
                        'Now the flames shall grow dark
and the fire destroy the sustainer of the warriors
who often endured the iron shower
1510 when, string-driven, the storm of arrows
sang over shield-wall, and the shaft did its work
urged on by its feathers, furthered the arrow-head.'
Then in his wisdom Weoxstan's son
called out from the company of the king's own thanes
1515 seven men in all, who excelled among them,
and, himself the eighth warrior, entered in beneath
that unfriendly roof. The front-stepping man
bore in his hand a blazing torch.

When the men perceived a piece of the hoard
1520 that remained unguarded, mouldering there
on the floor of the chamber, they did not choose by lot[†]
who should remove it; undemurring,
as quickly as they could, they carried outside
the precious treasures; and they pushed the dragon,
1525 the worm, over the cliff, let the waves take him
and the flood engulf the guardian of the treasures.
The untold profusion of twisted gold
was loaded onto a wagon, and the warrior prince
borne hoary-headed to Hronesness.

---

they . . . lot   understatement

1530 The Geat race then reared up for him
a funeral pyre. It was not a petty mound,
but shining mail-coats and shields of war
and helmets hung upon it, as he had desired.
Then the heroes, lamenting, laid out in the middle
1535 their great chief, their cherished lord.
On top of the mound the men then kindled
the biggest of funeral-fires. Black wood-smoke
arose from the blaze, and the roaring of flames
mingled with weeping. The winds lay still
1540 as the heat at the fire's heart consumed
the house of bone. And in heavy mood
they uttered their sorrow at the slaughter of their lord.

A woman of the Geats in grief sang out
the lament for his death. Loudly she sang,
1545 her hair bound up, the burden of her fear
that evil days were destined her
– troops cut down, terror of armies,
bondage, humiliation. Heaven swallowed the smoke.

Then the Storm-Geat nation constructed for him
1550 a stronghold on the headland, so high and broad
that seafarers might see it from afar.
The beacon to that battle-reckless man
they made in ten days. What remained from the fire
they cast a wall around, of workmanship
1555 as fine as their wisest men could frame for it.
They placed in the tomb both the torques and the jewels,
all the magnificence that the men had earlier
taken from the hoard in hostile mood.
They left the earls' wealth in the earth's keeping,
1560 the gold in the dirt. It dwells there yet,
of no more use to men than in ages before.

Then the warriors rode around the barrow,
twelve of them in all, athelings' sons.
They recited a dirge to declare their grief,
1565 spoke of the man, mourned their King.
They praised his manhood and the prowess of his hands,
they raised his name; it is right a man
should be lavish in honouring his lord and friend,
should love him in his heart when the leading-forth
1570 from the house of flesh befalls him at last.

This was the manner of the mourning of the men of the Geats,
sharers in the feast, at the fall of their lord:
they said that he was of all the world's kings
the gentlest of men, and the most gracious,
1575 the kindest to his people, the keenest for fame.

Elegies
?mid-8th–mid-9th centuries

The Old English Elegies, all found in the Exeter Book manuscript, have been given the following titles by editors: *The Ruin, The Wife's Complaint, The Husband's Message, Wulf and Eadwacer, The Wanderer* and *The Seafarer*. They are the most concentrated of Old English poems. In a dramatic situation, implied but not explained, an isolated speaker expresses loss and yearning, addressed to a source of consolation, sometimes Christian. Their composition seems to belong to a period later than that of *Beowulf*.

THE RUIN†

Well-wrought this wall: Weirds† broke it.
The stronghold burst....

Snapped rooftrees, towers fallen,
The work of the Giants, the stonesmiths,
5 Mouldereth.
            Rime scoureth gatetowers
            Rime on mortar.

Shattered the showershields, roofs ruined,
Age under-ate them.
            And the wielders and wrights?
Earthgrip holds them – gone, long gone,
10 Fast in gravesgrasp while fifty fathers
And sons have passed.

The Ruin is on the final fire-damaged leaves of the Exeter MS, and ends in tatters. Gaps are indicated in the translation by dots surrounded by reconstructions. The Anglo-Saxons, who built in wood, marvelled at the massive ruins left by the Romans, referring to them as the work of a previous race of giants. The hot baths mentioned at the end suggest Bath

Weirds the Fates personified

                        Wall stood,
        Grey lichen, red stone, kings fell often,
        Stood under storms, high arch crashed —
        Stands yet the wallstone, hacked by weapons,
15   By files grim-ground...
           ... shone the old skilled work
           ... sank to loam-crust.

        Mood quickened mind, and a man of wit,
        Cunning in rings, bound bravely the wallbase
20   With iron, a wonder.

        Bright were the buildings, halls where springs ran,
        High, horngabled, much throng-noise;
        These many meadhalls men filled
        With loud cheerfulness: Weird changed that.

25   Came days of pestilence, on all sides men fell dead,
        Death fetched off the flower of the people;
        Where they stood to fight, waste places
        And on the acropolis, ruins.
                                Hosts who would build again
        Shrank to the earth. Therefore are these courts dreary
30   And that red arch twisteth tiles,
        Wryeth from roof-ridge, reacheth groundwards....
        Broken blocks....
                          There once many a man,
        Mood-glad, goldbright, of gleams garnished,
        Flushed with wine-pride, flashing war-gear,
35   Gazed on wrought gemstones, on gold, on silver,
        On wealth held and hoarded, on light-filled amber,
        On this bright burg of broad dominion.

        Stood stone houses; wide streams welled
        Hot from source, and a wall all caught
40   In its bright bosom, that the baths were
        Hot at hall's hearth; that was fitting...

        ....

        Then hot streams, loosed, ran over hoar stone
        Unto the ring-tank....
           ... It is a kingly thing
45   ... city....

THE WIFE'S COMPLAINT[†]

I have wrought these words together out of a wryed existence,
The heart's tally, telling off
The griefs I have undergone from girlhood upwards,
Old and new, and now more than ever;
5   For I have never not had some new sorrow,
Some fresh affliction to fight against.

The first was my lord's leaving his people here:
Crossed crests. To what country I knew not,
Wondered where, awoke unhappy.
10 I left, fared any road, friendless, an outcast,
Sought any service to staunch the lack of him.

Then his kinsmen ganged, began to think
Thoughts they did not speak, of splitting the wedlock;
So – estranged, alienated – we lived each
15 Alone, a long way apart; how I longed for him!

In his harshness he had me brought here;
And in these parts there were new friendly-minded,
Worth trusting.
            Trouble in the heart now:
I saw the bitterness, the bound mind
20 Of my matched man, mourning-browed,
Mirk in his mood, murder in his thoughts.

Our lips had smiled to swear hourly
That nothing should split us – save dying –
Nothing else. All that has changed:
25 It is now as if it never had been,
Our friendship. I feel in the wind
That the man dearest to me detests me.
I was banished to this knoll knotted by woods
To live in a den dug beneath an oak.
30 Old is this earthen room; it eats at my heart.

The Wife's Complaint this is the lament of a woman whose lord, misled by one of his kinsmen, has banished her far away, apparently to a cave, although the landscape may be symbolic. Towards the end, she seems to curse the 'young man' (line 44) who has estranged her from her husband, whom she still loves. Editors differ in their reconstructions of this story

I see the thorns thrive up there in thick coverts
On the banks that baulk these black hollows:
Not a gay dwelling. Here the grief bred
By lordlack preys on me. Some lovers in this world
35 Live dear to each other, lie warm together
At day's beginning; I go by myself
About these earth caves under the oak tree.
Here I must sit the summer day through,
Here weep out the woes of exile,
40 The hardships heaped upon me. My heart shall never
Suddenly sail into slack water,
All the longings of a lifetime answered.

May grief and bitterness blast the mind
Of that young man! May his mind ache
45 Behind his smiling face! May a flock of sorrows
Choke his chest! He would change his tune
If he lived alone in a land of exile
Far from his folk.
     Where my friend is stranded
Frost crusts the cracked cliff-face,
50 Grey waves grind the shingle.
The mind cannot bear in such a bleak place
Very much grief.
     He remembers too often
Less grim surroundings. Sorrow follows
This too long wait for one who is estranged.

THE HUSBAND'S MESSAGE†

Now shall I unseal myself to yourself alone
... the wood kind, waxed from saplinghood;
On me ...   must in foreign lands
Set ...
5   Saltstreams.
              In the beak of ships
I have often been
Where my lord ...   me
Among high houses; and here am come now
On board a ship.
              You shall directly
10   Know how you may think of the thorough love
My lord feels for you. I have no fear in promising
You shall find him heart-whole, honour bright.

Hwaet!†
     The carver of this token entreats a lady
Clad in clear stones to call to mind
15   And hold in her wit words pledged
Often between the two in earlier days:
Then he would hand you through hall and yard
Lord of his lands, and you might live together,
Forge your love. A feud drove him
20   From this war-proud people.
                        That prince, glad now,
Gave me this word for you: when you shall hear
In the copse at the cliff's edge the cuckoo pitch
His melancholy cry, come over sea.

You will have listened long: leave then with no notice,
25   Let no man alive delay your going:
Into the boat and out to sea,
Seagull's range; southward from here
Over the paths in the foam you shall find your man,
Make landfall where your lord is waiting.

The Husband's Message the poem seems not to be related to *The Wife's Complaint*, and the message is to be imagined as written not upon vellum but inscribed in runes upon a wooden staff, which speaks the whole poem. The staff tells the lady that she may rejoin her husband in his now prosperous exile, as soon as she hears the cuckoo's cry. The poem ends with his runic signature. Dots indicate gaps caused by fire damage

Hwaet a formal call for attention: Listen!

30   He does not conceive, he said to me,
     That a greater happiness could be his in this world
     Than that all-wielding God should grant you both
     Days when together you may give out rings
     Among followers and fellows, free-handed deal
35   The nailed armbands. Of which he has enough,
     Of inlaid gold. . . .

     There lands are his, a hearth among strangers,
     Estate. . . .
                  . . . of men,
     Although my lord here . . .
40   When the need grew strait, steered his boat out
     Through steep breakers, and had singlehanded
     To run the deep ways, dared escape,
     Mingled saltstreams. The man has now
     Laid his sorrows, lacks no gladdeners;
45   He has a hoard and horses and hall-carousing
     And would have everything within an earl's having
     Had he my lady with him: if my lady will come:
     If she will hold to what was sworn and sealed in your youths.

     So I set together S and R† twinned,
50   EA, W, D.† The oath is named
     Whereby he undertakes until the end of his life
     To keep the covenants of companionship
     That, long ago, you delighted to repeat.

S R . . . D   The runes stand for words which
translated give the message: Go south (*sun's path*) across *ocean* to *joy* with your *man*

WULF AND EADWACER†

The men of my tribe would treat him as game:
If he comes to the camp they will kill him outright.
>   Our fate is forked.

Wulf is on one island, I on another.
5   Mine is a fastness: the fens girdle it
And it is defended by the fiercest men.
If he comes to the camp they will kill him for sure.
>   Our fate is forked.

It was rainy weather, and I wept by the hearth,
10   Thinking of my Wulf's far wanderings;
One of the captains* caught me in his arms.   *Eadwacer*
It gladdened me then; but it grieved me too.

Wulf, my Wulf, it was wanting you
That made me sick, your seldom coming,
15   The hollowness at heart; not the hunger I spoke of.

Do you hear, Eadwacer? Our whelp†
>   Wulf shall take to the wood.
What was never bound is broken easily,
>   Our song together.

THE WANDERER

[Translation by Richard Hamer, whose headnote is also reproduced in an abbreviated form]

It is now generally agreed that *The Wanderer* is a complete poem dealing in a consistently Christian manner with a coherent theme. [. . .] The paradox is propounded that despite the hardships of his life the lonely exile often feels the grace of God (ll. 1–5). Someone then narrates his personal experiences of exile (ll. 8–29), which he gives a more general application by appealing to others who have had similar experiences (ll. 29–57). This consideration leads

---

Wulf and Eadwacer a strophic poem with a refrain, like *Deor*, this is a series of compressed dramatic allusions. The first plausible solution was given by the editor Henry Bradley, who wrote in 1888 that the poem is 'a fragment of a dramatic soliloquy. The speaker, it should be premised, is shown by the grammar to be a woman, Wulf is her lover and an outlaw, and Eadwacer (I suspect, though it is not certain) is her tyrant husband.'

whelp presumably her son by Wulf

him to feel that he cannot understand why in the face of so much suffering and the general prospect of decay he is not depressed (ll. 58–63). Various precepts are advanced about how one should live, leading to the statement that one must understand the nature of the end of the world, of which the present signs of decline and the historical example of the Flood are tokens (ll. 64–87). He who has thought deeply about all this may well ask: 'Where have all the former glories of earth gone? Only ruins and the dark and cold remain. Everything earthly is transitory' (ll. 88–110). It will be well for those with faith, for all our security is with God (ll. 111–115).

     'Often the solitary man enjoys
     The grace and mercy of the Lord, though he
     Careworn has long been forced to stir by hand
     The ice-cold sea on many waterways,
5   Travel the exile's path; fate is relentless.'
     So spoke a wanderer who called to mind
     Hardships and cruel wars and deaths of lords.
     Frequently have I had to mourn alone
     My cares each morning; now no living man
10   Exists to whom I dare reveal my heart
     Openly; and I know it for a truth
     That in a man it is a noble virtue
     To hide his thoughts, lock up his private feelings,
     However he may feel. A weary heart
15   Cannot oppose inexorable fate,
     And anxious thoughts can bring no remedy.
     And so those jealous of their reputation
     Often bind fast their sadness in their breasts.
     So I, careworn, deprived of fatherland,
20   Far from my noble kin, have often had
     To tie in fetters my own troubled spirit,
     Since long ago I wrapped my lord's remains
     In darkness of the earth, and sadly thence
     Journeyed by winter over icy waves,
25   And suffering sought the hall of a new patron,
     If I in any land might find one willing
     To show me recognition in his mead-hall,
     Comfort my loneliness, tempt me with pleasures.
     He knows who has experienced it how bitter
30   Is sorrow as a comrade to the man
     Who lacks dear human friends; fair twisted gold
     Is not for him, but rather paths of exile,
     Coldness of heart for the gay countryside.
     He calls to mind receiving gifts of treasure

35　　And former hall-retainers, and remembers
　　　How in his younger years his lordly patron
　　　Was wont to entertain him at the feast.
　　　Now all that joy has gone. He understands
　　　Who long must do without the kind advice
40　　Of his beloved lord, while sleep and sorrow
　　　Together often bind him, sad and lonely,
　　　How in his mind it seems that he embraces
　　　And kisses his liege lord, and on his knee
　　　Lays hand and head, as when he formerly
45　　Received as a retainer in the hall
　　　Gifts from the throne; but then the joyless man
　　　Wakes up and sees instead the yellow waves,
　　　The sea-birds bathing, stretching out their wings,
　　　While snow and hail and frost fall all together.
50　　The heart's wounds seem by that yet heavier,
　　　Grief for the dear one gone: care is renewed,
　　　When memories of kinsmen fill the mind,
　　　He greets them gladly, contemplates them keenly,
　　　But his old friends swim frequently away;
55　　The floating spirits bring him all too few
　　　Of the old well-known songs; care is renewed
　　　For him who must continually send
　　　His weary spirit over icy waves.
　　　Therefore I see no reason in the world
60　　Why my heart grows not dark, when I consider
　　　The lives of warriors, how they suddenly
　　　Have left their hall, the bold and noble thanes,
　　　Just as this earth and everything thereon
　　　Declines and weakens each and every day.
65　　Certainly no man may be wise before
　　　He's lived his share of winters in the world.
　　　A wise man must be patient, not too hasty
　　　In speech, or passionate, impetuous
　　　Or timid as a fighter, nor too anxious
70　　Or carefree or too covetous of wealth;
　　　Nor ever must he be too quick to boast
　　　Before he's gained experience of himself.
　　　A man should wait, before he makes a vow,
　　　Until in pride he truly can assess
75　　How, when a crisis comes, he will re-act.
　　　The wise must know how awesome it will be
　　　When all the wealth of earth stands desolate,
　　　As now in various parts throughout the world

Stand wind-blown walls, frost-covered, ruined buildings.
80 The wine-halls crumble; monarchs lifeless lie,
Deprived of pleasures, all the doughty troop
Dead by the wall; some battle carried off,
Took from this world; one the dire bird removed
Over the ocean deep; one the grey wolf
85 Consigned to death; and one a tear-stained hero
Concealed from daylight in an earthy cave.
Just so in days long past mankind's Creator
Destroyed this earth, till lacking the gay sounds
Of citizens the ancient works of giants
90 Stood desolate. He who has wisely thought
And carefully considered this creation
And this dark life, experienced in spirit
Has often pondered many massacres
In far off ages, and might say these words:
95 'Where is the horse now, where the hero gone?
Where is the bounteous lord, and where the benches
For feasting? Where are all the joys of hall?
Alas for the bright cup, the armoured warrior,
The glory of the prince. That time is over,
100 Passed into night as it had never been.
Stands now memorial to that dear band
The splendid lofty wall, adorned with shapes
Of serpents; but the strong blood-greedy spear
And mighty destiny removed the heroes,
105 And storms now strike against these stony slopes.
The falling tempest binds in winter's vice
The earth, and darkness comes with shapes of night,
And from the north fierce hail is felt to fall
In malice against men. And all is hardship
110 On earth, the immutable decree of fate
Alters the world which lies beneath the heavens.
Here property and friendship pass away,
Here man himself and kinsmen pass away,
And all this earthly structure comes to nought.'
115 Thus spoke the thoughtful sage, he sat apart.
Blessed is he who keeps his faith; a man
Must never be too eager to reveal
His cares, unless he knows already how
To bring about a cure by his own zeal.
120 Well shall it be for him who looks for grace
And comfort from our father in the heavens,
Where is ordained all our security.

THE SEAFARER

[Translation by Richard Hamer, whose headnote is also given in an abbreviated form]

The Seafarer has a literature about as extensive as that of *The Wanderer*, with which it has certain similarities, on which however it would be dangerous to build too much. The main problems are, first that the poem appears to fall into two unconnected halves with a break in the middle of l. 64, all before being about seafaring while the rest is clearly homiletic, and second that within the first part there appear to be expressed two incompatible attitudes to the sea. The generally accepted answer to the first problem is that the first part of the poem gives a situation on which the homiletic section is based. This makes very good sense [...] The first part has variously been regarded as literal or allegorical, and related to such figures as the pilgrim.

   I sing my own true story, tell my travails,
   How I have often suffered times of hardship
   In days of toil, and have experienced
   Bitter anxiety, my troubled home
5 On many a ship has been the heaving waves,
   Where grim night-watch has often been my lot
   At the ship's prow as it beat past the cliffs.
   Oppressed by cold my feet were bound by frost
   In icy bonds, while worries simmered hot
10 About my heart, and hunger from within
   Tore the sea-weary spirit. He knows not,
   Who lives most easily on land, how I
   Have spent my winter on the ice-cold sea,
   Wretched and anxious, in the paths of exile,
15 Lacking dear friends, hung round by icicles,
   While hail flew past in showers. There heard I nothing
   But the resounding sea, the ice-cold waves.
   Sometimes I made the song of the wild swan
   My pleasure, or the gannet's call, the cries
20 Of curlews for the missing mirth of men,
   The singing gull instead of mead in hall.
   Storms beat the rocky cliffs, and icy-winged
   The tern replied, the horn-beaked eagle shrieked.
   No patron had I there who might have soothed
25 My desolate spirit. He can little know
   Who, proud and flushed with wine, has spent his time
   With all the joys of life among the cities,

Safe from such fearful venturings, how I
Have often suffered weary on the seas.
30   Night shadows darkened, snow came from the north,
Frost bound the earth and hail fell on the ground,
Coldest of corns. And yet the heart's desires
Incite me now that I myself should go
On towering seas, among the salt waves' play;
35   And constantly the heartfelt wishes urge
The spirit to venture, that I should go forth
To see the lands of strangers far away.
Yet no man in the world's so proud of heart,
So generous of gifts, so bold in youth,
40   In deeds so brave, or with so loyal lord,
That he can ever venture on the sea
Without great fears of what the Lord may bring.
His mind dwells not on the harmonious harp,
On ring-receiving, or the joy of woman,
45   Or wordly hopes, or anything at all
But the relentless rolling of the waves;
But he who goes to sea must ever yearn.
The groves bear blossom, cities grow more bright,
The fields adorn themselves, the world speeds up;
50   Yet all this urges forth the eager spirit
Of him who then desires to travel far
On the sea-paths. Likewise the cuckoo calls
With boding voice, the harbinger of summer
Offers but bitter sorrow in the breast.
55   The man who's blest with comfort does not know
What some then suffer who most widely travel
The paths of exile. Even now my heart
Journeys beyond its confines, and my thoughts
Over the sea, across the whale's domain,
60   Travel afar the regions of the earth,
And then come back to me with greed and longing.
The cuckoo cries, incites the eager breast
On to the whale's roads irresistibly,
Over the wide expanses of the sea,
65   Because the joys of God mean more to me
Than this dead transitory life on land.
That earthly wealth lasts to eternity
I don't believe. Always one of three things
Keeps all in doubt until one's destined hour.
70   Sickness, old age, the sword, each one of these
May end the lives of doomed and transient men.

Therefore for every warrior the best
Memorial is the praise of living men
After his death, that ere he must depart
75 He shall have done good deeds on earth against
The malice of his foes, and noble works
Against the devil, that the sons of men
May after praise him, and his glory live
For ever with the angels in the splendour
80 Of lasting life, in bliss among those hosts.
The great old days have gone, and all the grandeur
Of earth; there are not Caesars now or kings
Or patrons such as once there used to be,
Amongst whom were performed most glorious deeds,
85 Who lived in lordliest renown. Gone now
Is all that host, the splendours have departed.
Weaker men live and occupy the world,
Enjoy it but with care. Fame is brought low,
Earthly nobility grows old, decays,
90 As now throughout this world does every man.
Age comes on him, his countenance grows pale,
Grey-haired he mourns, and knows his former lords,
The sons of princes, given to the earth.
Nor when his life slips from him may his body
95 Taste sweetness or feel pain or stir his hand
Or use his mind to think. And though a brother
May strew with gold his brother's grave, and bury
His corpse among the dead with heaps of treasure,
Wishing them to go with him, yet can gold
100 Bring no help to the soul that's full of sins,
Against God's wrath, although he hide it here
Ready before his death while yet he lives.
Great is the might of God, by which earth moves;
For He established its foundations firm,
105 The land's expanses, and the sky above.
Foolish is he who does not fear his Lord,
For death will come upon him unprepared.
Blessed is he who humble lives; for grace
Shall come to him from heaven. The Creator
110 Shall make his spirit steadfast, for his faith
Is in God's might. Man must control himself
With strength of mind, and firmly hold to that,
True to his pledges, pure in all his ways.
With moderation should each man behave
115 In all his dealings with both friend and foe.

No man will wish the friend he's made to burn
In fires of hell, or on an earthly pyre,
Yet fate is mightier, the Lord's ordaining
More powerful than any man can know.
120 Let us think where we have our real home,
And then consider how we may come thither;
And let us labour also, so that we
May pass into eternal blessedness.
Where life belongs amid the love of God,
125 Hope in the heavens. The Holy One be thanked
That He has raised us up, the Prince of Glory,
Lord without end, to all eternity.
                                    Amen.

King Alfred
848–899

When Alfred, aged 23, came to the throne of Wessex in 871 the Vikings had destroyed all the other English kingdoms, and the knowledge of Latin was, he says, virtually dead. He arranged for the books 'most needful for all men to know' to be translated into English, including Bede's *Ecclesiastical History*. The *Anglo-Saxon Chronicle* also began under Alfred. Once this king, who could not read until he was 12 and learned Latin at the age of 35, had ensured the survival of his kingdom and of Christianity in England, he set about the renewal of morale and wisdom among the English by educating first the clergy and then, so he proposed, the free-born sons of the laity. He outlines his plan in the letter he writes to Bishop Waerferth of Worcester in preface to his own translation of Pope Gregory the Great's *Cura Pastoralis*, or *Pastoral Care*, written when he became Pope in 591 as a handbook for pastors.

This preface is preserved in a manuscript of Alfred's day in the Bodleian Library, Oxford, headed *Theos boc sceal to Wiogora ceastre* (This book is to go to Worcester). Besides its linguistic, cultural and historical interest, it reveals clearly the purposeful workings of the King's mind, and suggests something of the character of the first named English writer of English prose whom we can study. He opens in the third person but soon changes to the first, and then speaks of the inhabitants of Angelcynn (the people of the Angles) as 'we'.

The last of Alfred's translations was the *Soliloquia* (*Soliloquies*) which St Augustine of Hippo, Bishop of Carthage, left uncompleted at his death in 430. They concern the immortality of the soul. Alfred translated Augustine's two books and added a third, adapting and adding from other sources. In the preface, not long before his own death in 899, he describes his forays into the wisdom of the Fathers of the Church in terms of a man choosing timber in a forest with which to build and adorn his house.

From PREFACE TO THE PASTORAL CARE

[Trans. M. Swanton]

King Alfred sends greetings to Bishop Wærferth with his loving and friendly words, and would declare to you that it has very often come to my mind what wise men there were formerly† throughout the English people, both in sacred and in secular orders; and how there were happy times then throughout England; and how the kings who had rule over the people in those days were obedient to God and his messengers, and both maintained their peace and their morality and their authority at home, and also enlarged their territory abroad; and how they prospered both in warfare and in wisdom; and also how zealous the sacred orders were both about teaching and about learning and all the services which they had to perform for God; and how men from abroad came here to this land in search of knowledge and instruction, and how we should now have to get them from abroad, if we were to have them. So complete was its decay among the English people that there were very few this side of the Humber† who could comprehend their services in English, or even translate a letter from Latin into English; and I imagine that there were not many beyond the Humber. There were so few of them that I cannot even remember a single one south of the Thames when I succeeded to the kingdom.† Thanks be to Almighty God that now we have any supply of teachers. And therefore I command you to do, as I believe you wish, that you disengage yourself as often as you can from the affairs of this world, so that you can apply the wisdom which God has given you wherever you are able to apply it. Think what punishments then came upon us in this world when we neither loved it ourselves nor allowed it to other men – we loved only to be called Christians,† and very few loved the virtues.

When I remembered all this, then I also remembered how, before it was all ravaged† and burnt, I had seen how the churches throughout all England stood filled with treasures and books, and there was also a great multitude of God's servants – they had very little benefit from those books, because they could not understand anything of them, since they were not written in their own language. As if they had said: 'Our forefathers who formerly held these places loved knowledge, and through it they acquired wealth and left it to us. One can see their footprints here still, but we cannot follow after them and therefore we

---

formerly during the seventh century as described by Bede
Humber river dividing Northumbria from Mercia
kingdom Wessex, the northern border of which was the Thames valley
called Christians monasticism decayed in the eighth and ninth centuries
ravaged Danes sacked Lindisfarne in 793, and raids increased thereafter

have now lost both the wealth and the knowledge because we would not bend our mind to that course.' When I remembered all this, then I wondered greatly at those good wise men who formerly existed throughout the English people and had fully studied all those books, that they did not wish to translate any part of them into their own language. But then I immediately answered myself and said: 'They did not imagine that men should ever become so careless and learning so decayed; they refrained from it by intention and hoped that there would be the greater knowledge in this land the more languages we knew.'

Then I remembered how the law† was first found in the Hebrew language, and afterwards, when the Greeks learned it, they translated it all into their own language, and all the other books as well. And afterwards in the same way the Romans, when they had learned them, they translated them all into their own language through learned interpreters. And all other Christian nations also translated some part of them into their own language. Therefore it seems better to me, if it seems so to you, that we also should translate certain books which are most necessary for all men to know, into the language that we can all understand, and also arrange it, as with God's help we very easily can if we have peace, so that all the youth of free men now among the English people, who have the means to be able to devote themselves to it, may be set to study for as long as they are of no other use, until the time they are able to read English writing well; afterwards one may teach further in the Latin language those whom one wishes to teach further and wishes to promote to holy orders.

Then when I remembered how the knowledge of Latin had previously decayed throughout the English people, and yet many could read English writing, I began amidst other various and manifold cares of this kingdom to translate into English the book which is called *Pastoralis* in Latin and 'Shepherd's Book' in English, sometimes word for word, sometimes in a paraphrase, as I learned it from my archbishop Plegmund,† and my bishop Asser,† and my priest Grimbold† and my priest John.† When I had learned it, I translated it into English as I understood it and as I could interpret it most intelligibly; and I will send one to every bishopric in my kingdom; and in each there will be a book-marker worth fifty mancuses. And in the name of God I command that no one remove the book-marker from the book, nor the book from the minster; it is uncertain how long there may be such learned bishops, as now, thanks be to God, there are almost everywhere; therefore I desire that they should always lie at that place, unless the bishop want to have it with him, or it be anywhere on loan, or anyone be copying it.

---

the law the Bible
Plegmund Archbishop of Canterbury 890–914
Asser Bishop of Sherborne c. 892–909
Grimbold a Frankish monk from St Omer
John a native of continental Saxony whom Alfred made abbot of Athelney

From PREFACE TO ST AUGUSTINE'S SOLILOQUIES

[Trans. M. Swanton]

Then I gathered for myself staves and posts and tie-beams, and handles for each of the tools I knew how to use, and building-timbers and beams and as much as I could carry of the most beautiful woods for each of the structures I knew how to build. I did not come home with
5 a single load without wishing to bring home the whole forest with me, if I could have carried it all away; in every tree I saw something that I needed at home. Wherefore I advise each of those who is able, and has many waggons, to direct himself to the same forest where I cut these posts; let him fetch more there for himself, and load his waggons with
10 fair branches so that he can weave many a neat wall and construct many an excellent building, and build a fair town, and dwell therein in joy and ease both winter and summer, as I have not done so far. But he who taught me, to whom the forest was pleasing, may bring it about that I dwell in greater ease both in this transitory wayside habitation
15 while I am in this world, and also in that eternal home which he has promised us through St Augustine and St Gregory† and St Jerome,† and through many other holy fathers; so I also believe that for the merits of them all, he will both make this road easier than it was hitherto, and also enlighten the eyes of my mind so that I can find out the straight
20 road to the eternal home and to the eternal glory and to the eternal rest which is promised to us through those holy fathers. So be it.

It is no wonder, though, that one should labour for such material, both in the carrying and in the building; but every man, after he has built a cottage on land leased by his lord, with his help, likes to rest in
25 it sometimes, and go hunting and fowling and fishing, and from that lease to provide for himself in every way, both on sea and on land, until the time when, through his lord's favour, he should merit chartered land† and a perpetual inheritance. So may the rich benefactor, who rules both these transitory habitations and those eternal homes bring it
30 about. May he who created both and rules both grant that I may be fit for each; both to be useful here and especially to attain thither.

Augustine, Bishop of Carthage, made two books about his own meditations; those books are called Soliloquia, that is, concerning the

---

Gregory Pope from 590 to 604, he sent Augustine 'of Canterbury' to England in 597
Jerome Latin writer and Father of the Church (c. 348–420); translator into Latin of what became the standard version of the Bible, the Vulgate
chartered land bocland granted by royal charter

deliberation and doubts of his mind – how his reason answered his
35 mind when his mind was uncertain about anything, or it wished to
know anything that it could not clearly understand before.

Brunanburh
937

Brunanburh is a celebration of the mighty victory won by Wessex over its enemies in 937, and is the first poem to appear in the *Anglo-Saxon Chronicle*. King Athelstan and his brother Edmund, with Mercian help, defeated a combined invading force of Scots, Picts, Strathclyde British and the formidable Dublin-based Vikings at a place called Brunanburh, which cannot be identified with certainty. It was one of the first great *English* victories; its patriotic appeal may have recommended it to Tennyson, for it is the only Old English poem he translated.

In *Brunanburh* the old oral formulaic poetry is put to new purposes: it is the first royal panegyric, the first court poem, the first heroic poem to mention historiography and the reading of books, and the last piece of correct versification in Old English. It is the epitome of the old battle poetry, using all its proper devices, but it was also to be its epitaph.

BRUNANBURH

    Athelstan† the King, captain of men,
    Ring-giver of warriors – and with him his brother
    Edmund† the Atheling – unending glory
    Won in that strife by their swords' edges
5   That there was about Brunanburh. The board-wall they cut through,
    Cleft the lindens† with the leavings of hammers,†
    Edward'†s offspring, answering the blood
    They had from their forebears: that in the field they should often
    Against every foe defend the land,
10 Hoard and homes. The hated ones fell,

Athelstan   King of Wessex, Mercia and England, 924–39
Edmund   Ironside, aged 16 at the time of the battle, King 939–46
lindens   limewood shields
leavings of hammers   swords
Edward   the Elder, Alfred's eldest son, King 899–924

The people of the Scots and the shipmen* too,   vikings
Fell as was fated. The field was running
With the blood of soldiers from the sun's rise
At the hour of the morning when that marvellous star,
15   God's bright candle, glided over the lands,
To the time when the creature of the eternal Lord
Sank to rest. Then sated with battle
And weary lay many there, men of the Northerners*   vikings
Shot above their shields, and Scots men likewise,
20   Wasted by spears. The West Saxons
Rode in troop right through the day
Hard on the heels of the hated peoples,
Pursuing hewed fiercely at the fleeing warriors
With mill-sharpened swords. The Mercians did not refuse
25   The hard hand-play to any hero among those
Who with Anlaf† over the ocean's courses
In the bosom of a ship had sought our land
And their doom in that fight. There were five kings†
Who in their youth lay low on that battlefield,
30   Slain by the sword; and seven earls†
Of Anlaf's also; others without number
Of shipmen and Scots. With scant† retinue
The prince* of the Northmen was put to flight   Anlaf
By stark need to the stern of his craft:
35   The long ship drove out across the dark waters;
The king slipped away,† saved his life.
The old king† likewise came away also,
The grey-haired campaigner, Constantine, fled
To the North he knew. He had no need to rejoice
40   In that meeting of swords where he was shortened of kinsmen
And deprived of friends on the field of assembly,
Plucked on the battlefield: on that place of slaughter
He left his son brought low by wounds,
Young on the battlefield. The yield† of the swords
45   Gave no ground for boasting to the grey-haired chieftain,*   Constantine
The old enemy; to Anlaf neither.
They had no cause to laugh with those left from the war,
That they had been the better in battle-accomplishment
On the field of strife when the standards clashed,

Anlaf Olaf Guthfrithson of Dublin
five kings other annals confirm this
earls Norse *jarls*
scant that is, no

slipped away that, is disgracefully
The old king Constantine III of Scots
yield that is, the slaughter

50 At the spear-meeting when men came together
    In the exchange of weapons: when with Edward's sons
    They had played together in the place of slaughter.
           The nailed ships of the Norsemen took off
    What spears had spared, a spattered remnant,
55 Across deep Dingsmere† to Dublin once more,
    To seek again Ireland in shame.
    The brothers also, both of them together,
    The King and the Atheling,* came away to their own,   prince
    The West-Saxon land, in war-triumph.
60 The corpse-sharers, shadowy-coated,
    They left behind them: the black raven
    With its horny beak; the brown eagle
    Of white tail-feather, to feast on the slain
    – Greedy war-hawk; and the grey one,
65 The wolf of the weald.
                No worse slaughter
    In this island has ever yet
    Before these days befallen a people
    By the edge of the sword – so say the books,
70 The wise men of old – since† from the East came
    Angles and Saxons up to these shores,
    Seeking Britain across the broad seas,
    Smart for glory, those smiths of war
    That overcame the Welsh, and won a homeland.

Dingsmere   the Irish Sea   *since*   that is, since the fifth century

Maldon
991

The Battle of Maldon took place on 10 or 11 August 991 near Maldon in Essex. The Parker version of the *Anglo-Saxon Chronicle* reads:

> 993 [991]. In this year came Anlaf with ninety-three ships to Folkestone, and harried outside, and sailed thence to Sandwich, and thence to Ipswich, overrunning all the countryside, and so on to Maldon. Ealdorman Byrhtnoth came to meet them with his levies and fought them, but they slew the ealdorman there and had possession of the place of slaughter.

The Laud version of the *Chronicle* adds the great consequence of the defeat:

> In this year it was decided for the first time to pay tribute to the Danes because of the great terror they inspired along the sea coast. On this first occasion it amounted to ten thousand pounds.
> (trans. G. N. Garmonsway)

This tribute became known as Danegeld.

The poem is incomplete at its beginning and its end, but it turns historic defeat into ethical victory. Bryhtnoth (Old English Byrhtnoth), however excessive his *ofermod* (line 88), is a magnanimous lord who dies a Christian death, and his retainers all utter exemplary heroic and loyal sentiments before dying – except for the cowards who run away. The conduct of the East Saxons follows the archetypes of northern battle poetry: defence of a narrow place, high taunting words, suspense before fateful decision, deliberate courage, fidelity unto death. But the heathen enemy are unheroically (almost devilishly) cunning, mean and anonymous. The East Saxons mentioned are all known to the author and audience, and this local actuality makes the poem's archaic ideal believable. The place where vows were made, the legendary mead-hall in *Beowulf*, has become the historical council-place in *Maldon*; but the birds of prey, the death of the first Dane, the wait for the turn of the tide and the conduct of Bryhtnoth all conform to the old heroic style: this is how battles should be. *Maldon* is indeed a noble, simple poem; its elegiac ethos places it between the triumphal *Brunanburh* and the outrage of Wulfstan's *Sermo Lupi Ad Anglos* (*Wulf's Word to the Angles*). It is a clearer, if thinner, narrative playing-out of the Beowulfian code in historical action.

THE BATTLE OF MALDON

[Translation by Richard Hamer, notes by the editor]

He† ordered then that each young warrior
Should leave his horse and drive it far away,
Advance, and think on arms and noble valour.
Then first did Offa's† kinsman understand
5 That the earl would not suffer indolence,
And made his pet hawk fly out of his hands
Towards the wood, and stepped himself to battle;
Thus could be known that when the young man took
Up arms he would not weaken in the fight.
10 And Eadrich too resolved to serve his prince,
His lord in battle, and he started forth,
Bearing his spear. His heart remained heroic
As long as he might hold broad sword and shield.
Now that the time had come for him to fight
15 Before his lord, he duly kept his vow.
Then Byrhtnoth started to arrange his troops,
Rode and advised, and showed the warriors
How they should stand and hold their place, and bade
That they should hold their shields up properly,
20 Firm in their fists, and should not be afraid.
When he had all his troops correctly placed
He left his horse and joined the army where
His own most dear and loyal hearth-troop stood.
A viking messenger stood on the bank,
25 Called clearly forth and made his declaration,
Proudly proclaimed the message of the seamen
To Byrhtnoth as he stood upon the shore.
'Bold seamen send me to you, order me
To tell you that you speedily must send

---

he Bryhtnoth the Ealdorman (ruler) of the East Saxons   *Offa* the second-in-command

30　　Rings for defence; it would be better for you
　　　To buy off this armed onslaught with your tribute
　　　Than that our hardy men should deal out war.
　　　We need not fight if you can come to terms.
　　　We will establish with that gold a truce.
35　　If you who are in charge here will agree
　　　That you are willing to protect your people,
　　　And pay the seamen at their own demand
　　　Money for peace, and take a truce from us,
　　　We with that treasure will embark again,
40　　Go back to sea, and keep the peace with you.'
　　　Byrhtnoth replied, he raised his shield aloft,
　　　Brandished his slender spear, and spoke these words,
　　　Angry and resolute he answered him:
　　　'Do you hear, seaman, what this people says?
45　　They plan to give you nought but spears for tribute,
　　　Poisonous point and edge of tried old sword,
　　　War-tax that will not help you in the fight.
　　　Go, viking herald, answer back again,
　　　Tell to your men a much more hostile tale:
50　　Here stands an earl undaunted with his troop,
　　　One who intends to save this fatherland,
　　　Ethelred's† kingdom, and my liege lord's land
　　　And people. It shall be the heathen host
　　　That falls in fight. It seems to me too shameful
55　　That you should take our tribute to your ships
　　　Without a fight, now that you have advanced
　　　So far onto our soil. You shall not win
　　　Treasure so easily; but spear and sword
　　　Must first decide between us, the grim sport
60　　Of war, before we pay our tribute to you.'
　　　He then commanded all his men to take
　　　Their shields and stand along the river bank.
　　　But neither side might there approach the other
　　　For water: the tide rose after the ebb,†
65　　The streaming waters joined. It seemed too long
　　　Before they could engage in deadly combat.
　　　And so they lined the waters of the Pante,
　　　The troops of Essex and the viking army

Ethelred Ethelred II ('the Unready'), King 975–1016

ebb The Danes had beached their ships on Northey Island at the mouth of the river on which Maldon stands, the Pante or Blackwater. In order to gain the mainland they had to cross a causeway (here, 'bridge') which is at this point covered by the tide

In fine array; but none could give a wound,
70 Unless an arrow's flight should take its toll.
The tide receded, seamen ready stood,
A host of vikings eager to start battle.
The earl then called a hardened warrior
To guard the causeway, Wulfstan, Ceola's son,
75 Of a brave family a kinsman brave,
And with his spear he shot the foremost man
That boldly stepped upon the causeway there.
There stood with Wulfstan dauntless warriors,
Maccus and Alfere, two doughty men,
80 Who would not at that ford resort to flight,
But stoutly fought against the enemy
As long as they survived to wield their weapons.
When they perceived and clearly understood
That fierce defenders met them on the causeway,
85 Then did the hateful strangers turn to guile,
Asked that safe passage might be granted them
So that their infantry could cross the ford.
Then in his over-confidence† the earl
Yielded to the invaders too much land.
90 The soldiers stood and listened as the son
Of Byrhtelm called across the cold clear water:
'Now room is made for you; come quickly to us,
Men to the war; and God alone can tell
Who at the end may hold this battlefield.'
95 The wolves of war advanced, the viking troop,
Unmoved by water, westward over Pante,
Over the gleaming water bore their shields.
The seamen brought their linden-shields to land.
There Byrhtnoth and his warriors stood ready
100 To meet their enemies. He told his troops
To make a shield-wall and to hold it fast
Against their foes. So battle with its glory
Drew near. The time had come for fated men
To perish in that place. A cry went up.
105 The ravens† wheeled above, the fateful eagle
Keen for his carrion. On earth was uproar.
They let the file-hard spears fly from their fists,

---

over-confidence *ofermod* seems to imply an excess of noble courage, leading to the decision to allow the Danes to cross and not leave without a fight (see line 56)

ravens harbingers of battle

　　　　Grimly-ground darts; and bows were busy too,
　　　　Shield received spear-point; savage was the onslaught.
110　　Fighters fell dead, young men on either side.
　　　　Wulfmar was wounded, Byrhtnoth's sister's son
　　　　Chose death in battle, he was utterly
　　　　Cut down by swords. But there at once was vengeance
　　　　Paid to the vikings, for I heard that Edward
115　　Struck one of them so fiercely with his sword,
　　　　Restraining not the stroke, that at his feet
　　　　The fated warrior fell to the earth.
　　　　For this his prince, as soon as he had time,
　　　　Gave grateful thanks to his bold chamberlain.
120　　So the stout-hearted warriors stood firm
　　　　In battle, and the young men eagerly
　　　　Competed who might first with point of spear
　　　　Deprive a fated soldier of his life;
　　　　And all around the slaughtered fell to earth.
125　　Steadfast they stood, as Byrhtnoth stirred them on,
　　　　Bade every soldier concentrate on war
　　　　Who wished to win renown against the Danes.
　　　　A warlike viking soldier then advanced,
　　　　His weapon raised, his shield up in defence,
130　　And strode towards the earl, who in return
　　　　Marched resolutely forth to meet the churl.
　　　　They each intended evil to the other.
　　　　The seaman hurled a Frankish javelin
　　　　So that the leader of the troops was wounded.
135　　He thrust out with his shield so that the shaft
　　　　Was shattered and the spear sprang back again.
　　　　Enraged, the hero seized his spear and stabbed
　　　　The proud, rash viking who had wounded him.
　　　　No novice was the earl, he made his spear
140　　Pass through the young man's neck, guided his hand
　　　　So that he pierced the pirate fatally.
　　　　Then speedily he shot another man
　　　　So that his corslet cracked and through the chainmail
　　　　His breast was wounded, and the deadly point
145　　Stood at his heart. This made the earl more glad;
　　　　The bold man laughed, and said thanks to the Lord
　　　　For the day's work that God had granted him.
　　　　A pirate hurled a dart then from his hand
　　　　So that it pierced Ethelred's noble thane.

150	Beside him stood a lad not fully grown,
	A boy in battle, who right bravely drew
	The bloody spear out of the warrior's wound.
	He was the son of Wulfstan, young Wulfmar.
	He threw the hardened weapon back again;
155	Its point passed in, and he lay on the ground
	Who had before so sorely hurt his prince.
	A well-armed viking then approached the earl,
	He planned to take possession of his rings,
	His ornate sword and all his other booty.
160	Then Byrhtnoth drew his broad and bright-edged sword
	Out of its sheath, and smote upon his corslet.
	Too fast one of the pirates hindered him,
	Smashing the earl's right arm. So fell to earth
	The golden-hilted sword. Now could the earl
165	No longer hold the weapon or make use
	Of his sharp sword. But still he urged them on,
	The grey-haired chief encouraged the young men,
	Told them to carry on in fellowship.
	He could not stand firm on his feet much longer.
170	He looked to heaven, humbly made his prayer:
	'I wish to thank You, Ruler of the nations,
	For all the earthly joys that I have had.
	And now, mild God, I have most need that You
	Should grant grace to my spirit, that my soul
175	May come to You, into Your power, O Prince
	Of angels, journey forth in peace. I pray
	You will not let the devils harm my soul.'
	Then heathen soldiers cut him to the earth,
	And both the warriors who stood beside him,
180	Alfnoth and Wulfmar both lay on the ground,
	Gave up their lives beside their prince and lord.
	They then departed from the battlefield
	Who did not wish to be there: Odda's sons
	Were first in flight, as Godrich quit the field
185	And left the hero who so frequently
	Had given him a horse. He leapt upon
	The very steed his lord had owned, his saddle,
	Which was not right at all, and both his brothers
	Godwin and Godwig galloped after him.
190	They did not care for war, but turned away
	And sought the woods, fled to a safer place
	And saved their lives, and many soldiers more
	Than should have done if they had called to mind

        The many kindnesses that he had shown them.
195   So Offa warned him in the meeting-place,
        That very day, when he had held his council,
        That many there spoke boldly who at need
        Would not endure. Then was the leader fallen,
        Ethelred's earl, and all his household saw
200   Their prince lie slain. Then gallant thanes went forth,
        Men hastened eagerly who were not cowards.
        They all intended one of two results;
        To lose their lives or to avenge their dear one.
        Thus Alfwin son of Alfrich urged them on,
205   A hero young in years addressed them boldly:
        'Remember all the speeches that we uttered
        Often when drinking mead, when we made vows
        Upon the benches, heroes in the hall,
        About hard strife. Now may whoever has
210   True courage show it. Here will I reveal
        My genealogy to all. I come
        From a great family in Mercia;
        Alderman Ealhelm was my grandfather,
        Wise, prosperous, and honoured in this world.
215   The thanes among that race shall not reproach me
        That I intend to leave this troop and go
        Home to my land now that my lord lies dead,
        Cut down in battle. My grief is the greatest,
        For he was both my kinsman and my lord.'
220   Then he advanced, and set his mind on war,
        Until among that host he stabbed a sailor
        With spear-point, so that to the ground he fell
        Killed by his weapon. He encouraged all
        His colleagues, friends and comrades to advance.
225   Then Offa spoke, and shook his ash-wood spear:
        'Alfwin, you have encouraged all the thanes
        In time of need. Now that our prince, our earl,
        Lies on the ground the need for all is great
        That each of us should urge on every other
230   Soldier to battle, for as long as he
        May hold and keep his weapons, his sharp spear
        And trusty sword. Godrich the coward son
        Of Odda has been traitor to us all.
        When he rode on that horse, on that proud steed,
235   Full many a man thought that it was our lord.
        Thus was our force divided in the field,
        The shield-wall broken. May he come to grief,

That he put here so many men to flight.'
Leofsunu spoke, he raised his linden-shield
240 Aloft, and answered thus that warrior:
'I promise this, that I will not from here
Flee one foot's space, but rather will go forward,
Avenge my lord and patron in the throng.
No cause shall steadfast men of Sturmere have
245 To blame me with their words now that my prince
Lies dead, that I shall lordless travel home,
Turn from the fight. Rather shall weapons take me,
Spear-point and blade.' He went full angry on,
Fought with tenacity and scorned to flee.
250 Then Dunnere spoke out, brandished his dart,
A simple churl, he called out over all,
Said every man should take revenge for Byrhtnoth:
'He who among this people would avenge
His lord must weaken not nor care for life.'
255 So they advanced, and cared not for their lives.
The household troop then started fighting fiercely,
Furious spearmen, and they prayed to God
That they might take revenge for their loved lord,
Achieve the slaughter of their enemies.
260 The hostage† started eagerly to help them.
He was of bold Northumbrian family,
The son of Edglaf, Ashferth was his name.
He never weakened in the battle-play,
But sent forth darts fast and continuously.
265 Sometimes he struck a shield, sometimes he pierced
A man, and constantly he gave some wound,
As long as he survived to wield his weapons.
Edward the tall still stood among the troop,
Ready and eager; he spoke vaunting words
270 That he would never flee a foot of land,
Retreat at all, now that his lord lay dead.
He broke the ranks and fought against those men
Until he had avenged his patron nobly
Among their foes before he too lay dead.
275 Likewise did Atherich, a valiant comrade,
Forceful and keen; the brother of Sibirht
Fought earnestly, and very many others,
They cleft the rounded shield, and boldly strove.

---

hostage in heroic tradition hostages are even
more loyal than retainers. Compare the
Mercian nobleman Alfwin (line 204)

	The shield's rim burst, the smitten corslet sang	
280	A doleful dirge. Then Offa struck in battle	
	A seaman so that the earth he fell;	
	There too Gad's kinsman* tumbled to the ground,	Offa
	Offa was quickly cut down in the throng;	
	Nevertheless he had fulfilled the vow	
285	Which he had made his generous ring-giver,	
	That either they should both ride back to town,	
	Go home unharmed, or die among that army,	
	Perish of wounds upon the battle-field.	
	He lay like true retainer by his lord.	
290	There was a clash of shields. The Vikings came,	
	Enraged by battle. Many a spear passed through	
	The life-house of the doomed. Wistan went forth,	
	The son of Thurstan fought against those men.	
	Already in the throng he had slain three	
295	Before the son of Wigelm fell in death.	
	That was a fierce encounter. Warriors	
	Stood fast in battle, though their comrades fell	
	Weary with wounds. Dead men dropped to the earth.	
	All this time Oswold and his brother Eadwold	
300	Inspired the warriors, and bade their kinsmen	
	That in that grim necessity they should	
	Endure and use their weapons without weakness.	
	Byrhtwold spoke out, he raised his shield aloft	
	And shook his spear; an elderly retainer,	
305	Courageously he taught the warriors:	
	'Mind† must be harder, spirit must be bolder,	
	And heart the greater, as our might grows less.	
	Here lies our leader in the dust, the hero	
	Cut down in battle. Ever must he mourn	
310	Who thinks to go home from this battle-play.	
	I am an aged man. Hence will I not,	
	But I intend to die beside my lord,	
	Give up my life beside so dear a chief.'	
	So too did Godrich, son of Athelgar,	
315	Encourage them to war. Often he hurled	
	A murderous spear among the viking host.	
	Thus foremost he advanced among the people.	
	He slashed and smote, until he died in battle.	
	But that was not the Godrich who had fled.	

Mind ... less Lines often taken as the epitome
of the heroic code

Cynewulf
? 9th century

The Exeter Book manuscript begins with *Christ*, a sequence of three long poems known as *Christ I, II* and *III* but also as the *Advent Lyrics, Ascension* and *Doomsday*. *Ascension* is signed 'Cynewulf', as are three other poems including *Elene*. Cynewulf was probably a ninth-century monk, but nothing is known for certain about him; he subscribed his name, hidden under a simple runic disguise, in order to gain his readers' prayers rather than literary fame. Cynewulf was, like Aelfric after him, a skilful, orthodox writer. His *Juliana* and *The Fates of the Apostles* are representative hagiography, but *Ascension* and *Elene* are finely organised works of theological and human interest.

Elene tells the legend of the miraculous finding of the True Cross by Helena, the mother of the early fourth-century Emperor Constantine, and makes it a story of very great interest. At its conclusion the poet adds a self-portrait, here given in C. W. Kennedy's translation, which offers interesting comparisons with *The Dream of the Rood* and with the Elegies.

Cynewulfian, if not signed by him, are the *Advent Lyrics*, based upon antiphons from the Advent liturgy. The seventh of these deserves excerpting as the first piece of dramatic writing in English, an exchange between Mary and Joseph. She begins by asking why Joseph rejects her. Joseph's reply (*Advent Lyrics* 167–76), an expansion of Matthew 1. 18, is touching.

From ELENE

[*From the conclusion*]

                May hell's door be closed
And the entrance to heaven,   the angels' realm
And eternal bliss,   be open for ever,
And his lot appointed   with the Lady Mary
5   For every man   who keepeth in mind
The most hallowed feast,   under heaven, of the Cross
Which the Great Lord of all   clasped with His arms. Finit.
        Thus, old and death-bound   through this doomed flesh,
I have wondrously gathered   and woven this lay.
10 At times I have pondered   and patterned my thought
In the anxious night-watches.   I knew not the truth
Concerning the Rood   till with radiant power
Wisdom made wider   the thoughts of my mind.
Soiled by past deeds   and shackled with sin
15 I was vexed with sorrows,   bitterly bound,
Burdened with cares,   till the King of might
Through His radiant grace   granted me knowledge
To comfort old age, a glorious gift;
Instilled it in mind,   made steadfast its light,
20 Made it more ample,   unfastened the flesh,
Unlocked the spirit,   gave the gift of song
Which I've used in the world   with gladness and glee.
Full oft I took thought   of the Tree of glory,
Not once alone,   ere I learned the truth
25 Of the radiant Cross   as I read it in books,
In the fullness of time   to set forth in writing
The tale of that Standard.

                          Until then was strife,
    C The *hero*† perishing   haunted with care,
30   Though he shared in the mead-hall   many a treasure
    Y And appled gold.   He bewailed his *woe*;
    N A *death-bound* soul   he suffered sorrow,
    E Secret fear,   while his *horse* before him
       Measured the mile-paths,   proudly prancing,
35 W Decked with jewels.   *Joy* has fled,
       Mirth, with the years.   Youth has vanished
    U And olden pride.   *Our* portion was once
       The splendour of youth;   now the days of our years
       After time appointed   have passed away.
40 L Life's joy has waned   as the *waters* flow,
       The hurrying floods.   For all under heaven
    F *Wealth* is transient.   The treasures of earth
       Wane 'neath the clouds   most like to the wind
       When it rises loud   in the hearing of men,
45   Ranging the heavens,   faring in fury,
       And then all suddenly   is barred in silence,
       In its narrow prison   strictly constrained.

From ADVENT LYRICS VII

[Joseph's Reproach]

[Trans. J. J. Campbell]

          'I suddenly am
deeply disturbed, despoiled of honour,
for I have for you heard many words,
many great sorrows and hurtful speeches,
5 much harm, and to me they speak insult,
many hostile words. Tears I must
shed, sad in mind. God easily may
relieve the inner pain of my heart,
comfort the wretched one. O young girl,
10 Mary the virgin!'

---

hero the word translated as *hero* is represented in the MS by a rune which is to be taken as *cen*: keen, the keen one. The other letters of Cynewulf's name are italicised in the translation

The Phoenix
10th century

The Phoenix is an anonymous expansion of *De Phoenice,* an exotic poem sometimes attributed to the Latin Christian writer of the fourth century, Lactantius. The Old English tenth-century adaptation continues by adding a commentary based upon a Latin one by St Ambrose. *The Phoenix* is an allegorisation of the life, death and rebirth of the fabulous oriental bird as a type of Christ's resurrection. The initial description of the bird, and of the paradisal land where it dwells, appeals directly to the sensory imagination, uniquely in Anglo-Saxon verse which is normally in economical black-and-white.

From THE PHOENIX
lines 71–89

The groves are hung with growing fruit,
Bright to look upon; the burden of those woods
Favoured by heaven does not fail ever.
Nor does blossom, the beauty of trees,
5   Lie waste upon the ground; wonderfully rather,
The branches of the trees bear always
Perpetual plenty of fruit
And stand out green above the grassy plain.
It is the most glorious of groves, its gay adornment
10   The work of the Holy One. The woods' canopy
Is not to be broken, and it breathes out incense
Through that happy land. This shall last unchanging
For ever and ever, until the Ancient One
Shall ordain an end to all He first created.

15   Beautiful is the bird abiding in that wood,
Fair and feathered strongly: Phoenix is his name.
There he lives alone looking out upon his homeland,
Dauntless he surveys it. Death shall not touch him
On that lovely plain, for as long as the world shall be.

Aelfric
?955–1016

Aelfric has been called the father of English prose, and he is certainly the most prolific of Old English writers. Over a hundred sermons survive, including two cycles of forty *Catholic Homilies* and a volume of saints' lives, together with Bible translations, commentaries, canonical and liturgical handbooks, and a Latin grammar, glossary and an attractive language-practice manual, the *Colloquy*. Born about 955, Aelfric attended the school at Winchester set up by Aethelwold and became schoolmaster for novices at Cerne Abbas in Dorset, where over fifteen years he composed all his major scholarly and educational works. After he was made the first abbot of Eynsham, near Oxford, in 1005, he had little time for writing, and died in 1016. He gave scholarly assistance to Archbishop Wulfstan in his writings.

Aelfric was a graceful stylist and a gifted interpreter and translator of intellectual distinction. He was the easiest, clearest and most influential writer of Old English and the largest contributor to our vernacular culture, as his works were used widely throughout the English Church, which the Benedictines renewed during his lifetime, and were still being copied in the twelfth century. They are the object of increasing study today.

The text chosen to represent him comes from a sermon from his first volume of *Catholic Homilies* (*c*. 1000), on Easter, which shows his clarity in allegorical exposition. The translation by Benjamin Thorpe (1840) has a suitable smoothness and rhythmical balance and a clerical *suavitas* which would be hard for a modern translator to emulate successfully.

From SERMON ON EASTER DAY

[Easter Sunday]

Ye have often heard concerning the Saviour's resurrection, how he on this day arose from death; but we will remind you that it may not pass from your memory.

SERMON ON EASTER DAY

When Christ was buried, the Jews said to their governor Pilate, 'O Sir, the deceiver, who hath here been slain, said often times, while he was living, that he would arise from death on the third day,' etc.

We say now, if any one had stolen his corpse, he would not have stript him, for theft loves no delay. Christ appeared on the same day to Peter and to two others his disciples, and comforted them. 'Then at last Jesus came to his disciples, where they were assembled, and said to them, Peace be unto you; it is I, be ye not afraid. Then they were afraid, and weened it were a ghost. Then said he to them, Why are ye afraid, and think divers things of me? Behold my hands and my feet, that were pierced with nails. Grasp and behold: If I were a ghost, I should not have flesh and bones,' etc.

Jesus then frequently appeared to his disciples, and directed them to doctrine and to faith, how they should teach all mankind; and on the fortieth day of his resurrection he ascended bodily to heaven to his Father. But we have now said much more of the tenour of the book of Christ than this present day's gospel requires for the confirmation of your faith. We will now give you the explanation of this day's gospel, according to the exposition of the holy pope Gregory.†

My dearest brothers, ye have heard that the holy women, who followed the Lord in life, came with precious ointment to his sepulchre, and him whom they had loved in life they would when dead serve with human devotion. But this deed betokens something to be done in God's church. We who believe in the resurrection of Christ come assuredly to his sepulchre with precious ointment, if we are filled with the breath of holy virtues, and if we with the fame of good works seek our Lord. The women who brought the ointment saw angels; for they see the heavenly angels, who with the breath of good works yearn after the upward journey. The angel rolled the lid from the tomb; not that he would make way for Christ's departure, but he would manifest to men that he was risen. He who came mortal to this world, born of the closed womb of the virgin, he, without doubt, might, when he arose immortal, though in a closed tomb, depart from the world. The angel sat on the right side of the sepulchre. The right hand betokens the eternal life, and the left this present life. Rightly sat the angel on the right hand, for he manifested that Jesus had surmounted the corruptions of this present life, and was then dwelling immortal in eternity. The messenger was clad in a shining garment, because he announced the happiness of this festival-tide, and our glories. But we ask, ours or the angels? We say verily, both ours and theirs. The resurrection of Jesus is our festival

---

Gregory Pope 590–604, St Gregory the Great, who sent Augustine to convert the Angles. His biblical commentaries were regarded as authoritative throughout the Anglo-Saxon period

tide, for by his resurrection he led us to the immortality for which we were created. His resurrection was bliss to the angels, because God fills up their number[†] when he brings us to heaven.

The angel cheered the women, thus saying, 'Be ye not afraid:' as if he had said thus, Let those fear who love not the advent of angels; let those be terrified who are beset with fleshly lusts, and have no joy in the host of angels. Why fear ye, ye who see your companions? 'His countenance was like lightning, and his raiment as white as snow.' Verily in lightning is terror, and in snow the mildness of brightness. Rightly was the messenger of Christ's resurrection so figured; for when he himself shall come to the great doom, he will be very awful to the sinful, and very mild to the righteous. He said, 'Ye seek Jesus: he is risen: he is not here.' He was not then bodily in the sepulchre, who is everywhere through his divine power. There lay the garment behind in which he had been wrapt, for he recked not of an earthly garment, after he had arisen from death. Though a dead man be wrapt in a garment, that garment does not the sooner rise again with the man, but he will be clad with the heavenly garment after his resurrection.

It is well said of Jesus, that he would meet his companions in Galilee. Galilee is interpreted, *Passing over*. Jesus passed over from passion to resurrection, from death to life, from torment to glory. And if we pass from sins to holy virtues, then may we see Jesus after our passage from this life. For there are two lives: the one we know, the other one unknown to us before Christ's advent. The one life is mortal, the other immortal. But Jesus came and assumed the one life, and made manifest the other. The one life he manifested by his death, and the other by his resurrection. If he to us mortal men had promised resurrection and life eternal, and yet had not been willing to manifest them in himself, who would have believed in his promises? But when he would become man, then he also voluntarily humbled himself to death, and he arose from death through his divine power, and manifested in himself that which he had promised to us.

Now will some man say in this thoughts, 'Easily might he arise from death, because he is God: death could not hold him captive.' Let the man who imagines this hear an answer to his imagination. Christ departed at that time alone, but he arose not from death alone, but arose with a great host. The evangelist Matthew[†] wrote in the book of Christ, that many holy men, who had died in the old law, arose with Christ; and all wise doctors have said that they have effected their resurrection to eternal life, as we all shall do at the end of this world. Those doctors said, that the raised men would not truly have been

---

fills up ... number replacing the fallen angels, traditionally one-third of the original number   *Matthew* Matthew 27.52

witnesses of Christ's resurrection, if they had not been raised for ever. Now are extinguished all infidelities, so that no man may despair of his own resurrection, when the evangelist wrote that many arose with Christ, who were simple men, although Christ be God.

Now said the expounder Gregory, that it came to his mind, how the Jews cried out concerning Christ, when he was fastened on the cross. They said, 'If he be† the king of Israel, then let him now descend from the cross, and we will believe in him.' If he had then descended from the cross, and would not have borne their mockery, he had certainly not given us any example of his patience: but he remained a while, and bare their mockery, and had patience. But he who would not break from the cross, arose from the sepulchre. A greater miracle it was, that he arose from death, than that he living should have broken from the cross. A greater miracle it was, that he brake death in pieces, through his resurrection, than that he should have preserved his life by descending from the cross. But when they saw that he descended not from the cross, for their mockery, but thereon awaited death, they believed that he was vanquished and his name extinguished: but it so fell out, that from death his name sprang forth over the whole earth. Then was their joy turned to the greatest pain; for their sorrow shall be endless. . . .

If he be Matthew 27.42. Compare the Harrowing of Hell in *The Dream of the Rood* and *Piers Plowman*, Passus 18

Wulfstan
before 970–1023

Wulfstan was Bishop of London and then of Worcester, and Archbishop of York from 1002 to 1023. The leading statesman and jurist of his time, which spanned the humiliating reverses of Aethelred's reign (975–1016) and the beginning of Cnut's, he was the author of law codes in both reigns, and a score of his homilies survive. *Sermo Lupi* is the Word of the Wolf (*Lupus* was Wulfstan's pen-name), a thunderous sermon preached in 1014 to rally the English against moral collapse and against the Danes. As this selection shows, it is a catalogue of the nation's sins and of their punishment by the outrages of the invader. Wulfstan constantly identifies civil loyalties with Christian duties, and there is in his jeremiad as much of the jurist, who saw laws as the 'Institutes of Polity' (the title of his most profound work), as of the prophet. The style is oratorical and strongly stressed, trenchantly moral but also sober and realistic.

From SERMO LUPI AD ANGLOS

[Trans. M. Swanton]

Beloved men, recognize what the truth is: this world is in haste and it is drawing near the end,† and therefore the longer it is the worse it will get in the world. And it needs must thus become very much worse as a result of the people's sins prior to the advent of Antichrist; and then,
5 indeed, it will be terrible and cruel throughout the world. Understand properly also that for many years now the Devil has led this nation too far astray, and that there has been little loyalty among men although they spoke fair, and too many wrongs have prevailed in the land. And there were never many men who sought a remedy as diligently as they
10 should; but daily they added one evil to another, and embarked on many wrongs and unlawful acts, all too commonly throughout this

---

the end Revelation 20.7 was commonly taken to mean that the world would end 1000 years after Christ's birth or death

whole nation. And on that account, we have also suffered many injuries and insults. And if we are to expect any remedy then we must deserve better of God than we have done hitherto. Because we have earned the miseries which oppress us by great demerit, we must obtain the cure from God, if it is to improve henceforth by very great merit. Indeed, we know full well that a great breach requires a great repair and a great conflagration no little water if one is to quench the fire at all. And the necessity is great for every man henceforth to observe God's law diligently and pay God's dues properly. Among heathen peoples one dare not withhold little or much of what is appointed for the worship of false gods, and we everywhere withhold God's dues all too frequently. And among heathen peoples one dare not diminish, inside or out, any of the things which are brought to the false gods and are made over as gifts, and we have completely despoiled the houses of God inside and out. And God's servants are everywhere deprived of respect and protection; and with the heathen peoples one dare not in any way abuse the ministers of false gods, as one now does the servants of God, too commonly where Christians ought to keep God's law and protect God's servants. But it is true what I say; there is need of a remedy, because God's dues† have for too long dwindled away in every region within this nation, and the laws of the people have deteriorated all too much, and sanctuaries are commonly violated, and the houses of God are completely despoiled of ancient rights, and stripped of everything decent inside. And widows are wrongfully forced to take a husband. And too many are harassed and greatly humiliated, and poor men are painfully deceived and cruelly enslaved and, completely innocent, commonly sold out of this country into the power of foreigners, and through cruel injustice children in the cradle are enslaved for petty theft commonly throughout this nation, and the rights of freemen are taken away and the rights of slaves restricted, and the right to alms diminished; and, to be brief, God's laws are hated and his teachings scorned. And therefore, through God's anger, we are all frequently put to shame; let him realize it who can. And although one might not imagine so, the harm will become common to this entire nation, unless God defend us.

For it is clear and evident in us all that we have hitherto more often transgressed than we have atoned, and therefore many things fall upon this nation. For long now, nothing has prospered here or elsewhere, but in every region there has been devastation and famine, burning and bloodshed over and again. And stealing and slaughter, plague and pestilence, murrain and disease, slander and hatred, and the plundering of robbers have damaged us very severely; and excessive taxes have greatly oppressed us, and bad weather has very often caused us crop-

---

God's dues church tithes

failures; wherefore for many years now, so it seems, there have been in this country many injustices and unsteady loyalties among men everywhere. Now very often kinsman will not protect a kinsman any more than a stranger, nor a father his son, nor sometimes a son his own father, nor one brother another. Nor has any of us regulated his life just as he ought, neither clerics according to rule, nor laymen according to the law. But all too frequently, we have made lust a law to us, and have kept neither the teachings nor the laws of God or man just as we ought; nor has anyone intended loyally towards another as justly as he ought, but almost all men have betrayed and injured others by word and deed; and in any case, almost all men wrongfully stab others in the back with shameful attack; let him do more if he can. For there are here in the land great disloyalties towards God and towards the state, and there are also many here in the country who are betrayers of their lords in various ways. And the greatest betrayal in the world of one's lord is that a man betray his lord's soul; and it is also a very great betrayal of one's lord in the world, that a man should plot against his lord's life or, living, drive him from the land; and both have happened in this country. They plotted against Edward† and then killed, and afterwards burnt him. And they have destroyed too many godfathers and godchildren widely throughout this nation, as well as too many other innocent people who have been all too commonly slain. And all too many religious foundations have commonly been undone because previously certain men have been placed there, as they should not have been if one wished to show respect to God's sanctuary; and too many Christian people have been sold out of this country all the time now. And all that is hateful to God, let him believe it who will. And it is shameful to speak of what has too commonly happened, and it is dreadful to know what many too often do, who practice that wretchedness that they club together and buy one woman in common as a joint purchase, and with the one commit filth one after another and each after the other just like dogs who do not care about filth; and then sell for a price out of the land into the power of enemies the creature of God and his own purchase that he dearly bought.

Also we know well where the wretchedness has occurred that father has sold son for a price, and son his mother, and one brother has sold another into the power of foreigners; and all these are grave and dreadful deeds, let him understand who will. And yet what is injuring this nation is greater and also more multifarious. Many are forsworn and greatly perjured, and pledges are broken over and again; and it is

---

Edward the young King Edward, half-brother to Aethelred, was ambushed and killed at Corfe in Dorset in 978

evident in this nation that the wrath of God violently oppresses us, let him realize it who can.

And indeed, how can more shame befall men through the wrath of God than frequently does us on account of our own deeds? If any slave escape from his lord, and, leaving Christendom, becomes a Viking, and after that it happens that an armed encounter occurs between thegn and slave; if the slave should slay the thegn outright he will lie without payment to any of his family; and if the thegn should slay outright the slave whom he previous owned, he will pay the price of a thegn.† Over-cowardly laws and shameful tributes are, through the wrath of God, common among us, understand it who can; and many misfortunes befall this nation over and again. For long now nothing has prospered, within or without, but there has been devastation and persecution in every part, over and again. And for long now the English have been entirely without victory and too much cowed because of the wrath of God, and the pirates so strong with God's consent, that in battle often one will put to flight ten, and sometimes less sometimes more, all because of our sins. And often ten or twelve, one after another, will disgracefully insult the thegn's wife, and sometimes his daughter or near kinswoman, while he who considered himself proud and powerful and brave enough before that happened, looks on. And often a slave will bind very fast the thegn who was previously his lord, and make him a slave through the wrath of God. Alas for the misery, and alas for the public disgrace which the English now bear, all because of the wrath of God! Often two pirates, or sometimes three, will drive herds of Christian men out through this people from sea to sea, huddled together as a public shame to us all, if we could in earnest properly feel any. But all the disgrace we often suffer we repay with honour to those who bring shame on us. We pay them continually, and they humiliate us daily. They ravage and they burn, plunder and rob, and carry away on board; and indeed, what else is there in all these events but the wrath of God clear and visible towards this nation? . . .

---

the price . . . thegn the *wergild* (legal compensation) payable for a thane was many times that for a slave. Alfred's treaty of Wedmore (886) extended *wergild* to include Viking freemen as well as English, but runaway slaves were to have been excluded

MIDDLE ENGLISH LITERATURE

Edited by
Felicity Riddy

The Peterborough Chronicle
?late 9th century–1155

England is one of the small handful of European countries in which the vernacular language – as distinct from Latin – was used for historical writing before 1200. The *Anglo-Saxon Chronicle*, which records events in England from before the coming of the Angles and Saxons, was probably begun in the reign of Alfred the Great in the late ninth century, and from then on it was kept up to date in various centres until the Norman Conquest in 1066. At Peterborough Abbey, in Cambridgeshire, however, the monks maintained their version of the *Chronicle* for nearly a century after the Conquest. The following extract, which deals with the anarchic reign of William the Conqueror's grandson Stephen, was written in 1155, that is, retrospectively after Stephen's death in the previous year. The lawlessness of the nineteen-year period described was made possible because of the power struggle between Stephen, who was the nephew of his predecessor Henry I, and Henry's daughter Matilda, who regarded herself as the rightful heir. The prose of the anonymous monk who wrote this part of the *Chronicle* is plain and artless, at times even clumsy, but it conveys all the more forcefully the horrors suffered by ordinary people caught up in the violent ambitions of the powerful.

The text is from Bodleian Library, MS Laud Misc. 636, ed. Cecily Clark, *The Peterborough Chronicle 1070–1154* (1958).

1–5 1137. This year King Stephen went across the sea to Normandy and was welcomed there, because they thought he would be like his uncle and because he had acquired the royal treasury; but he dispersed it, squandering it foolishly. King Henry had amassed a great deal of gold
6–10 and silver, and it was not used for the benefit of his soul. When King Stephen arrived in England he held his council at Oxford, and there he seized Roger, bishop of Salisbury, and his nephews, Alexander, bishop of Lincoln and the chancellor Roger, and put them all in prison until they surrendered their castles. When the traitors realized that he was a
11–15 mild, soft-hearted, good-natured man who did not pursue vengeance, then all of them committed acts of atrocity. They had done him homage and sworn oaths, but they did not keep any pledges. They all perjured themselves and broke their pledges, because every powerful man established his castles and held them against Stephen; and they filled
16–20 the country full of castles. They bitterly oppressed the miserable people of the country with their castle-building. When the castles were built, then they filled them with fiends and evil men. Then they seized those people whom they thought had any goods, both by night and by day,
21–6 men and women, and put them in prison and tortured them for their gold and silver with indescribable tortures, for never were martyrs tortured as they were. They were hung up by the feet and smoked with foul smoke. They were hung by the thumbs or the head, and coats of mail were hung on their feet. Knotted strings were tied around their heads and twisted so that it went into the brains.

From THE PETERBOROUGH CHRONICLE

[The Reign of Stephen, 1135–54]

1137. This gære for the king Stephne ofer sæ to
Normandi and ther wes underfangen, forthi that hi wenden
that he sculde ben alswic alse the eom[†] wes, and for he hadde
get his tresor; ac he todeld it and scatered sotlice. Micel
5 hadde Henri king gadered gold and sylver, and na god ne dide
me for his saule[†] tharof. Tha the king Stephne to Englaland
com, tha macod he his gadering æt Oxeneford.[†] And thar he
nam the biscop Roger of Seresbyri and Alexander biscop of
Lincol and te canceler Roger, hise neves,[†] and dide ælle in
10 prisun til hi yafen up here castles. Tha the swikes[†]
undergæton that he milde man was[†] and softe and god, and ne
justise ne dide, tha diden hi alle wunder. Hi hadden him
manred maked and athes sworen, ac hi nan treuthe ne heolden.
Alle he wæren forsworen and here treothes forloren, for
15 ævric rice man his castles makede and agænes him
heolden; and fylden the land ful of castles. Hi swencten
swythe[†] the wrecce men of the land mid castelweorces. Tha the
castles waren maked, tha fylden hi mid deovles and yvele men.
Tha namen hi tha men the hi wenden that ani god hefden, bathe
20 be nihtes and be dæies, carlmen and wimmen, and diden heom
in prisun and pined heom efter gold and sylver untellendlice
pining, for ne wæren nævre nan martyrs swa pined alse hi
wæron. Me henged up bi the fet and smoked heom mid ful
smoke. Me henged bi the thumbes other bi the hefed and
25 hengen bryniges on her fet. Me dide cnotted strenges abuton
here hæved and wrythen it that it gæde to the hærnes.

---

the eom Stephen's maternal uncle, King Henry I of England (1100–1135), who had also been duke of Normandy since 1106
na god . . . his saule i.e. Henry's treasure was not used for the charitable purposes which he seems to have intended
his gadering æt Oxeneford in June 1139
neves the chancellor Roger le Poer was Bishop Roger's illegitimate son, not his nephew. These churchmen all lived like powerful and wealthy magnates (hence their castles)
swikes the barons, such as Geoffrey de Mandeville (d. 1144), who deserted Stephen for Matilda. Mandeville inflicted appalling cruelties on the people of Cambridgeshire, in the vicinity of Peterborough, which the chronicler seems to have in mind
he milde man was Stephen's firm but ill-judged action in arresting the bishops was followed by a more characteristic period of indecision. He was not stern enough to deal with the anarchy provoked by Matilda's invasion
swencten swythe i.e. with forced labour

They put them in prison where there were adders and snakes and toads, and killed them in this way. Some they put into a torture-chamber — that is, into a chest that was short and narrow and shallow — and they put sharp stones in it and pressed the person inside so that they broke all his limbs. In many of the castles there was a headband and noose that were of chains, a single one of which was enough for two or three men to carry. It was made like this, that is, fastened to a beam, and they put a sharp iron about the man's throat and his neck so that he could not turn in any direction, neither sit, nor lie, nor sleep, but was burdened with all that iron. They starved many thousands to death. I do not know how to, nor am I able to tell all the outrages nor all the atrocities that they inflicted on the miserable people of this country. And that lasted nineteen years while Stephen was king, and all the time it got worse and worse. They imposed taxes on the villages every so often and called it 'protection money'. When the miserable people had no more to give them they plundered and burned all the villages, so that you could easily go a whole day's journey and you would never find anyone living in a village, or land that had been tilled. Corn was expensive then, and so were meat and cheese and butter, because there was none in the country. The miserable people died of hunger. Some, who had once been rich men, lived by begging. Some fled out of the country. Never before was a country in greater misery, nor did heathens ever behave worse than they did; for too often they spared neither church nor churchyard, but seized all the goods that were in them and then burned the church and everything along with it. Nor did they respect the territory of bishops or abbots or priests, but robbed monks and clerks; and everyone who had the power to do it, robbed the next man. If two or three men came riding to a village, the whole township fled for fear of them, believing that they were robbers. The bishops and clergy kept on excommunicating them, but that was nothing to them, because they were all accursed and faithless and damned. Wherever the earth was tilled, it did not bear any corn, for the land was completely destroyed by actions such as these. And they said openly that Christ and his saints slept. Such things, and more than we can say, we suffered because of our sins for nineteen years.

Hi diden heom in quarterne thar nadres and snakes and pades[†]
wæron inne, and drapen heom swa. Sume hi diden in
crucethus – that is, in an cheste that was scort and nareu
and undep – and dide scærpe stanes therinne and threngde
the man thærinne that him bræcon alle the limes. In
mani of the castles wæron lof and grin: that wæron
rachenteges that twa other thre men hadden onoh to bæron
onne. That was swa maced, that is, fæstned to an beom, and
diden an scærp iren abuton tha mannes throte and his hals,
that he ne myhte nowiderwardes, ne sitten ne lien ne slepen,
oc bæron al that iren. Mani thusen hi drapen mid hungær.
I ne can ne I ne mai tellen alle the wunder ne alle the pines
that hi diden wrecce men on this land. And that lastede tha
xix wintre[†] wile Stephne was king, and ævre it was werse and
werse. Hi læiden gældes on the tunes ævre um wile, and
clepeden it 'tenserie'. Tha the wrecce men ne hadden nammore
to gyven, tha ræveden hi and brendon alle the tunes, that
wel thu myhtes faren al a dæis fare, sculdest thu nevre
finden man in tune sittende ne land tiled. Tha was corn
dære, and flesc, and cæse and butere, for nan ne wæs o
the land. Wrecce men sturven of hungær. Sume yeden on
ælmes the waren sum wile rice men. Sum flugen ut of
lande. Wes nævre gæt mare wreccehed on land ne nævre
hethen men werse ne diden than hi diden; for over sithon ne
forbaren hi nouther chirche ne chyrcheyærd, oc namen
al the god that tharinne was and brenden sythen the
chyrche and al tegædere. Ne hi ne forbaren biscopes
land ne abbotes ne preostes, ac ræveden munekes and
clerekes; and ævric man other the overmyhte. Gif twa men
other iii coman ridend to an tun, al the tunscipe flugæn for
heom, wenden that hi wæron ræveres. The biscopes and
lered men heom cursede ævre, oc was heom naht tharof, for
hi weron al forcursæd and forsworen and forloren. War sæ
me tilede, the erthe ne bar nan corn, for the land was al
fordon mid swilce dædes. And hi sæden openlice that
Crist slep and his halechen. Swilc and mare thanne we cunnen
sæin we tholeden xix wintre for ure sinnes.

---

pades toads were believed to be poisonous
xix wintre 1135–54

Layamon
fl. c. 1200

Layamon (Lawman) was a parish priest of the church at King's Arely in Worcestershire, probably around the turn of the twelfth century. His *Brut* (*c.* 1200), which is over 32,000 lines, is one of the longest poems in English. It is an account of the legendary history of Britain from its founding by Brutus to the reign of Cadwallon, last of the British (i.e. Welsh) kings, after which the kingdom falls into the hands of the Angles and Saxons. It derives largely from the *Roman de Brut* (Romance of Brutus, 1155) of the Jerseyman Wace, itself a translation into Anglo-Norman of Geoffrey of Monmouth's Latin *Historia Regum Britanniae* (History of the Kings of Britain, 1135) which Layamon also consulted directly. He knew Bede's *Historia Ecclesiastica Gentis Anglorum* (History of the English Church and People, 731) as well.

It is in the pages of the *Brut* that the legendary King Arthur, already well-known in Welsh, French, German and Latin, makes his first entry into English literature. According to the structure created by Geoffrey and followed by Layamon, during Arthur's reign Britain reaches its apogee as the Britons conquer their enemies at home and abroad. Nevertheless, Arthur's final triumph – the defeat of the Roman emperor – ushers in his downfall when news reaches him in Burgundy that his nephew, Modred, has usurped his throne and taken his wife, Guinevere. Arthur returns to England, and the extract below deals with the last two of his three battles against Modred, and the deaths of them both.

In writing 'national' history Layamon has created a new poetic form which draws on native poetry, presumably preserved in monastic libraries in his own part of the country, as well as on French versification. The *Brut* combines the alliteration and rhymes of late Old English poetry – already freer than 'classical' Old English verse – with the rhyming couplets of his French source. The echoing effects of his occasional rhymes are reinforced by the use of repetition and of formulaic lines and half-lines. The relations between Layamon's versification and the long alliterative line used by the poets of the fourteenth-century Alliterative Revival are obscure. Nevertheless the *Brut* provides evidence of the survival of the native alliterative tradition long after the Norman Conquest.

The text is from British Library, MS Cotton Caligula A. ix, ed. G. L. Brook, *Selections from Layamon's Brut* (1963).

1–8   And Arthur besieged the city of Winchester very closely and slew all the inhabitants – there was great sorrow. Young and old, he killed them all. When the people were all dead and the city burnt, then he commanded all the walls to be utterly destroyed. Then what Merlin said of old came to pass there: 'Wretched shalt thou be, Winchester! The earth shall consume thee!' Thus spoke Merlin, who was a great seer.

9–22   The queen remained in York; she had never been so unhappy; that was Queen Guinevere, most wretched of women. She heard very true words spoken: how Modred kept on fleeing and how Arthur pursued him. Misery was hers as long as she lived. She went out of York by night and fled towards Caerleon as swiftly as she could. Two of her knights brought her there by night, and her head was covered with a holy veil and she became a nun there, most sorrowful woman. Then no-one knew what had become of the queen, nor for many years after was it known for certain whether she were dead . . ., when she herself was sunk in the water.

23–30   Modred was in Cornwall and assembled many knights. He despatched his messengers to Ireland; he despatched his messengers to Saxony; he

From BRUT
(lines 3988–4090)

[The Death of Arthur]

And Arthur Winchestre† tha burh bilai wel faste
And al that moncun ofsloh – ther wes sorwen inoh!
Tha yeonge and tha alde alle he aqualde.
Tha that folc wes al ded, tha burh al forswelde,
5   Tha lette he mid alle tobreken tha walles alle.
Tha wes hit itimed there that Merlin seide while:
'Ærm wurthest thu, Winchæstre! Thæ eorthe the scal forswalwe!'
Swa Merlin† sæide – the witeye wes mære.
Tha quene† læi inne Eouwerwic, næs heo nævere swa sarlic;
10 That wes Wenhaver tha quene, særyest wimmonne.
Heo iherde suggen, soththere worden,
Hu ofte Modred† flah and hu Arthur hine bibah;
Wa wes hire there while that heo wes on life.
Ut of Eouerwike bi nihte heo iwende
15 And touward Karliun tuhte swa swithe swa heo mahte.
Thider heo brohten bi nihte of hire cnihten tweiye
And me hire hafd biwefde mid ane hali rifte
And heo wes ther munechene, karefullest wife.
Tha nusten men of there quene war heo bicumen weore;
20 No feole yere seoththe nuste hit mon to sothe
Whather heo weore on dethe . . .
Tha heo hireseolf weore isunken in the watere.†
Modred wes i Cornwale and somnede cnihtes feole:
To Irlonde he sende aneoste his sonde;
25 To Sexlonde† he sende aneouste his sonde;

---

1 *Winchestre* Modred has fled to Winchester after his army has been routed by Arthur's on the coast. When Arthur attacks the city, however, Modred treacherously slips away from the siege
8 *Merlin* son of a princess and an incubus, and instrumental in Arthur's birth. To Merlin are attributed the widely-read *Prophecies of Merlin* which were incorporated by Geoffrey of Monmouth into his *History of the Kings of Britain* (1135). The prophecy of the fall of Winchester is among them
9 *quene* Arthur's wife, Guinevere, who has betrayed her husband with Modred while Arthur has been away on a war of European conquest; hence her panic on hearing of Arthur's return
12 *Modred* Arthur's nephew, son of his sister Anna and King Loth of Lothian, to whom Arthur has entrusted his kingdom while he is abroad. Modred has usurped his uncle's throne and taken his wife during Arthur's absence
21–2 *Whather heo . . . the watere* the text is defective at this point. In Geoffrey and Wace Guinevere dies in the convent, but Layamon may have been aware of another tradition in which she is drowned
25 *Sexlonde* the Saxons are old enemies of the Britons, and have previously been defeated by Arthur

despatched his messengers to Scotland. He ordered all those who wanted to have land to come directly — silver or gold or goods or land. He took every precaution, as any wise man does when necessity overtakes him.

31–40   Arthur, most wrathful king, heard that Modred was in Cornwall with a great army and intended to wait there until Arthur rode up. Arthur sent messengers throughout his whole kingdom and ordered every living man who was fit for battle to come and take up arms; and whosoever resisted the king's command, the king would burn alive on the spot. Numberless men came to the court, riding and marching, like hoar-frost drifting down.

41–56   Arthur went to Cornwall with a huge army. Modred heard of it and advanced to meet him with numberless followers; many were doomed to die there. They came together on the Tamar; the place was called Camelford; that name will endure for ever. And at Camelford sixty thousand were assembled, and thousands more as well; Modred was their commander. Then the noble Arthur rode there with innumerable followers, although they were doomed. On the Tamar they came together; they raised battle-standards, advanced on one another, drew long swords, laid on helmets; sparks sprang forth, spears clashed, shields broke, shafts splintered; countless soldiers fought there altogether. Tamar was awash with blood.

57–68   It was impossible to identify any fighting-man in that battle, or know who did worse or who better, so confused was the fighting, for every man killed outright, whether he were servant or knight. Modred was slain there, and the days of his life ended, and all his knights were slain in that battle. All the brave retinue of Arthur was slain there, high and low, and all the Britons of Arthur's Round Table and all his foster-sons

To Scotlonde he sende aneouste his sonde.
He hehten heom to cume alle anan that wolde lond habben,
Other seolver other gold other ahte other lond;
On ælchere wisen he warnede hine seolven,
30 Swa deth ælc witer mon tha neode cumeth uvenan.
Arthur that iherde, wrathest kinge,
That Modred wæs i Cornwale mid muchele monweorede
And ther wolde abiden that Arthur come riden.
Arthur sende sonde yeond al his kinelonde
35 And to cumen alle hehte that quic wes on londe
Tha to vihte oht weoren, wepnen to beren,
And whaswa hit forsete that the king hete
The king hine wolde a folden quik al forbernen.
Hit læc toward hirede, fold unimete,
40 Ridinde and ganninde swa the rim falleth adune.
Arthur for to Cornwale mid unimete ferde.
Modred that iherde and him toyeines heolde
Mid unimete folke; ther weore monie væie.
Uppen there Tambre[†] heo tuhten togadere;
45 The stude hatte Camelford,[†] evermare ilast that ilke weorde.
And at Camelforde wes isomned sixti thusend
And ma thusend therto; Modred wes heore elder.
Tha thiderward gon ride Arthur the riche
Mid unimete folke, væie thah hit weore.
50 Uppe there Tambre heo tuhte tosomne;
Heven here-marken; halden togadere;
Luken sweord longe; leiden o the helmen;
Fur ut sprengen; speren brastlien;
Sceldes gonnen scanen; scaftes tobreken;
55 Ther faht al tosomne fold unimete.
Tambre wes on flode mid unimete blode.
Mon i than fihte non ther ne mihte ikenne nenne kempe
No wha dude wurse no wha bet, swa that wither wes imenged,
For ælc sloh adunriht, weore he swein weore he cniht.
60 Ther wes Modred ofslawe and idon of lif-dawe
And all his cnihtes islawene in than fihte;
There weoren ofslawe alle tha snelle
Arthures hered-men, heye and lowe,
And tha Bruttes[†] alle of Arthures borde

---

44 *Tambre* the river Tamar in Cornwall
45 *Camelforde* in Cornwall, on the river Camel (for which Tamar may be an error)
64 *Bruttes* Arthur is king of the Britons (ancestors of the modern Welsh), eventually to be dispossessed by the Angles and Saxons

from many kingdoms, and Arthur was mortally wounded with a broad deadly spear. He had fifteen terrible wounds; two gloves could be thrust into the least of them.

69–88 Afterwards, out of two hundred thousand men who lay there cut to pieces, no more were left in the battle except King Arthur alone and two of his knights. Arthur was atrociously wounded. A youth who was his kindred came to him there; he was the son of Cador, earl of Cornwall; the youth was called Constantine – he was dear to the king. Arthur, lying on the earth, looked at him and said these words with a sorrowful heart: 'Constantine, you are welcome. You were Cador's son; here I give you my kingdom. Guard my Britons as long as you live and preserve for them all the laws that have stood in my days and all the good laws that stood in Uther's days. And I will go to Avalon, to the fairest of all maidens, to the Queen Argante, most beautiful elvish-woman. And she shall make my wounds all whole and restore me with healing potions, and then I shall come to my kingdom and dwell among the Britons with great joy.'

89–103 After these words there came sailing from the sea a small boat, driven by the waves, and two women in it, marvellously clad, and they lifted Arthur up at once and quickly carried him, and laid him down gently and sailed away. Then what Merlin said of old came to pass: that there would be immeasurable grief at Arthur's passing. Britons still believe that he is alive and dwells in Avalon with the most beautiful of all the elvish-women, and Britons always look forward still to the time when Arthur shall come again.

65	And alle his fosterlinges of feole kineriches
	And Arthur forwunded mid wal-spere brade;
	Fiftene he hafde feondliche wunden;
	Mon mihte i thare laste twa gloven ithraste.
	Tha nas ther na mare i than fehte to lave
70	Of twa hundred thusend monnen, tha ther leien tohauwen,
	Buten Arthur the king ane and of his cnihtes tweien.
	Arthur wes forwunded wunder ane swithe.
	Ther to him com a cnave, the wes of his cunne;
	He wes Cadores† sune, the eorles of Corwaile;
75	Constantin† hehte the cnave; he wes than kinge deore.
	Arthur him lokede on, there he lai on folden,
	And thas word seide mid sorhfulle heorte:
	'Costæntin, thu art wilcume! Thu weore Cadores sone.
	Ich the bitache here mine kineriche,
80	And wite mine Bruttes a to thines lifes
	And hald heom alle tha lawen tha habben istonden a mine dawen
	And all tha lawen gode tha bi Utheres† dawen stode.
	And ich wulle varen to Avalun,† to vairest alre maidene,
	To Argante† there quene, alven swithe sceone,
85	And heo scal mine wunden makien alle isunde,
	Al hal me makien mid haleweiye drenchen.
	And seothe ich cumen wulle to mine kineriche
	And wunien mid Brutten mid muchelere wunne.'
	Æfne than worden ther com of se wenden
90	That wes an sceort bat lithen, sceoven mid uthen,
	And twa wimmen† therinne, wunderliche idihte,
	And heo nomen Arthur anan and aneouste hine vereden
	And softe hine adun leiden and forth gunnen liven.
	Tha wes hit iwurthen that Merlin seide whilen
95	That weore unimete care of Arthures forthfare.
	Bruttes ileveth† yete that he bon on live
	And wunnien in Avalun mid fairest alre alven,
	And lokieth evere Bruttes yete whan Arthur cumen lithe.

---

74 *Cadores sune* Arthur's kinsman Cador, earl of Cornwall, has figured previously as one of his leading supporters
75 *Constantin* Arthur's throne passes to Constantine, later to be struck down by God for the sacrilegious murder of Modred's sons
82 *Utheres* Uther Pendragon, Arthur's father
83 *Avalun* the magical isle of Avalon
84 *Argante* in other versions this is Arthur's sister Morgan le Fay (the Fairy), for which Argante may be a misreading
91 *twa wimmen* the mysterious women are Layamon's addition to the story
96 *Brutes ileveth* the persistent legend of Arthur's return, supposedly prophesied by Merlin, is recorded from the early twelfth century

There is no man born of woman, excellent though she be, who can say more of the truth about Arthur. But once there was a seer named Merlin; he foretold in words – his sayings were true – that an Arthur should come yet as the saviour of the English.

Nis naver the mon iboren, of naver nane burde icoren,
100　The cunne of than sothe of Arthure sugen mare.
Bute while wes an witeye, Mærlin ihate;
He bodede mid worde – his quides weoren sothe –
That an Arthur sculde yete cum Anglen† to fulste.

---

103 *Anglen* although Arthur is king of the Britons, nevertheless Layamon presents him here as the saviour of the English (descendants of Arthur's enemies). By 1200 Arthur had been assimilated into English, as well as Welsh, history

The Owl and the Nightingale
late 12th–early 13th century

The Owl and the Nightingale was written in the reign either of Richard I (1189–99) or his brother John (1199–1216). It takes the form of a debate, the poet chancing to overhear a protracted argument between the two birds as to the merits of their respective outlooks: the owl is sombre, stern and markedly clerical; the nightingale is a light-hearted spokeswoman (both birds are female) for lawful pleasure. Much of the poem – it is nearly eighteen hundred lines long – is in direct speech and the style is strikingly flexible. The four-stress couplets (an innovative borrowing from French verse) are used to create a varied and even complex rhetoric deploying proverbs, colloquialisms, exclamations, questions and *exempla* (exemplary narratives). The argument is not conducted in abstractions – English was not yet the language for abstract thought – but is constantly specific and physical; beyond the secluded nook in which owl and nightingale debate the reader is made aware of the busy worlds of farm, village, town and castle. The author of *The Owl and the Nightingale* was perhaps the Master Nicholas of Guildford to whose judgement the birds finally agree to submit, and whose talents are remarked on in the course of the poem. The title 'Master' signifies a graduate, and the whole poem bears in its fluid dialectic the impress of the twelfth-century university mind, trained to juxtapose arguments and delighting in irresolution. Neither side wins. The poem ends with owl and nightingale flying off to find Nicholas and the poet claiming not to have heard the outcome.

In the passage below the temperamental differences between the two birds are enlarged into a debate between summer and winter. This is also a debate about different kinds of poetry: the nightingale's version of summer is itself a literary *topos* or set-piece. A hundred years later the Harley lyrics 'When the Nightingale Sings' and 'Winter Wakens All My Care' (pp. 154 and 157) show the dialectic still unresolved.

The text is from British Library, MS Cotton Caligula A. ix.

1–12 And then, although the Nightingale was afraid, she spoke boldly: 'Owl,' she said,'why do you do this? In winter you sing "Woe is me!" You sing like a hen in the snow: everything that she sings is out of sheer misery. In winter you sing crossly and gloomily, and in summer you are always dumb. Thanks to your nasty spite you won't share our enjoyment, because you are almost eaten up with envy when our
13–23 happiness is here. You behave like the bad-tempered man to whom every pleasure is disagreeable; grumbling and glowering both come naturally to him when he sees that people are happy. He'd like to see tears in everyone's eyes, and he would not mind if knotted lumps were caught up in fine carded wool and hair. You do the same on your part, for when the snow lies thick all around and everyone is miserable, you
24–38 sing from evening until morning. But I bring every happiness with me; everybody is cheerful because of me and rejoices when I arrive, looking forward to my coming. The blossom begins to shoot and grow, both on the tree and in the field. The lily with her fair face welcomes me, I'd have you know, entreating me, with her fair complexion, to fly to her. The rose also, who comes out of the briar with her red hue, entreats me to sing a song of delight for love of her.

From THE OWL AND THE NIGHTINGALE
(lines 409–544)

[Summer and Winter]

An forthi, thegh the Nightingale
Were aferd, ho spac bolde tale:
  'Hule,' ho seide, 'wi dostu so?
Thu singest a winter "wolawo";
5 Thu singest so doth hen a snowe:
Al that ho singeth hit is for wowe.
A wintere thu singest wrothe an yomere,
An evre thu art dumb a sumere.
Hit is for thine fule nithe
10 That thu ne might mid us bo blithe,
For thu forbernest wel negh for onde
Whane ure blisse cumeth to londe.
Thu farest so doth the ille:
Evrich blisse him is unwille;
15 Grucching an luring him both rade
Yif he isoth that men both glade;
He wolde that he iseghe
Teres in evrich monnes eghe,
Ne roghte he thegh flockes were
20 Imeind bi toppes an bi here,
Also thu dost on thire side,
For wanne snou lith thicke an wide
An alle wightes habbeth sorwe,
Thu singest from eve fort amorwe.
25 Ac ich alle blisse mid me bringe;
Ech wight is glad for mine thinge
An blisseth hit wanne ich cume,
An highteth ayen mine kume.
The blostme ginneth springe an sprede
30 Bothe ine tro an ek on mede.
The lilie mid hir faire wlite
Wolcumeth me – that thu hit wite –
Bid me mid hire faire blo
That ich shulle to hire flo.
35 The rose also, mid hire rude
That cumeth ut of the thornewode,
Bit me that ich shulle singe
For hire luve one skentinge.

39-50 And I do so night and day – the more I sing the more I am able to – delighting them with my song, but nevertheless, not for too long. When I see that people are happy, I don't want them to become sated. When what I came for is done, I go again, and I act wisely. When a man's thoughts turn to his sheaves and the green leaves wither, I go home and
51-8 take my leave. I do not care at all for winter's plunder; when I see that hard time coming I go home to my own country, and I receive both love and gratitude for having come and laboured here. When my task is done, should I remain? No! Why? For he who stays longer than he need is neither clever nor wise.'
59-82 This Owl listened, storing up all this argument word by word, and then considered how she might, with justice, find the best answer: for he who fears procedural trickery must take very careful thought. 'You ask me', said the Owl, 'why I sing and cry out in winter. It is customary with good men – and has been since the beginning of the world – that each one cherishes his friend and celebrates with him for a time in his house, at his table, with pleasant talk and pleasant conversation; and especially at Christmas when rich and poor, mighty and humble, sing carols night and day, I help them in whatever way I can. And I also think about other things than having a good time and singing. I have a reply to this ready, straight away, all prepared: for summer time is much too free and easy, and makes a man's thoughts go astray.

      An ich so do thurgh night an dai –
40   The more ich singe the more I mai –
      An skente hi mid mine songe,
      Ac notheles noght overlonge.
      Wane ich iso that men both glade
      Ich nelle that hi bon to sade;
45   Wan is ido for wan ich com
      Ich fare ayen, an do wisdom.
      Wane mon howeth of his sheve
      An falew icumeth on grene leve,
      Ich fare hom an nime leve.
50   Ne recche ich noght of winteres reve;
      Wan ich iso that cumeth that harde
      Ich fare hom to min erde
      An habbe bothe luve an thonc
      That ich her com an hider swonk.
55   Than min erende is ido
      Sholde ich bileve? Nai! Warto?
      For he nis nother yep ne wis
      That longe abid thar him nod nis.'
        Thos Hule luste an leide an hord
60   Al this mot, word after word,
      An after thoghte hu he mighte
      Answere finde best mid righte;
      For he mot hine ful wel bithenche
      That is aferd of plaites wrenche.
65   'Thu aishest me,' the Hule sede,
      'Wi ich a winter singe an grede.
      Hit is gode monne iwone –
      An was from the worlde frome –
      That ech god man his frond icnowe
70   An blisse mid hom sume throwe
      In his huse, at his borde,
      Mid faire speche an faire worde;
      An hure an hure to Cristes masse
      Thane riche an poure, more an lasse,
75   Singeth cundut night an dai,
      Ich hom helpe what ich mai.
      An ek ich thenche of other thinge
      Thane to pleien other to singe.
      Ich habbe herto gode answare
80   Anon iredi an al yare.
      For sumeres tide is al to wlonc
      An doth misreken monnes thonk;

83-98 For he pays no attention to chastity but thinks only of lechery, because not one animal ever holds back, but each one rides another. The very horses in the stud are frisky and mad after the mares as well. And you yourself are in the midst of it, because your song is of nothing but lechery, and in anticipation of breeding you are bold and forward. As soon as you have trodden, you can't utter a word more, but peep like a mouse, squeaking with your hoarse voice. Yet you sing worse than the hedge-sparrow which flies along the ground among the stubble; when
99-118 your desire has gone, then your voice has gone as well. In summer the peasants go mad, writhing and contorting themselves. Nevertheless it isn't for love; it's the common man's violent urge; for when he has performed, all his cockiness disappears. If he has poked beneath a skirt, his love lasts no longer. It is the same with your mood: as soon as you are hatching, you forget all your songs. You do the same on your branch: when you have had your fun, your voice is immediately done for. And when the long nights come, bringing sharp, hard frosts, then it is clear at once where the active and the bold are. In that hard season
119-26 you can tell who goes out in front and who stays behind. You find out in times of need who can be given the difficult tasks. Then I am bold and have a good time singing, and rejoice with my songs of delight. I do not pay any heed to winter, because I am not a wretched weakling.

For he ne recth noght of clennesse –
Al his thoght is of golnesse;
85 For none dor no leng nabideth,
Ac evrich upon other rideth.
The sulve stottes ine the stode
Both bothe wilde an merewode;
An thu sulf art tharamong
90 For of golnesse is al thi song,
An ayen thet thu wult teme
Thu art wel modi an wel breme.
Sone so thu havest itrede
Ne mightu leng a word iquethe,
95 Ac pipest also doth a mose
Mid chokeringe mid stevne hose.
Yet thu singst worse thon the heisugge
That flighth bi grunde among the stubbe;
Wane thi lust is ago
100 Thanne is thi song ago also.
A sumere chorles awedeth
An forcrempeth an forbredeth.
Hit nis for luve notheles,
Ac is the chorles wode res;
105 For wane he haveth ido his dede
Ifallen is his boldhede.
Habbe he istunge under gore,
Ne last his luve no leng more.
Also hit is on thine mode:
110 So sone so thus sittest a brode,
Thu forlost al thine wise.
Also thu farest on thine rise:
Wane thus havest ido thi gome,
Thi stevne goth anon to shome.
115 Ac wane nightes cumeth longe
An bringeth forstes starke an stronge,
Thanne erest hit is isene
War is the snelle, war is the kene.
At than harde me mai afinde
120 Wo geth forth, wo lith bihinde.
Me mai ison at thare node
Wan me shal harde wike bode.
Thanne ich am snel an pleie an singe
An highte me mid mi skentinge.
125 Of non wintere ich ne recche,
For ich nam non asunde wrecche.

127–36 And I bring comfort to many people who do not have strength of their own. They are anxious and utterly miserable, and look desperately for a warm place. I often sing more for them, in order to reduce their suffering a little. What do you think? Do you give in? Are you defeated by the truth?' 'No, no,' said the Nightingale. 'You shall hear a different story . . .'

        An ek ich frouri fele wight
        That mid hom nabbed none mightte.
        Hi both hohfule an wel arme
130   An secheth yorne to the warme.
        Oft ich singe for hom the more
        For lutli sum of hore sore.
        Hu thincth the? Artu yut inume?
        Artu mid righte overcume?'
135   'Nay, nay,' sede the Nightingale,
        'Thu shalt ihere an other tale . . .'

Ancrene Wisse
?early 13th century

Ancrene Wisse (Anchoresses' Guide) is a version of a manual of spiritual guidance otherwise known as *Ancrene Riwle* (Anchoresses' Rule). It was probably written in the West Midlands in the early thirteenth century for three noble sisters who had become anchoresses, or recluses. In order to remove themselves completely from the temptations of the world and to devote themselves in solitude wholly to God, anchoresses were enclosed in cells, often built on to the sides of churches. An anchoress was not allowed to leave her cell; indeed, sometimes the door was sealed behind her when she entered it. The rites that were performed at her enclosure often included a mass for the dead, since she was regarded as dead to the world. This *Anchoresses' Guide* was written by an unknown cleric who was the sisters' spiritual counsellor. His purpose in writing was to furnish them with a daily routine of prayer, but also, and more importantly, to explain to them the basis on which the reclusive life is lived. He teaches them that it is not merely a life of privation and penance, but of love.

This passage is from Part Seven, which contains an extended discussion of love, and the writer makes clear that the extreme asceticism of the sisters' lives is not in itself what gives them spiritual value. Their solitariness is a means to the single-minded love of God which is a giving of the whole self and which reflects God's own love for mankind. The crucifixion is the supreme act of loving generosity: Christ is seen as a lover wooing and dying for his beloved, who is besieged by enemies in her earthen castle (at once a twelfth-century earth-work and a metaphor for the body). He is a knight at a tournament fighting for his lady; he is himself the knight's shield, the shape of which can be traced in his body on the cross. The prose of the *Anchoresses' Guide* is energetic and supple, a vehicle both for the self-consciously elaborated parable of the wooing king and for the shifting series of metaphors which conclude this excerpt. This passage can be compared with *The Dream of the Rood*, with Passus 18 of *Piers Plowman*, and with 'In a Valley of this Restless Mind' (all in this anthology) for its treatment of Christ as warrior and lover.

The text is from Corpus Christi College, Cambridge, MS 402, ed. J. R. R. Tolkien, EETS, OS 249 (1962).

1–5	And so, my dear sisters, strive above all else to have a pure heart. What is a pure heart? I have said it before: it is that you neither desire nor love anything but God alone, and those things, for God's sake, which help you toward him – love them for God's sake, I say, and not
6–10	for themselves – such as food or clothing, or the manservant or woman with whom you are provided. For as St Augustine says, speaking thus to our Lord: *He loves you the less who loves anything apart from you which he does not love on account of you*; that is: 'Lord, they love you the less who love anything but you, except they love it for your sake.'
11–15	Purity of heart is the love of God alone. In this is the strength of all religious professions, the end of all religious orders. *The fulfilment of the law is love*: love fulfils the law, says saint Paul. *Whatever is commanded, is made fast in love alone*: all God's commandments, as saint Gregory says, are grounded in love. Love alone shall be led along
16–20	saint Michael's way. Those who love most shall be most blessed, not those who lead the hardest life; for love outweighs that. Love is the steward of heaven because of her great bounteousness, for she keeps nothing back, but gives all that she has and even herself; otherwise God would set no store by what is hers.
21–4	God has earned our love in all sorts of ways. He has done much for us and promised more. A great gift draws love forth, but he gave us, in our fore-father Adam, all the world; and all that is in the world – beasts and birds – he set beneath our feet before we were found guilty of sin.
25–30	*Thou hast put all things under his feet: all sheep and oxen, as well as the animals of the plain, the birds of the air and the fish of the sea, which traverse the sea's paths*. And so the whole of creation, as has already been said, ministers to the righteous, to the soul's advantage; yet earth, sea and sun serve the purposes of the wicked also. He did even more: gave us, not only what is his, but all of himself. So high a

From ANCRENE WISSE
[On Love]

Forthi, mine leove sustren, over alle thing beoth bisie
to habben schir heorte. Hwet is schir heorte? Ich hit habbe
iseid ear: thet is thet ye na thing ne wilnin ne ne luvien bute
Godd ane ant te ilke thinges, for Godd, the helpeth ow toward
5   him – for Godd, ich segge, luvien ham ant nawt for ham seolven –
as is mete other clath, mon other wummon† the ye beoth of igodet.
For ase seith seint Austin and speketh thus to ure Lauerd:
*Minus te amat, qui, preter te, aliquid amat quod non propter
te amat*;† thet is, 'Lauerd, leasse ha luvieth the the luvieth eawt
10 bute the, bute ha luvien hit for the.' Schirnesse of heorte is
Godes luve ane. I this is the strengthe of all religiuns, the
ende of alle ordres. *Plenitudo legis est dilectio*:† luve
fulleth the lahe, seith seinte Pawel. *Quicquid preciptur, in
sola caritate solidatur*:† alle Godes heastes, as sein Gregoire
15 seith, beoth i luve irotet. Luve ane schal beon ileid i seinte
Mihales weie.† Theo the meast luvieth schulen beo meast
iblisset, nawt theo the leadeth heardest lif; for luve hit
overweieth. Luve is heovene stiward† for hire muchele freolec,
for heo ne edhalt na thing, ah yeveth al thet ha haveth, ant ec
20 hire seolven; elles ne kepte Godd nawt of thet hiren were.
    Godd haveth ofgan ure luve on alle cunne wise. He haveth
muchel idon us, ant mare bihaten. Muchel yeove ofdraheth luve,
me al the world he yef us in Adam, ure ald-feader; ant al thet
is i the world he weorp under ure fet – beastes ant fuheles –
25 ear we weren forgulte.† *Omnia subiecisti sub pedibus eius,
oves et boves universas, insuper et pecora campi, volucres
celi, et pisces maris, qui perambulant semitas maris.*† Ant
yet al thet is, as is thruppe iseid, serveth the gode to sawle
biheve; yet te uvele servith eorthe, sea ant sunne. He dude
30 yet mare: yef us nawt ane of his, ah dude al him seolven. Se

---

mon other wummon   a friend had provided each of the sisters with a maidservant to supply their physical needs
Minus te amat . . . te amat   Augustine, *Confessions*, bk 10, ch. 29
Plenitudo . . . dilectio   Romans, 13.10
Quicquid . . . solidatur   Gregory the Great, *Homilies on the Gospels*, bk 2, Homily 27
seinte Mihales weie   St Michael was believed to conduct the souls of the dead to heaven (as in the song, 'Michael, row the boat ashore')
stiward   a steward in a lord's household had charge of provisions and supplies
ear we weren forgulte   according to the doctrine of original sin, all mankind participates in the guilt of Adam for his sin of disobedience in Eden
oves et boves . . . semitas maris   Psalm 8, 7–8

gift was never given to such lowly wretches. *The Apostle says: Christ loved the church, and gave himself for it.* Christ, says saint Paul, so loved his beloved that he gave her the gift of himself. Now mark well, my dear sisters, the reason why he should be loved. First, like a man who goes courting, like a king who loved a poor noblewoman from a foreign land, he sent his messengers ahead – who were the patriarchs and the prophets of the Old Testament – with sealed-up letters. Finally he came himself and brought the gospel, as letters patent, and wrote greetings to his beloved with his own blood; a salutation of love, to woo her with and to enjoy her love. There is a story that goes with this, a parable with a hidden meaning.

A lady was surrounded on all sides by her enemies, her lands laid waste and she herself completely destitute, inside a castle of earth. A mighty king's love was directed towards her with such extravagance that he sent his messengers to her in order to woo her, one after another, often many together; he sent her many fine jewels, provisions to sustain her, help from his noble army to defend her castle. She accepted it all as if uncaring, and was so hard-hearted that he was never able to come closer to her love. What more would you have? He came himself in the end, showed her his fair face, as one who was the fairest of all men to look upon, spoke, so very sweetly, words so pleasing that they could raise the dead to life, performed many wondrous things and did great deeds of power before her very eyes, showed her his might, told her of his kingdom, promised to make her queen of all he possessed. All this counted for nothing. Was this not an extraordinary disdain? For she was never worthy to be his handmaid. But, because of his graciousness, love had so conquered him that in the end he said: 'Lady, you are attacked and your enemies are so strong that without my help you cannot escape from their power by any means, or avoid their putting you shamefully to death after all your suffering. I shall, for love of you, take that fight upon myself and deliver you from those who seek your death. Nevertheless I know for certain that I shall receive my death-wound in their midst; and I will do it gladly in order to win your heart. Now accordingly, I beseech you, for the love I show you, that you at least love me after that deed, dead, even though you would not while I lived.' This king did everything thus: delivered her from her enemies and was himself treated barbarically and finally killed; through a miracle he then arose from death to life. Would not this same lady be

hehe yeove nes neaver iyeven to se lahe wrecches. *Apostolus: Christus dilexit ecclesiam, et dedit semet ipsum pro ea*:†
Crist, seith seinte Pawel, luvede swa his leofmon thet he yef for hire the pris of himseolven. Neometh nu gode yeme, mine
35 leove sustren, for hwi me ah him to luvien. Earst, as a mon the woheth, as a king thet luvede a gentil poure leafdi of feorrene londe, he sende his sonden bivoren – thet weren the patriarches ant te prophetes of the Alde Testament – with lettres isealet. On ende he com him seolven ant brohte the godspel as leattres i-
40 openet† ant wrat with his ahne blod† saluz to his leofmon; luve-gretunge, forte wohin hire wit ant hire luve wealden. Herto falleth a tale, a wrihe forbisne.

A leafdi wes mid hire fan biset al abuten, hire lond al destruet ant heo al poure, inwith an eorthene castel. A
45 mihti kinges luve wes thah biturnd up on hire swa unimete swithe thet he for wohlech sende hire his sonden, an efter other, ofte somet monie; sende hire beawbelez bathe feole ant feire, sucurs of liveneth, help of his hehe hird to halden hire castel. Heo underfeng al as on unrecheles, ant swa wes
50 heard-iheortet thet hire luve ne mahte he neaver beo the neorre. Hwet wilt tu mare? He com himseolf on ende, schawde hire his faire neb, as the the wes of alle men feherest to bihalden, spec se swithe swoteliche ant wordes se murie thet ha mahten deade arearen to live, wrahte feole wundres ant dude muchele
55 meistries bivoren hire ehsihthe, schawde hire his mihte, talde hire of his kinedom, bead to makien hire cwen of al thet he ahte. Al this ne heold nawt. Nes this hoker wunder? For heo nes neaver wurthe forte beon his thuften. Ah swa, thurh his deboneirte, luve hefde overcumen him thet he seide on ende:
60 'Dame, thu art iweorret and thine fan beoth se stronge thet tu ne mahte nanesweis withute mi sucurs edfleon hare honden, thet ha ne don the to scheome death efter al thi weane. Ich chulle, for the luve of the, neome thet feht upo me ant arudde the of ham the thi death secheth. Ich wat thah to sothe thet ich
65 schal bituhen ham neomen deathes wunde; ant ich hit wulle heorteliche forte ofgan thin heorte. Nu thenne ich biseche the, for the luve that ich cuthe the, thet tu luvie me lanhure efter the ilke dede, dead, hwen the naldest, lives.' Thes king dude al thus: arudde hire of alle hire fan ant wes him seolf to
70 wundre ituket ant islein on ende; thurh miracle aras thah from

---

Apostolus . . . ipsum pro ea Ephesians, 5.23 and Galatians, 2.20
lettres i-openet letters patent were intended for public proclamation
wrat with his ahne blod i.e. through his crucifixion

71-5 wicked by nature, if she did not love him more than anything else after this?

This king is Jesus, God's son, that in all these ways has wooed our soul, to which devils have laid siege. And he, like a noble lover, after many messengers and numerous acts of kindness, came to prove his
76-80 love and showed through knighthood that he was worthy of love, as knights of old used to do; he entered the tournament and, for the love of his beloved, had his shield in the fight, like a fierce knight, pierced on either side. His shield, which hid his Godhead, was his dear body that was spread on the cross; like a shield, broad at the top with his
81-5 outstretched arms, narrow below, with one foot placed upon the other, as many believe. That this shield has no supporters is a sign that his disciples, who should have stood by him and been his supporters, all fled from him and left him as if he were a stranger, as the gospel says: *Then all the disciples forsook him, and fled*. This shield is given to us
86-90 against all temptations, as Jeremiah bears witness: *You shall give the shield of the heart, your labour*. Not only does this shield keep us from all evil, but it does even more: it crowns us in heaven *with the shield of good will*. 'Lord,' says David, 'with the shield of your good will you have crowned us': 'shield', he says, 'of good will', because all that he
91-2 suffered, he suffered willingly. *Isaiah: He has been offered up because he himself willed it.*

deathe to live. Nere theos ilke leafdi of uveles cunnes cunde,
yef ha over alle thing ne luvede him herefter?
   Thes king is Jesu, Godes sune, thet al o thise wise
wohede ure sawle the deoflen hefden biset. Ant he, as noble
75 wohere, efter monie messagers and feole goddeden, com to pruvien
his luve and schawde thurh cnihtschipe the he wes luvewurthe, as
weren sumhwile cnihtes iwunet to donne; dude him i turneiment
and hefde for his leoves luve, his scheld i feht as kene cniht
on euche half ithurlet. His scheld the wreah his Goddhead wes
80 his leove licome thet wes ispread o rode, brad as scheld buven
in his istrahte earmes, nearow bineothen, as the an fot – efter
monies wene – set up o the other. Thet this scheld naveth
siden[†] is for bitacnunge thet his deciples, the schulden stonden
bi him ant habben beon his siden, fluhen alle from him ant
85 leafden him as fremede, as the gospel seith: *Relicto eo, omnes
fugerunt.*[†] This scheld is iyeven us ayein alle temptatiuns, as
Jeremie witneth: *Dabis scutum cordis, laborem tuum.*[†] Nawt
ane this scheld ne schilt us from alle uveles, ah deth yet mare:
cruneth us in heovene *scuto bone voluntatis.*[†] 'Lauerd', he
90 seith, Davith, 'with the scheld of thi gode wil thu havest us
icrunet': 'scheld', he seith, 'of god wil', for willes he
tholede al thet he tholede. *Isaias: Oblatus est quia voluit.*[†]

---

siden   lit. sides. Heraldic supporters are the figures on either side of a coat of arms (like the lion and the unicorn in the English arms)
Relicto ... fugerunt   Matthew, 26.56
Dabis ... laborem tuem   Lamentations, 3.65 (vulgate version only)
scuto ... voluntatis   Psalm 5, 121
Isaias ... voluit   Isaiah, 53.7

Lyrics by Unknown Poets

'I CANNOT COME TO MY LOVE'
(13th century)

Some lines between 2 and 3 may be missing from this fragment, preserved in Worcester Cathedral Library, MS F.64, though the lack of rhyme is possibly deliberate.

> Hi ne may cume to mi lef
>   Bute by the watere.
> Wanne me lust slepen
>   Thanne mot I wakie.
> 5   Wnder is that hi livie.

I cannot come to my love except by the water. When I want to sleep, then I must lie awake. It is a wonder that I live.

'MERRY IT IS WHILE SUMMER LASTS'
(13th century)

This lyric, and the music to which it was set, have been preserved on a single leaf which also contains Anglo-Norman verses, now bound into Bodleian Library, Rawlinson MS G 22.

Mirie it is while sumer ilast*	lasts
With fugheles* song,	birds'
Oc* nu* necheth* windes blast	but now draws near
And weder strong.*	hard
5 Ei, ei! what* this nicht is long,	how
And ich with* muchel* wrong	because of great
Soregh* and murne and fast.	sorrow

'WHEN I SEE ON ROOD'
(13th century)

At least five other versions of this poem survive. The repetition of the final line in this text, from British Library, Royal MS 12 E 1, may indicate that it was set to music.

	†Quanne hic se on rode	
	Jhesu, my lemman,*	beloved
	An besiden him stonden*	stand
	Marie an Johan,*	John
5	And his rig* iswongen*	back beaten
	And his side istungen*	pierced
	For the luve of man –	
	†Wel ou hic to wepen	
	And sinnes forleten*	forsake
10	†Yif hic of luve kan,	
	Yif hic of luve kan,	
	Yif hic of luve kan.	

Stanzas from 'WHERE BETH THEY BEFORE US WEREN?'
(13th century)

These are the first four of ten stanzas, in the version of this poem preserved in Bodleian Library, Digby MS 86. The *ubi sunt* ('where are they now?') theme occurs in a variety of forms in writings of the Middle Ages. The answer is not always, as here, 'in hell'.

	Were beth* they biforen* us weren,	are (who) before
	Houndes ladden* and hauekes* beren*	led hawks carried
	And hadden feld and wode?	
	The riche levedies* in hoere* bour*	ladies their bower
5	That wereden* gold in hoere tressour*	wore head-dresses
	With hoere* brightte rode*	their complexions

---

1 *Quanne ... rode* When I see on the cross [*hic se* the speaker conjures up the traditional crucifixion scene, as depicted in painting and sculpture, in which Jesus on the cross is flanked by his mother, Mary, and St John. Meditating on images of the Passion was a common devotional practice]

8 *Wel ... wepen* I surely ought to weep
10 *Yif hic ... kan* if I understand love

Eten and drounken and maden hem glad;†
Hoere lif was al with gamen ilad;†
Men keneleden* hem* biforen.   kneeled them
10   They beren hem* wel swithe heye†   themselves
And in a twincling of an eye
Hoere soules weren forloren.*   lost

Were is that lawing* and that song,   laughter
That trayling† and that proude yong,*   youth
15   Tho* hauekes and tho houndes?   those
Al that joy is went away,
That wele* is comen te weylaway,*   contentment to grief
To manie harde stoundes.*   times

Hoere paradis hy nomen* here   they took
20   And nou they lien in helle ifere* –   together
The fuir* hit brennes* hevere.*   fire burns continually
Long is 'ay!'† and long is 'ho!'†
Long is 'wy?'† and long is 'wo!'†
†Thennes ne cometh they nevere.

---

7   *maden hem glad*   made merry
8   *with gamen ilad*   spent in enjoyment
10 *wel swithe heye*   very proudly indeed
14 *trayling*   trailing of long garments
22 *ay* ever, ah   *ho* cease, oh
23 *wy* why, alas   *wo* misery, woe   [*ay* ... *ho* ... *wy* ... *wo* editors often interpret these words simply as onomatapoeic cries of pain]
24 *Thennes ... nevere*   they never return from there

'ALAS, HOW SHOULD I SING?'
(early 14th century)

This fragment of a *chanson de mal mariée* (song of an unhappily married woman) is recorded in a collection of religious songs composed by Richard de Ledrede, bishop of Ossory in Ireland from 1317 to 1360. The bishop used old tunes, for which he supplied new words; these lines appear at the beginning of a Latin hymn to the Virgin as an indication of the tune to which it was to be sung.

> Alas, how shold I synge?
> Yloren* is my playinge.*   gone delight
> How shold I with that olde man
> To leven* and let* my lemman,*   live leave beloved
> 5   Swettist of all thinge?

'I AM OF IRELAND'
(early 14th century)

This enigmatic little poem is evidently an early carol: a song with a refrain or burden, sung to dancing. It is preserved, with eleven other lyrics in English and French, on a strip of parchment bound in Bodleian Library, Rawlinson MS D. 913.

> Icham* of Irlaunde   I am
> Ant of the holy londe
> Of Irlaunde.
>
> Gode sire, pray ich the,*   I pray you
> 5   For of saynte charité,*   out of holy charity
> Come ant daunce wyt me
> In Irlaunde.

Harley Lyrics
early 14th century

The following four lyrics are from British Library, Harley MS 2253, an anthology of verse and prose writings in English, French and Latin probably compiled in Ludlow, Shropshire, in the 1330s. The lyrics were presumably written in the early years of the thirteenth century. The poets must have known French or Provençal love poetry, with its complex stanzas and traditional forms such as the *reverdie* (celebration of spring) and *chanson d'aventure* (encounter-poem) which are used in the first three lyrics. The poet of 'Between March and April' evidently knew native, post-'classical' alliterative verse as well, and married English and French traditions with exuberant experimentalism. The bleak 'Winter Wakens All My Care', like the opening stanza of 'Now Shrink Rose and Lily Flower', is an anti-*reverdie* and may be compared with William Dunbar's 'Into these Dark and Drublie Days' (p. 553).

'BETWEEN MARCH AND APRIL'

    Bytwene Mersh* ant Averil*   *March April*
      When spray* biginneth to springe,*   *twigs bud*
    †The lutel foul hath hire wyl
      †On hyre lud to synge.
5   Ich libbe* in love-longinge   *live*
    For semlokest* of alle thynge;   *the fairest*
    He* may me blisse bringe: *she*
      Icham* in hire baundoun.*   *I am thrall*

      †An hendy hap ichabbe yhent
10   Ichot* from hevene it is me sent;   *I know*
    From alle wymmen mi love is lent*   *removed*
      Ant lyht* on Alysoun.   *is set*

---

3 *The lutel ... hire wyl* the little bird takes pleasure
4 *On hyre ... synge* in singing in her own language
9 *An hendy ... yhent* I have received a piece of wondrous good fortune

†On heu hire her is fayr ynoh,
　　Hire browe broune, hire eye blake;
15　†With lossum chere he on me loh,
　　With middel smal† ant wel ymake.*　　　　　　　proportioned
　†Bote he me wolle to hire take
　†For te buen hire owen make,
　Longe to lyven ichulle forsake†
20　　　Ant feye* fallen adoun.　　　　　　　　　　dead

　†Nihtes when I wende ant wake
　　†– Forthi myn wonges waxeth won –
　Levedi,* al for thine sake　　　　　　　　　　　lady
　　Longinge is ylent me on.†
25　In world nis non so wyter mon†
　　That al hire bounté* telle con;†　　　　　　　excellence
　Hire swyre* is whittore then the swon,　　　　　neck
　　Ant† feyrest may* in toune.　　　　　　　　　　maiden

　†Icham for wowyng al forwake,
30　　Wery so* water in wore;†　　　　　　　　　　as
　Lest eny reve me my make†
　　†Ichabbe y-yirned yore.
　†Betere is tholien whyle sore
　　Then mournen evermore.
35　†Geynest under gore,
　　　†Herkne to my roun.

13　*On heu ... ynoh*　Her hair is very fair in colour
15　*With lossum ... me loh*　she smiled at me with a delightful expression
16　*middel smal*　trim waist
17　*Bote he ... take*　Unless she will take me to her
18　*For te ... make*　to be her own lover
19　*ichulle forsake*　I shall refuse
21　*Nihtes ... wake*　At night when I toss and turn and lie awake
22　*Forthi ... won*　my cheeks turn pale because of it
24　*is ylent me on*　I feel
25　*wyter mon*　wise man
26　*telle con*　knows how to describe
28　*Ant*　and (she is)
29　*Icham ... forwake*　I am worn out with wakefulness caused by love
30　*wore*　troubled pool
31　*reve me my make*　deprive me of my beloved
32　*Ichabbe ... yore*　(whom) I have desired for so long
33　*Betere ... sore*　It is better to suffer greatly for a time
35　*Geynest ... gore*　Kindest of women (lit., under petticoat)
36　*Herkne ... roun*　Listen to my song

>   An hendy hap ichabbe yhent,
>   Ichot from hevene it is me sent;
>   From alle wymmen mi love is lent
> 40   And lyht on Alysoun.

'WHEN THE NIGHTINGALE SINGS'

> When the nyhtegale singes the wodes waxen* grene;   become
> Lef ant gras ant blosme springes* in Averyl,* I wene,*   grow April believe
> Ant love is to myn herte gon with one spere* so kene,   a spear
> Nyht ant day my blod hit drynkes: myn herte deth me tene.†
>
> 5 Ich have loved al this yer, that* I may love namore.*   so that no more
> †Ich have siked moni syk, lemmon, for thin ore.
> †Me nis love never the ner, ant that me reweth sore.
> Swete lemmon, thench* on me, ich have loved the yore.†   think
>
> Swete lemmon, I preye the of love one speche:
> 10 Whil I lyve in world so wyde other nulle I seche.†
> With thy love, my swete leof,* mi blis thou mihtes eche;*   darling increase
> A swete cos* of thy mouth mihte be my leche.*   kiss healer
>
> Swete lemmon, I preye the of a love bene:†
> Yef* thou me lovest ase men says, lemmon, as I wene,   If
> 15 †Ant yef hit thi wille be, thou loke that hit be sene;
> So muchel* I thenke upon the that al I waxe grene.*   much pale
>
> Bitwene Lyncolne ant Lyndeseye, Norhamptoun ant Lounde,
> †Ne wot I non so fayr a may as I go fore ybounde.
> Swete lemmon, I preye the thou lovie* me a stounde.†   love
> 20   †I wole mone my song
>   †On wham that hit ys on ylong.

---

4 *deth me tene* causes me pain
6 *Ich have ... thin ore* I have sighed many a sigh, beloved, for your favour
7 *Me nis ... reweth sore* Love is no nearer me and I bitterly regret that
8 *yore* for a long time
10 *other nulle I seche* I will not seek any other
13 *love bene* lover's petition
15 *Ant yef ... be sene* and if that is what you want, make sure it is apparent
18 *Ne wot ... ybounde* I do not know any woman so fair as the one I am in fetters for
19 *a stounde* a little while
20 *I wole ... song* I will sing my complaint
21 *On wham ... ylong* to the one who has caused it

'NOW SHRINK ROSE AND LILY FLOWER'

Nou skrinketh* rose ant lylie flour   wither
That whilen ber† that swete savour
   In somer, that swete tyde.*   time
Ne is no quene so stark ne stour,†
5   Ne no levedy* so bryht in bour*   lady bower
   That ded* ne shal by glyde.*   death overtake
†Whose wol fleysh lust forgon
   Ant hevene blis abyde,*   wait for
On Jesu be is thoht anon,*   at once
10   †That therled was ys side.

From Petresbourh in o morewenyng,†
†As I me wende o my pleyghyng,
   On mi folie* I thohte;   misdeeds
†Menen I gon my mournyng
15 To hire that ber the hevene kyng,
   †Of merci hire bysohte.
Ledy, preye thi sone for ous
   †That us duere bohte,
Ant shild* us from the lothe* hous   protect hateful
20   †That to the fend is wrohte.

Myn herte of dedes wes fordred*   terrified
Of synne that I have my fleysh fed
   Ant folewed al my tyme,
That I not whider† I shal be led
25 When I lygge* on dethes bed,   lie
   †In joie ore into pyne.
On o ledy* myn hope is,   one lady
   Moder ant virgyne;

---

2 *whilen ber* formerly bore
4 *stark ne stour* powerful or mighty
7 *Whose ... forgon* Whosoever wishes to forgo physical desire
10 *That ... ys side* whose side was pierced
11 *in o morewenyng* one morning
12 *As I ... pleyghyng* as I pursued my pleasure
14 *Menen ... mournyng* I made my lamentation
16 *Of merci ... bysohte* begged her for mercy
18 *That ... bohte* who bought us dearly
20 *That to ... wrohte* that is built for the devil
24 *That I not whider* so that I do not know whither
26 *In joie ... pyne* to joy or misery

> We shulen† into hevene blis
> 30   Thurh hire medicine.
>
> Betere is hire medycyn
> Then eny mede* or eny wyn;   mead
>   Hire erbes smulleth swete.
>   †From Catenas into Dyvelyn
> 35 Nis ther no leche* so fyn   healer
>   †Oure serewes to bete.
>   †Mon that feleth eni sor
>   †Ant his folie wol lete,
> Withoute gold other eny tresor
> 40 He mai be sound ant sete.*   content
>
> Of penaunce is his plastre† al,
> Ant ever serven hire I shal,
>   Nou ant al my lyve.
> Nou is fre that er* was thral†   formerly
> 45 †Al thourh that levedy gent ant smal:
>   Heried* be hyr joies fyve!   praised
> Wherso* eny sek* ys,   wherever sick
>   †Thider hye blyve;
>   †Thurh hire beoth ybroht to blis
> 50 Bo* mayden ant wyve.   both
>
> For he that dude is† body on tre†
> Of oure sunnes* have pieté*   sins mercy
>   †That weldes heovene boures.
> Wymmon, with thi jolyfté,*   light-heartedness
> 55 Thou thench on* Godes shoures.*   consider sufferings
>   †Thah thou be whyt ant bryth on ble
>   Falewen* shule* thy floures.   wither must

---

29 *We shulen* we shall go
34 *From . . . Dyvelyn* From Caithness to Dublin
36 *Oure . . . to bete* to assuage our griefs
37 *Mon . . . sor* He who feels any pain
38 *Ant . . . lete* and wants to leave his misdeeds
41 *plastre* soothing remedy
44 *thral* in bondage
45 *Al thourh . . . smal* all because of that lady noble and slender
48 *Thider hye blyve* let him go there directly
49 *Thurh . . . blis* through her are brought to bliss
51 *dude is* placed his *tre* tree, cross
53 *That . . . boures* who rules the bowers of heaven
56 *Thah thou . . . on ble* Though you are pale and fair of face

Jesu, have merci of us,
That al this world honoures.

'WINTER WAKENS ALL MY CARE'

    Wynter wakeneth al my care,
    Nou this* leves waxeth* bare.   these become
    Ofte I sike* ant mourne sare*   sigh bitterly
    When hit cometh in* my thoht   into
5   Of* this worldes joie, hou hit geth al to noht.†   concerning

    †Nou hit is ant nou hit nys,
    †Also hit ner nere, ywys.
    †That moni mon seith soth hit ys:
    †Al goth bote Godes wille;
10   Alle we shule deye* thah us like ylle.†   die

    †Al that grein me graveth grene,
    Nou hit faleweth* al bydene.*   withers quickly
    Jesu, help that hit be sene,*   clearly understood
    Ant shild* us from helle,   protect
15   †For I not whider I shal, ne hou longe her dwelle.

---

5 *geth al to noht*   all turns to nothing
6 *Nou hit . . . nys*   Now it is and now it is not
7 *Also . . . ywys*   as if, indeed, it had never been
8 *That . . . hit ys*   What many men say is true
9 *Al goth . . . wille*   everything passes except for God's will
10 *thah us like ylle*   although we do not want to
11 *Al that . . . grene*   All the grain which is planted unripe
15 *For I . . . dwelle*   for I do not know where I shall go, nor how long I shall remain here

Sir Orfeo
early 13th century

Sir Orfeo draws in part on classical legend: the names of the hero and his wife are taken from the story of Orpheus and Eurydice, as told by the Roman poets Virgil (*Georgics* 4, 453 ff.) and Ovid (*Metamorphoses* 10, 8 ff.), and moralised by the late Latin writer Boethius in his *Consolation of Philosophy* (c. 524). According to this legend the lute-player, Orpheus, goes to the underworld in pursuit of his dead wife, Eurydice. Having won her release from Pluto, king of Hades, through the power of his music, he loses her again by disobeying the injunction not to look back at her as they leave. The Middle English poem, however, also has Celtic affiliations, which have radically affected the story. According to the prologue, *Sir Orfeo* derives, like Chaucer's 'Franklin's Tale', from a Breton lay, a short narrative poem sung to the accompaniment of the harp. The poet of *Sir Orfeo*, or of the lost French source from which it was apparently translated in the early fourteenth century, has amalgamated the classical story with Celtic fairy lore, from which the happy ending probably derives. In this version of the story Heurodis is not dead, but has been taken by the fairies and is recovered from their power by her husband, although only after much suffering. Moreover the experience of Orfeo is paralleled by that of his steward, who also remembers and stays true. The poem makes powerful use of a series of contrasts – between humans and fairies, present and past, isolation and belonging, outcast and king – in order to express the tension between loss and recovery on which, as in Shakespeare's last plays, the comic understanding of things rests.

The earliest of the three surviving texts of *Sir Orfeo* is in the Auchinleck manuscript (National Library of Scotland, Advocates' MS 19.2.1), which was compiled for a wealthy Londoner around 1330. A page is missing from this manuscript at the beginning of the poem, so the first thirty-eight lines have been supplied from British Library, Harley MS 3810. Fragments survive of a sixteenth-century Scottish romance of *King Orphius*, in four-stress couplets like *Sir Orfeo*, and possibly a retranslation of the same French source, while a Shetland ballad telling a similar story was collected in the nineteenth century.

SIR ORFEO

We redyn* ofte and fynde ywryte,*   *read   written*
†As clerkes don us to wyte,
The layes that ben of harpyng
Ben yfounde* of frely* thing: *discovered   noble*
5   Sum ben of wele* and sum of wo,   *prosperity*
And sum of joy and merthe also;
Sum of bourdys* and sum of rybaudy,*   *jokes   ribaldry*
And sum ther ben* of the feyré;*   *are   fairies*
Sum of trechery and sum of gyle,
10   And sum of happes† that fallen by whyle;†
Of alle thing that men may se
Moost o love, forsothe,* they be.   *indeed*
In Brytayn* this layes arne ywrytt,   *Brittany*
Furst yfounde and forthe ygete,†
15   †Of aventures that fallen by dayes,
Wherof Brytouns made her* layes.   *their*
When they myght owher* heryn*   *anywhere   hear*
Of aventures that ther weryn,*   *were*
They toke her harpys with game,*   *delight*
20   Maden layes and yaf* it name.   *gave*
Of aventures that han befalle†
I can sum telle, but nought all.
Herken, lordyngys* that ben trewe,*   *lords   constant*
And I wol you telle of Syr Orfewe.
25   Orfeo most of ony thing
Lovede the gle* of harpyng.   *music*
Syker* was every gode harpure   *certain*
Of* him to have moche honour.   *from*
Hymself loved for to harpe
30   †And layde theron his wittes scharpe.
He lerned so, ther nothing was†
A better harper in no plas.†
In the world was never man born
That* onus* Orfeo sat byforn,   *who   once*

---

2   *As clerkes ... wyte* as learned men tell us
10   *happes* unforeseen events   *by whyle* from time to time
14   *forthe ygete* brought forth
15   *Of aventures ... dayes* of deeds that happened in olden times
21   *han befalle* have taken place
30   *And layde ... scharpe* and set his quick wits to it
31   *ther nothing was* that there was by no means
32   *in no plas* anywhere

35	And* he mygth of his harpyng her*	if hear
	He schulde thinke that he wer	
	In one of the joys of Paradys,	
	Suche joy and melody in his harpyng is.	
	Orfeo was a king,	
40	In Inglond an heighe* lording;	high
	†A stalworth man and hardi bo,	
	Large* and curteys† he was also.	open-handed
	His fader was comen of† King Pluto,†	
	And his moder of King Juno,†	
45	That sumtime* were as godes yhold*	formerly held
	For* aventours that thei dede and told.	because of
	This king sojournd* in Traciens†	lived
	That was a cité of noble defens,	
	(For Winchester was cleped* tho*	called then
50	Traciens, withouten no).*	for sure
	The king hadde a quen of priis*	precious
	That was ycleped* Dame Herodis,	called
	The fairest levedi,* for the nones,*	lady indeed
	That might gon* on* bodi and bones;	walk in
55	Ful of love and of godenisse,	
	Ac* no man may telle hir fairnise.	but
	Bifel† so in the comessing* of May –	beginning
	When miri and hot is the day	
	And oway* beth* winter schours	away are
60	And everi feld is ful of flours	
	And blosme breme* on everi bough	brilliant
	†Overal wexeth miri anough –	
	This ich* quen, Dame Heurodis,	same
	Tok* to* maidens of priis	took two
65	And went in an undrentide*	morning
	To play bi an orchard side,	
	To se the floures sprede* and spring*	burgeon flourish
	And to here the foules* sing.	birds

41 *A stalworth ... bo* a stalwart man and bold as well
42 *curteys* noble, courteous
43 *comen of* descended from [*King Pluto* in Greek mythology, the king of the underworld. The classical Orpheus was the son of Oeagrus and the Muse, Calliope *King Juno* a mistake; Juno was queen of the Roman goddesses, wife of Jupiter]
47 [*Traciens* the classical Orpheus was from Thrace (adj. Thracian, French *Traciens*) in northern Greece]
57 *Bifel* it happened
62 *Overal ... anough* becomes very delightful everywhere

	Thai sett them* doun, al thre,	sat
70	Under a fair ympe-tre,†	
	And wel sone* this fair quene	very quickly
	Fel on slepe opon the grene.	
	The maidens durst hir nought awake†	
	Bot lete hir ligge* and rest take.	lie
75	So sche slepe* til after none,†	slept
	That* undertide* was al ydone.*	so that morning finished
	Ac as sone as sche gan awake*	awoke
	Sche crid and lothli bere gan make.†	
	Sche froted* hir honden* and hir fet,*	chafed hands feet
80	And crached* hir visage:* it bled wete.	scratched face
	Hir riche robe hye* al torett*	she ripped
	And was reveyd* out of hir witt.	driven
	The two maidens hir biside	
	No durst† with hir no leng* abide,*	longer remain
85	Bot ourn* to the palays ful right*	run straight
	And told bothe squier and knight	
	That her* quen awede wold.†	their
	And bad hem† go and hir at-hold.*	restrain
	Knightes urn* and levedis* also,	run ladies
90	Damisels* sexti and mo.*	maidens more
	In the orchard to the quen hye* come	they
	†And her up in her armes nome,	
	And brought hir to bed atte* last	at the
	And held hir there fine fast.†	
95	†Ac ever sche held in o cri	
	†And wold up and owy.	
	When Orfeo herd that tiding*	news
	†Never him nas wers for no thing.	
	He come* with knightes tene	came
100	To chaumber, right bifor the quene,	

---

70 *ympe-tre* grafted tree. [The grafted (and thus cultivated) tree under which Heurodis lies perhaps represents civilisation, in contrast with the wilderness into which Orfeo retreats]
73 *durst ... awake* did not dare awake her
75 [*after none* notoriously, fairies are abroad in the mid-day sun]
78 *lothli ... make* made a terrible outcry
84 *No durst* did not dare
87 *awede wold* would go mad
88 *bad hem* told them
92 *And her ... nome* and took her up in their arms
94 *fine fast* very firmly
95–6 *Ac ever ... owy* But she kept on with one cry / and wanted to get up and be off
98 *Never him ... thing* he had never been more distressed by anything

And biheld and seyd with grete pité:
'O lef liif,† what is te,†
That* ever yete hast ben so stille*   (you) who quiet
And now gredest* wonder schille?*   cry out piercingly
105   Thi bodi, that was so white ycore,*   choicely
With thine nailes is al totore.*   torn
Allas, thi rode,* that was so red,   face
Is all wan as thou were ded,
And also thine fingres smale*   slender
110   Beth* al blodi and al pale.   are
Allas, thi lovesom eyghen to†
Loketh so* man doth on his fo.   as
A, dame, ich beseche merci!†
Lete ben* al this reweful* cri   cease pitiful
115   And tel me what the is,† and hou,
And what thing may the help now.'
Tho* lay sche stille atte last   then
And gan to wepe swithe* fast   very
And seyd thus the king to:
120   'Allas, mi lord Sir Orfeo,
Seththen* we first togider were   since
†Ones wroth never we nere,
Bot ever* ich* have yloved the   always I
As mi liif, and so thou me,
125   Ac now we mot delen ato.†
Do thi best, for I mot* go.'   must
'Allas,' quath* he, 'forlorn ich am.   said
Whider* wiltow go and to wham?   whither
Whider thou gost ichil† with the,
130   And whider I go thou schalt with me.'
'Nay, nay, sir, that nought nis!†
Ichil* the telle al hou it is.   I shall
As ich lay this undertide*   morning
And slepe under our orchard side,
135   Ther come to me to* fair knightes,   two
†Wel y-armed al to rightes,

---

102   *lef liif* dear loved one   *what is te* what is the matter with you
111   *lovesom eyghen to* two beautiful eyes
113   *ich beseche merci* mercy, I implore
115   *what the is* what is the matter with you
122   *Ones . . . nere* we have never once been angry
125   *delen ato* separate (in two)
129   *ichil* I shall (go)
131   *that nought nis* that is not so
136   *Wel y-armed . . . rightes* well armed in the proper way

	And bad* me comen an heighing*	told quickly
	And speke with her lord the king.	
	And ich answerd at* wordes bold,	with
140	†I no durst nought, no I nold.	
	Thai priked† ogain as thai might drive.*	hurry
	Tho com her* king, also blive,†	their
	With an hundred knightes and mo*	more
	And damissels an hundred also,	
145	Al on snowe-white stedes*	horses
	As white as milke were her wedes.*	clothes
	I no seighe* never yete bifore	saw
	So fair creatours ycore.*	choice
	The king hadde a croun on hed;	
150	It nas* of silver, no of gold red,	was not
	Ac* it was of a precious ston:	but
	As bright as the sonne it schon.	
	And as son* as he to me cam,	soon
	†Wold ich, nold ich, he me nam	
155	And made me with him ride	
	Opon a palfray* bi his side,	riding horse
	And brought me to his palays,	
	†Wele atird in ich ways,	
	And schewed me castels and tours,	
160	Rivers, forestes, frith* with flours,	woodland
	And his riche stedes* ichon;*	places each one
	And seththen* me brought ogain hom	afterwards
	Into our owhen* orchard	own
	And said to me thus afterward:	
165	'"Loke, dame, tomorwe thatow* be	that you
	Right here under this ympe-tre,	
	And than thou schalt with ous go	
	And live with ous ever mo.	
	†And yif thou makest ous ylet,	
170	Whar* thou be, thou worst yfet†	wherever
	†And totore thine limes al,	
	That* nothing help the no schal.	so that

---

140 *I no durst ... nold* I neither dared nor wished to
141 *priked* spurred their horses
142 *also blive* straight away
154 *Wold ich ... me nam* whether I wanted it or not, he snatched me
158 *Wele ... ways* well adorned in every way
169 *And yif ... ylet* and if you cause us to be prevented
170 *worst yfet* will be fetched
171 *And totore ... al* and your limbs all torn to pieces

	And thei* thou best* so totorn,	though you are
	†Yete thou worst with ous yborn.".'	
175	When King Orfeo herd this cas,*	circumstance
	'O we!'* quath he, 'Allas, allas!	woe
	Lever me were† to lete* mi liif	give up
	Than thus to lese* the quen mi wiif.'	lose
	He asked conseyl* at* ich man,	advice from
180	Ac no man him help no can.	
	Amorwe* the undertide is come	next day
	And Orfeo hath his armes* ynome*	weapons taken
	And wele* ten hundred knightes with him,	fully
	Ich* y-armed, stout* and grim,	each fierce
185	And with the quen wenten he*	they went
	Right unto that ympe-tre.	
	Thai made scheltrom* in ich a* side	formation on either
	And sayd thai wold there abide*	remain
	And dye ther everichon,*	each one
190	Er* the quen schuld fram hem gon.	before
	†Ac yete amiddes hem ful right	
	The quen was oway ytwight,†	
	With fairi forth ynome.*	snatched
	Men wist* never wher sche was bicome.	knew
195	Tho* was ther criing, wepe* and wo.	then weeping
	The king into his chaumber is go*	has gone
	And oft swoned* opon the ston	swooned
	And made swiche diol† and swiche mon*	grieving
	That neighe* his liif was yspent.	almost
200	Ther was non amendement.*	cure
	He cleped* togider his barouns,	called
	Erls, lordes of renouns,*	famous
	And when thai al ycomen were,†	
	'Lordinges,' he said, 'bifor you here	
205	Ich ordainy* min heighe steward	appoint
	To wite* mi kingdom afterward.	rule
	In mi stede* ben* he schal	place be
	To kepe mi londes overal.*	everywhere
	For now ichave* mi quen ylore,*	I have lost
210	The fairest levedi* that ever was bore,*	lady born

174 *Yete thou ... yborn* nevertheless you shall be carried off with us
177 *Lever me were* I would rather
191 *Ac yete ... right* But nevertheless right from in the middle of them
192 *oway ytwight* taken away
198 *swiche diol* such lamentation
203 *ycomen were* had arrived

	Never eft* I nil† no woman se.	again
	Into wildernes ichil te†	
	And live ther evermore	
	With wilde bestes in holtes hore.†	
215	And when ye understond that I be spent,*	am dead
	Make you than a parlement	
	And chese* you a newe king.	choose
	Now, doth* your best with al mi thing.'	do
	Lo, was ther wepeing in the halle,	
220	And grete cri among hem alle.	
	Unnethe* might old or yong	scarcely
	For wepeing speke a word with tong.	
	Thai kneled adoun al yfere†	
	And praid him, yif* his wille were,	if
225	That he no schuld nought fram hem go.	
	'Do way,'* quath he, 'it schal be so.'	enough
	Al his kingdom he forsoke;	
	Bot a sclavin† on him he toke.	
	He no hadde kirtel* no hode,*	coat hood
230	Schert, no nother gode,*	possessions
	Bot his harp he tok algate*	at any rate
	And dede him* barfot out atte yate† –	went
	No man most with him go.	
	O way,* what* ther was wepe* and wo,	alas how weeping
235	When he that hadde ben king with croun	
	Went so poverlich* out of toun!	poorly
	Thurth* wode and over heth,	through
	Into the wildernes he geth.*	goes
	Nothing he fint* that him is ays†	finds
240	Bot ever he liveth in gret malais.*	discomfort
	He that hadde ywerd* the fowe and griis†	worn
	And on bed the purper biis,†	
	Now on hard hethe he lith,*	lies
	With leves and gresse he him writh.†	
245	He that hadde had castels and tours,	
	River, forest, frith* with flours,	woodland

211 *I nil* I do not want to
212 *ichil te* I shall go
214 *holtes hore* grey woods
223 *al yfere* all together
228 *sclavin* pilgrim's cloak
232 *atte yate* at the gate
239 *him is ays* is a comfort to him
241 *fowe and griis* variegated and grey furs
242 *purper biis* purple linen
244 *him writh* wraps himself

Now, thei* it comenci* to snewe and frese,	though	begin
This king mot* make his bed in mese.*	must	moss
He that had yhad knightes of priis*		prized
250 Bifor him kneland,* and levedis,*	kneeling	ladies
Now seth* he nothing that him liketh,†		sees
Bot wilde wormes* bi him striketh.*	snakes	glide
He that had yhad plenté		
Of mete* and drink, of ich* deynté,	food	every
255 Now may he al day digge and wrote*		grub
Er* he finde his fille of rote.*	before	roots
In somer he liveth by wild frut		
And berien,* bot gode lite;†		berries
In winter may he nothing finde		
260 Bot rote, grases and the rinde.*		bark
Al his bodi was oway dwine*		wasted
For missays,* and al tochine.*	hardship	scarred
Lord, who may telle the sore*		pain
This king sufferd ten yere and more?		
265 His here of his berd, blac and rowe,*		rough
To his girdel-stede* was growe.		waist
His harp, whereon was al his gle,*		delight
He hidde in an holwe* tre		hollow
And when the weder was clere and bright		
270 He toke his harp† to him wel right		
And harped at his owhen wille.		
Into alle the wode the soun gan schille,*		rang
That* alle the wilde bestes that ther beth		so that
For joie abouten him thai teth,*		approach
275 And alle the foules* that ther were		birds
Come and sete* on ich a brere†		sat
To here his harping a fine:†		
So miche melody was therin.		
And when he his harping lete* wold,		stop
280 †No best bi him abide nold.		

---

251 *him liketh* pleases him
258 *gode lite* precious few
270–4 [*He toke his harp ... him thai teth* the classical Orpheus goes into the wilderness after his loss of Eurydice, and charms animals, trees and even stones with his lyre-playing]
276 *ich a brere* every briar
277 *a fine* to the end
280 *No best ... nold* no creature would remain by him

	He might se him bisides,†	
	Oft in hot undertides,*	mornings
	The king o fairy with his rout	
	Com to hunt him al about	
285	With dim* cri and bloweing,	faint
	And houndes also with him berking.	
	Ac* no best thai no nome,*	but caught
	No never he nist† whider thai bicome.	
	And other while he might him se	
290	As a gret ost* bi him te,*	army approach
	Wele atourned,* ten hundred knightes,	equipped
	†Ich y-armed to his rightes,	
	Of cuntenance stout* and fers,*	bold fierce
	With many desplaid* baners,	unfurled
295	And ich his swerd ydrawe* hold;	drawn
	Ac never he nist whider thai wold.*	would go
	And other while he seighe* other thing:	saw
	Knightes and levedis com daunceing	
	In queynt* atire, gisely,*	elegant skilfully
300	Queynt pas* and softly;	steps
	Tabours* and trumpes yede hem bi†	drums
	And all maner menstraci.*	minstrelsy
	And on a day† he seighe him biside	
	Sexti levedis on hors ride,	
305	Gentil and jolif* as brid* on ris* –	gay bird twig
	†Nought o man amonges hem ther nis.	
	And ich a faucoun* on hond bere*	falcon bore
	And riden on haukin† bi o rivere.	
	Of game thai founde wel gode haunt:*	plenty
310	Maulardes,* hayroun* and cormeraunt.	mallard heron
	The foules of* the water ariseth;	from
	The faucouns hem wele deviseth:*	observe
	Ich faucoun his pray slough.*	killed
	That seighe* Orfeo and lough:*	saw laughed
315	'Parfay,'* quath he, 'ther is fair game –	indeed
	Thider ichil,* bi Godes name!	I shall go

---

281 *him bisides* near him. [The traditional activities of the fairies which Orfeo witnesses in the following lines – the hunt, the mounted soldiers, the dancing and hawking – are all aristocratic or courtly, offering reminders of the world he has lost]
288 *nist* did not know
292 *Ich y-armed . . . rightes* each armed as he should be
301 *yede hem bi* went by them
303 *on a day* one day
306 *Nought . . . ther nis* there is not one man among them
308 *on haukin* hawking

	Ich was ywon* swiche werk† to se.'	accustomed
	He aros and thider gan te.*	approach
	To a levedi he was ycome,	
320	Biheld and hath wel undernome*	understood
	And seth* bi al thing that it is	sees
	His owhen quen, Dam* Heurodis.	lady
	Yern* he biheld hir and sche him eke,*	eagerly also
	Ac noither* to other a word no speke.	neither
325	For messais* that sche on him seighe,*	hardship saw
	That had ben so riche and so heighe,*	exalted
	The teres fel out of her eighe.	
	The other levedis this yseighe*	saw
	And maked* hir oway to ride:	made
330	Sche most with him no lenger abide.	
	'Allas,' quath he, 'now me is wo!†	
	Whi nil* deth now me slo?*	will not slay
	Allas, wroche,* that I no might	wretch
	Dye now after this sight.	
335	Allas, to* long last mi liif,	too
	When I no dar nought with mi wiif,	
	No* hye* to me, o* word speke.	nor she one
	Allas, whi nil* min hert breke?	will not
	Parfay,' quath he, 'tide wat bitide,†	
340	Whider so this* levedis ride,	these
	The selve* way ichil streche* –	same proceed
	Of liif no deth me no reche.'†	
	†His sclavain he dede also spac	
	And henge* his harp opon his bac	hung
345	And had wel gode wil† to gon;	
	He no spard* noither stub* no ston.	stopped for tree-trunk
	In at a roche* the levedis rideth†	rock
	And he after, and nought abideth.†	
	When he was in the roche ygo*	gone
350	Wele thre mile other mo,*	or more

---

317 *swiche werk* such matters
331 *me is wo* I am grief-stricken
339 *tide wat bitide* whatever happens
342 *me no reche* I take no heed
343 *His sclavain ... spac* He quickly put on his pilgrim's cloak
345 *wel gode wil* very strong desire
347 [*In at roche ... rideth* a detail drawn from Celtic lore; Walter Map in *De Nugis Curialium* (Courtly Trifles) (ll 81–93) tells a Welsh story of how the ancient British king Herla entered the otherworld through a cave in a cliff]
348 *nought abideth* does not wait at all

He com into a fair cuntray
As bright so sonne on somers day,
Smothe and plain and al grene;
Hille no dale nas ther non ysene.* — visible
355 Amidde† the lond a castel he sighe,* — saw
Riche and real* and wonder* heighe. — royal wondrously
Al the utmast* wal — outer
Was clere and schine* as cristal; — bright
An hundred tours ther were about,* — around
360 Degiselich* and bataild stout.† — wonderful
The butras* com out of the diche* — buttress moat
Of rede gold y-arched* riche. — vaulted
The vousour* was avowed* al — vaulting adorned
†Of ich maner divers aumal.
365 Within ther wer wide* wones* — spacious buildings
Al of precious stones;
†The werst piler on to biholde
Was al of burnist gold.
Al that lond was ever* light, — always
370 For when it schuld be therk* and night — dark
The riche stones light gonne†
As bright as doth at none* the sonne. — noon
No man may telle, no thenche* in thought, — think
The riche werk that ther was wrought.
375 Bi al thing him think† that it is
The proude court of Paradis.
In this castel the levedis* alight; — ladies
He wold* in after yif he might.* — wanted to (go) could
Orfeo knokketh atte gate;
380 The porter was redi* therate — at hand
And asked what he wold have ydo.* — done
'Parfay,'* quath he, 'icham* a minstrel, lo! — indeed I am
To solas* thi lord with mi gle,* — entertain music
Yif his swete wille be.'
385 The porter undede the gate anon* — immediately
And lete him into the castel gon.* — go
    Than he gan bihold about al* — all around
And seighe ful* liggeand* within the wal — indeed lying

---

355 *Amidde* in the middle of
360 *bataild stout* strongly crenellated
364 *Of ich ... aumal* with every different kind of enamelling
367 *The werst ... biholde* the worst pillar that might be seen
371 *light gonne* shone
375 *Bi al ... think* because of all this it seems to him

	Of* folk that were thider ybrought	some
390	And thought dede, and nare nought.†	
	Sum stode withouten hade,*	head
	And sum non armes nade,†	
	And sum thurth* the bodi hadde wounde,	through
	And sum lay wode,* ybounde,	mad
395	And sum armed on hors sete,*	sat
	And sum astrangled as thai ete,	
	And sum were in water adreynt,*	drowned
	And sum with fire al forschreynt.*	shrivelled up
	Wives ther lay on child-bedde,	
400	Sum ded and sum awedde;†	
	And wonder fele† ther lay bisides,	
	Right* as thai slepe her undertides.†	exactly
	Eche was thus in this warld ynome,*	snatched
	With fairi thider ycome.	
405	Ther he seighe his owhen wiif,	
	Dame Heurodis, his lef liif,†	
	Slepe under an ympe-tre;	
	Bi her clothes he knewe that it was he.*	she
	And when he hadde bihold this mervails alle	
410	He went into the kinges halle;	
	Than seighe he ther a semly* sight,	fair
	A tabernacle† blisseful and bright.	
	Therin her maister† king sete,	
	And her quen fair and swete.	
415	Her crounes, her clothes schine so bright	
	That unnethe* bihold he hem might.	scarcely
	When he hadde biholden al that thing	
	He kneled adoun bifor the king:	
	'O lord,' he seyd, 'yif it thi wille were,	
420	Mi menstraci thou schust* yhere.'	should(st)
	The king answerd: 'What man artow*	are you
	That art hider ycomen now?	
	Ich, no non that is with me,	
	No sent never after the.	

390 *nare nought* are not at all. [The Celtic belief that many people thought to be dead have in fact been 'taken' by the fairies, survived in Ireland until the nineteenth century at least]
392 *nade* did not have
400 *awedde* out of their minds
401 *wonder fele* an extraordinary number
402 *her undertides* in the (lit. their) mornings
406 *lef liif* dear loved one
412 *tabernacle* canopied throne
413 *her maister* their lord

425	†Seththen that ich here regni gan	
	I no fond* never so fole-hardi† man	encountered
	That hider to ous durst wende,†	
	†Bot that ichim wald of-sende.'	
	'Lord,' quath he, 'trowe* ful wel,	believe
430	I nam bot a pover* menstrel,	poor
	And, sir, it is the maner of ous†	
	To seche* mani a lordes hous;	seek out
	Thei* we nought welcom no be	though
	Yete we mot proferi forth† our gle.'	
435	Bifor the king he sat adoun	
	And tok his harp so miri of soun	
	And tempreth* his harp as he wele can*	tunes knows how
	And blisseful notes he ther gan,*	began
	That* al that in the palays were	so that
440	Com* to him for to here	came
	And liggeth* adoun to* his fete,	lie at
	Hem thenketh† his melody so swete.	
	The king herkneth* and sitt ful stille;	listens
	To here his* gle he hath gode wille.	Orfeo's
445	Gode bourde* he hadde of his gle –	pleasure
	The riche quen also hadde he.*	she
	When he hadde stint* his harping,	ceased
	Than seyd to him the king:	
	'Menstrel, me liketh† wele thi gle.	
450	Now aske of me what it be,†	
	†Largelich ichil the pay.	
	Now speke and tow* might asay.'†	you
	'Sir,' he sayd, 'ich biseche the	
	Thatow woldest yive* me	give
455	That ich* levedi, bright on ble,†	same
	That slepeth under the ympe-tre.†	

---

425 *Seththen . . . gan* Ever since I began to reign here
426 *fole-hardi* foolhardy
427 *durst wende* dared come
428 *Bot that . . . of-sende* without my sending him away
431 *the maner of ous* our custom
434 *mot proferi forth* must proffer
442 *Hem thenketh* seems to them
449 *me liketh* pleases me
450 *what it be* whatever it may be
451 *Largelich . . . pay* I shall pay you generously
452 *asay* make an attempt
455 *on ble* in complexion
456 *ympe-tre* grafted tree

'Nay,' quath* the king, 'that nought nere!†   *says*
†A sori couple of you it were,
For thou art lene, rowe* and blac   *rough*
460   And sche is lovesum,* withouten lac.*   *beautiful   blemish*
A lothlich* thing it were,† forthi,*   *grotesque   indeed*
To sen* hir in thi compayni.'   *see*
'O sir,' he seyd, 'gentil* king,   *noble*
Yete were it a wele fouler† thing
465   To here a lesing* of* thi mouthe.   *lie   from*
So, sir, as ye seyd nouthe*   *now*
What* ich wold aski,† have I schold,   *whatever*
And nedes† thou most thi word hold.'*   *keep*
The king seyd: 'Seththen* it is so,   *since*
470   Take hir bi the hond and go –
†Of hir ichil thatow be blithe.'
He kneled adoun and thonked him swithe.*   *immediately*
His wiif he tok bi the hond
And dede him* swithe out of that lond   *went*
475   And went him out of that thede.*   *country*
†Right as he come the wey he yede.
So long he hath the way ynome*   *taken*
To Winchester he is ycome,
That was his owhen cité,
480   Ac* no man knewe that it was he.   *but*
†No forther than the tounes ende
†For knoweleche no durst wende,
Bot with a begger, ybilt ful narwe,†
Ther he tok his herbarwe*   *lodging*
485   To* him and to his owhen wiif,   *for*
As a minstrel of pover* liif,   *poor*
And asked tidinges of that lond
And who the kingdom held in hond.†

---

457 *nought nere* could not be
458 *A sori . . . were* You would make a miserable pair
461 *were* would be
464 *a wele fouler* a very much fouler
467 *wold aski* wanted to ask for
468 *nedes* necessarily
471 *Of hir . . . blithe* I wish you joy of her
476 *Right as . . . yede* He went by exactly the same path as he had come
481–2 *No forther . . . wende* He did not dare go further than the town's end for fear of being recognised
483 *ybilt ful narwe* very meanly housed
488 *held in hond* ruled over

	The pover begger in his cote*	cottage
490	Told him everich a grot:†	
	Hou her* quen was stole owy,*	their away
	Ten yer gon,* with fairy,	ago
	And hou her king en exile yede,†	
	Bot no man wist* in wiche thede,*	knew country
495	And hou the steward the lond gan hold,*	governed
	And other mani thinges him told.	
	Amorwe,† oyain* none-tide,	towards
	He maked his wiif ther abide.	
	The beggers clothes he borwed* anon	borrowed
500	And heng his harp his rigge* opon	back
	And went him into that cité	
	That men him might bihold and se.	
	Erls and barouns bold,	
	Burjays† and levedis him gun bihold:	
505	'Lo,' thai seyd, 'swiche a* man!	what a
	Hou long the here* hangeth him opan!*	hair upon
	Lo, hou his berd hongeth to his kne!	
	He is yclongen* also* a tre!'	gnarled like
	And as he yede in the strete	
510	With his steward he gan mete*	met
	†And loude he sett on him a crie:	
	'Sir steward,' he seyd, 'merci!	
	Icham an harpour of hethenisse† –	
	Help me now in this destresse!'	
515	The steward seyd, 'Com with me, come.	
	Of that ichave,* thou schalt have some.	I have
	Everich gode harpour is welcom me to	
	For mi lordes love,† Sir Orfeo.'	
	In the castel the steward sat atte mete†	
520	And mani lording* was bi him sete;*	lord seated
	Ther were trompours* and tabourers,*	trumpeters drummers
	Harpours fele,* and crouders.†	many
	Miche melody thai maked alle,	
	And Orfeo sat stille* in the halle	quiet

---

490 *everich a grot*   every detail
493 *en exile yede*   went into exile
497 *Amorwe*   next morning
504 *Burjays*   burgesses, citizens
511 *And loude ... crie*   And he cried out to him loudly
513 *of hethenisse*   from a heathen land
518 *For mi lordes love*   for the love of my lord
519 *atte mete*   at the meal
522 *crouders*   crwth (bowed lyre) players

525	And herkneth when thai ben al stille.	
	He toke his harp and tempred schille.*	piercingly
	The blisfulest notes he harped there	
	That ever ani man yherd with ere.	
	Ich man liked wele his gle.	
530	The steward biheld and gan yse†	
	And knewe the harp als blive.†	
	'Menstrel,' he seyd, 'so mot thou thrive,†	
	Where hadestow† this harp and hou?	
	I pray that thou me telle now.'	
535	'Lord,' quath he, 'in uncouthe thede,†	
	Thurth a wildernes as I yede,	
	Ther I founde in a dale	
	With lyouns a man totorn smale,†	
	And wolves him frete† with teth so scharp:	
540	Bi him I fond this ich* harp.	same
	†Wele ten yere it is ygo.'	
	'O,' quath the steward, 'now me is wo!†	
	That was mi lord, Sir Orfeo.	
	Allas, wreche, what schal I do	
545	That have swiche* a lord ylore?*	such lost
	A, way,* that ich was ybore,*	alas born
	†That him was so hard grace y-yarked	
	And so vile deth ymarked!'*	decreed
	Adoun he fel aswon† to grounde.	
550	His barouns him tok up in that stounde*	time
	And telleth him hou it geth:†	
	†It nis no bot of manes deth.	
	King Orfeo knewe wele bi than*	then
	His steward was a trewe* man	faithful
555	And loved him as he aught to do,	
	And stont* up and seyt* thus: 'Lo!	stands says

---

530 *gan yse* saw
531 *als blive* straight away
532 *so mot thou thrive* as you may hope to prosper
533 *Where hadestow* where did you get
535 *uncouthe thede* foreign land
538 *totorn smale* torn into little pieces
539 *frete* had chewed
541 *Wele ten . . . ygo* It is a good ten years past
542 *me is wo* I am grief-stricken
547 *That him . . . y-yarked* That such a cruel fate was allotted to him
549 *aswon* in a faint
551 *it geth* it goes, things are
552 *It nis . . . deth* there is no remedy for man's death

```
        Steward, herkne now this thing:
        Yif* ich were Orfeo the king                                    if
        And hadde ysuffred ful yore†
560     In wildernisse miche sore,†
        And hadde ywon* mi quen owy*                          regained  away
        Out of the lond of fairy
        And hadde ybrought the levedi hende†
        Right here to the tounes ende,
565     And with a begger her in ynome,†
        And were miself hider ycome
        Poverlich† to the, thus stille,*                             secretly
        For to asay* thi gode wille,                                      test
        And ich founde the thus trewe,
570     Thou no schust* it never rewe.*                     should(st)  regret
        Sikerlich,* for love or ay,*                            surely    fear
        Thou schust be king after mi day.
        And yif thou of* mi deth hadest ben blithe,*              at    happy
        Thou schust have voided† also swithe.†
575       Tho al tho† that therin sete*                                    sat
        That it was King Orfeo underyete,*                         understood
        And the steward him wele knewe.
        Over and over the bord* he threwe                              table
        And fel adoun to* his fet;                                        at
580     So dede everich lord that ther sete,
        And al thai seyd at o criing:†
        'Ye beth* our lord, sir, and our king.'                      you are
        Glad thai were of his live;*                                    life
        To chaumber thai ladde him als bilive†
585     And bathed him and schaved his berd
        And tired* him as a king apert.†                             dressed
        And seththen* with gret processioun                       afterwards
        Thai brought the quen into the toun
        With all maner menstraci.
590     Lord, ther was gret melody!
```

---

559 *ful yore* long since
560 *miche sore* great hardship
563 *levedi hende* gracious lady
565 *her in ynome* placed her
567 *Poverlich* dressed as a poor man
574 *voided* been banished   *also swithe* directly
575 *Tho al tho* then all those
581 *at o criing* with one cry
584 *als bilive* quickly
586 *apert* openly, publicly

For joie thai wepe with her* eighe *their*
†That hem so sounde ycomen seighe.
Now King Orfeo newe coround* is, *crowned*
And his quen, Dame Heurodis,
595 And lived long afterward,
And seththen was king the steward.
Harpours in Bretaine* after than* *Brittany that*
Herd hou this mervaile bigan
And made herof a lay of gode likeing* *pleasure*
600 And nempned* it after the king. *named*
That lay 'Orfeo' is yhote:* *called*
Gode is the lay, swete is the note.
Thus com* Sir Orfeo out of his care: *came*
God graunt ous* alle wele to fare.* *us proceed*

---

592 *That hem ... seighe* who saw them arrive so safely

Laurence Minot
fl. 1333–1352

The following poem is one of a group of eleven on political topics preserved in a mid-fifteenth-century manuscript, British Library, MS Cotton Galba E.ix, written in the north of England. They are presumably all by the same man, who identifies himself as 'Laurence Minot'. Nothing else is known of him, but he was probably a Yorkshireman who wrote at the time of the events he deals with, that is, between 1333 and 1352. For the Scottish counterpart to Minot's boisterous chauvinism, see the extract from John Barbour's *Bruce*, p. 188.

The text is from *The Poems of Laurence Minot*, ed. J. Hall (1914).

SCOTS OUT OF BERWICK

Skottes out of Berwik and of Abirdene,†
At the Bannok burn† war ye* to kene.*   *ye were fierce*
Thare slogh* ye many sakles,* als* it was sene,   *slew innocent as*
And now has King Edward wroken* it,† I wene.*   *avenged believe*
5   It is wroken, I wene, wele wurth the while;†
War yit with† the Skottes for thai er ful of gile.

Whare er ye, Skottes of Saint Johnes toune?†
The boste of your baner es betin all doune.
When ye bosting will bede,† Sir Edward is boune*   *ready*
10 For to kindel yow care† and crak yowre crowne.
He has crakked yowre croune, wele worth the while;
Schame bityde* the Skottes for thai er full of gile.   *befall*

---

1 [*Berwick . . . Abirdene* Berwick is in the extreme south and Aberdeen in the north of English-speaking Scotland]
2 [*Bannok burn* (*burn*: stream) the battle of Bannockburn, near Stirling, in which the Scots under Robert I (1306–29) defeated the English army of Edward II (1307–27) in 1314]
4 [*now has King Edward wroken it* the English victory under Edward III (1327–77) at Halidon Hill, near Berwick, in 1333 is regarded as revenge for Bannockburn]
5 *wele wurth the while* glad is the hour
6 *War yit with* still beware of
7 [*Saint Johnes toune* Perth, which was taken by the English in 1332]
9 *bede* offer (yourselves)
10 *kindel yow care* cause you misery

Skottes of Striflin† war steren and stout;†
Of God ne of gude men had thai no dout.*   *fear*
15   Now have thai, the pelers,* priked obout,†   *thieves*
Bot at the last Sir Edward rifild thaire rout.†
    He has rifild thaire rout, wele wurth the while,
    †Bot ever er thai under bot gaudes and gile.

Rughfute riveling,† now kindels thi care,
20   Berebag† with thi boste, thi biging* es bare.   *house*
Fals wretche and forsworn,* whider wiltou fare?†   *perjured*
Busk the* unto Brug† and abide thare;   *hasten*
    Thare, wretche, saltou won* and wery the while;†   *remain*
    †Thi dwelling in Dondé es done for thi gile.

25   The Skotte gase* in Burghes* and betes* the stretes,   *goes Bruges roams*
All thise Inglis men harmes* he hetes.*   *injury promises*
Fast* makes he his mone to men that he metes,   *earnestly*
Bot fone* frendes he findes that his bale betes:†   *few*
    Fune* betes his bale, wele wurth the while,   *few*
30   He uses all thretyng* with gaudes and gile.   *threatening*

Bot many man thretes* and spekes ful ill   *makes threats*
That sum tyme war better to be stane* still;   *stone*
The Skot in his wordes has wind for to spill,*   *waste*
For at the last Edward sall have all his will.
35   He had his will at Berwik, wele wurth the while;
    Skottes broght him the kayes,† bot get* for thaire gile.   *look out*

---

13 [*Striflin* Stirling; perhaps refers to the battle of Bannockburn, fought to establish control of Stirling Castle, or to the battle of Stirling Bridge, fought between Scots and English in 1297] *steren and stout* fierce and proud
15 [*Now have ... priked obout* possibly refers to the Scottish raiding parties which attempted to deflect the English army from the siege of Berwick in 1333, before Halidon Hill (*priked obout*: galloped about)]
16 *rifild thaire rout* plundered their company
18 *Bot ever ... gile* Yet underneath they are always only trickery and deception
19 [*Rughfute riveling* rough-footed brogue(-wearer): this long-standing insult refers to the Scottish soldiers' rough rawhide brogues]
20 [*Berebag* bag-carrier: each soldier in the Scottish army carried his own provisions, thus dispensing with the need for a slow-moving baggage-train]
21 *wiltou fare* will you go
22 [*Brug* Bruges, in Flanders, with which Scotland had close trading connections]
23 *wery the while* curse the hour
24 *Thi dwelling ... for thi gile* your sojourn in Dundee is at an end because of your guile
28 *bale betes* relieve his misery
36 [*broght him the kayes* Berwick, besieged by Edward III in 1333, was forced to surrender after the English victory at Halidon Hill]

Richard Rolle
c. 1300–49

Richard Rolle was born around 1300 in Thornton Dale, in North Yorkshire, the son of a small householder. At the age of eighteen he gave up his studies at Oxford, where he had been supported by Thomas Neville, archdeacon of Durham, in order to return to the north and become a hermit. Hermits, unlike recluses, lived solitary but not enclosed lives; their vocation, like that of the friars, was to the world. Though they might inhabit caves and cells in remote places, hermits also frequently lived near bridges and fords which they maintained, collecting the tolls, or else they travelled the roads, living on alms. Rolle seems to have been caught between the desire for solitude and the need for financial security; an early patron gave him a cell in his own house, while later a great lady supported him in more seclusion on her estate. The form of eremitical life pursued by Rolle did not prevent his continued contact with the world of books; he may have studied briefly in Paris, and he wrote a number of mystical works in Latin and English which were widely read and imitated. In his solitude Rolle experienced the joy of the contemplative's love of God, which is the subject of the two poems below. The prose passage is from *The Form of Living*, one of his last works, which – like *Ancrene Wisse* – was written to provide an anchoress, Margaret Kirkeby, with guidance on the life of the recluse. Towards the end of his life Rolle moved to Hampole, near Doncaster in south Yorkshire, where he died in 1349, possibly of the plague.

The text is from Cambridge University Library, MS Dd.v.64, pt iii, ed. H. E. Allen, *English Writings of Richard Rolle* (1931).

From THE FORM OF LIVING, Chapter 12
[Active and Contemplative Lives]

Twa* lyves thar er that Cristen men lyfes. Ane* es called actyve lyfe; for it es in mare bodili warke.† Another, contemplatyve lyfe; for it es in mare swetnes gastely.† Actife lyfe es mykel owteward,† and in mare travel,* and in mare peryle for the temptacions that er in the worlde. Contemplatyfe lyfe es mykel inwarde;* and for thi* it es lastandar† and sykerar,* restfuller, delitabiler,† luflyer, and mare medeful.† For it hase joy in Goddes lufe, and savowre* in the lyf that lastes ay,* in this present tyme if it be right ledde. And that felyng* of joy in the lufe of Jhesu passes* al other merites in erth; for it es swa* harde to com to, for† the freelte* of oure flesch and the many temptacions that we er umsett* with, that lettes* us nyght and day. All other thynges er lyght at come to in regarde tharof,† for that† may na man deserve, bot anely* it es gifen of Goddes godenes til* tham that verrayli* gifes tham† to contemplacion and til quiete for Cristes luf.

Til men or wymen that takes tham til actife lyfe, twa thynges falles.† Ane, for to ordayne thair meyné† in drede* and in the lufe of God, and fynd tham† thaire necaries, and thamself kepe enterely the comandementes of God, doand* til thar neghbur als* thai wil† that thai do til tham. Another es, that thai do at thar power†

two   one

exertion

internal
thus   surer

delight   for ever

sensation
surpasses
so   frailty

beset
hinder

only
to   truly

dread

doing   as

---

it es . . . warke   it is in more physical action
it es . . . gastely   it is in more spiritual sweetness
mykel owteward   largely external
lastandar   more lasting
delitabiler   more delightful
medeful   deserving of reward
for   because of
lyght at . . . tharof   easy to achieve by comparison with it
that   [joy in the love of Jesus]
tham   themselves
falles   are required
ordayne thair meyné   organise their households   [Rolle's definition of active life is intended for devout heads of household]
fynd tham   supply them with
wil   desire
at thar power   to the extent that they are able

25 the seven werkes of mercy:† the whilk* es, to fede the — which
    hungry, to gyf the thirsti a drynk, to cleth* the naked, — clothe
    to herbar† hym that has na howsyng,* to viset the seke,* — home sick
    to comforth tham that er in prysoun, and to grave* dede — bury
    men. Al that mai and hase cost:† thai may noght be
30 qwyt* with ane or twa of thir,* bot tham behoves† do — let off these
    tham al, if thai wil have the benyson* on domes day,† — blessing
    that Jhesu sal* til al* gyf that dose† tham; or els may — shall to all
    thai drede the malysoun* that al mon have that wil — curse
    noght do tham, when thai had godes* to do tham wyth. — money
35   Contemplatife lyf hase twa partyes,* a lower and a — parts
    heer.* The lower party es meditacion of haly wrytyng, — higher
    that es Goddes wordes, and in other gude thoghtes and
    swete, that men hase of* the grace of God abowt the — concerning
    lufe of Jhesu Criste, and also in lovyng* of God in — praising
40 psalmes and ympnes,* or in prayers. The hegher* party — hymns higher
    of contemplacion es behaldyng and yernyng of† the
    thynges of heven, and joy in the Haly Gaste, that men
    hase oft.† And if it be swa† that thai be noght prayand
    with the mowth, bot anely thynkand of God and of the
45 fairehede† of aungels and haly sawles,* than may I say — holy souls
    that contemplacion es a wonderful joy of Goddes luf,* — love
    the whilk* joy es lovyng of God, that may noght be — which
    talde; and that wonderful lovyng es in the saule, and
    for abundance of joy and swettenes it ascendes intil the
50 mowth, swa that the hert and the tonge acordes in ane,†
    and body and sawle joyes* in God lyvand.* — rejoices living
       A man or woman that es ordaynd* til contemplatife — called
    lyfe first God enspires tham to forsake this worlde and
    al the vanite and the covayties* and the vile luste* — covetise desire
55 tharof. Sythen* he ledes tham by thar ane,† and spekes — then

---

[*the sevene werkes of mercy* there are traditionally seven corporal (physical) and seven spiritual works of mercy, which are held to be actions performed for the love of God and one's neighbour. Rolle lists the seven corporal works, six of which (the exception is burying the dead) derive directly from Matthew 25.35–6]
herbar give shelter
mai and hase cost can and have the wherewithal
tham behoves it is necessary for them
domes day judgement day
dose perform
yernyng of longing for
hase oft often have
swa so, the case
fairehede fairness
acordes in ane come together
by thar ane on their own

til thar hert, and als* the prophete says, 'He gifes tham — *as*
at sowke† the swetnes of the begynnyng of lufe.' And
than he settes tham in wil to gyf tham haly† to prayers
and meditacions and teres. Sithen, when thai have
60 sufferd many temptacions, and foule noyes† of thoghtes
that er ydel* and of vanitees,† the whilk wil comber* — *idle   encumber*
tham, that can noght destroy tham, er passand away,
he gars* tham geder til tham thair hert,† and fest* anely — *makes   settle*
in hym; and opens til the egh* of thair sawls the yates* — *eyes   gates*
65 of heven, swa that the ilk* egh lokes intil heven. And — *same*
than the fire of lufe† verrali ligges* in thair hert and — *lies*
byrnes tharin, and makes clene of al erthly filth. And
sithen forward† thai er contemplatife men, and ravyst* — *ravished*
in lufe. For contemplacion† es a syght, and thai se intil* — *into*
70 heven with thar gastly* egh. Bot thou sal witt,† that na — *spiritual*
man hase perfite syght of heven whils thai er lifand
bodili here,† bot als sone als† thai dye, thai er broght
before God, and sese* hym face til face and egh til egh, — *see*
and wones* with hym withouten ende. For hym thai — *dwell*
75 soght, and hym thai covayted,* and hym thai lufed in — *desired*
al thar myght.

Loo,* Margarete,† I have schortly sayde the† the — *behold*
forme* of lyvying, and how thou may come til perfec- — *best way*
cion, and to lufe hym that thou hase taken the til.† If it
80 do the gude,* and profit til the, thank God, and pray — *good*
for me. The grace of Jhesu Criste be with the and kepe
the. *Amen.*

---

at sowke that suck
settes tham ... haly makes them want to surrender themselves entirely
foul noyes evil afflictions
vanitees worthless things
gars tham ... hert makes them take heart
[*the fire of luf ... makes clene of al erthly filth* Rolle's own experience of mystical rapture (recorded in his *Incendium Amoris* (Fire of Love)) was accompanied by 'a heat, more sweet than words can say'. But here he is also following St Bernard of Clairvaux (1090–1153), who writes that 'the Lord comes [to the contemplative] as a consuming fire' which purifies the soul of the 'stain of sin' (*Sermons on the Canticle* 57.7)]
sithen forward thenceforward
[*For contemplacion ... gastly egh* for Rolle contemplation at its highest is a mystical experience of God's being and presence]
witt know
thai er lifand bodili here they are living here in the flesh
als sone als as soon as
[*Margarete* see headnote]
sayde the told you
taken the til committed yourself to

JESU, GOD'S SON, LORD OF MAJESTY

Jhesu, God sonn, Lord of magesté,
 Send wil* to my hert anly* to covayte* the.   *desire   only   covet*
 †Reve me lykyng of this land, my lufe that thou may be.
 Take my hert intill* thi hand, sett me in stabylté.*   *into   stability, rest*

5 Jhesu, the mayden sonn, that wyth thi blode me boght,
 Thyrl* my sawule* wyth thi spere, that mykel*   *pierce   soul   great*
  luf in men hase wroght.*   *created*
 Me langes,* lede me to thi lyght, and festen* in the al my   *I languish   fix*
  thoght.
 In thi swetnes fyll my hert, my wa* make wane till noght.†   *misery*

 Jhesu, my God, Jhesu my keyng,* forsake noght my desyre.   *king*
10 My thoght* make it to be meke, I hate bath pryde and ire.*   *mind   anger*
 Thi wil es my yhernyng;* of lufe* thou kyndel the fyre,   *longing   love*
 That I in swet lovyng* with aungels take my hyre.†   *praising*

 Wounde my hert within, and welde* it at thi wille.   *control*
 On blysse, that never sal blyn,* thou gar me fest me skylle.†   *cease*
15 That I thi lufe may wyn, of grace my thoght thou fylle,
 And make me clene of syn, that I may come the tylle.*   *to*

 Rote* it in my hert, the memor* of thi pyne;*   *root   memory   suffering*
 In sekenes and in qwert* thi lufe be ever myne.   *health*
 My joy es al of the; my sawle, take it as thine.
20 My lufe ay waxand be,† sa that it never dwyne.*   *grow less*

 My sang es in syghyng, whil I dwel in this way.
 My lyfe es in langyng that byndes me, nyght and day,
 Til I come til my kyng, that I won* with hym may,   *dwell*
 And se his fayre schynyng,* and lyfe that lastes ay.*   *brightness   for ever*

---

3 *Reve me . . . thou may be* Take away from me pleasure in this world, so that you may be my love
8 *wane tille noght* disappear to nothing
12 *take my hyre* receive my reward
14 *gar me . . . skylle* make me fix my mind
20 *My lufe ay waxand be* may my love always be increasing

25 Langyng es in me lent,† for lufe that I ne kan lete.†
My lufe, it hase me schent,* that ilk a bale† may bete. — hurt
Sen* that my hert was brent* in Cryste lufe sa swete, — since burnt
Al wa fra me es went,† and we sal* never mete. — shall

I sytt and syng of lufe-langyng, that in my hert es bred.
30 Jhesu, my keyng and my joyng,* why ne war* I to the led? — delight was
Ful wele I wate* in al my state,* in joy I sulde — know condition
be fed.* — nourished
Jhesu, me bryng til thi wonyng,* or blode that thou hase — dwelling-place
sched.

Demed* he was to hyng,* the faire aungels fode.* — judged hang food
Ful sare* thai gan hym swyng,† when that he bunden stode.† — grievously
35 His bak was in betyng,† and spylt hys blissed blode;
The thorn corond* the keyng, that nayled was on the — crowned
rode.* — cross

Whyte was his naked breste, and rede his blody syde;
Wan* was his faire face, his woundes depe and wyde. — pale
The Jewyis wald not wande* to pyne† hym in that tyde;* — hesitate time
40 Als* streme dose of the strande,* his blode gan downe — as torrent
glyde.†

Blynded was his faire ene,* his flesch blody for-bette.† — eyes
His lufsum* lyf was layde ful low, and saryful umbesette.† — lovely
Dede* and lyf began to stryf whether myght maystre mare,† — death
When aungels brede† was dampned* to dede, to safe* — condemned save
oure sauls sare.†

---

25 *es in me lent* has alighted on me   *ne kan lete* do not know how to desist from
26 *ilk a bale* each misery
28 *Al wa fra me is went* all grief has gone from me
34 *gan hym swyng* beat him   *bunden stode* stood bound
35 *in betyng* beaten
39 *pyne* inflict suffering on
40 *gan down glyde* flowed down
41 *for-bette* cruelly beaten
42 *saryful umbesette* miserably surrounded
43 *stryf whether . . . mare* compete as to which might have greater power
44 *brede* bread, food
44 *sauls sare* souls' pain

45	Lyf was slayne, and rase* agayne; in fairehede* may we fare;*	rose splendour go forward
	And dede es broght til litel or noght,* and kasten* in endles kare.	nothing thrust
	On hym, that the boght, hafe al thi thoght, and lede the in his lare.*	teaching
	Gyf al thi hert til Crist thi qwert,* and lufe hym evermare.	joy

MERCY IS MOST IN MY MIND

	Mercy es maste* in my mynde, for mercy es that I mast prayse.	most
	Mercy es curtayse* and kynde; fra al mischeves* he mai* me rayse.	gracious evils can
	Allas, sa lang I have bene blynd, and walked will* alwayse.	directionless
	Mercy walde I fayne† fynd, to lede me in my last dayse.*	days
5	Mercy, lede me at the last, when I owt of this world sal wende;*	pass
	To the cryand* I trayst fast,† that thou save me fra* the fende.*	crying from devil
	Mercy es trew as any stele, when it es ryght up soght.†	
	Whasa will mercy fele,* seke it, for it fayles noght.†	experience
	Mercy es syght of al my hele,† therfore I have it mast in thoght.	
10	Mercy likes me† sa wele,* for thorogh mercy was I boght.†	well
	I ne wate† what I may do or say til* mercy, that es ay sa gode.	to
	Thou graunte mercy, that mercy may,† that es my solace and my fode.*	food
	Mercy walde I fayne honowre, it es sa swete unto my syght.	
	It lyes in my Creatoure,* that made us of his awen myght.	creator
15	Mercy es al my socoure,* til lede me to the land of lyght,	succour
	And bring me til the rial* toure, whare I mai se mi God sa bryght.	royal
	God of al, Lorde and Keyng,* I pray the, Jhesu, be my frende,	king
	Sa that I may thi mercy syng in thi blys withowten ende.	

4 *walde I fayne* I deeply desire to
6 *trayst fast* trust surely
7 *ryght up soght* sought for properly
8 *noght* not at all
9 *syght of al my hele* ground of all my well-being
10 *likes me* pleases me   *was I boght* I was bought
11 *ne wate* do not know
12 *that mercy may* who is able to be merciful

Mercy es sa hegh a poynt, thar may na syn it suppryse.†
20 To thi mercy es my hert joynt,* for therein al my likyng* lyse.   joined   pleasure
Lord, lat it noght be aloynt,* when thou sal sett thi gret assyse.†   far off
With thi mercy my sawle anoynt, when I sal come to thi jugise.*   judgement
Til the Juge sal I come, bot* I wate* noght my day.   but   know
Mercy es bath al and some;† tharin I trayst and after* pray.   for

---

19 *Mercy es ... suppryse* Mercy is so high a virtue, no sin can overcome it there
21 *gret assyse* great court; day of judgement
24 *al and some* the part and the whole

John Barbour
?1325–95

John Barbour was born in the 1320s, possibly in south-west Scotland, during the reign of Robert I (1306–29), whose stirring history he was to record in *The Bruce*. Barbour was a churchman who studied at Oxford and Paris in the 1350s and 60s, there being as yet no university in his native country, and by 1357 was archdeacon of Aberdeen. Robert Bruce's grandson, Robert II, awarded him pensions and gifts between 1378 and 1388; one of these may have been in recognition of his services in writing *The Bruce*, on which he says he was working in 1375. Barbour's other historical writings, a version of the *Brut* and *The Stewartis Original*, have not survived. He died in 1395.

The Bruce, which is almost 14,000 lines in short couplets and has been divided since the eighteenth century into twenty books, marks the beginning of Scottish literature. Although the language in which it was composed was not yet fully distinguishable from northern English, nevertheless its subject is nothing less than the revival under Robert Bruce of the independent kingdom of Scotland. Edward I of England (1272–1307) claimed the overlordship of Scotland and placed a vassal ruler on the throne, but in 1306 Robert Bruce, earl of Carrick, had himself crowned king. Edward II (1307–27) attempted to regain control of Scotland, and in 1314 an English army marched north to relieve Stirling Castle which had been in English hands since 1304. On June 23 the Scottish and English armies came together near the Bannock Burn ('stream'), just south of Stirling. The Battle of Bannockburn, which was fought the following day, was an overwhelming victory for the Scots.

The extract below (Book 12, lines 165ff.) contains the speech made by King Robert to his army on the eve of the battle. In the course of 23 June King Robert had killed Sir Humphrey de Bohun, nephew of one of the English commanders, in single combat and routed his men, while other Scots had put the English vanguard to flight. Now the king asks his men whether they want to press home these early triumphs, or disperse. (For an English view of the Scottish struggle for independence, see Laurence Minot's 'Scots out of Berwick', p. 177.)

The text is from National Library of Scotland, MS 19.2.2.

From THE BRUCE

[The Eve of Bannockburn]

And quhen the gud king† gan thaim se†
Befor him swa* assemblit be, — *thus*
Blyth and glaid that thar fayis* wer — *foes*
Rabutyt† apon sic* maner, — *such*
5 A litill quhill* he held him still, — *while*
Syne* on this wys* he said his will: — *then manner*
'Lordingis,† we aucht† to love* and luf* — *praise love*
Allmychty God that syttis abuf,* — *above*
That sendis us sa fayr begynnyng.
10 It is a gret discomforting* — *discouragement*
Till our fayis, that on this wis
Sa sone has bene rabutyt twis.* — *twice*
For quhen thai of thar ost* sall her,* — *army hear*
And knaw suthly* on quhat maner — *truly*
15 Thar vaward,* that wes sa stout,* — *vanguard formidable*
And syne yone* othyr joly* rout* — *that gallant band*
– That I trow* of the best men war* — *believe were*
That thai mycht get amang thaim thar –
War rabutyt sa sodanly,
20 I trow and knawis it all clerly
That mony ane hart sall waverand* be — *faltering*
That semyt* er* of gret bounté;* — *seemed before courage*
And fra* the hart be discumfyt — *once*
The body is nocht* worth a myt.* — *not mite*
25 Tharfor I trow that gud ending
Sall folow till our begynnyng.
The-quhethir,* I say nocht this yow till* — *nevertheless to*
For* that ye suld folow my will — *in order*
To fycht, bot in yow all sall be.†
30 For gyf* yow thinkis spedfull* that we — *if advantageous*
Fecht,* we sall; and gif ye will† — *fight*
†We leve, your liking to fulfill,
I sall consent on alkyn wis†
To do rycht as ye will dyvys.* — *decide*

---

1 [*the gud king* Robert Bruce, king of Scotland, 1306–29] *gan . . . se* saw
4 *Rabutyt* driven back
7 *Lordingis* lords *we aucht* it is our duty
29 *in yow all sall be* all shall be in your hands
31–2 *gif ye will† / . . . fulfill* if you want us to leave, in order to satisfy your wish
33 *on alkyn wis* wholly

35	Tharfor, sayis of† your will planly.'	
	And with a voce* than gan thai cry:	one voice
	'Gud king, forowtyn mar† delay,	
	To-morne* alsone* as ye se day	tomorrow as soon
	†Ordane yow hale for the bataill.	
40	For doute of dede† we sall not faill,	
	Na na* payn sall refusyt be	nor any
	Quhill* we haif maid our countre fre!'	until
	Quhen the king had hard so manlily*	courageously
	Thaim spak to fechting,† and so hardely,*	boldly
45	Sayand that nouther* dreid nor deid*	neither death
	To sic discomfort suld thame leid	
	That they suld eschew the fechting,	
	In hart he had greit rejoising	
	†And till him gret glaidschip can ta,	
50	And said, 'Lordingis, sen ye will swa,†	
	Schaip we us† tharfor in the mornyng	
	Swa that we, be* the sone rysing,	by
	Haf herd mes* and buskyt* weill,	mass made ready
	Ilk* man intill* his awn eschell,*	each into squadron
55	†Without the pailyownys arayit,	
	In bataillis* with baneris displayit,*	battalions unfurled
	And luk* ye na wis brek aray.†	see that
	And as ye luf me, I yow pray	
	That ilk man for his awne honour	
60	Purvay him† a gud baneour,*	banner
	And quhen it cummys to the fycht	
	Ilk man set hart, will and mycht	
	To stynt* our fayis mekill prid.†	check
	On hors thai will arayit rid	
65	And cum on yow in full gret hy.*	haste
	Mete thaim with speris hardely,	

---

35 *sayis of* declare
37 *forowtyn mar* without more
39 *Ordane ... bataill* Prepare yourself fully for the battle
40 *For doute of dede* for fear of death
44 *to fechting* of fighting
49 *And till him ... can ta* and drew to himself great happiness
50 *sen ye will swa* since this is what you want
51 *Schaip we us* let us prepare
55 *Without ... arayit* outside the tents drawn up
57 *brek aray* break ranks
60 *Purvay him* equip himself with
63 *mekill prid* great pride

	And think than on the mekill ill†	
	That thai and tharis* has done us till	theirs
	†And ar in will yeit for to do,	
70	Gif* thai haf mycht* to cum tharto.†	if power
	And certis,* me think† weill that ye,	assuredly
	Forowt abasing,† aucht* to be	ought
	Worthy and of gret vasselagis,†	
	For we haf thre gret avantagis:	
75	The fyrst is that we haf the rycht,*	right
	And for the rycht ay* God will fycht.	always
	The tothir* is that thai cummyn ar	other
	For lyppynyng of† thar gret powar	
	To sek us on our awne land,	
80	And has brocht her,* rycht till our hand,†	here
	Ryches into* sa gret quantité	in
	That the powrest of yow sall be	
	Bath rych and mychty tharwithall,*	thereby
	Gif* that we wyne, as weill may fall.*	if happen
85	The thrid* is that we for our lyvis	third
	And for our childir* and for our wyvis	children
	And for our fredome and for our land	
	Ar strenyeit* into bataill for to stand,*	forced be drawn up
	And thai for thar mycht anirly,*	only
90	†And for thai lat of us heychtly,	
	And for thai wald distroy us all	
	Mais* thaim to fycht; bot yeit may fall	makes
	That thai sall rew* thar barganying.*	regret fighting
	And, certis, I warne yow of a* thing:	one
95	That happyn thaim† (as God forbed)	
	Till fynd fantis* intill our deid*	faint-heartedness actions
	That* thai wyn* us opynly,	so that conquer
	Thai sall of us haf na mercy;	
	And sen* we knaw thar felone* will,	since savage
100	Me think it suld accord to skill†	

---

67 *mekill ill*   great evil
69 *And ar . . . to do*   And still intend to do
70 *cum tharto*   achieve it
71 *me think*   it seems to me
72 *Forowt abasing*   without faltering
73 *vasselagis*   deeds of prowess
78 *lyppynyng of*   confidence in
80 *till our hand*   within our reach
90 *And for . . . heychtly*   And because they regard us scornfully
95 *happyn thaim*   if it befall them
100 *accord to skill*   correspond with reason

	To set stoutnes* agayne felony*	valour savagery
	And mak sagat† a juperty.†	
	Quharfor,* I yow requer* and pray	wherefore request
	That with all your mycht that ye may,	
105	That ye pres yow† at the begynnyng,	
	But* cowardys or abaysing,	without
	To mete thaim at thar fyrst assemble*	encounter
	Sa stoutly that the henmaist† trymble	
	And menys of† your gret manheid,*	prowess
110	Your worschip* and your douchti* deid,	honour brave
	And of the joy that we abid*	expect
	Gif that us fall,† as weill may tid,*	happen
	Hap† to vencus* this gret battaill.	win
	In our handys without faile	
115	Ye ber honour, price* and riches,	glory
	Fredome, welth and blythnes,	
	Gyf ye contene yow† manlely.	
	And the contrar,* all halyly,*	opposite entirely
	Sall fall gif ye lat cowardys	
120	And wykytnes yow suppris.*	overcome
	Ye mycht haf lyvyt* into threldome,*	lived bondage
	Bot for* ye yarnyt* till have fredome	because desired
	Ye ar assemblyt her with me.	
	Tharfor is nedfull that ye be	
125	Worthy and wycht,* but abaysing,†	strong
	And I warne yow weill of a thing:	
	That mar* myschef may fall us nane*	greater none
	Than in thar handys to be tane,*	taken
	For thai suld sla* us, I wate* weill,	kill know
130	Rycht as thai did my brothyr Nele.†	
	Bot quhen I mene of† your stoutnes,	
	And of the mony gret prowes†	
	That ye haf doyne* sa worthely,	done
	†I trayst and trowis sekyrly	

---

102 *sagat* in this way   *juperty* daring enterprise
105 *pres yow* advance eagerly
108 *henmaist* those to the rear
109 *menys of* bemoan
112–13 *Gif that us fall . . . / Hap* if good fortune befall us
117 *contene yow* bear yourselves
125 *but abaysing* without faltering
130 [*Nele* King Robert's brother, Neil Bruce, was executed by the English in 1306, shortly after Robert Bruce seized the Scottish throne]
131 *mene of* think of
132 *prowes* feats of courage
134 *I trayst . . . sekyrly* I trust and believe for certain

135	To haf plane victour† in this fycht.	
	For thoucht* our fayis haf mekill mycht,	though
	Thai have the wrang, and succudry*	arrogance
	And covatys* of senyowry*	greed sovereignty
	Amovys* thaim, forowtyn mor.†	motivates
140	†Na us thar dreid tham bot befor;	
	For strenth of this place, as ye se,	
	†Sall let us enveronyt to be.	
	And I pray yow als specially,	
	Bath mar and les,† commonaly,*	together
145	That nane of yow for gredynes	
	Haf ey† to tak of thar riches,	
	Na prisoneris for to ta,*	take
	Quhill* ye se thaim contraryit* sa†	until opposed
	That the feld anirly* yowris be.	alone
150	And than at your liking† may ye	
	Tak all the riches that thar is.	
	Gif ye will wyrk* apon this wis,†	proceed
	Ye sall haf victour* sekyryly.*	victory surely
	I wate nocht† quhat mar* say sall I,	
155	Bot all wate ye† quhat honour is;	
	Contene yow† than on sic a wis	
	That your honour ay* savyt* be,	always safeguarded
	And Ik hycht† her in leauté:†	
	Gif ony deys* in this bataille	die
160	†His ayr, but ward, relef or taile,	
	On the fyrst day sall weld,†	
	All be he† never sa young of eild.*	age

135 *plane victour* clear victory
139 *forowtyn mor* nothing else
140 *Na us . . . bot befor* Nor need we fear them except in front
142 *Sall let . . . to be* shall prevent our being surrounded
144 *mar and les* greater and lower in rank
146 *Haf ey* have as your object
148 *sa* in such a way
150 *at your liking* freely
152 *apon this wis* in this way
154 *wate nocht* do not know
155 *all wate ye* you all know
156 *Contene yow* conduct yourselves
158 *Ik hycht* I vow *leauté* in good faith
160 *His ayr . . . relef or taile* His heir, without wardship, relief or tallage [The heirs of those killed in battle are promised exemption from the usual feudal levies (wardship, relief and tallage) on inheritance]
161 *weld* have possession
162 *Al be he* although he be

Now makys yow redy for to fycht.
God help us, that is maist of mycht!†
165 I rede* armyt all nycht that we be, advise
Purvayit* in bataill, swa that we equipped
To mete our fayis ay be boune.'* ready
Than answeryt thai all with a soune:* one shout
'As ye dyvys,* all sall be done!' propose
170 Than till thar innys* went thai sone lodgings
And ordanyt thaim† for the fechting,
Syne assemblyt in the evynnyng.
And swagat* all the nycht bad* thai, in this way remained
Till on the morn that it wes day.

---

164 *maist of mycht* greatest in power
171 *ordanyt thaim* prepared themselves

William Langland
?c. 1330–?1386

According to a marginal note in an early manuscript of *Piers Plowman*, its author was an Oxfordshire gentleman's son named William Langland. Internal evidence suggests that he was a married clerk; that is, he had a clerical education, wore the tonsure and assisted at religious services but was not a priest. He seems to have lived both in London and Worcestershire, where his poem begins.

Langland was probably a slightly older contemporary of Chaucer, perhaps born in the early 1330s. He seems to have worked on *Piers Plowman* for most of his adult life, obsessively writing and rewriting it. He probably began it in the early 1360s and may have been still revising it when he died, probably before 1399. The manuscripts – there are over fifty of them – preserve different states of the poem which have traditionally been divided into three groups, representing the original A text and the expanded and revised B and C versions. Recently another, the Z text, has been added to these and it has begun to look as if the old classification is too rigid; the process of revising and rewriting may have been more or less continuous.

Piers Plowman is a vision poem in which the dreamer has a sequence of dreams – not always clearly ordered – through which he explores the state of his society and pursues his own search for salvation. The poem is written in alliterative long lines, though Langland does not use the poetic diction of, say, *Sir Gawain and the Green Knight* or *Morte Arthure*; the language of his symbolic and inward poetry is at once more particular and more abstract. Langland knew the Latin liturgy of the church and parts of the Bible intimately; his Latin quotations from these and other sources are often woven inextricably with his English into the structure of his thought, as in the opening of Passus 18.

The first of the extracts below is the Prologue to the poem, in which the dreamer falls asleep for the first time and has a vision of contemporary society which is expressed in a mixture of modes, literal and allegorical, that may at first be disconcerting. Reading the Prologue is a good preparation for the profounder and more complex Passus 18. This section explores, through its shifting symbolism and its triumphantly dramatic representation of the crucifixion and the harrowing of hell, the ways in which it is possible to experience and describe both human and divine love.

The texts are taken from W. W. Skeat's 1886 edition of Bodleian Library, Oxford, MS Laud Misc. 581, corrected against the variants listed in Kane and Donaldson's 1975 edition of the B-text.

2 I put on outer clothing as if I were a sheep
[*shepe*: possibly *shep* 'shepherd' is intended, though *shepe* means 'sheep'. Presumably the dreamer is wearing a garment of sheep's wool, like a hermit's (l. 3). There may also be a metaphorical sense in which the 'heremite unholy of workes' is a wolf in sheep's clothing]
5 [*Malverne hulles* the Malvern Hills are in Worcestershire, in the west of England. Although the dreamer falls asleep in the country, the vision of society which follows is as much urban as rural]
6 An amazing thing happened to me, from fairyland, it seemed.
7 *wery forwandred* tired out with wandering

10 I fell into a sleep, it flowed so sweetly
1–10 [The May-morning setting of the dream is an adaptation of the conventional prelude to a love-vision, as in the influential thirteenth-century French *Le Roman de la Rose* (The Romance of the Rose) of Guillaume de Lorris and Jean de Meung. There are similar openings, in which the dreamer falls asleep in the countryside, in other fourteenth-century alliterative dream-poems]
13 *bihelde into* looked towards
14 I saw a tower on a hillock choicely built
14–15 [*toure ... dongeon* the meanings of tower and dungeon are explained in Passus 1. The tower is where God as Truth lives, as is hinted in l. 13 by its location in the east, the place of resurrection. In Psalm 60(61).4 the psalmist says to God 'thou hast been ... a strong tower from the enemy'. The dungeon (a place of dishonourable imprisonment for felons) is explained in Passus 1 as 'the castle of care' (l. 61) inhabited by the devil]
16 *dredful of sight* terrifying to look at

20 *putten hem* set themselves   *ful selde* very rarely

22 *wonnen that* produce what   *with glotonye destruyeth* with gluttony destroy
23 Some devoted themselves to pride, dressed themselves accordingly.

28 *holden hem ... here selles* remain in their cells
[*ancres and heremites* anchorites lived in strict enclosure; hermits also lived solitary lives but were less cut off from their fellows. (See headnote on Richard Rolle, p. 179)]
29 *coveiten nought* do not desire at all
30 In order to gratify their bodies with easy living
31 *chaffare* commerce   *cheven* get on

33–7 [The dreamer distinguishes between harmless musicians ('mynstralles') who play for a living, and other travelling entertainers who lie, cheat and deceive]
34 *giltles, I leve* guiltlessly, I believe
35–7 But jesters and story-tellers, the offspring of Judas, make up outlandish tricks and play the fool, and yet have intelligence at their disposal, if only they wanted to work.
38–9 What St Paul preaches about them I do not wish to demonstrate here: namely, that 'He who speaks filth' is the devil's servant
[*Qui ... loquitur* probably derived from Ephesians 5.4]

From PIERS PLOWMAN
B-Version, Prologue

    In a somer seson, whan soft was the sonne,
   †I shope me in shroudes as I a shepe were,
    In habite* as an heremite unholy of workes,*   dress conduct
    Went wyde in this world wondres to here.
5 †Ac* on a May mornynge on Malverne hulles   but
   †Me byfel a ferly, of fairy me thoughte;
   †I was wery forwandred and went me to reste
    Under a brode* banke bi a bornes* side,   broad stream's
    And as I lay and lened and loked in the wateres,
10 †I slombred in a slepyng, it sweyved so merye.
        Thanne gan I to meten* a merveilouse swevene,*   dream dream
    That I was in a wildernesse, wist* I never where.   knew
   †As I bihelde into the est,* and hiegh* to the sonne,   east upwards
   †I seigh a toure on a toft trielich ymaked;
15 A depe dale binethe, a dongeon thereinne
   †With depe dyches and derke* and dredful of sight.   dark
    A faire felde* ful of folke fonde* I there bytwene,   field found
    Of alle maner* of men, the mene* and the riche,   kinds humble
    Worchyng* and wandryng as the worlde asketh.*   working requires
20 †Some putten hem to the plow, pleyed ful selde,
    In settyng* and in sowyng swonken* ful harde,   planting labour
   †And wonnen that wastours with glotonye destruyeth.
   †And some putten hem to pruyde, apparailed hem thereafter,
    In countenaunce* of clothyng comen disgised.*   display dressed up
25 In prayers and in penance putten hem manye,
    Al for love of Owre Lorde lyveden ful streyte,*   very strictly
    In hope forto have heveneriche* blisse: of heaven
   †As ancres* and heremites that holden hem in here selles   anchorites
   †And coveiten nought in contré to kairen* aboute   travel
30 †For no likerous liflode her lykam to plese.
   †And somme chosen chaffare; they cheven the bettere,
    As it semeth to owre syght that suche men thryveth;
   †And somme murthes* to make as mynstralles   entertainment
        conneth,*   know how
    And geten gold with here glee* – giltes, I leve.   music
35 †Ac japers and jangelers, Judas chyldren,
    Feynen hem fantasies, and foles hem maketh,
    And han here witte at wille to worche yif thei sholde.
   †That Poule precheth of hem I nel nought preve it here:
   †*Qui turpiloquium loquitur* is Luciferes hyne.

42 *Fayteden* shammed (hardship) *atte ale* at the ale-house

44 *ribaudye* debauchery *roberdes knaves* vagabonds
45 *sori sleuthe* miserable sloth
46 [*palmers* originally pilgrims to the Holy Land, though here almost synonymous with *pylgrymes*] *plighted hem* pledged themselves
47 [*Seynt James* the shrine of St James at Compostella, in Spain]
48 [*wise tales* the ironic adjective points to the fact that telling tall stories is a well-known travellers' pastime, which Chaucer exploits in *The Canterbury Tales*]
49 *hadden leve to lye* were free to lie

51 *ech a* every

54 *and here wenches after* and their women after [them]
[*Walsyngham* the shrine of Our Lady of Walsingham, Norfolk; one of England's major centres of pilgrimage]

56 *copis* copes (priestly vestments)
57 *shopen hem* made themselves into
58 [*foure ordres* Augustinians, Carmelites, Dominicans and Franciscans. Friars, unlike monks, were not enclosed in monasteries, but worked among the people as preachers and confessors, and were not supposed to own possessions but to live on charity]

62 *maistres freris* graduate friars *at lykyng* as they like
63 For the money (they get) and what they have to sell go together
64 For since charity has become a huckster and the leader (of those who) hear lords' confessions
65 *ferlis* amazing things *han fallen* have happened
66 Unless Holy Church and they are more united
67 *moste myschief* greatest evil
68 [*pardoner* pardoners – who were not necessarily priests – were licensed to issue indulgences or pardons to penitents. These indulgences remitted the temporal punishment for sin which was due to be exacted in purgatory. In return, the receiver of an indulgence would make a free donation to a specified charity. The system was obviously open to abuse, and pardoners frequently sold indulgences and also offered absolution or forgiveness, which they had no authority to do. For another fourteenth-century portrait of a corrupt pardoner, see Chaucer's *Pardoner's Tale*]
69 [*bulle* letter of authorisation bearing a seal]

74 *bonched hem* struck them *brevet* letter of indulgence

76 *glotones to kepe* to maintain gluttons

78 If the bishop were holy and paid attention to what is happening

40	Bidders* and beggeres fast aboute yede,*	scroungers went
	With her* bely and her bagge of bred ful ycrammed;	their
	†Fayteden for here fode, foughten atte ale.	
	In glotonye, God it wote,* gon hii* to bedde,	knows they go
	†And risen with ribaudye, tho roberdes knaves;	
45	†Slepe and sori sleuthe seweth* hem evre.*	follow always
	† Pilgrymes and palmers plighted hem togidere	
	†To seke Seynt James and seyntes in Rome.	
	†Thei went forth in here* wey with many wise tales,	their
	†And hadden leve to lye al here lyf* after.	life
50	I seigh* somme that seiden thei had ysought seyntes:	saw
	†To eche a tale that thei tolde here tonge* was tempred* to lye,	tongue tuned
	More than to sey soth,* it semed by here speche.	truth
	Heremites on an heep* with hoked* staves	in a crowd hooked
	†Wenten to Walsyngham, and here wenches after;	
55	Grete lobyes* and longe* that loth* were to swynke*	louts tall unwilling work
	†Clotheden hem in copis to ben knowen fram othere,*	others
	†And shopen hem heremites here ese* to have.	comfort
	† I fonde there freris,* alle the foure ordres,	friars
	Preched the peple for profit of hemselven,*	their own profit
60	Glosed* the gospel as hem good lyked,*	interpreted as they pleased
	For coveitise* of copis construed it* as thei wolde.	greed interpreted
	†Many of his maistres freris mowe* clothen hem at lykyng,	can
	†For here money and marchandise marchen togideres.	
	†For sith charite hath be chapman and chief to shryve lordes	
65	†Many ferlis han fallen in a fewe yeris.	
	†But Holy Chirche and hii holde better togideres	
	†The moste myschief on molde* is mountyng wel faste.	earth
	† There preched a pardonere as* he a prest were:	as if
	†Broughte forth a bulle with bishopes seles,	
70	And seide that hymself* myghte assoilen* hem alle	he himself absolve
	Of falshed* of fastyng, of vowes ybroken.	deception
	Lewed* men leved* hym wel and lyked his wordes,	ignorant believed
	Comen up knelyng to kissen his bulles;	
	†He bonched hem with his brevet and blered* here eyes,	dazzled
75	And raughte* with his ragman* rynges and broches.	acquired roll (official document)
	†Thus they geven here golde glotones to kepe,	
	And leneth it* such loseles* that lecherye haunten.*	give to idlers practise
	†Were the bischop yblissed and worth bothe his eres,	
	His seel shulde nought be sent to deceyve the peple.	

80 *naught by* not on behalf of

82 *poraille* poor people   *if thei nere* were it not for them

84 [*pestilence tyme* there were outbreaks of the plague in 1348–9, 1361–2, 1369 and 1375–6. Here, parish priests complain that they can no longer live on the tithes from their parishioners because so many have died in the plague, and seek permission to go to the more populous city]
86 *syngen there for symonye* sing masses there for payment
[*symonye* the sale of ecclesiastical offices; called after Simon Magus (Acts 8.9–24). Priests who have deserted their parishes come to London to sing masses for the dead (in chantries endowed for the purpose) in return for payment]
87 [*maistres and doctours* university graduates who have proceeded to Masters' and Doctors' degrees]
88 *han cure* have the cure of souls [i.e. have a responsibility for the spiritual welfare of their flocks]
[*crounyng* the tonsure, or shaven crown, which was a sign of the clerical calling]
89 *shryven here paroschienes* hear their parishioners' confessions
91 *Lenten an elles* Lent and other times
93 In the Exchequer and the Chancellor's court lay claim to what is owed him
[Many university-trained clerics made careers as civil servants in the Exchequer or the Chancellor's court, neglecting the ecclesiastical offices from which they derived incomes]
94 From wardships and ward meetings, waifs and strays
[*wardes* The king had the right to claim wardship (including the income from property) over the heir of a royal tenant-in-chief who inherited while still a minor   *wardmotes* meetings held in wards or sections of a city to determine monies due to the crown   *weyves and streyves* lost property of different kinds which came into the ownership of the crown]
96 *demen* pass judgement
[*stuwardes* a steward was a manorial official who could preside over a manor court]
97 *Here messe* their masses   *matynes* morning services   *oures* canonical hours
[*messe . . . matynes . . . oures* church services here heedlessly performed by priests whose concerns are with temporal affairs]
98 Are said without devotion; it is to be feared at the end
99 *consistorie* consistory or bishop's court   [The court of a bishop in which cases involving churchmen were tried, or a council of cardinals; here used metaphorically for the Last Judgement]
100–1 [Matthew 16.19; Jesus gave Peter, chief of the disciples, 'the keys of the kingdom of heaven: and whatsoever thou shalt bind on earth shall be bound in heaven: and whatsoever thou loose on earth shall be loosed in heaven']
104 [*cardinales* the four cardinal virtues: Fortitude, Prudence, Temperance and Justice   *closyng yatis* alludes to the derivation of 'cardinal' from Latin *cardo* 'hinge']
106 *hem* them [the virtues]
107 [*cardinales atte courte* members of the *curia* (court or consistory) of cardinals, the papal assistants and advisers who have the power to elect the pope]
108 *presumed in hem* took upon themselves presumptuously
109 *inpugnen I nelle* I do not want to find fault [i.e. with the cardinals]
110 *eleccioun* (papal) election
108–10 [In 1179 the responsibility of electing the pope became that of the cardinals alone. The ironic tone of these lines may cloak an allusion to the election in 1378 of an antipope by a group of French cardinals, which split the western church]
113 *comunes* common people
114 *Kynde Wytte* Natural Intelligence

116 *Clergye bothe* learned men together

117 *hem communes fynde* provide food for them

120 To till and labour, as honest living requires

80	†Ac it is naught by the bischop that the boy* precheth,	scoundrel
	For the parisch prest and the pardonere parten* the silver	share
	†That the poraille of the parisch sholde have, if thei nere.	
	Persones* and parisch prestes pleyned hem* to the bischop	parsons complained
	†That here parisshes were pore* sith* the pestilence tyme,	poor since
85	To have a lycence and a leve* at London to dwelle,	permission
	†And syngen there for symonye, for silver is swete.	
	†Bischopes and bachelers,* bothe maistres and doctours	graduates
	†(That han cure under Criste, and crounyng in tokne*	as a mark
	†And signe that thei sholden shryven here paroschienes,	
90	Prechen and prey for hem, and the pore fede)	
	†Liggen* in London in Lenten an elles.	reside
	Somme serven the kyng and his silver tellen;*	count
	†In Cheker and in Chancerye chalengen his dettes	
	†Of wardes and wardmotes, weyves and streyves.	
95	And some serven as servantz lordes and ladyes,	
	†And in stede* of stuwardes sytten and demen.	place
	†Here messe and here matynes and many of here oures	
	†Arn don undevoutlych; drede is at the laste	
	†Lest Crist in consistorie acorse* ful manye!	damn
100	†I parceyved of* the power that Peter had to kepe,	understood
	To bynde and to unbynde, as the boke telleth;	
	How he it left with love, as Owre Lorde hight,*	commanded
	Amonges foure vertues, the best of alle vertues,	
	†That cardinales ben called and closyng yatis,*	gates
105	There Crist is in kyngdome, to close and to shutte,	
	†And to opne it to hem and hevene* blisse shewe.*	heaven's show
	†Ac* of the cardinales atte courte that caught of* that name	but obtained
	†And power presumed in hem a pope to make,	
	†To han* that power that Peter hadde, inpugnen I nelle:	have
110	†For in love and letterure* the eleccioun bilongeth;	learning
	Forthi* I can and can naughte of courte speke more.	therefore
	Thanne come there a Kyng: Knyghthod* hym ladde;*	Knighthood led
	†Might of the comunes made* hym to regne.*	caused reign
	†And thanne cam Kynde Wytte and clerkes* he made,	clerics
115	For to conseille* the Kyng and the Comune save.*	advise preserve
	†The Kyng and Knyghthode and Clergye bothe	
	†Casten* that the Comune shulde hem communes fynde.	decide
	The Comune contreved* of* Kynde Wytte craftes,*	devised by skills
	And for profit of alle the poeple plowmen ordeygned*	established
120	†To tilie and travaile, as trewe lyf asketh.	

123 [*lunatik* in the world in which educated men do not put their learning to proper use, it is left to the lunatic to speak *clergealy*, i.e. with the voice of learning]

126 And grant you to govern your country so that justice may love you

129 *Lowed* came down *ne coude* did not know how to
130 Argue or judge that which should vindicate them

132–8 'I am King, I am Prince', but perhaps in future you shall be neither. O you who administer the supreme laws of Christ the king: in order to do it better, as you are just, be merciful. Naked justice requires to be clothed by you in mercy; as you wish to reap, so must you sow. If the law is stripped bare by you, may it be measured out to you with the same stark justice. If mercy is sown, may you reap mercy.
[These anonymous lines also appear in an early fourteenth-century sermon MS. The angel delivers his message about the need for kings to be both merciful and just in Latin, the language of power. Compare *Piers Plowman*, Passus 18, lines 188 ff., on the relation between justice and mercy]

139 *greved hym* became angry   *goliardeys* former clerk, joker   [Strictly one who has forsaken the clerical life, but used elsewhere in ME to denote a joker or buffoon. Both senses are relevant here]
141–2 Since a king is said to derive his name from ruling, he has the name without the thing itself if he does not seek to maintain the law. [A variant version of an anonymous couplet]

144 *construe hoso wolde* if anyone wishes to interpret them
145 The precepts of the King are the bonds of our law
[A well-known principle of Roman law. The enigmatic 'construe hoso wolde' (l. 144) perhaps implies that the 'bonds of the law' both hold anarchy in check and curtail freedom]
146 ff. [The dreamer's story of the attempt of the rats and mice to bell the cat is a version of a well-known fable. The rats and mice seem to represent different orders of society or perhaps different groups in Parliament. The cat is either the king (probably Edward III [1327–77] rather than his grandson Richard II [1377–99]) or possibly a predatory nobleman. There may be an allusion to the Good Parliament of 1376 when the House of Commons and members of the House of Lords jointly demanded the removal from power of certain of Edward III's courtiers, who were charged with corruption; nevertheless, in 1377 Edward's brother, John of Gaunt, reasserted the authority of the crown, motivated, it seems, by a belief in the necessity of strong central government. The conclusion of the tale, conveyed in the mouse's speech, is that even a ruthless central authority is better than no law at all]
148 *here comune profit* their general good
152 For fear of various dangers we do not dare show our faces
153 *grucche of* complain about

155 So that our life becomes a torment, before he lets us go

            The Kynge and the Comune   and Kynde Witte the thridde*   third
            Shope* lawe and lewte,*   eche man to knowe his   established justice
            owne.
            †Thanne loked up a lunatik,   a lene* thing withalle,*   lean moreover
            And knelyng to the Kyng   clergealy* he seyde: learnedly
125   'Crist kepe* the, sire Kyng, and thi kyngriche,*   preserve kingdom
            †And lene the lede thi londe   so leuté the lovye,
            And for thi rightful rewlyng   be rewarded in hevene!'
            And sithen* in the eyre* an hiegh* an angel of hevene   then air on high
            †Lowed to speke in Latyn   – for lewed* men ne coude   unlearned
130   †Jangle ne jugge   that justifie hem shulde,
            But suffren* and serven – forthi* seyde the angel: endure therefore
            †' "Sum Rex, sum Princeps", neutrum fortasse deinceps;
            O qui iura regis   Christi specialia regis,
            Hoc quod agas melius, iustus es, esto pius!
135   Nudum ius a te   vestiri vult pietate;
            Qualia vis metere   talia grana sere.
            Si ius nudatur   nudo de iure metatur;
            Si seritur pietas   de pietate metas!'
            †Thanne greved hym a goliardeys, a glotoun* of wordes,   glutton
140   And to the angel an heigh   answeres after,
            †'Dum rex a regere   dicatur nomen habere,
            Nomen habet sine re   nisi studet iura tenere.'
            And thanne gan alle the Comune   crye in vers* of Latin   verses
            †To the kynges conseille,   construe hoso wolde:
145   †'Precepta Regis   sunt nobis vincula legis.'
            †With that ran there a route* of ratones* at ones,   crowd rats
            And smale mys* myd* hem,   mo* then a thousande,   mice with more
            †And comen to a conseille*   for here comune profit;   council
            For a cat of a courte   cam whan hym lyked,*   he wanted to
150   And overlepe* hem lyghtlich   and laughte* hem at   pounced on caught
            his wille,
            And pleyde with hem perilouslych*   and possed*   dangerously tossed
            hem aboute.
            †'For doute of dyverse dredes   we dar noughte wel loke;
            †And yif we grucche of his gamen*   he wil greve* us alle –   sport vex
            Cracche* us, or clowe* us   and in his cloches*   scratch claw claws
            holde,
155   †That us lotheth the lyf   or he lete us passe.
            Myghte we* with any witte*   his wille withstonde, if we could contrivance
            We myghte be lordes aloft*   and lyven at owre ese.'   above
            A raton of renon,*   most renable* of tonge,   distinguished persuasive
            Seide for a sovereygne*   help to hem alle: powerful

WILLIAM LANGLAND

160 *ysein segges*   seen men
161 *Beren bighes*   wear necklaces
162 And some [wear] collars of skilful work; they go about off the leash
[Probably an allusion to the livery-collars or chains worn as badges of allegiance to a lord by his retainers. For a fifteenth-century view of the depredations of noblemen's followers, see *The Second Shepherds' Play*, p. 440]
163 *waste*   waste ground   *hem leve liketh*   they please
165 *here beigh*   their necklace   *as me thynketh*   it seems to me

167 *me sheweth*   suggests to me

170 *here we mowen*   we can hear
171 *ritt*   moves around   *rest*   stays still
172 And if he wants to play, then we can look out
173 and appear in his presence as long as he wants to play
174 and if he grows angry, beware and keep out of his way

176 *beighe*   collar

180 *helden hem unhardy*   (they) regarded themselves as timid
181 *here longe studye*   their lengthy deliberation
182 *moche good couthe*   had much good sense
183 *Stroke forth sternly*   pushed forward firmly

190 *fet hym*   feeds himself   *defame we hym never*   let us not dishonour him

192 (For better is) the turmoil among us all, though we fail to stop a villain
193 *is seven yere ypassed*   seven years ago
194 *ful elyng*   very miserable
194 [Richard II came to the throne in 1377 at the age of 10; his predecessor Edward III had also inherited the crown as a minor fifty years previously]
195 *whoso wil it rede*   whoever wants to read it
196 Woe to the land where a boy is king   [A well-known dictum, from Ecclesiastes 10.16]

160 †'I have ysein segges,' quod he, 'in the cité of London
†Beren bighes ful brighte abouten here nekkes,
†And some colers of crafty werk; uncoupled thei wenden
†Bothe in wareine* and in waste where hem leve lyketh, — warren
And otherwhile* thei aren elleswhere, as I here telle. — sometimes
165 †Were there a belle on here beigh, bi Jesu, as me thynketh,
Men myghte wite* where thei went and awei renne!* — know run
†And right* so,' quod that ratoun, 'reson me sheweth, — just
To bugge* a belle of brasse or of brighte sylver, — buy
And knitten* it on a colere for owre comune profit — fix
170 †And hangen it upon the cattes hals;* thanne here we mowen — neck
†Where he ritt or rest or renneth* to playe. — runs
†And yif him list for to laike, thenne loke we mowen
†And peren in his presence therewhile hym plaie liketh,
†And yif him wrattheth, be ywar and his weye shonye.'
175 Alle this route* of ratones to this reson* thei — crowd argument
assented.
†Ac tho* the belle was ybought and on the beighe hanged — but when
There ne was ratoun in alle the route, for alle the rewme* of — kingdom
Fraunce,
That dorst* have ybounden* the belle aboute the cattis — dared tied
nekke,
Ne hangen it aboute the cattes hals al Engelonde to wynne;
180 †And helden hem unhardy and here conseille feble,
†And leten* here laboure lost and alle here longe studye. — considered
†A mous that moche good couthe, as me thoughte,
†Stroke forth sternly and stode biforn* hem alle, — before
And to the route of ratones rehersed* these wordes: — uttered
185 'Though we culled* the catte, yut sholde ther come another, — killed
To cracchy* us and al owre kynde,* though we — scratch species
croupe* under benches. — crept
Forthi* I conseille alle the comune to lat the catte — therefore
worthe,* — be
And be we* never so bolde the belle hym to shewe. — and let us be
The while he caccheth conynges* he coveiteth* — rabbits desires
nought owre caroyne,* — flesh
190 †But fet hym al with venesoun: defame we hym nevere.
For better is a litel losse than a longe sorwe,
†The mase amonge us alle, though we mysse a schrewe.
†For I herde my sire seyn, is sevene yere ypassed,
†There* the catte is a kitoun the courte is ful elyng; — where
195 †That witnisseth Holi Write, whoso wil it rede:
†*Ve terre ubi puer rex est*
For may no renke* there rest have for ratones bi nyghte. — man

200 *Nere* were it not for *overlepe* pounce on
201 For if you rats could do what you wanted, you would not know how to govern yourselves
202 *se so mykel after* see so far ahead

204 *costed me nevre* never cost me anything
205 *biknowen it I nolde* I would not reveal it
206–7 But (would prefer) to let him do as he wishes, according to his whim, to catch what they can, with or without restraint

210 *Devine ye* interpret *ne dar* dare not
211 *hoved* stood around *houves of selk* coifs of silk
212 *Serjauntz* sergeants-at-law; barristers *atte barre* at the bar
[Sergeants-at-law were senior barristers in the employment of the king; their silk caps ('houves', l. 211) were the badge of their profession (like modern barristers' wigs)]
214 *unlese here lippis ones* once unlock their lips

217 *an burgeis* and burgesses *bondemen als* serfs as well

223 Some of all the kinds of labourers on earth ran forward
224 Like ditchers and diggers who perform their tasks badly
225 *dryven forth* pass *Dieu vous save, Dame Emme* God save you, Mistress Emma.
[A popular song]

For many mannus* malt   we mys* wolde destruye,*   men's mice destroy
And also ye route of ratones   rende* mennes clothes,   tear to pieces
200 †Nere that cat of that courte   that can yow overlepe;
†For had ye rattes yowre wille   ye couthe nought reule yowreselve.
†I sey for me,' quod the mous,   'I se so mykel after,
Shal never the cat ne the kitoun   bi my conseille be greved,*   harmed
†Ne carpyng* of this coler   that costed me nevre.   talking
205 †And though it had coste me catel,*   biknowen it I nolde,   wealth
†But suffre as hymself wolde   to do as hym liketh,
Coupled and uncoupled,   to cacche what thei mowe.
Forthi uche a* wise wight* I warne: wite* wel   every person know
   his owne.'
What this meteles* bemeneth,*   ye men that be merye,   dream means
210 †Devine ye, for I ne dar,   bi dere God in hevene.
†Yit hoved there an hondreth*   in houves of selke,   hundred
†Serjauntz, it semed,   that serveden atte barre,
Plededen* for penyes   and poundes* the lawe,   pleaded pummel
†And nought for love of Owre Lorde   unlese here lippes onis.
215 Thow myghtest better mete* the myste   on Malverne hulles   measure
Than gete a 'momme'* of her mouthe,   but* money   mumble unless
   were shewed.
†Barones an burgeis   and bondemen als
I seigh* in this assemblé,   as ye shul here* after.   saw hear
Baxsteres* and brewesteres*   and bocheres*   bakers brewers butchers
   manye,
220 Wollewebsteres* and weveres of lynnen,   woolweavers
Taillours and tynkeres   and tolleres* in marketes,   toll-collectors
Masons and mynours*   and many other craftes.*   miners craftsmen
†Of alkin libbyng laboreres   lopen forth somme,
†As dykers and delveres   that doth here dedes ille,
225 †And dryven forth the longe day   with *Dieu vous save, Dame
   Emme!'*
Cokes* and here knaves*   crieden, 'Hote pies, hote!   cooks their servants
Gode gris* and gees!   Go we dyne, go we!   pigs
Taverners until hem*   tolde the same: to them
230 'White wyn of Oseye*   and red wyn of Gascoigne,*   Alsace Gascony
Of the Ryne* and of the Rochel,*   the roste to   Rhine La Rochelle
   defye!*   digest
— Al this seigh I slepyng   and sevene sythes* more.   times

208   WILLIAM LANGLAND

1   *Wolleward*   wearing wool next to the skin
2   Like a heedless man who takes no thought of hardship

5   *lened me to a Lenten*   lay around until Lent
6   *Reste me*   rested myself   *ramis palmarum*   Palm Sunday   ['with palm branches'; from the eighth antiphon of the procession before the mass on Palm Sunday, the Sunday before Easter, which commemorates Christ's last entry into Jerusalem: 'As the Lord was entering the holy city, the Jewish children ['gerlis'] ... carrying palm branches, cried: Hosanna in high heaven']
7   *gloria, laus*   glory, praise   ['glory, praise'; chorus from the processional hymn for Palm Sunday, in which the congregation re-enacts Christ's reception by the people of Jerusalem]
8   [*osanna*   Matthew 21.9; 'Hosanna' is the opening word of the ceremony of the blessing of palms that precedes the procession and mass on Palm Sunday, and is frequently repeated during the service. See note to l. 6 above]   *by orgonye*   to the organ
9   [*Crystes passioun*   the crucifixion]   *that ofraughte*   which reached out to
10   [*Samaritan*   Luke 10.30–7; the Good Samaritan, whose story is told by Christ to exemplify the love of one's neighbour, is used in the previous Passus as a figure for Christ himself.   *Piers the Plowman*   Piers Plowman has appeared earlier in the poem working on behalf of his fellows, and by the end becomes the object of the Dreamer's search. In lines 23, 26 and 34 Piers represents humankind and, like the Samaritan, is identified with Christ's love for man]
11   [*on an asse bakke*   Matthew 21.5–7; Christ made his final journey into Jerusalem on an ass]   *botelees*   without boots   *cam prykye*   came riding
13   [*knyghte*   Christ, suffering and dying on the cross for mankind, is symbolised as a newly-dubbed knight at a joust. For other versions of this theme, see *Ancrene Wisse*, p. 147, and 'In a Valley of this Restless Mind', p. 417. The crowds receiving Christ into Jerusalem, the congregation at a Palm Sunday service and the audience at a joust dissolve into one another in this passage]
14   *galoches ycouped*   slashed shoes
15   *A! Fili David!*   Ah, son of David!   [From the seventh antiphon of the Palm Sunday procession: 'Hail, our King, son of David']
18   Blessed is he who comes in the name of the Lord
19   *fraynd at*   asked of   *fare bemente*   commotion signified
21   *Piers fruit the Plowman*   the fruit of Piers Plowman   [Piers' fruit is redeemed mankind]

24   *haberjoun*   coat of mail   *humana natura*   human nature
25   So that Christ might not be recognised here as almighty God
26   *Piers paltok the Plowman*   Piers Plowman's tunic
27   *in deitate Patris*   in his divine nature (lit., in the divinity of the Father)
28   [*Juwes or scribes*   not mutually exclusive terms; the gospels mention the Jewish chief priests and scribes as leading the opposition to Jesus]

32   *leyth his lif to wedde*   lays his life as a pledge
33   [*thre dayes*   Christ was crucified on Good Friday and rose from the dead on Easter Sunday]

35   *there hym lyketh*   where he pleases
[*Lucifer*   'light-bearer'; Satan]

From PIERS PLOWMAN
B-Version, Passus 18

†Wolleward and weteshoed* went I forth after,   *wet-shod*
†As a reccheles renke that of no wo recchetth,
And yede* forth lyke a lorel* all my lyf tyme,   *went tramp*
Tyl I wex* wery of the worlde and wylned* eft* to slepe,   *grew longed again*
5 †And lened me to a Lenten, and long tyme I slepte;
†Reste me there, and rutte* faste tyl *ramis palmarum*,   *snored*
†Of gerlis* and of *gloria, laus* gretly me dremed,   *children*
†And how *osanna* by orgonye olde* folke songen,   *hosannah of old*
†And of Crystes passioun and penaunce the peple that ofraughte.
10 †One semblable to* the Samaritan, and somedel* to Piers the Plowman,   *resembling partly*
†Barfote on an asse bakke botelees cam prykye,
Wythoute spores other spere; spakliche* he loked,   *eager*
†As is the kynde* of a knyghte that cometh to be dubbed,   *nature*
†To geten hem gylte spores* or galoches ycouped.   *spurs*
15 †Thanne was Faith in a fenestre* and cryde 'A! *fili David!*'   *window*
As doth an heraude of armes whan auntrous* cometh to justes.   *(a) bold knight*
Olde Juwes of Jerusalem for joye thei songen,
†*Benedictus qui venit in nomine domini.*
†Thanne I frayned at Faith what al that fare bemente,
20 And who sholde jouste in Jherusalem. 'Jesus,' he seyde,
†'And fecche that* the fende claymeth: Piers fruit the Plowman.'   *what*
'Is Piers in this place?' quod I, and he preynte* on me,   *fixed his eye*
'This Jesus of his gentrice* wole juste in Piers armes,   *nobility*
†In his helme and in his haberjoun, *humana natura*;
25 †That Cryst be nought biknowe here for *consummatus Deus*,
†In Piers paltok the Plowman this priker* shal ryde;   *horseman*
†For no dynte shal hym dere* as *in deitate Patris*.'   *harm*
†"Who shal juste with Jesus?' quod I, 'Juwes or scribes?'
'Nay,' quod he, 'the foule fende* and Falsdome* and Deth.   *devil falsehood*
30 Deth seith he shal fordo,* and adown brynge   *destroy*
Al that lyveth or loketh* in londe or in watere.   *looks*
†Lyf seyth that he lieth, and leyth his lif to wedde
†That, for al that Deth can do, within thre dayes to walke
And fecche fro the fende Piers fruite the Plowman
35 †And legge* it there hym lyketh, and Lucifer bynde,   *place*

37   O death, I shall be your death   [*O mors*   Hosea 13.14]
38   [*Pilatus*   Pontius Pilate, the Roman governor of Judea, who presided over Jesus' trial] *sedens pro tribunali*   sitting in the judgement seat
39   *deme her botheres righte*   judge the rights of them both

41   *Crucifige*   crucify him [John 19.6]
42   *Tho put hym forth a piloure*   then a thief thrust himself forward
43   [*owre Jewes temple*   Matthew 26.61; at Jesus' trial witnesses accused him of having said he could destroy the temple of God and rebuild it in three days; in fact Jesus had been speaking symbolically of his own death and resurrection]
45   *Edefye it eft*   build it again
46   *al manere pyntes*   in every detail

48   'Crucify him', said an officer of the court, 'I swear he is a sorcerer!'
49   *Tolle, tolle*   away with him [John 19.15]
50   [*of grene ... gerelande*   Matthew 27.29; before Jesus was taken away to be crucified, Roman soldiers put a crown of thorns on his head in a mock coronation]
52   *Ave, rabby*   hail, master   [Matthew 26.49 and 27.29; the words of the 'ribaude' echo Judas' greeting to Jesus when he betrayed him]
53   [*thre nailles*   medieval crucifixions frequently represent Jesus with a nail in either hand and one through his crossed feet]
54   [*poysoun*   Matthew 27.43: 'They gave him vinegar to drink mingled with gall']
55   *deth-yvel*   deadly draught

59   [*Consummatum est*   'it is finished'; Jesus' last words (John 19.30)]

61   *tho leyed his eyen togidres*   then closed his eyes
62   [*The daye ... withdrowe*   as Jesus was dying 'there was darkness over all the earth. ... And the sun was darkened ...' (Luke 23.44–5)]

67   *her one fordoth her other*   one of them destroys the other
68   *wite witterly*   know for certain   *maystrye*   upper hand
69   [*Sondey aboute sonne-rysynge*   The three Maries came 'as it began to dawn toward the first day of the week [Sunday]', and found Jesus' tomb empty (Mark 28.1–8)]

71   [*Vere filius ... iste*   'Truly this was the son of God' (Mark 27.54)]

And forbete* and adown brynge   bale* and deth for evere: beat   sorrow
†*O mors, ero mors tua!*
†Thanne cam *Pilatus* with moche* peple,   *sedens pro tribunali*,   many
†To se how doughtilich* Deth sholde do,   and deme her   bravely
    botheres righte.
40 The Juwes and the justice   ayeine* Jesu thei were,   against
†And al her* courte on hym cryde   'Crucifige!' sharpe.*   their   harshly
†Tho put hym forth a piloure   bifor Pilat and seyde,
†'This Jesus of owre Jewes temple   japed* and dispised,   mocked
    To fordone* it on o* day,   and in thre dayes after   destroy   in one
45 †Edefye it eft newe   (here he stant that seyde it)
†And yit maken it as moche*   in al manere poyntes,   great
    Bothe as longe and as large*   bi loft* and by   broad   above
      grounde.'*   below
†'*Crucifige!*' quod a cacchepole   'I warante hym a wicche!'
†'*Tolle, tolle!*' quod another,   and toke of kene* thornes,   some sharp
50 †And bigan of grene thorne   a gerelande to make,
    And sette it sore* on his hed   and seyde in envye,   painfully
†'*Ave, rabby!*' quod that ribaude,*   and threw redes*   villain   reeds, rods
    at hym,
†Nailled hym with thre nailles   naked on the rode,*   cross
†And poysoun on a pole   thei put up to his lippes,
55 †And bede* hym drynke his deth-yvel;   his dayes were ydone.   ordered
    'And yif* that thow sotil* be,   help now thi-selven.   if   clever
    If thow be Cryst and kynges sone,   come downe of* the rode;   from
    Thanne shul we leve* that Lyf the loveth   and wil nought lete   believe
      the dye!'
†'*Consummatum est*,' quod Cryst   and comsed* forto   began
      swowe;*   swoon
60 Pitousliche* and pale,   as a prisoun* that deyeth;   pitiably   prisoner
†The lorde of lyf and of light   tho leyed his eyen togideres.
†The daye for drede* withdrowe   and derke bicam the sonne.   fear
    The wal wagged* and clef*   and al the worlde   shook   split
      quaved.*   trembled
    Ded men for that dyne   come out of depe graves
65 And tolde whi that tempest   so long tyme dured;*   lasted
    'For* a bitter bataille,'   the ded bodye sayde;   because of
†'Lyf and Deth in this derknesse,   her one fordoth her other;
†Shal no wighte* wite witterly   who shal have the maystrye   person
†Er* Sondey aboute sonne-rysynge',   and sank with   before
      that* til erthe.   thereupon
70 Some seyde that he was Goddes sone   that so faire deyde:
†*Vere filius dei erat iste*;
    And somme saide he was a wicche: 'Good is that we assaye,*   test

73 *doun er he be taken* before he is taken down
74 [*Two theves also* Mark 27.38]

82 [*Longeus* According to John 19.34, 'one of the soldiers with a spear pierced [Jesus'] side, and forthwith came there out blood and water'. In the apocryphal *Gospel of Nicodemus* (c. 400) the soldier is named Longeus or Longinus; in the 13th-century *Golden Legend* he becomes a blind man who is converted when his sight is miraculously restored as Jesus' blood falls on his eyes]
84 *Maugre his many tethe* despite his protests

90 *cryed hym mercy* begged for mercy from him

92 *Sore it me athynketh* I bitterly regret it
93 *do me in* commit myself to

95 Then Faith fiercely reviled the false Jews

98 To make the blind man beat him, bound – that was a knave's scheme
99 Cursed villains! It was never a knightly deed

103 *Yelt hym recreaunt rennyng* acknowledges himself as defeated in the lists
104 *be this derkenesse ydo* when this darkness is ended
105 *han ylost* are defeated *maistrye* upper hand

107 *cherles* ignoble creatures

	†Where* he be ded or noughte ded, doun er he be taken.'	whether
	†Two theves also tholed* deth that tyme	suffered
75	Uppon a crosse bisydes Cryst; so was the comune lawe.	
	A cacchepole cam forth and craked* bothe her* legges	broke their
	And her armes after of eyther* of tho theves.	each
	Ac* was no boy* so bolde Goddes body to touche;	but rascal
	For* he was knyghte and kynges sone, Kynde* foryaf* that tyme	because nature granted
80	That non harlot* were so hardy* to leyne* hande uppon hym.	menial bold lay
	Ac there cam forth a knyghte with a kene spere ygrounde,*	sharp
	†Highte* *Longeus*, as the lettre* telleth, and longe had lore* his sighte.	called scripture lost
	Bifor Pilat and other peple in the place he hoved;*	came
	†Maugre his many tethe he was made that tyme	
85	To take the spere in his honde and justen* with Jesus;	joust
	For alle thei were unhardy,* that hoved on hors or stode,	afraid
	To touche hym or to taste* hym or take hym down of* rode.	feel from
	But this blynde bacheler* thanne bar* hym thorugh the herte;	knight pierced
	The blode spronge down by the spere and unspered* the knightes eyen.*	unstopped eyes
90	†Thanne fel the knyghte upon knees and cryed him mercy;	
	'Ayeyne* my wille it was, Lorde, to wownde yow so sore!'	against
	†He seighed* and sayde, 'Sore it me athynketh;	sighed
	†For the dede that I have done I do me in yowre grace;*	mercy
	Have on me reuth,* rightful Jesu!' and right with that he wept.	pity
95	†Thanne gan Faith felly the fals Juwes dispise,	
	Called hem caytyves,* acursed for evere.	villains
	'For this foule vyleynye* venjaunce to yow falle!	contemptible action
	†To do the blynde bete hym ybounde, it was a boyes conseille.	
	†Cursed caytyves! Knighthod was it nevere	
100	To mysdo* a ded body, by day or by nyghte.	mutilate
	The gree* yit hath he geten,* for all his grete wounde,	prize won
	For yowre champioun chivaler,* chief knyght of yow alle,	warrior, knight
	†Yelt hym recreaunt rennyng, right at Jesus wille.	
	†For be this derkenesse ydo, his deth worth* avenged;	will be
105	†And ye, lordeynes,* han ylost, for Lyf shal have the maistrye.	cowards
	And yowre fraunchise,* that fre* was, fallen is in thraldome,*	freedom unconstrained bondage
	†And ye, cherles, and yowre children, chieve* shal ye nevre,	prosper
	Ne have lordship in londe, ne no* londe tylye,*	nor any till

109 [*usurye usen* In the middle ages Christians were not allowed to lend each other money at interest. In many Christian communities, therefore, money-lending was practised by Jews, who were forbidden by the Old Testament to exact interest from fellow Jews]
111 [*Danyel* The Old Testament prophet Daniel foretold the history of the Jews]
112 *her* their (the Jews')
113 [*Cum veniat sanctus sanctorum* . . . 'When the holy of holies comes, your anointing shall cease'; based on Daniel 9.24]
114 *What for fere* through fear
115 to *descendit ad inferna* to [where] 'he descended into hell' [From the Apostles' creed]
116 [*secundum scripturas* 'in accordance with the scriptures'; from the Nicene creed, said in the mass: 'And on the third day he rose again from the dead, in accordance with the scriptures']
117 *me thoughte* it seemed to me
118 *in the wey* along *to helle-ward* towards hell
119ff. [*Mercy . . . Truth . . . Righteousness . . . Peace* these allegorical figures derive from Psalm 84 [85].10: 'Mercy and truth are met together; righteousness and peace have kissed each other' (cf. l. 441). In the *Chasteau d'Amour* (Castle of Love) of Robert Grosseteste (*c.* 1175–1253) they are identified as the four daughters of God and debate, as here, whether mankind should be redeemed]

131 *myrthe it bytokneth* it signifies joy
132 [*Marye* Christ's mother, the Blessed Virgin Mary]

133–4 [*conceyved thorw speche / And grace . . . Goste* Luke 1.28–38]

137 [*thritti wynter* a round figure; traditionally Jesus is held to have lived thirty-three years]

140 *In menynge* as a sign

142 *patriarkes* patriarchs; Old Testament leaders

144 [*And that . . . wynne* mankind was condemned because Adam and Eve ate the fruit of the tree of knowledge; mankind was saved by Christ's crucifixion on the tree of the cross]

	†But al bareyne* be and usurye usen,	barren
110	Which is lyf that Owre Lorde in alle lawes acurseth.	
	†Now yowre good dayes ar done, as Danyel propecyed;	
	†Whan Cryst cam, of her kyngdom the croune shulde cesse:	
	†*Cum veniat sanctus sanctorum, cessabit unxio vestra.*'	
	†What for fere of this ferly* and of the fals Juwes,	marvel
115	†I drowe me* in that derkenesse to *descendit ad inferna*	withdrew
	†And there I sawe sothely,* *secundum scripturas*,	truly
	†Out of the west coste,* a wenche,* as me thoughte;	region woman
	†Cam walkynge in the wey; to helle-ward she loked.	
	†Mercy hight* that mayde, a meke thynge* was called creature	
	withalle,*	moreover
120	A ful benygne* buirde* and boxome* of speche. gracious lady gentle	
	Her suster,* as it semed, cam softly walkynge	sister
	Evene* out of the est, and westward she loked.	straight
	A ful comely creature, Treuth she highte;	
	For* the vertue that hir folwed, aferd* was she nevere. because of afraid	
125	Whan this* maydenes mette, Mercy and Treuth,	these
	Eyther* axed* other of this grete wonder,	each asked
	Of the dyne* and of the derknesse and how the daye	noise
	rowed,*	dawned
	And which* a lighte and a leme* lay befor helle.	what gleam
	'Ich* have ferly* of this fare* in feith,' seyde	I marvel commotion
	Treuth,	
130	'And am wendyng* to wyte* what this wonder meneth.' going discover	
	†'Have no merveille,' quod Mercy, 'myrthe it bytokneth.	
	†A mayden that hatte* Marye, and moder without	is called
	felyng*	experience
	Of any kynnes* creature, conceyved thorw speche	kind of
	†And grace of the Holy Goste; wex* grete with childe;	became
135	Withouten wem* into this worlde she brought hym;	flaw
	And that my tale be trewe I take God to witnesse.	
	†Sith* this barn* was bore* ben thritti wynter passed, since child born	
	Which* deyde and deth tholed* this day aboute mydday, who endured	
	And that is cause of this clips* that closeth* now the	eclipse encloses
	sonne,	
140	†In menynge that man shal fro merkenesse* be drawe* darkness led	
	The while this lighte and this leme shal Lucyfer ablende.*	blind
	†For patriarkes and prophetes han preched herof often,	
	That man shal man save thorw a maydenes helpe,	
	†And that* was tynt* thorw tre, tree shal it wynne, that which lost	
145	And that deth doun broughte, deth shal releve.'*	restore
	'That thow tellest,' quod Treuth, 'is but a tale of waltrot!*	nonsense

147–8 [*Adam and Eve and Abraham . . . in peyne* those who lived before the birth of Christ were believed to have awaited his coming in hell (or in limbo), to which he descended after his crucifixion and from where he led them to heaven]

151 *wote the sothe* know the truth

153 [*Job the prophete patriarke* author of the Old Testament Book of Job]
154 ['Since from hell there is no release'; based on Job 7.9: 'he that goeth down to the grave shall come up no more']

160 *do therto* placed upon that spot

163 *fordyd furste* destroyed first

165 *make a good sleighte* play a benign trick [Jesus' resurrection from death is seen as a benign trick, a counterpart to the guile of the devil in persuading Eve to eat the fruit of the Tree of Knowledge]
166 Art to deceive art [Echoes the easter hymn *Pange, Lingua* (Sing, my tongue) by Venantius Fortunatus, line 8]
167 *suffre we* let us be patient
168 *nippe* piercing cold   *ful fer hennes* very far from here
169 *the while* in the meantime

176 *hem tweyne* the two of them
177 *reverenced* greeted courteously

179 *grete thoughte* intended to greet

183 [*Moyses and many mo* Moses, as one of the patriarchs, awaits Jesus' coming with Adam and Eve; other versions of the harrowing regularly depict Isaiah, John the Baptist and Simeon as well]

†For Adam and Eve   and Abraham with other
　　Patriarkes and prophetes　　that in peyne liggen,*　　　　　　　　lie
　　Leve* thow nevere that yone* lighte　　hem* alofte　　believe yonder them
　　　brynge,
150　Ne have hem* out of helle.　　Holde thi tonge, Mercy!　　　　nor let them
　　†It is but a trufle* that thow tellest;　　I, Treuth, wote the　　nonsense
　　　sothe.
　　For that* is ones* in helle　　out cometh it nevere;　　that which once
　　†Job the prophete patriarke　　reproveth* thi sawes:*　　disproves words
　　†*Quia in inferno nulla est redempcio.*'
155　Thanne Mercy ful myldly　　mouthed* thise words:　　　　　uttered
　　'Thorw experience,' quod she,　　'I hope* thei shal be saved.　　believe
　　For venym fordoth* venym,　　and that I prove by resoun.　　destroys
　　For of alle venymes　　foulest is the scorpioun;
　　May no medcyne helpe　　the place there* he styngeth,　　　　where
160　†Tyl he be ded and do therto;　　the yvel he destroyeth,
　　The fyrst venymouste,*　　thorw venym of hymself.*　　poison its own
　　So shal this deth fordo,*　　I dar my lyf legge,*　　　　destroy wager
　　†Al that Deth fordyd furste　　thorw the develles entysynge;*　enticements
　　And right* as thorw gyle*　　man was bigyled,　　　just guile, deception
165　†So shal grace that bigan al　　make a good sleighte;
　　†*Ars ut artem falleret.*'
　　　　†'Now suffre we!' seyde Treuth,　　'I se, as me thinketh,
　　†Out of the nippe of the north,　　nought ful fer hennes,
　　†Rightwisnesse* come rennynge;　　reste we the while,　　　righteousness
170　For she wote* more than we;　　she was* er* we　　knows existed before
　　　bothe.'
　　'That is soth,'* seyde Mercy,　　'and I se here bi southe*　true to the south
　　Where Pees cometh playinge,*　　in pacience yclothed;　desporting herself
　　Love hath coveyted* hir longe,　　leve* I none other　　desired believe
　　But* he sent hir some lettre;　　what this lighte　　　　　but that
　　　bymeneth*　　　　　　　　　　　　　　　　　　　　　　signifies
175　That overhoveth* helle thus,　　she us shal telle.'　　　hangs over
　　†Whan Pees, in pacience yclothed,　　approched nere hem tweyne,
　　†Rightwisnesse her reverenced　　for* her riche clothyng,　　because of
　　And preyed Pees to telle hir　　to what place she wolde,*　wanted to go
　　†And in her gay garnementz　　whom she grete thoughte.
180　'My wille is to wende,'* quod she,　　'and welcome hem alle　　go
　　That many day myghte I noughte se　　for merkenesse*　　darkness
　　　of synne:
　　Adam and Eve　　and other moo* in helle,　　　　　　others as well
　　†Moyses* and many mo*　　mercy shal have,　　　　Moses more
　　And I shal daunce therto.　　Do thow so, sustre!
185　For* Jesus justed wel,　　joye bygynneth dawe;*　　because to dawn

186   In the evening weeping shall have place and in the morning gladness   [Psalm 29(30).6]

191–2   'Behold, here is the licence:' said Peace, ' "in peace in the self-same", and [as a guarantee] that this document shall last: "shall I sleep and take my rest." '
[The texts that Peace cites as guarantees of the role in man's salvation given to her and Mercy by Love (i.e. God) come from Psalm 4.9: 'I will both lay me down in peace and sleep', sung at matins on Holy Saturday]
193   *ravestow*   are you mad?
194   *Levestow*   do you believe
196–9   [Genesis 3.3: 'But of the fruit of the tree which is in the midst of the garden, God hath said [to Adam and Eve], Ye shall not eat of it, neither shall ye touch it, lest ye die.']

200   *ayeines his defence*   against his prohibition

203   *felawes wille*   desire of his companion [Eve]

206   *chyde we nought*   let us not quarrel

207   *botelees bale*   irremediable sorrow
208   *her peyne*   their suffering

209   And in the end grief can turn into joy

211   *no wighte wote*   no-one knows
212   *had ... defaute*   knew deprivation
213   *If no nyghte ne were*   if there were no night
214   *witterly*   for certain   *is to mene*   means

216   *ne were the deth of kynde*   if there were not mortality

219   [*solde*   Judas betrayed Jesus to the chief priests and Pharisees for thirty pieces of silver]

222   *is ynough to mene*   a sufficiency means

†*Ad vesperum demorabitur fletus, et ad matutinum leticia.*
Love, that is my lemman,*   suche lettres me sente   beloved
That Mercy, my sustre, and I   mankynde shulde save;
And that God hath forgyven   and graunted me, Pees, and Mercy,
190   To be mannes meynpernoure*   for everemore after.   surety
†'Lo! here the patent!' quod Pees,   '*in pace in idipsum* –
And that this dede shal dure,   *dormiam et requiescam.*'
†'What, ravestow?' quod Rightwisnesse,   'or thow art right dronke!
†Levestow that yonde* lighte   unlouke* myghte helle   yonder   unlock
195   And save mannes soule?   Sustre, wene* it nevre!   believe
†At the bygynnynge, God gaf   the dome* hymselve,   judgement
That Adam and Eve   and alle that hem suwed*   followed
Shulde deye dounerighte,*   and dwelle in pyne* after,   outright   torment
If that thei touched a tre   and the fruite eten.
200   †Adam afterward   ayeines his defence,
Frette* of that fruit   and forsoke, as it were,   ate
The love of Owre Lorde   and his lore* bothe,   teaching
†And folwed that* the fende* taughte   and his felawes wille,   what   devil
Ayeines resoun; I, Rightwisness,   recorde thus with treuth
205   That her* peyne be perpetuel   and no preyere hem helpe.   their
†Forthi* late hem chewe* as thei chose,   and chyde we   therefore   eat
    nought, sustres,
†For it is botelees bale,   the bite that thei eten.'
†'And I shal preve,'* quod Pees,   'her peyne mote* have   show   can
    ende,
†And wo into wel   mowe wende atte laste;
210   For had thei wist* of no wo,   wel* had thei noughte   known   joy
    knowen.
†For no wighte wote what wel is   that nevere wo suffred,
†Ne what is hote* hunger   that had never defaute.   called
†If no nyghte ne were,   no man, as I leve,*   believe
†Shulde wite witterly   what day is to mene;
215   Shulde nevere righte riche man   that lyveth in reste and ese
†Wyte what wo is,   ne were the deth of kynde.
So God that bygan al   of his good wille
Bycam man of a mayde   mankynde to save,
†And suffred* to be solde,   to see the sorwe* of   allowed (himself)   sorrow
    deyinge,
220   The which unknitteth* al kare   and comsynge* is of   unravels   beginning
    reste.
For til *modicum* * mete with us,   I may it wel avowe,   a small amount
†Wote* no wighte, as I wene,*   what is ynough to mene.   knows   believe
    Forthi* God, of his goodnesse,   the fyrste gome*   therefore   man
Adam,

224 *sovereigne myrthe* highest joy
225 *sorwe to fele* to experience sorrow

229 *thynketh* intends (to go)

231 *fare bi* happen to *her foly* their folly, wrongdoing
232 *lere hem* teach them *langour* suffering
233–4 No-one knows what war is, where peace reigns, nor what is truly joyful, till 'alas' teaches him

235 *brode eyen* wide eyes [The Old and New Testaments, or the literal and figurative intepretations of scripture]
236 *Boke highte that beupere* that reverend man was called Book [The Bible]

238 [Matthew 2.9–11]

239 [*alle the wyse* includes the Magi, or wise men, who, according to Matthew 2.7–10, followed the star in the east] *in o witte acordeden* were of one mind

245 *tendeden hir* lit it

247–8 [*he went on it – Peter the apostel* ... *gate* Jesus walked on the waters of the Sea of Galilee, watched by the disciples, including Peter, who called out to him (Matthew 14.22–32)]

249 *wel hym knewe* recognised him
250 Bid me come to you on the waters [Matthew 14.28]
251–4 [See note to l. 62. At the moment of Jesus' death 'the earth did quake and the rocks rent' (Matthew 27.45 and 51)]

254 *al biquashte* split to pieces

256 [According to the *Gospel of Nicodemus*, the two sons of Simeon were released from death by Jesus and returned to the world to record the harrowing. Their father was the 'just and devout' man of Luke 2.25 who, having seen the child Jesus, was able to 'depart in peace']
257 *hym loth thinke* it seems hateful to him
258 [*Gygas the geaunt* in Psalm 18(19).6, God 'rejoiceth as a strong man ('*gigas*') to run a race'; as a 'strong man', Jesus is also prefigured by the mighty Samson, who broke open the gates of Gaza as Jesus breaks those of hell (Judges 16.3)] *gynne* siege machine
261 *his moder gladye* bring joy to his mother

263 *Juwen* of the Jews

	†Sette hym in solace* and in sovereigne myrthe;	comfort
225	†And sith* he suffred* hym synne, sorwe to fele,	afterwards allowed
	To wite what wel was, kyndelich* to knowe it.	naturally
	And after, God auntred* hymself and toke Adames kynde,*	ventured nature
	To wyte what he hath suffred in thre sondri* places,	different
	†Bothe in hevene and in erthe, and now til* helle he thynketh,	to
230	To wite what al wo is, that* wote of al joye.	he who
	†So it shal fare bi this folke: her foly and her synne	
	†Shall lere hem what langour is, and lisse* withouten ende.	joy
	†Wote no wighte what werre is there that pees regneth,	
	Ne what is witterly wel til "weyllowey" hym teche.'	
235	†Thanne was there a wighte* with two brode eyen;	person
	†Boke highte that beupere, a bolde man of speche.	
	'By Godes body,' quod this Boke, 'I wil bere witnesse,	
	†That tho* this barne* was ybore,* there blased a sterre	when child born
	†That alle the wyse* of this worlde in o witte acordeden,	wise men
240	That such a barne was borne in Bethleem citee	
	That mannes soule sholde save and synne destroye.	
	And all the elementz,' quod the Boke, 'herof* bereth witnesse:	to it
	That he was God that al wroughte* the walkene* firste shewed;	created heaven
	Tho* that weren in hevene token* *stella comata*	those took comet
245	†And tendeden hir as a torche to reverence his birthe;	
	The lyghte folwed the Lorde into the lowe erthe.	
	†The water witnessed that he was God, for he went on it —	
	Peter the apostel parceyved his gate,*	passage
	†And as he went on the water wel hym knewe, and seyde,	
250	†"*Iube me venire ad te super aquas*" —	
	†And lo! how the sonne gan louke* her lighte in herself,	closed up
	Whan she seye* hym suffre, that* sonne and se made!	saw who
	The erthe for hevynesse* that he wolde suffre	grief
	†Quaked as quykke* thinge and al biquashte the roche;*	living rock
255	Lo! helle mighte noughte holde but opened tho* God tholed,*	when suffered
	†And lete oute Symondes sones to seen hym hange on rode.	
	†And now shal Lucifer leve* it, thowgh hym loth thinke;	believe
	†For *Gygas* the geaunt with a gynne engyned*	contrived
	To breke and to bete doune that ben* ayeines Jesus.	those who are
260	And I, Boke, wil be brent,* but* Jesus rise to lyve	burned unless
	†In alle myghtes* of man and his moder gladye.	powers
	And conforte al his kynne* and out of care brynge,	kindred
	†And al the Juwen joye unjoignen* and unlouken;*	disperse undo

266 *Suffre we*   let us be patient
267 *unspere the yatis*   unlock the gates
268 Lift up [your heads], o ye gates   [Psalm 23(24).7 and 9]

273 *ayeines owre leve*   against our will   [*Lazar* Lazarus, whom Jesus raised from the dead (John 19.1–44)]

276 *ther hym lyketh*   where he pleases   *lyghtlych*   without difficulty

282 *ac war hym*   but let him beware
283 *reve me*   deprive me of   *by maistrye*   by force

290–1 And since I was in possession seven thousand years, I believe that law will not grant him the least of them   [*seven thousand wyntre*   the B-version MSS all read 'hundred', but the length of time between the creation and the resurrection was usually reckoned as at least four thousand years]
292 *I me sore drede*   I am very much afraid
293 *gete hem*   acquired them   *breke*   broke into
[*his gardyne breke, / and in . . . serpent*   Satan, disguised as a serpent, entered the Garden of Eden and tempted Eve to eat the forbidden fruit of the Tree of Knowledge (Genesis 3.1–6)]

298 Things are not fairly come by where deception is the source
299 [*Gobelyn*   traditional name for a devil]

302 *This thretty winter*   these thirty years
303–4 *assailled hym with*   incited him to   *some tyme*   on one occasion   [The devil came to Jesus in the wilderness and tempted him to prove that he was the Son of God by performing miracles (Matthew 4.1–11)]

	And but thei reverencen* his rode* and his resurexioun,	honour cross
265	And bileve on* a newe lawe, be lost, lyf and soule.'	in
	†'Suffre we,' seide Treuth, 'I here and se bothe,	
	†How a spirit speketh to helle and bit* unspere the yatis:	bids
	†"*Attollite portas.*"	
	A voice loude in that lighte to Lucifer cryeth,	
270	"Prynces of this place, unpynneth* and unlouketh,*	unbolt unlock
	For here cometh with croune that kynge is of glorie."'	
	Thanne syked* Sathan and seyde to hem alle,	sighed
	†'Suche a lyghte, ayeines owre leve, Lazar it fette;*	took away
	Care and combraunce* is comen to us alle.	trouble
275	If this kynge come in, mankynde wil he fecche	
	†And lede it ther hym lyketh and lyghtlych me bynde.	
	Patriarkes and prophetes han parled* herof* longe,	spoken of this
	That such a lorde and a lyghte shulde lede hem alle hennes.'	
	'Lysteneth,' quod Lucifer, 'for I this lorde knowe,	
280	Bothe this lorde and this lighte; is* longe ago I knewe hym.	it is
	May no deth hym dere,* ne no develes queyntise,*	harm trickery
	†And where he wil, is his waye; ac war hym of the periles.	
	†If he reve me my righte, he robbeth me by maistrye;	
	For by right and bi resoun, tho renkes* that ben here	those men
285	Bodye and soule ben myne, bothe gode and ille.	
	For hymself seyde, that sire* is of hevene,	lord
	Yif Adam ete the apple alle shulde deye	
	And dwelle with us develes; this thretynge* he made.	threat
	And he that sothenesse* is seyde thise wordes;	truth
290	†And sitthen I seised sevene thousand wyntre,	
	I leve that lawe nil naughte lete hym the leest.'	
	†'That is sothe,* seyde Sathan, 'but I me sore drede;	true
	†For thow gete hem with gyle and his gardyne breke,	
	And in semblaunce* of a serpent sat on the appeltre,	likeness
295	And eggedest* hem to ete, Eve by hirselve,	urged
	And toldest hir a tale, of tresoun were the wordes;	
	And so thow haddest* hem oute and hider atte laste.	took
	†It is nought graythely geten there gyle is the rote.'	
	†'For God wil nought be bigiled,'* quod* Gobelyn,	deceived said
	'ne bijaped;*	outwitted
300	We have no trewe title* to hem, for thorwgh tresoun were thei dampned.'	just claim
	'Certes,* I drede me,' quod the Devel, 'leste Treuth wil hem fecche.	indeed
	†This thretty wynter, as I wene,* hath he gone and preched;	believe
	†I have assailled hym with synne, and some tyme y-asked	

305 [*two and thretty wynter*   traditionally, Jesus is believed to have been crucified at the age of thirty-three. Cf. l. 137]

306–7 [*I went/To warne ... wyf*   Pontius Pilate's wife warned him to have nothing to do with the trial of Jesus 'for I have suffered many things this day in a dream because of him' (Matthew 27.19). Medieval elaborations attributed her dream to the devil, who was attempting to thwart man's redemption by preventing the crucifixion]

311   *on bones yede*   remained in the flesh   *aboute was evere*   was continually concerned
312   *yif hemself wolde*   if they wanted it themselves

315   *rede we*   advise that we

318 [*thorw the ... so heighe*   as in Milton's *Paradise Lost*, Lucifer is presented as the ringleader of the rebel angels cast out of heaven into hell]

321   *a londe and a water*   by land and sea
322   Now shall the ruler of this world be cast out   [John 12.31]
323   *bad unlouke*   ordered [the door to be] unlocked
324–5   *Quis est iste*   who is this   *Rex glorie*   the king of glory   [Psalm 23(24).8 The psalmist's question: Who is the king of glory? has been divided into Lucifer's question and Jesus' response]

327   Lord of power and might

330 [*Beliales*   Belial was a traditional term for a devil, deriving from e.g. Judges 19.22]

331   *For any wye or ward*   regardless of every guard or watchman
332   *populus in tenebris*   the people that sat in darkness   [Matthew 4.16]
333   *Ecce agnus dei*   behold the lamb of God   [The words of St John the Baptist, recorded by St John the Evangelist (John 1.36)]
334   *loke ne myghte*   could not see

336   *to amendes*   as ransom

339   Although reason and my own justice require

      Where* he were God or Goddes sone?   He gaf me shorte   *whether*
         answere,
305 †And thus hath he trolled forth* this two and thretty   *gone about*
         wynter.
      †And whan I seighe* it was so, slepyng I went   *saw*
      To warne Pilates wyf   what done man* was Jesus,   *make of man*
      For Juwes hateden hym   and han done hym to deth.
      I wolde have lengthed* his lyf,   for I leved,* yif he   *prolonged believed*
         deyede,
310 That his soule wolde suffre   no synne in his syghte.
      †For the body, whil it on bones yede,   aboute was evere
      †To save men fram synne   yif hemself wolde.
      And now I se where a soule   cometh hiderward seyllynge*   *hastening*
      With glorie and with grete lighte: God it is, I wote wel.*   *I am sure*
315 †'I rede we flee,' quod he,   'faste alle hennes;*   *hence*
      For us were better noughte be   than biden* his syghte.   *await*
      For thi lesynges,* Lucifer,   loste is al owre praye.*   *lies prey*
      †Firste thorw* the we fellen   fro hevene so heighe;*   *through high*
      For* we leved thi lesynges   we loupen* oute alle with   *because leaped*
         the,
320 And now for thi last lesynge,   ylore* we have Adam   *lost*
      †And al owre lordeship, I leve,   a londe and a water:
      †*Nunc princeps huius mundi eicietur foras.*'
      †   Efte* the lighte bad unlouke,   and Lucifer answered,   *then*
      †'What lorde artow?' Quod Lucifer: '*Quis est iste?*'
325 '*Rex glorie,*' the lighte sone* seide,   *directly*
      'And lorde of myghte and of mayne*   and al manere vertues;   *power*
      †*Dominus virtutum.*
      Dukes* of this dym place,   anon* undo this yates,   *lords immediately*
      That Cryst may come in,   the kynges sone of hevene.'
330 †And with that breth* helle brake*   with Beliales   *sound broke open*
         barres;
      †For any wye or warde   wide opene the yatis.
      †Patriarkes and prophetes, *populus in tenebris,*
      †Songen Seynt Johanes songe,   '*Ecce agnus dei.*'
      †Lucyfer loke ne myghte,   so lyghte hym ableynte;*   *blinded*
335 And tho* that owre lorde loved,   into his lighte he   *those*
         laughte,*   *caught up*
      †And seyde to Sathan, 'Lo! here   my soule to amendes
      For alle synneful soules,   to save tho that ben worthy.
      Myne thei be and of me: I may the bette* hem clayme.   *better*
      †Although resoun recorde,   and right of myself,
340 That if thei ete the apple   alle shulde deye,
      I bihyghte* hem nought here   helle for evere.   *promised*

342 *dede that thei dede* deed they performed

346 [*lusarde with a lady visage* ME 'lusarde' can mean 'serpent' but is usually 'lizard'. The Tempter is often portrayed in art as a creature with legs and a female face]
347 *Thevelich* like a thief
[*Olde Lawe* the Old Testament *lex talionis* (law of punishment in kind)]
349 A tooth for a tooth and an eye for an eye [Matthew 5.38, quoting Exodus 21.24, Leviticus 24.19–20]
350 [*synne to synne wende* the sin of the crucifixion will counter the sin of Adam]

351 *misdo* done wrong *amende* make amends for

355 And what death destroyed in them, my death shall restore
356 *quykke* bring to life *queynte* quenched
357 And good faith requires that grace should destroy guile

360 I do not come to destroy the Law, but to fulfil it [Matthew 5.17]

369–70 [See line 144 and note]

372 And he fell into the hole which he had made [Psalm 7.16]

379 *me threstes* I thirst
381 *vendage fall* grape-harvest come
[*the vale of Josephath* God's words in Joel 3.12–13 were taken to refer to the Last Judgement: 'Let the heathen be wakened, and come up to the valley of Jehoshaphat: for there I will sit to judge all the heathen ... Put ye in the sickle, for the harvest is ripe: come, get you down; for the press is full, the fats overflow']

†For the dede that thei dede, thi deceyte it made;
With gyle thow hem gete,* agayne* al resoun. *acquired* *against*
For in my paleys, paradys, in persone of an addre,
345 Falseliche thow fettest* there thynge that I loved. *took*
†Thus ylyke a lusarde* with a lady visage, *reptile*
†Thevelich thow me robbedest; the Olde Lawe graunteth
That gylours* be bigiled,* and that is gode resoun: *deceivers* *deceived*
†*Dentem pro dente, et oculum pro oculo.*
350 †*Ergo,* soule shal soule quyte* and synne to synne wende* *therefore* *pay for* *counter*
†And al that man hath mysdo, I, man, wyl amende.
Membre* for membre bi the Olde Lawe was amendes,* *limb* *compensation*
And lyf for lyf also, and by that lawe I clayme it –
Adam and al his issue at my wille herafter.
355 †And that deth in hem fordid, my deth shal releve,
†And bothe quykke and quyte* that queynte was thorw synne; *redeem*
†And that grace gyle destruye, good feith it asketh.
So leve* it noughte, Lucifer, ayeine the lawe I fecche hem, *believe*
But bi right and by resoun raunceoun* here my lyges:* *ransom* *followers*
360 †*Non veni solvere legem, sed adimplere.*
Thow fettest* myne in my place ayeines al resoun, *took away*
Falseliche and felounelich;* gode faith me it taughte *wickedly*
To recovre hem thorw raunceoun, and bi no resoun elles,
So that* with gyle thow gete, thorw grace it is ywone.* *what* *retrieved*
365 Thow, Lucyfer, in lyknesse of a luther* addere, *treacherous*
Getest by gyle tho* that God loved; *those*
And I, in lyknesse of a leode,* that lorde am of hevene, *man*
Graciousliche thi gyle have quytte: go gyle ayeine gyle!
†And as Adam and alle thorw a tre deyden,* *died*
370 Adam and alle thorwe a tree shal torne ayeine to lyve;
And gyle is bigyled and in his gyle fallen:
†*Et cecidit in foveam quam fecit.*
Now bygynneth thi gyle ageyne the* to tourne, *against you*
And my grace to growe ay* gretter and wyder. *always*
375 The bitternesse that thow hast browe,* brouke* it thiselven, *brewed* *drink*
That art doctour of deth, drynke that thow madest!
For I, that am lorde of lyf, love is my drynke,
And for that drynke to-day I deyde upon erthe.
†I faughte* so, me threstes yet, for mannes soule sake; *fought*
380 May no drynke me moiste ne my thruste* slake *thirst*
†Tyl the vendage falle in the vale of Josephath,

382 *resureccio mortuorum* resurrection of the dead

391 Against thee only have I sinned [Psalm 50(51).6]
392 *It is nought used* it is not the custom
392–6 [A hanged person who by some chance survived execution was given a royal pardon]

395 *thole sholde deth* is about to suffer death
396 *Lawe wolde* law has it that

398 *al wikked* all the wicked
399 *wil I* wishes me to
400 *that thei deden ille* what they did wrong
401–2 If the arrogance of their sins has been paid for at all, I can, in justice, be merciful and everything I have said remain true
403 *I be wroke of* I be revenged on

404 No evil will go unpunished [From the *De Contemptu Mundi* (In Contempt of the World) of Pope Innocent III (1160–1216)]

406 [*purgatorie* the place of punishment for unforgiven sins and for sins which, though forgiven, have not been wholly expiated on earth. Unlike those of hell, the pains of purgatory are finite, and are a preparation for heaven]
parce it hote the order is given to spare them [*parce* 'forgive, spare']
408 *suffre* allow
409 *but hym rewe* without pitying him
410 And I heard secret words which it is not granted to man to utter [II Corinthians 12.4; the 'I' must be the dreamer, not Jesus; his poetic vision at this moment is felt to have the mysterious authority of the revelation of paradise granted to St Paul, to which the passage in Corinthians refers]
413 *but I my kynde holpe* if I did not help my kindred
414 And especially in such a time of need when, necessarily, help is required
415 Enter not into judgement with thy servant, O Lord [Psalm 142(143).2]
416–17 [Support for the belief that Jesus led out of hell the souls of the righteous who had died in the expectation of his coming was found in Psalm 67(68).19: 'Thou hast ascended on high, thou hast led captivity captive']

419 *abye it bittre* pay dearly for it
420 [*Astaroth* the Babylonian 'queen of heaven' worshipped as a false god in Jeremiah 8.10, and thus a devil in medieval lore]

	†That I drynke righte* ripe must,* *resureccio mortuorum,*	absolutely	new wine
	And thanne shal I come as a kynge crouned, with angeles,		
	And han* out of helle alle mennes soules.		take
385	Fendes and fendekynes* bifor me shulle stande,		fiendlings
	And be at my biddynge wheresoevre me lyketh.*		I please
	And to be merciable to man thanne, my kynde it asketh;		
	For we beth* bretheren* of blode, but noughte in baptesme alle.	are	brothers
	Ac* alle that beth myne hole* bretheren, in blode and in baptesme,	but	full
390	Shal noughte be dampned to the deth that is withouten ende;		
	†*Tibi soli peccavi.*		
	†It is nought used in erthe to hangen a feloun*		wrongdoer
	Ofter than ones, though he were a tretour.*		traitor
	And yif the kynge of that kyngedome come in that tyme,		
395	†There* the feloun thole sholde deth other juwise,*	where	punishment
	†Lawe wolde he yeve* hym lyf, if he loked on hym.		grant
	And I, that am kynge of kynges, shal come suche a tyme		
	†There* dome* to the deth dampneth al wikked;	when	judgement
	†And yif* lawe wil I loke on hem, it lithe* in my grace	if	lies
400	†Whether thei deye or deye noughte for that thei deiden ille.		
	†Be it any thinge abought, the boldnesse of her synnes,		
	I may do mercy thorw rightwisnesse, and alle my wordes trewe.		
	†And though Holi Writ wil* that I be wroke of hem that deden ille,		demands
	†*Nullum malum inpunitum.*		
405	Thei shul be clensed clereliche* and wasshen of her synnes		completely
	†In my prisoun purgatorie, til *parce* it hote.		
	And my mercy shal be shewed to manye of my bretheren;		
	†For blode may suffre blode bothe hungry and akale,*		(to be) cold
	†Ac* blode may nought se blode blede, but hym rewe.'		but
410	†*Audivi archana verba, que non licet homini loqui.*		
	'Ac my rightwisnesse and right shal reulen* al helle,		govern
	And mercy al mankynde bifor me in hevene.		
	†For I were an unkynde kynge but I my kynde holpe,		
	†And namelich at such a nede there nedes helpe bihoveth:		
415	†*Non intres in judicium cum servo tuo, domine.*		
	†Thus bi lawe,' quod Owre Lorde, 'lede I wil fro hennes		
	Tho that me loved and leved* in my comynge.		believed
	And for thi lesynge,* Lucifer, that thow lowe* til Eve,	lie	lied
	†Thow shalt abye it bittre!' – and bonde* hym with cheynes.		bound
420	†Astaroth and al the route* hidden hem in hernes,*	rabble	corners
	They dorste noughte loke on Owre Lorde, the boldest of hem alle,		

422 *lete what hym liste* leave what he wanted

424 Flesh sins, flesh atones for sin; God's flesh reigns as God [From the Ascension Day hymn, *Aeterne rex altissime*]
425 *of poysye a note* a song in verse
426–7 The sun is always brighter after thick cloud, and love is brighter after enmity [Alanus de Insulis (?1128–1202), *Liber Parabolum*, 581–2]

433 that Love, if he wanted to, did not turn to laughter

436 Let us embrace as a sign of agreement, and each of us kiss the others

440 *and Pees here* and Peace [kissed] her   *per secula seculorum* world without end
[The phrase *per omnia saecula saeculorum* concludes the prayer immediately preceding the kiss of peace in a solemn mass]
441 Mercy and Truth are met together; Justice and Peace have kissed each other [Psalm 84(85).11]
442 *tromped tho* blew a trumpet then   *Te deum laudamus* We praise you, God [The opening words of the hymn *Te Deum*]
443 *luted* played on a lute
444 Behold how good and joyful [it is]   [Psalm 132(133).1]
445 *this damaiseles* these maidens
446 *rongen to resurexioun* rang the church bells for the Easter Sunday mass
right with that thereupon
447 [*Kitte . . . Kalote* In the C-text, Passus 5, 1.3 (not in A or B) the dreamer refers again to his wife as 'Kitte', but he elsewhere uses 'Kitte' as a generic name for a wife. 'Kitte' and 'Calote' are proverbially linked in ME (like 'Tom, Dick and Harry'), so they are probably not intended as real names, but suggest members of a typical, lower-class family. The dreamer presents himself as a married man and thus as a clerk in minor orders, not a priest in major orders]

452 *grysly gost* evil spirit   *there it shadweth* under its shade

†But leten* hym lede forth what hym lyked   and lete what hym liste.   *let*
Many hundreth* of angeles   harpeden and songen,   *hundreds*
†'*Culpat caro, purgat caro;   regnat deus dei caro.*'
425 †Thanne piped Pees   of poysye a note:
†'*Clarior est solito post maxima nebula phebus,*
Post inimicitias clarior est et amor.
After sharpe shoures,' quod Pees, 'moste shene* is the sonne;   *bright*
Is no weder warmer   than after watery cloudes;
430 Ne no love levere,*   ne lever frendes,   *dearer*
Than after werre and wo,   whan Love and Pees be maistres.*   *rule*
Was nevere werre* in this worlde   ne wykkednesse so kene,*   *war   fierce*
†That Love, and hym luste,   to laughynge ne broughte,
And Pees, thorw pacience,   alle perilles stopped.'
435 'Trewes,'* quod Treuth,   'thow tellest us soth,* bi Jesus!   *truce   true*
†Clippe we in covenaunt,   and uch of us cusse other!'
'And lete no peple,' quod Pees, 'perceyve that we chydde!*   *quarrelled*
For inpossible is no thyng   to hym that is almyghty.'
'Thow seist soth,' seyde Ryghtwisnesse,   and reverentlich hir kyste
440 †Pees, and Pees here, *per secula seculorum.*
†*Misericordia et Veritas obviaverunt sibi; Justicia et Pax osculate sunt.*
†Treuth trompod tho, and songe* '*Te deum laudamus*';   *sang*
†And thanne luted Love   in a loude note,
†'*Ecce quam bonum et quam iocundum.*'
445 †Tyl the daye dawed*   this damaiseles daunced,   *dawned*
†That men rongen to the resurexioun,   and right with that I waked,
†And called Kitte my wyf   and Kalote my doughter:
'Ariseth and reverenceth   Goddes resurrexioun,
And crepeth to the cross on knees   and kisseth it for a juwel!
450 For Goddes blissed body   it bar* for owre bote,*   *bore   salvation*
And it afereth* the fende,*   for suche is the myghte.*   *terrifies   devil   its power*
†May no grysly gost   glyde there it shadweth!'

Robert of Sicily
c. 1350–75

Robert of Sicily was composed by an unknown author in the southeast midlands, probably in the third quarter of the fourteenth century. It seems to have been one of the most widely read Middle English narratives, apart from those of Chaucer and Gower, since as many as ten copies of it have survived. Although it is often classed as a romance, *Robert of Sicily* does not deal with the traditional romance themes of love or war, and criticises princely pride. Like *Patience*, it teaches that 'They are happen [blessed] also that haunt mekenesse, / For thay schall welde [rule] this worlde and alle her wylle have'. There are a number of analogous tales in different languages of kings losing their status and power, but no direct source for this version is known. The text below is the earliest, from the late fourteenth-century Bodleian Library, Eng. Poet. MS A.1, the 'Vernon' manuscript, compiled in the west midlands, possibly for a household of devout ladies or nuns. It is taken from *Middle English Metrical Romances*, ed. W. H. French and C. B. Hale (1930).

ROBERT OF SICILY

Princes proude that beth in pres,†
I wol ou* telle thing not lees*   *you false*
In Cisyle* was a noble kyng,   *Sicily*
Fair and strong and sumdel yyng;*   *quite young*
5 He hedde a brother in grete Roome,
Pope of al Cristendome;
Another he hedde in Alemayne,*   *Germany*
An emperour† that Sarazins wroughte payne.†
The kyng was hote* Kyng Robert;   *called*
10 †Never mon ne wuste him fert.

---

1 *that beth in pres* who are among the crowd
8 [*emperour* the Holy Roman Emperor] *Sarazins wroughte payne* inflicted suffering on the Saracens [*Sarazins* originally applied to Arabs, but later to all infidels. Perhaps here the Mongols who threatened the borders of the Empire in the thirteenth century]
10 no one ever knew him afraid

He was kyng of gret honour
For that he was conquerour.
In al the world nas* his peer, ·was not
Kyng ne prince, fer ne neer;* ·far or near
15 And for he was of chivalrie flour,
His brother was mad emperour;
His other brother, Godes vikere,* ·vicar
Pope of Rome, as I seide ere.* ·before
The pope was hote Pope Urban;†
20 He was good to God and man.
The emperour was hote Valemounde;
A strengur* weorreour nas non founde ·stronger
After his brother of Cisyle,
Of whome that I schal telle a while.
25   The Kyng thoughte he hedde no peer
In al the world, fer no neer,
And in his thought he hedde pryde
For he was nounpeer* in uch a* syde. ·peerless on every
At midsomer, a Seynt Jones Niht,†
30 The Kyng to churche com ful riht* ·directly
For to heeren his evensong.†
Hym thouhte† he dwelled ther ful* long; ·very
He thouhte more in* worldes honour ·on
Then in Crist, ur* saveour. ·our
35 In *Magnificat*† he herde a vers;
He made a clerk hit him rehers* ·repeat
In langage of his owne tonge –
In Latyn he nuste† what heo songe.* ·they sang
The vers was this, I telle the:
40 †'*Deposuit potentes de sede,
Et exaltavit humiles.*'
This was the vers, withouten les.* ·falsehood
  The clerk seide anon riht;†
'Sire, such is Godes miht

---

19 [*Urban* there were several medieval popes of this name: Urban II (1088–99) launched the First Crusade; Urban V (1362–70) may have been pope when this poem was written]
29 *Seynt Jones Niht* Saint John's Night [23 June (eve of St John's Day, 24 June)]
31 [*evensong* the evening office, Vespers, which includes psalms, hymns and prayers]
32 *Hym thouhte* it seemed to him
35 [*Magnificat* a song of praise, known from the first word of the Latin text, sung by the Blessed Virgin Mary in response to her cousin Elizabeth's acknowledgement that she was carrying the Lord (Luke 1.46–55). The Magnificat is sung at Vespers]
37 *nuste* did not know
40–1 'He hath put down the mighty from their seats, and exalted them of low degree' [Luke 1.52]
43 *anon riht* straight away

45	That he may make heyghe* lowe	high
	And lowe heighe, in luytel throwe.†	
	God may do, withoute lyghe,*	lie
	His wil in twynklying of an eighe.'*	eye
	The Kyng seide with herte unstable:	
50	'Al yor song is fals and fable.*	fiction
	What mon hath such pouwer	
	Me to bringe lowe in daunger?†	
	I am flour of chivalrye;	
	Myn enemys I may distruye.*	destroy
55	No mon lyveth in no londe	
	That me may withstonde.	
	Then is this a song of nouht!'*	worthless
	This errour he hedde in thought	
	And in his thouht a sleep him tok*	seized him
60	In his pulput,* as seith the bok.	royal pew
	Whon that evensong was al don,	
	A kyng ilyk* him out gan gon*	like went
	And alle men with hym gan wende;*	went
	Kyng Robert lafte* out of mynde.†	left
65	The newe kyng was, as I ou telle,	
	Godes angel, his pruide* to felle.*	pride cut down
	The angel in halle joye made	
	And alle men of hym weore* glade.	were
	The Kyng wakede that lay in churche.	
70	†His men he thouhte wo to worche	
	For he was laft* ther alon	left
	And derk niht him fel uppon.	
	He gan crie after his men;	
	Ther nas non† that spak agen.*	replied
75	But the sexteyn,† atten* eende	at the
	Of the churche to him gan wende	
	And seide, 'What dost thou nouthe her,†	
	Thou false thef,* thou losenger?*	thief parasite
	Thou art her with felenye,	
80	Holy churche to robbye!'*	rob

46 *luytel throwe* moment
52 *in daunger* in (his) dominion
64 *out of mynde* forgotten
70 He planned to punish his men
74 *nas non* was no-one
75 [*sexteyn* sexton, a church official responsible for cleaning, ringing the bells and digging graves]
77 *nouthe her* now here

He seide, 'Foule gadelyng,*   scoundrel
I am no thef, I am a kyng!
Opene the churche-dore anon,*   straight away
That I mowe* to my paleis gon.'*   may go
85   The sexteyn thouhte anon with-than*   thereupon
      That he was sum wood* man   mad
      And wolde* the chirche dilyveret* were   wished that rid
      Of hym, for he hedde fere,*   was afraid
      And openede the chirche-dore in haste.
90   The Kyng bygon to renne out faste,
      As a mon that was wood.
      At his paleys gate he stood
      And heet* the porter 'gadelyng',   called
      And bad hym come in highing*   quickly
95   Anon the gates up to do.*   to unbar
      The porter seide, 'Ho clepeth* so?'   who calls
      He onswerde anon tho:*   then
      'Thou schalt witen* ar* I go.   know before
      Thi kyng I am: thou schalt knowe!
100 In prison thou schalt ligge* lowe   lie
      And ben anhonged and todrawe†
      As a traytur bi the lawe.
      Thou schalt wel witen I am kyng.
      Open the gates, gadelyng!'
105 The porter seide, 'So mot I the,†
      The Kyng is mid his meyné!†
      Wel I wot,* withoute doute,   know
      The Kyng nis not* now withoute.'*   is not outside
      The porter com into halle,
110 Bifore the newe kyng aknes gan falle†
      And seide 'Ther is atte* gate   at the
      †A nyce fool icome late.
      He seith* he is lord and kyng   says
      And clept* me foule gadelyng.   called
115 †Lord, what wol ye that I do:
      Leten him in or leten him go?'
      The angel seide in haste:
      'Do* him come in swithe faste,†   make

---

101 *anhonged and todrawe* hanged and drawn
105 *So mot I the* as I hope to prosper
106 *mid his meyné* with his followers
110 *aknes gan falle* fell to his knees
112 A silly fool arrived just now
115 Lord, what do you want me to do
118 *swithe faste* very quickly

	For my fol* I wole him make	fool
120	Forte* he the nome* of kyng forsake.'	until title
	The porter com to the gate	
	And him he called, in to late.*	let
	He smot* the porter whon he com in	hit
	That* blod barst* out of mouth and chyn.	so that burst
125	The porter yeld him his travayle;†	
	Him smot ageyn,† withouten fayle,	
	That neose and mouth barst a-blood:*	bleeding
	Thenne he semed almost wod.*	mad
	The porter and his men in haste	
130	Kyng Robert in a podel* caste.	puddle
	Unsemely* heo maden* his bodi than,	unpleasing they made
	That* he nas lyk non other man,	so that
	And brouht him bifore the newe kyng	
	And seide: 'Lord, this gadelyng	
135	Me hath smyte† withoute decert.*	deserving
	He seith he is ur kyng apert!*	publicly
	This harlot* oughte, for his sawe,*	rascal speech
	Ben ihonged* and todrawe,*	hanged drawn
	For he seith non other word	
140	Bote that he is bothe kyng and lord.'	
	The angel seide to Kyng Robert:	
	'Thou art a fol, that art not fert*	afraid
	Mi men to don such vilenye.†	
	†Thi gult thou most nede abuye.	
145	What art thou?' seide the angel.	
	Qwath* Robert: 'Thou schalt wite* wel	said know
	That I am kyng, and kyng wol be!	
	†With wronge thou hast my dignité.	
	The Pope of Roome is my brother,	
150	And the Emperour myn other.	
	Heo* wol me wreke,* for soth* to telle;	they avenge truth
	†I wot heo nulle not longe dwelle!'	
	'Thow art my fol,' seide the angel.	
	'Thou schal be schoren* everichdel,*	shaved completely
155	Lych* a fool, a fool to be.	like
	Wher is now thi dignité?	

125 *yeld him his travayle* repaid his efforts
126 *Him smot ageyn* hit him back
135 *Me hath smyte* has hit me
143 *don such vilenye* insult in this way
144 You will have to atone for your offence
148 You wrongfully usurp my state
152 I know they will not delay long

	Thi counseyler schal ben an ape	
	†And o clothing ou worth ischape:	
	I schal him clothen as thi brother	
160	Of o clothing; hit is non other.†	
	He schal beo thin owne feere:*	companion
	Sum wit* of him thou miht lere!*	wisdom learn
	Houndes, how so hit falle,†	
	Schulen eten with the in halle.	
165	Thou schalt eten on the ground;	
	Thin assayour† schal ben an hound,	
	To assaye* thi mete* bifore the.	test food
	Wher is now thi dignité?'	
	He heet* a barbur him bifore	called
170	That* as a fool he schulde be schore*	so that shaved
	Al around, lich* a frere,*	like friar
	†An honde-brede bove either ere,	
	And on his croune make a crois.*	cross
	He gan crie and make nois.	
175	He swor thei schulde alle abuye*	pay for
	†That him dude such vileynye,	
	And evere* he seide he was lord,	always
	And uche mon† scorned him for that word;	
	And uche mon seide he was wod.	
180	That proved wel he couthe no good,†	
	†For he wende in none wyse	
	†That God Almihti couthe devyse	
	†Him to bringe to lower stat –	
	†With o drauht he was chekmat!	
185	With houndes everi niht he lay	
	And ofte he crighede weylaway†	
	That he evere was ibore,*	born
	For he was a mon forlore.†	

---

158 And the same clothes shall be made for you both
160 *hit is non other*   it shall not be otherwise
163 *how so hit falle*   whatever happens
166 [*assayour*   one who tests the food for a great man, to ensure that it is not poisoned]
172 A hand's width above either ear
176 Who insulted him in this way
178 *uche mon*   each man
180 *couthe no good*   had no sense
181–4 Because he did not believe that Almighty God could in any way contrive to bring him to a lower condition – with one move he was checkmated
186 *crighede weylaway*   uttered lamentations
188 *mon forlore*   lost man

	Ther nas in court grom* ne* page	groom nor
190	†That of the Kyng ne made rage;	
	For no mon ne mihte him knowe† –	
	He was defygured* in a throwe.†	altered
	So lowe er* that was never kyng.	before
	Allas, her was a deolful* thing,	grievous
195	That him* scholde for his pryde	to him
	Such hap* among his men betyde.*	ill luck befall
	Hunger and thurste he hedde grete,	
	For he ne moste* no mete ete	was obliged
	But houndes eeten of his disch,	
200	Whether hit weore flesch or fisch.	
	He was to dethe neigh* ibrouht*	near brought
	For hunger, ar* he miht eten ouht*	before anything
	With houndes that beth* in halle.	are
	†How might him hardore bifalle?	
205	†And whon hit nolde non othur be,	
	He eet with houndes gret plenté.	
	The angel was kyng, him thhoughte long.†	
	In his tyme was never wrong,	
	Tricherie,* ne falshede, ne no gyle*	treason deceit
210	Idon* in the lond of Cisyle.	done
	Alle goode ther was gret plenté;	
	Among men love and charité.	
	In his tyme was never strif	
	Bitwene mon and his wyf;	
215	Uche* mon lovede wel other;	each
	Beter love nas nevere of brother.	
	Thenne was that a joyful thing	
	In londe to have such a kyng.	
	Kyng he was threo* yeer and more –	three
220	Robert yeode* as mon forlore.	went
	Seththe* hit fel* uppon a day	afterwards it befell
	A luytel* bifore the moneth of May,	little
	Sire Valemound the Emperour	
	Sende* lettres of gret honour	sent
225	To his brother, of Cisyle Kyng,	
	And bad him come withouten lettyng,*	delay

190 Who did not make sport of the king
191 *mihte him knowe*   could recognise him
192 *in a throwe*   in an instant
204 How could things turn out worse for him?
205 And when there was no alternative
207 *him thhoughte long*   it seemed long to him

	†That heo mihten beo bothe isome	
	With heore* brother, Pope of Rome.	their
	†Hym thhoughte long heo weore atwinne;	
230	†He bad him lette for no wynne,	
	†That he neore of good aray	
	†In Roome an Holy Thoresday.	
	The angel welcomede the messagers	
	And gaf hem clothes riche of pers,*	sky-blue cloth
235	Furred al with ermyne;	
	In Cristendom is non so fyne;	
	And al was chouched mid perré.†	
	Better was non in Cristianté.	
	†Such cloth, and hit weore to dihte,	
240	†Al Cristendom hit make ne mihte.	
	Of that wondrede al that lond,	
	Hou that cloth was wrought* with hond;	made
	Wher such cloth was to selle,	
	Ne ho* hit maade, couthe* no mon telle.	who knew how to
245	The messagers wenten with the Kyng	
	To grete* Rome, withoute lettyng.	great
	The fool Robert also went,	
	Clothed in lodly garnement,†	
	With foxes tayles† mony aboute:	
250	Men miht him knowen in the route!*	crowd
	The angel was clothed al in whit;	
	Nas never seyghe* such samyt;*	seen silk
	And al was chouched myd* perles riche:	with
	Never mon seigh* none hem liche.*	saw like them
255	Al was whit, atyr* and steede;	attire
	The steede was feir ther he yede,*	went
	†So feir a steede as he on rod	
	†Nas never mon that ever bistrod.	
	The angel com to Roome sone,*	soon
260	†Real, as fel a kyng to done;	

---

227 So that they might be both together
229 It seemed to him that they had been apart for a long time
230–2 He told him not to delay, for any consideration, their being in Rome, in all their magnificence, on Holy Thursday   [Thursday of Easter Week]
237 *chouched mid perré* adorned with jewels
239–40 Such cloth, if it were arrayed, all Christendom could not match
248 *lodly garnement* hideous attire
249 [*foxes tayles* part of the traditional attire of the fool]
257–8 No man ever bestrode as fair a steed as he rode upon
260 Royally, as befitted a king

So real* kyng com nevere in Rome;   *royal*
Alle men wondrede whethen* he come.*   *whence came*
His men weore realliche diht:†
†Heore richesse con seye no wiht
265 Of clothus, gurdeles, and other thing.
Everiche sqygher thhoughte a* kyng,   *seemed*
And alle ride of riche aray
Bote Kyng Robert, as I ow* say: *you*
Alle men on him gon pyke,*   *peer*
270 †For he rod al other unlyke:
An ape rod of his clothing,†
In tokne* that he was underlyng.   *as a sign*
The Pope and the Emperour also
And other lordes mony mo*   *more*
275 Welcomede the angel as for kyng,
And made joye of his comyng.
Theose threo bretheren made cumfort;*   *merriment*
The angel was brother mad bi sort.*   *fate*
Wel was the Pope and Emperour
280 That hedden* a brothur of such honour!   *had*
Forth con sturte† Kyng Robert
As fol and mon that nas not fert,*   *afraid*
And crighede with ful egre* speche   *angry*
To his bretheren to don him wreche†
285 Of* him that hath with queynte gyle†   *on*
His coroune and lond of Cisyle.
The Pope ne the Emperour nouther*   *neither*
The fol ne kneugh* not for heor* brother.   *recognised their*
Tho* was he more fol iholde,*   *then held*
290 More then er* a thousend folde,   *before*
To cleyme such a bretherhede:
†Hit was holde a foles dede.
Kyng Robert bigon to maken care,†
Muche more then he dude are,†

---

263 *weore realliche diht* were royally clad
264 no-one can describe their splendour
270 Because he rode, quite unlike the rest
271 *of his clothing* dressed as he was
281 *con sturte* bounded
284 *don him wreche* avenge him
285 *with queynte gyle* through a cunning ruse
292 It was regarded as the action of a fool
293 *maken care* lament
294 *dude are* did before

295	Whon his bretheren nolde* him knowe;	were unable
	'Allas,' quath* he, 'nou am I lowe!'	said
	For he hopede,* bi eny thing,†	trusted
	His bretheren wolde ha* mad him kyng;	have
	And whon his hope was al ago,*	gone
300	He seide 'allas and weilawo!'	
	He seide 'allas' that he was bore,*	born
	For he was a mon forlore:*	lost
	He seide 'allas' that he was mad,*	made
	For of his lyf he was al sad.*	tired
305	'Allas! allas!' was al his song:	
	His heer he tar,† his hondes wrong,	
	And evere he seide, 'Allas, allas!' –	
	And thenne he thoughte on his trespas:*	wrongdoing
	He thoughte on Nabugodonosore,†	
310	A noble kyng was him bifore:	
	In al the world nas his peer,†	
	Forte acounte,† fer ne neer.	
	With him was Sire Olyferne,*	Holofernes
	Prince of knihtes stout and steorne.†	
315	Olyferne swor evermor	
	By God Nabugodonosor,	
	And seide ther nas no* God in londe	was not any
	But Nabugodonosor, ich understonde;	
	Therfore Nabugodonosor was glad	
320	That he the name of God had,	
	And lovede Olofern the more;	
	†And seththe hit greved hem bothe sore.	
	Olofern dyghede in dolour:†	
	He was slaye* in hard schour.*	killed battle
325	Nabugodonosor lyvede in desert;	
	†Dorst he noughwher ben apert;	

---

297 *bi eny thing* at all cost
306 *His heer he tar* he tore his hair
309 *Nabugodonosore* Nebuchadnezzar [In the Book of Judith (Old Testament apocrypha), the Assyrian king Nebuchadnezzar sends his army, under Holofernes, to attack Jerusalem. Holofernes tells the Jews that his master is the only god; he is murdered by Judith and the Assyrians flee in ignominy. This story has been conflated with that told in Daniel 4.25–34 of the Babylonian king Nebuchadnezzar who is punished by God for his pride by being driven from his kingdom into the wilderness]
311 *nas his peer* there was not his equal
312 *forte acounte* according to the record
314 *stout and steorne* bold and strong
322 And later it distressed them both deeply
323 *dyghede in dolour* died in torment
326 he dared not go anywhere openly

Fyftene yer he livede thare,
With rootes, gras, and evel fare,
And al of mos* his clothing was; — moss
330 'Al com that bi Godes gras:* — grace
He crighede merci with delful chere:* — woeful demeanour
God him restored as he was ere!* — formerly
Nou am I in such caas,* — predicament
And wel* worse then he was. — much
335 Whon God gaf me such honour
That I was clepet* conquerour, — styled
In everi lond of Cristendome
Of me men speke wel ilome,* — often
And seiden noughwher was my peer
340 In al the world, fer ne neer.
For that name I hedde pride:
And angels that gonne from joye glyde,†
And in twynklyng of an eighe
†God binom heore maystrie,
345 So hath he myn, for my gult;* — guilt
Now am I wel lowe ipult,* — brought down
And that is riht that I so be!
Lord, on thi fool thow have pité!
I hedde an errour in myn herte,
350 And that errour doth me smerte;†
Lord, I leeved* not on the. — believed
On thi fol thou have pité!
Holy Writ I hedde in dispyt;†
For that is reved* my delyt* – — snatched away joy
355 For that is riht a fool I be!
Lord, on thi fool thou have pité!
Lord, I am thi creature;
This wo is riht that I dure,* — endure
†And wel more, gif hit may be.
360 Lord, on thi fool thou have pité!
Lord, I have igult* the sore!* — offended grievously
Merci, Lord: I nul no more;†
Evere thi fol, Lord, wol I be.
Lord, on thi fol thou have pité!

---

342 *gonne from joye glyde* fell from heaven
344 God took away their eminence
350 *doth me smerte* causes me pain
353 *hedde in dispyt* despised
359 And even more, if it were possible
362 *I nul no more* I do not wish for more

365	'Blisful Marie, to the I crie,	
	As thou art ful of cortesye,*	graciousness
	Preye thi Sone, that dyed for me;	
	On me, his fol, thow have pité.	
	Blisful Marie, ful of graas,*	grace
370	To the I knowe* my trespas;	acknowledge
	Prey thi Sone, for love of the,	
	On me, his fool, he have pité!'	
	He seide no more, 'Allas, allas!'	
	But thonked Crist of his gras,	
375	And thus he gon himself stille,†	
	And thonked Crist mid* good wille.	with
	Then Pope, Emperour, and Kyng	
	†Fyve wikes made heore dwellyng.	
	Whon fyve wykes weore agon,	
380	To heore owne lond heo wolden anon,†	
	Bothe Emperour and the Kyng;	
	There was a feir departyng.*	leave-taking
	The angel com to Cisyle,	
	He and his men in a while.†	
385	Whon he com into halle,	
	The fool anon he bad forth calle;†	
	He seide, 'Fool, art thow kyng?'	
	'Nay, sire,' quath he, 'withoute lesyng.'†	
	'What artou?' seide the angel.	
390	'Sire, a fol; that wot* I wel,	know
	And more then fol, gif* hit may be;	if
	Kep* I non other dignité.'*	retain rank
	The angel into chaumbre went,	
	And after the fol anon he sent;	
395	He bad his men out of chaumbre gon:*	go
	Ther lafte* no mo but he alon	remained
	And the fol that stod him bi.	
	To him he seide, 'Thou hast merci:	
	Thenk, thou weore lowe ipult,*	brought down
400	And al was for thin owne gult.*	wrongdoing
	A fool thou weore to Hevene-kyng;*	king of heaven
	Therfore thou art an underlyng.	

---

375 *gon himself stille* calmed himself
378 remained for five weeks
380 *heo wolden anon* they wished to go immediately
384 *in a while* after a time
386 *bad forth calle* ordered to be summoned forth
388 *withoute lesyng* truly

	God hath forgiven thi mysdede;	
	Evere herafter thou him drede!	
405	I am an angel of renoun,*	famous
	Isent* to kepe* thi regioun;	sent protect
	More joye me schal falle*	befall
	In hevene, among my feren* alle,	companions
	In an houre of a day,	
410	Then in eorthe,* I the say,	earth
	In an hundred thousend yeer,	
	Theigh* al the world fer and neer,	though
	Weore myn at my lykyng!†	
	I am an angel, thou art kyng.'	
415	He went in twynklyng of an eghe;	
	No more of him ther nas seghe.†	
	Kyng Robert com into halle;	
	His men he bad anon forthe calle.	
	†And alle weore at his wille	
420	†As to heore lord, as hit was skille.	
	He lovede God and holi churche,	
	And evere he thouhte wel to worche.†	
	He regned after two yer and more,	
	And lovede God and his lore.*	teaching
425	The angel gaf him in warnyng†	
	Of the tyme of his dighing.	
	Whon tyme com to dyghe son,	
	†He let write hit riht anon –	
	Hou God myd his muchel miht†	
430	Made him lowe, as hit was riht.	
	This storie he sende everidel*	completely
	To his bretheren under his seel;*	seal
	And the tyme whon he schulde dye	
	That tyme he dighede as he gon seye.†	
435	Al this is writen, withouten lyghe,*	lie
	At Roome, to ben in memorie	
	At Seint Petres Chirche, I knowe;	
	And thus is Godes miht isowe,*	spread

---

413 *at my lykyng* as I please
416 *nas seghe* was seen
419–20 And all acknowledged his authority as their lord, as was right
422 *wel to worche* perform good deeds
425 *gaf him in warning* forewarned him
428 He had it written down precisely
429 *myd his muchel miht* with his great power
434 *as he gon seye* as he said

†That heighe beoth lowe, theigh hit be ille,
And lowe heighe,* at Godes wille.   *high*
Crist, that for us gon dye,*   *died*
In his kynereche* let* us ben heighe,   *kingdom allow*
Evermore to ben above,
Ther* is joye, cumfort, and love.   *where there*

---

439 That the high are low, though it is painful

Sir John Mandeville
later 14th century

The author of the book of *Travels* from which this extract comes says in his introduction that his name is John Mandeville, knight ('thoughe it so be that I be nat worthy'), that he was born in St Albans, and that he began his extensive journeys through the Holy Land and beyond in 1332. All of this is a fiction. The writer seems in fact to have been a French cleric – the *Travels* was originally written in French in the late 1350s – who had access to a good library of travel literature, encyclopaedias, Alexander romances and other writings, out of which he concocted one of the most widely read books of the later middle ages. By 1400 *The Travels of Sir John Mandeville* had been translated into English and all the other major European languages, and it has been continuously in print in England since Pynson's first edition of *c*. 1496. This extract, in which 'Mandeville' describes the Earthly Paradise far in the east, is taken from the earliest of the three Middle English prose translations, preserved in British Library, MS Cotton Titus c.xvi. For once the author does not make his narrator claim first-hand knowledge of what he describes. The route to the Earthly Paradise – the Garden of Eden from which Adam and Eve were expelled – was believed to be almost impassable and to have been achieved by only the occasional superhuman adventurer like Alexander the Great, so on this occasion 'Mandeville' acts as recorder, not as eye-witness.

The text is from British Library, MS Cotton Titus c.xvi, ed. M. C. Seymour, *Mandeville's Travels* (1967).

From TRAVELS
[The Earthly Paradise]

And beyonde the lond and the yles and the desertes of Prestre Johnes lordschipe† in goynge streight towardes the est men fynde nothing but montaynes and roches† fulle† grete. And there is the derke regyoun where no man may see nouther† be day ne be nyghte, as thei of the
5 contree seyn.† And that desert and that place of derknesse duren† fro this cost unto Paradys Terrestre,† where that Adam oure formest† fader and Eve weren putt that dwelleden there but lytylle while, and that is towardes the est† at the begynnynge of the erthe. But that is not that est that we clepe† oure est on this half where the sonne riseth to us.
10 For whanne the sonne is est in tho partyes† toward Paradys Terrestre, it is thanne mydnyght in oure parties o† this half for† the roundeness of the erthe, of the whiche I have towched to you of† before. For oure lord God made the erthe alle rownd in the mydde place of the firmament. And there as mountaynes† and hilles ben and valeyes, that is not but
15 only of Noes Flode that wasted the softe ground and the tendre and felle doun into valeyes. And the harde erthe and the roche abyden† mountaynes, whan the soft erthe and tendre wax nessche† thorgh the water and felle and becamen valeyes.

Of Paradys ne can I not speken propurly, for I was not there. It is fer
20 beyonde, and that forthinketh† me, and also I was not worthi. But as I have herd seye of† wyse men beyonde, I schalle telle you with gode wille. Paradys Terrestre, as wise men seyn, is the highest place of erthe that is in alle the world, and it is so high that it toucheth nygh to the cercle of the mone,† there as† the mone maketh hire torn.† For sche is

---

Prestre Johnes lordschipe   the kingdom of Prester John [mythical Christian emperor of India]
roches   rocks   *fulle*   very
nouther   neither   *seyn*   say
duren   extend   *Paradys Terrestre*   Earthly Paradise
formest   original   *est*   east
clepe   call   *tho partyes*   those parts
o   of   *for*   because of
towched to you of   touched on to you
And there as mountaynes . . . doun into valeyes   And where there are mountains and hills and valleys, that is simply from Noah's flood which washed away the soft and pliable earth and (it) fell down into the valleys
abyden   remain as
forthinketh   grieves   *wax nessche*   softened
                               of   from
cercle of the mone   in Ptolemaic (pre-Copernican) cosmology, the course of the moon round the earth
there as   where   *maketh hire torn*   revolves

so high that the Flode of Noe ne myght not come to hire that wolde have covered alle the erthe of the world alle abowte† and aboven and benethen, saf† Paradys only allone. And this Paradys is enclosed alle aboute with a walle, and men wyte† not wherof it is,† for the walles ben covered alle over with mosse, as it semeth. And it semeth not that the walle is ston of nature ne of non other thing that the walle is. And that walle streccheth fro the south to the north, and it hath not but on† entree that is closed with fyre brennynge,† so that no man that is mortalle ne dar not entren.†

And in the most high place of Paradys, evene in the myddel place, is a welle that casteth out the four flodes† that rennen be† dyverse† londes; of the whiche the firste is clept† Phison or Ganges, that is alle on,† and it renneth thorghout Ynde† or Emlak,† in the whiche ryvere ben manye precious stones and mochel† of *lignum aloes*† and moche gravelle of gold. And that other ryvere is clept Nilus or Gyson, that goth be Ethiope and after be Egypt. And that other is clept Tigris, that renneth be Assirye† and be Armenye the Grete.† And that other is clept Eufrate,† that renneth also be Medee† and be Armonye and be Persye. And men there beyonde seyn that alle the swete watres of the world aboven and benethen taken hire† begynnynge of that welle of Paradys, and out of that welle alle watres comen and gon.

The firste ryvere is clept Phison, that is to seyne in hire langage Assemblee, for manye othere ryveres meten hem† there and gon into that ryvere. And sum men clepen it Ganges, for a kyng that was in Ynde that highte† Gangeres and that it ran thorghout his lond. And that water is in sum place clere and in sum place trouble,† in sum place hoot and in sum place cold.

---

abowte around
wyte know
And it semeth not . . . walle is And it does not look as if the wall is stone in composition, nor as if it is of anything else
not but on only one
fyre brennynge burning fire [this detail probably derives from Genesis 3.24: '[God] placed at the east of the garden of Eden . . . a flaming sword which turned every way']
ne dar not entren dare enter
[*four flodes* for the four rivers of Paradise, see Genesis 2.10–11]
rennen be flow through
clept called
Ynde India
mochel a large amount
[*lignum aloes* a precious medicinal wood, believed to come from Paradise]
Assirye Assyria
Eufrate Euphrates
hire their
highte was called

saf except
whereof it is what it is made of

dyverse different
alle on all the same
Emlak Havilah [a biblical name for India]

Armenye the Grete Greater Armenia
Medee Medea
meten hem come together
trouble troubled

The second ryvere is clept Nilus or Gyson, for it is allewey trouble and Gyson in the langage of Ethiope is to seye Trouble and in the langage of Egipt also.

The thridde ryvere that is clept Tigris is as moche for to seye as Faste Rennynge,† for he renneth† more faste than ony of the tothere,† and also there is a best† that is cleped Tigris that is faste rennynge.

The fourthe ryvere is clept Eufrates, that is to seyne Wel Berynge, for there growen many godes upon that ryvere, as cornes, frutes, and othere godes ynowe plentee.†

And yee schulle understonde that no man that is mortelle ne may not approchen to that Paradys. For be londe no man may go for wylde bestes that ben in the desertes and for the high mountaynes and grete huge roches that no man may passe by for the derke places that ben there and that manye. And be† the ryveres may no man go, for the water renneth so rudely† and so scharply because that it cometh doun so outrageously from the high places aboven that it renneth in so grete waves that no schipp may not rowe ne seyle agenes† it. And the water roreth so and maketh so huge noyse and so gret tempest that no man may here other† in the schipp, though he cryede with alle the craft† that he cowde in the hiest† voys that he myghte. Many grete lordes han assayed† with gret wille many tymes for to passen be tho† ryveres toward Paradys with fulle grete companyes, but thei myght not speden† in hire viage.† And manye dyeden† for werynesse of rowynge ayenst tho stronge waves. And many of hem becamen blynde and many deve† for the noyse of the water. And summe weren perisscht and loste withinne the waves. So that no mortelle man may approche to that place withouten specyalle grace of God, so that of that place I can sey you no more. And thefore I schalle holde me stille† and retornen to that that I have seen.

Rennynge running	*renneth* runs
tothere others	*best* beast
ynowe plentee extremely abundant	*be* by
rudely roughly	*agenes* against
other another	*craft* strength
hieste loudest	*assayed* tried
tho those	*speden* succeed
viage journey	*dyeden* died
deve deaf	*holde me stille* keep silent

John Gower
c. 1340–1408

John Gower was probably born around 1340 or slightly earlier. He seems to have come from a Kentish landowning family with Yorkshire roots, and he may have received a legal training in London. Like his friend Geoffrey Chaucer, Gower had connections with the court. He dedicated his major English poem *Confessio Amantis* (The Lover's Confession) first to Richard II (1377–99) and then, in 1393, revised it and presented it to Henry Bolingbroke, later Henry IV (1399–1413). Gower married late in life, perhaps not for the first time, and by 1398 was living in the Southwark priory of St Mary Overy. Two years later, in 1400, he alludes to himself as blind, and seems to have stopped writing poetry. He died in 1408.

Gower's writings reflect more obviously than Chaucer's the conflicting claims of English, French and Latin among the learned and well-to-do in the second half of the fourteenth century. His first long moral poem, *Mirour de l'Omme* (The Mirror of Mankind) was written in French, and was followed by *Vox Clamantis* (The Voice of One Crying), a complaint on the times that deals with, among other things, the Peasants' Revolt of 1381. It may have been the example of Chaucer's early poems and *Troilus and Criseyde* (which includes a dedication to 'moral Gower') that impelled him to turn to English for *Confessio Amantis*.

This poem, from which the following extracts are taken, is a tale-collection of over 33,000 lines. The fiction which holds it together is that of the lover's confession: the unhappy lover goes out on a May morning and meets Venus, who tells him to confess his sins against Love to her priest Genius. Genius leads the lover through the deadly sins and their branches, in the manner in which real-life penitents were taught to examine their consciences, and illustrates them with over one hundred and thirty stories drawn from classical and medieval sources, especially from the Roman poet Ovid (43 BC–AD 18). In the end the lover is made to face what has been concealed from the reader hitherto – that he is growing old and so must renounce sexual love – and receives absolution from Genius when he finally accepts this. The *Confessio Amantis* does not have the formal or stylistic variety of Chaucer's *Canterbury Tales*, with which it is almost directly contemporary, but Gower's staple octosyllabic couplet is nevertheless an instrument whose delicacy, subtlety and range are sometimes underestimated.

In the passage below the lover replies to Genius' warning against somnolence (a branch of the deadly sin of sloth), by describing his sleeplessness. This introduces Genius' tale of Ceix and Alceone, which Chaucer had already used in *The Book of the Duchess*. Both poets take the story from Ovid.

The text is taken from G. C. Macaulay's edition of Bodleian Library, MS Fairfax 3, EETS, ES 81 (1901).

From CONFESSIO AMANTIS
Book 4, lines 2771–3132

[Ceix and Alceone]

THE LOVER:
    'For certes,* fader Genius,   truly
    †Yit into nou it hath be thus,
    At alle time* if it befelle*   occasions happened
    †So that I mihte come and dwelle
5   In place ther my ladi were,
    I was noght slow ne* slepi there: nor
    For thanne I dar wel undertake,†
    †That whanne hir list on nyhtes wake
    In chambre as to carole† and daunce,
10 †Me thenkth I mai me more avaunce,
    If I mai gon upon hir hond,†
    Thanne if I wonne a kinges lond.
    For whanne I mai hire hand beclippe,*   clasp
    With such gladnesse I daunce and skippe,
15 Me thenkth* I touche noght the flor;   it seems to me
    The ro, which renneth* on the mor,*   runs   moor

2 Up to now it has been like this
4 That I was allowed to come and remain
7 *I dar wel undertake* I declare
8 That when it pleases her to stay up at night
9 *to carole* to perform a dance with sung accompaniment
10 It seems to me that I spend my time more profitably
11 *gon upon hir hond* take her by the hand

JOHN GOWER

<pre>
         Is thanne noght so lyht as I:
         †So mow ye witen wel forthi,
         That for the time† slep I hate.
20   And whanne it falleth othergate,†
         So that hire like noght† to daunce,
         †Bot on the dees to caste chaunce
         Or axe* of love som demande,*   ask   question
         †Or elles that hir list comaunde
25   †To rede and here of Troilus,
         †Riht as sche wole or so or thus,
         I am al redi to consente.
         And if so is* that I mai hente*   it comes about   seize
         Sometime among† a good leisir,*   opportunity
30   So as* I dar of mi desir   as far as
         I telle a part; bot whanne I preie,*   beseech (her)
         †Anon sche bidt me go mi weie
         And seith* it is ferr in the nyht;   says
         And I swere it is even* liht.   still
35   Bot as* it falleth ate laste,*   just as   in the end
         Ther mai no worldes joie laste,
         †So mot I nedes fro hire wende
         And of my wachche* make an ende: wakefulness
         And if sche thanne hiede* toke,   heed
40   Hou pitousliche* on hire I loke,   pitiably
         Whan that I schal my leve take,
         †Hire oghte of mercy forto slake
         †Hire daunger, which seith evere nay.
              Bot he seith often, 'Have good day,'*   good-bye
45   That loth* is forto take his leve: unwilling
         Therfore, while I mai beleve,*   remain
         I tarie forth* the nyht along,*   delay   throughout
         For it is noght on me along†
</pre>

---

18 So you can see clearly from this
19 *for the time* for the moment
20 *it falleth othergate* things happen differently
21 *hire like noght* she does not want
22 But to try her luck at dice
24–5 Or else it pleases her to have the story of Troilus read and listened to   [*Troilus* the hero of Chaucer's poem *Troilus and Criseyde*, completed by 1387, to which this may be an allusion]
26 Whether she wants this or that
29 *among* in the midst (of this)
32 She immediately tells me to be on my way
37 Similarly, I am obliged to go from her
42–3 She ought, out of mercy, to abate her remoteness, which always denies me.
[*daunger* see note to Chaucer, *Parliament of Fowls*, line 136]
48 *on me along* up to me

	To slep that I so sone go,	
50	Til that I mot algate† so;	
	And thanne I bidde Godd hire se,†	
	And so doun knelende* on mi kne	kneeling
	I take leve, and if I schal,*	must
	I kisse hire, and go forth withal.*	therewith
55	And otherwhile,* if that I dore,*	sometimes dare
	Er I come fulli to the dore,*	door
	I torne ayein* and feigne a thing,†	back
	As thogh I hadde lost a ring	
	Or somwhat elles, for I wolde	
60	Kisse hire eftsones,* if I scholde,*	again might
	Bot selden* is that I so spede.†	seldom
	And whanne I se that I mot nede†	
	Departen, I departe, and thanne	
	With al myn herte I curse and banne*	swear
65	That evere slep was mad for yhe;*	eye
	For, as me thenkth, I mihte dryhe†	
	Withoute slep to waken* evere,	stay awake
	So that I scholde noght dissevere*	part
	Fro hire, in whom is al my liht:	
70	And thanne I curse also the nyht	
	With al the will of mi corage,*	heart
	And seie, 'Awey, thou blake ymage,	
	Which of thi derke cloudy face	
	Makst al the worldes lyht deface,†	
75	And causest* unto slep a weie,*	provides passage
	Be which I mot* nou gon aweie*	must away
	Out of mi ladi compaignie.	
	O slepi nyht, I thee defie,	
	†And wolde that thou leye in presse	
80	With Prosperine† the goddesse	
	And with Pluto† the helle king:	
	For til I se the daies spring,*	beginning

---

50 *mot algate* am nevertheless obliged to
51 *Godd hire se* God protect her
57 *feigne a thing* make pretence
61 *so spede* succeed in this
62 *mot nede* am obliged
66 *mihte dryhe* could endure
74 *Makst ... deface* obliterates
79 and would like you to lie down below
80–1 [*Prosperine ... Pluto* Proserpina, Roman goddess of the underworld, and wife of Pluton or Dis, god of the underworld]

	†I sette slep noght at a risshe.'	
	And with that word I sike* and wisshe,	sigh
85	And seie, 'Ha, whi ne were† it day?	
	For yit mi ladi thanne* I may	then
	Beholde, thogh I do nomore.'*	nothing more
	And efte I thenke forthermore,	
	To som man hou the niht doth ese,*	relieves
90	Whan he hath thing* that mai him plese	something
	The longe nyhtes be his side,	
	Where as I faile* and go beside.†	weaken
	Bot slep, I not wherof it serveth,†	
	†Of which noman his thonk deserveth	
95	†To gete him love in eny place,	
	Bot is an hindrere of* his grace	hindrance to
	And makth him ded as for a throwe,†	
	Riht as a stok were overthrowe.†	
	And so, mi fader, in this wise*	manner
100	The slepi nyhtes I despise,	
	And evere amiddes* of mi tale*	in the middle speech
	I thenke upon the nyhtingale,	
	Which slepeth noght be weie of kinde†	
	For love, in bokes as I finde.	
105	Thus ate* laste I go to bedde,	at the
	And yit min herte lith to wedde†	
	With hire, wher as I cam fro;*	from
	Thogh I departe, he* wol noght so,	my heart
	Ther is no lock mai schette* him oute,	shut
110	†Him nedeth noght to gon aboute,	
	That perce* mai the harde wall;	pierce
	Thus is he with hire overall,*	in every way
	†That be hire lief, or be hire loth,	
	Into hire bedd myn herte goth,*	goes
115	And softly takth* hire in his arm	takes
	And fieleth* hou that sche is warm,	feels

83 *I do not set any store at all by sleep*
85 *whi ne were* why is it not
92 *go beside* miss my way
93 *I not . . . serveth* I do not know what use it is
94–5 From whom no-one, thanks to him, deserves to win love anywhere
97 *as for a throwe* for a while
98 *stok were overthrowe* dead log
104 *be weie of kinde* naturally
106 *lith to wedde* lies in pawn
110 He does not need to go round and round
113 So that whether she wants it or not

	And wissheth that his body were	
	To fiele that* he fieleth there.	what
	And thus miselven* I tormente,	myself
120	Til that the dede slep me hente:*	siezes
	Bot thanne be a thousand score	
	Wel more* than I was tofore*	much more before
	I am tormented in mi slep,	
	Bot that* I dreme is noght of schep;*	what sheep
125	For I ne thenke noght on wulle,*	wool
	Bot I am drecched* to the fulle	tormented
	Of love, that I have to kepe,*	in my keeping
	That nou I lawhe* and nou I wepe,	laugh
	And nou I lese* and nou I winne,	lose
130	And nou I ende and nou beginne.	
	And otherwhile I dreme and mete*	dream, imagine
	That I al one with hire mete*	meet
	And that danger* is left behinde;	(her) remoteness
	And thanne in slep such joie I finde,	
135	†That I ne bede nevere awake.	
	Bot after, whanne I hiede* take,	heed
	And schal arise upon the morwe,†	
	Thanne is al torned into sorwe,*	sorrow
	Noght for the cause† I schal arise,	
140	†Bot for I mette in such a wise,	
	And ate laste I am bethoght*	meditate
	That al is vein and helpeth noght:	
	†Bot yit me thenketh be my wille	
	I wolde have leie* and slepe* stille,	lain slept
145	†To meten evere of such a swevene,	
	For thanne I hadde a slepi hevene.'	

CONFESSOR:

	'Mi Sone, and for* thou tellest so,	since
	A man mai finde of time ago†	
	That many a swevene* hath be certein,	dream
150	Al be it† so, that som men sein*	say

135 That I never ask to wake up
137 *upon the morwe*   the next morning
139 *for the cause*   because
140 But because I dreamed in such a manner
143 But yet it seems to me that if I had had my way
145 In order to keep on dreaming such a dream
148 *of time ago*   in the old days
150 *Al be it*   although it may be

That swevenes ben of no credence.†
Bot forto schewe* in evidence — show
That thei ful ofte sothe* thinges — true
Betokne,* I thenke in my wrytinges — represent
155 To telle a tale therupon,
Which fell be* olde daies gon.* — in past

This finde I write* in poesie:† — written
Ceïx the king of Trocinie†
Hadde Alceone to his wif,
160 Which as hire oghne* hertes lif — own
Him loveth; and he hadde also
A brother, which was cleped tho†
Dedalion, and he per cas†
Fro kinde* of man forschape* was — nature transformed
165 Into a goshauk of liknesse;* — in form
Wherof the king gret hevynesse* — sadness
Hath take, and thoghte in his corage* — heart
To gon upon a pelrinage* — pilgrimage
Into a strange regioun,
170 Wher he hath his devocioun* — devout wish
To don* his sacrifice and preie, — make
If that he mihte in eny weie
Toward the goddes finde grace
His brother hele† to pourchace,* — bring about
175 So that he mihte be reformed* — changed back
Of* that he hadde be transformed. — from
To this pourpos and to this ende
This king is redy forto wende,* — go
As he which wolde go be schipe;
180 And forto don him felaschipe†
His wif unto the see him broghte,
With al hire herte and him besoghte,* — prayed
That he the time hire wolde sein* — tell
Whan that he thoghte come ayein:* — back
185 'Withinne,' he seith, 'two monthe day.'
And thus in al the haste he may

---

151 *ben of no credence* have no credibility
157 *in poesie* poetry [Ovid, *Metamorphoses*, 9.410–78]
158 [*Trocinie* Trachis, in northern Greece]
162 *cleped tho* called then
163 *per cas* as luck would have it
174 *brother hele* brother's well-being
180 *don him felaschipe* keep him company

	He tok his leve, and forth he seileth	
	Wepende, and sche hirself beweileth,	
	And torneth hom,* ther* sche cam fro.	home where
190	Bot whan the monthes were ago,*	gone
	The whiche he sette of his comynge,	
	And that sche herde no tydinge,	
	†Ther was no care forto seche:	
	Wherof the goddes to beseche*	beseech
195	Tho sche began in many wise,*	ways
	And to Juno† hire sacrifise	
	Above alle othre most sche dede,*	made
	And for hir lord sche hath so bede*	prayed
	To wite* and knowe hou that he ferde,*	learn fared
200	That Juno the goddesse hire herde,	
	Anon* and upon this matiere*	directly matter
	Sche bad Yris† hir messagere	
	To Slepes† hous that sche schal wende,	
	And bidde him that he make an ende	
205	Be swevene* and schewen al the cas†	dream
	Unto this ladi, hou it was.	
	This Yris, fro the hihe stage†	
	Which undertake hath the message,	
	†Hire reyny cope dede upon,	
210	The which was wonderli begon*	decorated
	With colours of diverse hewe,	
	An hundred mo* than men it knewe;	more
	The hevene lich* unto a bowe	like
	Sche bende,* and so she cam doun lowe,	bent
215	The god of slep wher that sche fond.*	found
	And that was in a strange lond,	
	Which marcheth upon† Chymerie:†	
	For ther, as seith the poesie,	
	The god of Slep hath mad his hous,	
220	Which of entaille* is merveilous.	shape, appearance

---

193 no sorrow was absent (lit., to be sought for)
196 [*Juno* Roman queen of the gods and protector of women]
202 [*Yris* personification of the rainbow, and as such aptly seen as a messenger between the gods, especially Juno and Jupiter, and man]
203 [*Slepe* Hypnus, personification of sleep]
205 *al the cas* the entire circumstance
207 *hihe stage* high places, abode of the gods
209 put on her rainy mantle [*cope* Iris was traditionally depicted wearing a silk garment which had the colours of the rainbow]
217 *marcheth upon* lies alongside [*Chymerie* the country of the Cimmerians, on which the sun never rose]

	Under an hell* ther is a cave,	hill
	†Which of the sonne mai noght have,	
	So that noman mai knowe ariht*	properly
	The point betwen the dai and nyht:	
225	There is no fyr, ther is no sparke,	
	There is no dore, which mai charke,*	creak
	Wherof an yhe* scholde unschette,*	eye open
	So that inward* there is no lette.*	inside hindrance
	And forto speke of that withoute,*	outside
230	Ther stant* no gret tree nyh aboute*	stands nearby
	Wher on ther myhte crowe or pie*	magpie
	Alihte,* forto clepe* or crie:	alight, settle call
	Ther is no cok to crowe day,	
	No beste non which noise may†	
235	The hell, bot al aboute round	
	Ther is growende* upon the ground	growing
	Popi,* which berth* the sed of slep,	poppy bears
	With othre herbes suche an hep.*	quantity
	A stille* water for the nones†	silent
240	Rennende* upon the smale stones,	running
	Which hihte* of Lethes† the rivere,	is called
	Under that hell in such manere	
	Ther is, which yifth* gret appetit	gives
	To* slepe. And thus full of delit*	for delight
245	Slep hath his hous; and of his couche	
	Withinne his chambre if I schal touche,*	touch on
	Of hebenus* that slepi tree†	ebony
	The bordes* al aboute be,*	boards are
	And for* he scholde slepe softe,	so that
250	Upon a fethrebed alofte*	on top
	He lith* with many a pilwe* of doun:	lies pillow
	The chambre is strowed* up and doun	strewn
	With swevenes* many thousendfold.	dreams
	Thus cam Yris into this hold,*	stronghold
255	And to the bedd, which is al blak,	
	Sche goth, and ther with Slep sche spak,*	spoke
	And in the wise as sche was bede*	bidden
	The message of Juno sche dede.*	carried out

222 Which cannot receive any sunlight
234 *noise may* can make a noise in
239 *for the nones* assuredly
241 [*Lethes* Lethe, the river of oblivion in the underworld]
247 [*hebenus that slepi tre* ebony is a dark wood, and thus may be associated with night]

	Ful ofte* hir wordes sche reherceth,*	frequently repeats
260	Er* sche his slepi eres perceth	before
	With mochel* wo, bot ate* laste	much at the
	†His slombrende yhen he upcaste	
	And seide hir that it schal be do.*	done
	Wherof among a thousand tho,*	then
265	Withinne his hous that slepi were,	
	In special* he ches* out there	especially chose
	Thre, whiche scholden do this dede:	
	The ferste of hem,* so as I rede,	them
	Was Morpheüs,† the whos nature	
270	Is forto take the figure†	
	Of what persone that him liketh,*	he pleases
	Wherof that he ful ofte entriketh*	deceives
	†The lif which slepe schal be nyhte.	
	And Ithecus† that other hihte,*	was called
275	Which hath the vois of every soun,*	sound
	The chiere* and the condicioun	look
	Of every lif, what so it is:	
	The thridde suiende* after this	following
	Is Panthasas,† which may transforme	
280	Of every thing the rihte* forme,	proper
	And change it in an other kinde.	
	†Upon hem thre, so as I finde,	
	†Of swevenes stant al thapparance,	
	Which otherwhile* is evidence*	sometimes true indication
285	And otherwhile bot a jape.†	
	Bot natheles* it is so schape,*	nevertheless arranged
	That Morpheüs be nyht alone	
	Appiereth until Alceone	
	In liknesse of hir housebonde	
290	Al naked ded upon the stronde,*	shore
	And hou he dreynte* in special*	drowned particular
	These othre two it schewen* al.	show
	The tempeste of the blake cloude,	
	The wode see,† the wyndes loude,	

---

262 He turned his sleeping eyes upwards
269 [*Morpheus* one of the sons of Sleep, who was able to take on human shape]
270 *take the figure* assume the appearance
273 the living person who must sleep at night
274 [*Ithecus* Icelos, Sleep's second son, who could assume animal forms]
279 [*Panthasas* Phantasos, Sleep's third son, who could assume the shapes of inanimate things]
282–3 On the three of them rests the entire illusion of dreams, I find
285 *bot a jape* only a trick
294 *wode see* raging sea

295	Al this sche mette,* and sih* him dyen,*	dreamed saw die
	Wherof that sche began to crien,	
	Slepende abedde ther* sche lay,	where
	And with that noise of hire affray*	terror
	Hir wommen sterten up† aboute,*	around (her)
300	Whiche of here* ladi were in doute,*	their fear
	And axen* hire hou that sche ferde;*	ask fared
	And sche, riht as sche syh* and herde,	saw
	Hir swevene hath told hem everydel.*	in every detail
	And thei it halsen* alle wel	greet
305	And sein* it is a tokne* of goode;	say sign
	Bot til sche wiste* hou that it stode,*	knew things stood
	Sche hath no confort in hire herte.	
	Upon the morwe* and up sche sterte,	morning
	And to the see, wher that sche mette*	dreamed
310	The bodi lay, withoute lette*	delay
	Sche drowh,* and whan that sche cam nyh,	drew near
	Stark ded, hise armes sprad, sche syh	
	Hire lord flietende* upon the wawe.*	floating wave
	†Wherof hire wittes ben withdrawe,	
315	And sche, which tok of deth no kepe,†	
	Anon* forth lepte into the depe	immediately
	And wolde have cawht him in hire arm.	
	This infortune* of double harm*	misfortune grief
	The goddes fro the hevene above	
320	Behielde, and for the trowthe* of love,	constancy
	Which in this worthi ladi stod,*	was
	Thei have upon the salte flod	
	Hire dreinte* lord and hire also	drowned
	From deth to lyve* torned so,	life
325	That thei ben schapen* into briddes*	fashioned birds
	Swimmende upon the wawe* amiddes.†	wave
	And whan sche sih* hire lord livende*	saw living
	In liknesse of a bridd swimmende,	
	And sche was of the same sort,	
330	So as sche mihte do desport,†	
	Upon the joie which sche hadde	
	Hire wynges bothe abrod* sche spradde,	wide

---

299 *sterten up* jump up
314 Because of this she went out of her mind
315 *which tok . . . no kepe* who paid no heed of death
326 *amiddes* in the middle (of the sea)
330 *do desport* give pleasure

	And him, so as sche mai suffise,†	
	Beclipte* and keste* in such a wise,	embraced kissed
335	As sche was whilom* wont* to do:	formerly accustomed
	Hire wynges for hire armes two	
	Sche tok, and for hire lippes softe	
	Hire harde bile, and so ful ofte	
	Sche fondeth* in hire briddes forme,	tries
340	If that sche mihte hirself conforme†	
	†To do the plesance of a wif,	
	As sche dede* in that other lif:	did
	For thogh sche hadde hir pouer* lore,*	capability lost
	Hir will stod* as it was tofore,*	remained before
345	And serveth him so as sche mai.	
	Wherof into* this ilke* day	until very
	Togedre upon the see thei wone,*	live
	Wher many a dowhter and a sone	
	Thei bringen forth of briddes kinde;*	species
350	And for* men scholden take* in mynde	because bear
	This Alceoun the trewe queene,	
	Hire briddes yit,* as it is seene,	still
	Of Alceoun† the name bere.	
	Lo thus, mi sone, it mai thee stere*	guide
355	Of swevenes forto take kepe,*	heed
	For ofte time a man aslepe	
	Mai se what after* schal betide.*	afterwards happen
	Forthi* it helpeth at som tyde*	therefore occasion
	A man to slepe, as it belongeth,†	
360	†Bot slowthe no lif underfongeth	
	†Which is to love appourtenant.'	

---

333   *so as sche mai suffise*   so far as she is able
340   *hirself conforme*   adapt herself
341   To perform the pleasurable duties of a wife
353   [*Alceoun*   Alceone gave her name to the halcyon, or kingfisher, into which she was transformed]
359   *as it belongeth*   when it is appropriate
360–1   But Sloth does not accept a person who is committed to love

Julian of Norwich
1343–?1429

Julian of Norwich was born in 1343 and was thus an almost exact contemporary of Chaucer. At the age of thirty she had a series of revelations or 'shewings' during an illness from which she nearly died. After her recovery she recorded her experiences and then, over fifteen years later, returned to them again in an expanded version which was copied in the mid-seventeenth-century British Library MS, Sloane 2499, from which this extract comes. Julian's method is both autobiographical and meditative; she describes her visions of Christ and the Blessed Virgin simply and directly, and then proceeds to explore the meanings which they have acquired for her over the years. Thus in this passage she moves from the bloody figure of Christ to the Trinity which he represents, and whose presence is also expressed through the hazelnut which signifies all creation: made by the Father, loved by the Son, sustained by the Spirit. Julian is widely read in the Bible and in devotional literature, both English and Latin, though where she received her education, and what form it took, we do not know. She seems to have become an anchoress in Norwich, where she was visited by Margery Kempe in 1413; the fact that Margery refers to her as 'Dame' suggests that she was of gentle birth. She possibly lived until well into her eighties.

The text is from *A Book of Shewings to the Anchoress Julian of Norwich*, ed. E. Colledge and J. Walsh (1978).

From REVELATIONS OF DIVINE LOVE
[The First Showing]

And when I was thirty yere old and a halfe, God sent me a bodily sicknes in the which I ley three daies and three nyghtes; and on the fourth nyght I toke all my rightes of holie church,† and went not to have leven† tyll day. And after this I lay two daies and two nightes;

[*rightes of holie church* Extreme Unction, the sacrament of the sick. The sick person is anointed with oil and receives the eucharist]
went not to have leven believed I would not live

5   and on the third night I weenied† often tymes to have passed,† and so
wenyd thei that were with me. And yet in this I felt a great louthsomnes†
to die, but for nothing† that was in earth that me lyketh† to leve† for,
ne for no payne that I was afrayd of, for I trusted in God of his mercie.
But it was for† I would have leved† to have loueved† God better and
10 longer tyme, that I might by the grace of that levyng† have the more
knowing and lovyng of God in the blisse of heaven. For my thought†
all that tyme that I had leved heer so litle and so shorte in regard of†
that endlesse blesse,† I thought: 'Good Lorde, may my levyng no longer
be to thy worshippe?' And I understode by my reason and by the
15 feelyng of my paynes that I should die; and I ascentyd† fully with all
the will of myn hart to be at Gods will.
  Thus I indured till day, and by then was my bodie dead from the
miedes† downward, as to my feeling. Then was I holpen† to be set
upright, undersett† with helpe, for to have the more fredom of my hart
20 to be at Gods will, and thinkyng on God while my life laste. My curate†
was sent for to be at my ending, and before he cam I had set up† my
eyen and might not speake. He set the crosse before my face, and sayd:
'I have brought the image of thy saviour; looke ther upon and comfort
thee ther with.' My thought I was well, for my eyen† was sett upright
25 into† heaven, where I trusted to come by the mercie of God; but
nevertheles I ascentyd to sett my eyen in the face of the crucyfixe, if I
might, and so I dide, for my thought I might longar dure to looke even
forth then right up.† After this my sight began to feyle.† It waxid† as
darke aboute me in the chamber as if it had ben nyght, save in the
30 image of the crosse, wher in held† a comon† light; and I wiste† not
how. All that was beseid† the crosse was oglye and ferfull to me as† it
had ben much occupied with fiendes.

---

weenied believed
louthsomnes aversion
me lyketh I wish
for because
loueved loved
my thought it seemed to me
blesse bliss
miedes middle
undersett supported
set up raised
sett upright into raised towards
I might longar ... then right up I would be able to continue looking straight ahead longer than upwards
feyle fail
held remained
wiste knew
as as if

passed died
for nothing not for anything
leve live
would have leved wanted to live
levyng living
in regard of in comparison with
ascentyd assented
holpen helped
curate priest
eyen eyes

waxid grew
comon general
All that was beseid everything beside

After this the over† part of my bodie began to die so farforth† that unneth† I had anie feeling. My most† payne was shortnes of breth and faielyng of life. Then went I verily to have passed.† And in this sodenly all my paine was taken from me, and I was as hole,† and namely† in the over parte of my bodie, as ever I was befor. I merveiled of this sodeyn change, for my thought that it was a previe† working of God, and not of kynd;† and yet by feeling of this ease I trusted never the more to have lived,† ne† the feeling of this ease was no full ease to me, for me thought I had lever have ben delivred of† this world, for my hart was wilfully† set ther to.

Then cam sodenly to my mynd that I should desyer the second wound† of our Lordes gifte and of his grace, that my bodie might be fulfilled with mynd† and feeling of his blessed passion† as I had before praied, for I would† that his paynes were my paynes, with compassion† and afterward langyng to† God. Thus thought me† that I might with his grace have the woundes that I had before desyred; but in this I desyred never no bodily sight ne no maner schewing of God,† but compassion as me thought that a kynd† sowle might have with our Lord Jesu, that for love would become a deadly† man. With him I desyred to suffer, livyng in my deadly bodie, as God would give me grace.

And in this sodenly I saw the reed bloud rynnyng downe from under the garlande† hote and freyshely, plentuously† and lively,† right as it was in the tyme that the garland of thornes was pressed on his blessed head. Right so, both God and man, the same that sufferd for me, I conceived truly and mightly that it was him selfe that shewed it me without anie meane.†

---

over upper
unneth scarcely
went I ... passed I truly believed I had died
namely especially
kynd nature
I trusted ... lived I believed that I had never been more alive
ne and (with following negative)
I had lever ... delivred of I would rather have been set free from
wilfully unshakeably
[*the second wound* Julian had previously prayed that she might share the suffering of Christ]
mynd recollection
would desired
langyng to longing for
no maner ... God no revelation of any kind from God
kynd loving
[*garlande* the crown of thorns placed on Christ's head at his crucifixion]
plentuously plentifully
meane intermediary

so farforth to such an extent
most greatest
hole sound
previe secret

passion suffering, crucifixion
compassion shared suffering
thought me it seemed to me

deadly mortal

lively brightly

60   And in the same shewing† sodeinly the Trinitie† fulfilled my hart most of joy, and so I understode it shall be in heaven without end to all that shall come ther. For the Trinitie is God, God is the Trinitie. The Trinitie is our maker, the Trinitie is our keper, the Trinitie is our everlasting lover, the Trinitie is our endlesse joy and our bleisse,† by
65 our lord Jesu Christ, and in our lord Jesu Christ. And this was shewed in the first syght and in all, for wher Jhesu appireth the blessed Trinitie is understand,† as to† my sight. And I sayd: '*Benedicite dominus.*'† This I sayd for reverence in my menyng,† with a mightie voyce, and full greatly was I astonned† for wonder and marvayle that I had that he
70 that is so reverent† and so dreadfull† will be so homely† with a synnfull creature liveing in this wretched flesh.

    Thus I toke it for that tyme that our Lord Jhesu of his curteys† love would shewe me comfort before the tyme of my temptation; for me thought it might well be that I should by the sufferance of God† and
75 with his keping be tempted of† fiendes before I should die. With this sight of his blessed passion, with the Godhead that I saw in my understanding, I knew well that it was strenght† inough to me, ye, and to all creaturs livyng that sould be saved, against all the fiendes of hell, and against all ghostely† enemies.

80   In this he brought our ladie sainct Mari to my understanding. I saw her ghostly† in bodily lykenes, a simple mayden and a meeke, yong of age, a little waxen† above a chylde, in the stature as she was when she conceivede. Also God shewed me in part the wisdom and the truth of her sowle, wher in I understode the reverent beholding, that she beheld
85 her God, that is her maker, marvayling with great reverence that he would be borne of her that was a symple† creature of his makyng. And this wisdome and truth, knowing the greatnes of her maker and the littlehead† of her selfe that is made, made her to say full meekely to

---

shewing revelation
[*the Trinitie* Julian understands that her vision is not of Christ only but, through him, of the Trinity: God the Father, Son and Holy Spirit]
bleisse bliss
as to according to
for reverence in my menyng with a reverent intention
astonned astonished
dreadfull awesome
curteys courteous
by the sufferance of God with God permitting it
of by
ghostely spiritual
waxen grown [According to popular medieval tradition, Mary was fourteen when she conceived]
symple humble

understand understood
Benedicite dominus the Lord bless you
reverent worthy of devotion
homely gracious
strenght protection
ghostly spiritually
littlehead smallness

Gabriell: 'Loo me† here, Gods handmayden'.† In this syght I did understand verily† that she is more then all that God made beneth her in wordines† and in fullhead;† for above her is nothing that is made but the blessed manhood of Christ, as to my sight.

In this same tyme that I saw this sight of the head bleidyng, our good Lord shewed a gostly sight of his homely lovyng. I saw that he is to us all thing that is good and comfortable to our helpe. He is oure clothing, that for love wrappeth us and wyndeth† us, halseth† us and all becloseth† us, hangeth about us for tender love, that he may never leeve us. And so in this sight I saw that he is all thing that is good, as to my understanding.

And in this he shewed a little thing, the quantitie† of an haselnott,† lying in the palme of my hand, as me semide,† and it was as rounde as a balle. I looked theran† with the eye of my understanding, and thought: 'What may this be?' And it was answered generaelly thus: 'It is all that is made.' I marvayled how it might laste,† for me thought it might sodenly have fallen to nawght† for littlenes. And I was answered in my understanding: 'It lasteth and ever shall, for God loveth it; and so hath all thing being by the love of God.'

In this little thing I saw three propreties.† The first is that God made it,† the secund that God loveth it, the thirde that God kepyth it. But what behyld† I ther in? Verely, the maker, the keper, the lover. For til I am substantially† unyted to him I may never have full reste ne verie† blisse; that is to say that I be so fastned to him that ther be right nought that is made betweene my God and me.

This little thing that is made, me thought it might have fallen to nought for littlenes. Of this nedeth us† to have knowledge, that us lyketh nought all thing that is made,† for to love and have God that is unmade. For this is the cause why we be not all in ease of hart and of

---

Loo me behold me
Gods handmayden [For the story of the Angel Gabriel's annunciation to Mary that she would bear the son of God, see Luke 1.26–38]
verily truly
fullhead plenitude
halseth embraces
quantetie size
me semide it seemed to me
laste continue in being
propreties characteristics
wordines merit
wyndeth winds about
becloseth encloses
haselnott hazel-nut
theran thereon
nawght nothing
[*God made it . . . God loveth it . . . God kepyth it* according to Trinitarian teaching, God the Father is the creator, God the Son the lover, and God the Holy Spirit the preserver]
behyld beheld
verie true
that us lyketh . . . made so that everything that is made does not please us at all
substantially entirely
nedeth us we need

sowle, for we seeke heer† rest in this thing that is so little, wher no reste is in, and we know not our God, that is almightie, all wise and all good, for he is verie reste. God will be knowen, and him lyketh† that we rest us in him; for all that is beneth him suffyseth not to us.† And this is the cause why that no sowle is in reste till it is noughted of† all things that is made. When she is wilfully noughted for love, to have him that is all, then is she able to receive ghostly† reste.

And also our good Lord shewed that it is full great plesannce† to him that a sely† sowle come to him naked, pleaynly† and homly.† For this is the kynde yernyng† of the sowle by the touchyng of the Holie Ghost, as by the understandyng that I have in this schewying: 'God of thy goodnes geve me thy selfe, for thou art inough to me, and I maie aske nothing that is lesse that maie be full worshippe to thee. And if I aske anie thing that is lesse, ever me wanteth;† but only in thee I have all.'

And these wordes of the goodnes of God be full lovesum† to the sowle, and full neer† touching the will of our Lord, for his goodnes fulfillith all his creaturs and all his blessed workes and overpassith† without end. For he is the endlesshead† and he made us only to him selfe and restored us by his precious passion, and ever kepeth us in his blessed love; and all this is of his goodnes.

---

heer here, in this world
suffyseth not to us is not sufficient for us
ghostly spiritual
sely blessed
homly intimately
ever me wanteth I am always deficient
full neer very closely
endlesshead endlessness

him lyketh it pleases him
noughted of set free from
plesannce delight
pleaynly openly
kynde yernying natural longing
lovesum pleasing
overpassith endures

The 'Gawain-Poet'
late fourteenth century

A modest manuscript in the British Library, Cotton Nero A.X, contains the only texts we have of four poems, probably all written by the same person, who was one of the greatest poets of the late fourteenth century. We do not know his name or anything about him, except what we can deduce from his work. The manuscript was written around 1400 in the north-west midlands on the border between Cheshire and Staffordshire (a region not far from that through which Gawain travels in the passage below); this language area also seems to have been that of the poet himself. Since he clearly knew the Latin Bible well, he was probably a cleric. He may have been employed in a secular household – he is also familiar with French romances and with the manners and *mores* of courtly society – but the nature of his audience is still a matter of conjecture and debate.

The four poems are *Sir Gawain and the Green Knight*, a knightly romance, from which lines 491–810 are printed below; *Pearl*, a dream-vision poem in which the dreamer is visited by his dead daughter, transfigured in heaven, who teaches him to accept his loss of her; *Purity* (or *Cleanness*), a homily on that virtue, conveyed through a series of biblical narratives; and *Patience*, the simplest of the four, which is also homiletic and which uses the story of Jonah and the whale as an illustration of the need for accepting God's will without complaint. The poet evidently knew the Old Testament Book of Jonah which he greatly expands, turning Jonah himself into a comic figure and incorporating him into a world in which God's purposes are not always easy to discern.

The works of the 'Gawain-poet' (or 'Pearl-poet' as he is also called) are all alliterative, though they use some variety of stanzaic or strophic forms as well. *Sir Gawain and the Green Knight* is written in stanzas of irregular length in which most of the lines are long and unrhymed, but which have an additional, short, rhyming 'bob and wheel' at the end. *Patience* is less clearly stanzaic: there are marks in the margin of the manuscript every four lines, and this pattern seems to be reflected in the syntax, but there are no rhymes and some editors print the poem without breaks.

The passage from *Sir Gawain and the Green Knight*, the opening of the second fitt (or section), describes the passage of the seasons, and then Gawain's departure from Arthur's court and his journey through a wild region in winter weather to keep his appointment with the Green Knight. It shows the way in which the poet is able to relate internal and external worlds by means of a poetic language which constantly grounds abstract moral discriminations in intensely physical experiences and activities.

The text and translation of *Sir Gawain and the Green Knight* are from W. R. J. Barron's 1974 edition, to which notes have been added. The text of *Patience* is from the 1983 edition of the works of the 'Gawain-poet' by A. C. Cawley and J. J. Anderson; the translation and notes are by the editor of this section of the Anthology.

II

1–25   This foretaste of adventures Arthur received at the beginning of the new year, for he ever longed to hear of bold deeds. Though matter for discussion was lacking when they went to table, now they are fully occupied with serious business, their hands are cram-full. Gawain was happy to begin those sports in the hall, but do not be surprised if the end should be sad; for though men may be light-hearted when they have drunk strong drink, a year passes very quickly, and never brings back like circumstances, the beginning is very seldom like the end. And so this Yuletide passed by, and the year after it, and each season in turn followed after the other: after Christmas there came meagre Lent, which tries the flesh with its fish and plainer fare; but then the weather everywhere contends against winter, cold shrinks down into the earth, the clouds lift, bright falls the rain in warm showers, falls upon the fair plain where flowers appear, the fields and groves alike are clothed in green, birds make haste to build, gaily singing their delight in the mild summer which follows next upon the hillsides; and blossoms swell into bloom along hedgerows richly overgrown, while many glorious songs are heard in the lovely wood.

26–45   With the coming of the summer season with its gentle breezes, when the West Wind breathes himself into seeds and grasses, there springs from them the most lovely growth,

From SIR GAWAIN AND THE GREEN KNIGHT

[Gawain's Journey]

II

This hanselle has Arthur of aventurus† on fyrst
In yonge yer, for he yerned yelpyng to here.
Thagh hym wordes were wane when thay to sete wenten,
Now ar thay stoken of sturne werk, stafful her hond.
5 Gawan was glad to begynne those gomnes in halle,
Bot thagh the ende be hevy haf ye no wonder;
For thagh men ben mery in mynde quen thay han mayn drynk,
A yere yernes ful yerne, and yeldes never lyke,
The forme to the fynisment foldes ful selden.
10 Forthi this Yol† overyede, and the yere after,
And uche sesoun serlepes sued after other:
After Crystenmasse com the crabbed lentoun,†
That fraystes flesch wyth the fysche and fode more symple;
Bot thenne the weder of the worlde wyth wynter hit threpes,
15 Colde clenges adoun, cloudes uplyften,
Schyre schedes the rayn in schoweres ful warme,
Falles upon fayre flat, flowres there schewen,
Bothe groundes and the greves grene ar her wede,
Bryddes busken to bylde, and bremlych syngen
20 For solace of the softe somer that sues therafter
      bi bonk;
   And blossumes bolne to blowe
   Bi rawes rych and ronk,
   Then notes noble innoghe
25   Ar herde in wod so wlonk.

After the sesoun of somer wyth the soft wyndes
Quen Zeferus syfles hymself on sedes and erbes,
Wela wynne is the wort that waxes theroute,

---

1 *hanselle ... of aventurus* the foretaste which Arthur has received is the arrival in his hall during the Christmas festivities of a green knight on a green horse who challenges one of Arthur's knights to give him a blow from his axe, in return for which he will give the knight a blow in a year's time. Arthur's nephew, Gawain, takes up the challenge and strikes the strange knight a blow which severs his neck. The green knight picks up his head, confirms the agreement that Gawain must come to his green chapel next New Year's Day, and rides out
10 *Yol* from Christmas Day to Twelfth Night
12 *crabbed lentoun* so called because it is a season of fasting, in which meat was not eaten

when the moistening dew drips from the leaves, and it enjoys a pleasant glance from the bright sun. But then autumn hastens on, and matures it quickly, warning it to grow fully ripe in readiness for winter; by drought he drives the dust to rise, to fly far, far up from the face of the earth; in the heavens above a wild wind wrestles with the sun, the leaves fly from the linden tree and light upon the ground, and the grass which once was green becomes quite grey; then all that sprang up in the beginning ripens and decays, and so the year runs by in many passing days, and winter returns again, as is, to be sure, the way of the world, until the Michaelmas moon was come with forewarning of winter. Then Gawain all at once recalls his difficult quest.

46–75 Yet until All Saints' Day he remained with Arthur; and he made a feast on that festival for the knight's sake, with much splendid revelry of the Round Table. Courteous knights and lovely ladies were in distress, all for love of that man, but yet they were nonetheless ready to speak only of pleasant things: many there made jests who were sad at heart for that gentle knight. For after dinner he spoke with concern to his uncle, and talked of his journey, and said frankly, 'Now, sovereign lord of my life, I ask your leave to go. You know the nature of this affair, and I do not care to speak to you further about the difficulties involved, it would only be a waste of breath; but I am to set out for the return blow tomorrow without fail, to seek the Green Knight, as God shall guide me.' Then the best knights in the castle came together, Ywain, and Erec, and very many others, Sir Dodinel de Savage, the Duke of Clarence, Lancelot, and Lionel, and the good Sir Lucan, Sir Bors, and Sir Bedivere, both eminent men, and many other nobles, including Mador de la Port. All this courtly company gathered round the king to advise the knight, with grief in their hearts.

When the donkande dewe dropes of the leves,
30 To bide a blysful blusch of the bryght sunne.
Bot then hyghes hervest, and hardenes hym sone,
Warnes hym for the wynter to wax ful rype;
He dryghes wyth droght the dust for to ryse,
Fro the face of the folde to flyghe ful hyghe;
35 Wrothe wynde of the welkyn wrasteles with the sunne,
The leves lancen fro the lynde and lyghten on the grounde,
And al grayes the gres that grene was ere;
Thenne al rypes and rotes that ros upon fyrst,
And thus yirnes the yere in yisterdayes mony,
40 And wynter wyndes ayayn, as the worlde askes,
   no fage,
  Til Meghelmas† mone
  Was cumen wyth wynter wage.
  Then thenkkes Gawan ful sone
45   Of his anious vyage.

Yet quyl Al-hal-day† with Arther he lenges;
And he made a fare on that fest for the frekes sake,
With much revel and ryche of the Rounde Table.
Knyghtes ful cortays and comlych ladies
50 Al for luf of that lede in longynge they were,
Bot never the lece the later thay nevened bot merthe:
Mony joyles for that jentyle japes ther maden.
For aftter mete with mournyng he meles to his eme,
And spekes of his passage, and pertly he sayde,
55 'Now, lege lorde of my lyf, leve I yow ask.
Ye knowe the cost of this cace, kepe I no more
To telle yow tenes therof, never bot trifel;
Bot I am boun to the bur barely to-morne,
To sech the gome of the grene, as God wyl me wysse.'
60 Thenne the best of the burgh bowed togeder,
Aywan, and Errik, and other ful mony,†
Sir Doddinaval de Savage, the duk of Clarence,
Launcelot, and Lyonel, and Lucan the gode,
Sir Boos, and Sir Bydwer, big men bothe,
65 And mony other menskful, with Mador de la Port.†
Alle this compayny of court com the kyng nerre
For to counseyl the knyght, with care at her hert.

---

42 *Meghelmas* the feast of St Michael (Michaelmas), 29 September
46 *Al-hal-day* 1 November
61–5 *Aywan, and Errik . . . Mador de la Port* these knights of the Round Table are all drawn from French, or in some cases possibly English, romances

Much secret sorrow was felt in the hall that one so distinguished as Gawain should have to go on that mission, to suffer a grievous blow, and strike none in return with his sword. The knight remained cheerful throughout, and said, 'What should I shrink from? What can one do but plumb to the depths what Fate holds in store, painful and pleasant alike?'

76–99 He remained there all that day, and next day prepared himself, asked early for his arms, and they were all brought. First a silken carpet was spread over the floor, on which much gilded armour gleamed. The bold man stepped on to it, and handled the arms, clad in a tunic of costly Tharsian silk, and over that a hooded cape, skilfully made, fastened at the neck, and trimmed inside with a pure white fur. Then they put the steel shoes upon the knight's feet, his legs were lapped in steel by handsome greaves, to which were attached knee-pieces, very brightly polished, fastened about his knees with ties of gold; next fine thigh-pieces, which elegantly encased his stout muscular thighs, and were fastened with thongs; and then the linked corslet of bright steel rings enveloped the knight, covering his splendid clothing, and well burnished arm-pieces on his two arms, with good, bright elbow-pieces, and gauntlets of plate, and all the fine equipment which would be of use to him on that occasion; together with a costly surcoat, his gold spurs fastened on with ceremony, a trusty sword girt about his waist by a silken girdle.

100–28 When he was encased in armour, his gear was splendid: the smallest lace or loop shone with gold. Armed thus as he was he heard his mass, offered and celebrated at the high altar. Then he came to the king and to his companions at court, courteously took his leave of the lords and ladies, and they kissed him and escorted him out, commending him to Christ. By that time Gryngolet was ready, and girt with a saddle

There was much derne doel driven in the sale
That so worthé as Wawan schulde wende on that ernde,
70 To dryghe a delful dynt, and dele no more
                        wyth bronde.
            The knyght mad ay god chere,
            And sayde, 'Quat schuld I wonde?
            Of destinés derf and dere
75   What may mon do bot fonde?'

He dowelles ther al that day, and dresses on the morn,
Askes erly hys armes, and alle were thay broght.
Fyrst a tulé tapit tyght over the flet,
And miche was the gyld gere that glent theralofte.
80 The stif mon steppes theron, and the stel hondeles,
Dubbed in a dublet of a dere tars,
And sythen a crafty capados, closed aloft,
That wyth a bryght blaunner was bounden withinne.
Thenne set thay the sabatouns upon the segge fotes,
85 His leges lapped in stel with luflych greves,
With polaynes piched therto, policed ful clene,
Aboute his knes knaged wyth knotes of golde;
Queme quyssewes then, that coyntlych closed
His thik thrawen thyghes, with thwonges to tachched;
90 And sythen the brawden bryné of bryght stel rynges
Umbeweved that wyy, upon wlonk stuffe,
And wel bornyst brace upon his bothe armes,
With gode cowters and gay, and gloves of plate,
And alle the godlych gere that hym gayn schulde
95   that tyde;
            Wyth ryche cote-armure,
            His gold spores spend with pryde,
            Gurde wyth a bront ful sure
            With silk sayn umbe his syde.

100 When he was hasped in armes, his harnays was ryche:
The lest lachet other loupe lemed of golde.
So harnayst as he was he herknes his masse,
Offred and honoured at the heghe auter.
Sythen he comes to the kyng and to his cort-feres
105 Laches lufly his leve at lordes and ladyes,
And they hym kyst and conveyed, bikende hym to Kryst.
Bi that was Gryngolet† grayth, and gurde with a sadel

---

107 *Gryngolet* name given to Gawain's horse in earlier French romances

that shone gaily with many gold fringes, newly studded all over, specially prepared for that occasion; the bridle was ringed round, bound with bright gold; the decoration of the breast-trappings and of the magnificent saddle-flaps, the crupper and the horse-cloth, matched that of the saddle-bows; and everywhere, set upon a red ground, were splendid gold nails, which all glittered and glinted like rays of sunlight. Then he took up and quickly kissed the helmet, which was stapled strongly and padded inside. It sat high on his head, secured behind, with a band of fine silk above the chain-mail neck-guard, embroidered and set with the best gems on its broad silken hem, and along the seams, birds such as parrots depicted amongst periwinkle plants, turtle-doves and true-love flowers embroidered as closely as if many ladies at court had been engaged on it for seven years. The circlet which encompassed his brow was more precious still, composed of flawless diamonds which were both clear and clouded.

129–49 Then they displayed for him the shield, which was of bright gules with the pentangle picked out in the colour of pure gold. He seized the shield by the baldrick and slung it about his neck; it suited the knight fittingly and well. And just why the pentangle is appropriate to that noble lord I am bent on telling you, even though it should delay me: it is a symbol that Solomon devised once upon a time as a token of fidelity, appropriately, for it is a figure which contains five points, and each line overlaps and interlocks with another, and it is unbroken anywhere; and all over England, so I hear, it is called the endless knot. And so it is appropriate to this knight and to his unblemished arms; because he was always trustworthy in five respects and fivefold in each, Gawain was known to be a good knight, and like refined gold, free from every imperfection, graced with chivalric virtues.

That glemed ful gayly with mony golde frenges,
Ayquere naylet ful nwe, for that note ryched;
110 The brydel barred aboute, with bryght golde bounden;
The apparayl of the payttrure and of the proude skyrtes,
The cropore and the covertor, acorded wyth the arsounes;
And al was rayled on red ryche golde nayles,
That al glytered and glent as glem of the sunne.
115 Thenne hentes he the helme, and hastily hit kysses,
That was stapled stifly, and stoffed wythinne.
Hit was hyghe on his hede, hasped bihynde,
Wyth a lyghtly urysoun over the aventayle,
Enbrawden and bounden wyth the best gemmes
120 On brode sylkyn borde, and bryddes on semes,
As papjayes paynted perwyng bitwene,
Tortors and trulofes entayled so thyk
As mony burde theraboute had ben seven wynter
        in toune.
125   The cercle was more o prys
    That unbeclypped hys croun,
    Of diamauntes a devys,
    That bothe were bryght and broun.

Then they schewed hym the schelde, that was of schyr goules,†
130 Wyth the pentangel† depaynt of pure golde hwes.
He braydes hit by the bauderyk, aboute the hals kestes,
That bisemed the segge semlyly fayre.
And quy the pentangel apendes to that prynce noble
I am in tent yow to telle, thof tary hyt me schulde:
135 Hit is a synge that Salamon† set sumquyle
In bytoknyng of trawthe, bi tytle that hit habbes
For hit is a figure that haldes fyve poyntes,
And uche lyne umbelappes and loukes in other,
And ayquere hit is endeles; and Englych hit callen
140 Overal, as I here, the endeles knot.
Forthy hit acordes to this knyght and to his cler armes;
For ay faythful in fyve and sere fyve sythes,
Gawan was for gode knawen, and as golde pured,
Voyded of uche vylany, wyth vertues ennoured
145   in mote.

---

129 *goules* heraldic red
130 *pentangel* a five-pointed star, drawn with a single continuous line (thus 'the endeles knot', line 140)
135 *Salamon* in the middle ages the pentangle was identified with the seal of the biblical Solomon because it was used in Jewish as well as cabbalistic and Christian symbolism

For this reason he bore the pentangle newly painted upon shield and surcoat, as being a man most true to his word and in bearing the noblest of knights.

150–79 First, he was proved faultless in his five senses, and secondly the knight was never at fault through his five fingers, and all his trust on this earth was in the five wounds which Christ received on the cross, as the Creed tells. And wherever this man was beset in battle, his steadfast thought was upon this, above all else – that he should draw all his fortitude from the five joys which the gracious Queen of Heaven had in her child; for this reason the knight appropriately had her image depicted on the inner side of his shield, so that when he looked at it his courage never failed. The fifth group of five which I find the man displayed was generosity and love of his fellow men above all else, his purity and his courtesy were never at fault, and compassion, which surpasses all other qualities, these five virtues were more firmly attached to that man than to any other. Now all these five groups were, in truth, conjoined in this knight, each one linked to another, so that none had an end, established upon five points that were ever fixed, none coinciding anywhere nor separating either, and all without end at any place I can find anywhere, wherever the tracing process began or came to an end. Accordingly there was fashioned upon his bright shield, splendid in red gold upon the crimson gules, the device which is called by learned men the perfect pentangle. Now Gawain was finely arrayed, and there and then he took his lance and bade them all good day – for ever, as he thought.

180–200 He set spurs to the horse and sprang on his way, so vigorously that sparks were struck from the stones behind him. All who saw that splendid sight sighed in their hearts, and all the people alike said quietly to each other,

Forthy the pentangel nwe
He ber in schelde and cote,
As tulke of tale most trwe
And gentylest knyght of lote.

150 Fyrst he was funden fautles in his fyve wyttes,
And efte fayled never the freke in his fyve fyngres,
And alle his afyaunce upon folde was in the fyve woundes
That Cryst kaght on the croys, as the crede telles.
And quere-so-ever thys mon in melly was stad,
155 His thro thoght was in that, thurgh alle other thynges,
That alle his forsnes he fong at the fyve joyes†
That the hende heven-quene had of hir chylde;
At this cause the knyght comlyche hade
In the inore half of his schelde hir ymage depaynted,
160 That quen he blusched therto his belde never payred.
The fyft fyve that I finde that the frek used
Was fraunchyse and felawschyp forbe al thyng,
His clannes and his cortaysye croked were never,
And pité, that passes alle poyntes, thyse pure fyve
165 Were harder happed on that hathel then on any other.
Now alle these fyve sythes, for sothe, were fetled on this knyght,
And uchone halched in other, that non ende hade,
And fyched upon fyve poyntes that fayld never,
Ne samned never in no syde, ne sundred nouther,
170 Withouten ende at any noke I oquere fynde,
Whereever the gomen bygan or glod to an ende.
Therfore on his schene schelde schapen was the knot
Ryally wyth red golde upon rede gowles,
That is the pure pentaungel wyth the peple called
175   with lore.
       Now graythed is Gawan gay,
       And laght his launce ryght thore,
       And gef hem alle goud day –
       He wende for evermore.

180 He sperred the sted with the spures and sprong on his way,
So stif that the ston-fyr stroke out therafter.
Al that sey that semly syked in hert,
And sayde sothly al same segges til other,

---

156 *the fyve joyes* the Annunciation, the Nativity, the Resurrection of Christ, his Ascension, and Mary's Assumption (or sometimes the third, fourth and fifth are Ascension, Assumption and Coronation of Mary)

grieving for that fair knight: 'By Christ, it is a pity that you, sir, who are so noble in your life are to perish! To find his equal on this earth, truly, is not easy. It would have been wiser to have acted with more caution, and to have appointed that noble man to be a duke; to be a brilliant leader of men in this land would well befit him, and he had better have been so than be destroyed utterly, beheaded by an elvish man because of excessive pride. Who ever knew any king to take such counsel as knights give in quibbling over Christmas games!' Much warm water gushed from their eyes when that fair knight went out from the castle that day. He made no delay, but went on his way swiftly; he rode by many a devious path, as I have heard the story say.

201-22 Now the knight goes riding through the realm of Logres, Sir Gawain rides in God's name, though no mere game it seemed to him. Often, companionless, he spent the night alone where he found no food to his liking set before him. He had no company save his horse among the woods and hills, and no one but God to speak with by the way, till he drew very close to north Wales. Keeping all the islands of Anglesey on his left hand, and passing over the fords at the coastal promontories, he crossed over at the Holy Head, till he gained the shore once more in the wilderness of Wirral; few lived there who loved either God or man wholeheartedly. And ever as he rode, he inquired of the people whom he met whether they had heard any talk of a Green Knight of the Green Chapel in any region thereabouts; and they all denied it, saying no, that never in their lives had they seen any man who was of such a colour as green.

Carande for that comly: 'Bi Kryst, hit is scathe
185 That thou, leude, schal be lost, that art of lyf noble!
To fynde hys fere upon folde, in fayth, is not ethe.
Warloker to haf wrogt had more wyt bene,
And haf dyght yonder dere a duk to have worthed;
A lowande leder of ledes in londe hym wel semes,
190 And so had better haf ben then britned to noght,
Hadet wyth an alvisch mon, for angardes pryde.
Who knew ever any kyng such counsel to take
As knyghtes in cavelaciouns on Crystmasse gomnes!'
Wel much was the warme water that waltered of yyen
195 When that semly syre soght fro tho wones
 thad daye.
  He made non abode,
  Bot wyghtly went hys way;
  Mony wylsum way he rode,
200 The bok as I herde say.

Now rides this renk thurgh the ryalme of Logres,†
Sir Gawan, on Godes halve, thagh hym no gomen thoght.
Oft leudles alone he lenges on nyghtes
Ther he fonde noght hym byfore the fare that he lyked.
205 Hade he no fere bot his fole bi frythes and dounes,
Ne no gome bot God bi gate wyth to karp,
Til that he neghed ful neghe into the Northe Wales.
Alle the iles of Anglesay† on lyft half he haldes,
And fares over the fordes by the forlondes,
210 Over at the Holy Hede,† til he hade eft bonk
In the wyldrenesse of Wyrale;† wonde ther bot lyte
That auther God other gome wyth goud hert lovied.
And ay he frayned, as he ferde, at frekes that he met,
If thay hade herde any karp of a knyght grene,
215 In any grounde theraboute, of the grene chapel;
And al nykked hym wyth nay, that never in her lyve
Thay seye never no segge that was of suche hwes
 of grene.

---

201 *Logres* roughly, England; in Geoffrey of Monmouth's *Historia Regum Britanniae* ('History of the Kings of Britain', 1135) Britain is divided into Loegria, Cambria (Wales) and Albany (Scotland)
208 *alle the iles of Anglesay* Anglesey itself and the smaller islands close to it, off the north-west coast of Wales
210 *the Holy Hede* this location is unidentifiable; it is clearly not the Holyhead on Anglesey since it is at a crossing of the river Dee
211 *Wyrale* the promontory between the rivers Mersey and Dee, south of Liverpool; known in the middle ages as a wild region

The knight took unfamiliar paths among many dreary hills; his mood changed many times before he came to see that chapel.

223–49 He clambered up many a cliff in strange regions; having wandered far from his friends, he rode as a stranger. At every ford or stream where the knight crossed over, it was a wonder if he did not find a foe facing him, and one so evil and so fierce that he was compelled to fight. The man encountered so many strange things there among the hills, that it would be too difficult to recount the tenth part of them. Sometimes he fought with dragons, and with wolves also, sometimes with forest trolls, who lived in the rocks, with bulls and bears too, and at other times with boars, and ogres who pursued him from the fells above; had he not been bold and unflinching and served God, without doubt he would have been struck down and killed many a time. Yet fighting did not so greatly trouble him, the winter weather was worse, when the cold, clear rain was shed from the clouds, and froze before it could fall on the faded earth. Almost slain by the sleet, he slept in his armour night after night amongst the naked rocks, where the cold burn came crashing down from the cliff-top, and hung high above his head in hard icicles. So through pain and peril and the greatest hardships this knight went riding across the country until Christmas Eve, all alone. Then the knight duly made his prayer to Mary, that she would direct his course and guide him to some dwelling.

250–72 On the morning of that day he rode in good heart over a mountain and deep into a forest that was wonderfully wild, and high hills on every side, and woods at their feet of hundreds of great, grey oaks; the hazel and the hawthorn were all tangled together, hung all over with rough, shaggy moss, with many mournful birds upon their bare branches, piping pathetically there, in pain from the cold. The knight upon Gryngolet passed beneath them, through many a bog and mire, a man all alone, concerned about his religious duties, lest he should not manage

             The knyght tok gates straunge
220   In mony a bonk unbene;
             His cher ful oft con chaunge,
             That chapel er he myght sene.

        Mony klyf he overclambe in contrayes straunge;
        Fer floten fro his frendes fremedly he rydes.
225   At uche warthe other water ther the wyye passed
        He fonde a foo hym byfore, bot ferly hit were,
        And that so foule and so felle that feight hym byhode.
        So mony mervayl bi mount ther the mon fyndes,
        Hit were to tore for to telle of the tenthe dole.
230   Sumwhyle wyth wormes he werres, and with wolves als,
        Sumwhyle wyth wodwos that woned in the knarres,
        Bothe wyth bulles and beres, and bores otherquyle,
        And etaynes that hym anelede of the heghe felle;
        Nade he ben dughty and dryye, and Dryghtyn had served,
235   Douteles he hade ben ded and dreped ful ofte.
        For werre wrathed hym not so much, that wynter was wors,
        When the colde cler water fro the cloudes schadde,
        And fres er hit falle myght to the fale erthe.
        Ner slayn wyth the slete he sleped in his yrnes
240   Mo nyghtes then innoghe in naked rokkes,
        Ther as claterande fro the crest the colde borne rennes,
        And henged heghe over his hede in hard iisse-ikkles.
        Thus in peryl and payne and plytes ful harde
        Bi contray caryes this knyght tyl Krystmasse even,
245   al one.
             The knyght wel that tyde
             To Mary made his mone,
             That ho hym red to ryde
             And wysse hym to sum wone.

250   Bi a mounte on the morne meryly he rydes
        Into a forest ful dep, that ferly was wylde,
        Highe hilles on uche a halve, and holtwodes under
        Of hore okes ful hoge a hundreth togeder;
        The hasel and the haghthorne were harled al samen,
255   With roghe raged mosse rayled aywhere,
        With mony bryddes unblythe upon bare twyges,
        That pitosly ther piped for pyne of the colde.
        The gome upon Gryngolet glydes hem under,
        Thurgh mony misy and myre, mon al hym one,
260   Carande for his costes, lest he ne kever schulde

to see the service of the Lord, who on that very night was born of a virgin to end our troubles. And so, sighing, he said, 'I beseech you, Lord, and Mary, your most dear and gentle mother, for some shelter where I may devoutly hear Mass and the matins of your feast day tomorrow, meekly I ask it, and in preparation I here and now recite my Paternoster and Ave Maria and Creed.' He rode on as he prayed and lamented his sins; he crossed himself repeatedly and said, 'Christ's cross be my aid!'

273–94 Scarcely had the knight crossed himself three times, when he became aware of a dwelling in the wood surrounded by a moat, on a knoll above a glade, shut in under the boughs of many massive trees round about the defensive ditches: the fairest castle that ever a knight owned, erected in a meadow, surrounded by a park, set about by a palisade of close-set spikes, which enclosed many trees in its circuit of more than two miles. The knight gazed at the castle from his side of the moat, as it shimmered and shone through the lovely oaks; then he reverently removed his helmet, and devoutly thanked Jesus and St Julian, who are both gracious, for having shown him courtesy and listened to his cry for help. 'Now I beseech you,' said the knight, 'grant me good lodging.' Then he urged on Gryngolet with his gilded spurs, and as he had most fortunately taken the main path, it directly and speedily brought the knight to the end of the drawbridge. The bridge was firmly drawn up, the gates were securely shut, the walls were well constructed and feared no tempest blast.

295–320 The knight remained on his horse, which came to a halt on the bank of the deep double ditch which surrounded the building; the wall went down into the water extremely deep, and it also rose up above to a very great height,

To se the servyse of that syre, that on that self nyght
Of a burde was borne oure baret to quelle.
And therfore sykyng he sayde, 'I beseche the, lorde,
And Mary, that is myldest moder so dere,
265 Of sum herber ther heghly I myght here masse
Ande thy matynes to-morne, mekely I ask,
And therto prestly I pray my pater and ave†
    and crede.'
    He rode in his prayere
270   And cryed for his mysdede;
    He sayned hym in sythes sere
    And sayde, 'Cros Kryst me spede!'

Nade he sayned hymself, segge, bot thrye,
Er he was war in the wode of a won in a mote,
275 Abof a launde, on a lawe, loken under boghes
Of mony borelych bole aboute bi the diches:
A castel the comlokest that ever knyght aghte,
Pyched on a prayere, a park al aboute,
With a pyked palays pyned ful thik,
280 That umbeteye mony tre mo then two myle.
That holde on that on syde the hathel avysed,
As hit schemered and schon thurgh the schyre okes;
Thenne has he hendly of his helme, and heghly he thonkes
Jesus and sayn Gilyan,† that gentyle ar bothe,
285 That cortaysly hade hym kydde and his cry herkened.
'Now bone hostel,' cothe the burne, 'I beseche yow yette!'
Thenne gederes he to Gryngolet with the gilt heles,
And he ful chauncely has chosen to the chef gate,
That broght bremly the burne to the bryge ende
290   in haste.
    The bryge was breme upbrayde,
    The gates wer stoken faste,
    The walles were wel arayed,
    Hit dut no wyndes blaste.

295 The burne bode on blonk, that on bonk hoved
Of the depe double dich that drof to the place;
The walle wod in the water wonderly depe,
Ande eft a ful huge heght hit haled upon lofte,

---

267 *pater and ave* opening words in Latin (and thus titles) of the 'Our Father' and 'Hail Mary'
284 *saint Gilyan* Julian 'the hospitaller' who, according to legend, succoured travellers and poor people

built of hard cut stone up to the cornices, with courses of masonry projecting under the battlements in the best style; and then elegant turrets constructed at intervals along the wall, with many fine loopholes that were neatly shuttered: a better barbican the knight had never seen. And further in he saw the lofty hall, towers set up here and there, thickly pinnacled, handsome turrets in matching style, and wonderfully tall, with carved tops ingeniously and skilfully made. He perceived there many chimneys pale as chalk gleaming whitely upon the tower roofs; so many painted pinnacles were scattered everywhere, clustering so thickly amongst the embrasures of the castle, that it looked just as if cut out of paper. The noble knight on his horse thought it handsome enough, if only he could manage to get inside the bailey, to lodge in that pleasant dwelling while the holy season lasted. He called aloud, and at once there came a very civil porter, who from the wall inquired his business, and greeted the knight errant.

PATIENCE

1–4 Patience is a virtue, though it often displeases. When heavy hearts are hurt by scorn or anything else, patience may soothe them and ease the sore, for she obliterates every evil and puts malice out.

5–8 For if one could bear misfortune, happiness would ensue, and he who, out of impatience, cannot endure, suffers more deeply. So it is better to bear the brunt occasionally than to keep giving vent to my impatience, painful though I find it.

          Of harde hewen ston up to the tables,
300   Enbaned under the abataylment, in the best lawe;
          And sythen garytes ful gaye gered bitwene,
          Wyth mony luflych loupe that louked ful clene:
          A better barbican that burne blusched upon never.
          And innermore he behelde that halle ful hyghe,
305   Towres telded bytwene, trochet ful thik,
          Fayre fylyoles that fyyed, and ferlyly long,
          With corvon coprounes craftyly sleye.
          Chalkwhyt chymnees ther ches he innoghe
          Upon bastel roves, that blenked ful quyte;
310   So mony pynakle payntet was poudred ayquere,
          Among the castel carneles clambred so thik,
          That pared out of papure purely hit semed.
          The fre freke on the fole hit fayr innoghe thoght,
          If he myght kever to com the cloyster wythinne,
315   To herber in that hostel whyl halyday lested,
                    avinant.
                He calde, and sone ther com
                A porter pure plesaunt,
                On the wal his ernd he nome,
320   And haylsed the knyght erraunt.

PATIENCE
Prologue

          Pacience is a poynt, thagh hit displese ofte.
          When hevy herttes ben hurt wyth hethyng other elles,
          Suffraunce may aswagen hem and the swelme lethe,
          For ho quelles uche a qued and quenches malyce.

5   For quo-so suffer cowthe syt, sele wolde folwe,
          And quo for thro may noght thole, the thikker he sufferes.
          Then is better to abyde the bur umbestoundes
          Then ay throw forth my thro, thagh me thynk ylle.

9–12 I heard on a holy day, at a high mass, how Matthew said that his master taught his disciples; he promised them eight beatitudes, and each one a reward, individually, for its merit, of a different kind.

13–16 They are blessed who have poverty in their hearts, for theirs is the kingdom of heaven to keep for ever. They are blessed also who practise humility, for they shall possess this world and have all that they desire.

17–20 They are blessed also who weep for their sins, for they shall obtain comfort in many lands. They are blessed also who hunger after righteousness, for they shall be fed abundantly on all good things.

21–4 They are blessed also who have pity in their hearts, for their reward shall be mercy in all forms. They are blessed also who are pure of heart, for they shall see with their own eyes their Saviour on his throne.

25–8 They are blessed also who keep their peace, for they shall be called fittingly the sons of God. They are blessed also who can control their hearts, for theirs is the kingdom of heaven, as I said before.

29–32 These are all the beatitudes that were promised to us, if we would only love these ladies in imitation of their virtues: Dame Poverty, Dame Pity, Dame Penance the third, Dame Humility, Dame Mercy and fair Purity,

33–6 And then Dame Peace and Patience put in as well; he who had one would be blessed; all would be better still. But since I am placed in a condition which is called poverty, I shall procure patience for myself and take pleasure in both.

I herde on a halyday, at a hyghe masse,
10 How Mathew† melede that his mayster his meyny con teche;
Aght happes he hem hyght, and ucheon a mede
Sunderlupes for hit dissert upon a ser wyse.

Thay arn happen that han in hert poverté,
For hores is the hevenryche to holde for ever.
15 Thay ar happen also that haunte mekenesse,
For thay schall welde this worlde and alle her wylle have.

Thay ar happen also that for her harme wepes,
For thay schal comfort encroche in kythes ful mony.
Thay ar happen also that hungeres after ryght,
20 For thay schal frely be refete ful of alle gode.

Thay ar happen also that han in hert rauthe,
For mercy in alle maneres her mede schal worthe.
Thay ar happen also that arn of hert clene,
For thay her Savyour in sete schal se with her yyen.

25 Thay ar happen also that halden her pese,
For thay the gracious Godes sunes schal godly be called.
†Thay are happen also that con her hert stere,
For hores is the hevenryche, as I er sayde.

These arn the happes alle aght that uus bihyght weren,
30 If we thyse ladyes wolde lof in lyknyng of thewes:
Dame Povert, dame Pitee, dame Penaunce the thrydde,
Dame Mekenesse, dame Mercy and miry Clannesse.

And thenne dame Pes and Pacyence put in therafter;
He were happen that hade one, alle were the better.
35 Bot syn I am put to a poynt that poverté hatte,
I schal me porvay pacyence and play me with bothe.

---

10 *Mathew* for the Beatitudes, of which lines 13–28 are a version, see Matthew 5.3–10
27–8 This is a reinterpretation, with greater relevance to the story of Jonah, of the eighth Beatitude: 'Blessed are they which are persecuted for righteousness' sake'

37–40 For in the passage where these two are discussed, they are presented in a single series, the first and the last, and, by the judgement of their Wisdom, receive one reward; and also, in my opinion, they are of one nature,

41–4 for where poverty presses her suit, she will not be cast out, but stays where she pleases, like it or not; and where poverty is burdensome, a man has no choice but to suffer greatly, say what he will, though it seem a torment.

45–8 So poverty and patience are necessarily playfellows; since I am beset by them both together, I have to endure. Then it is better for me to like it and to praise their ways, than to resist and be angry and suffer defeat.

49–52 If it is ordained to me to have an appointed destiny, what good does indignation do me, or resistance? Or if my liege lord wished to command me to go to Rome on horseback or foot on an errand for him,

53–6 what would complaining achieve, apart from inviting more trouble? Lucky if he did not compel me, despite my efforts, and then I would have to endure misery and displeasure as a reward, who should have complied with his order in accordance with my charge.

57–60 Did not Jonah in Judea once perform such an act of folly? To keep himself safe, he brings misery on himself. If you are willing to stop for a moment and attend to me for a while, I shall tell you about it as Holy Writ records.

I

61–4 It happened once within the boundaries of Judea that Jonah was appointed prophet to the Gentiles there. The voice of God came to him, which made him unhappy, whispered in his ear with an unpleasing sound:

65–8 'Rise quickly,' He says, 'and go forth at once; take the way to Nineveh without further talk, and spread all around in that city the teachings of mine which, when the time comes, I shall put into your heart in that place.

For in the tyxte there thyse two arn in teme layde,
Hit arn fettled in on forme, the forme and the laste,
And by quest of her quoyntyse† enquylen on mede;
40 And als, in myn upynyoun, hit arn of on kynde,

For ther as povert hir proferes ho nyl be put utter,
Bot lenge wheresoever hir lyst, lyke other greme;
And there as povert enpresses, thagh mon pyne thynk,
Much, maugré his mun, he mot nede suffer.

45 Thus poverté and pacyence arn nedes playferes;
Sythen I am sette with hem samen, suffer me byhoves.
Thenne is me lyghtloker hit lyke and her lotes prayse
Thenne wyther wyth and be wroth and the wers have.

Yif me be dyght a destyné due to have,
50 What dowes me the dedayn other dispit make?
Other yif my lege lorde lyst on lyve me to bidde
Other to ryde other to renne to Rome in his ernde,

What graythed me the grychchyng bot grame more seche?
Much yif he me ne made, maugref my chekes,
55 And thenne thrat moste I thole and unthonk to mede,
The had bowed to his bode bongré my hyure.

Did not Jonas in Judé† suche jape sumwhyle?
To sette hym to sewrté, unsounde he hym feches.
Wyl ye tary a lyttel tyne and tend me a whyle,
60 I schal wysse yow therwyth as Holy Wryt telles.

I

Hit bitydde sumtyme in the termes of Judé
Jonas joyned was therinne jentyle prophete.
Goddes glam to hym glod that hym unglad made,
With a roghlych rurd rowned in his ere:

65 'Rys radly,' he says, 'and rayke forth even;
Nym the way to Nynyve† wythouten other speche,
And in that ceté my sawes soghe alle aboute
That in that place, at the poynt, I put in thi hert.

---

39 *quoyntyse* possibly an allusion to Christ, often identified with Wisdom, who preached the Beatitudes in the sermon on the mount
57 *Judé* Judea (Judah); the southern kingdom of the Jewish people. Jonah is a native of the northern kingdom, Israel (see lines 205 and 463)
66 *Ninyve* Nineveh, Assyrian city on the river Tigris

69–72 For indeed those who live in that city are so wicked, and their evil is so great, I cannot endure it, but will avenge myself on their evil and malice immediately. Now hasten there quickly and proclaim this message for me.'

73–6 When that voice, which stunned his comprehension, ceased, he became enraged in his mind and thought rebelliously: 'If I comply with His bidding and bring them this message, and I am caught in Nineveh, then my troubles will begin.

77–80 He tells me those traitors are out-and-out villains; I arrive with that news, they take me straight away, shut me up in a prison, put me in the stocks, torture me in a foot-shackle, pluck out my eyes.

81–4 This is a wonderful message for a man to preach among so many enemies and cursed malefactors, unless my gracious God wished me such harm that I should be killed in punishment for some crime.

85–8 Whatever the risks,' says the prophet, 'I am going no closer; I will proceed some other way which He does not watch over. I shall go into Tarshish and stay there for a while, and perhaps when I am lost He will leave me alone.'

89–92 Then Jonah gets up quickly and goes straight away towards port Jaffa, always muttering in indignation that he would not put up with those torments for anything, even if the Father who created him were indifferent about his well-being.

93–6 'Our Lord sits,' he says, 'so high on His throne in His shining glory and is hardly concerned, though I am taken in Nineveh and stripped naked, torn apart miserably on a cross by a lot of ruffians.'

97–100 Thus he makes his way to that port to seek his passage; he finds a fair ship ready for the voyage, comes to an agreement with the sailors and gives them payment to take him to Tarshish as quickly as they can.

For iwysse hit arn so wykke that in that won dowelles,
And her malys is so much, I may not abide,
Bot venge me on her vilanye and venym bilyve.
Now sweye me thider swyftly and say me this arende.'

When that steven was stynt that stowned his mynde,
Al he wrathed in his wyt and wytherly he thoght:
'If I bowe to his bode and bryng hem this tale,
And I be nummen in Nunive, my nyes begynes.

He telles me those traytoures arn typped schrewes;
I com wyth those tythynges, thay ta me bylyve,
Pynes me in a prysoun, put me in stokkes,
Wrythe me in a warlok, wrast out myn yyen.

This is a mervayl message a man for to preche
Amonge enmyes so mony and mansed fendes,
Bot if my gaynlych God such gref to me wolde,
For desert of sum sake, that I slayn were.

At alle peryles,' quoth the prophete, 'I aproche hit no nerre;
I wyl me sum other waye that he ne wayte after.
I schal tee into Tarce† and tary there a whyle,
And lyghtly when I am lest he letes me alone.'

Thenne he ryses radly and raykes bilyve,
Jonas toward port Japh,† ay janglande for tene
That he nolde thole for no thyng non of those pynes,
Thagh the Fader that hym formed were fale of his hele.

'Oure Syre syttes,' he says, 'on sege so hyghe,
In his glowande glorye, and gloumbes ful lyttel
Thagh I be nummen in Nunnive and naked dispoyled,
On rode rwly torent with rybaudes mony.'

Thus he passes to that port his passage to seche,
Fyndes he a fayr schyp to the fare redy,
Maches hym with the maryneres, makes her paye
For to towe hym into Tarce as tyd as thay myght.

---

87 *Tarce* Tarshish is variously identified in the Old Testament, but is often associated with 'the ends of the earth'. Jonah is fleeing as far as possible
90 *Japh* Jaffa (Joppa), the port of Jerusalem

101-4 Then he stepped on board and they make their tackle ready, hoist the mainsail, fasten cables, quickly weigh the anchors on the windlass, smartly hitch the spare bowline to the bowsprit,

105-8 heave at the guy-ropes, the great canvas falls. They lay in their oars on the larboard side and gain the luff. Behind them the merry wind finds the belly of the sail; he swiftly swings this fair ship out of the harbour.

109-12 There was never as joyful a Jew as Jonah was then, who had escaped so boldly from God's control. He firmly believed that that being who created all the world had no power to harm anyone in that sea.

113-16 Look, the silly wretch, because he did not want to suffer at all, has now put himself into a state of much greater danger. It was a foolish hope that revolved in his mind that, though he might be gone from Samaria, God saw no further.

117-20 Yes, He looked far and wide: Jonah should have known that for sure. The speech which the king made told him that often: worthy David on high, who uttered these words in a psalm which he put into the psalter:

121-4 'Oh, fools among the people, have some sense now and then and understand occasionally, though you are deep in folly. Do you imagine that He who made all the ears does not hear? It is not possible that He is blind who created every eye.'

125-8 But he, foolish in his old age, fears no blow, because he was far into the sea, hurrying to Tarshish. But I believe that he was very quickly overtaken, so that he shot ignominiously short of his mark.

129-32 For the master of wisdom, who knows all things, who is ever vigilant and watchful, has resources at His command. He called on that very power He formed with His hands; they wakened much the more angrily because He called in anger:

Then he tron on tho tres and thay her tramme ruchen,
Cachen up the crossayl, cables thay fasten,
Wight at the wyndas weyen her ankres,
Spynde spak to the sprete the spare bawelyne,

105 Gederen to the gyde-ropes – the grete cloth falles.
Thay layden in on laddeborde and the lofe wynnes;
The blythe brethe at her bak the bosum he fyndes,
He swenges me thys swete schip swefte fro the haven.

Was never so joyful a Jue as Jonas was thenne,
110 That the daunger of Dryghtyn so derfly ascaped.
He wende wel that that wyy that al the world planted
Hade no maght in that mere no man for to greve.

Lo, the wytles wrechche, for he wolde noght suffer,
Now has he put hym in plyt of peril wel more.
115 Hit was a wenyng unwar that welt in his mynde,
Thagh he were soght fro Samarye, that God sey no fyrre.

Yise, he blusched ful brode, that burde hym by sure;
That ofte kyd hym the carpe that kyng sayde,
Dyngne David on des that demed this speche
120 In a psalme that he set the Sauter withinne:

'O foles in folk, feles otherwhyle,
And understondes umbestounde, thagh ye be stape in folé.†
Hope ye that he heres not that eres alle made?
Hit may not be that he is blynde that bigged uche yye.'

125 Bot he dredes no dynt that dotes for elde,
For he was fer in the flod foundande to Tarce.
Bot I trow ful tyd overtan that he were,
So that schomely to schort he schote of his ame.

For the welder of wyt that wot alle thynges,
130 That ay wakes and waytes, at wylle has he slyghtes.
He calde on that ilk crafte he carf with his hondes;
Thay wakened wel the wrotheloker for wrothely he cleped:

---

122 *stape in folé* the MS reads *stape fole*, which Anderson suggests may mean 'crazy-mad'. Other editors emend as here

133-6 'Eurus and Aquilon who sit in the east, blow, both of you, upon the dark waters at my command.' Then there was no delay between His words and their action, so prompt were they both to do His bidding.

137-40 Immediately out of the north-east the din begins, when both winds blew upon the dark waters. Rough storm-clouds came up, with a red glare beneath them; the sea roared very violently, awesome to hear.

141-4 The winds wrestle with each other so on the dark water that the waves in their madness rolled so high, and plunged back into the depths, that the terrified fish did not dare remain motionless anywhere at the bottom because of the turbulence.

145-8 When the wind and the sea and the boat came together, it was an unhappy craft that Jonah was in, because it twisted about on the rough waves; the blast struck it abaft, so that all their tackle broke.

149-52 Then the tiller and the stern crashed in a heap; first many ropes snapped, and then the mast; the sail collapsed on to the sea; then the ship had to drink the cold water, and then the cry arises.

153-6 Yet they cut the ropes and threw them all out of there; many a fellow leapt forward to bale out and toss overboard; wanting to escape, they scooped out the dangerous water, for however burdensome a man's load, life is always sweet.

157-60 There was a bustling about to throw packages overboard – their bags and their feather-beds and their many-coloured clothes, their chests and their boxes and all their casks – and all to lighten that ship, in case calm should ensue.

161-4 But the noise of the winds was unremittingly loud, and the water ever angrier and the seas wilder. Then the men, exhausted with their labours, thought that there was no remedy, but each one called on the god that profited him the most.

'Ewrus† and Aquiloun† that on est sittes,
Blowes bothe at my bode upon blo watteres.'
135 Thenne was no tom ther bytwene his tale and her dede,
So bayn wer thay bothe two his bone for to wyrk.

Anon out of the north-est the noys bigynes,
When bothe brethes con blowe upon blo watteres.
Rogh rakkes ther ros, with rudnyng anunder;
140 The see soughed ful sore, gret selly to here.

The wyndes on the wonne water so wrastel togeder
That the wawes ful wode waltered so highe,
And efte busched to the abyme, that breed fysches
Durst nowhere for rogh arest at the bothem.

145 When the breth and the brok and the bote metten,
Hit was a joyles gyn that Jonas was inne,
For hit reled on roun upon the roghe ythes;
The bur ber to hit baft, that braste alle her gere.

Then hurled on a hepe the helme and the sterne;
150 Furst tomurte mony rop, and the mast after;
The sayl sweyed on the see; thenne suppe bihoved
The coge of the colde water, and thenne the cry ryses.

Yet corven thay the cordes and kest al theroute;
Mony ladde ther forth lep to lave and to kest,
155 Scopen out the scathel water that fayn scape wolde,
For be monnes lode never so luther, the lyf is ay swete.

Ther was busy overborde bale to kest,
Her bagges and her fether-beddes and her bryght wedes,
Her kysttes and her coferes, her caraldes alle,
160 And al to lyghten that lome, yif lethe wolde schape.

Bot ever was ilyche loud the lot of the wyndes,
And ever wrother the water and wodder the stremes.
Then tho wery forwroght wyst no bote,
Bot uchon glewed on his god that gayned hym beste.

---

133 *Ewrus ... Aquiloun* Eurus is an east or south-east wind; Aquilo is usually a north wind

165-8 Some made their solemn vows there to Vernagu, some to holy Diana and to mighty Neptune, to Mahomet and Margot, the moon and the sun, and every man accordingly as he loved and had placed his affections.

169-72 Then the wisest spoke, very near despair: 'I believe some traitor is here, some lawless wretch, who has offended his god and is travelling here among us. Look, everyone is sinking because of his sin and perishing on his account.

173-6 I recommend that we give out lots to each man, and whoever the losing one falls to, throw him overboard; and when the guilty person has gone, what may a man believe but that He who rules the storm may have pity on the rest?'

177-80 This was agreed and they were assembled, chivvied out of each nook to take what is coming; a helmsman quickly leapt below deck to search out more men and bring them to the casting of lots.

181-4 But he could find no-one missing except Jonah the Jew, who lay sleeping out of sight; he had fled for fear of the roaring of the sea into the bottom of the boat, and lay on a board,

185-8 huddled by the rudder-band, for fear of the vengeance of heaven, fallen into a deep sleep, he snores, slobbering. The man kicked him with his foot and told him to get up quickly; where Ragnel in his chains may shake him out of his dreams!

189-92 Then he grabs him by the hasp-head, and picked him up by the breast and put him on the deck, asked him very roughly what reason he had for sleeping so soundly in such dire straits.

193-6 Soon they have prepared the lots and dealt them out separately, and the lot in the end always fell to Jonah. Then they immediately cried out upon him and asked very loudly: 'What the devil have you done, you mad wretch?

165 Summe to Vernagu† ther vouched avowes solemne,
Summe to Diana† devout and derf Neptune,†
To Mahoun† and to Mergot,† the mone and the sunne,
And uche lede as he loved and layde had his hert.

Thenne bispeke the spakest, dispayred wel nere:
170 'I leve here be sum losynger, sum lawles wrech,
That has greved his god and gos here amonge uus.
Lo, al synkes in his synne and for his sake marres.

I louve that we lay lotes on ledes uchone,
And who-so lympes the losse, lay hym theroute;
175 And quen the gulty is gon, what may gome trawe,
Bot he that rules the rak may rwe on those other?'

This was sette in asent, and sembled thay were,
Heryed out of uche hyrne to hent that falles;
A lodesmon lyghtly lep under hachches
180 For to layte mo ledes and hem to lote bryng.

Bot hym fayled no freke that he fynde myght,
Saf Jonas the Jwe, that jowked in derne;
He was flowen, for ferde of the flode lotes,
Into the bothem of the bot, and on a brede lyggede,

185 Onhelde by the hurrok, for the heven wrache,
Slypped upon a sloumbe-selepe, and sloberande he routes.
The freke hym frunt with his fot and bede hym ferk up;
Ther Ragnel† in his rakentes hym rere of his dremes!

Bi the hasp-hede he hentes hym thenne,
190 And broght hym up by the brest and upon borde sette,
Arayned hym ful runyschly what raysoun he hade
In such slaghtes of sorwe to slepe so faste.

Sone haf thay her sortes sette and serelych deled,
And ay the lote upon laste lymped on Jonas.
195 Thenne ascryed thay hym sckete and asked ful loude:
'What the devel has thou don, doted wrech?

---

165 *Vernagu* a Saracen giant in Charlemagne romances, whose name has here been appropriated to a pagan god
166 *Diana* Roman goddess of the moon   *Neptune* Roman god of the sea
167 *Mahoun* common name for a pagan god, derived from 'Mohammed'   *Mergot* Margot, a pagan god in Charlemagne romances, perhaps derived from 'Magog'
188 *Ragnel* name for a devil

197–200 Why are you seeking, you sinful villain, to lose each one of us on the sea with your vices so terrible? Man, have you no lord or god to call on, that you fall asleep in this way when you are about to be killed?

201–4 What country have you come from? What are you looking for here? Where in the world do you want to go, and what is your errand? Look, your fate is ordained for you, because of your evil deeds; give glory to your god before you go from here.'

205–8 'I am a Hebrew,' he said, 'born in Israel; the One I worship, certainly, [is He] who made all things, all the world with the sky, the wind and the stars, and all that dwells therein, with a single word.

209–12 All this trouble has been made on this occasion because of me, for I have offended my God and am found guilty; therefore carry me to the ship's side and plunge me overboard; until then you will have no luck, I truly believe.'

213–16 He showed them by signs which they understood that he had fled from the face of the most high Lord. Then such a fear possessed them, terrifying them inwardly, that they make haste to row and let the man alone.

217–20 Men hurried at speed to row at the ship's sides with very long oars since their sail had got away from them; they heave and haul with all their might to help themselves; but it was all useless effort that would not avail.

221–4 In the seething water of the dark sea their oars snapped; then they had nothing in their hands that could help them; then there was no comfort to be had, or any other counsel, except to consign Jonah to his fate immediately.

225–8 First they pray to the Prince whom prophets serve, that he might give them grace never to offend Him should they steep their hands there in innocent blood, even though the man was His that they killed here.

What seches thou on see, synful schrewe,
With thy lastes so luther to lose uus uchone?
Has thou, gome, no governour ne god on to calle,
200 That thou thus slydes on slepe when thou slayn worthes?

Of what londe art thou lent, what laytes thou here,
Whyder in worlde that thou wylt, and what is thyn arnde?
Lo, thy dom is the dyght, for thy dedes ille;
Do gyf glory to thy godde, er thou glyde hens.'

205 'I am an Ebru,' quoth he, 'of Israyl† borne;
That wyye I worchyp, iwysse, that wroght alle thynges,
Alle the worlde with the welkyn, the wynde and the sternes,
And alle that wones ther withinne, at a worde one.

Alle this meschef for me is made at thys tyme,
210 For I haf greved my God and gulty am founden;
Forthy beres me to the borde and bathes me theroute;
Er gete ye no happe, I hope forsothe.'

He ossed hym by unnynges that thay undernomen
That he was flawen fro the face of frelych Dryghtyn.
215 Thenne such a ferde on hem fel and flayed hem withinne
That thay ruyt hym to rowwe, and letten the rynk one.

Hatheles hyyed in haste with ores ful longe,
Syn her sayl was hem aslypped, on sydes to rowe,
Hef and hale upon hyght to helpen hymselven.
220 Bot al was nedles note, that nolde not bityde;

In bluber of the blo flod bursten her ores.
Thenne hade thay noght in her honde that hem help myght;
Thenne nas no coumfort to kever, ne counsel non other
Bot Jonas into his juis jugge bylyve.

225 Fyrst they prayen to the prynce that prophetes serven
That he gef hem the grace to greven hym never
That thay in baleles blod ther blenden her handes,
Thagh that hathel wer his that thay here quelled.

---

205 *Israyl* Israel, the northern kingdom of the Jewish people

229-32 Then they quickly seized him by the hair of the head and the toe, and they toss him straight away into that dreadful sea. No sooner was he thrown in than the tempest ceased; at that the sea became calm as quickly as could be.

233-6 Then though the tackle of those who lurched on the waves was torn, strong controlling currents took hold of them for a while, which drove them down relentlessly in the mastery of the deep until a gentler current swiftly sped them to shore.

237-40 Praises were sung to heaven when they reached land, to our merciful God in the manner of Moses, with sacrifice raised and solemn vows, acknowledging Him alone to be God and truly no-one else.

241-4 Though they rejoice for joy, Jonah is still terrified; though he did not want to suffer any harm, his well-being is in jeopardy; for what became of that man after he plunged into the water would be hard to believe were it not Holy Writ.

II

245-8 Now Jonah the Jew is condemned to drown; he was quickly pushed off that damaged ship. As fate then decreed, a wild whale, rolling about, that was driven from the depths, floated past that boat

249-52 and saw that man who went into the water, and swiftly swung round to swoop on him and opened its gullet. With the people still holding his feet, the fish quickly grabs him; without contact with any tooth he tumbled down its throat.

253-6 Then the whale swings and sweeps back and forth to the sea bottom, past many very rough rocks and surging currents with the man in his belly dazed with terror – it was not at all surprising if he suffered agony.

257-60 Because if the high King of heaven, through the power of His hands, had not guarded this wretched man in the monster's guts, who could believe that by any natural law he could be granted life for so long inside the whale?

Tyd by top and bi to thay token hym synne,
230 Into that lodlych loghe thay luche hym sone.
He was no tytter outtulde that tempest ne sessed;
The se saghtled therwith as sone as ho moght.

Thenne thagh her takel were torne that totered on ythes,
Styffe stremes and streght hem strayned a whyle,
235 That drof hem dryylych adoun the depe to serve,
Tyl a swetter ful swythe hem sweyed to bonk.

Ther was lovyng on lofte, when thay the londe wonnen,
To oure mercyable God, on Moyses wyse,
With sacrafyse upset and solempne vowes,
240 And graunted hym on to be God, and graythly non other.

Thagh thay be jolef for joye, Jonas yet dredes;
Thagh he nolde suffer no sore, his seele is on anter;
For what-so worthed of that wyye fro he in water dipped,
Hit were a wonder to wene, yif Holy Wryt nere.

II

245 Now is Jonas the Jwe jugged to drowne;
Of that schended schyp men schowved hym sone.
A wylde walterande whal, as wyrde then schaped,
That was beten fro the abyme, bi that bot flotte,

And was war of that wyye that the water soghte,
250 And swyftely swenged hym to swepe and his swolw opened.
The folk yet haldande his fete, the fysch hym tyd hentes;
Withouten towche of any tothe he tult in his throte.

Thenne he swenges and swayves to the se bothem,
Bi mony rokkes ful roghe and rydelande strondes,
255 Wyth the mon in his mawe malskred in drede —
As lyttel wonder hit was, yif he wo dreyed,

For nade the hyghe heven-kyng, thurgh his honde myght,
Warded this wrech man in warlowes guttes,
What lede moght lyve, bi lawe of any kynde,
260 That any lyf myght be lent so longe hym withinne?

261–4 But he was sustained by the Lord who sits so high, though he was without hope of salvation in the belly of that fish, driven through the deep as well, and rolling about in the dark. Lord, cold was his comfort and great his misery!

265–9 For he acknowledged every misfortune and trouble that befell him, how from the boat he was snatched into the seething water by a beast and tossed down its throat without more ado, like a speck of dust in a cathedral doorway, so huge were its jaws.

270–2 He passes in by the gills through the slimy filth, rolling in down an intestine which seemed to him a highway, always tumbling about head over heels till he fetched up in an enclosure as wide as a hall.

273–6 And there he finds his feet and gropes about, and stood up in the whale's stomach that stank like the devil. There in grease and filth that smelled like hell, was the bower provided for him who would suffer no harm.

277–80 And then he crouches down and looks for where the best shelter is, in each corner of the whale's bowels, but nowhere does he find either rest or safety but muck and filth, whichever intestine he goes into – but God is always kind.

281–4 And in the end he stayed there and called out to God: 'Now, Prince, have pity on your prophet. Though I am foolish and fickle and false in my heart, now forgo your vengeance through the power of mercy.

285–8 Though I am guilty of deception, the scum of the prophets, you are God and all good things are truly your own; have mercy on your man and his crimes, and effortlessly show yourself a lord in land and sea.'

289–92 With that he went into a corner and stayed there where there was no stain of any filth close to him. There he remained as safe, apart from a single mark, as in the bulkhead of the ship where he slept before.

293–6 So he remains alive in the bowel of that beast, three days and three nights, always thinking of the Lord, his power and his mercy, and then his compassion; now he acknowledges Him in sorrow who did not acknowledge Him in prosperity.

Bot he was sokored by that Syre that syttes so highe,
Thagh were wanles of wele in wombe of that fissche,
And also dryven thurgh the depe, and in derk walteres.
Lorde, colde was his cumfort, and his care huge!

265 For he knew uche a cace and kark that hym lympled,
How fro the bot into the blober was with a best lachched,
And threw in at hit throte withouten thret more,
As mote in at a munster dor, so mukel wern his chawles.

He glydes in by the giles thurgh glaymande glette,
270 Relande in by a rop, a rode that hym thoght,
Ay hele over hed hourlande aboute,
Til he blunt in a blok as brod as a halle.

And ther he festnes the fete and fathmes aboute,
And stod up in his stomak that stank as the devel.
275 Ther in saym and in sorwe that savoured as helle,
Ther was bylded his bour that wyl no bale suffer.

And thenne he lurkkes and laytes where was le best
In uche a nok of his navel, bot nowhere he fyndes
No rest ne recoverer bot ramel ande myre,
280 In wych gut so-ever he gos — bot ever is God swete.

And ther he lenged at the last and to the lede called:
'Now, prynce, of thy prophete pité thou have.
Thagh I be fol and fykel and falce of my hert,
Dewoyde now thy vengaunce, thurgh vertu of rauthe.

285 Thagh I be gulty of gyle, as gaule of prophetes,
Thou art God, and alle gowdes ar graythely thyn owen;
Haf now mercy of thy man and his mysdedes,
And preve the lyghtly a lorde in londe and in water.'

With that he hitte to a hyrne and helde hym therinne,
290 Ther no defoule of no fylthe was fest hym abute.
Ther he sete also sounde, saf for merk one,
As in the bulk of the bote ther he byfore sleped.

So in a bouel of that best he bides on lyve,
Thre dayes and thre nyght, ay thenkande on Dryghtyn,
295 His myght and his merci, his mesure thenne;
Now he knawes hym in care that couthe not in sele.

297–300 And the whale keeps on plunging along the savage depths and through many a rough region, through the pride of its will, because that speck in its throat made it, I believe – though that was tiny compared with itself – feel sick at its heart.

301–4 And as the man sailed on, assuredly he kept on hearing the mighty ocean on the whale's back, beating on its sides. Then the prophet sent up a prayer there very quickly; something like this, I believe, went his long speech:

III

305–8 'Lord, I have called to you in my bitter sorrows; you heard me out of the pit of the belly of hell. I called and you recognized my feeble voice. You plunged me into the dim heart of the deep sea.

309–12 The great flow of your ocean wrapped around me; all the currents of your depths and your bottomless pools, and your restless streams of so many tides pour over me in one rushing flood.

313–16 And yet I said as I sat on the sea bottom: "I am miserable, cast out from your clear eyes and separated from your sight; yet I confidently hope to walk in your temple and belong to you."

317–20 I am encircled in water till my misery stuns me; the abyss envelopes the body that I reside in; the foaming surge itself plays on my head. To the utmost limit of each mountain, sir, am I fallen.

321–4 The bars of every shore hold me very firmly so that I am unable to reach land, and you control my life; you must sustain me, Lord, while your justice sleeps, through the power of your mercy which is greatly to be trusted.

325–8 For when the fit of anguish was hidden in my soul then I duly recalled my noble Lord, beseeching him for pity to hear His prophet, that my prayer might enter His holy house.

Ande ever walteres this whal bi wyldren depe,
Thurgh mony a regioun ful roghe, thurgh ronk of his wylle;
For that mote in his mawe mad hym, I trowe,
300 Thagh hit lyttel were hym wyth, to wamel at his hert.

Ande as sayled the segge, ay sykerly he herde
The bygge borne on his bak and bete on his sydes.
Then a prayer ful prest the prophete ther maked;
On this wyse, as I wene, his wordes were mony:

III

305 'Lorde, to the haf I cleped in cares ful stronge;
Out of the hole thou me herde of hellen wombe;
I calde, and thou knew myn uncler steven.
Thou diptes me of the depe se into the dymme hert;

The grete flem of thy flod folded me umbe;
310 Alle the gotes of thy guferes and grundeles powles,
And thy stryvande stremes of stryndes so mony,
In on daschande dam dryves me over.

And yet I sayde, as I seet in the se bothem:
"Careful am I, kest out fro thy cler yyen,
315 And deseuered fro thy syght; yet surely I hope
Efte to trede on thy temple and teme to thyselven."

I am wrapped in water to my wo stoundes;†
The abyme byndes the body that I byde inne;
The pure poplande hourle playes on my heved;
320 To laste mere of uche a mount, man, am I fallen.

The barres of uche a bonk ful bigly me haldes,
That I may lachche no lont, and thou my lyf weldes;
Thou schal releve me, renk, whil thy ryght slepes,
Thurgh myght of thy mercy that mukel is to tryste.

325 For when th'acces of anguych was hid in my sawle,
Thenne I remembred me ryght of my rych Lorde,
Prayande him for peté his prophete to here,
That into his holy hous myn orisoun moght entre.

---

317 *to my wo stoundes* this puzzling phrase translates Jonah 2.6: *usque ad animam* ('even to the soul')

329–32 I have spoken with your learned men many a long day, but now I know for sure that those ignoramuses who pledge themselves to vanity and trifling matters renounce their forgiveness for a thing that amounts to nothing.

333–6 But I, who am regarded as a man of my word, devoutly promise to do solemn sacrifice to You when I am safe, and offer You a completely perfect gift for my well-being and regard what You command me as good: here receive my pledge.'

337–40 Then our Father fiercely tells the fish that it should spit him out quickly on bare dry land. The whale proceeds at His bidding and finds a shore, and there it spews up the man as our Lord commanded.

341–4 Then Jonah swept on to the sand in filthy clothes; it may well be that he needed to wash his cloak. The shore that he beheld lying round about him was of the very region that he had rejected.

345–8 Then a breath of God's speech upbraids the man again: 'Will you never go to Nineveh, by any route whatever?' 'Yes, Lord,' said the man, 'grant me grace to go at your pleasure; nothing else profits me.'

349–52 'Rise, then draw near the city, lo, to preach here. See, my teaching is locked in you: release it in there.' Then the man rose as quickly as he could and that night he came straight to Nineveh.

353–6 It was a vast city and marvellous in extent; just to pass straight through it was the work of three days. Jonah went without stopping on one day's journey before he uttered any word to anyone he met,

357–60 and then he called out in such a clear voice that everyone could understand; he described in this way the true purport of his subject: 'Forty days from now shall be completed, and then Nineveh shall be seized and utterly destroyed.

I haf meled with thy maystres mony longe day,
330 Bot now I wot wyterly that those unwyse ledes,†
That affyen hym in vanyté and in vayne thynges,
For think that mountes to noght her mercy forsaken.

Bot I dewoutly awowe, that verray bes halden,
Soberly to do the sacrafyse when I schal save worthe,
335 And offer the for my hele a ful hol gyfte,
And halde goud that thou me hetes, haf here my trauthe.'

Thenne oure Fader to the fysch ferslych biddes
That he hym sput spakly upon spare drye.
The whal wendes at his wylle and a warthe fyndes,
340 And ther he brakes up the buyrne as bede hym oure Lorde.

Thenne he swepe to the sonde in sluchched clothes;
Hit may wel be that mester were his mantyle to wasche.
The bonk that he blosched to and bode hym bisyde
Wern of the regiounes ryght that he renayed hade.

345 Thenne a wynde of Goddes worde efte the wyye bruxles:
'Nylt thou never to Nunive bi no kynnes wayes?'
'Yisse, Lorde,' quoth the lede, 'lene me thy grace
For to go at thi gre; me gaynes non other.'

'Ris, aproche then to prech, lo, the place here!
350 Lo, my lore is in the loke, lauce hit therinne!'
Thenne the renk radly ros as he myght,
And to Ninive that naght he neghed ful even.

Hit was a ceté ful syde and selly of brede;
On to threnge therthurghe was thre dayes dede.
355 That on journay ful joynt Jonas hym yede,
Er ever he warpped any worde to wyye that he mette,

And thenne he cryed so cler that kenne myght alle;
The trwe tenor of his teme he tolde on this wyse:
'Yet schal forty dayes fully fare to an ende,
360 And thenne schal Ninive be nomen and to noght worthe.

---

330 *unwyse ledes* presumably the 'ignoramuses' are not the same as the 'learned men' of the previous line

361-4 Truly, this town shall fall to the ground; you shall plunge upside down deep into the abyss, to be swiftly swallowed up by the dark earth, and everything that lives here shall lose its life.'

365-8 These words leaped forth into that place and spread all around to the burgesses and the young men that lived in that city. Such a terror seized them and a fierce dread that their demeanour changed and they were chilled at the heart.

369-72 The man still did not stop but kept on repeating: 'The true vengeance of God shall destroy this city.' Then the people mourned pitifully in silence, and in terror of God they grieved in their hearts.

373-6 They seized rough hair shirts that chafed sharply, and they bound them to their backs and their naked sides, poured dust on their heads and faintly pleaded that that penance would satisfy Him who complains of their evil.

377-80 And still Jonah cries out in that country until the king heard; and he quickly got up and ran from his throne. He tore his rich robe from his naked back and sat in the middle of a heap of ashes.

381-4 He urgently demands a hair shirt and fixed it round himself, sewed a sackcloth on top of it and sighed very woefully. He was stunned there in the dust, with tears falling down, bewailing all his evil deeds in a way to be marvelled at.

385-8 Then he said to his officers: 'Assemble quickly; proclaim a decree issued by myself, that all the beings who are alive in this city – both men and beasts, women and children,

389-92 every prince, every priest and all the bishops – all fast willingly for their evil deeds. Remove children from the breast, however distressed they are, and let no beast feed on any broom nor on any grass either;

393-6 let them go to no pasture and crop no plants, nor shall any ox go to the hay or horse to water. We must all cry out, racked with hunger, with all possible strength; the sound must rise to Him who shall have mercy.

Truly this ilk toun schal tylte to grounde;
Up so doun schal ye dumpe depe to the abyme,
To be swolwed swyftly wyth the swart erthe,
And alle that lyvyes hereinne lose the swete.'

365 This speche sprang in that space and spradde alle aboute
To borges and to bacheleres that in that burgh lenged.
Such a hidor hem hent and a hatel drede
That al chaunged her chere and chylled at the hert.

The segge sesed not yet, bot sayde ever ilyche:
370 'The verray vengaunce of God schal voyde this place.'
Thenne the peple pitosly pleyned ful stylle,
And for the drede of Dryghtyn doured in hert.

Heter hayres thay hent that asperly bited,
And those thay bounden to her bak and to her bare sydes,
375 Dropped dust on her hede, and dymly bisoghten
That that penaunce plesed him that playnes on her wronge.

And ay he cryes in that kyth tyl the kyng herde;
And he radly upros and ran fro his chayer.
His ryche robe he torof of his rigge naked,
380 And of a hep of askes he hitte in the myddes.

He askes heterly a hayre and hasped hym umbe,
Sewed a sekke therabof, and syked ful colde.
Ther he dased in that duste, with droppande teres,
Wepande ful wonderly alle his wrange dedes.

385 Thenne sayde he to his serjauntes: 'Samnes yow bilyve;
Do dryve out a decré, demed of myselven,
That alle the bodyes that ben withinne this borgh quyk,
Bothe burnes and bestes, burdes and childer,

Uch prynce, uche prest, and prelates alle,
390 Alle faste frely for her falce werkes.
Seses childer of her sok, soghe hem so never,
Ne best bite on no brom, ne no bent nauther,

Passe to no pasture, ne pike non erbes,
Ne non oxe to no hay, ne ho horse to water.
395 Al schal crye, forclemmed, with alle oure clere strenthe;
The rurd schal ryse to hym that rawthe schal have;

397–400	Who knows or can find out whether it will be pleasing to God, who is gracious in the exaltation of His nobility? I know His power is so great, though He be displeased, that in His mild gentleness He can find mercy.
401–4	And if we forsake the pursuit of our detestable sins and walk undisturbed in the path which He marks out Himself, He will turn aside from His fury and leave His anger, and forgive us this guilt, if we believe in Him as God.'
405–8	Then they all accepted his decree and forsook their sins, performed all the penance that the prince counselled. And God through His goodness forgave as the king said He would; though He had threatened otherwise, He withheld His vengeance.

IV

409–12	Great sorrow then descended upon the man Jonah; he became as angry as the wind towards our Lord. Such resentment has seized his heart that he summons up a prayer to the high Prince, because of his anguish, in this way:
413–16	'I beseech You, Sir, now judge Yourself: was not this which has now come about exactly what I spoke of in my country when You issued your command that I should go to this city to preach Your purpose?
417–20	I knew Your graciousness well, Your wise forbearance, the generosity of Your kindness and Your gentle grace, Your long-suffering in the face of injury, Your slow vengeance; and Your mercy is always sufficient, however great the crime.
421–4	I knew very well, when I had said whatever I could to threaten all these proud men who live in this city, that they might get their pardon with a prayer and a penance, and for that reason I wanted to flee far into Tarshish.
425–8	Now, Lord, take my life; it lasts too long; give me my death agony quickly and bring me to my end. For it would be sweeter for me to die at once, I think, than to teach Your doctrine any longer, You who make me a liar.'

What wote other wyte may yif the wyye lykes,
That is hende in the hyght of his gentryse?
I wot his myght is so much, thagh he be myssepayed,
400   That in his mylde amesyng he mercy may fynde.

And if we leven the layk of oure layth synnes,
And stylle steppen in the styye he styghtles hymselven,
He wyl wende of his wodschip, and his wrath leve,
And forgif uus this gult, yif we hym God leven.'

405   Thenne al leved on his lawe and laften her synnes,
Parformed alle the penaunce that the prynce radde.
And God thurgh his godnesse forgef as he sayde;
Thagh he other bihyght, withhelde his vengaunce.

IV

Muche sorwe thenne satteled upon segge Jonas;
410   He wex as wroth as the wynde towarde oure Lorde.
So has anger onhit his hert, he calles
A prayer to the hyghe prynce, for pyne, on thys wyse:

'I biseche the, Syre, now thou self jugge,
Was not this ilk my worde that worthen is nouthe,
415   That I kest in my cuntré, when thou thy carp sendes
That I schulde tee to thys toun thi talent to preche?

Wel knew I thi cortaysye, thy quoynt soffraunce,
Thy bounté of debonerté, and thy bene grace,
Thy longe abydyng wyth lur, thy late vengaunce;
420   And ay thy mercy is mete, be mysse never so huge.

I wyst wel, when I hade worded quat-so-ever I cowthe
To manace alle thise mody men that in this mote dowelles,
Wyth a prayer and a pyne thay myght her pese gete,
And therfore I wolde haf flowen fer into Tarce.

425   Now, Lorde, lach out my lyf, hit lastes to longe;
Bed me bilyve my bale stour and bryng me on ende;
For me were swetter to swelt as swythe, as me thynk,
Then lede lenger thi lore, that thus me les makes.'

429-32 The voice of our Sovereign then resounded in his ear, sternly upbraiding this man: 'Listen, man, is it right to rage so arrogantly on account of any action that I have taken or decreed for you up to now?'

433-6 Jonah, utterly miserable, grumbling, gets up and goes out on the east side of the noble town, and he settles down conveniently to wait in a field, in order to watch what would happen afterwards in that city.

437-40 There he made a bower for himself as best he could, out of hay and fern and a few grasses, for that place was bare of bending trees to provide shelter from the bright sun or cast any shade.

441-4 He curled up under his little arbour, his back to the sun, and there he fell asleep and slept soundly all night, while out of His kindness God made the fairest woodbind ever known to man grow above him from the soil.

445-8 When the Lord sent the daybreak, then the man woke up beneath the woodbind, looked upwards at the shimmering green leaves. No one ever had such a fine bower,

449-52 for it was broad at the bottom, vaulted above, shut in on either side as if it were a house, an opening on the north side and nowhere else, but all enclosed in a thicket that provided a cool shade.

453-6 The man looked at the pleasant green leaves which a wind shook continually, so mild and so cool. The bright sun shone round it though no ray, even the size of a tiny speck, could shine on that man.

457-60 Then the man was so delighted with his pretty shelter, he lies luxuriating inside it, looking towards the town; so happy with his woodbind which he sprawls underneath, that he gave no thought that day to any food – the devil take it!

The soun of oure Soverayn then swey in his ere,
430 That upbraydes this burne upon a breme wyse:
'Herk, renk, is this ryght so ronkly to wrath
For any dede that I haf don other demed the yet?'

Jonas al joyles and janglande upryses,
And haldes out on est half of the hyghe place,
435 And farandely on a felde he fetteles hym to bide,
For to wayte on that won what schulde worthe after.

Ther he busked hym a bour, the best that he myght,
Of hay and of everferne and erbes a fewe,
For hit was playn in that place for plyande greves,
440 For to schylde fro the schene other any schade keste.

He bowed under his lyttel bothe, his bak to the sunne,
And ther he swowed and slept sadly al nyght,
The whyle God of his grace ded growe of that soyle
The fayrest bynde hym abof that ever burne wyste.

445 When the dawande day Dryghtyn con sende,
Thenne wakened the wyy under wodbynde,
Loked alofte on the lef that lylled grene.
Such a lefsel of lof never lede hade,

For hit was brod at the bothem, boghted on lofte,
450 Happed upon ayther half, a hous as hit were,
A nos on the north syde and nowhere non elles,
Bot al schet in a schawe that schaded ful cole.

The gome glyght on the grene graciouse leves,
That ever wayved a wynde so wythe and so cole.
455 The schyre sunne hit umbeschon, thagh no schafte myght
The mountaunce of a lyttel mote upon that man schyne.

Thenne was the gome so glad of his gay logge,
Lys loltrande therinne likande to toune;
So blythe of his wodbynde he balteres therunder
460 That of no diete that day – the devel haf! – he roght.

461-4 And he kept on laughing as he looked all round the arbour and wished it was his own country, where he ought to be, high upon Mount Ephraim and the hills of Mount Hermon. 'Indeed, I never wanted to possess a finer house.'

465-8 And when nightfall drew on, he had to sleep; he falls slowly into a slumber under the leaves, while God sent a worm that dug up the root and the woodbind was withered by the time that the man awoke.

469-72 And then He orders the west wind to waken very gently, and commands Zephyr to blow warmly so that no cloud should form in front of the bright sun, which is to rise and shine far and wide, and burn like a candle.

473-6 Then the man woke from his sweet dreams and looked at the woodbind which was suddenly ruined. Those splendid leaves were all withered and wasted; the bright sun had destroyed them before the man was aware of it.

477-80 Then the sun rose and burned fiercely; the warm wind from the west makes the grass tremble; the man was in distress on the earth which was unable to hide him; his woodbind was gone, he wept for sorrow.

481-4 With bitter, blazing anger he calls out roughly: 'O You maker of man, what triumph does it seem to You, to ruin your servant in this way, more than anyone else? With all the trouble that You are capable of, You never spare me.

485-8 I procured for myself a source of comfort that now is taken from me, my woodbind so fair that sheltered my head. But now I see You are determined to take away my pleasure. Why do You not put me to death? I endure too long.'

489-92 Yet our Lord uttered a speech to the man: 'Is all this proud clamour of yours just, O man – to become so angry for a woodbind so quickly? Why are you so bad-tempered, man, about so little?'

And ever he laghed as he loked the loge alle aboute,
And wysched hit were in his kyth ther he wony schulde,
On heghe upon Effraym other Ermonnes hilles.†
'Iwysse, a worthloker won to welde I never keped.'

465 And quen hit neghed to naght nappe hym bihoved;
He slydes on a sloumbe-slep sloghe under leves,
Whil God wayned a worme that wrot upe the rote,
And wyddered was the wodbynde bi that the wyye wakned.

And sythen he warnes the west to waken ful softe,
470 And sayes unto Zeferus† that he syfle warme,
That ther quikken no cloude bifore the cler sunne,
And ho schal busch up ful brode and brenne as a candel.

Then wakened the wyye of his wyl dremes,
And blusched to his wodbynde that brothely was marred.
475 Al welwed and wasted tho worthelych leves;
The schyre sunne hade hem schent er ever the schalk wyst.

And then hef up the hete and heterly brenned;
The warm wynde of the weste wertes he swythes.
The man marred on the molde that moght hym not hyde;
480 His wodbynde was away, he weped for sorwe.

With hatel anger and hot heterly he calles:
'A, thou maker of man, what maystery the thynkes
Thus thy freke to forfare forbi alle other?
With alle meschef that thou may, never thou me spares.

485 I kevered me a cumfort that now is caght fro me,
My wodbynde so wlonk that wered my heved.
Bot now I se thou art sette my solace to reve;
Why ne dyghttes thou me to diye? I dure to longe.'

Yet oure Lorde to the lede laused a speche:
490 'Is this ryghtwys, thou renk, alle thy ronk noyse,
So wroth for a wodbynde to wax so sone?
Why art thou so waymot, wyye, for so lyttel?'

---

463 *Effraym . . . Ermonnes hilles* the highlands of Ephraim and the Mount Hermon range were in the northern kingdom of Israel
470 *Zeferus* the west wind

493–6 'It is not little,' said the man, 'but a matter of justice, more like; I wish I were out of this world, buried in my grave.' 'Then consider, man: if you are bitterly aggrieved, do not be surprised if I wanted to help my handiwork.

497–500 You have become so angry on account of your woodbind, and yet you never worked for the space of an hour to tend it; but at one stroke it grew here and was gone at another, and yet you are so upset you want to give up living.

501–4 Then do not blame me for my creation, that I wanted to help it and have mercy on those wretched people who cry out against their sin. In the beginning I made them myself from my own primal matter and then I watched over them for a very long time and had them under my governance.

505–8 And if I should destroy my work of so long duration, and overthrow that city when it had repented, the suffering of such a sweet place must penetrate my heart, there being so many sinful men lamenting within it.

509–12 And moreover there are some, such foolish simpletons as little children at the breast who never did any harm and ignorant women who could not distinguish one hand from the other for all this great world.

513–15 [They cannot tell the side of the ladder from the rung, nor what rule mysteriously separates the right hand from the left, though their lives depended on it.]

516–19 And also there are many dumb beasts in the city that cannot do any evil to their own detriment. Why should I be angry with them, when men want to repent and come to acknowledge me as king and believe in my words?

520–3 Were I as hasty as you, sir, disaster would have befallen; if I could only put up with things in the way you do, very few would have prospered there. I cannot be so harsh and still be counted gentle, because severity is not to be maintained without mercy within.'

'Hit is not lyttel,' quoth the lede, 'bot lykker to ryght;
I wolde I were of this worlde, wrapped in moldes.'
495 'Thenne bythenk the, mon, if the forthynk sore,
If I wolde help my hondewerk, haf thou no wonder.

Thou art waxen so wroth for thy wodbynde,
And travayledes never to tent hit the tyme of an howre,
Bot at a wap hit here wax and away at an other;
500 And yet lykes the so luther, thi lyf woldes thou tyne.

Thenne wyte not me for the werk, that I hit wolde help,
And rwe on tho redles that remen for synne.
Fyrst I made hem myself of materes myn one,
And sythen I loked hem ful longe and hem on lode hade.

505 And if I my travayl schulde tyne, of termes so longe,
And type doun yonder toun when hit turned were,
The sor of such a swete place burde synk to my hert,
So mony malicious mon as mournes therinne.

And of that soumme yet arn summe, such sottes formadde,
510 As lyttel barnes on barme that never bale wroght,
And wymmen unwytte, that wale ne couthe
That on hande fro that other for alle this hyghe worlde.

†[Bitwene the stele and the stayre disserne noght cunen,
What rule renes in roun bitwene the ryght hande
515 And his lyfte, thagh her lyf schulde lost be therfor.]

And als ther ben doumbe bestes in the burgh mony,
That may not synne in no syt hemselven to greve.
Why schulde I wrath wyth hem, sythen wyyes wyl torne,
And cum and cnawe me for kyng, and my carpe leve?

520 Wer I as hastif as thou, heere, were harme lumpen;
Couthe I not thole bot as thou, ther thryved ful fewe.
I may not be so malicious and mylde be halden,
For malyse is nogh to mayntyne boute mercy withinne.'

513–15 Some editors regard these lines (which repeat the sense of line 512) as a cancellation by the poet which has found its way by mistake into the MS

524–7 Do not be so angry, master, but go on your way. Be reticent and patient in pain and in joy; because he who is too hasty in tearing his clothes, afterwards has to sit in greater discomfort sewing them together.

528–31 Therefore when poverty bears down on me and many hardships, it behoves me to become reconciled very meekly with patience. Therefore penance and hardship make it quite plain that patience is a noble virtue, though it often displeases.

                                                              Amen

†Be noght so gryndel, godman, bot go forth thy wayes,
525　Be prevé and be pacient in payne and in joye;
For he that is to rakel to renden his clothes
Mot efte sitte with more unsounde to sewe hem togeder.

Forthy when poverté me enpreces and paynes innoghe,
Ful softly with suffraunce saghttel me bihoves.
530　Forthy penaunce and payne topreve hit in syght
That pacience is a nobel poynt, thagh hit displese ofte.

　　　　　　　　　　　　　　　　　　　　　　　　Amen.

524–7 These lines, here treated as addressed to the reader by the poet, may also be read as a continuation of God's speech to Jonah

Geoffrey Chaucer
c. 1343–1400

Geoffrey Chaucer was probably born in the early 1340s, the son of a prosperous London wine-merchant. He may well have attended a city grammar-school, at which the medium of instruction would presumably have been French and where he would have received a grounding in Latin language and literature. There is no record of this exceptionally widely read poet having proceeded to Oxford or Cambridge, though he knew these university towns well, or of his having received a legal training at the Inns of Court like other boys of his class. Chaucer's father was clearly ambitious for him: by the time he was fourteen or so he had secured a place in the household of the Countess of Ulster, later amalgamated with that of her husband Prince Lionel, son of Edward III (1327–77). Chaucer took part in the war with France before he was twenty, and by 1367 was in the service of the king. It seems that his knowledge of languages (he knew Italian as well as French and Latin) was among the skills which singled him out for diplomatic missions to Spain in 1366 and to Italy in 1372–3 and 1378. He married a woman called Philippa who was in the Countess of Ulster's household, and who may have been the sister of Katherine Swynford, mistress and later wife of John of Gaunt, duke of Lancaster. Between 1374 and 1386 Chaucer held senior positions in customs and excise, then a royal prerogative, which must have entailed constant dealings with both city and court. In the late 1380s and 1390s he held other posts in the patronage of the king, Richard II (1377–99), in what would today be the civil service. He died in 1400, the same year as the deposed Richard.

Chaucer's earliest long poem, *The Book of the Duchess* (an elegaic dream-vision probably written between 1368 and 1372 after the death of John of Gaunt's first wife), shows the detachment which characterises all his later poetry. It is not an unfeeling detachment; quite the reverse. Chaucer's command of language is such that he is able to project a range of attitudes and sentiments with deep sympathy. Nevertheless, he constantly juxtaposes one style with another, shifting from seriousness to humour, from pathos to irony. He characteristically uses literary forms which are open-ended or unresolved, as with the later dream-visions *The House of Fame* (? late 1370s) and *The*

THE PARLIAMENT OF FOWLS

Parliament of Fowls. If his forms are closed – as with the courtly romance *Troilus and Criseyde* (completed by 1387) – they are disconcertingly so.

The Parliament of Fowls, included here in full, was written in the late 1370s or early 1380s, and may have been composed for a St Valentine's Day celebration at court. If so, the poem is typically ambivalent about the central purpose of the feast, which always seems to have been associated with love and the choosing of partners. It is Chaucer's earliest poem in rhyme royal, the French-derived stanza he used for *Troilus and Criseyde* and some of the *Canterbury Tales*. It is also one of the first English poems to show the influence of the Italian poets Dante and Boccaccio (whose work Chaucer may have encountered during the Italian journeys of the 1370s). Around 1380 it must have been *avant-garde*.

The Parliament of Fowls is a tapestry of competing voices, as is, though on a much larger scale, *The Canterbury Tales*. In this, his masterpiece of detachment, Chaucer claims to be reporting a series of stories as he heard them during a pilgrimage to Canterbury. His self-presentation in the poem is characteristically ironic: when his own turn comes to tell a tale it is such doggerel that the other pilgrims beg him to stop. Chaucer's *persona* as pilgrim is a mask, as is his use of the other pilgrims for the expression of continually changing and self-contradictory outlooks. The indirection of this method is its meaning: we do not have to look behind the tales, or try to reconcile them, or choose one of them, to see if we can find what Chaucer himself believed. As a public servant Chaucer was probably good at regulating and harmonising matters; as a poet, on the other hand, he was uniquely conscious of the irreconcilability of things.

The text of *The Parliament of Fowls* is taken from W. W. Skeat's 1899 edition of Bodleian Library, Oxford, MS Fairfax 16, corrected against the variants listed in D. S. Brewer's 1960 edition.

The texts of the Pardoner's, Shipman's and Nun's Priest's Tales are from National Library of Wales, MS Peniarth 392D (Hengwrt MS).

THE PARLIAMENT OF FOWLS

The lyf so short, the craft so long to lerne,
Th'assay* so hard, so sharp* the conquering,   *the attempt painful*
The dredful* joy, that alwey slit* so yerne,*   *frightening passes quickly*
Al this mene I by love, that my feling*   *senses*
5   Astonyeth* with his wonderful worching*   *bewilders operation*
So sore, ywis,* that whan I on him thinke,   *indeed*
Nat wot* I wel wher that* I wake or winke.*   *know whether sleep*

For al be* that I knowe not Love† in dede,   *although*
Ne wot how that he quyteth folk hir hyre,†
10   Yet happeth me* ful ofte in bokes rede   *I happen to*
Of his miracles, and his cruel yre;
Ther rede I wel he wol* be lord and syre;   *wants to*
I dar not seyn* (his strokes been so sore),   *say*
But* God save swich* a lord! I can no† more.   *other than such*

15   †Of usage, what for luste, what for lore,
On bokes rede I ofte, as I yow tolde.
But wherfor that I speke al this? Not yore*   *long*
Agon,* hit happed me* for to beholde   *ago I happened*
Upon a boke, was write* with lettres olde;   *written*
20   And therupon, a certeyn thing to lerne,
The longe day ful faste I radde* and yerne.*   *read eagerly*

For out of olde feldes, as men seith,
Cometh al this newe corn fro yeer to yere;
And out of olde bokes, in good feith,
25   Cometh al this newe science* that men lere.*   *wisdom learn*
But now to purpos* as of this matere: *to the point*
To rede forth hit gan me so delyte,†
That al the day† me thoughte but a lyte.*   *little [space of time]*

---

1   [A reinterpretation of a proverb, well known in its Latin form: 'Ars longa, vita brevis est' – Art is long (= enduring), life is short]
8   [*Love* the god of love, who later appears as Cupid (see note to l. 212)]
9   *quyteth folk hir hyre* repays people
14   *can no* do not know any
15   Customarily, partly for pleasure, partly for knowledge
27   *gan ... delyte* delighted
28   *al the day* the whole day

    This book of which I make mencioun,
30 Entitled was al thus, as I shal telle,
    †'Tullius of the Dreme of Scipioun';
    Chapitres seven hit hadde, of hevene and helle
    And erthe, and soules that therinne dwelle,
    Of whiche, as shortly as I can hit trete,*   summarise
35 Of his sentence* I wol you seyn the grete.*   meaning substance

    First telleth hit, whan Scipioun was come
    †In Afrik, how he mette Massinisse,
    That him for joye in armes hath ynome.*   taken
    Than telleth hit hir* speche and al the blisse   their
40 That was betwix hem,* til the day gan misse;†   between them
    And how his auncestre, African* so dere,   Africanus
    Gan in his slepe that night to him appere.

    Than telleth hit that, fro* a sterry place,   from
    How African hath him Cartage* shewed,   Carthage
45 And warned him before* of al his grace,*   in advance fortune
    And seyde him, what* man, lered other lewed,†   whatever
    That loveth comun profit,† wel ythewed,*   well instructed
    He shal unto a blisful place wende,*   go
    Ther as* joye is that last withouten ende.   where

50 Than asked he if folk that heer be dede
    Have lyf and dwelling in another place;
    And African seyde, 'Ye,* withoute drede,'*   yes doubt
    †And that our present worldes lyves space
    Nis but* a maner* deth, what wey we trace,*   is only kind of tread
55 And rightful* folk shal go, after they dye,   righteous
    To heven; and shewed him the galaxye.†

---

31 *'Tullius . . . Scipioun'* 'Cicero on Scipio's Dream' [The *Somnium Scipionis* ('Dream of Scipio') was originally part of the *De Republica* ('Concerning the State') of the Roman lawyer and statesman M. Tullius Cicero ('Tully') (106–43 BC). The *Somnium Scipionis* was extracted around AD 400 from the extended work by the Late Latin writer Macrobius, who wrote an extended commentary on it in which he discussed the nature of dreams. It was Macrobius' edition of Cicero's *Somnium Scipionis* which was known in the Middle Ages]
36–7 [The *Somnium Scipionis* (see previous note) describes an occasion in 150 BC when the Roman general Cornelius Scipio Africanus the Younger ('Scipioun') visited Masinissa, king of Numidia in north Africa, who had been an ally of Scipio's adoptive grandfather, Scipio Africanus the Elder ('African'). The younger Scipio and Masinissa reminisced at length about Africanus, and that night Africanus appeared to Scipio in a dream, the substance of which Chaucer gives in lines 43–84, though with a Christian gloss]
40 *gan misse* came to an end
46 *lered other lewed* learned or ignorant
47 *comun profit* the common good
53 And that the extent of our life in the present world
56 [*galaxye* the Milky Way]

Than shewed him he the litel erthe that heer is,
At regard of⁺ the hevenes quantité;* — size
And after shewed he* him the nyne speres,⁺ — Scipio
60 And after that the melodye⁺ herde he* — Scipio
That cometh of thilke speres thryes* three, — thrice
That welle is of musyke and melodye
In this world heer, and cause of armonye.

Than bad he him, sin* erthe was so lyte, — since
65 And ful of torment and of harde grace,* — fortune
That he ne shulde him in the world delyte.
Than tolde he him, in certeyn yeres space,⁺
That every sterre shulde come into his place
Ther* hit was first; and al shulde* out of minde — where would (pass)
70 That in this worlde is don of* al mankinde. — by

Than prayde him Scipioun⁺ to telle him al
The wey to come unto that hevene blisse;
And he seyde, 'Know thyself first immortal,
And loke ay besily thou werke and wisse* — give instruction
75 To comun profit, and thou shalt nat misse* — fail
To comen swiftly to that place dere,
That ful of blisse is and of soules clere.* — pure

But brekers* of the lawe, soth to seyne,⁺ — breakers
And lecherous folk, after that they be dede
80 Shul alwey whirle aboute th'erthe in peyne,
Til many a world be passed, out of drede,* — without doubt
And than, foryeven* alle hir wikked dede, — forgiven
Than shul they come unto that blisful place,
⁺To which to comen God thee sende his grace!'

---

58 *At regard of* by comparison with
59 [*nyne speres* according to Ptolemaic (pre-Copernican) cosmology, the earth is encircled by nine concentric spheres bearing the Moon, Mercury, Venus, the Sun, Mars, Jupiter, Saturn, the fixed stars and, finally, the unmoving sphere of the *Primum Mobile* (first mover)]
60 [*melodye* musical notes made by the spheres as they rotate]
67 *in certeyn yeres space* after the duration of a fixed number of years
71 *prayde him Scipioun* Scipio asked him
78 *soth to seyne* to speak truthfully
84 To come to which, may God send you his grace

he doesn't receive awwre answers from Scipio's dream. The dream is an awthoratuie contribution to theme of love

THE PARLIAMENT OF FOWLS

85	The day gan failen,* and the derke night,	grew dim
	That reveth* bestes† from hir besinesse,*	takes away activities
	Berafte me* my book for lakke of light,	deprived me of
	And to my bedde I gan me for to dresse,*	get ready
	Fulfild of* thought and besy hevinesse;†	filled with
90	For bothe I hadde thing* which that I nolde,*	something did not want
	And eek* I ne hadde that thing that I wolde.*	also wanted

poet 90 — it is sfied

But fynally my spirit, at the laste,
Forwery of* my labour al the day,   exhausted by
Took rest, that made me to slepe faste,
95 And in my slepe I mette,* as I lay,   dreamed
How African, right in that selfe* aray   identical
That Scipioun him saw before that tyde,*   time
Was comen, and stood right at my beddes syde.

The wery hunter, slepinge in his bed,
100 To wode ayein* his minde goth anoon;   back
The juge dremeth how his plees ben sped;†
The carter dremeth how his cartes goon;*   go
The riche, of gold; the knight fight with his foon,*   enemies
†The seke met he drinketh of the tonne;
105 The lover met he hath his lady wonne.

Can I nat seyn if that the cause were
For* I had red of African beforn,   because
That made me to mete* that he stood there;   dream
But thus seyde he: 'Thou hast thee so wel born†
110 In loking of myn olde book totorn,*   tattered
†Of which Macrobie wroghte* nat a lyte,*   composed   not a little
That somdel* of thy labour wolde I quyte!'*   part   repay

The garden is idealised

---

86 *bestes* beasts, living creatures
89 *besy hevinesse* anxious depression
101 *plees ben sped* lawsuits have succeeded
104 The sick man dreams he drinks from the cask
109 *thee ... born* conducted yourself
111 [See note to l. 31. 'Macrobie' is Macrobius]

GEOFFREY CHAUCER

    'Citherea!† thou blisful lady swete,
    That with thy fyrbrand dauntest* whom thee lest,†   *subdues*
115 And madest me this sweven* for to mete,   *vision*
    Be thou my help in this, for thou mayst* best;   *are able to do*
    As wisly* as I saw thee north-north-west†   *surely*
    When I began my sweven for to wryte,
    So yif* me might* to ryme hit and endyte!*   *give power compose*

120 This forseid African me hent* anoon,*   *seized straight away*
    And forth with him unto a gate broghte
    Right of* a parke, walled with grene stoon,   *just by*
    And over the gate, with lettres large ywroghte,*   *worked*
    Ther weren vers* ywriten, as me thoghte,   *verses*
125 On eyther halfe, of ful gret difference,†
    Of which I shal yow sey the pleyn sentence:*   *clear meaning*

    'Thorgh me men goon† into that blisful place
    Of hertes hele* and dedly woundes cure;   *well-being*
    Thorgh me men goon unto the welle of grace,
130 Ther* grene and lusty May shal ever endure;   *where*
    This is the wey to al good aventure;*   *fortune*
    Be glad, thou reder, and thy sorwe* ofcaste,*   *sorrow cast off*
    Al open am I; passe in, and hy the* faste!'   *hasten*

    'Thorgh me men goon,' than spak that other syde,
135 'Unto the mortal strokes of the spere,
    Of which Disdayn and Daunger† is the gyde,
    Ther* tree shal never fruyt ne* leves bere.   *where nor*
    This streem you ledeth to the sorwful were,†
    Ther as* the fish in prison is al drye;   *where*
140 †Th'eschewing is only the remedye.'

---

113 *Citherea* Venus [The planetary goddess of love]
114 *thee lest* it pleases you
117 [*I saw thee north-north-west* the planet Venus was visible in the north-north-west (more or less) in May 1382, and this is often taken as an indication of the date of the poem's composition]
125 *of ful gret difference* very different indeed
127 [*Thorgh me men goon* an echo of the warning inscribed over the gate of hell at the beginning of Canto 3 of Dante's *Inferno* (the first part of the *Divine Comedy*): 'Through me one goes to the sorrowful city'. Chaucer seems to have become acquainted with the Italian writer's work when he visited Italy in the 1370s (see headnote)]
136 *Daunger* distance [In the code of manners practised in medieval courtly society, a woman of refinement was not expected to give her favours easily or quickly; the *daunger* of the beloved – her coolness or standoffishness – was both required by the courtly lover as an indication of her good breeding and yet tirelessly complained of]
138 *sorwful were* sorrowful weir
140 The only remedy is abstinence

Thise vers of gold and blak ywriten were,
The whiche I gan astoned* to beholde,   astonished
For with that oon* encresed ay my fere,   one
And with that other gan myn herte bolde;*   embolden
145 That oon me hette,* that other did me colde,*   warmed   cool
No wit* had I, for errour,* for to chese*   judgement perplexity choose
To entre or flee, or me* to save or lese.*   myself   lose

Right as, betwixen adamauntes two†
Of even* might, a pece of iren yset*   equal placed
150 That hath no might to meve* to ne fro –   move
For what that on* may hale,* that other   one draw forward
    let* –   holds back
†Ferde I, that niste whether me was bet
To entre or leve, til African my gyde
Me hente,* and shoof* in at the gates wyde,   seized shoved

155 And seyde: 'Hit stondeth* writen in thy face,   stands
Thyn errour,* though thou telle it not to me;   confusion
But dred thee nat* to come into this place,   do not fear
For this wryting is nothing ment by thee,†
Ne by noon,† but* he Loves servant be;   unless
160 For thou of love hast lost thy tast, I gesse,
As seek* man hath of swete and bitternesse.   sick

But natheles,* although that thou be dulle,   nevertheless
Yit that* thou canst not do, yit mayst thou see;   what
For many a man that may not stonde a pulle†
165 Yit lyketh him* at the wrastling for to be,   likes
†And demeth yit wher he do bet or he;
And if thou haddest cunning* for t'endyte,   skill
I shal thee shewen mater* of to wryte.'   material

---

148 [*betwixen adamuntes two* the adamant or lodestone is magnetic]
152 I was frightened, so that I did not know whether it was better for me
158 *is nothing ment by thee* is not intended for you at all
159 *Ne by noon* nor for anyone
164 *stonde a pulle* withstand a bout of wrestling
166 And still judges whether this one or that does better

	With that my hond in his he took anoon,	
170	Of which I comfort caughte, and wente in faste;	
	But Lord! so I was glad and wel begoon,*	happy
	For over al* wher that I myn eyen* caste	everywhere eyes
	Were trees clad with leves that ay shal laste,	
	Eche in his kinde, of colour fresh and grene	
175	As emeraude, that joye was to sene.	

	The bilder* ook, and eek the hardy asshe;	for building
	The piler* elm, the cofre unto careyne;†	vine-prop
	The boxtree piper,* holm* to whippes lasshe;†	for making pipes holm-oak
	The sayling† firr; the cipres, deth to pleyne;*	for mourning
180	The sheter† ew, the asp* for shaftes pleyne;†	aspen, poplar
	The olyve of pees, and eek the drunken vyne,	
	†The victor palm, the laurer* to devyne.*	laurel for foretelling

	A garden saw I, ful of blosmy bowes,*	flowery boughs
	Upon a river in a grene mede,	
185	†Ther as that swetnesse evermore ynow is,	
	With floures whyte, blewe, yelowe, and rede,	
	And colde welle-stremes, nothing dede,†	
	That swommen ful of† smale fisshes lighte,	
	With finnes rede and scales silver brighte.	

190	On every bough the briddes* herde I singe	birds
	With voys of aungel in hir* armonye,	their
	Som besyed hem hir briddes forth to bringe;	
	The litel conyes* to hir pley gunne hye,*	rabbits hurried
	And further al aboute I gan espye	
195	The dredful roo,* the buk, the hert and hinde,	timid roe-deer
	Squerels, and bestes smale of gentil kinde.*	superior species

---

177 *cofre unto careyne* coffin for a corpse
178 [*to whippes lasshe* for whip handles]
178 *sayling* for sailing [i.e. masts]
180 *sheter* for shooting [with bows]   *shaftes pleyne* smooth arrow-shafts
182 [The palm is an emblem of victory; the laurel leaf was believed, when eaten, to give prophetic powers]
185 Where there is abundant sweetness all the time
187 *nothing dede* not at all lifeless
188 *swommen ful of* were aswim with

	Of instruments of strenges in acord*	harmony
	Herde I so pleye a ravisshing swetnesse,	
	That God, that maker is of al and lord,	
200	Ne herde never better, as I gesse;	
	Therwith a wind, unnethe* hit might be lesse,	scarcely
	Made in the leves grene a noise softe	
	Acordant to† the foules songe onlofte.*	above

	The air of that place so attempre* was	temperate
205	That never was grevaunce* of hoot ne cold;	discomfort
	Ther wex* eek every holsom* spyce and gras,	grew health-giving
	Ne no man may ther wexe seek ne old;	
	Yet was ther joye more a thousand fold	
	Then man can telle; ne never wolde it nighte,†	
210	But ay cleer day to any mannes sighte.	

	Under a tree, besyde a welle, I say*	saw
	Cupyde our lord† his arwes* forge and fyle;	arrows
	And at his fete his bowe al redy lay,	
	And Wil* his doghter† tempred al the whyle	Desire
215	The hedes in the welle, and with hir wyle*	ingenuity
	She couched hem after as† they shulde serve,*	be put to use
	Som for to slee,* and som to wounde and kerve.*	kill cut

	Tho was I war* of Plesaunce* anonright,*	aware Delight immediately
	And of Aray,* and Lust,* and Curtesye;	Display Pleasure
220	And of the Craft† that can* and hath the might	knows how to
	†To doon by force a wight to do folye –	
	Disfigurat* was she, I nil not* lye;	deformed do not want to
	And by him self, under an oke, I gesse,	
	Sawe I Delyt, that stood with Gentilnesse.*	Graciousness

---

203 *Acordant to* in harmony with
209 *wolde it nighte* would it grow dark
212 [*Cupyde our lord* Cupid, son of the goddess Venus, whose arrows were believed to cause the joys and pains of love. This lordly and unfeeling figure (compare line 11) derives from a different iconographic tradition from that in which Cupid is depicted as a blind child]
214 [*Wil, his doghter* Cupid's allegorical daughter Will (and many of the other allegorical figures in lines 218–45) derive from the description of Venus' temple in Bk 7 of the *Teseida* by the Italian writer Giovanni Boccaccio (? 1313–1375)]
216 *couched hem after as* arranged them accordingly as
220 *Craft* artifice [Probably means 'dissembling skills']
221 Forcibly to compel a person to commit sin

225	I saw Beautee withouten any atyr,*	clothing
	And Youthe ful of game* and jolyte,	playfulness
	Foolhardinesse, Flatery, and Desyr,	
	Messagerye,† and Mede,* and other three –	Bribery
	Hir names shul noght here be told for me –	
230	And upon pilers grete of jasper longe	
	I saw a temple of bras yfounded* stronge.	erected
	Aboute the temple daunceden alway	
	Wommen ynowe,* of whiche somme ther were	many
	Faire of hemself,* and somme of hem were gay;	in themselves
235	In kirtels,* al disshevele,† wente they there –	tunics
	That was hir office* alwey, yeer by yere –	function
	And on the temple of doves whyte and faire	
	Saw I sittinge many a hundred paire.	
	Before the temple dore ful soberly	
240	Dame Pees sat with a curteyn in hir hond:	
	And hir besyde, wonder discretly,*	soberly
	Dame Pacience sitting ther I fond*	encountered
	With face pale, upon an hille of sond,*	sand
	And aldernext,* within and eek withoute,	nearest of all
245	Behest* and Art, and of hir folke a route.*	Promise crowd
	Within the temple, of syghes hote as fyr	
	I herde a swogh† that gan aboute renne;†	
	Which syghes were engendred with desyr,	
	That maden every auter* for to brenne*	altar burn
250	Of newe flaume; and wel aspyed I thenne	
	That al the cause of sorwes that they drye*	suffer
	Com of* the bitter goddesse Jalousye.	came from

---

228 *Messagerye* sending of messages
235 *al disshevele* with their hair all hanging loose
247 *swogh* sound like wind   *gan . . . renne* ran

	The god Priapus† saw I, as I wente,	
	Within the temple, in soverayn place* stonde,	highest position
255	In swich* aray as whan the asse him shente*	such put to shame
	With crye by night, and with his ceptre* in honde;	sceptre
	Ful besily men gunne assaye* and fonde*	attempted tried
	Upon his hede to sette, of sondry hewe,*	various colours
	Garlondes ful of fresshe floures newe.	
260	And in a privee* corner, in disporte,*	private recreation
	Fond I Venus† and hir porter* Richesse,*	door-keeper Wealth
	That was ful noble and hauteyn* of hir porte;*	proud demeanour
	Derk was that place, but afterward lightnesse	
	I saw a lyte,* unnethe* hit might be lesse,	little scarcely
265	And on a bed of golde she lay to reste,	
	Til that the hote sonne gan to weste.†	
	Hir gilte heres* with a golden threde	tresses
	Ybounden were, untressed* as she lay,	with hair loose
	And naked fro the breste unto the hede	
270	Men might hir see; and, sothly* for to say,	truly
	The remenant* wel kevered* to my pay†	rest covered
	Right with a subtil kerchef of Valence,†	
	†Ther was no thikker cloth of no defence.	
	The place yaf* a thousand savours swote,*	gave sweet
275	And Bachus, god of wyn, sat hir besyde,	
	And Ceres† next, that doth of hunger bote;†	
	And, as I seide, amiddes* lay Cipryde,†	in the middle
	To whom on knees two yonge folkes cryde	
	To ben hir* help; but thus I leet* hir lye,	their let
280	And ferther in the temple I gan espye	

253 [*Priapus* Priapus was a fertility god who, according to legend, tried to seduce a sleeping nymph but was forestalled at the crucial moment by the braying of an ass. 'In swich array' and 'with his ceptre in honde' presumably refer to his erect penis; Priapus was regularly portrayed with enlarged genitalia]
261 [*Venus* Roman goddess of love]
266 *weste* move towards the west
271 *to my pay* to my satisfaction
272 *subtil kerchef of Valence* delicately-woven bedspread
273 There was no less transparent cloth as a protection
276 [*Ceres* Roman goddess of the fruits of the earth]   *doth of hunger bote* provides a remedy for hunger
277 [*Cipryde* Venus, who, when she was born of the sea, was carried by winds to Cyprus which became a centre of her cult]

That, in dispyte of* Diane the chaste,† — in defiance of
Ful many a bowe ybroke* heng* on the wal — broken hung
Of maydens, suche as gunne hir tymes waste
In hir servyse; and peynted over al
285 Of many a story, of which I touche* shal — touch on
A fewe, as of Calixte† and Athalaunte,†
And many a mayde, of which the name I wante;* — lack

Semyramus,† Candace,† and Ercules,†
Biblis,† Dido,† Tisbe and Piramus,†
290 Tristram, Isoude,† Paris,† and Achilles,†
Eleyne,† Cleopatre,† and Troilus,†
Silla,† and eek* the moder of Romulus† – — also
Alle these were peynted on that other syde,
And al hir love, and in what plyte* they dyde. — plight

281–2 [*Diane . . . bowe* the Roman goddess Diana was a perpetual virgin and devoted herself to hunting with the bow]
286 *Calixte* Callisto [virgin follower of Venus; seduced by Jupiter and changed into a she-bear by Juno, she became the constellation, the Great Bear] *Athalaunte* Atalanta [originally dedicated to virginity, was turned into a lion with her husband when they desecrated a shrine by having sexual intercourse there]
288 [*Semyramis* legendary queen of Babylon, who, according to medieval tradition, committed incest with her son] [*Candace* had a child by her brother and was ordered to kill herself by their father] [*Ercules* Hercules' wife, jealous of his mistress, sent him a shirt steeped in what she thought was a love-potion, but which was in fact poison. Hercules burned to death]
289 [*Biblis* was in love with her brother and when he rejected her, went mad with grief and killed herself] [*Dido* killed herself when her lover Aeneas, hero of Virgil's *Aeneid*, left her] [*Tisbe and Piramus* Babylonian lovers; Pyramus killed himself in the mistaken belief that Thisbe was dead; she, finding his body, followed suit]
290 [*Tristram, Isoude* Tristram and Isolde, whose story is told in several medieval romances, drank a love-potion that bound them irrevocably; Tristram was killed by Isolde's husband, who was his uncle] [*Paris* a Trojan prince whose seduction of the Greek princess Helen led to the Trojan War, in which he died] [*Achilles* according to one tradition, the Greek hero Achilles fell in love with a Trojan princess and came unarmed to a meeting where he was killed by her brother, Paris]
291 [*Eleyne* Helen of Troy (see note to *Paris*, line 290); according to one tradition she eventually hanged herself] [*Cleopatra* queen of Egypt, who killed herself in 30 BC, after the defeat and suicide of her lover, the Roman general Mark Antony] [*Troilus* Trojan prince who, according to medieval legend, was killed in the Trojan War after being betrayed by his mistress, Criseyde. Their story is the subject of Chaucer's long poem *Troilus and Criseyde*]
292 [*Silla* Scylla betrayed her father and country for love of Minos of Crete; Minos repaid her by drowning her] [*the moder of Romulus* Rhea Silvia, a Vestal virgin who became secretly pregnant with the twins Remus and Romulus (founder of Rome), and died soon after their birth]

THE PARLIAMENT OF FOWLS

295	Whan I was come ayen* into the place	back
	That I of spak, that was so swote and grene,	
	Forth welk* I tho,* myselven to solace.*	walked then comfort
	Tho was I war* wher that ther sat a quene	aware
	†That, as of light the somer sonne shene	
300	†Passeth the sterre, right so over mesure	
	She fairer was than any creature.	
	And in a launde,* upon an hille of floures,	clearing
	Was set this noble goddesse Nature;	
	Of braunches were hir halles and hir boures,	
305	Ywrought* after† hir craft and hir mesure;*	constructed measurement
	Ne ther nas† foul* that cometh of engendrure,†	bird
	That they ne were prest* in hir presence,	ready
	To take hir doom* and yeve hir audience.*	judgement a hearing
	For this was on seynt Valentynes day,†	
310	Whan every foul cometh ther to chese* his make,*	choose mate
	Of every kinde,* that men thenke* may;	species conceive of
	And that so huge a noyse gan they make	
	That erthe and see and tree and every lake	
	So ful was, that unnethe* was ther space	scarcely
315	For me to stonde, so ful was al the place.	
	And right as Aleyn, in the 'Pleynt of Kinde',†	
	Devyseth* Nature of aray and face,	describes
	In swich* aray men mighten hir ther finde.	such
	This noble emperesse,* ful of grace,	empress
320	Bad* every foul to take his owne place,	commanded
	As they were wont* alwey fro yeer to yere,	accustomed
	Seynt Valentynes day, to stonden there.	

299–300 Who, just as the bright summer sun surpasses the star, so, immeasurably
305 *after* in accordance with
306 *Ne ther nas* Nor was there   *of engendrure* from the procreative act
309 [*seynt Valentynes day* 14 February. The idea that birds choose their mates on this day was a courtly fiction which is alluded to elsewhere in Chaucer and in *Le Songe Saint Valentin* by his French contemporary, Oton de Grandson. There may be a play on the words 'Valentine' and 'volantine' (= birds). The birds' final song 'Now welcom somer, with thy sonne softe' (lines 680–692) ignores the realities of an English February]
316 [*Aleyn, in the 'Pleynt of Kinde'* Alanus de Insulis (? 1128–1202) was the author of *De Planctu Naturae* ('The Complaint of Nature') which contains an immensely influential presentation of the goddess Natura]

That is to sey, the foules of ravyne* *prey*
Were hyest set; and than the foules smale
325 That eten as hem nature wolde enclyne,†
As worm, or thing of whiche I telle no tale;
But water-foul sat lowest in the dale;
And foul that liveth by seed sat on the grene,
And that so fele* that wonder was to sene. *many*

330 There mighte men the royal egle finde,
†That with his sharpe look perceth the sonne;
And other egles of a lower kinde
Of which that clerkes* wel devysen conne.† *learned men*
Ther was the tyraunt with his fethres donne* *grey-brown*
335 And greye, I mene the goshauk, that doth pyne* *inflicts torment*
To briddes for his outrageous ravyne.†

The gentil faucon,† that with his feet distreyneth†
The kinges hond; the hardy sperhauk† eke,* *as well*
The quayles foo,* the merlion* that peyneth* *foe merlin, falcon exerts*
340 Himself ful ofte the larke for to seke;
Ther was the douve with hir eyen meke;
The jalous swan, ayens* his deth that singeth; *approaching*
The oule* eek that of dethe the bode* bringeth; *owl warning*

The crane the geaunt,* with his trompes soune;* *giant trumpet's noise*
345 The theef, the chogh,* and eek the jangling pye;* *chough chattering magpie*
The scorning* jay; the eles* foo, the heroune; *mocking eel's*
†The false lapwing, ful of trecherye;
The stare,* that the counseyl* can bewrye;* *starling secret betray*
The tame ruddok;* and the coward kyte; *robin redbreast*
350 The cok, that orloge* is of thorpes lyte;† *clock*

---

325 *as hem ... enclyne* as nature wished to dispose them
330–1 [The eagle, traditionally the king of birds, was believed to be able to gaze directly at the sun]
333 *devysen conne* know how to describe
336 *outrageous ravyne* excessive violence
337 *gentil faucon* noble falcon *distryneth* holds fast to [Falconry – the art of training falcons to kill other birds – was an aristocratic pursuit]
338 *hardy sperhauk* bold sparrow-hawk
347 [The tradition of the lapwing's treachery may derive from classical myth: Tereus, who raped his sister-in-law Philomela and cut out her tongue, was changed into a lapwing]
350 *thorpes lyte* little villages

The sparow, Venus sone;† the nightingale,
That clepeth* forth the fresshe leves newe;   calls
The swalow, mordrer* of the flyës smale   murderer
That maken hony of* floures fresshe of hewe;   from
355 The wedded turtel,† with hir herte trewe;
The pecok, with his aungels fethres brighte;
The fesaunt,* scorner of the cok by nighte;   pheasant

The waker* goos; the cukkow† ever unkinde;*   watchful   unnatural
The popinjay,* ful of delicasye;*   parrot   wantonness
360 The drake, stroyer* of his owne kinde;   destroyer
The stork, the wreker of avouterye;†
The hote cormeraunt of glotonye;*   gluttony
The raven wys, the crow with vois of care;
The throstel olde; the frosty feldefare.*   thrush

365 What shulde I seyn? of foules every kinde
That in this worlde han fethres and stature,*   form
Men mighten in that place assembled finde
Before the noble goddesse Nature.
And everich of hem* did his besy cure*   each of them   care
370 Benignely to chese or for to take,
By hir acord,* his formel* or his make.*   agreement   female   mate

But to the poynt – Nature held on hir honde
A formel egle, of shap the gentileste
That ever she among hir werkes fonde,
375 The most benigne and the goodlieste;
In hir was every vertu at his reste,†
So ferforth,† that Nature hir self had blisse
To loke on hir, and ofte hir bek* to kisse.   beak

---

351 [*The sparow, Venus sone*   the sparrow was notorious for its lechery]
355 [*The wedded turtel*   the turtle dove was renowned for its fidelity]
358 [*the cukkow ever unkynde*   the cuckoo's unnaturalness stems from the fact that it lays its eggs in the nests of other birds; when hatched, the young cuckoo ejects the other occupants]
361 *wreker of avouterye*   avenger of adultery
376 *at his reste*   in its proper place
377 *So ferforth*   to such an extent

†Nature, the vicaire* of th'almyghty lorde,   *vicar, representative*
380 That hoot, cold, hevy, light, and moist and dreye
     Hath knit by even* noumbre of acorde,   *equal*
     In esy vois began to speke and seye:
     'Foules, tak hede of my sentence,* I preye,   *opinion*
     And, for your ese, in furthering of your nede,
385 As faste as I may speke, I wol me spede.*   *make haste*

     Ye know wel how, seynt Valentynes day,
     By my statut and through my governaunce,*   *rule*
     Ye come for to chese – and flee* your way –   *fly*
     Your makes, as I prik* yow with plesaunce.*   *stimulate   desire*
390 But natheles,* my rightful ordenaunce*   *nevertheless   dispensation*
     May I not lete,* for al this world to winne,   *abandon*
     That he that most is worthy shal beginne.

     The tercel egle,* as that ye knowen wel,   *male eagle*
     The foul royal above yow in degree,
395 The wyse and worthy, secree,* trewe as stel,*   *discreet   steel*
     The which I formed have, as ye may see,
     In every part as hit best lyketh me,†
     Hit nedeth noght his shap* yow to devyse,*   *form   describe*
     He shal first chese and speken in his gyse.*   *manner*

400 And after him by* order shul ye chese,   *in*
     After your kinde, everich* as yow lyketh,*   *each one   you please*
     And as your hap* is shul ye winne or lese;*   *fortune   lose*
     But which of yow that love most entryketh,*   *ensnares*
     God sende him hir that sorest for hir syketh.'*   *sighs*
405 And therwithal* the tercel gan she calle,   *thereupon*
     And seyde: 'My sone, the choys is to thee falle.†

     But natheles, in* this condicioun   *on*
     Mot* be the choys of everich that is here: *must*
     That she agree to his eleccioun,*   *choice*
410 Whoso* he be that shulde been hir fere.*   *whoever   mate*
     This is our usage* alwey, fro yeer to yere;   *custom*
     And who so may at this time have his grace,†
     In blisful tyme he com into this place.'

379–81 [Nature, as God's representative on earth, holds in balance the discordant elements of which the physical world is composed]
397 *hit best lyketh me* it pleases me best
406 *is . . . falle* has . . . fallen
412 *have his grace* receive favour

speech = summary of medieval courtly love. — Love is a subject of rhetorical display → creates theme of reflective + argumentative poetry.

With hed enclyned and with ful humble chere
415 This royal tercel spak and taried nought:
'Unto my sovereyn lady, and noght my fere,
I chese,* and chese with wille and herte and thought,   *choose*
The formel on your hond so wel ywrought,*   *fashioned*
Whos I am al and ever wol hir serve,
420 Do what hir list,† to do* me live or sterve.*   *make die*

Beseching hir of mercy and of grace,
As she that is my lady sovereyne,
Or let me dye present* in this place;   *immediately*
For certes,* long may I not live in peyne,   *indeed*
425 For in myn herte is corven* every veyne;   *cut*
Having reward* only to my trouthe,*   *regard constancy*
My dere herte, have on my wo* som routhe.*   *misery pity*

And if that I to hir be founde untrewe,
Disobeysaunt,* or wilful negligent,†   *disobedient*
430 Avauntour,* or in proces† love a newe,*   *boaster a new [love]*
I pray to you this be my jugement:
That with* these foules I be al torent†   *by*
That ilke* day that ever she me finde   *same*
To hir untrewe, or in my gilte unkinde.*   *cruel*

435 And sin* that noon loveth hir so wel as I,   *since*
Al be* she never of love me behette,*   *although promised*
Than oghte she be myn thourgh hir mercy,
For other bond can I noon on hir knette.*   *fasten*
For never, for no* wo, ne shal I lette*   *any cease*
440 To serven hir, how fer so† that she wende;*   *goes*
Sey what yow list,† my tale is at an ende.'

Right* as the fresshe, rede rose newe   *just*
Ayen* the somer sonne coloured is,   *in*
Right so for shame al wexen gan* the hewe   *became*
445 Of this formel, whan she herde al this;

---

420 *Do what hir list* whatever it may please her to do
429 *wilful negligent* perversely neglectful
430 *proces* course of events
432 *al torent* torn all to pieces
440 *how fer so* however far
441 *what yow list* whatever you like

She neyther answerde wel, ne seyde amis,*   *the wrong thing*
So sore* abasshed was she, til that Nature   *grievously*
Seyde: 'Doghter, drede yow* noght, I yow assure.'   *fear*

    Another tercel egle spak anoon
450 Of lower kinde,† and seyde: 'That shal not be!'
I love hir bet* than ye do, by seynt John,   *better*
Or atte leste* I love hir as wel as ye   *at least*
And lenger* have served hir, in my degree;   *longer*
And if she shulde have loved for long loving,
455 To me allone had been the guerdoning.*   *reward*

I dar eek* seye, if she me finde fals,   *also*
Unkinde, jangler,* or rebel any wyse,   *gossip*
Or jalous, do me hongen by the hals!†
And but* I bere me* in hir servyse   *unless conduct myself*
460 As wel as that my wit* can me suffyse,*   *reason allow*
Fro poynt to poynt,† hir honour for to save,*   *preserve*
Tak ye my lyf, and al the good* I have.'   *possessions*

The thridde* tercel egle answerde tho,   *third*
'Now, sirs, ye seen the litel leyser* here;   *time*
465 For every foul cryeth out to been ago*   *gone*
Forth with his make, or with his lady dere;
And eek Nature hirself ne wol nought here,
For† tarying here, noght half that I wolde seye;
And but* I speke, I mot* for sorwe* deye.*   *unless must sorrow die*

470 Of long servyse avaunte* I me no thing,*   *boast not at all*
But as possible is me* to dye today   *for me*
For wo, as he* that hath ben languisshing   *one*
Thise twenty winter,* and wel happen may†   *years*
A man may serven bet* and more to pay,*   *better pleasingly*
475 In half a yere, although hit were no more,
Than som man doth that hath served ful yore.†

---

450 *lower kinde*   less exalted species
458 *do me hongen by the hals*   have me hanged by the neck
461 *Fro poynt to poynt*   from beginning to end
468 *For*   in order to avoid
473 *wel happen may*   it may well come about that
476 *ful yore*   for a very long time

I say not this by me,† for I ne can
Do no servyse that may my lady plese;
But I dar seyn I am hir trewest man
480 As to my dome,† and feynest* wolde hir ese;*   most gladly   please
At shorte wordes,† til that deth me sese,*   put an end to
I wol ben hires, whether I wake or winke,*   sleep
And trewe in al that herte may bethinke.'*   imagine

Of al my lyf, sin that day I was born,
485 So gentil plee* in love or other thing   refined appeal
Ne herde never no man me beforn,
Whoso that* hadde leyser and cunning*   whoever   skill
For to rehers* hir chere* and hir speking;   relate   their demeanour
And from the morwe* gan this speche laste   morning
490 Til dounward drow* the sonne wonder faste.   moved

The noyse of foules for to ben delivered*   released
So loude rong: 'Have doon and let us wende!'*   go
That wel wende I* the wode had al toshivered.*   I believed   splintered
'Come of!'* they cryde, 'Allas! ye wil us shende!'*   hurry up   ruin
495 Whan shal your cursed pleding* have an ende?   argument
How shulde a juge eyther party leve,*   believe
For yee or nay,† withouten any preve?'*   proof

The goos, the cokkow, and the doke also
So cryden 'Kek, kek!' 'Kukkow!' 'Quek, quek!' hye*   loudly
500 That thorgh myn eres the noyse wente tho.*   then
The goos seyde, 'Al this nis not worth a flye!
But I can shape hereof† a remedye,
And I wol sey my verdit faire and swythe*   promptly
†For water-foul, whoso be wrooth or blythe.'

---

477 *by me*   on my own account
480 *As to my dome*   in my opinion
481 *At short wordes*   to speak briefly
497 *For yee or nay*   in order to say yes or no
502 *shape hereof*   devise for this
504 On behalf of water birds, like it or not
504 ff. [Chaucer's division of the birds into birds of prey, water fowl, worm-eaters and seed-eaters, derives from medieval encyclopaedic lore, and parallels the divisions in his own society]

505   'And I for worm-foul,' seyde the fool* cukkow,   foolish
       'For I wol, of myn owne auctorité,*   authority
       For comune spede,† take the charge now,
       For to delivere* us is gret charité.'   release
       'Ye may abyde* a whyle yet, pardé,'*   stay for sure
510   †Seide the turtel, 'If hit be your wille
       †A wight may speke, him were as good be stille.

       I am a seed-foul, oon* the unworthieste,   one of
       That wot* I wel, and litel of kunninge,*   know knowledge
       But bet* is that a wightes tonge reste   better
515   Than entremeten him of* such doinge   meddle with
       Of which he neyther rede can nor singe.
       And who so doth, ful foule* himself acloyeth,* shamefully overloads
       †For office uncommitted ofte anoyeth.'

       Nature, which that alway had an ere
520   To murmour of the lewednes* behinde,   foolishness
       With facound* voys seide: 'Hold your tonges there!   eloquent
       And I shal sone,* I hope, a counseyl* finde   shortly plan
       You to delivere, and fro this noyse unbinde;
       I juge, of every folk† men shal oon calle
525   To seyn the verdit for you foules alle.'

       Assented were to this conclusioun
       The bridddes alle; and foules of ravyne*   prey
       Han chosen first, by pleyn eleccioun,*   open choice
       The tercelet of the faucon,† to diffyne*   state
530   †Al hir sentence, and as him list, termyne;
       And to Nature him gonnen to presente,†
       And she accepteth him with glad entente.*   gladly

---

507   *comune spede*   for the advantage of everyone
510–11   The turtle-dove said, 'If (the rest of) you will allow a person to speak, (I think) he [i.e. the cuckoo] should remain silent
518   For (performing) a duty not entrusted to one often causes trouble
524   *of every folk*   from every species
529   *tercelet of the faucon*   male falcon
530   The views of them all, and to set them out as he saw fit
531   *gonnen to presente*   they presented

THE PARLIAMENT OF FOWLS

The tercelet seide than in this manere:
'Ful hard* were hit to preve hit by resoun   *very difficult*
535 Who loveth best this gentil formel here;
For everich* hath swich replicacioun,†   *each one*
That noon by skilles* may be broght adoun;   *arguments*
I can not seen that arguments avayle;
Than semeth hit ther moste be batayle.'†

540 'Al redy!' quod these egles tercels tho.
'Nay, sirs!' quod he, 'If that I dorste* it seye,   *dared*
Ye doon me wrong, my tale is not ydo.*   *finished*
For sirs, ne taketh noght agref,† I preye,
It may noght gon* as ye wolde in this weye;   *proceed*
545 Oure is the voys that han the charge in honde,†
And to the juges dome* ye moten* stonde;   *decision must*

And therfor pees! I seye, as to my wit,*   *as I understand it*
Me wolde thinke* how that the worthieste   *it would seem to me*
Of knighthode, and lengest hath used hit,†
550 Moste of estat,† of blode the gentileste,*   *most noble*
Were sittingest* for hir, if that hir leste;†   *most fitting*
And of these three she wot* hirself, I trowe,*   *knows believe*
Which that he be, for hit is light* to knowe.'   *easy*

The water-foules han her hedes leyd
555 Togeder, and of short avysement,*   *consultation*
Whan everich had his large golee* seyd,   *mouthful*
They seyden sothly,* al by oon assent,*   *truly unanimously*
How that 'the goos, with hir facounde gent,*   *graceful eloquence*
That so desyreth to pronounce* our nede,   *declare*
560 Shal telle our tale,' and preyde 'God hir spede.'*   *help*

---

536 *swich replicacioun* such an answer
539 [*ther moste be batayle* the eagles, who represent the nobility, turn instinctively to the judicial duel, for which their class is specifically trained]
543 *ne taketh noght agref* do not take it amiss
545 *han the charge in honde* have the matter in hand
549 *lengest hath used it* [the one who] has practised it longest
550 *Moste of estat* highest in rank
551 *hir leste* it is agreeable to her

And for these water-foules tho* began — then
The goos to speke, and in hir cakelinge
She seyde, 'Pees! now tak kepe* every man, — pay heed
†And herkeneth which a reson I shal bringe;
My wit is sharp, I love no taryinge; (565)
I seye, I rede* him, though he were my brother, — advise
But* she wol love him, lat him love another!' — unless

'Lo here! a parfit* reson of a goos!' — perfect
Quod the sperhauk; 'Never mot she thee!†
Lo, swich hit is† to have a tonge loos! (570)
Now pardé,* fool, yet were hit bet* for thee — indeed better
Have holde thy pees, than shewed thy nyceté!* — foolishness
Hit lyth* not in his wit* nor in his wille, — rests intelligence
But sooth* is seyd, "a fool can noght be stille."' — truly

The laughter aroos of gentil foules alle, (575)
And right anoon* the seed-foul chosen hadde — straight away
The turtel trewe, and gunne hir to hem calle,
And preyden hir to seye the sothe sadde* — plain truth
Of this matere, and asked what she radde;* — advised
And she answerde, that pleynly hir entente* — opinion (580)
She wolde shewe, and sothly what she mente.

'Nay, God forbede a lover shulde chaunge!'
The turtel seyde, and wex* for shame al reed; — became
'Thogh that his lady evermore be straunge,* — distant
Yet let him serve hir ever, til he be deed; (585)
For sothe, I preyse noght the gooses reed;* — advice
For thogh she deyde,* I wolde† non other make,* — died mate
I wol ben hires, til that the deth me take.'

---

564 And listen to what argument I shall put forward
569 *Never mot she thee* may she never thrive
570 *swich it is* this is what it's like
587 *wolde* would not want

'Wel bourded,'† quod* the doke,* 'by my hat!   *said*   *duck*
590   That men shulde alwey* loven, causeles,*   *always*   *for no reason*
     Who can a reson* finde or wit in that?   *sense*
     Daunceth he mury* that is mirtheles?   *happily*
     †Who shulde recche of that is reccheles?
     Ye, quek!' yit quod the doke, ful wel and faire,
595   'There been mo* sterres, God wot,* than a paire!'   *more*   *knows*

     'Now fy, cherl!'* quod the gentil tercelet,   *boor*
     'Out of the dunghil com that word ful right,
     Thou canst noght see which* thing is wel beset:*   *what*   *employed*
     Thou farest by† love as oules doon by light,
600   The day hem blent,* ful wel they see by night;   *blinds them*
     Thy kind* is of so lowe a wrechednesse,*   *species*   *baseness*
     That what love is, thou canst nat see ne gesse.'

     Tho gan the cukkow putte him forth in prees†
     For foul that eteth worm, and seide blyve,*   *quickly*
605   'So I,'* quod he, 'may have my make in pees,   *so long as I*
     I recche not how longe that ye stryve;*   *quarrel*
     Lat ech of hem be soleyn* al hir lyve,   *single*
     This is my reed,* sin* they may not acorde;   *advice*   *since*
     This shorte lesson nedeth noght recorde.'*   *repeat*

610   †"Ye! have the glotoun fild ynogh his paunche,
     Than are we wel!' seyde the merlioun;*   *merlin, falcon*
     'Thou mordrer of the heysugge† on the braunche
     That broghte thee forth, thou reufulles* glotoun!   *pitiless*
     Live thou soleyn, wormes corrupcioun!
615   †For no fors is of lakke of thy nature;
     Go, lewed* be thou, whyl the world may dure!'*   *ignorant*   *last*

---

589   *Wel bourded*   what a good joke
593   Who should pay heed to what is heedless?
599   *farest by*   act in respect of
603   *putte him forth in presse*   thrust forward
610   Yes, if the glutton has filled his stomach enough
612   *mordrer of the heysugge*   murderer of the hedge-sparrow
615   For the lack of your species is of no consequence

    'Now pees,' quod Nature, 'I comaunde here;
    For I have herd al your opinioun,
    And in effect yet be we never the nere;*   *closer*
620 But fynally, this is my conclusioun,
    That she hirself shal han the eleccioun*   *choice*
    Of whom hir list,† whoso* be wrooth* or blythe,   *whoever angry*
    Him that she cheest,* he shal hir have as swythe.*   *chooses directly*

    For sith* hit may not here discussed* be   *since settled*
625 Who loveth hir best, as seide the tercelet,
    Than wol I doon* hir this favour, that she   *do*
    Shal have right* him on whom hir herte is set,   *just*
    And he hir that his herte hath on hir knet.*   *fastened*
    This juge I, Nature, for I may not lyë;
630 To noon estat* I have non other yë.†   *rank*

    But as for counseyl* for to chese a make,   *advice*
    If I were Reson, certes,* than wolde I   *assuredly*
    Counseyle yow the royal tercel take,
    As seide the tercelet ful skilfully,*   *reasonably*
635 As for the gentilest and most worthy,
    Which I have wroght* so wel to my plesaunce;*   *fashioned delight*
    That to yow oghte been a suffisaunce.'*   *enough*

    With dredful* vois the formel hir answerde,   *timid*
    'My rightful lady, goddesse of Nature,
640 Soth* is that I am ever* under your yerde,*   *true always authority*
    Lyk as is everiche other creature,
    And moot* be youres whyl my lyf may dure;   *must*
    And therfor graunteth me my firste bone,*   *boon, request*
    And myn entente* I wol yow sey right sone.'   *opinion*

645 'I graunte it you,' quod she; and right anoon
    This formel egle spak in this degree,*   *manner*
    'Almighty quene, unto* this yeer be doon*   *until ended*
    I aske respit* for to avysen me,*   *respite consider*
    And after that to have my choys al free;
650 This al and som,* that I wolde speke and seye;   *the entirety*
    Ye gete no more, although ye do me deye.†

---

622 *hir list*   she pleases
630 *have non other yë*   pay any particular regard
651 *do me deye*   put me to death

†I wol noght serven Venus ne Cupyde
For sothe as yet, by no manere wey.'*   in any way at all
'Now sin* it may non other wyse betyde,'*   since   happen
655 Quod tho Nature, 'here is no more to sey;
Than wolde I that these foules were awey
Ech with his make, for tarying* lenger here' –   to avoid delaying
And seyde hem thus, as ye shul after here.

'To you speke I, ye tercelets,' quod Nature,
660 'Beth* of good herte and serveth, alle three;   be
A yeer is not so longe to endure,
And ech of yow peyne him,* in his degree,   take pains
For to do wel; for, God wot, quit* is she   free
Fro yow this yeer; what after so befalle,†
665 This entremes* is dressed* for you alle.'   interval   arranged

And whan this werk* al broght was to an ende,   business
To every foule Nature yaf* his make   gave
By even acorde,* and on hir* wey they wende. exact agreement their
A! lord! the blisse and joye that they make!
670 For ech of hem gan other in winges take,
And with hir nekkes ech gan other winde,
Thanking alwey the noble goddesse of kinde.*   nature

But first were chosen foules for to singe,
As yeer by yere was alwey hir usaunce*   custom
675 To singe a roundel at hir departinge,
To do Nature honour and plesaunce.
The note,* I trowe,* maked was in Fraunce;   tune believe
The wordes wer swich* as ye may heer finde,   such
The nexte vers, as I now have in minde.

680 †'Now welcom somer, with thy sonne softe,
That hast this wintres wederes* overshake,*   storms shaken off
And driven awey the longe nightes blake!

652–3 ['In truth, I do not want to have anything at all to do with love yet'. The formel seems to be implying that she is still too young for love]
664 *what after so befalle* whatever happens later
680–92 [the birds sing a roundel, a French lyric form in which the opening lines recur at the middle and end. It may, as line 677 suggests, have been written for an already existing French tune, as were many court songs]

GEOFFREY CHAUCER

      Seynt Valentyn, that art ful hy onlofte;* —   *above*
      Thus singen smale foules for thy sake —
685   *Now welcom somer, with thy sonne softe,*
      That hast this wintres weders overshake.

      Wel han* they cause for to gladen* ofte,   *have rejoice*
      Sith ech of hem recovered hath his make;
      Ful blisful may they singen whan they wake;
690   *Now welcom somer, with thy sonne softe,*
      That hast this wintres weders overshake,
      And driven awey the longe nightes blake.'

      And with the showting, whan hir song was do,*   *done*
      That foules maden at hir flight away,
695   I wook,* and other bokes took me to   *awoke*
      To rede upon, and yet I rede alway;
      I hope, ywis, to rede so som day
      That I shal mete* som thing for to fare*   *dream do*
      The bet,* and thus to rede I nil not spare.*   *better cease*

The Pardoner's Prologue and Tale

A pardoner – who was usually a cleric but not necessarily a priest – was licensed by the ecclesiastical authorities to issue indulgences or pardons to people who had confessed their sins to a priest and been absolved, but who still faced punishment after death in purgatory. A pardon, guaranteed by the pope, could remit that punishment. The person who received a pardon would in return give the pardoner a free donation to a specified charity. It was not the intention that pardons should be directly sold but the system was obviously open to abuse. Chaucer's Pardoner sells spurious relics for which he claims magical powers; he also sells absolution or forgiveness for sin (at lines 57–60, for example). He uses preaching as his salesman's patter, designed to make gullible and ignorant people buy his shoddy goods.

The Pardoner's Prologue is modelled in part on the self-revealing monologue of Faux Semblant (False Seeming) in the thirteenth-century *Le Roman de la Rose* (The Romance of the Rose) by Guillaume de Lorris and Jean de Meung. The Tale itself has the structure of a sermon on the sins of the tavern; the text is 'Covetousness is the root of all evil', and the embedded tale of the young men's quest for death is used as an *exemplum*, or extended moral lesson.

In the General Prologue to the *Canterbury Tales* the Pardoner is described as having a thin, goat-like voice and being unable to grow a beard; the narrator comments: 'I trow he were a gelding or a mare'. At the end of the Pardoner's Tale (lines 618 ff.) the Host's violently obscene response to the Pardoner's attempt to peddle his wares among the pilgrims (just after having boasted to them of his fraudulence) has to do in part with the ambivalence of the Pardoner's gender.

THE PARDONER'S PROLOGUE AND TALE

[*The Pardoner addresses the other pilgrims.*]

    'Lordynges,'* quod he, 'in chirches whan I preche   *lords*
†I peyne me to han an hauteyn speche
And rynge it out as round as gooth a belle,
For I kan* al by rote* that I telle.   *know   by heart*
5 My theme is alwey oon* and evere was: *the same*
†*Radix malorum est cupiditas.*
    'First I pronounce* whennes* that I come   *declare whence*
And thanne my bulles† shewe I alle and some.*   *one and all*
Oure lige-lordes* seel on my patente,†   *feudal superior's*
10 That shewe I first my body* to warente*   *myself protect*
That* no man be so boold, ne preest ne clerk,*   *so that cleric*
Me to destourbe of* Cristes holy werk.   *distract from*
And after that thanne telle I forth my tales;
Bulles of popes and of cardynales,
15 Of patriarkes† and bisshopes I shewe,
And in Latyn I speke a wordes fewe
To saffron* with my predicacioun*   *flavour preaching*
And for to stire hem* to devocioun.   *them*
    'Thanne shewe I forth my longe, cristal stones*   *jars*
20 Ycrammed ful of cloutes* and of bones: *bits of cloth*
†Relikes been they, as wenen they echon.
Thanne have I in a latoun* a shulder-bon   *brass*
Which that was of an holy Jewes sheep.
"Goode men," I seye, "tak of my wordes keep:†
25 If that this boon be wasshe* in any welle,   *washed*
If cow or calf or sheep or oxe swelle*   *puff up*

---

2 I take pains to speak resonantly
6 Covetousness is the root of all evil   [I Timothy 6.10]
8 [*bulles* originally a seal attached to an official document, then used of the document itself, especially of an edict issued by the pope or other ecclesiastical authority]
9 [*lige-lordes seel ... patente* the Pardoner's 'patente' or licence to carry out his work bears the royal seal, which protects him from harassment]
15 *patriarkes* patriarchs   [members of the ecclesiastical hierarchy]
21 They are relics, as each one of them believes   [*Relikes* material objects derived from or associated with saints were collected and venerated from the early Christian era, but especially from the twelfth century. The list of relics held, for example, at Glastonbury Abbey during Chaucer's lifetime includes part of Moses' rod, some of the gold the Magi offered to the Lord and some of blessed Mary's milk. However, if fraud was widespread (as it must have been) so too was scepticism]
24 *tak of my wordes keep* pay attention to my words

	That any worm* hath ete* or worm ystonge,*	snake bitten stung
	Taak water of that welle and wassh his tonge	
	And it is hool anoon;* and forthermoor	immediately healthy
30	Of pokkes* and of scabbe and every soor*	pox sore
	Shal every sheep be hool that of this welle	
	Drynketh a draughte. Taak kepe eek* what I telle:	also
	If that the goode man† that the bestes oweth*	owns
	Wol every wike,* er that* the cok hym croweth,	week before
35	Fastynge drynken of this welle a draghte,	
	As thilke* holy Jew† oure eldres* taghte,	that forefathers
	Hise bestes and his stoor* shal multiplie.	stock
	'"And, sire, also it heeleth jalousie,	
	For thogh a man be falle* in jalous rage,	fallen
40	†Lat maken with this water his potage	
	And nevere shal he moore his wyf mystriste*	suspect
	Thogh he the soothe* of hir defaute* wiste,*	truth fault knew
	Al* hadde she taken preestes two or thre.	although
	'"Heere is a miteyn* eek that ye may se;	glove
45	He that his hand wol putte in this mitayn,	
	He shal have multiplyyng of his grayn	
	Whan he hath sowen be it whete or otes –	
	So that* he offre pens or ellis grotes.†	as long as
	'"Goode men and wommen, o* thyng warne I yow:	one
50	If any wight* be in this chirche now	person
	That hath doon synne horrible that he	
	Dar* nat for shame of it yshryven be,†	dare
	Or any womman, be she yong or old,	
	That hath ymaked hir housbond cokewold,*	cuckold
55	Swich* folk shal have no power ne no grace	such
	To offren* to my relikes in this place.	make offerings
	And whoso fyndeth hym out of* swich blame*	free from guilt
	He wol come up and offre a* Goddes name,	in
	†And I assoille* hym by the auctoritee*	absolve authority
60	Which that by bulle ygraunted was to me."	
	'By this gaude* have I wonne,* yeer by yeer,	trick gained
	An hundred mark* sith* I was pardoner.	6 shillings 8 pence since

---

33 *goode man* head of the household
36 [*thilke holy Jew* presumably one of the Old Testament prophets]
40 Have his broth made with this water
48 *grotes* groats, fourpenny pieces
52 *yshryven be* make his confession
59 [*I assoille hym* a pardoner's licence did not give him the authority, claimed here, to forgive sin]

I stonde lyk a clerk† in my pulpet
And whan that lewed* peple is doun yset,*   *ignorant seated*
65 I preche so as ye han herd bifore
And telle an hundred false japes* more.   *tricks*
Thanne peyne I me to strecche forth the nekke
And est and west upon the peple I bekke*   *nod*
As dooth a dowve* sittyng on a berne;*   *dove barn*
70 Myne handes and my tonge goon* so yerne*   *work briskly*
That it is joye to se my bisynesse.*   *activity*
Of avarice and of swich cursednesse
Is al my prechyng, for to make hem free*   *generous*
To yeven* hir pens and namely* unto me.   *give especially*
75 †For myn entente is nat but for to wynne
And nothyng* for correccioun of synne.   *not at all*
I rekke* nevere, whan that they been beryed,*   *care buried*
Thogh that hir soules goon a blakeberyed.†
For, certes,* many a predicacioun*   *indeed sermon*
80 †Comth ofte tyme of yvel entencioun;
Som for plesance* of folk and flaterye,   *pleasing*
To* been avanced by ypocrisie,*   *in order to hypocrisy*
And som for veyne glorie,* and som for hate.   *empty pride*
'For whan I dar noon ootherweyes† debate,*   *argue*
85 Thanne wol I stynge hym with my tonge smerte*   *sharply*
In prechyng, so that he shal nat asterte*   *escape*
To been diffamed* falsly if that he   *being slandered*
Hath trespased to* my bretheren or to me.   *offended against*
For though I telle noght his propre name,
90 Men shal wel knowe that it is the same
By signes and by othere circumstances.
Thus quyte* I folk that doon us displesances;†   *pay back*
Thus spete* I out my venym under hewe*   *spit colour, guise*
Of holynesse, to seme holy and trewe.
95 But shortly myn entente I wol devyse:*   *describe*
I preche of nothyng but for coveitise*   *covetousness, greed*
Therfore my theme is yet and evere* was: *always*
Radix malorum est cupiditas.

---

63 [*clerk* member of the clergy. The Pardoner here is only 'lyk a clerk'; in the General Prologue he is described as a 'noble ecclesiaste' who participates in the mass. His exact status is debatable]
75 For my intention is only to make a profit
78 *goon a blakeberyed* go blackberry-picking
80 Often stems from an evil intention
84 *noon ootherweyes* in no other way
92 *doon us displesances* make trouble for us

	'Thus kan I preche agayn* that same vice	against
100	Which that I use, and that is avarice.	
	But though myself be gilty in that synne,	
	Yet kan I make oother folk to twynne*	part
	From avarice and soore* to repente;	painfully
	But that is nat my principal entente.	
105	I preche nothyng but for coveitise;	
	Of this matere it oghte ynow* suffise.	enough
	'Thanne telle I hem ensamples† many oon	
	Of olde stories longe tyme agoon,*	past
	For lewed* peple loven tales olde;	ignorant
110	Swiche thynges kan they wel reporte* and holde.*	relate retain
	What, trowe* ye that whiles I may preche	believe
	And wynne gold and silver for* I teche	because
	That I wol lyve in poverte wilfully?*	voluntarily
	Nay, nay, I thoghte* it nevere trewely,	considered
115	For I wol preche and begge in sondry* landes;	various
	I wol nat do no labour with myne handes,	
	Ne make baskettes and lyve therby,	
	†By cause I wol nat beggen ydelly* –	in idleness
	I wol none of the apostles countrefete.*	copy
120	I wol have moneye, wolle, chese and whete,	
	†Al were it yeven of the poverest page,†	
	Or of the povereste widwe* in a village –	widow
	Al* sholde hir children sterve for famyne.	although
	Nay, I wol drynke licour* of the vyne	juice
125	And have a joly wenche* in every toun.	mistress
	'But herkneth, lordynges, in conclusioun:	
	Youre likyng is† that I shal telle a tale.	
	†Now have I dronke a draghte* of corny* ale;	draught malty
	By God, I hope I shal yow telle a thyng	
130	That shal by resoun* been at* youre likyng.	fairly to
	For thogh myself be a ful vicious man,	
	A moral tale yet I yow telle kan	
	Which I am won* to preche for to wynne*	accustomed make money
	Now holde youre pees, my tale I wol bigynne:	

---

107 [*ensamples* medieval preachers were trained to interlard their sermons with *exempla*, moral stories designed to engage the interest of their audiences and illustrate their arguments]
118–19 [The Pardoner's implication is that the apostles' life of voluntary poverty – often held up in the middle ages as an ideal – was one of idleness, unlike his own busy life of preaching]
121 Even though it were given by the poorest boy
127 *Youre likyng is* it is your pleasure
128 [Before beginning his tale, the Pardoner has insisted on stopping at an inn for a drink and some bread]

Here bigynneth the Pardoners Tale.

135 In Flandres whilom† was a compaignye
Of yonge folk that haunteden folye,†
As riot,* hasard,* stewes* and tavernes,   *debauchery dicing brothels*
Where as with harpes, lutes and gyternes†
They daunce and pleyen at dees* bothe day and nyght,   *dice*
140 And ete also and drynke over hir myght,*   *beyond their capacity*
Thurgh which they doon the devel sacrifise†
Withinne that develes temple in cursed wise
By superfluytee abhomynable.
Hir* othes* been so grete and so dampnable   *their oaths*
145 That it is grisly* for to heere hem swere –   *terrible*
Oure blissed Lordes body they totere,*   *rend*
Hem thoughte† that Jewes rente* hym noght ynough –   *tore*
And eech of hem at otheres synne lough.*   *laughed*
And right anon* thanne coomen* tombesteres,†   *immediately come*
150 Fetys* and smale,* and yonge frutesteres,†   *graceful slender*
Syngeris with harpes, baudes,* waufereres,*   *pimps cake sellers*
Whiche been the verray* develes officers*   *true agents*
To kyndle and blowe the fyr of lecherye
That is annexed* unto glotonye.   *linked*
155 The holy writ* take I to my witnesse   *the Bible*
That luxure* is in wyn and dronkenesse.   *lust*
Lo, how that dronken Loth† unkyndely*   *unnaturally*
Lay by his doghtres two unwityngly;*   *unknowingly*
So dronke he was he nyste* what he wroghte.*   *did not know did*
160 †Herodes whoso* wel the stories soghte,*   *whoever looked for*
When he of wyn was replet* at his feste   *full*
Right at his owene table he yaf* his heste*   *gave promise*
To sleen* the Baptist John, ful giltelees.*   *slay completely innocent*
Senec† seith a good word doutelees:*   *undoubtedly*
165 He seith he kan no difference fynde

---

135 *whilom* formerly, in olden times
136 *haunteden folye* made a habit of sinful pastimes
138 *gyternes* citterns [stringed instruments]
141 *doon the devel sacrifise* offer sacrifice to the devil
147 *Hem thoughte* it seemed to them
149 *tombesteres* dancing girls
150 *frutesteres* fruit girls
157 [*Loth* Lot was made drunk by his two daughters who slept with him and bore his children (Genesis 19.30–8)]
160–3 [*Herodes . . . Baptist John* Herod, at a feast celebrating his birthday, promised his wife Herodias that she could have what she wanted, and she asked for the head of John the Baptist who had criticised their marriage (Mark 6.19–28)]
164 [*Senec* Lucius Annaeus Seneca the Younger, moral philosopher and dramatist (*c.* 4 BC–AD 65) wrote that 'drunkenness is nothing other than a willed madness' (*Epistolae* (Letters), 83.18)]

	Bitwix* a man that is out of his mynde	between
	And a man which that is dronkelewe,*	always drunk
	†But that woodnesse, yfallen in a sherewe,	
	Persevereth lenger* than dooth dronkenesse.	longer
170	O glotonye, ful of cursednesse!	
	O cause first of oure confusioun!	
	O original* of oure dampnacioun,	cause
	Til Crist hadde boght* us with his blood agayn!	redeemed
	Lo, how deere, shortly for to sayn,*	to speak briefly
175	Aboght* was thilke* cursed vileynye.*	bought that vice
	Corrupt was al this world for glotonye.	
	Adam,† oure fader, and his wyf also	
	Fro paradys to labour and to wo	
	Were dryven for that vice, it is no drede.*	without doubt
180	For whil that Adam fasted, as I rede,	
	He was in paradys, and whan that he	
	Eet of the frut defended* on a tree	forbidden
	Anon* he was out cast to wo and peyne.	immediately
	O glotonye, on thee wel oghte us pleyne.†	
185	O wiste a man† how manye maladies	
	Folwen of* excesse and of glotonyes,	follow from
	He wolde been the moore mesurable*	temperate
	Of his diete, sittyng at his table.	
	Allas, the shorte throte, the tendre mouth	
190	Maketh* that est and west and north and south	is the cause
	In erthe, in eyr, in water, men to swynke*	toil
	To gete a gloton deyntee mete* and drynke.	food
	†Of this matere, o Paul,* wel kanstow trete:†	St Paul
	Mete unto wombe* and wombe eek unto mete,	belly
195	Shal God destroyen bothe, as Paulus seith.	
	Allas, a foul thyng is it, by my feith,	
	To seye this word, and fouler is the dede	
	Whan man so drynketh of the white and rede†	
	†That of his throte he maketh his pryvee	
200	Thurgh thilk* cursed superfluité.	that

---

168 Except that madness, having lighted on an evil man
177 [*Adam . . . hys wyf* according to this application of the story, the sin of Adam and Eve in eating the fruit of the tree of the knowledge of good and evil was gluttony, not pride]
184 *on thee wel oghte us pleyne* we certainly ought to complain about you
185 *wiste a man* if a man knew
193–5 [*Paul* the apostle, who wrote I Corinthians 6.13: 'meat for the belly, and the belly for meats: but God shall destroy both it and them']   *kanstow trete* know how to speak of
198 *white and rede* white and red wines
199 That he makes his privy of his throat (by vomiting)

†The apostle,* wepyng, seith ful pitously:	St Paul
Ther walken manye of whiche yow toold have I,	
I seye it now wepying with pitous voys.	
Ther been enemys of Cristes croys,*	cross
205 Of whiche the ende is deth: wombe is hir* god.	their
O wombe, o bely, o stynkyng cod*	bag
Fulfilled of* dong* and of corrupcioun,	filled with dung
At either ende of thee foul is the soun;*	sound
†How greet labour and cost is thee to fynde.	
210 Thise cokes,* how they stampe and streyne and grynde	cooks
†And turnen substance into accident	
To fulfillen* al thy likerous* talent.*	satisfy lecherous inclination
Out of the harde bones knokke they	
The mary,* for they caste nat awey	marrow
215 That* may go thurgh the golet* softe and soote.*	what gullet sweet
Of spicerie,* of lief* and bark and roote,	spices leaf
Shal been his sauce ymaked* by delit*	made delightfully
To make hym yet a* newer appetit.	a still
†But, certes, he that haunteth swiche delices	
220 Is deed* whil that he lyveth in tho* vices.	dead those
†A lecherous thyng is wyn, and dronkenesse	
Is ful of stryvyng* and of wrecchednesse.	strife
O dronke man, disfigured is thy face,	
Sour is thy breeth, foul artow* to embrace,	art thou, are you
225 And thurgh thy dronke nose semeth the soun*	sound
As thogh thou seydest ay† 'Sampsoun, Sampsoun.'	
And yet God woot* Sampson† drank nevere no wyn!	knows
Thou fallest as it were a stiked swyn;†	
Thy tonge is lost and al thyn honest cure,†	
230 For dronkenesse is verray sepulture*	true grave

201-5 [Paul's epistle to the Ephesians 3.18–19: 'For many walk [who] ... are enemies of the cross of Christ: Whose end is destruction, whose God is their belly']
209 What a great effort and expense it is to provide for you
211-12 [Chaucer borrows here, as elsewhere in this section, from the *De Miseria Conditionis Humanae* (Concerning the Misery of the Human Condition) of Pope Innocent III (1160–1216), according to whom cooks 'convert substance into accident, change nature into art'. 'Substance' and 'accident' are philosophical terms distinguishing essential being from external characteristics]
219 But indeed he who makes a habit of such delicacies
219-20 ['She that liveth in pleasure is dead while she liveth' (I Timothy 5.6)]
221-2 ['Wine is a mocker [Latin: wanton], strong drink is raging' (Proverbs 20.1)]
226 *thou seydest ay* you kept on saying
227 [*Sampson* the drunkard's snorting recalls the name of the Old Testament hero, Samson, whose mother was commanded, in preparation for his birth, to 'drink not wine nor any strong drink' (Judges 13.4)]
228 *as it were a stiked swyn* as if you were a stuck pig
229 *honest cure* sense of decency

	Of mannes wit* and his discrecioun.	intelligence
	In whom* that drynke hath domynacioun	in (the person) whom
	He kan no conseil* kepe, it is no drede.†	secret
	Now kepe yow fro the white and fro the rede,	
235	And namely* fro the white wyn of Lepe†	particularly
	That is to selle* in Fisshstrete or in Chepe.†	for sale
	This wyn of Spaigne crepeth subtilly†	
	In* othere wynes growynge faste by,*	into near at hand
	Of* which ther riseth swich fumositee*	from vapour
240	That whan a man hath dronken draghtes thre	
	And weneth* that he be at hom in Chepe,	believes
	He is in Spaigne right at the toune of Lepe,	
	Nat at the Rochel ne at Burdeux† toun –	
	And thanne wol he seyn 'Sampson, Sampsoun.'	
245	But herkneth,* lordynges, o* word I yow preye:	listen one
	That alle the sovereyn actes* dar I seye,	greatest deeds
	Of victories in the Olde Testament	
	Thurgh verray God that is omnipotent	
	Were doon in abstinence and in prayere;	
250	Looketh* the bible and ther ye may it leere.*	look at learn
	Looke* Attilla,† the grete conquerour,	consider how
	Deyde in his sleep with shame and dishonour,	
	Bledyng at his nose in dronkenesse;	
	A capitayn* sholde lyve in sobrenesse.	general
255	And over* al this avyseth yow* right wel	above reflect
	What was comaunded unto Lamwel –†	
	Nat Samuel,† but Lamwel, seye I.	
	Redeth the bible and fynd it expresly,*	explicitly
	Of wyn-yevynge* to hem* that han justise.†	giving wine them
260	Namoore of this, for it may wel suffise.*	be adequate
	And now that I have spoken of glotonye,	
	Now wol I yow defende* hasardrye:*	forbid gambling

---

233 *it is no drede* there is no doubt
235 [*Lepe* a town in Spain]
236 [*Fisshstrete . . . Chepe* London streets: Fish Street, off Lower Thames Street (where Chaucer's father sold wine), and Cheapside, near St Paul's]
237 *crepeth subtilly* secretly creeps   [In other words, is surreptitiously mixed by the wine-merchant]
243 [*Rochel . . . Burdeux* La Rochelle and Bordeaux are French wine ports]
251 [*Attilla* Attila the Hun, scourge of the Roman empire, who died in 453 through choking to death on his own blood after falling in a drunken stupor]
256 [*Lamwel* 'The words of king Lemuel . . . that his mother taught him. . . . It is not for kings to drink wine; nor for princes strong drink' (Proverbs 31.1 and 4)]
257 [*Samuel* Old Testament prophet]
259 *han justise* are responsible for justice

	Hasard is verray moder* of lesynges*	mother lies
	And of deceite and cursed forswerynges,*	perjuries
265	Blaspheme of Crist, manslaughtre, and wast* also	waste
	Of catel* and of tyme; and forthermo	goods
	It is reprove* and contrarie of honour	shame
	For to ben holden* a commune hasardour.	held, regarded as
	And evere the hyer he is of estaat,*	in rank
270	The moore is he holden desolat.*	vile
	If that a prynce useth hasardrye,	
	In alle governance and policye	
	He is as by commune opynyoun	
	Yholde* the lasse in reputacioun.	held
275	Stilbon† that was a wys embassadour,	
	Was sent to Corynthe† in ful gret honour	
	Fro Lacedomye,* to make hir alliaunce.†	Lacedæmon
	And whan he cam, hym happed† parchaunce*	by chance
	That alle the gretteste that were of that lond	
280	Pleiynge at the hasard* he hem fond.*	dicing found them
	For which, as soone as it myghte be,	
	He stal hym* hom agayn to his contree	went secretly
	And seyde: 'Ther wol I nat lese my name,†	
	Ne I wol nat* take on me so greet defame*	nor will I ignominy
285	Yow for to allie unto none hasardours.	
	Sendeth othere wise embassadours,	
	For, by my trouthe, me were levere* dye	I would rather
	Than I yow sholde to hasardours allye.	
	For ye that been so glorious in honours	
290	Shal nat allye yow with hasardours,	
	†As by my wyl, ne as by my tretee.'	
	This wise philosophre thus seyde he.	
	Looke eek* that to the kyng Demetrius.†	also
	The kyng of Parthes,* as the book seith* us,	Parthia tells
295	Sente hym a paire of dees of gold in scorn	
	For he hadde used hasard† therbiforn,*	before then

---

275 [*Stilbon* an error for Chilon of Sparta (or Lacedaemon, see l. 277), of whom this story is told by John of Salisbury (d. 1180) in his *Policraticus* 1.5.1]
276 [*Corynthe* a Greek city-state renowned for its profligacy and licentiousness]
277 *hir alliance* alliance between them
278 *hym happed* it befell him
283 *lese my name* lose my good name
291 Neither by my wish, nor by my treaty
293 [*Demetrius . . . Parthes* Demetrius Nicator, king of Syria, who was captured by the Parthians. This story is associated with the previous one in John of Salisbury's *Policraticus*]
296 *used hasard* practised gambling with dice

For which he heeld his glorie or his renoun
At no value or reputacioun.
Lordes may fynden oother manere pley†
300 †Honeste ynow to dryve the day awey.
　　Now wol I speke of oothes false and grete
A word or two, as olde bokes trete:
Greet sweryng is a thyng abhomynable
And fals sweryng is yet moore reprevable.*   reprehensible
305 The heighe God forbad sweryng at al –
Witnesse on Mathew† – but in special*   especially
Of sweryng seith the holy Jeremye:†
Thow shalt swere sooth* thyne othes and nat lye,   truly
And swere in doom† and eek in rightwisnesse,*   justice
310 But ydel sweryng is a cursednesse.
　　Bihoold and se that in the firste table†
Of heighe Goddes hestes* honurable,   commandments
How that the seconde heste† of hym is this:
Take nat my name in ydel* or amys.*   in vain wrongly
315 Lo, rather* he forbedeth* swich sweryng   sooner forbids
Than homycide or many a cursed thyng.
I seye that as by ordre* thus it standeth;   in sequence
†This knoweth that hise hestes understandeth
How that the seconde heste of God is that.
320 And, fortherover,* I wol thee telle al plat*   moreover quite bluntly
That vengeance shal nat parten from* his hous   leave
That of hise othes is to* outrageous: too
'By Goddes precious herte' and 'By his nayles'
And 'By the blood of Crist that is in Hayles,†
325 †Sevene is my chance and thyn is cynk and treye',*   five and three
'By Goddes armes, if thow falsly pleye

---

299 *oother manere pley*   other kinds of amusement
300 Honourable enough to pass the time with
306 [*Mathew*   'But I say unto you, Swear not at all; neither by heaven; for it is God's throne' (Matthew 5.34)]
307 [*Jeremye*   'And thou shalt swear, The Lord liveth, in truth, in judgment, and in righteousness' (Jeremiah 4.2)]
309 *in doom*   in making a judgement
311 [*the firste table*   the ten commandments were given to Moses by God on two tables of stone; the first table contains those which govern man's relation to God]
313 [*seconde heste*   according to the division sanctioned by the Vulgate version of the Bible (used in the middle ages), the second commandment is 'Thou shalt not take the name of the Lord thy God in vain']
318 he who knows his commandments knows this
324 [*Hayles*   Hailes Abbey, Gloucestershire, possessed among its relics a phial of what was believed to be Christ's blood]
325 [A gambler's exclamation; the numbers refer to dice]

	This dagger shal thurghout thyn herte go'.	
	This frut cometh of the bicche* bones two:	cursed
	Forsweryng,* ire, falsnesse, homycide.	perjury
330	Now for the love of Crist that for us dyde,	
	Lete* youre othes bothe grete and smale.	leave
	But, sires, now wol I telle forth my tale.	
	Thise riotours* thre, of whiche I telle,	debauched youths
	Longe erst er pryme† ronge of any belle	
335	Were set hem* in a taverne to drynke.	seated
	And as they sat, they herde a belle klynke*	tinkle
	Biforn† a cors* was* caryed to his grave.	corpse which was
	That oon* of hem gan callen to his knave:*	one servant
	†'Go bet,' quod he, 'and axe redily	
340	What cors is this that passeth heer forby,*	by
	And looke that thow reporte his name wel.'	
	'Sire,' quod* this boy, 'it nedeth never-a-del;†	said
	It was me told er* ye cam heer two houres.	before
	He was, pardee,† an old felawe* of youres,	companion
345	And sodeynly he was yslayn tonyght,	
	Fordronke* as he sat on his bench upright.	very drunk
	Ther cam a privee* theef men clepeth* deeth,*	stealthy call death
	That in this contree al the peple sleeth,*	kills
	And with his spere he smoot* his herte atwo*	smote, cut in two
350	And wente his wey withouten wordes mo.*	more, further
	He hath a thousand slayn this pestilence.†	
	And, maister, er ye come in his presence	
	Me thynketh† that it were necessarie	
	For to be war* of swich an adversarie.	beware
355	Beeth redy for to meete hym everemoore:*	continually
	Thus taughte me my dame* – I sey namoore.'	mother
	'By seinte Marie,'* seyde this taverner,	the Blessed Virgin
	'The child seith sooth,* for he hath slayn this yer,	the truth
	Henne* over a myle withinne a greet village,	from here
360	Bothe man and womman, child and hyne* and page;	servant
	I trowe* his habitacioun be there.	believe
	†To been avysed greet wisdom it were,	

---

334 *erst er pryme* before prime [the first to third hours of the day]
337 *Biforn* in front of
339 'Go as quickly as you can,' said he, 'and ask at once ...'
342 *it nedeth never-a-del* it is quite unnecessary
344 *pardee* to be sure [by God]
351 [*pestilence* there were outbreaks of plague in 1349–50, 1361–2, 1369 and 1375–6]
354 *Me thyketh* it seems to me
362 It would be very prudent to be careful

  Er that he dide a man a dishonour.'
   'Ye, Goddes armes,' quod this riotour,
365 'Is it swich* peril with hym for to meete?   such
  I shal hym seke by wey and eek by strete,
  I make avow* to Goddes digne* bones.   vow worthy
  Herkneth,* felawes, we thre been al ones;*   listen in agreement
  Lat ech of us holde up his hand to oother
370 And ech of us bicome ootheres brother,
  And we wol sleen* this false traytour deeth.   slay
  He shal be slayn, he that so manye sleeth,
  By Goddes dignytee, er* it be nyght.'   before
   Togidres* han thise thre hir trouthes plyght*   together pledged
375 To lyve and dyen ech of him with oother
  As thogh he were his owene ybore* brother.   born, natural
  And up they stirte,* al dronken in this rage,   jumped
  And forth they goon towardes that village
  Of which the taverner hadde spoke biforn;
380 And many a grisly ooth thanne han they sworn
  And Cristes blessed body they torente,*   lacerated
  Deeth shal be deed if they may hym hente.*   catch
   Whan they han goon nat fully half a myle,
  Right as they wolde han treden* over a style   stepped
385 An old man and a poure† with hem mette.
  This olde man ful mekely hem grette*   greeted
  And seyde thus: 'Now, lordes, God yow se.'†
   The proudeste of thise riotours thre
  †Answerde agayn: 'What, carl, with sory grace,
390 Why artow* al forwrapped* save thy face?   are you wrapped up
  Why lyvestow* so longe in so greet age?'   do you live
   This olde man gan looke in his visage*   face
  And seyde thus: 'For I ne kan nat fynde
  A man, thogh that I walked into Inde,*   India
395 Neither in citee ne in no village,
  That wolde chaunge his youthe for myn age.
  And therfore moot* I han* myn age stille   must keep
  As longe tyme as it is Goddes wille;
  Ne* deeth, allas, ne wol nat have my lyf.   nor
400 Thus walke I lyk a restelees caytyf,*   captive

---

385 *An old man and a poure* a poor old man [This figure has been variously identified as,
e.g., Death, fallen Man, Old Age, the Wandering Jew]
387 *God yow se* may God watch over you
389 Replied: 'Hey, fellow, bad luck to you . . .'

	And on the ground which is my modres* gate	mother's
	I knokke with my staf, bothe erly and late,	
	And seye: "Leeve* moder, leet me in!	dear
	Lo, how I vanysshe, flessh and blood and skyn.	
405	Allas, whan shal my bones been at reste?	
	Moder, with yow wolde I chaunge* my cheste†	exchange
	That in my chambre longe tyme hath be,	
	Ye,* for an heyre clowt† to wrappe me."	yes, indeed
	But yet to me she wol nat do that grace,*	kindness
410	For which ful pale and welked* is my face.	withered
	'But, sires, to yow it is no curteisye*	good breeding
	To speken to an old man vileynye,*	shame
	But* he trespase* in word or ellis in dede.	unless do wrong
	In holy writ† ye may yourself wel rede:	
415	Agayns an old man hoor* upon his heed	with white hairs
	Ye shal arise; wherfore I yeve yow reed.*	give you advice
	Ne dooth* unto an old man noon harm now,	do not
	Namoore* than that ye wolde men dide to yow	any more
	In age, if that ye so longe abyde.*	last
420	And God be with yow, wher ye go or ryde;	
	I moot go thider as I have to go.'	
	'Nay, olde cherl,* by God, thow shalt nat so,'	fellow
	Seyde this oother hasardour* anon.	gambler
	'Thow partest nat so lightly, by Seint John.	
425	Thow speeke right now of thilke* traytour deeth	that
	That in this contree alle oure freendes sleeth* –	slays
	Have here my trouthe,* as thow art his espye,*	pledge spy
	Tel wher he is or thow shalt it abye,*	pay for
	By God and by the holy sacrament.	
430	For soothly thow art oon of his assent†	
	To sleen us yonge folk, thow false theef.'	
	'Now, sires,' quod he, 'if that yow be so leef†	
	To fynde deeth, turn up this croked wey,	
	For in that grove I lafte hym, by my fey,*	faith
435	Under a tree and ther he wol abyde;*	wait
	†Nat for youre boost he wol hym nothyng hyde.	
	Se ye that ook,* right ther ye shal hym fynde.	oak

---

406 *cheste* coffer [suggesting coffin]
408 *heyre clowt* haircloth [both shroud and penitential garment]
414 [*In holy writ* 'Thou shalt rise up before the hoary head, and honour the face of the old man' (Leviticus 19.32)]
430 *oon of his assent* in league with him
432 *yow be so leef* it is so desirable to you
436 He will not hide himself at all for all your bluster

	God save yow, that boghte agayn* mankynde,	redeemed
	And yow amende.' Thus seyde this olde man.	
440	And everich* of thise riotours* ran	each one debauched youths
	Til he cam to that tree, and ther they founde	
	Of floryns† fyne of gold ycoyned* rounde	made into coins
	Wel ny an eighte busshels, as hem thoughte.	
	No lenger thanne* after deeth they soughte,	then
445	But ech of hem so glad was of the sighte,	
	For that the floryns been so faire and brighte,	
	That doun they sette hem* by this precious hoord.	themselves
	The worste of hem, he spak the firste word:	
	'Bretheren,' quod he, 'taak kepe† what that I seye,	
450	My wit is greet thogh that I bourde* and pleye.*	jest fool around
	This tresor hath fortune unto us yeven*	given
	In myrthe and jolitee oure lyf to lyven,	
	And lightly* as it cometh so wol we spende.	easily
	By Goddes precious dignytee, who wende*	expected
455	Today that we sholde han so fair a grace?*	such good luck
	But myghte this gold be caried fro this place	
	Hoom to myn hous or ellis unto youres –	
	For wel ye woot* that al this gold is oures –	know
	Thanne were we in heigh felicitee.*	great happiness
460	But trewely by daye it may nat be;	
	Men wolde seyn* that we were theves stronge*	say out-and-out
	And for oure owene tresor doon us honge.†	
	This tresor moste ycaried be by nyghte,	
	As wisly* and as sleyly* as it myghte.	discreetly cunningly
465	Therfore I rede* that cut* amonges us alle	advise lots
	Be drawe,* and lat se wher the cut wol falle.	drawn
	And he that hath the cut, with herte blithe,	
	Shal renne* to towne and that ful swithe,*	run very quickly
	And brynge us breed and wyn ful prively.*	secretly
470	And two of us shal kepen* subtilly*	guard cleverly
	This tresor wel, and if he wol nat tarye,	
	Whan it is nyght we wol this tresor carye	
	By oon assent† wher as us thynketh* best.'	it seems
	That oon of hem the cut broghte in his fest*	fist
475	And bad hem* drawe and looke wher it wol falle;	told them
	And it fel on the yongeste of hem alle,	

---

442 *floryns* coins worth 6 shillings
449 *taak kepe* pay attention to
462 *doon us honge* have us hanged
473 *oon assent* mutual agreement

And forth toward the town he wente anon.* — immediately
And also* soone as that he was agon, — as
That oon of hem spak thus unto that oother:
480 'Thow knowest wel thow art my sworn brother,
Thy profit wol I telle thee anon.
Thow woost* wel that oure felawe is agon — know
And heere is gold, and that ful greet plentee,
That shal departed* been among us thre. — shared
485 But, nathelees,* if I kan shape* it so — nevertheless arrange
That it departed were among us two,
Hadde I nat doon a freendes torn* to thee?' — turn
　　That oother answerde: 'I noot* how that may be; — do not know
He woot* that the gold is with us tweye.* — knows two
490 What shal we doon? What shal we to hym seye?'
　　'Shal it be conseil?'* seyde the firste shrewe,* — secret villain
'And I shal telle in a wordes fewe
What we shul doon, and brynge it wel aboute.'
　　'I graunte,'* quod that oother, 'out of doute,† — agree
495 That by my trouthe I wol thee nat biwreye.'* — betray
　　'Now,' quod* the firste, 'thow woost* wel we be tweye, — said know
And two of us shul strenger* be than oon. — stronger
Looke whan that he is set,* that right anon* — seated straight away
Arys* as though thow woldest with hym pleye, — get up
500 And I shal ryve* hym thurgh the sydes tweye — stab
Whil that thow strogelest* with hym as in game; — wrestle
And with thy daggere looke thow* do the same. — see that you
And thanne shal al this gold departed be,
My deere freend, bitwixe* thee and me. — between
505 Thanne may we bothe oure lustes* al fulfille — desires
And pleye at dees* right at oure owene wille.'† — dice
And thus acorded been* thise sherewes* tweye — are agreed villains
To sleen* the thridde,* as ye han herd me seye. — kill third
　　This yongeste which that wente to the toun,
510 Ful ofte in herte he rolleth up and doun
The beautee of thise floryns, newe and brighte.
'O lord,' quod he, 'if so were* that I myghte — if it might be
Have al this tresor to myself allone,
Ther is no man that lyveth under the trone* — throne
515 Of God that sholde lyve so myrie* as I.' — happy
And at the laste the feend,* oure enemy, — devil

494 *out of doute*　wholeheartedly
506 *at our owene wille*　as much as we like

	Putte in his thoght that he sholde poyson beye*	buy
	With which he myghte sleen* his felawes tweye;*	kill two
	Forwhy* the feend foond* hym in swich lyvynge†	because found
520	That he hadde leve* hym to sorwe* brynge,	permission sorrow
	For this was outrely* his ful entente:*	utterly intention
	To sleen hem bothe, and nevere to repente.	
	And forth he goth – no lenger* wolde he tarye –	longer
	Into the toun unto a pothecarye*	apothecary
525	And preyed hym that he hym wolde selle	
	Som poyson, that he myghte his rattes quelle.*	kill
	And eek* ther was a polcat in his hawe*	also yard
	That, as he seyde, his capons* hadde yslawe.*	chickens killed
	†And fayn he wolde wreke hym if he myghte	
530	On vermyn that destroyed hym by nyghte.	
	The pothecarie answerde: 'And thow shalt have	
	A thyng that, also* God my soule save,	as
	In al this world ther is no creature	
	†That ete or dronke hath of this confiture,	
535	Nat but the montaunce* of a corn of whete,	quantity
	†That he ne shal his lyf anoon forlete.	
	Ye,* sterve* he shal, and that in lasse while	yes die
	Than thow wolt goon a paas* nat but a myle,	step
	The poyson is so strong and violent.'	
540	This cursed man hath in his hand yhent*	seized
	This poyson in a box, and sith* he ran	then
	Into the nexte strete unto a man	
	And borwed hym* large botels thre.	borrowed
	And in the two his poison poured he;	
545	The thridde* he kepte clene for his drynke,	third
	For al the nyght he shoop hym* for to swynke*	planned toil
	In cariyng of the gold out of that place.	
	And whan this riotour,* with sory grace,†	debauched youth
	Hadde filled with wyn hise grete botels thre,	
550	To hise felawes agayn repaireth* he.	returns
	What nedeth it to sarmone* of it moore,	speak
	For right as they hadde cast* his deeth bifore,	planned
	Right* so they han* hym slayn and that anon?*	just have immediately
	And whan this was doon thus spak that oon:*	one

519 *lyvynge* state of life
529 And he wanted to avenge himself if he could
534 Who has eaten or drunk of this mixture
536 Who will not lose his life immediately
548 *sory grace* misfortune

555 'Now lat us sitte and drynke and make us merye,
And afterward we wol his body berye.'
And with that word it happed hym, par cas,†
To take the botel ther* the poyson was, — *in which*
And drank and yaf* his felawe drynke also, — *gave*
560 For which anon they storven* bothe two. — *died*
But certes I suppose that Avycen†
Wroot* nevere in no *Canon** ne in no fen — *wrote Rule*
Mo wonder* signes of empoysonyng* — *more amazing poisoning*
Than hadde thise wrecches two er* hir endyng. — *before*
565 Thus ended been thise homicides two
And eek the false empoysoner also.
O cursed synne of alle cursednesse!
O traytours* homicide, o wikkednesse! — *treacherous*
O glotonye, luxure,* and hasardrye,* — *lust gambling*
570 Thou blasphemour of Crist with vileynye* — *vicious conduct*
And othes grete of usage* and of pryde! — *habitual*
Allas, mankynde, how may it bityde* — *come about*
That to thy creatour,* which that thee wroghte* — *creator made*
And with his precious herte-blood the boghte,
575 Thow art so fals and so unkynde, allas?
Now, goode men, God foryeve* yow youre trespas — *forgive*
And ware yow fro* the synne of avarice. — *beware of*
Myn holy pardoun may yow alle warisse,* — *save*
So that* ye offre nobles† or starlynges* — *provided that silver coins*
580 Or ellis silver broches, spones,* rynges. — *spoons*
Boweth your heed under this holy bulle;
Cometh up, ye wyves, offreth of youre wolle.†
Youre name I entre here in my rolle anon:
Into the blisse of hevene shul ye gon.* — *go*
585 I yow assoille* by myn heigh power, — *absolve*
Ye that wol offre, as clene and eek as cler* — *pure*
As ye were born – and lo, sires, thus I preche.
And Jesu Crist, that is oure soules leche,* — *physician*
So graunte yow his pardoun to receyve,
590 For that is best, I wol yow nat deceyve.
But, sires, o* word forgat I in my tale: — *one*
I have relikes and pardon in my male* — *bag*

---

557 *it happed hym, per cas* he chanced
561–2 [*Avycen ... Canon* the Arab philosopher and physician Avicenna (980–1037) wrote a work called *The Book of the Canon in Medicine*, which is divided into 'fens' or chapters]
579 *nobles* 6 shillings 8 pence
582 *of your wolle* some of your wool

	As faire as any man in Engelond,	
	Whiche were me yeven* by the popes hond.	given
595	If any of yow wol of* devocioun	out of
	Offren and han* myn absolucioun,	have
	Com forth anon and kneleth here adoun	
	And mekely receyveth my pardoun;	
	Or ellis taketh pardoun as ye wende,*	go
600	Al newe and fressh at every myles ende,	
	So that* ye offren alwey, newe and newe,	so long as
	Nobles or pens whiche that been goode and trewe.	
	It is an honour to everich* that is heer	each one
	That ye mowe* have a suffisant* pardoner	may capable
605	T'assoille yow in contree as ye ryde,	
	For aventures* whiche that may bityde.	accidents
	Paraventure* ther may falle oon or two	perhaps
	Doun of his hors and breke his nekke atwo.*	in two
	Looke which a seuretee* is it to yow alle	security
610	That I am in your felaweship yfalle,*	fallen
	That may assoille yow, bothe moore and lasse,*	high and low
	Whan that the soule shal fro the body passe.	
	I rede* that oure hoost† shal bigynne,	advise
	For he is moost envoluped* in synne.	enwrapped
615	Com forth, sire hoost, and offre first anon	
	And thow shalt kisse the relikes everychon;*	each one
	Ye, for a grote* unbokele* anon thy purs.'	fourpenny piece unbuckle
	'Nay, nay,' quod he, 'thanne have I Cristes curs.	
	Lat be,' quod he. 'It shal nat be, so thee ich,†	
620	Thow woldest make me kisse thyn olde breech*	pants
	And swere it were a relyk of a seint,	
	Thogh it were with thy fondement* depeynt.*	anus stained
	†But by the croys which that seint Eleyne foond,	
	I wold I hadde thy coylons* in myn hond	testicles
625	In stide* of relikes or of seintuarie.*	stead sacred object
	Lat cutte hem of;† I wol thee hem carie –	
	They shul be shryned* in an hogges toord!*	enshrined turd
	This pardoner answerde nat a word.	

---

613 [*oure hoost* the host of the Tabard Inn at Southwark, in London, where the pilgrims assemble at the start of their journey. It is he who proposes the story-telling contest of which the *Canterbury Tales* is ostensibly a record, and joins the group as their guide]
619 *so thee ich* as [I hope] to prosper
623 [*by the croys ... foond* according to legend, Saint Helena (*c*. 255–320), mother of the Emperor Constantine, found the cross on which Jesus was crucified in the Holy Land]
626 *Lat cutte hem of* have them cut off

So wrooth* he was, no word ne wolde he seye. — angry
'Now,' quod oure hoost, 'I wol no lenger pleye* — joke
With thee, ne with noon oother angry man.'
But right anon the worthy knyght† bigan,
Whan that he saugh* that al the peple lough:* — saw laughed
'Namoore of this, for it is right ynough.* — quite sufficient
Sire pardoner, be glad and murye of cheere.†
And sire hoost, that been to me so deere,
I pray yow that ye kisse the pardoner,
And, pardoner, I pray thee drawe thee neer
†And as we diden lat us lawe and pleye,'
Anon they kiste and ryden forth hir* weye. — their

---

632 [*knyght* the highest in social status of the pilgrims and thus naturally able to assert authority]
635 *murye of cheere* enjoy yourself
639 And let us laugh and joke as we did before

The Shipman's Tale

A shipman is a sailor; as he is described in the General Prologue this Shipman seems to be piratical and unscrupulous, though the narrator calls him 'a good felawe' (a phrase which in Chaucer's usage often has a derogatory edge). The Shipman's Tale is a *fabliau*, that is, a short, low-life story using stock characters – lecherous priests, gullible husbands, deceitful wives – in realistic settings, in which the emphasis is on action, usually involving some kind of trickery. The amorality of the Tale, with its insistent linking of money and sex, can be read as a comment not only on 'good fellowship' but also on late fourteenth-century mercantilist values.

This tale may have originally been intended for the Wife of Bath, since the speaker appears initially to be a woman. (See lines 12, 14, 18–19 below.)

THE SHIPMAN'S TALE

Here bigynneth the shipmannes tale.

	A marchant whilom* dwelled at Seint Denys†	once
	That riche was, for which men helde hym wys.	
	A wyf he hadde of excellent beautee,	
	And compaignable* and revelous* was she,	sociable party-loving
5	Which is a thyng that causeth moore dispence*	expense
	†Than worth is al the cheere and reverence	
	That men hem doon at festes and at daunces.	
	Swiche* salutacions and contenances*	such glances
	Passen as dooth a shadwe* upon the wal,	shadow
10	But wo is hym that payen moot* for al!	has to pay
	The sely* housbonde algate* he moot paye:	poor always
	He moot us clothe and he moot us arraye,	

---

1 *Seint Denys* St Denis, outside Paris
6–7 Than all the attentions and flattery that men show them at feasts and dances are worth

	Al for his owene worship* richely,	honour
	In which array we dauncen jolily.	
15	And if that he noght may, paraventure,†	
	Or ellis list no swich dispense endure,†	
	But thynketh it is wasted and ylost,	
	Thanne moot another payen for oure cost	
	Or lene* us gold, and that is perilous.	lend
20	This noble marchant heeld* a worthy hous,	kept
	For which he hadde alday so greet repair†	
	For his largesse, and for his wyf was fair,	
	That wonder is – but herkneth* to my tale.	listen
	Amonges alle hise gestes grete and smale†	
25	Ther was a monk, a fair man and a bold –	
	I trowe* a thritty wynter* he was old –	believe years
	That evere in oon* was drawyng to that place.	always
	This yonge monk, that was so fair of face,	
	Aqueynted was so with the goode man,*	master of the house
30	Sith* that hir* firste knewliche* bigan,	ever since their acquaintance
	That in his hous as famulier* was he	intimate
	As it is possible any freend to be.	
	And for as muchel* as this goode man	in as much
	And eek* his monk, of which that I bigan,	also
35	Were bothe two yborn in o* village,	one
	The monk hym claymeth as for cosynage;†	
	And he* agayn* he seith nat ones nay,	the merchant in return
	But was as glad therof as fowel* of day	bird
	For to his herte it was a gret plesance.*	delight
40	Thus been they knyt with eterne* alliance,	eternal
	And ech of hem gan oother for t'assure†	
	Of bretherhede whil that hir lyf may dure.*	last
	Free† was daun* John and manly* of dispence	Father generous
	As in that hous, and ful of diligence	
45	To doon plesance* and also greet costage.†	give pleasure
	He nat forgat to yeve* the leeste* page	give most humble
	In al that hous; but after* hir degree	according to
	He yaf* the lord and sith* al his meynee,*	gave then, afterwards household

---

15 *noght may, paraventure* cannot afford it, perhaps
16 *list no swich dispense endure* does not want to stand any expenditure of this kind
21 *alday so greet repair* always so many visitors
24 *gestes grete and smale* guests of higher and lower rank
36 *as for cosynage* as a relation [with a possible pun on cozen 'to defraud']
41 *gan oother for t'assure* promised the other
43 *Free* open-handed
45 *greet costage* a great deal of money

	Whan that he cam, som manere* honeste* thyng,	kind of suitable
50	For which they were as glad of his comyng	
	As fowel is fayn* whan that the sonne up riseth.	pleased
	Namoore* of this as now, for it suffiseth.	no more
	But so bifel† this marchant on a day*	one day
	Shoop hym* to make redy his array*	prepared baggage
55	Toward the town of Brugges† for to fare,*	travel
	To byen there a porcion of ware;*	goods
	For which he hath to Parys sent anon*	directly
	A messager, and preyed hath daun John	
	That he sholde come to Seint Denys and pleye*	enjoy himself
60	With hym and with his wyf a day or tweye,*	two
	Er* he to Brugges wente, in alle wise.*	before in every way
	This noble monk, of which I yow devyse,*	tell
	Hath of his abbot, as hym list,† licence,*	permission
	By cause he was a man of heigh* prudence	high
65	And eek* an officer,* out for to ryde	also monastic official
	To seen hir granges* and hir bernes* wyde,	granaries barns
	And unto Seint Denys he comth anon.	
	Who was so welcome as my lord daun John,	
	Oure deere cosyn, ful of curteisye?*	courtesy
70	With hym broghte he a jubbe* of malvesye*	jar malmsey, sweet wine
	And eek another ful of fyn vernage*	an Italian wine
	And volatil,* as ay was his usage.*	poultry custom
	And thus I lete hem* ete and drynke and pleye,	them
	This marchant and this monk, a day or tweye.	
75	The thridde* day this marchant up ariseth	third
	†And on his nedes sadly hym avyseth;	
	And up into his countour-hous* goth he	counting-house
	To rekene* with* hymself, wel may be,	calculate by
	Of* thilke* yeer how that it with hym stood,	for that
80	And how that he despended* hadde his good,*	spent goods
	And if that he encressed were* or noon.*	were richer not
	Hise bokes and his bagges many oon	
	He leyth biforn hym on his countyng-bord.	
	Ful riche was his tresor and his hord,	
85	For which ful faste* his countour-dore he shette,*	firmly shut
	And eek he nolde* that no man sholde hym lette*	did not want hinder

53 *so bifel* it so happened
55 *Brugges* Bruges, in Flanders
63 *as hym list* as he wants
76 And applies himself soberly to his affairs

	Of* his acountes for the mene tyme;*	from time being
	And thus he sit* til it was passed prime.†	sits
	Daun John was risen in the morwe* also	morning
90	And in the gardyns walketh to and fro,	
	And hath his thynges seyd† ful curteisly.	
	This goode wyf† cam walkyng prively*	stealthily
	Into the gardyn ther* he walketh softe,*	where quietly
	And hym salueth* as she hath doon ofte.	greets
95	A mayde child cam in hir compaignye,	
	Which as hir list† she may governe and gye,*	direct
	For yet under the yerde† was the mayde.	
	'O deere cosyn myn, daun John,' she sayde,	
	'What eyleth yow† so rathe* for to ryse?'	early
100	'Nece,' quod* he, 'it oghte ynow suffise†	said
	Fyve houres for to slepe upon a nyght,	
	But* it were for an old, apalled* wight,*	unless enfeebled creature
	As been thise wedded men that lye and dare*	doze off
	As in a forme sit a wery hare	
105	†Were al forstraught with houndes grete and smale.	
	But, deere nece, why be ye so pale?	
	I trowe,* certes,* that oure goode man	believe indeed
	Hath yow laboured* sith the nyght bigan	put to work
	That* yow were nede to resten hastily.'	so that
110	And with that word he lough* ful myrily,	laughed
	And of his owene thoght he weex* al reed.*	grew red
	This faire wyf gan for to shake hir heed	
	And seyde thus: 'Ye, God woot al,'† quod she.	
	'Nay, cosyn myn, it stant* nat so with me,	stands
115	For by that God that yaf* me soule and lyf,	gave
	In al the reawme* of France is ther no wyf	kingdom
	That lasse lust† hath to that sory* pley.	miserable
	For I may synge "allas and weilawey*	alack
	That I was born". But to no wight,'* quod she,	nobody
120	'Dar I nat telle how that it stant with me.	

---

88 *prime* the first division of the day: 6 to 9 a.m.
91 *his thynges seyd* said his breviary
92 *goode wyf* mistress of the house
96 *as hir list* as she pleases
97 *under the yerde* under her authority
99 *eyleth yow* is the matter with you
100 *ynow suffise* to be sufficient
105 Who has been agitated by hounds great and small
113 *Ye, God woot al* to be sure, God knows everything
117 *lasse lust* less desire

	Wherfore I thynke out of this land to wende*	go
	Or ellis of myself to make an ende,	
	So ful am I of drede and eek of care.'	
	This monk bigan upon this wyf to stare	
125	And seyde: 'Allas, my nece, God forbede	
	That ye, for any sorwe or any drede,	
	Fordo* your self; but telleth* me your grief.	do away with tell
	Paraventure* I may in youre meschief*	perhaps distress
	Conseille* or helpe, and therfore telleth me	advise
130	Al youre anoy,* for it shal been secree.*	trouble secret
	For on my porthors* I make an oth	breviary, prayer-book
	That nevere in my lif, for lief or loth,†	
	Ne shal I of no conseil* yow biwreye.'*	secret reveal
	'The same agayn to yow,' quod she, 'I seye.	
135	By God and by this porthors I swere,	
	Thogh men me wolde al into peces tere,	
	Ne shal I nevere, for to gon to helle,	
	Biwreye a word of thyng that ye me telle,	
	†Nat for no cosynage ne alliance	
140	†But verraily for love and affiance.'	
	Thus been they sworn and herupon they keste,*	kissed
	And ech of hem tolde oother what hem leste.*	pleased them
	'Cosyn,' quod she, 'if that I hadde a space,	
	As I have noon, and namely* in this place,	especially
145	Thanne wolde I telle a legende* of my lyf,	story
	What I have suffred sith I was a wyf	
	With myn housbonde, al be he* youre cosyn.'	although he is
	'Nay,' quod this monk, 'by God and seint Martin,	
	He is namore* cosyn unto me	no more
150	Than is this leef that hangeth on the tree.	
	I clepe* hym so, by seint Denys of France,	call
	To han* the moore cause of aqueyntance	have
	Of yow, which I have loved specially	
	Aboven alle wommen, sikerly;*	truly
155	This swere I yow on my professioun.*	vow
	Telleth youre grief, lest that he come adoun;	
	And hasteth yow* and goth awey anon.'†	hurry
	'My deere love,' quod she, 'O my daun John,	

---

132 *for lief or loth* willingly or unwillingly
139–40 Not because of any relationship or alliance, but truly out of love and trust
157 *goth awey anon* go away quickly

>   Ful lief were me† this conseil* for to hyde,   secret
> 160   But out it moot;* I may namoore abyde.*   must come   endure
>   'Myn housbonde is to me the worste man
>   That evere was sith that the world bigan.
>   But sith I am a wyf it sit* nat me   becomes
>   To tellen no wight of oure privetee,*   intimate matters
> 165   Neither abedde* ne in noon oother place.   in bed
>   God shilde* I sholde it tellen, for his grace!   forbid
>   A wyf ne shal nat seyn of hir housbonde
>   But al honour,† as I kan understonde.
>   Save unto yow thus muche I tellen shal:
> 170   As help me God, he is noght worth at al,
>   In no degree,† the value of a flye.
>   But yet me greveth* moost his nygardye.*   vexes me   meanness
>   And wel ye woot* that wommen naturelly   know
>   Desiren thynges sixe as wel as I:
> 175   They wolde that hir housbondes sholde be
>   Hardy* and wise and riche and therto free,*   strong   open-handed
>   And buxom* unto his wyf and fressh abedde.†   obedient
>   But by that ilke* lord that for us bledde,   same
>   For his honour myself for to arraye,
> 180   A* Sonday next I moot nedes* paye   on   have to
>   An hundred frankes,* or ellis* am I lorn.*   francs else   lost
>   Yet were me levere† that I were unborn
>   †Than me were doon a sclaundre or vileynye.
>   And if myn housbonde eek myghte it espye†
> 185   I nere but lost,† and therfore, I yow preye,
>   Lene* me this somme or ellis moot I deye.*   lend   die
>   Daun John, I seye, lene me thise hundred frankes.
>   Pardee,* I wol noght faile yow my thankes   By God
>   If that yow list to doon that† I yow praye,
> 190   For at a certeyn day I wol yow paye
>   And doon to yow* what plesance and servyse   provide you with
>   That I may doon, right as yow list devyse.†

---

159 *Ful lief were me* I should very much like
168 *But al honour* anything except what is entirely to his credit
170–1 *noght worth at al, / In no degree* not even remotely worth
177 *fressh abedde* vigorous in bed
182 *were me lever* I would rather
183 Than I was disgraced or shamed
184 *might it espye* were to discover it
185 *I nere but lost* I would be quite lost
189 *yow list to doon that* are willing to do what
192 *right as yow list devyse* exactly as it pleases you to suggest

	And but I do,* God take on me vengeance	if I do not
	As foul as evere hadde Genelon of France.'†	
195	This gentil* monk answerde in this mannere:	courteous
	'Now trewely, myn owene lady deere,	
	I have,' quod he, 'on yow so gret a routhe*	pity
	That I yow swere and plighte yow my trouthe†	
	That whan youre housbonde is to Flandres fare,*	gone
200	I wol delivere yow out of this care,	
	For I wol brynge yow an hundred frankes.'	
	And with that word he caughte hir by the flankes	
	And hir embraceth harde and kiste hir ofte.	
	'Goth now youre wey,' quod he, 'al stille* and softe,	quietly
205	And lat us dyne as soone as that ye may,	
	For by my chilyndre† it is pryme of day.	
	Goth now and beth* as trewe as I shal be.'	be
	'Now ellis* God forbede, sire,' quod she,	otherwise
	And forth she goth as jolif as a pye,†	
210	And bad the cokes* that they sholde hem hye*	cooks hurry
	†So that men myghte dyne, and that anon.	
	Up to hir housbonde is his wyf ygon*	gone
	And knokketh at his countour boldely.	
	'Qi la?'† quod he. 'Peter,* it am I,'	by St Peter
215	Quod she. 'What, sire, how longe wol ye faste?†	
	How longe tyme wol ye rekene and caste*	calculate
	Youre sommes and youre bokes and youre thynges?	
	The devel have part on† alle swiche rekenynges!	
	Ye have ynogh, pardee, of Goddes sonde;*	gifts
220	Com doun today and lat youre bagges stonde.	
	Ne be ye nat* ashamed that daun John	are you not
	Shal fastynge al this day elenge* gon?*	miserable go
	What, lat us heere a masse and go we dyne.'	
	'Wyf,' quod this man, 'litel kanstow devyne*	guess
225	The curious bisynesse† that we have,	
	For of us chapmen* – also God me save†	merchants, businessmen

---

194 [*Genelon of France*   Ganelon betrayed Roland, hero of the twelfth-century French *Chanson de Roland* (Song of Roland), and was torn to pieces by four horses]
198   *plighte yow my trouthe*   give you my word
206   [*chilyndre*   a modish portable sundial]
209   *jolif as a pye*   cheerful as a magpie
211   So that people could have dinner, and quickly
214   *Qi la*   who is there
215   *wol ye faste?*   do you want to do without food?
218   *The devel have part on*   My the devil have a share in
225   *curious bisynesse*   abstruse responsibilities
226   *also God me save*   may God save me

        And by that lord that clepid* is seint Yve† — *called*
        Scarsly amonges twelve ten shul thryve
        Continuelly, lastyng unto oure age.
230 †We may wel make cheere and good visage
        †And dryve forth the world, as it may be,
        †And kepen oure estat in pryvetee
        †Til we be dede, or ellis that we pleye
        †A pilgrymage, or goon out of the weye.
235 And therfore have I gret necessitee
        Upon this queynte* world t'avyse me,* *strange to deliberate*
        For evermo* we mote* stonde in drede *continually must*
        Of hap* and fortune in oure chapmanhede.* *mischance trade*
          To Flandres wol I go tomorwe at day,
240 And come agayn* as soone as evere I may. *back*
        For which, my deere wyf, I thee biseke* *pray*
        As be to every wight buxom* and meke, *agreeable*
        †And for to kepe oure good be curious
        And honestly governe wel oure hous.
245 Thow hast ynow,* in every maner wise,† *enough*
        †That to a thrifty houshold may suffise.
        Thee lakketh† noon array* ne no vitaille;* *clothing food*
        Of silver in thy purs shaltow nat faille.'†
        And with that word his countour-dore he shette* *shut*
250 And doun he goth, no lenger wolde he lette.* *delay*
        But hastily a masse was ther seyd,
        And spedily the tables were yleyd,* *laid*
        And to the dyner* faste they hem spedde,* *dinner hurried*
        And richely this monk the chapman fedde.†
255   At after-dyner daun John sobrely
        This chapman took apart,* and prively *aside*
        He seyde hym thus: 'Cosyn, it standeth so†
        That wel I se to Brugges wol ye go.
        †God and seint Austyn spede yow and gyde;
260 I pray yow, cosyn, wysly that ye ryde.

---

227 *seint Yve* St Ivo [perhaps Yves of Kermartin (1303–47), lawyer and bishop]
230–4 We can certainly keep up appearances, put a good face on things, and face life as best we can, attending to our affairs discreetly, until we are dead, or enjoy a pilgrimage or disappear from view
243 And take care to look after our property
245 *in every maner wise* in every possible way
246 That a decent household needs
247 *Thee lakketh* you lack
248 *shaltow nat faille* you shall not want
254 *this monk the chapman fedde* the merchant fed this monk
257 *it standeth so* the circumstances are
259 May God and St Augustine help and guide you

Governeth yow* also of youre diete   regulate
Atemprely,* and namely* in this hete.   moderately   especially
Bitwix* us two nedeth no strange fare;†   between
Farewel, cosyn, God shilde* yow fro care.   protect
265 And if that any thyng, by day or nyght,
      If it lye in my power and my myght
      That ye me wol comande in any wise,*   way
      It shal be doon right* as ye wol devyse.*   exactly   instruct
        'O* thyng, er that ye goon,† if it may be: one
270 I wold preye yow for to lene me
      An hundred frankes for a wyke* or tweye   week
      For certeyn bestes* that I moste beye,*   livestock   buy
      †To store with a place that is oures.
      God help me so, I wolde it were youres.
275 I shal nat faille seurely* of my day,*   for certain   due date
      Nat for a thousand frankes, a myle way.†
      But lat this thyng be secree, I yow preye,
      For yet tonyght thise bestes moot I beye.
      And fare now wel, myn owene cosyn deere;
280 Grant mercy of† youre cost* and of youre cheere.'* expenditure   hospitality
        This noble marchant gentilly anon
      Answerde and seyde: 'O cosyn myn, daun John,
      Now sikerly* this is a smal requeste.   indeed
      My gold is youres whan that it yow leste,†
285 And nat oonly my gold but my chaffare.*   merchandise, goods
      Tak what yow list, God shilde† that ye spare.*   do without
      But o thyng is, ye knowe it wel ynow,
      Of chapmen, that hir moneye is hir plow.†
      We may creance* whil we han a name,†   borrow on credit
290 †But goldlees for to been, it is no game.
      Pay it agayn* whan it lyth in youre ese;†   back
      After my myght ful fayn† wol I yow plese.'
        Thise hundred frankes he fette* forth anon   fetched
      And prively he took hem to daun John.

---

263 *nedeth no strange fare*   no reserve is necessary
269 *er that ye goon*   before you go
273 To stock one of our properties
276 *a myle way*   by the time it takes to walk a mile
280 *Grant mercy of*   thank you for
284 *whan that yow leste*   whenever you want it
286 *God shilde*   God forbid
288 *hir plow*   their plough (the tools of their trade)
289 *han a name*   are regarded as financially sound
290 But to be without money is no joke
291 *lyth in your ese*   it is convenient for you
292 *After my myght ful fayn*   according to my capabilities very gladly

295	No wight* in al this world wiste* of this lone,	nobody knew
	Savyng this marchant and daun John allone.	
	They drynke and speke and rome† a while and pleye,*	amuse themselves
	Til that daun John rideth to his abbeye.	
	The morwe cam and forth this marchant rydeth	
300	To Flandres-ward;† his prentys* wel hym gydeth	apprentice
	Til he cam into Brugges murily.*	in good spirits
	Now goth this marchant faste and bisily	
	Aboute his nede,* and byeth and creaunceth.	business affairs
	He neither pleyeth at the dees* ne daunceth,	dice
305	But as a marchant, shortly for to telle,	
	He let his lyf,† and ther I lete hym dwelle.*	stay
	The Sonday next* the marchant was agon,*	after gone
	To Seint Denys ycomen is daun John,	
	With crowne† and berd al fressh and newe shave.	
310	In al the hous ther nas* so litel* a knave*	was not humble servant
	†Ne no wight ellis, that he nas ful fayn	
	That my lord daun John was come agayn.	
	And shortly to the poynt right for to gon,*	get
	This faire wyf acorded with† daun John	
315	That for thise hundred frankes he sholde al nyght	
	Have hire in his armes bolt upright,†	
	And this acord* parfourned* was in dede.	agreement performed
	In myrthe al nyght a bisy lyf they lede	
	Til it was day, that daun John wente his way	
320	And bad the meynee* farewel, have good day.	household
	For noon* of hem, ne no wight* in the town,	none nor anybody
	Hath of daun John right* no suspecioun.	at all
	And forth he rydeth hom* til his abbeye	home
	Or where hym list;† namoore* of hym I seye.	no more
325	This marchant, whan that ended was the faire,*	market
	To Seint Denys he gan for to repaire,†	
	And with his wyf he maketh feste and cheere,†	
	And telleth hir that chaffare* is so deere*	goods expensive

297 *rome* stroll about
300 *To Flandres-ward* towards Flanders
306 *let his lyf* passed his time
309 *crowne* tonsure [Priests shaved the crowns of their heads as a sign of their clerical calling]
311 Nor anyone else who was not very glad
314 *acorded with* came to an agreement with
316 *bolt upright* flat on [her] back
324 *where hym list* wherever he pleases
326 *gan for to repaire* returned
327 *maketh feste and cheere* rejoices and celebrates

	†That nedes moste he make a chevyssance,	
330	For he was bounden in a reconyssance*	bond
	To paye twenty thousand sheeld† anon.	
	For which this marchant is to Parys gon	
	To borwe of certeyne freendes that he hadde	
	A certeyn frankes,† and somme with hym he ladde.*	brought
335	And whan that he was come into the town,	
	For greet chiertee* and greet affeccioun,	fondness
	Unto daun John he first goth hym to pleye;*	to enjoy himself
	Nat for to axe* or borwe of hym moneye,	ask
	But for to wite* and seen of his welfare	find out about
340	And for to tellen hym of his chaffare,*	trade
	As freendes doon whan they been met yfeere.*	together
	Daun John hym maketh feste and murye cheere,†	
	And he hym tolde agayn* ful specially†	in return
	How he hadde wel yboght* and graciously,†	bought
345	Thanked be God, al hool his marchandise,†	
	Save that he moste in all maner wyse*	at all costs
	†Maken a chevyssance as for his beste,	
	And thanne he sholde been in joye and reste.	
	Daun John answerde: 'Certes,* I am fayn*	indeed delighted
350	That ye in heele* ar comen hom agayn.	safe and sound
	And if that I were riche, as have I blisse,†	
	Of twenty thousand sheeld sholde ye nat mysse,†	
	For ye so kyndely this oother day	
	Lente me gold, and as I kan and may†	
355	I thanke yow, by God and by seinte Jame.*	St James of Compostella
	But nathelees,* I took unto oure dame,†	nevertheless
	Yowre wyf at hom, the same gold agayn	
	Upon youre bench; she woot it wel,† certayn,	
	By certeyn toknes* that I kan yow telle.	proofs
360	Now, by youre leve, I may no lenger dwelle;*	stay

---

329 That he is obliged to raise a loan
331 *sheeld*   écus [French coins]
334 *A certeyn frankes*   a certain quantity of francs
342 *maketh feste and murye cheere*   welcomes him hospitably
343 *ful specially*   in great detail
344 *graciously*   on favourable terms
345 *al hool his marchandise*   all the goods he had purchased
347 Raise money to secure his interests
351 *as I have blisse*   I swear
352 *mysse*   feel the want
354 *as I kan and may*   to the best of my abilities
356 *dame*   mistress of the household
358 *woot it wel*   knows it for sure

Oure abbot wol* out of this town anon,* — wants to go straight away
And in his compaignye moot* I gon. — must
Greet wel oure dame, myn owene nece swete,
And farewel, deere cosyn, til we meete.'

365 This marchant, which that was ful war* and wys, — cautious
Creanced* hath and payed eek* in Parys — borrowed also
To certeyn Lombardes,† redy* in hir hond, — in cash
The somme of gold, and gat of hem† his bond
And hoom he gooth murye as a papynjay,* — parrot
370 For wel he knew he stood in swich array* — condition
That nedes moste he wynne* in that viage* — gain enterprise
A thousand frankes aboven al his costage.* — outlay
His wyf ful redy mette hym at the gate,
†As she was wont of old usage algate,
375 And al that nyght in myrthe they bisette,* — spent
For he was riche and cleerly out of dette.
Whan it was day, this marchant gan embrace
His wyf al newe and kiste hir on hir face,
And up he goth and maketh it ful tough.†
380 'Namoore,' quod she, 'by God, ye have ynough.'
And wantownely agayn with hym she pleyde,
Til at the laste this marchant seyde:
'By God,' quod he, 'I am a litel wroth* — angry
With yow, my wyf, althogh it be me looth,†
385 And woot ye* why? By God, as that I gesse,* — do you know think
That ye han maad a manere strangenesse†
Bitwixen* me and my cosyn, daun John. — between
Ye sholde han warned me er* I had gon — before
That he yow hadde a hundred frankes payed
390 †By redy tokne; and heeld hym yvele apayed,
For that* I to hym spak of chevyssance;† — because
†Me semed so as by his contenance.
But nathelees,* by God oure hevene kyng, — nevertheless
†I thoghte nat to axe of hym nothyng.†

---

367 *Lombardes* Lombards (Italian bankers)
368 *gat of hem* received from them
374 As she had always been accustomed to doing for a long time
379 *maketh it ful tough* is very pressing
384 *it be me looth* it is distasteful to me
386 *a manere strangenesse* a kind of coldness
390 With unmistakable signs of proof; and he esteemed himself ill-pleased
391 *chevyssance* raising a loan
392 It seemed so to me, from his expression
394 I did not intend to ask anything of him

395	I pray thee, wyf, ne do namoore so.†	
	Tel me alwey, er that I fro thee go,	
	If any dettour hath in myn absence	
	Ypayed thee, lest thurgh thy necligence	
	I myghte hym axe* a thyng that he hath payed.'	demand
400	This wyf was nat afered* ne afrayed,*	disturbed abashed
	But boldely she seyde, and that anon:	
	'Marie,† I diffye* the false monk, daun John.	reject
	†I kepe nat of his toknes never-a-del;	
	He took* me certeyn gold, this woot* I wel.	gave know
405	What yvel thedam* on his monkes snowte!	bad luck
	For God it woot, I wende* withouten dowte	believed
	That he hadde yeve* it me by cause of yow,	given
	†To doon therwith myn honour and my prow,	
	For cosynage† and eek for bele cheere*	hospitality
410	That he hath had ful ofte tymes heere.	
	†But sith I se it stant in this disjoynt,	
	I wole answere yow shortly to the poynt:	
	Ye han mo slakker* dettours than am I,	more dilatory
	For I wol paye yow wel and redily	
415	Fro day to day; and if so be I fayle,	
	I am youre wyf, score it upon my tayle.†	
	And I shal paye as soone as evere I may.	
	For, by my trouthe, I have on myn array,*	clothes
	And nat in wast,* bistowed every del.*	extravagance entirely
420	And for I have bistowed it so wel	
	For youre honour, for Goddes sake, I seye,	
	As be nat wrooth,* but lat us laughe and pleye.	don't be angry
	Ye shal my joly body han to wedde;*	for a pledge
	By God, I wol noght paye yow but abedde.*	except in bed
425	Forgyve it me, myn owene spouse deere.	
	Turn hiderward* and maketh bettre cheere.'*	this way cheer up
	This marchant saugh* ther was no remedye,	saw
	And for to chide it nere but folye,†	

---

395 *ne do namoore so* don't do it again
402 *Marie* By saint Mary [the Blessed Virgin]
403 I don't care a hoot for his signs of proof
408 to advance my honour and profit with
409 *For cosynage* because of kinship
411 But since I see this difficulty has arisen
416 *score it upon my tayle* mark it up on my tally [*tayle* there is a pun here on *taile* 'genitals' which is picked up again in l. 434. The wife pays her financial debt by paying her marital debt (obligation to have intercourse with her husband; see Margery Kempe, 'The Vow of Chastity', p.435)]
428 *nere but foly* would be nothing but foolishness

Syn* that the thyng may nat amended be. — since
430 'Now, wyf,' he seyde, 'and I foryeve it thee;
But by thy lyf, ne be namoore so large.* — liberal
Keep bet thy good;† this yeve I thee in charge.'* — as a duty
  Thus endeth my tale, and God us sende
Taillynge* ynough unto oure lyves ende. — tallying

---

432 *Keep bet thy good* look after your property better

The Nun's Priest's Tale

The Nun's Priest is not described in the General Prologue, where we are simply told that the Prioress is accompanied by three priests. At the conclusion of the Monk's gloomy Tale, which is brought to an end by the Knight, the Host invites the Nun's Priest to tell 'swich thyng as may our hertes glade'. The Nun's Priest, described by the narrator as 'This sweete preest, this goodly man, Sir John', promises to oblige.

His Tale is an Aesopic beast fable drawn from the cycle of stories associated with Reynard the Fox which were composed in France in the late twelfth and early thirteenth centuries. The story of Reynard, Chantecler and Chantecler's wife Pinte occurs in Branch Two of the Reynard cycle, with the major difference from Chaucer's version that in the French Pinte is fearful of Chantecler's dream, and it is he who refuses to take it seriously. The Nun's Priest's version of the tale is an exuberant literary parody whose mock-heroics send up chivalric, learned, preacherly and rhetorical discourses, as well as the dreamlore which Chaucer treats seriously in *The Parliament of Fowls*. In its diversity of styles the Nun's Priest's Tale can be seen as a paradigm of Chaucer's method in *The Canterbury Tales* as a whole.

THE NUN'S PRIEST'S TALE

A poore widwe,* somdel* stape* in age,	widow somewhat advanced
Was whilom* dwellynge in a narwe* cotage	once small
Biside a grove, stondyng in a dale.	
This widwe, of which I telle yow my tale,	
5 Syn thilke* day that she was last a wyf	that
In pacience ladde a ful symple lyf,	
For litel was hir catel* and hir rente.*	property income
By housbondrye* of swich* as God hir sente	management such

	She foond[†] hirself and eek* hir doghtren* two.	also daughters
10	Thre large sowes hadde she and namo,*	no more
	Thre kyn* and eek a sheep that highte* Malle.	cows was called
	Ful sooty was hir bour* and eek hir halle,	bower
	In which she eet ful many a sklendre* meel.	frugal
	Of poynaunt* sawce hir neded never a deel;*	pungent none at all
15	No deyntee morsel passed thurgh hir throte.	
	Hir diete was acordant to hir cote;*	gown
	Repleccioun* ne made hir nevere syk.	surfeit
	Attempree* diete was al hir phisyk,*	moderate medicine
	And exercise and hertes suffisaunce.*	heart's sufficiency
20	The gowte lette hir nothyng for to daunce,[†]	
	N'apoplexie shente* nat hir heed.*	hurt head
	No wyn ne drank she, neither whit ne reed.	
	Hir bord* was served moost* with whit and blak –	table mostly
	Milk and broun breed – in which she foond no lak,*	nothing lacking
25	Seynd* bacoun, and somtyme an ey* or tweye,*	grilled egg two
	For she was, as it were, a maner deye.[†]	
	A yeerd* she hadde, enclosed al aboute	yard
	With stikkes and a drye dych withoute,*	outside
	In which she hadde a cok heet* Chauntecler.	called
30	In al the land of crowyng nas* his peer;	was not
	His voys was murier* than the myrie orgon	more tuneful
	On massedayes that in the chirche gon.*	play(s)
	Wel sikerer[†] was his crowyng in his logge*	shed
	Than is a clokke or any abbey orlogge.*	clock
35	By nature he krew ech ascencioun[†]	
	Of equinoxial in thilke town;	
	For whan degrees fiftene were ascended	
	Thanne krew he, that it myghte nat ben amended.*	improved upon
	His komb was redder than the fyn coral	
40	And batayled* as it were a castel-wal.	crenellated
	His byle was blak and as the jeet* it shoon;	jet
	Lyk asure were hise legges and his toon.*	toes
	Hise nayles whitter than the lylye-flour	
	And lyk the burned gold was his colour.	

9 *foond* provided for
20 *lette hir nothyng for to daunce* did not stop her dancing at all
26 *maner deye* sort of dairywoman
33 *Wel sikerer* much more reliable
35–8 [According to medieval astronomy, the equinoctial is an imaginary line round the earth on the plane of the equator which revolves westwards, completing the circle every 24 hours. An imaginary point on the equinoctial will thus travel through 15 degrees an hour, taking 24 hours to pass through 360 degrees. Chauntecleer is naturally able to reckon when such a point has ascended 15 degrees above the horizon and thus when an hour has passed, and crow accordingly]

45	This gentil* cok hadde in his governaunce*	noble control
	Sevene hennes for to doon al his plesaunce,†	
	Whiche were hise sustres* and his paramours*	sisters concubines
	And wonder lyke* to hym as of colours,	remarkably similar
	Of whiche the faireste hewed* on hire throte	coloured
50	Was clepid* faire damoysele* Pertelote.	called lady, mistress
	Curteys* she was, discret and debonaire*	courteous gracious
	†And compaignable, and bar hirself so faire	
	Syn thilke day that she was seven nyght oold	
	That trewely she hath the herte in hoold*	in her keeping
55	Of Chauntecler, loken* in every lyth.*	locked limb
	He loved hir so that wel was hym therwith.†	
	But swich a joye was it to here hem* synge,	them
	Whan that the brighte sonne gan to sprynge,*	rise
	In swete acord: 'My leef is faren in londe';†	
60	For thilke tyme, as I have understonde,	
	Beestes and briddes* kouden* speke and synge.	birds knew how to
	And so bifel that in a dawenynge,*	early one morning
	As Chauntecler among hise wyves alle	
	Sat on his perche that was in the halle	
65	And next hym sat this faire Pertelote,	
	This Chauntecler gan gronen* in his throte	began to groan
	As man that in his dreem is drecched* soore.	disturbed
	And whan that Pertelote thus herde hym rore	
	She was agast, and seyde: 'Herte deere,	
70	What eyleth* yow to grone in this manere?	ails
	Ye ben a verray* sleper, fy for shame!'	true
	And he answerde and seyde thus: 'Madame,	
	I prey yow that ye take it nat agrief.†	
	By God, me mette* I was in swich meschief*	I dreamed such trouble
75	Right now that yet myn herte is soore afright.*	terrified

---

46 *doon al his plesaunce*   perform all his desires
52 and sociable, and behaved herself so beautifully
56 *wel was hym therwith*   he was happy because of it
59 *My leef is faren in londe*   My love has gone away
[A single stanza of this lover's lament has survived:

> My lefe ys faren in lond;
>   Allas, why is she so?
> And I am so sore bound
>   I may nat come her to.
> She hath my hert in hold
>   Wherever she ryde or go
> With trew love a thousandfold.

The fifth line is echoed in l. 54]
73 *take it nat agrief*   are not upset

Now God,' quod he, 'my swevene* recche* aright — dream interpret
And kepe my body out of foul prisoun.
Me mette how that I romed up and doun
Withinne oure yeerd, where as I say* a beest — saw
80 Was lyk an hound and wolde han maad arest* — seized
Upon my body and han* had me ded. — have
His colour was bitwixe* yelow and red, — between
And tipped was his tayl and bothe hise erys* — ears
With blak, unlik the remenaunt* of hise herys;* — rest hair
85 His snowte smal,* with glowyng eyen* tweye;* — slender eyes two
Yet of his look for fere almoost I deye.* — die
This caused me my gronyng doutelees.'* — undoubtedly
  'Avoy,'* quod* she, 'fy on yow, hertelees!* — come said feeble creature
Allas,' quod she, 'for by that God above,
90 Now han ye lost myn herte and al my love.
I kan nat love a coward, by my feith!
For certes,* whatso* any womman seith, — indeed whatever
We alle desiren if it myghte be
To han housbondes hardy,* wise and fre,* — bold generous
95 And secree* and no nygard* ne* no fool, — discreet miser nor
Ne hym that is agast* of every tool,* — afraid weapon
Ne noon avauntour.* By that God above, — boaster
How dorste* ye seyn for shame unto youre love — dared
That anythyng myghte make yow aferd?* — afraid
100 Have ye no mannes herte and han a berd?* — beard
Allas, and konne* ye ben agast of swevenys?* — can dreams
  'Nothyng, God woot,* but vanytee* in swevene is. — knows nonsense
Swevenes engendren of* replexions* — breed from surfeit
And ofte of fume,* and of complexions* — vapour temperaments
105 Whan humours† ben* to habundant in a wight.* — are person
Certes, this dreem which ye han met* tonyght — dreamed
Comth of the grete superfluitee
Of youre rede colera,* pardee,* — bile indeed
Which causeth folk to dreden* in hir* dremes — fear their
110 Of arwes* and of fyr with rede lemes,* — arrows flames
Of rede bestes that they wol hem byte,
Of contek* and of whelpes grete and lyte;* — strife small
Right* as the humour of malencolie — just
Causeth ful many a man in sleep to crie

---

105 [*humours* according to medieval theory, the human body is a blending ('complexioun') of four humours: blood, choler, phlegm and melancholy. Pertelote diagnoses Chauntecleer's dream of the red and black fox as being caused by a superfluity of choler, which is associated with red, and also of melancholy, associated with black. Her remedy is a laxative (ll. 126–7)]

115	For fere of blake beres* or boles* blake,	bears	bulls
	Or ellis* blake develes wol hem take.		else
	Of othere humours koude I telle also		
	That werken many a man in sleep ful wo,†		
	But I wol passe as lightly* as I kan.		quickly
120	Lo, Catoun,† which that was so wys a man,		
	Seyde he nat thus: "Ne do no fors of† dremes"?		
	'Now, sire,' quod she, 'whan we fle* fro* thise bemes,	fly	from
	For Goddes love, as taak som laxatif.		
	Up* peril of my soule and of my lif,		upon
125	I conseile* yow the beste, I wot nat lye,		advise
	That bothe of coler and of malencolye		
	Ye purge yow; and for* ye shal nat tarye,		so that
	Thogh in this town is noon* apothecarye,		there is no
	I shal myself to herbes techen* yow		instruct
130	That shul ben for youre heele* and for youre prow.*	health	advantage
	And in oure yerd tho* herbes shal I fynde		those
	The whiche han of hir propretee* by kynde*	peculiarity	nature
	To purge yow bynethe and eek above.		
	Foryet* nat this, for Goddes owene love!		forget
135	Ye ben ful colerik of complexioun;		
	Ware* the sonne in his ascencioun		beware
	Ne fynde yow nat replet* of humours hote.†		full
	And if it do, I dar wel leye* a grote*	lay	fourpenny piece
	That ye shul have a fevere terciane*		tertian (recurrent)
140	Or an agew* that may be youre bane.*	ague	death
	A day or two ye shul han degestyves		
	Of wormes, er ye take youre laxatyves		
	†Of lauriol,* centaur,* and fumetere,*	spurge laurel centaury	fumitory
	Or ellis of ellebor* that groweth there,		hellebore
145	Of katapuce* or of gaytrys beryis,†		caper-spurge
	Of herbe yve† growyng in oure yerd ther merye is.		
	Pekke hem up right as they growe and ete hem in.		
	Be myrie, housbonde, for youre fader kyn!*		father's family
	Dredeth* no dreem! I kan sey yow namoore.'		fear

118 *werken ... ful wo* do ... much harm
120 [*Catoun* Dionysus Cato, author of the fourth-century *Disticha Catonis* (Distichs of Cato), a collection of maxims which was widely read in Latin and in English translation. The quotation is from book 2.32]
121 *Ne do no fors of* pay no heed to
137 [*humours hote* choler is formed out of the contraries hot and dry, and Pertelote fears that Chauntecleer's choleric temperament will be aggravated by the heat of the sun]
143–6 [The herbs recommended by Pertelote were all known in the middle ages for their purgative powers]
145 *gaytrys beryis* ?buckthorn ?honeysuckle berries
146 *herbe yve* ?buck's horn plantain

150	'Madame,' quod he, 'grant mercy of youre loore.*	teaching
	But nathelees, as touchyng daun* Catoun	master
	That hath of wisdom swich a gret renoun:*	reputation
	Thogh that he bad* no dremes for to drede,	commanded
	By God, men may in olde bokes rede	
155	Of many a man moore of auctoritee*	authority
	Than evere Caton was, so mote I thee,†	
	That al the revers* seyn* of his sentence,*	opposite says opinion
	And han wel founden by experience	
	That dremes ben signyficaciouns	
160	As wel of joye as tribulaciouns	
	That folk enduren in this lyf present.	
	†Ther nedeth make of this noon argument –	
	The verray preve* sheweth it in dede.*	proof in fact
	†'Oon* of the gretteste auctour* that men rede	one authors
165	Seith thus: that whilom* two felawes* wente	once companions
	On pilgrymage in a ful good entente,†	
	And happed* so they coomen in a town	it chanced
	Where as ther was swich congregacioun	
	Of peple, and eek so streit* of herbergage,*	short accommodation
170	That they ne founde as muche as o* cotage	one
	In which they bothe myghte ylogged* be.	lodged
	Wherfore they mosten* of necessitee	must
	As for that nyght departe* compaignye;	part
	And ech of hem gooth to his hostelrye*	lodging
175	And took his loggyng as it wolde falle.†	
	That oon* of hem was logged in a stalle	one
	Fer* in a yeerd with oxen of the plow;	at a distance
	That oother man was logged wel ynow,*	enough
	As was his aventure,* or his fortune	luck
180	That us governeth alle as in commune.*	generally
	And so bifel* that longe er* it were day	it happened before
	This man mette* in his bed ther as* he lay	dreamed where
	How that his felawe gan upon hym calle	
	And seyde: "Allas, for in an oxes stalle	
185	This nyght I shal be mordred ther* I lye.	where
	Now help me, deere brother, or I dye!	

156 *so mote I thee* as I hope to prosper
162 It is not necessary to dispute this
164 [Possibly Marcus Tullius Cicero (106–43 BC) in *De Divinatione* (On Divination); or Valerius Maximus in *Facta et Dicta Memorabilia* (Memorable Deeds and Sayings) (*c.* AD 15); or Robert Holcot (d.1349) in *Libri Sapientiae* (Books of Wisdom). All these authors tell both stories]
166 *in a ful good entente* with the best of intentions
175 *as it wolde falle* as things turned out

In alle haste come to me," he sayde.
   'This man out of his sleep for feere abrayde,* started
But whan that he was wakned of his sleep
190 He turned hym and took of this no keep:†
Hym thoughte his dreem nas* but a vanytee.* was trifle
Thus twies* in his slepyng dremed he, twice
And atte* thridde* tyme yet his felawe at the third
Cam, as hym thoughte,† and seyde: "I am now slawe.* slain
195 Bihoold my blody woundes depe and wyde.
Arys up erly in the morwe tyde* morning
And atte west gate of the town," quod* he, said
"A carte ful of donge ther shaltow* se you shall
In which my body is hyd ful prively.* secretly
200 Do thilke cart aresten* boldely. stop that cart
My gold caused my mordre,* sooth to seyn,"† murder
And tolde hym every poynt* how he was sleyn, detail
With a ful pitous* face pale of hewe. pitiful
And truste wel, his dreem he fond* ful trewe, found
205 For on the morwe as soone as it was day
To his felawes in* he took the way, lodging
And whan that he cam to this oxes stalle
After his felawe he bigan to calle.
   'The hostiler* answerde hym anon* innkeeper straight away
210 And seyde: "Sire, youre felawe is agon.* gone
As soone as day he wente out of the town."
   'This man gan fallen in suspecioun,†
Remembrynge on hise dremes that he mette.
And forth he goth – no lenger wolde he lette* – delay
215 Unto the west gate of the town and fond
A dong-carte wente* as it were to donge lond† [that] went
That was arrayed* in that same wise* equipped way
As ye han herd the dede man devyse.* describe
And with an hardy herte he gan to crye:
220 "Vengeaunce and justice of* this felonye! for
My felawe mordred is this same nyght,
And in this cart heere he lyth* gapyng upright.* lies face upwards
I crye on the mynystres,"* quod he, officers
"That sholde kepe* and rulen this citee: maintain

---

190 *took of this no keep* paid no attention to this
194 *hym thoughte* it seemed to him
201 *sooth to seyn* to tell the truth
212 *gan fallen in suspecioun* began to be suspicious
216 *donge lond* dung heap

225	Harrow,* allas, heere lyth my felawe slayn!"	help
	What sholde I moore unto this tale sayn?	
	The peple up sterte* and caste the cart to grounde.	rushed
	And in the myddel of the dong they founde	
	The dede man that mordred was al newe.*	recently
230	'O blisful* God, that art so just and trewe,	full of blessings
	Lo, how that thow biwreyest* mordre alway.	reveal
	Mordre wol out, that se we day by day.	
	Mordre is so wlatsom* and abhomynable	heinous
	To God, that is so just and resonable,	
235	That he ne wol nat suffre it helyd* be	hidden
	Though it abyde a yeer or two or thre.	
	Mordre wol out, this my conclusioun.	
	And right anon* ministres of that town	straight away
	Han hent* the cartere and so soore hym pyned,*	seized tortured
240	And eek the hostiler so sore engyned,*	racked
	That they biknewe* hir wikkednesse anon	confessed
	And they were anhanged* by the nekke-bon.	hanged
	Heere may men sen that dremes ben to drede.*	to be feared
	'And certes, in the same book I rede,	
245	Right in the nexte chapitre after this	
	†— I gabbe nat, so have I joye or blys! —	
	Two men that wolde han passed over see	
	For certeyn cause into a fer contree,	
	If that the wynd ne hadde ben contrarie	
250	That made hem in a citee for to tarie	
	That stood ful myrie upon an haven syde.	
	But on a day, agayn* the even-tyde,	towards
	The wynd gan chaunge and blew right as hem leste.*	they wanted
	Jolif* and glad, they wenten unto reste	light-hearted
255	And casten hem* ful erly for to sayle.	decided
	But herkneth, to that o* man fil* a gret mervaille.	one befell
	'That oon of hem in slepyng as he lay	
	Hym mette* a wonder dreem agayn the day.	dreamed
	Hym thoughte a man stood by his beddes syde	
260	And hym comanded that he sholde abyde,*	stay (there)
	And seyde hym thus: "If thow tomorwe wende,*	go
	Thow shalt be dreynt.* My tale is at an ende."	drowned
	'He wook and tolde his felawe what he mette	
	And preyde hym his viage* to lette;*	journey delay

---

246 I do not talk idly — may I be saved

265	As for that day he preyde hym to byde.	
	'His felawe, that lay by his beddes syde,	
	Gan for to laughe and scorned hym ful faste.	
	"No dreem," quod he, "may so myn herte agaste*	terrify
	That I wol lette for to do my thynges.	
270	I sette nat a straw by† thy dremynges,	
	For swevenes* ben but vanytees* and japes.*	dreams trifles foolishness
	Men dreme al day of owles or of apes,	
	And of many a maze* therwithal –	delusion
	Men dreme of thyng that nevere was ne shal.	
275	But sith* I see that thow wolt here abyde	since
	And thus forslewthen* wilfully thy tyde,*	waste time
	God woot,* it reweth me,* and have good day."	knows I am sorry
	And thus he took his leve and wente his way.	
	But er* that he hadde half his cours* yseyled,	before journey
280	†Noot I nat why ne what meschaunce it eyled,	
	But casuelly* the shippes botme* rente	by chance bottom
	And ship and man under the water wente	
	In sighte of othere shippes it bisyde,	
	That with hem seyled at the same tyde.	
285	'And therfore, faire Pertelote so deere,	
	By swiche ensamples olde maystow leere*	learn
	That no man sholde ben to recchelees*	too heedless
	Of dremes, for I sey* thee, doutelees,	tell
	That many a dreem ful soore is for to drede.	
290	†'Lo, in the lyf of seint Kenelm I rede,	
	That was Kenulphus sone, the noble kyng	
	Of Mercenrike,† how Kenelm mette* a thyng	dreamed
	A lite* er he was mordred on a day.	little
	His mordre in his avysion* he say.*	dream saw
295	His norice* hym expowned* every del*	nurse interpreted part
	His swevene and bad hym for to kepe* hym wel	protect
	For traysoun, but he nas but sevene yeer old	
	And therfore litel tale hath he told†	
	Of any dreem, so holy was his herte.	
300	By God, I hadde levere* than my sherte	rather

270 *I sette . . . by* I not give a straw for
280 I do not know why or what misfortune afflicted it
290–2 [*seint Kenelm . . . Kenulphus . . . Mercenrike* according to legend the seven-year-old Cenhelm (*Kenelm*), son of Cenwulf (*Kenulphus*) king of Mercia (d.821), dreamed that he climbed a tree which was cut down by one of his friends, whereupon he flew to heaven in the form of a bird. This dream foretold his murder]
292 *Mercenrike* the kingdom of Mercia
298 *tale hath he told* notice has he taken

That ye hadde rad* his legende as have I.   *read*
Dame Pertelote, I sey yow trewely:
†Macrobeus, that writ the avysioun
In Affrike of the worthy Cipioun,
305 Affermeth* dremes and seith that they ben   *confirms the value of*
Warnynge of thynges that men after* sen.   *afterwards*
   'And forthermoore, I pray yow looketh wel
In the Olde Testament of Danyel,†
If he heeld dremes any vanytee.*   *trifle*
310 †Rede eek of Joseph, and there shul ye see
Wher dremes be somtyme, I sey nat alle,
Warnynge of thynges that shul after falle.*   *come about*
Looke of Egipte the kyng, daun* Pharao,   *lord*
His bakere and his butiller also
315 Wher* they ne felte noon effect in* dremes.   *whether   from*
   'Whoso wol seke actes of sondry* remes*   *various   kingdoms*
May rede of dremes many a wonder thyng.
Lo, Cresus,† which that was of Lyde* kyng,   *Lydia*
Mette he nat that he sat upon a tree
320 Which signyfide he sholde anhanged be?
†Lo here, Andromacha, Ectores wyf,
That day that Ector sholde lese* his lyf   *lose*
She dremed on the same nyght biforn
How that the lyf of Ector sholde be lorn*   *lost*
325 If thilke* day he wente into bataille.   *that*
She warned hym but it myghte nat availle;
He wente for to fighte nathelees,*   *nevertheless*
But he was slayn anon* of* Achilles,   *directly   by*
   'But thilke tale is al to long to telle,
330 And eek it is ney* day; I may nat dwelle.   *almost*
Shortly I seye, as for conclusioun,
That I shal han* of* this avysioun   *have   from*
Adversitee; and I seye, forthermoor,
That I ne telle of laxatyves no stoor,†

303–4 [*Macrobeus* around AD 400 Macrobius wrote a commentary on the *Somnium Scipionis* (Dream of Scipio) which was originally part of the *De Republica* (On the State) of Marcus Tullius Cicero (106–43 BC). The Scipio ('Cipioun') of the title had his dream while visiting north Africa]
308 [*Danyel* the Old Testament book of Daniel, chapters 7–12, consists of a series of visions]
310–15 [Joseph earned his freedom from captivity in Egypt through his ability to interpret the prophetic dreams first of Pharaoh's butler and baker, and then of Pharaoh himself. See Genesis 41 and 42]
318 [*Cresus* the story of Croesus is told in the thirteenth-century French *Roman de la Rose* (*Romance of the Rose*), which Chaucer translated]
321–8 [*Andromacha, Ectores wyf . . . Achilles* Andromache, wife of Hector, son of king Priam of Troy and leader of the Trojan army, presaged her husband's death at the hands of the Greek hero, Achilles. This story is not in Homer's *Iliad*, but is a medieval development]
334   *telle of . . . stoor*   set no store by

335	For they ben venymes,* I woot* it wel.	poisons know
	I hem deffie,* I love hem never a del.†	reject
	'Now lat us speke of myrthe, and stynte* al this.	cease
	Madame Pertelote, so have I blys,	
	Of o thyng God hath sent me large grace.*	bountiful favour
340	For whan I se the beautee of youre face	
	– Ye ben so scarlet reed aboute youre eyen –	
	It maketh al my drede for to dyen.	
	†For also siker as *In principio,*	
	†*Mulier est hominis confusio.*	
345	Madame, the sentence* of this Latyn is:	meaning
	Womman is mannes joye and al his blys.	
	For whan I feele a* nyght youre softe syde,	by
	Al be it that I may nat on yow ryde	
	For that oure perche is maad* so narwe,* allas,	made narrow
350	I am so ful of joye and of solas*	delight
	That I deffie bothe swevene and dreem.'	
	And with that word he fley* doun fro the beem	flew
	For it was day, and eke hise hennes alle,	
	And with a chuk he gan hem for to calle	
355	For he hadde founde a corn lay† in the yerd.	
	Real* he was; he was namoore aferd.	royal
	He fethered Pertelote twenty tyme	
	And trad* as ofte er* it was pryme.	trod before
	He looketh* as it were a grym leoun,	appears
360	And on hise toos* he rometh* up and doun.	toes walks
	Hym deyned* nat to sette his foot to grounde	he deigned
	And chukketh whan he hath a corn yfounde,	
	And to hym rennen* thanne hise wyves alle.	run
	Thus real as a prince is in his halle	
365	Leve I this Chauntecler in his pasture,	
	And after wol I telle his aventure.	
	Whan that the monthe in which the world bigan,†	
	†That highte* March, whan God first maked man,	is called

---

336 *never a del* not a jot
343–4 For as sure as 'In the beginning', woman is man's undoing
[*In principio* (in the beginning) is the opening of St John's gospel, and therefore gospel truth. The popular Latin tag which Chauntecleer seeks to verify in this way means the opposite of what he claims]
355 *corn lay* piece of corn [which] lay
367 [*the monthe ... world bigan* medieval authorities taught that the world was created in March]
368–70 [*March .../... thirti dayes and two* May 3, the day after the completion of 32 days after the completion of March. ('Syn March bigan' is misleading)]

                Was complet and passed were also
370   Syn March bigan thirti dayes and two,†
      Bifel that Chauntecler in al his pryde,
      Hise sevene wyves walkyng hym bisyde,
      †Caste up hise eyen to the brighte sonne
      That in the signe of Taurus hadde yronne*   run
375   Twenti degrees and oon* and somwhat moore,†   one
      And knew by kynde* and by noon oother loore*   nature   teaching
      That it was pryme* and krew with blisful stevene.*   the first hour   voice
      †'The sonne,' he seyde, 'is clomben* upon hevene   has climbed
      Fourti degrees and oon and moore, ywis.*   indeed
380   Madame Pertelote, my worldes blys,
      Herkneth thyse blisful bryddes* how they synge,   birds
      And se the fresshe floures how they sprynge.*   grow
      Ful is myn herte of revel* and solas.'   pleasure
          But sodeynly hym fil* a sorweful cas,†   there befell him
385   For evere* the latter ende of joye is wo.   always
      God woot* that worldly joye is soone ago!*   knows   gone
      And if a rethor* koude faire endite,*   rhetorician   compose
      He in a cronycle saufly* myghte it write   with safety
      As for a sovereyn notabilitee.†
390   Now every wys man lat hym herkne* me: listen to
      This storie is also* trewe, I undertake,   as
      As is the book of Launcelot de Lake†
      That wommen holde in ful gret reverence.
      Now wol I torne agayn to my sentence.*   subject
395   A colfox,* ful of sley* iniquitee,   black fox   sly
      That in the grove hadde woned* yeres thre,   lived
      †By heigh ymaginacioun forncast,*   premeditated
      The same nyght thurghout the hegges* brast*   hedges   burst
      Into the yerd ther* Chauntecler the faire   where
400   Was wont and eek hise wyves to repaire;*   resort

373–5 [*the brighte sonne/ . . . Taurus . . ./ somwhat moore* if the sun has travelled rather more than 21 degrees into the zodiacal sign of Taurus (mid April to mid May), the date can be calculated as May 3]
378–9 [*The sonne . . ./. . . oon and moore* the sun's annual journey through all the signs of the zodiac is reckoned in degrees (as in line 375, and so, though on a different scale, is its daily journey across the sky. It is this latter calculation which Chauntecleer makes at line 379. On May 3, the sun is just past 41 degrees above the horizon at 9 a.m.]
384 *sorweful cas* grievous misfortune
389 *sovereyn notabilitee* supremely significant fact
392 [*Launcelot de Lake* the hero of the thirteenth-century French Arthurian romance *Lancelot du Lac*, which is not true at all]
397 [This line can be interpreted as referring to God's foreknowledge of events, or to Chauntecleer's dream, but the 'heigh imaginacioun' may be an ironic reference to the fox's machinations]

	And in a bed of wortes* stille he lay	cabbages
	Til it was passed undren* of the day,	midmorning
	Waitynge his tyme on Chauntecler to falle –	
	As gladly doon thise homycides alle	
405	That in awayt liggen* to mordre men.	lie
	O false mordrour lurkynge in thy den!	
	O newe Scariot†, newe Genylon!†	
	False dissimilour,* o Greek Synoun†	dissimulator
	That broghtest Troye al outrely* to sorwe!*	utterly grief
410	O Chauntecler, acursed be that morwe*	morning
	That thow into the yerd flaugh* from the bemys!	flew
	Thow were ful wel ywarned by thy dremys	
	That thilke day was perilous to thee.	
	But what that God forwoot† moot* nedes be,	must
415	After the opynyoun of certeyn clerkis.*	scholars
	Witnesse on hym that any parfit clerk is,	
	That in scole* is gret altercacioun*	universities argument
	In that matere, and gret disputisoun*	disputation
	And hath ben of an hundred thousand men.	
420	But I ne kan nat bulte it to the bren†	
	– As kan the holy doctour Augustyn†	
	Or Boece* or the bisshop Bradwardyn –	Boethius
	†Wheither that Goddes worthy forewityng*	foreknowledge
	Streyneth* me nedely* for to doon* a thyng	constrains necessarily do
425	(Nedely clepe* I symple necessitee);	call
	Or ellis if fre choys be graunted me	
	To do that same thyng or do it noght,	
	Thogh God forwoot it er* that I was wroght;*	before created
	Or if his wityng* streyneth never a del*	knowledge not at all
430	But* by necessitee condicionel.	except

---

407 [*Scariot* Judas Iscariot, betrayer of Christ   *Genyloun* Ganelon, who betrayed Roland, hero of the twelfth-century French epic, *Le Chanson de Roland* (The Song of Roland)]
408 [*Synoun* Sinon treacherously persuaded the Trojans to let into Troy the wooden horse containing Greek soldiers]
414 *forwoot* has foreknowledge of
420 *bulte it to the bren* sift it thoroughly
421–2 [*Augustyn ... Boece ... Bradwardyn* all wrote on the question of man's freedom and God's foreknowledge. St Augustine (354–430) wrote against the Pelagian heresy that man can freely will his own salvation; Boethius (*c.* 480–524) confronted the question of how far man is free in his *Consolatio Philosophiae* (Consolation of Philosophy), which Chaucer translated; Thomas Bradwardine (d.1349), Oxford theologian, argued that God has complete foreknowledge of events]
423–30 [The alternatives suggested are: that because God has foreknowledge of what I am going to do, I am bound to do it as a consequence of that foreknowledge (simple necessity); that God's foreknowledge of an event still leaves it open for me to choose whether or not to do it (free choice); that I will do what God foresees I will do, but not as a consequence of God's foreseeing it (conditional necessity)]

>   I wol nat han to do of swich* matere; *with such*
>   My tale is of a cok, as ye may heere,
>   That took his conseil* of his wyf with sorwe *advice*
>   To walken in the yerd upon that morwe
> 435   That he hadde met* the dreem that I yow tolde. *dreamed*
>   Wommens conseils be ful ofte colde;
>   Wommannes conseil broghte us first to wo
>   And made Adam fro paradys to go,
>   Ther as* he was ful myrie and wel at ese. *where*
> 440   But for* I noot* to whom it myghte displese *because   do not know*
>   If I conseil of wommen wolde blame,
>   Passe over, for I seyde it in my game.
>   Rede auctours* where they trete of swich matere *authors*
>   And what they seyn of wommen heere;
> 445   Thise ben the cokkes wordes and nat myne.
>   I kan noon harm on* no womman devyne.* *in   suppose*
>   Faire in the sond* to bathe hir myrily *sand*
>   Lyth* Pertelote and alle hir sustres* by *remains   sisters*
>   Agayn* the sonne, and Chauntecler so free *in*
> 450   Song myrier than the mermayde in the see
>   (For Phisiologus† seith sikerly
>   How that they syngen wel and myrily).
>   And so bifel that as he caste his eye
>   Among the wortes* on a boterflye *cabbages*
> 455   He was war of this fox that lay ful lowe.
>   Nothyng ne liste hym* thanne for to crowe, *he did not want at all*
>   But cryde anon, 'Cok, cok', and up he sterte
>   As man that was affrayd in his herte;
>   For naturelly a beest desireth flee
> 460   Fro his contrarie, if he may it see,
>   Though he nevere erst* hadde seye it with his eye. *before*
>   This Chauntecler whan he gan hym espye,
>   He wolde han fled but that the fox anon
>   Seyde: 'Gentil sire, allas, wher wol ye gon?
> 465   Be ye affrayd of me that am youre freend?
>   Now certes, I were worse than a feend* *devil*
>   If I to yow wolde harm or vileynye.* *injury*
>   I am nat come youre conseil* for t'espye,* *secrets   to spy on*
>   But trewely the cause of my comynge
> 470   Was oonly for to herkne* how that ye synge: *listen*

451 [*Phisiologus* 'one learned in natural history'; a Latin compilation, perhaps made in the fourth century, of the moral significations of natural objects and, particularly, of animals. Versified by one Thetbald in the eleventh century, it was the basis of many vernacular bestiaries]

	For trewely ye han as myrie a stevene*	voice
	As any angel hath that is in hevene.	
	Therwith ye han in musyk moore feelynge	
	Than hadde Boece† or any that kan synge.	
475	My lord youre fader (God his soule blesse!)	
	And eek youre moder of hir gentillesse*	good breeding
	Han in myn hous yben,* to my gret ese.*	been satisfaction
	And certes, sire, ful fayn* wolde I yow plese.	willingly
	'But for* men speke of syngynge, I wol seye,	because
480	†So mote I browke wel myne eyen tweye,	
	Save ye,* I herde nevere man so synge	except for you
	As dide youre fader in the morwenynge.*	morning
	Certes, it was of herte* al that he song,	from the heart
	And for to make his voys the moore strong	
485	He wolde so peyne hym* that with bothe hise eyen	exert himself
	He moste wynke,† so loude he wolde cryen,	
	And stonden on his typton* therwithal	tiptoes
	And strecche forth his nekke long and smal.	
	And eek he was of swich discrecioun*	good judgement
490	That ther nas no man in no regioun	
	That hym in song or wisdom myghte passe.*	surpass
	I have wel rad* in daun Burnell the asse,†	read
	Among hise vers,* how that ther was a cok;	verses
	For* a preestes sone yaf hym a knok	because
495	Upon his leg whil he was yong and nyce*	foolish
	He made hym for to lese* his benefice.	lose
	But certeyn, ther nys no comparisoun	
	Bitwix the wisdom and discrecioun	
	Of youre fader and of his subtiltee.	
500	Now syngeth,* sire, for seynte charitee;†	sing
	†Lat se konne ye youre fader countrefete.'	
	This Chauntecler hise wynges gan to bete	
	As man that koude his trayson nat espie,	
	So was he ravysshed with his flaterie.	
505	Allas, ye lordes, many a fals flatour*	flatterer
	Is in youre court and many a losengeour*	toady

474 [*Boece* Anicius Manlius Severinus Boethius (*c*. 480–524) wrote an influential treatise *De Musica* (On Music)]
480 May I have the use of my two eyes
485–6 *with both his eyen/ He moste wynke* He had to close both his eyes
492 [*daun Burnell the asse* the *Speculum Stultorum* (Mirror of Fools) by Nigel Wireker (late twelfth century), a satire recounting the adventures of Sir Brunel the Ass. It includes the story of the cock who avenges himself on a priest's son by failing to crow on the morning of the latter's ordination, which he misses by oversleeping]
500 *for seynte charitee* for holy charity's sake
501 Show how you can imitate your father

	That plesen yow wel moore, by my feyth,	
	Than he that soothfastnesse* unto yow seith.	truth
	Redeth Ecclesiaste† of flaterye;	
510	Beth war, ye lordes, of hir trecherye.	
	This Chauntecler stood hye upon his toos	
	Strecchynge his nekke, and heeld hise eyen cloos	
	And gan to crowe lowde for the nones.*	straight away
	And daun Russell the fox stirte* up atones*	jumped at once
515	And by the gargat* hente* Chauntecler	throat seized
	And on his bak toward the wode hym beer,*	bore
	For yet ne was ther no man that hym sewed.*	followed
	O destynee, that mayst nat ben eschewed!*	avoided
	Allas, that Chauntecler fly* fro the bemes!	flew
520	Allas, his wif ne roghte nat of† dremes,	
	And on a Friday fil al this meschaunce!*	misfortune
	†O Venus, that art goddesse of plesaunce,*	pleasure
	Syn* that thy servant was this Chauntecler	since
	And in thy servyce dide al his power	
525	Moore for delit than world to multiplie,*	increase the population
	Why woldestow suffre hym on thy day† to dye?	
	†O Gaufred,* deere maister soverayn,*	Geoffrey supreme
	That whan thy worthy kyng Richard was slayn	
	With shot compleynedest his deth so soore,	
530	Why ne hadde I now thy sentence and thy loore	
	The Friday for to chide as diden ye,	
	For on a Friday soothly* slayn was he?	truly
	Thanne wolde I shewe yow how that I kowde pleyne*	could mourn
	For Chaunteclerys drede and for his peyne.	
535	Certes, swich* cry ne lamentacioun	such
	Was nevere of ladyes maad* when Ylioun†	made
	Was wonne, and Pirrus with his streite swerd	
	Whanne he hadde hent* kyng Priam by the berd	seized
	And slayn hym, as seith us Eneydos,*	the Aeneid
540	As maden alle the hennes in the cloos*	yard

---

509 [*Ecclesiaste* possibly Ecclesiasticus 12.14–15. 'This false friend will be thy companion for an hour . . . ; all those honeyed words do but mask a plot to lure thee into some ditch']
520 *ne roghte nat of* paid no attention to
522–6 [*Venus . . . thy day* Friday; Latin *dies Veneris* 'day of Venus']
527–32 [*Gaufred* Geoffrey of Vinsauf whose early thirteenth-century manual of rhetoric, *Poetria Nova* (The New Poetry), contains a model lament on the death of Richard I on Friday 26 March 1199 which begins (in translation) 'O mournful Friday!']
536–9 [*Ylioun . . . Pirrus . . . Priam . . . Eneydos* when the citadel of Troy (*Ilioun*) fell, the Greek Pyrrhus (*Pirrus*) killed the Trojan king Priam, according to Virgil's *Aeneid* (*Eneydos*), book 2]

	Whan they hadde seyn of Chauntecler the sighte.	
	But sovereynly* dame Pertelote shrighte*	chiefly shrieked
	Ful louder than dide Hasdrubales wyf†	
	Whan that hire housbonde hadde ylost his lyf	
545	And that the Romayns hadden brend* Cartage.	burnt
	She was so ful of torment and of rage	
	That wilfully* unto the fyr she sterte	deliberately
	And brende hirselven with a stedefast herte.	
	O woful hennes, right so cryden ye	
550	As, whan that Nero† brende the citee	
	Of Rome, cryden the senatours wyves	
	For that* hir housbondes losten all hir lyves	because
	(Withouten gilt this Nero hath hem slayn).	
	Now wol I turne to my tale agayn.	
555	The sely widwe* and eek hire doghtres two	poor widow
	Herden thise hennes crye and maken wo,*	lament
	And out at dores stirten* they anon	rushed
	And seyen* the fox toward the grove gon*	saw go
	And bar upon his bak the cok away,	
560	And criden, 'Out, harrow and weilaway!†	
	Ha, ha, the fox!' And after hym they ran,	
	And eek with staves* many another man.	sticks
	Ran Colle, oure dogge, and Talbot and Gereland†	
	And Malkyn with a distaf in hir hand,	
565	Ran cow and calf and eek the verray hogges,	
	So fered for berkynge of the dogges	
	And showtynge of the men and wommen eek;	
	†They ronne so hem thoughte hir herte breek.	
	They yelleden as fendes doon in helle;	
570	The dokes* cryden as men wolde hem quelle;*	ducks kill
	The gees for feere flowen* over the trees;	flew
	Out of the hyve cam the swarm of bees.	
	So hydous was the noyse, a benedicite,*	ah, bless us

543–4 [*Hasdrubales wyf . . . Cartage* when the Romans razed Carthage in 146 BC, the wife of the Carthaginian leader Hasdrubal threw herself into the flames]
550 [*Nero* Boethius (c. 480–524) in his *Consolation of Philosophy*, book 2, attributes the burning of Rome in 64 AD to the emperor Nero's murderous inclinations]
560 *Out, harrow and weilaway* ah me, help and alas
563 [*Talbot . . . Gerelande . . . Malkyn* Talbot and Gerelande are evidently other dogs; Malkyn (short for Matilda) is a generic name for a servant girl]
568 They ran so that they thought their hearts would burst

>   Certes he, Jakke Straw, and his meynee*   followers
> 575   Ne made nevere showtes half so shrille
>   Whan that they wolden any Flemyng kille†
>   As thilke day was maad upon the fox.
>   Of bras they broghten bemys,* and of box,*   trumpets boxwood
>   Of horn, of boon,* in whiche they blewe and powped*   bone puffed
> 580   And therwithal they skryked* and they howped* –   shrieked whooped
>   It semed as that hevene sholde falle.
>   Now, goode men, I prey yow herkneth alle,
>   Lo, how fortune turneth sodeynly
>   The hope and pryde eek of hire* enemy.   her
> 585   This cok that lay upon the foxes bak,
>   In al his drede unto the fox he spak
>   And seyde: 'Sire, if that I were as ye
>   Yit sholde I seyn, as wys* God helpe me: wise
>   "Turneth ayein,* ye proude cherles* alle,   turn back fellows
> 590   A verray* pestilence* upon yow falle!   veritable plague
>   Now I am come unto this wodes syde,
>   Maugree youre heed† the cok shal here abyde.
>   †I wol hym ete in feith and that anon."'
>   The fox answerde: 'In feith it shal be don.'
> 595   And as he spak that word, al sodeynly
>   This cok brak from his mouth delyverly*   quickly
>   And hye* upon a tree he fley* anon.   high   flew
>   And whan the fox say that he was gon,
>   'Allas,' quod he, 'O Chauntecler, allas,
> 600   I have to yow,' quod he, 'ydon trespas*   done an injury
>   In as muche as I maked yow aferd
>   Whan I yow hente* and broghte into this yerd.   seized
>   But, sire, I dide it in no wikke* entente.   evil
>   Com doun, and I shal telle yow what I mente.
> 605   I shal seye sooth* to yow, God help me so.'   truth
>   'Nay, thanne,' quod he, 'I shrewe* us bothe two.   curse
>   And first I shrewe myself bothe blood and bones,
>   If thow bigile* me any ofter than ones.   deceive
>   Thow shalt namoore* thurgh thy flaterye   never again
> 610   Do* me to synge and wynken with myn eye.†   get

574–6 [*Jakke Straw . . . Flemyng* Jack Straw was one of the leaders of the Peasants' Revolt in June 1381, when mobs entered London and joined forces with citizens in attacking Flemish workers whose prosperity they resented]
592 *Maugree your heed* in spite of you
593 I shall eat him for sure and do it very quickly
610 *wynken with myn eye* close my eyes

For he that wynketh whan he sholde see
Al wilfully, God lat hym nevere thee.'*   *thrive*
 'Nay,' quod the fox, 'but God yeve* hym meschaunce*   *give bad luck*
That is so undiscret* of governaunce*   *undiscerning behaviour*
615 That jangleth* whan he sholde holde his pees.'   *chatters*
 Lo, swich* it is for to be recchelees*   *such heedless*
And necligent and truste on flaterye.
But ye that holden this tale a folye*   *piece of foolishness*
As of a fox or of a cok and hen,
620 Taketh the moralitee, goode men,
For seint Poul† seith that al that writen is
To oure doctryne it is ywrite, ywis:*   *indeed*
Taketh the fruyt and lat the chaf* be stille.   *chaff*
Now goode God, if that it be thy wille,
625 As seith my lord, so make us alle goode men
And brynge us to his heye* blisse. Amen.   *high*

---

621 [*seint Poul* 'For whatsoever things were written aforetime were written for our learning' (Romans 15.4)

Morte Arthure
c. 1400

Morte Arthure (often known as 'the alliterative *Morte*') was composed in the north-east midlands, possibly in Lincolnshire, around 1400 by an unknown author. Only one text has survived, in a manuscript copied around 1430 by Robert Thornton, a minor Yorkshire landowner, though we know that later in the century Sir Thomas Malory had access to another text which he used in writing his *Morte Darthur*. Like *Piers Plowman*, *Morte Arthure* is written in unrhymed alliterative long lines, though its diction is both more archaic and more extraordinary than that of Langland's poem. Its affinities in English lie with Layamon's *Brut*, which the poet of *Morte Arthure* is unlikely to have known, though both writers drew on Wace's twelfth-century French version of Geoffrey of Monmouth's *Historia Regum Britanniae* (History of the Kings of Britain, 1135).

The poet of *Morte Arthure* has extracted from the traditional account of Arthur's reign, as established by Geoffrey, the tragic story of Arthur's last and greatest campaign, against the Romans, which leads to his death. At the beginning of the poem Roman ambassadors demand tribute from Arthur, who is at the height of his powers and who responds by taking an army across to France and then to Italy, where he defeats the Roman emperor. As Arthur is about to assume the imperial crown, news comes from England of the treachery of his nephew Modred, who has been left in charge of the kingdom. Arthur and his knights, including Gawain who is Modred's brother, return to England where they encounter the fleet of Modred and his allies at Dover. A sea-battle ensues, which Arthur's force wins, but Modred himself is on land with another army. Gawain rashly wades ashore with a small band of men and rushes into the attack.

The passage below describes the violent fight between Gawain and Modred, Modred's grief at his brother's death, Arthur's discovery of the body on the shore and his vow of vengeance. The alliterative style is strongly physical; as with Layamon's *Brut*, there is an unsentimental acknowledgement of the brutality of warfare. Physical too is the poet's understanding of the blood-relationships between Gawain, Modred and Arthur which give this passage its power: Modred's sighing for his 'sybb blode' (line 79) is expanded in the grim scene in which the grieving Arthur, his beard stained with gore, scoops up Gawain's blood in a helmet. The presentation of Arthur is critical, as this passage shows: a figure of almost primitive passions, rendered hieratic and awesome by the poet's formulaic language.

The text is from Lincoln Cathedral Library, MS 91.

1 [*Sir Gawayne* Arthur's favourite nephew (son of his sister and the king of Orkney) and his leading knight]
2 *graythes him son* moves quickly

5 *wodewyse* berserk   *at the gaynest* directly
6 Injures some of the enemy with fearsome blows

8 *thofe him ware full woo* although it was very grievous for him

12 *rittes* cuts through   *mayles* mail-coats

17 *hedlyngis* headlong

19 *Letande* appearing

22 *woundis of thas wedirwyns* see l. 6   *wondirfull* prodigious
23 As one who would willingly destroy himself
24 *for wondsom and will* because of the difficulty and confusion

27 Every man may be on guard against injury from another
28 [*Sir Modrede* Gawain's brother, to whom his uncle Arthur has entrusted the kingdom while he is fighting in Europe. Modred has usurped the throne and taken Arthur's wife Guinevere. The poet of *Morte Arthure* does not follow the tradition, invented by the author of the thirteenth-century French *La Mort le Roi Artu* ('The Death of King Arthur'), that Modred is Arthur's son]
29 *myde-schelde* middle of the shield
30 *scharpe* sharp point   *schownttes* steps back
31 *a schaftmonde large* the width of a hand
32 *schire beryn* noble man

From MORTE ARTHURE
lines 3813–4051

[The Death of Gawain]

	†Than grymly Sir Gawayne gryppis hys wapyn,	
	†Agayne* that gret bataille* he graythes hym son.	towards army
	Radly* of his riche swerde he reghttes* the cheynys,	swiftly adjusts
	In he schokkes* his schelde, schountes* he no lengare;	draws delays
5	†Bot alls* unwyse,* wodewyse, he wente at the gayneste,	as reckless
	†Wondis of thas wedirwyns with wrakfull dynttys,	
	All wellys* full of blode thare* he aweye passes.	gushes where
	†And thofe hym ware full woo, he wondys* bot lyttill,	flinches
	Bot wrekys* at* his wirchip* the wrethe*	enacts through honour anger
	of hys lorde.	
10	He stekys* stedis* in stoure* and sterenefull*	stabs horses battle fierce
	knyghttes,	
	That* steryn* men in theire sterapes stone-dede thay	so that bold
	lygge;*	lie
	†He ryvys* the ranke* stele, he rittes the mayles;	splits stout
	Thare myghte no renke* hym areste,* his reson was passede.	man stop
	He fell in a fransye* for fersenesse of herte;	frenzy
15	He feghttis and fellis down that* hym before standis.	what(ever)
	Fell* never fay* man siche* fortune in erthe.	befell doomed such
	†Into the hale* bataile hedlyngs he rynys*	whole runs
	And hurts of* the hardieste that one the erthe lenges;*	some of dwell
	†Letande alls a lyon he lawnches* them thorowe,*	thrusts through
20	Lordes and ledars that one the launde* hoves.*	field ride
	Yit Sir Gawayne for wo wondis bot lyttill,	
	†Bot woundis of thas wedirwyns with wondirfull dyntes,*	blows
	†Alls he that wold wilfully wasten hym selfen.	
	†And for wondsom and will all his wit* failede,	mind
25	That* wode* alls a wylde beste he wente at the gayneste;	so that mad
	All walewede* one blode, thare* he aweye passede –	wallowed where
	†Iche a wy may be warre be wreke of another.	
	†Than he moves to Sir Modrede amange all his knyghttes	
	†And mett hym in the myde-schelde and mallis* hym thorowe,	strikes
30	†Bot the schalke* for the scharpe he schownttes a littill.	knight
	†He schare* hym one the schorte rybbys a shaftmonde large;	sliced
	†The schafte schoderede* and schotte in the schire beryn,	shuddered
	That* the schadande* blode over his schanke*	so that streaming leg
	rynnys	

34 *schynbawde* leg armour   *schire burneste* bright burnished

37 *akere-lenghe* furlong's distance   *full lothely* very grievously
38 *gyrde to the gome* sprang at the man   *one the groffe* face down
39 In the same way as his misfortune was sent to him, his good fortune was no better

41 *slottede* cut his throat
42 *o slante* slantwise

47 Without being rescued by knights, and greater is the pity

50 From Glamorgan, from Wales, these valiant knights
51 *glent of gloppynyng* terrible blow
52 [*Kyng Froderike of Fres* one of Modred's allies]
53 *Fraynes at* asks of

55 *Beknowe now the sothe* tell the truth now

57 [*gryffoune of golde* Gawain has a griffin, half lion and half eagle, on his shield. In *Sir Gawain and the Green Knight*, ll. 129–30 (see p. 277), Gawain's shield is red with a gold pentangle]

60 He was the fiercest that ever wore armour in battle
61 *stroyede* destroyed (it)

63 *makles* matchless
64 *gladdeste of othire* most joyful of all

66 The boldest man at fighting, the most fortunate in arms

68 *lordelieste of ledyng* noblest leader   *qwhylls* as long as

70 *kythe thare he lenged* country where he dwelled

73 You would have grief for his death as long as you live

	†And schewede* on his schynbawde that was schire burneste.	was seen
35	And so they schyfte* and schove,* he schotte to the erthe;	parry shove
	With the lussche* of the launce he lyghte* one hys schuldyrs,	blow landed
	†Ane akere-lenghe one a launde,* full lothely wondide.	field
	†Than Gawayne gyrde to the gome and one the groffe fallis –	
	†Alls his grefe was graythede, his grace was no bettyre.	
40	He schokkes* owtte a schorte knyfe schethede* with silvere	pulls sheathed
	†And scholde have slottede hym in, bot no slytte* happenede:	slit
	His hand sleppid and slode* o slante one the mayles,	slid
	And the tother sleyly* slynges hym* undire.	wilily throws himself
	With a trenchande* knyfe the traytoure hym hyttes	sharp
45	Thorowe the helme and the hede, one heyghe* one the brayne;	upward
	And thus Sir Gawayne es gon, the gude man of armes,	
	†Withowttyn reschewe of renke, and the rewthe es the more.	
	Thus Sir Gawayne es gon that gyede* many othire;	led
	Fro Gowere* to Gernesay,* all the gret lordys,	Gower [in Wales] Guernsey
50	†Of Glamour, of Galys londe, this galyarde knyghtes,	
	†For glent of gloppynyng glade be they never.	
	†Kyng Froderike of Fres* faythely* thareaftyre	Friesland indeed
	†Fraynes at* the false mane* of* owre ferse knyghte:	asks of man about
	'Knew thow ever this knyghte in thi kithe* ryche?	homeland
55	†Of whate kynde* he was comen? Beknowe now the sothe.	family
	Qwat gome* was he, this with the gaye armes,*	man weapons
	†With his gryffoune* of golde, that es one growffe* fallyn?	griffin face down
	He has grettly greffede* us, sa me Gode helpe,	harmed
	Gyrde* down oure gude men and grevede* us sore.	struck injured
60	†He was the sterynneste in stoure that ever stele werryde,	
	†For he has stonayede* oure stale* and stroyede for ever!'	stunned army
	Than Sir Mordrede with mouthe melis* full faire:	speaks
	†'He was makles one molde,* mane, be my trowthe,*	earth troth
	†This was Sir Gawayne the gude, the gladdeste of othire,	
65	And the graciouseste gome that undire God lyffede,*	lived
	†Mane hardyeste of hande, happyeste in armes,	
	And the hendeste* in hawle undire heven riche;	most gracious
	†The lordelieste of ledyng qwhylls he lyffe myghte,	
	For he was lyone* allossede* in londes inewe;*	lion renowned many
70	†Had thow knawen hym, sir kyng, in kythe thare he lengede –	
	His konynge,* his knyghthode, his kyndly werkes,*	wisdom deeds
	His doyng, his doughtynesse, his dedis of armes –	
	†Thow wolde hafe dole for his dede the dayes of thy lyfe.'	

76   *weries the stowndys*   curses the hour
77   That his fate should ever have been devised to bring about such misery

80   When that forsworn knight called to mind

86   *one the coste ligges*   lies on the coast

90   [*Tambire*   the river Tamar in Cornwall, near which the last battle between Arthur and Modred is fought in Layamon's *Brut*, though here the final encounter is to take place by the 'Treyntis']

92   [*Waynor*   Guinevere, Arthur's queen, who is treated here with much less sympathy than in other versions. The children mentioned in l. 95 are presumably hers by Modred (her marriage to Arthur is traditionally childless), and are the same children whom the dying Arthur orders to be killed. In the end Guinevere is faithful to neither husband nor lover, and her flight to the nunnery is motivated by terror and not by remorse, as in Layamon's *Brut*, ll. 10–22, p. 123.]
93   And what fair coast the king had reached
94   *felled them o lyfe*   killed them
95   *ferken oo ferre*   go far away
96   Until he could escape and get to speak to her

102   *chese hir the wayes*   made their way
103   *Dighte hir*   made herself ready
104   [*Karelyone*   Caerleon-on-Usk in Wales, frequently associated with Arthurian legend. In Layamon's version, Guinevere flees to Carlisle]   *kawghte hir a vaile*   took the veil

107   [*oure wiese kyng*   Arthur, who has remained with his fleet, unaware till now that Gawain has gone ashore]
108   *al towrythes for wo*   is in paroxysms of grief
109   has his boats launched on shallow water

111   Slips in to the muddy water sideways to the waist

	Yit that traytour alls tite* teris lete he fall,	readily
75	Turnes hym furthe tite,* and talkes no more,	abruptly
	†Went wepand awaye and weries the stowndys	
	†That ever his werdes ware wroghte siche wandrethe to wyrke.	
	Whene he thoghte on this thynge, it thirllede* his herte;	pierced
	For sake of his sybb* blode sygheande* he rydys.	kinsman's sighing
80	†When that renayede renke remembirde hym selven	
	Of reverence and ryotes* of the Rownde Table,	revelry
	He remyd* and repent hym of all his rewthe* werkes;	cried out disastrous
	Rode awaye with his rowte,* ristys* he no lengere,	followers remains
	For rade* of oure riche* kynge, ryve* that he scholde.	in fear mighty arrive
85	Thane kayres* he to Cornewaile, carefull* in herte,	heads sorrowful
	†Because of his kynsemane that one the coste ligges;	
	He taries* tremlande* ay, tydandis* to herken.	delays trembling tidings
	Than the traytoure treunted* the Tyseday tharaftyre,	departed
	Trynnys* in with a trayne* treson to wirke,	marches trick
90	†And by the Tambire that tide* his tentis he reris;*	time erects
	And thane in a mette-while* a messangere he sendes	short while
	†And wraite* unto Waynor how the werlde chaungede,	wrote
	†And what comliche coste the kyng was aryvede,	
	†One floode* foughten with his fleete and fellyd them o lyfe;	at sea
95	†Bade hir ferken oo ferre and flee with hir childire,*	children
	†Whills he myghte wile hym awaye and wyn to hir speche,	
	Ayere* into Irelande, into thas owte-mowntes,*	go those mountains
	And wonn* thare in wildernesse, within tha* wast landys.	stay those
	Than cho yermys* and yeghes* at Yorke in hir chambire,	she weeps cries out
100	Gronys full grysely* with gretand* teres,	terribly weeping
	Passes owte of the palesse with all hir pryce* maydenys;	excellent
	†Towarde Chestyre in a charre* thay chese hir the wayes,	cart
	†Dighte hir evyn for to dye, with dule* at hir herte.	grief
	†Scho kayres* to Karelyone and kawghte hir a vaile,	goes
105	Askes thare the habit* in the honoure of Criste,	(nun's) habit
	And all for falsede* and frawde and fere of hir louerde.*	falsehood lord
	†Bot whene oure wiese kyng wiste* that Gawayne was landede	knew
	†He al towrythes for woo and, wryngande his handes,	
	†Gers lawnche his botes appon a lawe watire,	
110	Londis* als a lyon with lordliche knyghtes,	lands
	†Slippes in in the sloppes o slante to the girdyll,	
	Swalters* upe swyftly with his swerde drawen,	wades
	Bownnys* his bataile* and baners displayes,	makes ready battalion
	Buskes* over the brode sandes with breth* at his herte,	sets off rage

115 Moves swiftly to the field where the dead lie
116 [*the traytours* Modred's]   *trappede stedes* caparisoned horses
117 *the trewthe to acownt*   to tell the truth

119 Together with their sovereign are left wounded
120 *comly* in a seemly way   *overkeste* turned over

129–30 Sees them all in a troop together by themselves, surrounded by the dead Saracens [*Sarazenes* The last attack by Gawain and his men had been on a group of 'Saracens', used loosely to denote pagan (and thus suitably ungodly) allies of Modred, in the centre of whom Modred himself stood]
132 Gripped the grass and fallen on his face

134 *blody beronen* wet with blood

136 *Ne that sanke hym so sade*   nor weighed on him so heavily

149 The king of all knights that lived under Christ

152 *witt one*   wisdom alone

156 *Why drawes thou so one dreghe*   why do you delay so long

115	†Ferkes frekkly one felde thare the feye lygges.	
	†Of the traytours men one trappede stedis,	
	†Ten thosandez ware tynte,* the trewthe to acownt,	destroyed
	And certane* on owre syde seven score knyghtes	certainly
	†In soyte with theire soverayne unsownde are belevede.	
120	†The kyng comly overkeste knyghtes and othire,	
	Erlles of Awfrike* and Estriche berynes,*	Africa Austrian knights
	Of Orgaile* and Orekenay,* the Iresche* kynges,	Argyll Orkney Irish
	The nobileste of Norwaye, nowmbirs full hugge,	
	Dukes of Danamarke* and dubbid knyghtes;	Denmark
125	And the Guthede* kynge in the gay armes	Gotland
	Lys gronande on the grownde and girde* thorowe even.*	struck straight
	The riche kynge ransakes* with rewthe* at his herte	searches pity
	And up rypes* the renkes* of all the Rownde Tabyll,	searches out knights
	†Ses them all in a soppe in sowte by them one	
130	†With the Sarazenes unsownde enserclede abowte;	
	And Sir Gawayne the gude in his gaye armes,	
	†Umbegrippede the girse and one grouffe fallen,	
	His baners brayden* down, betyn* of gowlles,*	flung embossed gules
	†His brand* and his brade* schelde all blody beronen.	sword broad
135	Was never oure semliche kynge so sorowfull in herte,	
	†Ne that sanke hym so sade bot that sighte one.*	alone
	Than gliftis* the gud kynge and glopyns* in herte,	looks up grieves
	Gronys* full grisely* with gretande* teris,	groans terribly weeping
	Knelis down to the cors* and kaught it in armes,	body
140	Kastys upe his umbrere* and kyssis hym sone,*	visor straight away
	Lokes one his eye-liddis, that lowkkide* ware faire,	closed
	His lippis like to the lede* and his lire falowede.*	lead complexion pale
	Than the corownde kyng cryes full lowde:	
	'Dere kosyn o kynde,* in kare am I levede,*	kinsman left
145	For nowe my wirchipe es wente* and my were* endide.	gone war
	Here es the hope of my hele,* my happynge* of armes —	well-being good fortune
	My herte and my hardynes* hale* one hym lengede,*	courage entirely belonged
	My concell, my comforthe, that kepide* myn herte.	sustained
	†Of all knyghtes the kynge that undir Criste lifede;	
150	Thou was worthy to be kyng, thofe* I the corown bare.*	though bore
	Me wele* and my wirchipe* of all this werlde riche	prosperity honour
	†Was wonnen* thourghe Sir Gawayne and thourghe his witt one.'	gained
	'Allas!' saide Sir Arthure, 'Nowe ekys* my sorowe —	increases
	I am uttirly undon in myn awen landes.	
155	A, dowttouse,* derfe* dede,* thou dwellis to longe!	fearful cruel death
	†Why drawes thou so one dreghe? Thow drownnes myn herte!'	

159 *burlich berde* thick beard   *blody berown* wet with blood
160 As if he had butchered beasts and put them to death
161 [*Sir Ewayne* Sir Ywain, son of Urien, a leading knight of the Round Table]
162 *brousten for bale* burst for sorrow
163 *blondirs thi selfen* are distracted

166 *it es no witt holden* is accounted no wisdom

168 *for Cristes lufe of heven* for the love of Christ in heaven

170 Either my brain shall burst or else my breast

174 He, guiltless, is attacked because of my own wrongdoing

177 *rewthe* object of pity

184 And moves forward with the body to the country where he belongs

187 *ryvaye* ride the river-banks   *racches uncowpyll* uncouple hounds

189 *late glyde* unleash

190 Nor ever see bird brought down that flies on the wing

195 *droupe and dare* languish and remain inactive   *qwylls* as long as

	Than sweltes* the swete kyng and in swoun* fallis,	collapses in a faint
	Swafres* up swiftely and swetly hym kysses	staggers
	†Till his burliche berde was blody berown,	
160	†Alls he had bestes birtenede and broghte owt of life.	
	†Ne had Sir Ewayne comen and othire grete lordys,	
	†His bolde herte had brousten for bale at that stownde.*	moment
	†'Blyne,'* sais thies bolde men, 'thow blondirs thi selfen.	cease
	This es botles bale,* for bettir bees* it never.	vain grief shall be
165	It es no wirchipe, iwysse,* to wryng thyn hondes;	indeed
	†To wepe als a woman it es no witt holden.	
	Be knyghtly of contenaunce,* als a kyng scholde,	bearing
	†And leve siche* clamoure, for Cristes lufe of heven!'	such
	'For blode,' said the bolde kyng, 'blyn* sall I never,	cease
170	†Or my brayne tobriste, or my breste other!	
	Was never sorowe so softe that sanke to my herte;	
	Itt es full sibb* to my selfe, my sorowe es the more.	very close
	Was never so sorowfull a syghte seyn* with myn eyghen:	seen
	†He es sakles supprysede for syn of myn one.'	
175	Down knelis the kyng and kryes full lowde;	
	With carefull contenaunce he karpes* thes wordes:	utters
	†'O rightwis,* riche Gode, this rewthe thow beholde,	righteous
	This ryall,* rede blode ryn appon erthe.	royal
	It ware worthy to be schrede* and schrynede* in golde,	preserved enshrined
180	For it es sakles* of syn, sa helpe me oure Lorde.'	innocent
	Down knelis the kyng with kare at his herte,	
	Kaughte it* upe kyndly with his clene handis,	the blood
	Keste it in a ketill-hatte* and coverde it faire	helmet
	†And kayres furthe with the cors in kythe thare he lenges.	
185	'Here I make myn avowe,'* quod the Kynge than,	vow
	'To Messie* and to Marie, the mylde quene of heven:	Messiah
	†I sall never ryvaye, ne racches uncowpyll	
	At roo* ne raynedere* that rynnes appone erthe;	roe reindeer
	†Never grewhownde* late glyde, ne gossehawke* latt flye,	greyhound goshawk
190	†Ne never fowle see fellide that flieghes with wenge;	
	Fawkon* ne formaylle* appon fiste handill,*	falcon female hawk handle
	Ne yitt with gerefawcon* rejoyse me* in erthe,	gerfalcon amuse myself
	Ne regne* in my royaltez,* ne halde my Rownde Table,	reign splendour
	Till thi dede,* my dere, be dewly* revengede;	death properly
195	†Bot ever droupe and dare qwylls my lyfe lastez,	
	Till Drighten* and derfe* dede hafe don qwate* them likes.'	God cruel what

199 [*Wynchestre* Gawain's body is left in the care of the prior and monks of Winchester Cathedral. Arthur never returns for the interment (ll. 210–11). In Layamon's *Brut* Modred flees to Winchester, which is razed to the ground by Arthur; (see ll. 1–7, p. 123)]

205 Prepared for requiem masses, as is fitting for the dead
206 Honoured with masses for the reward of the soul

209 If you hope your convent may gain any honour

211 Delay the interment until they be brought low

213 [*Sir Wychere* has been mentioned earlier in the poem as a companion of Gawain]
214 I advise you to act cautiously and do what is best
215 *semble thi berynes* assemble your knights

222 I pray you, do not be anxious, sir knight, nor forecast any dangers
223 Had I no man but myself alone under the sun

226 Before I move from this place the length of half a horse

230 I shall never remain untroubled or at peace in my heart

233 *yif any sleyghte happen* if any skill eventuate
235 Until I can injure and torment them, in the place I choose
236 *Thare durst no renke hym areste* no knight dared stop him

   Than kaughte* they upe the cors* with kare at theire   took body
    hertes,
   Karyed one a coursere* with the kynge selfen.*   war-horse himself
   †The waye unto Wynchestre thay wente at the gayneste,*   directly
200 Wery and wandsomdly,* with wondide* knyghtes.   sadly wounded
   Thare came the prior of the plas and professide monkes,
   Apas* in processione and with the prynce metys,   quickly
   And he betuke* tham the cors of the knyghte noble.   gave
   'Lokis it be clenly kepyd,'* he said, 'and in the kirke*   preserved church
    holden,*   kept
205 †Done for derygese, as to the ded fallys,
   †Menskede with messes for mede of the saule.
   Loke it wante no waxe,* ne no wirchipe ells,*   candles other honour
   And at* the body be bawmede* and one erthe holden.   that embalmed
   †Giff thou kepe thi covent encroche any wirchipe
210 At my comyng agayne, gif Crist will it thole,*   permit
   †Abyde of the beryeng till they be broughte undire,
   That has wroghte us this woo and this werre movede.'*   provoked
   †Than sais Sir Wychere the wy,* a wyese mane of armes: warrior
   †'I rede ye warely wende and wirkes the beste;
215 †Sojorne* in this ceté and semble thi berynes,   stay
   And bidde* with thi bolde men in thi burghe* riche;   remain stronghold
   Get owt knyghttez of contrés* that castells holdes,   regions
   And owt of garysons grete* gude men of armes,   welcome
   For we are faithely* to fewe to feghte* with them all,   truly fight
220 That we see in his sorte* appon the see bankes.'   company
   With krewell contenance thane the Kyng karpis* theis wordes: utters
   †'I praye the, kare noghte, sir knyghte, ne caste thou no dredis;
   †Hadde I no segge bot my selfe one undir sone
   And* I may hym see with sighte or one hym sette hondis,   if
225 I sall even amange* his mene malle* hym to dede.   amidst batter
   †Are I of the stede styre halfe a stede lenghe,
   I sall stryke hym in his stowre* and stroye hym for ever,   troop
   And thareto make I myn avowe devottly to Cryste
   And to Hys Modyre Marie, the mylde Qwene of Heven,
230 †I sall never sojourne sounde ne sawghte at myne herte
   In ceté ne in subarbe sette appon erthe,
   Ne yitt slomyre* ne slepe with my slawe eyghne,*   slumber heavy eyes
   †Till he be slayne that hym slowghe,* yif any sleyghte happen;   slew
   Bot ever pursue the payganys that my pople* distroyede,   people
235 †Qwylls I may pare them and pynne, in place thare me likes.'
   †Thare durste no renke hym areste of all the Rownde Table,
   Ne none paye* that prynce with plesande wordes,   placate
   Ne none of his ligemene* luke* hym in the eyghne,*   followers look eyes
   So lordely* he lukes for losse of his knyghttes.   imperiously

In a Valley of this Restless Mind
and
In a Tabernacle of a Tower
late 14th century

The following poems by unknown authors are often presented as a pair – indeed, they occur side by side in an early fifteenth-century manuscript – but although they share the same refrain and stanza form they were composed in different parts of England. Both were probably written around the turn of the fourteenth century but it is impossible to tell which is the earlier. The words of the refrain, *Quia amore langueo* ('because I am sick for love'), come from the Song of Solomon (or Song of Songs) 2.5. This Old Testament book was often interpreted allegorically by medieval commentators as an expression of the love of God for the human soul, and both poems use this tradition in expanding the mystical eroticism of the refrain.

In a Valley of this Restless Mind

In 'In a Valley of this Restless Mind' the wooer of man is the crucified Jesus, variously presented as king, knight, lover, mother and husband. The metaphors by means of which these shifting relationships are expressed are often striking, sometimes even 'witty'; they are the vernacular products of a learned Latin tradition in verse and prose. Like Lydgate's 'As a Midsummer Rose', this poem is deeply imbued with devotion to the Five Wounds inflicted on Jesus at the crucifixion, which was a very popular form of piety in the later middle ages. The text is taken from Lambeth Palace Library, MS 853.

IN A VALLEY OF THIS RESTLESS MIND

In a valey of this restles mynde
I soughte in mounteyne and in mede,
Trustynge a trewe love† for to fynde;
Upon an hil than I took hede.
5 A voice I herde, and neer I yede,*   *I went closer*
In huge dolour* complaynynge tho:*   *grief   then*
'Se, dere soule, how my sidis blede,
†*Quia amore langueo*.'

Upon this hil I fond* a tree,†   *found*
10 †Undir the tree a man sittynge;
From heed to foot woundid was he –
His herte blod I sigh* bledinge.   *saw*
A semeli* man to ben* a king,   *handsome   be*
A graciouse face to loken unto;*   *look upon*
15 I askide whi he had peynynge.*   *suffering*
He seide, '*Quia amore langueo*.

'I am true love that fals was nevere;
My sistyr, mannis soule, I loved hir thus:
Bicause we wolde in no wise discevere*   *separate*
20 †I lefte my kyngdom glorious.
I purveide* for hir a paleis† precious;   *provided*
Sche fleyth,* I folowe – I soughte hir so,   *flees*
I suffride this peyne pitevous,*   *pitiable*
Quia amore langueo.

---

3 [*a trewe love*   the flower herb Paris was known as 'true love', and the dual meaning of the words may be present in the inner landscape of these opening lines]
8 *Quia amore langueo*   because I am sick for love
9 [*hil ... tree*   the hill, which in the first stanza is contrasted with the valley (of despair?), is now also the hill of Calvary, where Jesus was crucified, while the tree suggests the cross]
10 [Medieval pictures of the Deposition from the Cross show Jesus in various reclining postures (though usually supported by his followers)]
20 [Alludes to Jesus' incarnation as man]
21 [*a paleis*   heaven]

25 'My fair spouse and my love bright,
    I saved hir fro betynge and sche hath me bet.*   beaten
    I clothid hir in grace and hevenli light,
    This bloodi scherte† sche hath on me sette.
    For longynge of love yit wolde I not lette.*   give up
30 Swete strokis are these, lo!
    I have loved hir evere as I hir het,*   promised
    Quia amore langueo.

    I crowned hir with blis and sche me with thorn,
    I ledde hir to chaumbir and sche me to die,
35 I broughte hir to worschipe and sche me to scorn,
    †I dide hir reverence and she me vilonye.
    †To love that loveth is no maistrie;
    †Hir hate made nevere my love hir foo.
    Axe* me no question whi,   ask
40 Quia amore langueo.

    Loke unto myn hondis, man:
    These gloves† were yove* me whan I hir soughte.   given
    Thei ben not white, but rede and wan;*   pale
    Onbroudrid* with blood, my spouse hem broughte.   embroidered
45 Thei wole not of,† I loose hem† noughte;
    I wowe* hir with hem where evere sche go.   woo
    These hondis for hir so freendli* foughte,   kindly
    Quia amore langueo.

    Merveille noughte, man, though I sitte stille:
50 Se, love hath schod† me wondir streite,*   tightly
    Boclid* my feet, as was hir wille,   buckled
    With scharp naile – lo, thou maiste waite:*   know
    In my love was nevere desaite;*   deceit
    Alle my membres I have opened hir to,
55 There my bodi hath maad hir hertis baite,*   enticement
    Quia amore langueo.

---

28 [*bloodi scherte* symbolically, Jesus' scourged back and wounded side]
36 I honoured her and she insulted me
37 To reciprocate love is not hard
37–8 [The sense of these lines is that it is easy to love when one is loved in return (and thus no hardship for man to love God). Jesus does something far more difficult: continues to love man despite the latter's rejection of him]
42 [*gloves* symbolically, Jesus' wounded hands]
45 *wole not of* will not come off   *loose hem* unloosen them
50 [*schod* shod   the constricting and painful 'shoes' are the wounds in Jesus' feet]

†In my side I have made hir neste.
Loke in, how wyde a wounde is heere!
This is hir chaumbir, heere schal sche reste,
60 That sche and I may slepe in fere.*   *together*
Here may sche waische if ony filthe were;
Here is sete* for al hir woo.   *comfort*
Come whanne sche wole, sche schal have chere,*   *be made welcome*
Quia amore langueo.

65 I wole abide til sche be redy,
I wole hir sue* if sche seie nay.   *entreat*
If sche be richilees* I wole be redi.*   *heedless   alert*
And if sche be daungerus* I wole hir praie;*   *distant   beseech*
If sche do wepe than byd I nay;†
70 Myn armes be spred† to clippe* hir me to.   *embrace*
Crie oonys,* I come – now, soule, asay,*   *once   try*
Quia amore langueo.

I sitte on this hil for to se fer,
I loke into the valey, my spouse to se:
75 †Now renneth sche awayward, yit come sche me neer,
For out of my sighte may sche not be.
Summe wayte hir* prai to make hir to flee: *their*
I renne bifore* and fleme* hir foo.   *run in front   banish*
Returne, my spouse, ayen* to me,   *back*
80 Quia amore langueo.

Fair love, lete us go pleye,
†Applis ben ripe in my gardayne.
†I schal thee clothe in a newe aray,
Thi mete schal be mylk, hony and wiyn.†
85 Fair love, lete us go digne:*   *dine*
Thi sustynaunce is in my crippe,* lo!   *pouch*
Tarie thou not, fair spouse myne,
Quia amore langueo.

---

57 [The haven of Jesus' wounded side was a common devotional theme]
69 *byd I nay*   I beg [her] to stop
70 [*Myn armes ben spred*   the posture of the crucifixion as well as that of embrace]
75 Now she runs away, yet she still approaches me
82 [See Song of Solomon 4.16: 'Let my beloved come into his garden, and eat his pleasant fruits']
83 [In Revelation 19.8 the wife of the Lamb is 'arrayed in fine linen, clean and white: for the white linen is the righteousness of saints']
84 [*mylk, hony and wiyn*   see Song of Solomon 5.1: 'I am come into my garden . . . I have eaten . . . my honey; I have drunk my wine with my milk']

>   If thou be foul, I schal thee make clene;
> 90 If thou be siik, I schal the hele;
>   If thou moorne ought,* I schal thee meene;*   at all   comfort
>   Whi wolt thou not, fair love, with me dele?
>   Foundist thou evere love so leel?*   faithful
>   What woldist thou, spouse, that I schulde do?
> 95 I may not unkyndeli thee appele,*   accuse
>   Quia amore langueo.
>
>   What schal I do with my fair spouse
>   But abide hir,* of my gentilnes,   wait for her
>   Til that sche loke out of hir house
> 100 Of fleischi affeccioun?† Love myn* sche is.   my love
>   Hir bed is maade, hir bolstir is blis,
>   Hir chaumbir is chosen. Is ther non moo?
>   Loke out at the window† of kyndenes,
>   Quia amore langueo.
>
> 105 My love is in hir chaumbir — holde youre pees!
>   Make ye no noise but lete hir slepe.
>   My babe I wolde not were in disese;*   discomfort
>   I wolde not heere my dere child wepe.
>   †With my pap* I schal hir kepe;   breast
> 110 Ne merveille ye not though I tende hir to:
>   This hole in my side had nevere be so depe,
>   But quia amore langueo.
>
>   Longe thou for love nevere so high,
>   My love is more than thin* may be.   thine
> 115 Thou wepist, thou gladist,* I sitte the bi,   rejoice
>   Yit woldist thou oonys, leef,* loke unto me!   beloved
>   Schulde I alwey fede thee
>   With children mete?* Nay, love, not so —   children's food
>   I wole preve* thi love with adversite,   test
> 120 Quia amore langueo.

99–100 [hir house / Of fleischli affeccioun allegorically, the body and its desires]
103 [the window possibly an allusion to Song of Solomon 2.9: 'behold . . . he looketh forth at the windows, shewing himself through the lattice']
109 [Jesus the lover becomes the mother; devotion to 'Jesus our mother' was a late medieval form of piety]

Wexe* not wery, myn owne wiif; — grow
What mede* is it to lyve evere in counfort? — reward
In tribulacioun I regne more riif†
Ofttymes than in disport.* — comfort
125   In wel and in woo† I am ay to supporte;
Myn owne wiif, go not me fro.
Thi meede is markid* whan thou art mort,* — assigned dead
Quia amore langueo.

In a Tabernacle of a Tower

'In a Tabernacle of a Tower' was written in a more northerly dialect than 'In a Valley of this Restless Mind'. In this poem the traditional *planctus* or complaint of the Blessed Virgin over the body of the dead Jesus – a very popular theme in art and literature – has been modified by elements from another tradition, that of Christ's complaints from the cross at man's hardheartedness. Here the Virgin appears as queen of heaven, ready to intercede with God on behalf of mankind: this is why she calls herself 'mediatrix'. As such, she is the spiritual mother of all humanity, whom she chides and for whom she grieves. She is also the earthly mother of Jesus and laments his sufferings as well – sufferings inflicted on one of her children by the others. The text below, which is closest to the original dialect of any of the surviving versions, has not been printed before. It is taken from British Library, Additional MS 37049, possibly compiled for the Carthusian monastery of Mount Grace in Yorkshire. This version is defective in places; the final stanza and some other readings, especially in lines 65–71, come from Bodleian Library Oxford, Douce MS 322.

---

123   *I regne more riif*   I am more readily found
125   *In wel and in woo*   in prosperity and misery

IN A TABERNACLE OF A TOWER

In a tabernakil† of a towre,
As I stode musand of* the mone,* — reflecting on   moon
A crowned qwene, most of honour,
†I sawe syttyng on a trone.* — throne
5 Sche complayned by hyr one* — on her own
For mans saule, so wrappyd in woo:
'I may not lefe mankynde allone,
†*Quia amore langueo*.

'I lang* for luf of man, my brother,† — pine
10 I am his vocate* to voyd* his vice; — advocate   set aside
I am his mediatryce† and his moder;* — mother
Why suld I my dere chyld dyspyse?
If he me wrathe* in dyvers wyse,† — anger
Thorow fleschly frellte* fal me fro,* — frailty   from
15 †Yitt bus me rewe to he wil ryse,
Quia amore langueo.

I byd,* I byde* in gret langyng, — entreat   wait
I luf, I loke when man wil crave,
I compleyne for pyté of his pynyng;* — suffering
20 Whald† he ask mercy, he suld it hafe.
†Pray to me and I sall the safe;* — save you
Byd me, my barne,* and I sal goo. — child
Thou prayed me never bot I forgafe,
Quia amore langueo.

---

1 *tabernakil* niche containing a statue
4 [Another version of this line is 'Appered in gostly syght ful sone' which makes explicit what is here left unsaid]
8 Because I am sick for love
9 [*brother* as a human being the Blessed Virgin Mary is man's sister as well as being, spiritually, his mother (l. 11)]
11 *mediatryce* mediatrix between God and man
13 *dyvers wyse* different ways
15 Yet it behoves me to have pity on him until he will rise
20 *Whald* if he wanted to
21 [Strictly, only God can save, but the emphasis here is on the Blessed Virgin's infallible intercessory powers, available to those who turn to her for help]

25	O wretche in the warld, I loke on the,	
	I se thi trespas day be day:	
	With lytchery agayn* my chastite,	against
	With pride agayne my pore aray.	
	My luf abydes, thinne is away;	
30	My luf the* cals, thou stels me fro.	thee
	Turne to me, synner, I the pray,	
	Quia amore langueo.	

	Moder of mercy I was for the made;	
	Who nedys it?* None bot thou allone.	mercy
35	To gyf the grace I am more glad	
	Than thou to ask it – why wil thou none?	
	Whan sayd I nay, telle me, tyl on?†	
	For sothe,* never yitt to frende ne foo.	truly
	Whan thou askes not, than make I mone,*	I lament
40	*Quia amore langueo.*	

	'I seke the in wele* and wretchydnes,	prosperity
	I seke the in ricches and poverte;	
	Than,* man, behold wher thi moder is.	then
	Why lufs thou not me as I luf the?	
45	Synful or sory however thou be,	
	So welcom to me ther ar no mo.	
	I am thi syster, thou traystes on* me,	rely on
	Quia amore langueo.	

	'My chyld† is outlawed for thi syn,	
50	My barne is bett* for thi trespas.	beaten
	It prykkes my hert that so nere my kynne	
	Suld be dysesed.† O son, allas!	
	Thou art his brother, thi moder I was,	
	Thou sowked* my pappe;* thou luf man so	sucked breast
55	Thou dyed for hym; my hert thou has,	
	Quia amore langueo.	

---

37 *tyl on*   to a single one
49 [*My chyld*   Jesus, to whom ll. 52–5 and 65–7 are addressed]
52 *dysesed*   afflicted with suffering

'Man, lefe thi syn for my sake.
Why suld I gyf the that thou not walde?†
And if thou syn, sum prayer take
60 And trayst on me as I haf talde.
Am I not thi moder cald?
Why suld thou flee? I luf the, lo!
I am thi frende; I helpe the, byhalde,
Quia amore langueo.

65 'Now sone,' she said, 'wil thou say nay,
Whan man walde mend hym of his mysse?†
Thou lete me never in veyne yet pray.
O synful man, I say the* this: to you
What* day thou comes, welcome thou is.   whatever
70 A hondreth* yere if thou war me fro*   hundred   away from me
I take the ful fayne,* I clyppe,* I kysse,   very gladly   embrace
Quia amore langueo.

'Now wil I syte* and sygh* no more;   mourn   grieve
Lefe,* and loke with grete langyng.   leave
75 When man wil calle, I wil restore;
I luf to safe him, he is my ofspryng.
No wonder if my hert on hym hyng:*   hangs
I am his moder – what may I doo?
For hym I hafe this worschyppyng,
80 *Quia amore langueo.*

†'Why was I crowned and made a qwene?
Why was I cald of mercy the welle?
Why suld any erthly woman bene
So hye in heven, abowve angell,
85 Bot for the, mankynde, the trewth to tell?
Therfore aske mercy and I sal doo
That* I was ordand:* to helpe the fro hell,   what   commanded
Quia amore langueo.

---

58 *that thou not walde* what you do not want
66 *walde mend hym of his mysse* would like to repent of his sin
81 [The Blessed Virgin's coronation as queen of heaven after her bodily assumption there was a major theme in devotional art and literature from the twelfth century on]

'Now, man, hafe mynde on me for ever;
90 Loke on thi luf† thus languysshyng;
    †Late us never fro othere dissevere;
    Myn helpe is thine owne, crepe under my wynge.
    Thy syster is a qwene, thy brother a kynge;
    Thy heritage is tayled† – son, come ther to.
95 Take me for thy wyfe and lerne to synge:
    Quia amore langueo.

---

90 [*thi luf* the Blessed Virgin, here and in l. 95, is presented as man's wooer (taking up the erotic implications of the refrain); at ll. 93 and 94 she is also his sister and his mother]
91 Let us never separate from one another
94 [*heritage is tayled* an entailed heritage is one that is vested in the eldest son; hence the emphasis on man's sonship in this line. Man is urged to seek his rightful place in heaven]

John Lydgate
?1470–1449/50

John Lydgate was born in Suffolk around 1470 and entered the Benedictine abbey at Bury St Edmunds as a boy. He was able to spend much of his adult life outside the monastery, and put his gifts as a prolific versifier at the disposal of various patrons at court, in the church and in the city. His *Troy Book* (1412–20), for example, was composed for Henry V; his translation of *The Pilgrimage of the Life of Man* (begun 1426) was undertaken for the earl of Salisbury; his very popular *Fall of Princes* (1431–9) was commissioned by Humphrey, duke of Gloucester. The abbot of St Edmunds asked him to write *The Life of SS Edmund and Fremund* in 1433, and he undertook *SS Alban and Amphibal* at the request of the abbot of St Albans. The London goldsmiths' and mercers' guilds procured his services for mummings performed in the presence of the mayor, and many of his other works were similarly utilitarian.

In all, Lydgate wrote around 145,000 lines of verse, much of it pedestrian and verbose. He was, nevertheless, an admirer of Chaucer and *The Siege of Thebes* (around 1420) is his own addition to the *Canterbury Tales*. His learned and pretentious manner was more imitable than Chaucer's, and he was influential in the fifteenth and early sixteenth centuries in Scotland as well as England. Lydgate spent the last fifteen years or so of his life back in the abbey at Bury, and died in 1449 or thereabouts.

'As a Midsummer Rose' is written in the 'Monk's stanza' (used by Chaucer in 'The Monk's Tale') with refrain which was a popular form for moral lyrics. Its expansiveness is typical of Lydgate; in the fifth line, for example, 'Provisioun, forsight, and providence' all mean the same thing. Nevertheless, the image of the rose is developed in the course of the poem with an unusually concentrated power.

The text is from *John Lydgate: Poems*, ed. J. Norton-Smith (1966).

AS A MIDSUMMER ROSE

    Lat no man booste* of konnyng* nor vertu,   *boast knowledge*
    Of tresour, richesse, nor of sapience,*   *wisdom*
    Of worldly support – al comyth of* Jhesu: *from*
    Counsayl,* confort, discresioun, prudence,   *advice*
5 Provisioun,* forsight, and providence,   *foresight*
    Like* as the Lord of grace list dispoose:†   *accordingly*
    Som* hath wisdam, som hath elloquence,   *one*
    †Al stant on chaung like a mydsomyr roose.

    †Holsom in smellyng be the soote flourys,
10 Ful delitable* outward to the sight,   *delightful*
    The thorn is sharp, curyd* with fressh colourys.   *covered*
    Al is nat gold that outward shewith bright;
    A stokfyssh boon† in dirknesse yevith* a light;   *gives*
    Twen* fair and foule, as God list dispoose,   *between*
15 †A difference atwixen* day and night: *between*
    Al stant on chaung like a mydsomyr roose.

    Floures open upon every grene,
    Whan the larke, messager of day,
    Salueth* th'uprist* of the sonne shene*   *greets rising bright*
20 Moost amerously* in Apryl and in May;   *amorously*
    And Aurora† ageyn* the morwe* gray   *at the approach of morning*
    Causith the daysye hir crown to uncloose:*   *open*
    Worldly gladnes is medlyd* with affray,*   *mixed fear*
    Al stant on chaung like a mydsomyr roose.

---

6 *list dispoose* is pleased to ordain
8 Everything rests on change like a midsummer rose
9 The sweet flowers are pleasing in scent
13 *stokfyssh boon* stockfish [cured cod] bone
14–15 [These elliptical lines possibly mean: 'Between fair and foul, as God is pleased to ordain, [there is] a difference [as] between day and night']
21 [*Aurora* the dawn]

25	Atwen the cokkow and the nightyngale†	
	Ther is a maner straunge* difference.	strange kind of
	On fressh braunchys syngith the woode-wale.*	golden oriole
	Jayes in mysyk have smal* experyence.	little
	Chateryng pyes* whan they come in presence	magpies
30	Moost malapert* ther verdite* to purpoose:*	cheekily opinion propound
	Al thyng hath favour,* breffly in sentence,†	inclination
	Of soffte or sharp like a mydsomyr roose.	

†The roial lioun lette calle a parlement,
Alle beests abowt hym enviroun,* — all around
35 The wolff of malys,* beyng ther present, — malicious
Upon the lamb compleyned, ageyn resoun,* — irrationally
Said he maad his watir unholsom,
His tendre stomak to hyndre* and undespoose.* — impede upset
Raveynours* reign, the innocent is bore doun, — plunderers
40 Al stant on chaung lyk a mydsomer roose.

Al worldly thynges braydeth* upon tyme: — change
The sonne chaungith, so doth the pale moone,
†The aureat noumbre in kalends set for prime.
Fortune is double,* doth favour for no boone,* — duplicitous prayer
45 †And who that hath with that queen to doone
Contrariously she wyl his chaunce* dispoose: — luck
Who sittith hihest* moost like* to fall soone. — highest is most likely
Al stant on chaung like a mydsomyr roose.

The golden chaar* of Phebus* in the ayr — chariot the sun
50 Chasith mysts blak that* thay dar not appeere, — so that
At whos uprist mounteyns be made so fayr
As* they were newly gilt with his beemys cleere; — as if
The nyht doth folwe,* appallith† al his cheere* — follow appearance
Whan western wawes* his streemys over-close.* — waves close over
55 Rekne* al bewté,* al fresshness that is heere: — consider beauty
Al stant on chaung lyke a mydsomyr roose.

---

25 [*the cukkow and the nightyngale* traditionally opposed because of the differences in their songs]
31 *breffly in sentence* to put it briefly
33–40 [The lion is king of beasts and thus has the power to summon a parliament. This stanza is an adaptation of an Aesopic fable in which a wolf accuses a lamb of fouling his drinking-water, even though the lamb has drunk downstream from the wolf]
lette calle a parlement had a parliament summoned
43 The golden number fixed in the calendar to reckon the date of Easter
[*aureat noumbre* the 'Golden Number' is used in fixing the date of Easter and other movable feasts of the church]
45 And he who has anything to do with that queen [Fortune]
53 *appallith* grows pale

Constreynt* of coolde makith floures dare* *agony droop*
With wyntir froosts that* they dar nat appeere. *so that*
Al clad in russet* the soyl of greene is bare.† *russet, grey*
60 Tellus and Jove† be dullyd* of ther cheere *diminished*
By revolucioun and turnyng of the yeere:
As gery* March his stoundys* doth disclose: *changeable different times*
Now reyn, now storm, now Phebus bright and cleere.
Al stant on chaung like a mydsomyr roose.

65 Wher is now David,† moost worthy kyng
Of al Juda, moost famous and notable?
Wher is Salomon† most sovreyn of konnyng,†
Richest of bildyng, of tresour incomparable?
Face of Absolon,† moost fair, moost amyable?* *agreeable*
70 Rekne up echon,† of trouthe make no gloose,* *specious rendering*
Rekne up Jonathas,† of frenship immutable,
Al stant on chaung lyke a mydsomyr roose.

Wher is Julius,† proudest in his empyre
With his tryumphes moost imperyal?
75 Wher is Porrus† that was lord and sire* *master*
Of al Ynde in his estat roial?* *royal dignity*
And wher is Alisaunder† that conqueryd al,
Failed leiser† his testament to dispoose?
†Nabugodonosor or Sardanapal?
80 Al stant on chaung like a mydsomyr roose.

---

59 *of greene is bare* is denuded of green
60 [*Tellus and Jove* earth and sky]
65–6 [*David . . . Juda* David, king of Judah (southern Palestine) and then of Israel, united the tribes of Israel, establishing his capital at Jerusalem and defeating the Philistines (I Samuel 16 – I Kings 2)]
67 [*Salamon* Solomon, David's son and successor as king of Israel, was renowned for the wisdom and knowledge given him by God (II Chronicles, 1.7–12)]
most sovreyn of konnyng supreme in understanding
69 [*Absolon* Absolom, the rebellious son of David, renowned for his beauty (II Samuel, 14.25)]
70 *Rekne up echon* consider each one
71 [*Jonathas* Jonathan, son of David's predecessor King Saul, who refused to betray his oath of friendship to David (I Samuel, 20)]
73 [*Julius* Julius Caesar (c. 100–44 BC), Roman commander (proconsul) of Gaul and subsequently dictator of Rome until his assassination]
75 [*Porrus . . . Ynde* Porrus of India was, according to legend, one of the defeated opponents of Alexander the Great]
77 [*Alisaunder* Alexander the Great (356–323 BC), king of Macedonia, whose empire extended as far as India. According to medieval tradition, he died of poisoning]
78 *Failed leiser* time was wanting
79 [*Nabugodonosor* Nebachudnezzar, king of Babylon, who was driven from his throne until he acknowledged the sovereignty of God (Daniel, chapters 1–4)   *Sardanapal* Sardanapalus, last king of Assyria, who burned himself to death in his citadel on his defeat by the king of the Medes]

JOHN LYDGATE

Wher is Tullius† with his sugryd* tonge? — sugared
Or Crisistomus† with his golden mouth?
The aureat ditees* that be red and songe — gilded compositions
Of Omerus† in Grece both north and south?
85 The tragedyes divers† and unkouth* — marvellous
Of moral Senek,† the mysteryis to uncloose?
By many example this matere is ful kouth:* — fully known
Al stant on chaung like a mydsomyr roose.

Wher been of Fraunce† al the dozepeers* — 'douzepeers', twelve companions
90 Which that in Gawle had the governaunce?
Vowes of the Pecok† with al ther proude cheers*? — looks
The worthy nyne† with al ther hih bobbaunce?* — lofty pride
Trojan knyhtis,† grettest of alliaunce?†
†The flees of gold, conqueryd in Colchoos?
95 Rome and Cartage,† moost sovereyn of puissaunce?* — power
Al stant on chaung like a mydsomyr roos.

Put in a som* al marcial policye, — reckon up
Compleet* in Affryk and boundys of Cartage, — performed
†The Theban legioun, example of chevalrye,
100 At Rodanus Ryver was expert* ther corage.* — experienced fighting spirit

---

81 [*Tullius* Marcus Tullius Cicero (106–43 BC), Roman statesman, moral philosopher and rhetorician]
82 [*Crisistomus* St John Chrysostom ('golden-mouthed') (c. 347–407), bishop of Constantinople, famous for his preaching]
84 [*Omerus* Homer (c. 700 BC), Greek author of the epics, the *Iliad* and the *Odyssey*]
85 *divers* of different kinds
86 [*Senek* Lucius Annaeus Seneca the younger (c. 4 BC–AD 65) Roman tragedian and moral philosopher]
89 [*of Fraunce al the dozepeers* the legendary twelve companions of the Frankish emperor Charlemagne (742–841), celebrated in many English and French romances]
91 [*Vowes of the Pecok* in the early fourteenth-century French romance *Les Voeux du Paon* ('The Vows of the Peacock'), by Jacques de Longuyon, Alexander's knights vow on a roast peacock served at a feast that they will perform martial deeds]
92 [*worthy nyne* the 'Nine Worthies', exemplary figures from the past, traditionally include three Jews (Joshua, David and Judas Maccabaeus); three pagans (Hector, Alexander and Julius Caesar); and three Christians (Arthur, Charlemagne and Godfrey de Bouillon)]
93 [*Trojan knyhtis* warriors who fought in the legendary war at Troy between the Greeks and the Trojans. Lydgate wrote a long poem, the *Troy Book*, on the subject]
93 *grettist of alliaunce* of most distinguished kindred
94 [In Greek legend, Jason won the Golden Fleece from the king of Colchis, on the Black Sea]
95 [*Rome and Cartage* Rome and Carthage (near modern Tunis) were both great imperial powers in the ancient world]
99–100 [*Theban legion . . . Rodanus Ryver* according to legend, a legion of Christian soldiers serving in the Roman army was massacred at Aganum on the River Rhone ('Rodanus') around AD 300 on the orders of the Roman emperor Maximian when they refused to offer pagan sacrifices]

Ten thousand knyhtes born of hih parage*   *birth*
Ther martirdam, rad* in metre and proose,   *read*
Ther golden crownys maad in hevenly stage,*   *station*
Fressher than lilies or ony somyr roose.

105   The remembraunce of every famous knyht,
Ground considerid,† is bilt on rihtwisnesse.*   *justice*
Race out* ech quarel that is not bilt on riht,   *eradicate*
Withoute trouth what vaileth* hih noblesse?   *avails*
Th'awtiers* of martirs foundid on hoolynesse: *altars*
110   Whit was maad red ther tryumphes to discloose:
The white lillye was ther chaast clennesse,†
Ther bloody suffraunce* was no somyr roose.   *martyrdom*

It was the Roose of the bloody feeld,†
†Roose of Jericho that greuh* in Beedlem:†   *grew*
115   The five Roosys† portrayed in the sheeld,
Splayed* in the baneer at Jerusalem.†   *displayed*
The sonne was clips* and dirk* in every rem*   *eclipsed dark realm*
Whan Christ Jhesu five wellys† lyst uncloose†
Toward Paradys, callyd the rede strem,
120   †Of whos five woundys prent* in your hert a roos.   *imprint*

---

106 *Ground considerid* bearing in mind (its) foundation
111 *ther chaast clennesse* their chaste purity
113 [*bloody feeld* metaphorically, the battlefield on which Christ the knight is slain; heraldically, the background on which an emblem is displayed on a shield (see line 115)]
114 [*Roose of Jericho* in Ecclesiasticus 24.17–18, Wisdom (often identified with Christ) says: 'I grew as a rose-plant in Jericho'. Jericho is north-east of Jerusalem and Bethlehem   *Beedlem* Bethlehem, birthplace of Jesus]
115 [*five Roosys* the five wounds received by Jesus at the crucifixion, seen here as a heraldic emblem displayed on a knight's shield and banner]
116 [*Jerusalem* the scene of Jesus' crucifixion which is presented as a knightly combat against death, as in *Piers Plowman*, Passus 18]
118 [*five wellys* Jesus' five wounds, from which flows his saving blood]
     lyst uncloose was pleased to reveal
120 [The rose finally provides the reader with an image of Jesus' suffering which can be internalised and meditated upon]

Margery Kempe
c. 1373–c. 1440

The Book of Margery Kempe is the first spiritual autobiography in English. Margery, daughter of John Brunham, burgess of King's Lynn, Norfolk, married John Kempe around 1393. During a period of mental crisis after the birth of the first of their fourteen children, Margery Kempe underwent a religious conversion, and believed thereafter that she was in constant communication with God, who appeared to her in visions. She insisted on wearing white clothes; she wept noisily and publicly, to the constant irritation of those with whom she came into contact; she travelled restlessly, both in England and on a series of pilgrimages, to Rome, Jerusalem, and Compostella. At the age of sixty she accompanied her widowed daughter-in-law back to the latter's home in Danzig, encountering many hardships (some of her own making) on the return journey. Turbulent, self-righteous and defensive, she reveals the strain imposed on those late medieval laywomen who could not conform to the conventional roles of wife and mother, for whatever reason, and yet who did not have the temperament for the reclusive life either. Her inability to conform led to frequent charges of heresy, though in fact her piety, extreme and hysterical though it may seem, was quite orthodox.

The *Book* was written in its final form in 1436. Margery Kempe was illiterate, and so dictated her first draft to an amanuensis who was probably her son. Four years later she persuaded a priest to rewrite and expand it. She gives a vivid account of their combined efforts: the priest struggling with the son's execrable handwriting and his own bad sight; she, refusing to accept excuses, urging him on with pious exhortations and explaining the bits he could not decipher.

In the extract below, which can be dated by inference to the summer of 1413, Margery finally succeeds in persuading her husband to let her take a vow of chastity so that she can be released from the obligation of marital sex, which she has found distasteful for many years. Some months earlier she had prayed that her husband might allow her to live in chastity, and had been told by Jesus that if she abstained from meat and drink on Fridays, her prayer would be granted. Shortly afterwards her husband tried to have intercourse with her but was miraculously restrained when she said the words 'Jesus, help me'. The events narrated here took place eight weeks after this occurrence, which clearly weighed on John Kempe's mind.

The text is from *The Book of Margery Kempe*, ed. S. B. Meech and H. E. Allen, EETS, OS 212 (1940).

From THE BOOK OF MARGERY KEMPE
[The Vow of Chastity]

It befel upon a Fryday on Mydsomyr Evyn† in rygth* very
hot wedyr,* as this creatur† was komyng fro Yorke- weather
ward† beryng a botel wyth bere† in hir hand and hir
husbond a cake in hys bosom,† he askyd hys wyfe this
5 qwestyon, 'Margery, yf her come a man† wyth a swerd
and wold smyte of† myn hed les than* I schulde comown unless
kendly† wyth yow as I have do* befor, seyth me trewth† done
of yowr consciens – for ye sey ye wyl not lye – whethyr
wold ye suffyr* myn hed to be smet of er ellys† suffyr allow
10 me to medele† wyth yow agen as I dede sumtyme?'†
'Alas, ser,' sche seyd, 'why meve ye† this mater and have
we ben chast this eight wekys?' 'For* I wyl wete† the because
trewth of yowr hert.' And then sche seyd wyth gret
sorwe,* 'Forsothe* I had levar† se yow be slayn than sorrow   indeed
15 we schuld turne agen to owyr unclennesse.' And he seyd
agen,* 'Ye arn no good wyfe.' And than sche askyd in reply
hir husbond what was the cawse that he had not medelyd
wyth hir eight wekys befor, sythen* sche lay wyth hym since
every nygth in hys bedde. And he seyd he was so made
20 aferde† whan he wold a* towchyd hir that he durst no have

Mydsomyr Evyn   23 June (1413)
creatur   creature [Margery's usual term for herself]
fro Yorke-ward   from the direction of York
botel wyth bere   bottle of beer
[*in hys bosom*   i.e. carried in the front of his shirt]
yf her come a man   if a man came here
wold smyte of   wanted to cut off
comown kendly   have sexual intercourse as nature urges
seyth me trewth   tell me the truth
smet of er ellys   cut off or else
medele   have sexual intercourse
sumtyme   at one time
meve ye   do you raise
wyl wete   want to know
levar   rather
so made aferde   made so frightened

mor don.† 'Now, good ser, amend yow* and aske God   *repent*
mercy, for I teld yow ner three yer sythen† that ye schuld
be slayn sodeynly, and now in this the thryd* yer, and   *third*
yet I hope I schal han my desyr. Good sere, I pray yow
25 grawnt me that* I schal askyn, and I schal pray for yow   *what*
that ye schul be savyd thorw the mercy of owyr Lord
Jhesu Cryst, and ye schul have more mede* in Hevyn   *reward*
than gyf ye weryd an hayr or an haburgon.† I pray yow,
suffer me to make a vow of chastyté in what* bysshopys   *whichever*
30 hand that God wele.'* 'Nay,' he seyd, 'that wyl I not   *wishes*
grawnt yow, for now may I usyn yow† wythowtyn dedly
synne and than mygth I not so.' Than sche seyd agen,
'Gyf* it be the wyl of the Holy Gost to fulfyllyn that* I   *if   what*
have seyd, I pray God ye mote* consent therto; and, yf   *may*
35 it be not the wyl of the Holy Gost, I pray God ye nevyr
consent therto.' Than went thei forth to-Brydlyngton-
ward† in rygth hoot wedyr, the fornseyd* creatur havyng   *aforesaid*
gret sorwe and gret dred for hyr chastité. And, as thei
cam be a cros,† hyr husbond sett hym down undyr the
40 cros, clepying* hys wyfe unto hym and seyng this wordys   *calling*
onto hir, 'Margery, grawnt me my desyr, and I schal
grawnt yow yowr desyr. My fyrst desyr is that we schal
lyn* stylle to gedyr in o* bed as we han do† befor; the   *lie   one*
secunde that ye schal pay my dettys er* ye go to   *before*
45 Jherusalem; and the thrydde that ye schal etyn and
drynkyn wyth me on the Fryday as ye wer wont to don.†
'Nay ser,' sche seyd, 'to breke the Fryday† I wyl nevyr
grawnt yow whyl I leve.'* 'Wel,' he seyd, 'than schal I   *live*
medyl yow ageyn.' Sche prayd hym that he wold geve
50 hir leve to make hyr praerys,† and he grawntyd it
goodlych.* Than sche knelyd down besyden a cros in   *gladly*
the feld and preyd in this maner wyth gret habundawns*   *abundance*
of teerys, 'Lord God, thou knowyst al thyng; thow
knowyst what sorwe I have had to be chast in my body

---

durst no mor don   did not dare do any more
teld yow ner three yer sythen   told you almost three years ago
gyf ye weryd . . . haburgon   than if you wore a hair-shirt or a penitential garment of mail
usyn yow   use you, have intercourse with you
to-Brydlyngton-ward   towards Bridlington
cros   cross [on a wayside shrine]
han do   have done
wont to don   accustomed to do
to breke the Fryday   break the Friday fast
geve hir leve . . . praerys   give her permission to say her prayers

55 to ye al this three yer, and now mygth I han† my wylle	
and I dar not for lofe of the. For, gyf I wold brekyn†	
that maner of fastyng whech thow comawndyst me to	
kepyn on the Fryday wythowtyn mete or drynk, I schuld	
now han my desyr. But, blyssyd Lord, thow knowyst I	
60 wyl not contraryen† thi wyl, and mekyl* now is my	great
sorwe les than* I fynde comfort in the. Now, blyssed	unless
Jhesu, make thi wyl knowyn to me unworthy that I may	
folwyn theraftyr† and fulfyllyn it wyth al my myghtys.'*	strength
And than owyr Lord Jhesu Cryst wyth gret swetnesse	
65 spak to this creatur, comawndyng hir to gon agen* to	go back
hir husbond and prayn hym to grawntyn hir that* sche	what
desyred. 'And he schal han that he desyreth. For, my	
derworthy* dowtyr, this was the cawse that I bad the	esteemed
fastyn for thu schuldyst the sonar opteyn and getyn thi	
70 desyr,† and now it is grawntyd the. I wyl no lengar†	
thow fast, therfor I byd the in the name of Jhesu ete and	
drynk as thyn husbond doth.' Than this creatur thankyd	
owyr Lord Jhesu Cryst of* hys grace and hys goodnes,	for
sythen* ros up and went to hir husbond, seyng unto	then
75 hym, 'Sere, yf it lyke yow,† ye schal grawnt me my desyr,	
and ye schal have yowr desyr. Grawntyth* me that ye	grant
schal not komyn* in my bed, and I grawnt yow to	come
qwyte* yowr dettys er* I go to Jerusalem. And makyth	repay before
my body fre to God so that ye nevyr make no chalengyng	
80 in† me to askyn no dett of matrimony† aftyr this day	
whyl ye levyn,* and I schal etyn and drynkyn on the	live
Fryday at yowr byddyng.'* Than seyd hir husbond agen	command
to hir, 'As fre mot* yowr body ben to God as it hath	may
ben to me.' Thys creatur thankyd God gretly, enjoyng	
85 that sche had hir desyr, preyng hir husbond that thei	
schuld sey three Pater Noster† in the worshep† of the	
Trinyté for the gret grace that he* had grawntyd hem.	God

---

mygth I han I might have
gyf I wold brekyn if I were willing to break
contraryen contradict
folwyn theraftyr follow [after] it
I bad the … getyn thi desyr I told you to fast in order that you should the sooner obtain and receive your desire
wyl no lengar no longer wish that
yf it lyke yow if it please you
chalengyng in demand of
dett of matrimony marital debt [sexual intercourse]
Pater Noster 'Our Fathers' [Lord's prayer]
in the worshep in honour

And so they ded, knelyng undyr a cros, and sythen thei
etyn and dronkyn togedyr in gret gladnes of spyryt. This
was on a Fryday on Mydsomyr Evyn. Than went thei
forth to-Brydlyngton-ward and also to many other
contrés* and spokyn wyth Goddys servawntys, bothen   regions
ankrys* and reclusys and many other of owyr Lordys   anchorites
loverys, wyth many worthy clerkys,* doctorys of dyvy-   learned men
nyte, and bachelers† also in many dyvers placys. And
this creatur to dyvers* of hem schewyd hir felyngys and   several
hyr contemplacyons,* as sche was comawndyd for to   meditations
don,† to wetyn* yf any dysseyt† were in hir felyngys.   find out

---

[*bachelers*   holders of bachelors' degrees]
for to don   to do
[*dysseyt*   deception. Margery was examined by the ecclesiastical authorities who suspected her of fraud and heresy]

Two Corpus Christi plays
15th century

The Wakefield *Second Shepherds' Play* and the York Butchers' *Play of the Death of Christ* both come from fifteenth-century Corpus Christi play cycles. It was customary in many towns in England and Scotland from the fourteenth to the mid-sixteenth centuries for play cycles to be performed as part of the civic celebrations that were held each summer on the feast of Corpus Christi, which falls on the Thursday after Trinity Sunday. This religious festival was instituted by the church in 1311 in order to remind ordinary Christians of the central meaning of the service of holy communion in the Roman Catholic mass, when the communion bread and wine are held to become the body and blood of Christ. (*Corpus Christi* is Latin for 'the body of Christ'.) The plays, performed in procession in the town streets, told the whole story of God's intervention in human affairs from the creation of the world to the last judgement, and included the story of Christ's birth, ministry, death and resurrection.

Only four complete Corpus Christi play-cycles survive from the late middle ages. The longest is that of York, which when complete consisted of fifty plays; the cycle from nearby Wakefield may have contained thirty-two. The plays – all short like the two below – were performed by different guilds, the trade or craft associations of the towns. Each guild was allocated a play and was responsible for organising and paying for its staging, including the provision of a mobile stage, or pageant wagon. This was a wheeled structure, manhandled or possibly horse-drawn – probably looking something like an old-fashioned hay-wain – which was basically a flat acting area with whatever additional features were necessary for the settings of particular plays. (For example, *The Second Shepherds' Play* may have required some kind of structure to represent Mak's cottage and, later, the stable at Bethlehem.) It is clear from surviving records that some of these pageant wagons were quite elaborately furnished and equipped.

Early in the morning of the feast day – the sixteenth-century Wakefield records say 5 a.m. – the guildsmen would assemble with their wagons on some open space outside the town to form a procession. The first pageant-wagon would then move into the town to the first playing place, the opening play would be performed and then the wagon would move on to the second playing place. Meanwhile the second wagon would move into the place vacated by the first, and so on. (The playing places were carefully regulated by the city fathers.) The audience could gather at one venue and the plays would, in turn, all come to them, or they could follow a particular play and watch it being performed more than once. People who lived round the playing areas were able to sell advantageous viewing positions from their windows and doorways, as well as from scaffold seating erected for the occasion. The mixture of colloquial informality and stylisation which characterises this drama seems to arise out of the need to develop a mode of presentation that is both accessible and commanding. The actors have to assert themselves over the comings and goings of the street: to contend with dogs, drunks, children, birds and weather.

The function of this drama as part of a festival controlled by civic authorities was to restate and celebrate the beliefs of the community; indeed, it was an expression of the idea of community itself. When those beliefs changed with the Reformation in the sixteenth century, the Corpus Christi plays lost their function and were suppressed.

The Wakefield *Second Shepherds' Play*

The Second Shepherds' Play is given this title to distinguish it from another Shepherds' (Nativity) Play in the same collection in the Towneley manuscript, after which this cycle is sometimes called. Both *Shepherds' Plays* seem to have been written by the same man, whose name has not come down to us but who also wrote another four plays in the cycle, presented, as far as we can tell, in the town of Wakefield in Yorkshire. He is now usually known as the Wakefield Master, and wrote in the first half of the fifteenth century. He is likely – because of his biblical knowledge – to have been a cleric of some kind.

The Second Shepherds' Play is written in nine-line stanzas (aaaa4b1ccc2b2), which are the hall-mark of the Wakefield Master's work, and which he uses to create strikingly flexible dialogue. Dramatically, this is one of the most complex and ambitious of all the surviving mystery plays, with its changes of location and period, the contrasts and parallels of its scenic design, and its use of Christian symbolism. In order to appreciate the mentality which can make the shepherds of the nativity story into fifteenth-century Yorkshiremen, we should look at Netherlandish paintings of the period, in which scenes from sacred history are depicted in realistic contemporary settings, and in which donors and their families can inhabit without strain the same pictorial space as the Virgin and Child.

The text is from Huntington Library, MS 1.

THE SECOND SHEPHERDS' PLAY

[*A field, on a stormy winter's night.* COLL *enters.*]
COLL: Lord, what† these weders† ar cold and I am yll happyd.†
I am nerehande dold,† so long have I nappyd;*   slept
My legys thay fold, my fyngers ar chappyd.
It is not as I wold,† for I am al lappyd*   wrapped
5   In sorow,
     In stormes and tempest,
     Now in the eest, now in the west –
   Wo is hym has* never rest   who has
   Mydday nor morow!*   morning

---

1   *what* how   *weders* storms   *happyd* clad
2   *nerehand dold* almost numb
4   *as I wold* as I would like it

10	Bot we sely husbandys† that walkys on the moore,	
	In fayth, we ar nerehandys outt of the doore.	
	No wonder, as it standys, if we be poore	
	For the tylthe* of oure landys lyys falow as the floore,	arable part
	As ye ken.*	know
15	†We ar so hamyd,*	hamstrung
	†Fortaxed and ramyd,	
	We ar mayde handtamyd	
	With* thyse gentlery-men.*	by gentry
	Thus thay refe† us oure rest, oure Lady theym wary!*	curse
20	These men that ar lord-fest,† thay cause the ploghe tary.	
	That* men say is for the best, we fynde it contrary.	what
	Thus ar husbandys opprest, in ponte to myscary†	
	On lyfe.*	in this life
	†Thus hold thay us hunder,	
25	Thus thay bryng us in blonder;*	distress
	It were greatte wonder	
	And* ever shuld we thryfe.*	if thrive
	For may he† gett a paynt slefe† or a broche* now-on-dayes,	brooch
	Wo is hym that hym grefe* or onys agane says.*	angers gainsays
30	Dar no man hym represe,* what mastry he mays;†	reprove
	And yit may no man lefe* oone word that he says –	believe
	No letter.	
	He can make purveance*	requisition goods
	With boste and bragance,*	arrogance
35	And all is thrugh mantenance	
	Of* men that ar gretter.	by

---

10 *sely husbandys* poor farmers
15–45 [The first shepherd complains of the exploitation of his class of small tenant-farmers at the hands of the lords. In the late fourteenth and fifteenth centuries powerful men attached to themselves groups of retainers whom they maintained in return for service. Such men, wearing badges of allegiance of the kind referred to in l. 28 and secure in their master's protection, became almost a law unto themselves. They usurped the king's privilege of purveying or requisitioning the goods needed to maintain his court as he travelled about the country (ll.33ff.). Statutes restricting maintenance were continually enacted in the late middle ages]
16 Over-taxed and beaten down
19 *refe* take away from
20 *lord-fest* bound to lords
22 *in ponte to miscary* in danger of failing
24 In this way they keep us down
28 *may he* if one can   *paynt slefe* painted sleeve
30 *what mastry he mays* whatever power he uses

    Ther shall com a swane* as prowde as a po* —   *serving-man peacock*
    He must borow my wane,* my ploghe also.   *cart*
    Then I am full fane† to graunt* or* he go.   *accede before*
40 Thus lyf we in payne, anger* and wo,   *suffering*
    By nyght and day.
    †He must have if he langyd,
    If* I shuld forgang* it;   *though forgo*
    I were better be hangyd
45 Then oones* say hym nay.   *once*

    It dos me good as I walk thus by myn oone†
    Of this warld for to talk in maner of mone.*   *complainingly*
    To my shepe wyll I stalk* and herkyn anone,*   *go listen now*
    Ther abyde on a balk,† or sytt on a stone
50 Full soyne.*   *straight away*
    For I trowe,* perdé,*   *believe by God*
    Trew men if thay be,
    We gett more compané
    Or* it be noyne.*   *before noon*

[GIB, *another shepherd, enters. He does not notice* COLL]
55 GIB: Bensté and Dominus,† what may this bemeyne?*   *signify*
    Why fares this warld thus? Oft have we not sene.†
    Lord, thyse weders ar spytus* and the wyndys full kene,   *pitiless*
    And the frostys so hydus* thay water myn eeyne* —   *hideous eyes*
    No ly.*   *truly*
60 Now in dry, now in wete,
    Now in snaw, now in slete,
    When my shone* freys* to my fete   *shoes freeze*
    It is not all esy.

---

39 *full fane* absolutely delighted
42 If he wants something, he must have it
46 *by myn oone* on my own
49 *abyde on a balk* wait on a ridge
55 *Bensté and Dominus* Lord bless us
56 *Oft have we not sene* we haven't often seen the like

	†Bot as far as I ken or yit as I go,	
65	†We sely wedmen dre mekyll wo.	
	We have sorow then and then;† it fallys* oft so.	happens
	Sely* Copyle, oure hen, both to and fro	poor
	She kakyls –	
	Bot begyn she to crok,*	croak
70	To groyne* or to clok,*	groan cluck
	†Wo is hym is oure cok,	
	For he is in the shakyls.*	shackles

	These men that ar wed have not all thare wyll;†	
	When they ar full hard sted,† thay sygh full styll.*	endlessly
75	God wayte* thay ar led* full hard and full yll;	knows treated
	In bowere nor in bed they say noght thertyll.†	
	†This tyde	
	My parte have I fun;*	found
	I know my lesson:	
80	Wo is hym that is bun,*	bound
	For he must abyde.*	endure

	Bot now late in oure lyfys† (a mervell to me,	
	That I thynk my hart ryfys* sich wonders to see –	breaks
	†What that destany dryfys it shuld so be)	
85	Som men wyll have two wyfys and som men thre†	
	In store!*	abundance
	Som ar wo* that has any.	miserable
	†Bot so far can I:	
	Wo is hym that has many,	
90	For he felys* sore.	feels

64–5 As far as I know or indeed as I range, we poor married men suffer great misery
66 *then and then* all the time
71 Woe betide him who is our cock
73 *have not all thare wyll* cannot do everything they want
74 *full hard sted* very hard pressed
76 *say noght thertyll* have no say at all in things
77 At this time
82 *late in oure lyfys* recently in our times
84 What destiny brings must come to pass
85 [*two wyfys . . . thre* these marriages are in succession, not simultaneously]
88 But I know this much

[*To the audience*]
  Bot, yong men, of wowyng,† for God that you boght,*   redeemed
  Be well war of wedyng† and thynk in youre thoght:
  'Had-I-wyst'† is a thyng that servys of noght.†
  †Mekyll styll mowrnyng has wedyng home broght,
95 And grefys,
  With many a sharp showre.*   hail [of blows]
  For thou may cach in an owre
  †That shall sow the full sowre
  As long as thou lyffys.

100 For as ever rede I pystyll,† I have oone to my fere†
  As sharp as thystyll, as rugh as a brere;*   briar
  She is browyd* lyke a brystyll, with a sowre-loten chere;†   has brows
  †Had she oones wett hyr whystyll, she couth syng full clere
  Hyr Paternoster.†
105 She is as greatt as a whall;
  She has a galon of gall;
  By hym that dyed for us all,
  I wald I had ryn to* I had lost hir.   run till

[COLL *has meanwhile been trying to signal to him.*]
  COLL [*To the audience*]: God looke over the raw!† Full defly*   deafly
  ye stand.
110 GIB: Yee, the devill in thi maw,* so tariand!†   belly
  †Sagh thou awre of Daw?
    COLL: Yee, on a ley-land*   pasture
  Hard* I hym blaw.† He commys here at hand,   heard
  Not far.
  Stand styll!

---

91 *of wowyng* as to wooing
92 *Be well war of wedyng* be on your guard against marriage
93 *Had-I-wyst* had I known   *servys of nought* is of no avail
94 Much endless sorrow has marriage brought home
98 What shall afflict you very bitterly
100 *pystyll* epistle [the Bible]   *to my fere* as my mate
102 *sowre-loten chere* sour-looking expression
103 Had she once taken a drink, she could sing loudly
104 *Paternoster* Our Father [Lord's prayer]
109 *God looke over the raw* May God take care of this assembly
110 *so tariand* loitering so long
111 Have you seen Daw anywhere?
112 *blaw* blow [his horn]

GIB: Qwhy?
115 COLL: For he commys, hope* I.   believe
GIB: He wyll make* us both a ly   tell
Bot if* we be war.   unless

[*Enter* DAW, *a shepherd-boy who is* GIB's *assistant. He does not see the others.*]

DAW: Crystys crosse me spede,* and Sant Nycholas!   help
Therof had I nede – it is wars* then it was.   worse
120 Whose* couthe take hede and lett the warld pas: whoever
It is ever in drede† and brekyll* as glas,   brittle
And slythys.*   slips away
†This warld fowre never so,
With mervels mo and mo;*   more and more
125 Now in weyll,* now in wo,   prosperity
And all thyng wrythys.†

Was never syn* Noe* floode sich* flodys seyn,   since Noah's such
Wyndys and ranys so rude,* and stormes so keyn;   rough
Som stamerd,* som stod in dowte,† as I weyn.*   stumbled think
130 Now God turne all to good! I say as I mene,†
For ponder:*   to ponder on it
These floodys so thay drowne
Both in feyldys and in towne,
And berys* all downe –   bear
135 And that is a wonder.

[*He sees* COLL *and* GIB, *and starts.*]
We that walk on the nyghtys, oure catell to kepe,
We se sodan* syghtys when othere men slepe.   sudden

---

121 *It is ever in drede* [would know that] it is always uncertain
123 This world has never been thus
126 *all thyng wrythys* everything changes
129 *in dowte* afraid
130 *as I mene* what I think

	†Yit me thynk my hart lyghtys:* I se shrewys pepe.†	lightens
	Ye ar two ill wyghtys†! I wyll gyf my shepe	
140	A turne.	
	[*To himself:*] †Bot full yll have I ment.	
	As I walk on this bent*	heath
	†I may lyghtly repent,	
	My toes if I spurne.*	stub
145	[*To* COLL *and* GIB:] A, syr, God you save, and master myne!	
	A drynk fayn wold I† have, and somwhat to dyne.†	
	COLL: Crystys curs, my knave, thou art a ledyr hyne!†	
	GIB: What, the boy lyst rave!† Abyde unto syne† —	
	We have mayde it.*	eaten
150	†Yll thryft on thy pate!	
	Though the shrew* cam late,	rascal
	Yit is he in state*	ready
	To dyne, if he had it.	
	DAW: Sich servandys as I that swettys and swynkys,*	toil
155	Etys oure brede full dry and that me forthynkys.†	
	We ar oft weytt and wery when master-men wynkys;†	
	Yit commys full lately both dyners and drynkys.	
	Bot nately*	firmly
	Both oure dame* and oure syre,*	mistress master
160	When we have ryn* in the myre,	run
	They can nyp* at oure hyre*	pinch pay
	And pay us full lately.*	belatedly

138–45 [The sense of these lines may be that Daw, who is frightened of the storm, is at first cheered to discern two figures ('my hart lyghtys'), then becomes nervous of them and says, with false nonchalance, that he will give his sheep a turn, in order to get out of the way of the 'ill wythtys' without looking foolish. As soon as he has said this he realises that walking around the dark moor may be more painful than staying. Finally, he recognises the figures, one of whom (presumably Gib) is his master]
138 *shrewys pepe* villains looking about.
139 *ill wyghtys* evil creatures
141 But that was the wrong thing to say
143 I may easily regret it
146 *fayn wold I* I would be glad to   *somwhat to dyne* to eat a little
147 *ledyr hyne* lazy servant
148 *lyst rave* likes to talk nonsense   *Abyde unto syne* wait till later
150 Bad luck to you
155 *me forthynkys* I regret
156 *when master-men wynkys* while the bosses sleep

	Bot here my trouth,† master: for the fayr* that ye make†	food
	I shall do therafter† – wyrk as I take.*	am paid
165	I shall do a lytyll, syr, and emang ever lake,†	
	For yit* lay my soper never on my stomake	so far
	In feyldys.	
	†Wherto shuld I threpe?	
	With my staf can I lepe,*	run away
170	And men say, 'Lyght chepe†	
	†Letherly foryeldys.'	

	COLL: †Thou were an yll lad to ryde on wowyng	
	†With a man that had bot lytyll of spendyng.	
	GIB: Peasse, boy, I bad.* No more janglyng†	told [you]
175	Or I shall make the full rad,† by the hevens kyng.	
	†With thy gawdys –	
	Where ar oure shepe, boy? – we skorne.†	
	DAW: Sir, this same day at morne	
	I thaym left in the corne,	
180	†When they rang lawdys.	

	Thay have pasture good, thay can not go wrong.	
	COLL: That is right. By the roode,* thyse nyghtys ar long.	cross
	†Yit I wold, or we yode, oone gaf us a song.	
	GIB: So I thoghte as I stode, to myrth us emong.†	
185	DAW: I grauntt.*	agree
	COLL: Lett me syng the tenory.*	tenor
	GIB: And I the tryble* so hye.	treble
	DAW: Then the meyne* fallys to me.	middle part
	Lett se how ye chauntt.*	sing

---

163 *trouth* promise   *make* provide
164 *do therafter* perform accordingly
165 *emang ever lake* in between, play all the time
168 Why should I haggle?
170–1 *Lyght chepe / Letherly foryeldys* A cheap bargain gives a poor return
172–3 You'd be the wrong lad to go courting with a man who hadn't much money
174 *janglyng* chattering
175 *make the full rad* very quickly make you [be quiet]
176-7 *With thy gawdys ... we skorne* we scorn ... your tricks
180 When the bells for matins were rung
183 Yet I would like, before we went, to be given a song
184 *myrth us emong* enjoy ourselves together

[*They sing. Enter* MAK†, *who is a local trouble-maker, wearing a cloak over his doublet.*]

190 MAK: Now, Lord, for thy naymes seven, that made both moyn*   moon
      and starnes*   stars
†Well mo then I can neven – thi will, Lorde, of me tharnys.
I am all uneven;* that moves oft my harnes.†   upset
Now wold God I were in heven, for ther wepe no barnes*   children
So styll.*   continually
195 COLL: Who is that pypys* so poore?*   cries pathetically
MAK: [*Putting on a southern accent*:] Wold God ye wyst* how   knew
      I foore!*   fared
Lo, a man that walkys on the moore,
And has not all hys wyll.†
GIB: Mak, where has thou gone? Tell us tythyng.*   news
200 DAW: †Is he commen? Then ylkon take hede to his thyng.

MAK: What, ich* be a yoman,* I tell you, of the kyng,   I yeoman
The self and the some,* sond* from a greatt   same messenger
      lordyng,*   lord
And sich.*   such
Fy on you! Goyth* hence   go
205 Out of my presence.
I must have reverence.
Why, who be ich?

COLL: Why make ye it so qwaynt?† Mak, ye do wrang.
GIB: †Bot, Mak, lyst ye saynt? I trow that ye lang.
210 DAW: I trow* the shrew can paynt,† the devyll myght hym hang!   believe
MAK: Ich shall make complaynt and make you all to thwang†

---

190 [Mak It is tempting, but possibly not plausible at this date, to think of Mak as the Scots 'Mac' (from the Gaelic *mac* 'son of') and the character as a Scotsman. See Laurence Minot's poems (pp. 177–8) for anti-Scottish feeling in the north of England a century earlier. Mak initially speaks with a southern accent and pretends to be the retainer of a great lord. The others know him of old for the thief he is, and Daw prudently relieves him of his cloak. (Later, at l. 396, Mak, asserting his innocence of sheep-stealing, tells them to check in his sleeves.)]
191 *Many more than I can name* – I don't know what you want of me, Lord
192 *moves oft my harnes* often disturbs my brain
198 *all his wyll* everything he wants
200 Has he come? Then everyone look after his things
208 *Why make ye it so qwaynt* Why are you putting on such airs
209 But Mak, do you want to play the saint? I think you do
210 *shrew can paynt* villain can talk speciously
211 *make you all to thwang* get you all flogged

At a worde,
And tell evyn how ye doth.†
COLL: Bot Mak, is that sothe?* — true
215 Now take outt that Sothren tothe†
And sett in a torde!* — turd

GIB: Mak, the devill in youre ee!* A stroke† wold I leyne† you. — eye
DAW: Mak, know ye not me? By God, I couthe teyn† you.
[MAK *finally realises that his pretence is useless.*]
MAK: God looke you all thre! Me thoght I had sene you.
220 Ye ar a fare compané.
COLL: Can ye now mene you?* — remember
GIB: †Shrew, pepe!
†Thus late as thou goys,
What wyll men suppos?* — suspect
And thou has an yll noys* — bad reputation
225 Of steyling of shepe.

MAK: And I am trew as steyll, all men waytt,* — know
Bot a sekenes I feyll that haldys me full haytt.†
My belly farys not weyll;* it is out of astate.* — well condition
DAW: †Seldom lyys the devyll dede by the gate.
230 MAK: Therfor
Full sore am I and yll,
If* I stande stone-styll; — even if
I ete not* an nedyll — I haven't eaten
Thys moneth and more.

235 COLL: How farys* thi wyff? By thi hoode, how farys she? — fares
MAK: Lyys walterying,* by the roode, by the fyere, lo! — sprawling
And a howse full of brude.* She drynkys well, to. — children
†Yll spede othere good that she wyll do!

---

213 *evyn how ye doth* just what you do
215 *Sothren tothe* southern tooth [accent]
217 *stroke* blow   *leyne* give
218 *couthe teyn* could hurt
221 Villain, snoop about
222 Going about late like this
227 *haldys me full haytt* that is giving me a bad time
229 The devil seldom lies dead by the wayside   [This proverb warns against being deceived by appearances; Daw means 'Watch out; he's at it again']
238 May any other good she will do go wrong

                Bot sho*   she
240   Etys as fast as she can
        And ilk* yere that commys to man   each
        She bryngys furth a lakan*   baby
        And, som yeres, two.

        Bot were I† now more gracyus* and rychere be far,   fortunate
245   I were† eten outt of howse and of harbar.*   home
        Yit is she a fowll dowse,* if ye com nar;*   trollop   close
        Ther is none that trowse† nor knowys a war*   worse
        Then ken I.*   Than I do
        Now wyll ye se what I profer?*   offer
250   To gyf all in my cofer*   money-box
        †To-morne at next to offer
        †Hyr hed-maspenny.

        GIB: I wote* so forwakyd* is none in this shyre.   know   weary
        I wold slepe, if I takyd les to my hyere.†
255   DAW: I am cold and nakyd and wold have a fyere.
        COLL: I am wery, forrakyd* and run in the myre.   exhausted
        †Wake thou!   [Lies down.]
        GIB: Nay, I wyll lyg downe by,†
        For I must slepe, truly.   [Lies down beside him.]
260   DAW: As good a mans son was I
        As any of you.
                                                    [Lies down with the others.]
        Bot, Mak, com heder!* Betwene* shall thou lyg downe.   here   between us
        MAK: Then myght I lett you bedene of that ye wold rowne,†
        No drede.*   no doubt

---

244 *were I* even if I were
245 *I were* I would be
247 *trowse* is acquainted with
251–2 To pay straight away tomorrow morning for her requiem mass   [He would give all he has to become chief mourner at his wife's funeral]
254 *if I takyd les to my hyere* even if I received less for my pay
257 You stay awake
258 *lyg downe by* lie down nearby
263 *lett you . . . wold rowne* keep you at once from whispering

265 Fro my top† to my too,*   toe
     †*Manus tuas commendo,*
     †*Poncio Pilato.*
     †Cryst-crosse me spede!

[MAK *lies down and then, as the shepherds fall asleep, gets up.*]
     Now were tyme for a man that lakkys what he wold†
270 To stalk prevely* than unto a fold*   secretly sheepfold
     And neemly* to wyrk* than and be not to bold,   nimbly act
     For he myght aby the bargan,† if it were told
     At the endyng.
     †Now were tyme for to reyll,
275 Bot he nedys good counsell
     †That fayn wold fare weyll.
     And has bot lytyll spendyng.*   money

[*He walks round the sleeping shepherds, casting a 'spell' on them.*]
     †Bot abowte you a serkyll* as rownde as a moyn,*   circle moon
     To* I have done that* I wyll, tyll that it be noyn,*   until what noon
280 †That ye lyg stone-styll to that I have doyne;
     And I shall say thertyll* of good wordys a foyne:*   thereto few
     'On hight,*   high
     Over youre heydys, my hand I lyft.
     Outt go youre een!* Fordo* youre syght!'   eyes destroy
285 Bot yit I must make better shyft*   efforts
     †And it be right.

     Lord, what* thay slepe hard! [*To the audience.*] That may ye   how
       all here.
     Was I never a shepard, bot now wyll I lere.*   learn
     If* the flok be skard* yit shall I nyp nere.†   even if scared

---

265 *top* the crown of my head
266–7 I commend your hands to Pontius Pilate
[Mak's bed-time 'prayer' is a mangled version of Jesus' last words: 'Pater, in manus tuas commendo spiritum meum' (Into your hands, Father, I commend my spirit), Luke 23.46]
268 Christ's cross preserve me
269 *lakkys what he wold* has not got what he wants
272 *aby the bargan* pay dearly for it
274 Now would be the time to move quickly
276 Who would like to do well
278–86 [Mak, the comic devil-figure, is a practitioner of sorcery]
280 So that you lie stock-still until I have done
286 If it is to be right
289 *nyp nere* grab tightly

THE SECOND SHEPHERDS' PLAY

290 †How, drawes hederward! [*He catches a sheep.*] Now mendys oure chere
From sorow
A fatt shepe, I dar say;
A good flese, dar I lay.*   I dare wager
†Eft-whyte when I may,
295 Bot this will I borow.

[*He crosses the stage with the sheep and knocks at the door of his house.*]
How, Gyll, art thou in? Gett us som lyght.
GILL: Who makys sich dyn this tyme of the nyght?
†I am sett for to spyn. I hope not I myght
Ryse a penny to wyn; I shrew them on hight!
300 So farys
A huswyff that has bene
To be rasyd thus betwene.
Here may no note be sene
For sich small charys.

305 MAK: Good wyff, open the hek!* Seys thou not†what I bryng?   door
GILL: †I may thole the dray the snek. [*She opens the door.*]
                              A, com in, my swetyng.
MAK: †Yee, thou thar not rek of my long standyng.
GILL [*seeing the sheep*]: By the nakyd nek art thou lyke for to hyng!†
MAK: Do way.*   Enough
310 †I am worthy my mete,
For in a strate* can I gett   tight corner
More then thay that swynke* and swette   toil
All the long day.

Thus it fell to my lott, Gyll – I had sich grace.*   such luck
315 GILL: It were a fowll blott† to be hanged for the case.
MAK: †I have skapyd, Jelott, oft as hard a glase.

290–2 *How, drawes . . . / . . . / fatt shepe* Hey! Come here! Now a fat sheep will cheer us up
294 I shall repay when I can
298–304 I am sitting spinning. I don't think that getting up can earn a penny; my curses on them! It's the same for any woman who has been a housewife, being got to her feet all the time. There's no work to be seen here because of petty chores like these
305 *Seys thou not* do you not see
306 I may let you draw the latch
307 Yes, you needn't worry about keeping me standing so long
308 *lyke for to hyng* likely to hang
310 I deserve my food
315 *It were a fowll blott* it would be a crying shame
316 Gilly, I have often escaped as hard a blow as this

	GILL: 'Bot* so long goys* the pott to the water', men says,	only goes
	'At last	
	Comys it home broken.'	
320	MAK: Well knowe I the token,*	saying
	Bot let it never be spoken!	
	Bot com and help fast.	

I wold he were flayn;* I lyst* well ete. *skinned   want*
This twelmothe was I not so fayn of oone shepe-mete.†
325 GILL: Com thay or he be slayn† and here the shepe blete –
MAK: Then myght I be tane;* that were a cold swette! *caught*
Go spar* *bar*
The gaytt-doore.* *outer door*
GILL: Yis, Mak,
For and* thay com at thy bak – *if*
330 MAK: Then myght I by,* for* all the pak, *get   from*
†The devill of the war!

GILL: †A good bowrde have I spied, syn thou can none:
Here shall we hym hyde to* thay be gone, *till*
In my credyll.* Abyde,* lett* me alone *cradle wait leave*
335 And I shall lyg besyde in chylbed and grone.
MAK: Thou red,* *get ready*
And I shall say thou was lyght†
Of a knave-childe* this nyght *baby boy*
GILL: †Now well is me day bright
340 †That ever was I bred.

This is a good gyse* and a far cast,* *disguise clever trick*
†Yit a woman avyse helpys at the last.
†I wote never who spyse; agane go thou fast.

---

324 *fayn of oone shepe-mete*   eager for a single meal of mutton
325 *Come they or he be slayn*   if they come before it is killed
331 Much the worst of it
332 I have spotted a good trick, since you don't know of any
337 *thou was lyght*   you were delivered
339–40 Now I rejoice in the bright day I was born
342 A woman's advice still helps in the end
343 I don't know who is watching; go back quickly

MAK: †Bot I com or thay ryse, els blawes a cold blast.
345 I wyll go slepe.
[*He leaves his cottage and goes over to where the shepherds are sleeping.*]
†Yit slepys all this meneye;
And I shall go stalk prevely* walk stealthily
As* it had never bene I as if
That caryed thare shepe.

[*He lies down again by the shepherds.*]
350 COLL [*waking up*]: †*Resurrex a mortruus*! Have hold my hand.
Judas carnas dominus! I may not well stand.
My foytt* slepys, by Jesus, and I water fastand.† foot
I thoght that we layd us full nere Yngland.
GIB: A, ye?
355 Lord, what* I have slept weyll! how
As fresh as an eyll,* eel
As lyght I me feyll
As leyfe on a tre.

DAW [*waking from a bad dream, and not knowing where he is*]:
Bensté* be herein! So me qwakys† blessed
360 My hart is outt of skyn, whatso it makys.†
Who makys all this dyn? So my browes blakys,†
To the dowore* wyll I wyn.* Harke, felows, wakys. door escape
We were fowre –
†So ye awre of Mak now?
365 COLL: We were up or* thou. before
GIB: Man, I gyf God a vowe,
†Yit yede he nawre.

---

344 If I don't come back before they get up, a cold blast will blow
346 The whole crowd are still sleeping
350–1 [*Resurrex a mortruus . . . / Judas carnas dominus* Coll's befuddled prayers are meaningless]
352 *water fastand* am faint with hunger
359 *So me qwakys* I tremble so much
360 *whatso it makys* whatever causes it
361 *so my browes blakys* my brows darken so [with fear]
364 Have you seen Mak anywhere?
367 He hasn't moved at all yet

DAW: Me thoght he was lapt* in a wolfe-skyn.   *wrapped*
COLL: †So ar many hapt now, namely within.†
370 DAW: When we had long napt,* me thoght with a gyn*   *slept   snare*
A fatt shepe he trapt, bot he mayde no dyn.*   *noise*
GIB: Be styll.*   *Be quiet*
Thi dreme makys the* woode* –   *thee, you   mad*
It is bot fantom,* by the roode.   *illusion*
375 COLL: Now God turne all to good,
If it be his wyll.

GIB: Ryse, Mak, for shame. Thou lygys* right lang.   *lie*
MAK: Now Crystys holy name be us emang!*   *in our midst*
What is this? For Sant Jame, I may not well gang.†
380 I trow I be† the same. A, my nek has lygen* wrang.   *lain*
[*The others straighten his neck.*]
Enoghe,
†Mekill thank! Syn yister even,
Now by Sant Stevyn,
I was flayd* with a swevyn;*   *frightened   dream*
385 My hart out of sloghe.†

I thoght Gyll began to crok* and travell full sad,†   *croak*
Wel ner* at the fyrst cok,* of a yong lad   *just about   cock-crow*
For to mend* oure flok. Then be I never glad –   *increase*
I have tow on my rok† more than ever I had.
390 A, my heede!*   *head*
A house full of yong tharmes,*   *bellies*
The devill knok outt thare harnes!*   *brains*
Wo is hym has many barnes*   *children*
And therto lytyll brede.*   *bread*

---

369 Many people are covered like that now, epecially inside   [*namely within* an allusion to wolves in sheep's clothing, or hypocrites; a common anti-clerical gibe]
379 *may not well gang* can't walk properly
380 *trow I be* hope I shall be
382 Many thanks! Since yesterday night
385 *out of sloghe* [jumped] out of its skin
386 *travell full sad* go into very difficult labour
389 *tow on my rok* flax-fibre on my distaff   [work on hand]

395	I must go home, by youre lefe, to Gyll, as I thoght.	
	I pray you looke* my slefe,* that I steyll noght.*	inspect sleeve nothing
	I am loth you to grefe* or from you take oght.*	anger anything

[*The shepherds search him, and let him go.*]

	DAW: Go furth, yll myght thou chefe!† Now wold I we soght,*	looked
	This morne,	
400	That we had all oure store.*	livestock
	COLL: Bot I will go before.*	ahead
	Let us mete.	
	GIB: Whore?*	where
	DAW: At the crokyd thorne.†	

[*They go off in different directions. MAK enters and crosses to his house.*]

	MAK: Undo this doore! Who is here? How long shall I stand?	
405	GILL: Who makys sich a bere?* Now walk in the wenyand!†	din
	MAK: A, Gyll, what chere?† It is I, Mak, youre husbande.	
	GILL: Then may we se here the devill in a bande,†	
	Syr Gyle.*	Guile
	Lo, he commys with a lote,*	noise
410	As* he were holden* in the throte.	as if held
	I may not syt at my note*	work
	A handlang* while.	little

	MAK [*To the audience*]: Wyll ye here what fare* she makys	commotion
	to gett hir a glose?†	
	And dos noght bot lakys† and clowse hir toose.†	
415	GILL: Why, who wanders?† Who wakys? Who commys? Who gose?	
	Who brewys? Who bakys? What makys me thus hose?*	hoarse
	And than	
	It is rewthe* to beholde,	a pity
	Now in hote, now in colde,	
420	Full wofull is the householde	
	That wantys* a woman.	lacks

---

398 *yll myght thou chefe* may you fare badly
403 [*crokyd thorne* possibly refers to the thorn that has given their names to the parishes of Thornhill and Thornes, near Horbury, south-west of Wakefield]
405 *wenyand* waning [The waning of the moon was believed to be an unlucky time; the expression seems to mean 'may you have bad luck']
406 *what chere* how are you
407 *the devill in a bande* a pack of devils
413 *gett hir a glose* put on a false show [of work]
414 *lakys* enjoys herself   *clowse hir toose* lounges about [lit., scratches her toes]
415 *wanders* goes here and there

†Bot what ende has thou mayde with the hyrdys, Mak?
MAK: The last worde that thay sayde when I turnyd my bak,
Thay wold looke that† thay hade thare shepe, all the pak.
425 I hope* thay wyll nott be well payde† when thay thare shepe lak,   *think
Perdé!*   *by God
†Bot howso the gam gose,
To me thay wyll suppose*   *suspect
And make a fowll noyse
430 And cry outt apon me.
Bot thou must do as thou hyght.*   *promised
GILL: I accorde me thertyll.†
I shall swedyll* hym right in my credyll.   *swaddle

[GILL *wraps up the sheep and puts it in the cradle.*]
GILL: If* it were a gretter slyght,† yit couthe* I help tyll.†*   *even if *could
I wyll lyg downe stright.* Com hap* me.   *at once *cover
MAK: I wyll.
435 GILL: Behynde!*   *at the back
Com Coll and his maroo,*   *mate
Thay will nyp* us full naroo.*   *pinch *hard
MAK: Bot I may cry 'out, haroo!'*   *help, help
The shepe if thay fynde.

440 GILL: Harken ay† when they call; thay will com onone.*   *very soon
Com and make redy all and syng by thyn oone.†
Syng 'lullay'† thou shall, for I must grone
And cry outt by the wall on Mary and John,†
For sore.*   *in pain
445 Syng 'lullay' on fast*   *quickly
When thou heris at the last,
And bot* I play a fals cast,*   *unless *trick
Trust me no more.

---

422 But what conclusion have you come to with the shepherds, Mak?
424 *wold looke that* would see if
425 *payde* pleased
427 But however the game turns out
431 *accorde me thertyll* agree to it
433 *slyght* deception   *tyll* towards [it]
440 *Harken ay* keep listening for
441 *by the oone* on your own
442 [*Syng 'lullay'* Mak is to sing a lullaby to the 'baby']
443 *on Mary and John* to the Blessed Virgin and St John

[*MAK begins to sing a lullaby. Meanwhile, back at the crooked thorn, the shepherds meet.*]

DAW: A, Coll, goode morne. Why slepys thou nott?

450 COLL: Alas, that ever was I borne! We have a fowll blott* —   *disgrace*
A fat wedir* have we lorne.*   *wether lost*
              Mary, Godys forbott!†

GIB: Who shuld do us that skorne?* That were a fowll   *insult*
  spott.*   *shame*

COLL: Som shrewe.*   *villain*
I have soght with my dogys
455 All Horbery† shrogys*   *shrubs*
And of* fifteene hogys*   *among young sheep*
Fond* bot oone ewe.   *found*

DAW: Now trow* me if ye will, by Sant Thomas of Kent,   *believe*
Ayther Mak or Gyll was at that assent.†

460 COLL: Peasse, man, be still! I sagh* when he went.   *saw*
Thou sklanders* hym yll; thou aght* to repent   *slander ought*
Goode spede.*   *straight away*

GIB: †Now as ever myght I the,
If I shuld evyn here de,*   *die*
465 I wold say it were he
That dyd that same dede.

DAW: Go we theder,* I rede,* and ryn on oure feete.   *thither advise*
Shall I never ete brede the sothe to I wytt.†

COLL: Nor drynk in my heede, with hym tyll I mete.
470 GIB: I wyll rest in no stede* tyll that I hym grete,   *place*
My brothere.
Oone* I will hight:*   *one thing promise*
Tyll I se hym in sight,
Shall I never slepe one nyght
475 Ther* I do anothere.   *where*

---

451 *Mary, Goddis forbot* By Our Lady, God forbid
455 [*Horbery* Horbury is three miles south-west of Wakefield]
459 *at that assent* a party to it
463 Now as ever I hope to prosper
468 *the sothe to I witt* till I know the truth

[*They cross the stage to* MAK's *cottage. Sounds of singing and groaning are audible.*]

DAW: Will ye here how they hak?* Oure syre lyst croyne.†   *trill*
COLL: Hard I never none crak† so clere out of toyne.*   *tune*
Call on hym.
   GIB: Mak, undo youre doore soyne!
MAK: Who is that spak* as it were noyne,*   [who] *spoke noon*
480 On loft?*   *loudly*
Who is that, I say?   [*He opens the door.*]
DAW: Goode felowes, were it day.†
MAK: As far as ye may,
Good,* spekys soft   *good men*

485 Over a seke* womans heede* that is at maylleasse.*   *sick   head   in pain*
I had lever* be dede or* she had any dyseasse.*   *rather   before   discomfort*
GILL: Go to anothere stede!* I may not well qweasse.*   *place   breathe*
Ich* fote that ye trede goys thorow my nese†   *each*
So hee.*   *piercingly*
490 COLL: Tell us, Mak, if ye may,
How fare ye,† I say?
MAK: Bot ar ye in this towne to-day?
Now how fare ye?

Ye have ryn in the myre and ar weytt yit.*   *still wet*
495 I shall make you a fyre if ye will sytt.
A nores* wold I hyre. Thynk ye on yit?†   *nurse*
Well qwytt is my hyre;† my dreme, this is itt,
A seson.* [*He points to the cradle.*]   *for a while*
I have barnes,* if ye knew,   *children*
500 Well mo* then enewe.*   *more   enough*
Bot we must drynk as we brew
And that is bot reson.*   *only reasonable*

---

476 *syre list croyne* master likes to croon
477 *Hard I never none crak* I never heard anyone bawling
482 *were it day* [as you would see] if it were day
488 *nese* nose [i.e. head]
491 *How fare ye* how are you doing
496 *Think ye on yit* do you still remember
497 *Well qwytt is my hire* I've been well paid

I wold ye dynyd or ye yode.† Me thynk that ye swette.
GIB: †Nay, nawther mendys oure mode drynke nor mette.
MAK: Why, syr, alys you oght bot goode?†
DAW: Yee, oure shepe that we gett
Ar stollyn as thay yode.* Oure los* is grette.   went loss
MAK: Syrs, drynkys!*   drink
Had I bene thore,*   there
Som shuld have boght it full sore.†
COLL: Mary, som men trowes* that ye wore*   believe were
And that us forthynkys.*   makes us angry

GIB: Mak, som men trowys that it shuld be ye.
DAW: Ayther ye or youre spouse, so say we.
MAK: Now if ye have suspowse to* Gill or to me,   suspicion of
Com and rype* oure howse and then may ye se   ransack
Who had hir.*   the wether
If I any shepe fott,*   stole
Ayther cow or stott* –   heifer
And Gyll, my wyfe, rose nott
Here syn she lade hir* –   was brought to bed

As I am true and lele,* to God here I pray   honest
That this be the fyrst mele that I shall ete this day.
[*The shepherds look round the house for their sheep.*]
COLL: †Mak, as have I ceyll, avyse the, I say.
†He lernyd tymely to steyll that couth not say nay.
GILL: I swelt!*   I'm dying
Outt, thefys, fro my wonys;*   home
Ye com to rob us for the nonys.†
MAK: Here ye not how she gronys?
Youre hartys shuld melt.

---

503 *I wold ye . . . yode* I'd like you to eat before you go
504 No, neither food nor drink will cheer us up
505 *alys you oght bot goode* is anything wrong with you
509 *boght it full sore* paid very dearly for it
523 Mak, as I hope for happiness, I say take heed
524 He who couldn't say no learned to steal early
527 *rob us for the nonys* on purpose to rob us

[*The shepherds approach the cradle.*]

530 GILL: Outt, thefys, fro my barne!* Negh hym not thor!†   *child*
MAK: Wyst ye† how she had farne,* youre hartys wold be sore.   *fared*
Ye do wrang, I you warne, that thus commys before
To† a woman that has farne;* bot I say no more.   *been in labour*
GILL: A, my medyll!*   *middle*
535 I pray to God so mylde,
If ever I you begyld,*   *deceived*
That I ete* this chylde   *eat*
That lygys* in this credyll.   *lies*

MAK: Peasse, woman, for Godys payn, and cry not so!
540 Thou spyllys* thy brane and makys me full wo.*   *destroy   miserable*
GIB: I trow* oure shepe be slayn. What fynde ye two?   *believe*
DAW: All wyrk we in vayn;† as well may we go.
Bot hatters,*   *confound it*
I can fynde no flesh,
545 Hard nor nesh,*   *soft*
Salt nor fresh,
Bot two tome* platers.   *empty*

[*Gestures towards the 'baby'.*]
†Whik catell bot this, tame nor wylde,
†None, as have I blys, as lowde as he smylde.
550 GILL: No, so God me blys and gyf me joy of my chylde!
COLL: †We have merkyd amys; I hold us begyld.
GIB: Syr, don.*   *completely*
Syr – oure Lady hym save! –
Is youre chyld a knave?*   *boy*
555 MAK: Any lord myght hym have,
This chyld, to his son.

---

530 *Negh him not thor* Don't come close to him there
531 *Wyst ye* if you knew
532–3 *before / To* in the presence of
542 *All wyrk we in vayn* we are achieving nothing
548–9 Upon my soul, no livestock, tame or wild, apart from this [baby], that smelt as high as he [the sheep] does
551 We have made a mistake; I think we've been deceived

	When he wakyns he kyppys,* that joy is to se.	reaches out
	DAW: †In good tyme to hys hyppys, and in celé!	
	Bot who was his gossyppys* so sone redé?*	god-parents at hand
560	MAK: †So fare fall thare lyppys!	
	COLL: [Aside]: Hark now, a le.*	lie
	MAK: So God thaym thank,	
	Parkyn and Gybon Waller, I say,	
	And gentill John Horne,† in good fay* –	faith
	He made all the garray* –	disturbance
565	With the greatt shank.*	long legs

	GIB: Mak, freyndys will we be, for we ar all oone.	
	MAK: We? Now I hald for me,† for mendys* gett I none.	amends
	Fare well all thre. All glad were ye gone.†	
	DAW: Fare wordys may ther be bot luf is ther none	
570	This yere.	

[*The shepherds leave the cottage, stopping at the threshold.*]

	COLL: †Gaf ye the chyld any thyng?	
	GIB: I trow not oone farthyng.	
	DAW: †Fast agane will I flyng.	
	Abyde ye me† there.	

[*He goes back into the house.*]

575	Mak, take it to no grefe† if I come to thi barne.	
	MAK: Nay, thou dos me greatt reprefe* and fowll has thou	shame
	farne.*	behaved
	DAW: The child will it not grefe,* that lytyll day-starne.*	hurt star
	Mak, with youre leyfe,* let me gyf youre barne	permission
	Bot six pence.	
580	MAK: Nay, do way,* he slepys.	enough
	DAW: †Me thynk he pepys.	
	MAK: Wen he wakyns he wepys. [GIB *and* COLL *go back into the house.*]	
	I pray you go hence.	

---

558 May he have a good and happy future
560 May good come to them
563 [*John Horne* the name of one of the shepherds in the First Shepherds' Play]
567 *Now I hald for me* I'm not joining in
568 *All glad were ye gone* [I'd be] very glad if you were gone
571–4 [It is still customary in Scotland to give a coin to a new-born baby]
573 I will dash back quickly
574 *Abyde ye me* wait for me
575 *take it to no grefe* don't take offence
581 I think he's looking around

DAW: Gyf me lefe hym to kys and lyft up the clowtt.*   cover
585 What the devill is this? He has a long snowte!
COLL: †He is merkyd amys. We wate ill abowte.
GIB: †Ill-spon weft, iwys, ay commys foull owte.
Ay, so.
He is lyke to oure shepe!
590 DAW: How, Gyb, may I pepe?
COLL: †I trow kynde will crepe
†Where it may not go.

GIB: This was a qwantt gawde† and a far cast.†
It was a hee* frawde.   high
DAW: Yee, syrs, wast.*   it was
595 Lett bren this bawde† and bynd hir fast.
A fals skawde* hang* at the last –   scold hanged
So shall thou.
Wyll ye se how thay swedyll*   wrap up
His foure feytt in the medyll?*   middle
600 Sagh* I never in a credyll   saw
A hornyd lad or* now.   before

MAK: Peasse, byd I.† What, lett be youre fare.*   fuss
I am he that hym gatt* and yond woman hym bare.*   sired bore
COLL: What devill shall he hatt,† Mak? Lo, God, Makys ayre!*   heir
605 GIB: Lett be* all that! Now God gyf hym care,*   stop sorrow
I sagh.
GILL: A pratty* child is he   pretty
As syttys on a wamans kne –
A dyllydowne,* perdé,*   darling by God
610 To gar* a man laghe.*   make laugh

---

586 He is deformed. We shouldn't be prying
587 Indeed, wrongly spun weft always comes out badly
591–2 I reckon nature will crawl where it cannot walk [i.e. find a way]
593 *qwantt gawde* crafty ruse   *far cast* clever trick
595 *Lett bren this bawde* burn this harlot
602 *byd I* I tell [you]
604 *What devill shall he hatt* what the devil shall he be called

DAW: I know hym by the eere-marke; that is a good tokyn.*   *sign*
MAK: I tell you, syrs, hark! – hys noyse was brokyn.
†Sythen told me a clerk that he was forspokyn.
COLL: This is a fals wark. I wold fayn be wrokyn.†

615   Gett wepyn!
GILL: He was takyn with* an elfe,   *by*
I saw it myself –
When the clok stroke twelf
Was he forshapyn.*   *transformed*

620   GIB: †Ye two ar well feft sam in a stede.
COLL: Syn thay manteyn thare theft, let do thaym to dede.†
MAK: If I trespas eft,* gyrd* of my heede.   *again chop*
†With you will I be left.
DAW: Syrs, do my reede:†
For this trespas
625   We will nawther ban* ne flyte,*   *swear quarrel*
Fyght nor chyte,*   *argue*
†Bot have done as tyte
†And cast* hym in canvas.   *toss*

[*The shepherds toss* MAK *up in a canvas sheet, and then leave the house.*]
COLL: Lord, what* I am sore, in poynt for to bryst!†   *how*
630   In fayth, I may* no more; therfor wyll I ryst.*   *can do rest*
GIB: As a shepe of seven skore* he weyd in my fyst.   *140 pounds*
†For to slepe aywhore me thynk that I lyst.
DAW: Now I pray you
Lyg downe on this grene.
635   COLL: On these thefys yit I mene.*   *think*
DAW: Wherto shuld ye tene?*   *be annoyed*
Do as I say you.

---

613   Afterwards a learned man told me he was bewitched
614   *wold fayn be wrokyn*   would like to be avenged
620   You two are in a fine predicament together
621   *let do thaym to dede*   put them to death
623   I am in your hands. [DAW] Sirs, take my advice
627   But finish it as quickly as possible
628   [*cast hym in canvas*   possibly parallels the old custom of tossing a woman in a blanket to induce labour]
629   *in poynt for to bryst*   on the point of bursting
632   I think I'd be pleased to sleep anywhere

[*They lie down. An* ANGEL *appears above. The* ANGEL *sings 'Gloria in Excelsis' and then says:*]
ANGEL: Ryse, hyrd-men heynd,† for now is He borne
That shall take fro* the feynd that* Adam had lorne;*   *from what lost*
640   That warloo* to sheynd,* his nyght is He borne.   *devil destroy*
God is made youre freynd now at this morne,
He behestys.*   *promises*
At Bedlem* go se   *Bethlehem*
†Ther lygys that fre
645   In a cryb full poorely,
Betwyx* two bestys. [*Exit. A star appears.*]   *between*

COLL: †This was a qwant stevyn that ever yit I hard.
It is a mervell to nevyn,* thus to be skard.*   *speak of frightened*
GIB: Of Godys son of hevyn he spak upward.*   *on high*
650   †All the wod on a levyn me thoght that he gard
Appere.
DAW: He spake of a barne*   *child*
In Bedlem, I you warne.*   *tell*
COLL: †That betokyns yond starne.
655   Let us seke hym there.

GIB: Say, what was his song? Hard ye not know he crakyd* it,   *sang*
Thre brefes* to a long?   *short notes*
DAW: Yee, Mary,† he hakt* it.   *trilled*
Was no crochett wrong, nor nothyng that lakt it.*   *it lacked*
COLL: †For to syng us emong, right as he knakt it,
660   I can.
GIB: Let se how ye croyne.*   *croon*
Can ye bark at the mone?
DAW: Hold youre tonges, have done!
COLL: †Hark after, than.   [*They sing the 'Gloria'.*]

---

638   *hyrd-men heynd*   gentle shepherds
644   Where that noble one lies
647   This was as strange a voice as ever I heard till now
650–1   It seemed to me that he made the whole wood appear in a flash of light
654   That [is what] that star signifies
657   *Mary*   by Our Lady
659–60   I know how to sing it among ourselves just as he trilled it
664   Listen, then

665	GIB:	To Bedlem he bad* that we shuld gang.*	said go
		I am full fard* that we tary to* lang.	afraid too
	DAW:	Be mery and not sad; of myrth is oure sang.	
		†Everlastyng glad to mede may we fang,	
		Withoutt noyse.*	vexation
670	COLL:	†Hy we theder forthy,	
		If* we be wete and wery,	even if
		To that chyld and that lady –	
		†We have it not to lose.	
	GIB:	We fynde by the prophecy – [*To the audience*] let be*	stop
		youre dyn! –	
675		Of David † and Isay† and mo then I myn,†	
		Thay prophecyed by clergy* that in a vyrgyn	learnedly
		Shuld he lyght* and ly, to slokyn† oure syn	come down
		And slake* it,	relieve
		Oure kynde,* from wo;	race
680		For Isay sayd so:	
		†*Ecce virgo*	
		Concipiet a chylde that is nakyd.	
	DAW:	Full glad may we be and abyde* that day	await
		That lufly* to se, that all myghtys may.†	lovely one
685		†Lord, well were me for ones and for ay,	
		Myght† I knele on my kne, som word for to say	
		To that chylde.	
		Bot the angell sayd	
		In a cryb was he layde;	
690		He was poorly arayd,	
		Both mener* and mylde.	more humble

---

668 May we have everlasting joy as a reward
670 Let's go there, then
673 We must not neglect it
675 [*David* King David, the psalmist, figures in the (incomplete) Prophets play which occurs earlier in the Wakefield cycle   *Isay* Isaiah 7.14: 'Behold, a virgin shall conceive, and bear a son'; cf. ll. 681–2]   *mo then I myn* more than I remember
677 *slokyn* do away with
681–2 Behold, a virgin shall conceive
684 *all myghtys may* is all-powerful
685 Lord, it would be well for me, now and for ever
686 *Myght* if I could

COLL: Patryarkes that has bene† and prophetys beforne,†
Thay desyryd to have sene this chylde that is borne.
Thay ar gone full clene; that have thay lorne.†
695 We shall se hym, I weyn,* or* it be morne,   think   before
To tokyn.*   as a sign
When I se hym and fele*   touch
Then wote* I full weyll   know
It is true as steyll
700 That* prophetys have spokyn: what

To so poore† as we ar that he wold appere,
Fyrst fynd and declare† by his messyngere.
GIB: Go we now, let us fare;† the place is us nere.
DAW: I am redy and yare.* Go we in fere*   prepared together
705 To that bright.*   bright one
Lord, if thi wylles be –
We ar lewde* all thre –   ignorant
†Thou grauntt us somkyns gle†
To comforth thi wight.*   creature

[They cross the stage to the stable. A curtain is drawn back, revealing MARY, JOSEPH *and the infant* JESUS.*]*
710 COLL: Hayll, comly and clene, hayll, yong child!
Hayll, maker, as I meyne,* of a madyn so mylde!   believe
Thou has waryd,* I weyne,* the warlo* so wylde; cursed think devil
†The fals gyler of teyn, now goys he begylde.
Lo, he merys,*   is happy
715 Lo, he laghys, my swetyng;*   sweet one
A wel fare metyng.
I have holden my hetyng;†
Have a bob of cherys.†

---

692 *Patryarkes that has bene* patriarchs who once lived   *beforne* at an earlier time
694 *that have they lorne* they have lost [the opportunity]
701 *To so poore* to men so poor
702 *Fyrst fynd, and declare* find [us] first and proclaim
703 *fare* make our way
708 *somkyns gle* a source of joy of some kind
708–9 [Daw asks God for the simple (but symbolic) gifts which they bring to the infant Jesus: cherries, bird and ball]
713 The false, malicious deceiver is now himself deceived
717 *holden my hetyng* kept my promise
718 [*bob of cherys* the midwinter fruit is a miraculous parallel to the virgin birth]

GIB: Hayll, sufferan* savyoure, for thou has us soght!†   sovereign
720   Hayll, frely foyde† and floure that all thyng has wroght!*   made
     Hayll, full of favoure that made all of noght!†
     Hayll, I kneyll and I cowre.* A byrd† have I broght   crouch
     To my barne.*   child
     Hayll, lytyll tyné mop!*   tiny moppet
725   Of oure crede* thou art crop.*   belief head
     †I wold drynk on thy cop,*   from your chalice
     Lytyll day-starne.*   star

DAW: Hayll, derlyng dere, full of godhede!
     I pray the be nere when that I have nede.
730   Hayll, swete is thy chere!* My hart wold blede   face
     To se the sytt here in so poore wede*   clothing
     With no pennys.
     Hayll, put furth thy dall!†
     I bryng the bot a ball.
735   †Have and play the withall
     And go to the tenys.†

MARY: The fader of heven, God omnypotent,
     That sett all on seven,† His son has He sent.
     †My name couth He neven and lyght or He went.
740   †I conceyvyd hym full even thrugh myght, as He ment,
     And now is He borne.
     He* kepe you fro wo –   may He
     I shall pray Hym so.
     Tell furth* as ye go   make known
745   And myn on* this morne.   remember

---

719 *thou has us soght* you have sought us
720 *frely foyde* noble child
721 *all of noght* everything from nothing
722 [*A byrd* possibly an allusion to the dove, symbol of the Holy Spirit]
726 [An allusion to the chalice of the Eucharist containing the wine which is Christ's blood]
733 *furth thy dall* out your hand
735 Take it and play with it
736 [*go to the tenys* real (royal) tennis, played on indoor courts, was a sport of kings. The ball suggests an orb, symbol of kingly power]
738 *That sett all on seven* who made everything in seven days
739 He called me by my name and descended into me before He went
740 I conceived Him indeed through God's power, as He intended

COLL: Fare well, lady, so fare to beholde,
With thy childe on thi kne.
GIB: Bot he lygys* full cold.   lies
[*He covers the baby*]
Lord, well is me! Now we go, thou behold.
DAW: Forsothe,* allredy it semys to be told   indeed
750 Full oft.*   very often
COLL: What grace we have fun.*   found
GIB: Com furth; now ar we won.*   saved
DAW: To syng ar we bun* –   bound
Let take on loft!*   Begin loudly
[*The shepherds go off the stage singing.*]

The York Butchers' Play of the Death of Christ

This play from the York cycle was performed, as the heading suggests, by the Butchers' guild. It is one of a sequence of eight plays, beginning with Judas' conspiracy to betray Jesus, which deal with the events leading up to the crucifixion. They use a variety of alliterative stanzas, and thus were probably originally written before the middle of the fifteenth century, when the taste for alliterative verse died out in England. They have been attributed to one man, known as the York Realist, though it is not certain that this play, the last of the sequence, is his work. Whoever he was, the author is likely to have been a cleric who was familiar not only with the gospel accounts of the crucifixion, but also with a version of the apocryphal *Gospel of Nicodemus* and with vernacular lyrics expressing the sorrows of the Virgin and Christ's reproaches from the cross.

The Death of Christ is less obviously varied than *The Second Shepherds' Play*; nevertheless, the juxtaposition of scenes of differing intensities of feeling is masterly. The play is written in a complex, alliterating, thirteen-line stanza (ababbcbc3d1eee2d3) with concatenation; that is, the words at the end of one stanza are picked up at the beginning of the next. The heightening of essentially plain language that is achieved by this elaboration goes along with the stylised simplicity of the visual images presented to the onlooker through the changing groups of characters.

The text is from British Library, MS Additional 35290.

THE YORK BUTCHERS' PLAY OF THE DEATH OF CHRIST

[*Jesus, bound to a cross, is on a raised part of the stage, flanked by the two thieves, also on crosses. John, Mary and Mary Cleophas are at the foot of the cross. Pilate, Annas and Caiaphas enter, accompanied by the Centurion, the Soldier, Longeus and the Boy.*]

PILATE:† Sees,* seniours,* and see what I saie,   *cease   masters*
†Takis tente to my talkyng enteere,
Devoyde* all this dynne here this day   *stop*
†And fallis to my frenschippe in feere.
5 Sir Pilate, a prince withowten pere,*   *equal*
My name is, full nevenly to neven,†
†And domisman full derworth and dere
Of gentillest Jewry full even*   *impartial*
Am I.
10 Who* makis oppressioun   *whoever*
Or dose transgressioun,
Be my discressioun
Shall be demed* dewly* to dye.   *judged   justly*

To dye schall I deme thame, to dede,*   *death*
15 Tho* rebelles that rewles thame unright.†   *those*
Who that to yone* hill† wille take heede,   *yonder, over there*
May se ther the soth* in his sight,   *truth*

---

1 [Pilate's opening call for attention is addressed both to the other characters on stage and – more importantly – to the crowd watching in the street]
2 Pay attention to everything I say
4 And together seek my friendship
6 *ful nevenly to neven* to speak very precisely
7 And a most esteemed and highly-prized judge
15 *rewles thame unright* conduct themselves unlawfully
16 [*yone hill* a raised part of the stage on which are erected the three crosses on which Jesus and the two thieves hang. (Or possibly the crosses are on the pageant wagon, and Pilate speaks from the street.) The previous play in the York cycle has been devoted to the crucifixion itself]

Howe doulful* to dede thei are dight†   *miserably*
That liste noght† owre lawes for to lere.*   *learn*
20 Lo, thus be* my mayne* and my myght,   *by* *power*
Tho churles* schalle I chasteise and cheere,†   *villains*
      Be lawe.
Ilke* feloune false   *each*
Shall hynge be the halse,†
25 Transgressours als*   *also*
      On the crosse schalle be knytte for to knawe.†

To knawe schall I knytte thame on crosse,
To schende* thame with schame schall I shappe.*   *disgrace* *contrive*
Ther liffis* for to leese* is no losse,   *lives* *lose*
30 †Suche tirrauntis with teene for to trappe.
Thus leelly* the lawe I unlappe†   *conscientiously*
And punyssh thame pitously.*   *miserably*
Of Jesu I holde it unhappe,†
That he on yone hill hyng so hye,
35   For gilte.
†His bloode to spille,
Toke ye you till;
Thus was youre wille,
      †Full spitously to spede he were spilte.

40 CAIAPHAS: To spille* hym we spake in a speede,*   *destroy* *in haste*
For falsed* he folowde in faie,*   *falsehood* *faith*
With fraudes oure folke gan he feede†

---

18 *dede thei are dight* put to death
19 *liste noght* do not care at all
21 *chasteise and cheere* restrain and punish
24 *hynge be the halse* hang by the neck
26 *knytte for to knawe* fastened in order to provide an example [lit., to make known]
30 To trap such brutes with affliction
31 *unlappe* unfold, disclose
33 *holde it unhappe* regard it as a misfortune. [According to Luke 23.4 and 14, Pilate was unable to find Jesus guilty as charged, and wanted merely to chastise and release him]
36–7 You took it upon yourselves to spill his blood
39 To accomplish his death in great misery
42 *gan he feede* he fed

And laboured to lere* thame his laye.*   *teach law*
ANNAS: Sir Pilate, of pees we youe praye,
45   Oure lawe was full lyke to be lorne.†
He saved* noght oure dere sabott* daye,   *set aside sabbath*
†And that for to scape it were a scorne,
    By lawe.
PILATE: Sirs, before youre sight,
50   With all my myght,
I examynde hym right
    †And cause non in hym cowthe I knawe.

CAIAPHAS: Ye knawe wele the cause, sir, in cace.*   *in this matter*
It touched treasoune untrewe:
55 †The tribute to take or to trace
Forbadde he, oure bale for to brewe.†
ANNAS: †Of japes yitt jangelid yone Jewe
And cursedly he called hym† a kyng;
†To deme hym to dede it is diewe,
60 For treasoune it touches,* that thyng,   *concerns*
    In dede.
CAIAPHAS: Yitt principall
And worste of all,
†He garte hym call
65   Goddes sonne, that foulle motte hyme speede!†

PILATE: †He spedis for to spille in space,
†So wondirly wrought is youre will.

---

45 *full lyke to be lorne* very likely to be lost sight of
47 And to get away with that would be an insult
52 And I was unable to discover in him any ground for complaint
55–6 He forbade us to exact or pursue the levy, in order to concoct our downfall
55–8 [See John 19.6]
57 That Jew chattered on about trickery
58 *hym* himself [see Luke 23.2]
59 To sentence him to death is fair
64 He had himself called
65 *that foulle motte hym spede* may he suffer for it
66–7 He is going to die in a short time, your decision having been carried out with such rare dispatch

His bloode schall youre bodis enbrace,†
†For that have ye taken you till.
70 ANNAS: †That forwarde ful fayne to fulfille,
In dede schall we dresse us bedene,†
†Yone losell hym likis full ille,
†For turned is his trantis all to teene,
        I trowe.*   reckon
75 CAIAPHAS: He called hym* kyng,   himself
†Ille joie hym wring!
Ya,* late hym hyng,   yes
    †Full madly on the mone for to mowe.

[*They move over to where Jesus and the two thieves are hanging on crosses.*]
ANNAS: †To mowe on the moone has he mente.
80 We!* fye on the, faitour,* in faye!*   yah deceiver indeed
†Who trowes thou to thi tales toke tente?
†Thou saggard, thi selffe gan thou saie,
†The tempill destroie thou todaye,
Be* the thirde day ware done ilk a dele*   by the time that completely
85 To rayse it thou schulde the arraye.*   equip yourself.
Loo, howe was thi falsed* to feele,*   falsehood to be seen
    Foule falle the!*   May you be cursed!
For thy presumpcyoune
Thou haste thy warisoune.*   reward
90 Do faste come doune,*   Come down quickly
    And a comely kyng schalle I calle thee.

CAIAPHAS: I calle the a coward to kenne,*   acknowledged
That mervaylles and mirakills made.

---

68 *your bodis enbrace* surround your bodies
69 Because of what you have taken upon yourselves
70 In order to fulfil that agreement most willingly
71 *dresse us bedene* go immediately
72–3 That wretched creature is feeling pretty sorry for himself for all his plots have come to grief
76 I hope he's thoroughly miserable
78 In order to pull foolish faces at the moon
79 He's already done his best to pull faces at the moon
81 Who do you imagine took any notice of your stories?
82–3 You boaster, you said yourself that if you should destroy the temple today
83–5 [See Matthew 26.61. This was one of the accusations made at Jesus' trial; symbolically, the temple of Jesus' body was destroyed at the crucifixion and raised three days later]

	Thou mustered* emange many menne	mumbled
95	†But, brothell, thou bourded to brede.	
	Thou saved thame fro sorowes, thai saide;	
	To save nowe thi selffe late us see.	
	†God sonne if you grathely be grayde,	
	Delyvere the† doune of* that tree	from
100	Anone.*	directly
	If thou be funne*	found [that]
	Thou be Goddis sonne,	
	We schalle be bonne*	obliged
	To trowe on* the trewlye, ilkone.*	believe in each one

105 ANNAS: Sir Pilate, youre pleasaunce* we praye,   indulgence
Takis tente to† oure talkyng this tide*   at this time
And wipe ye yone writyng† away,
It is not beste it abide.†
It sittis youe† to sette it aside,
110 And sette that† he saide in his sawe,*   own words
As he that was prente* full of pride: filled
'Jewes kyng am I,' comely to knawe,†
    Full playne.
PILATE: †*Quod scripci, scripci,*
115 Yone same wrotte I —
I bide therby,*   I stand by it
    †What gedlyng will grucche there agayne.

JESUS: Thou man† that of mys here has mente,†
†To me tente enteerly thou take:

---

95 But, you rascal, you played your tricks too freely
98 If you are properly made God's son
99 *Delivere the* release yourself
106 *Takis tente to* pay heed to
107 *yone writyng* yonder, that writing   [See John 19.19: 'And Pilate wrote a title, and put it on the cross. And the writing was JESUS OF NAZARETH, KING OF THE JEWS']
108 *it abide* that it should remain
109 *It sittis youe* it is appropriate for you
110 *sette that* put up what
110–12 [John 19.21]
112 *comly to knawe* beautiful to acknowledge
114 What I have written, I have written   [John 19.22]
117 Whatever scoundrel likes to complain against it
118 [*Thou man* Jesus' words are addressed to the audience and to all mankind, in the manner of contemporary crucifixion lyrics]   *that of mys here has mente* who has intended sin here
119 Pay attention to me wholly

120	On roode* am I ragged and rente,†	cross
	Thou synfull sawle, for thy sake.	
	For thy misse* amendis wille I make.	wrongdoing
	My bakke for to bende here I bide,*	remain
	This teene* for thi trespase I take.	suffering
125	Who couthe* the more kyndynes have kydde*	could shown
	Than I?	
	Thus for thy goode	
	I schedde my bloode.	
	Manne, mende thy moode,*	repent
130	†For ful bittir thi blisse mon I by.	

	MARY: †Allas for my swete sonne, I saie,	
	†That doulfully to dede thus is dight.	
	Allas, for full lovely thou laye	
	In my wombe, this worthely wight.*	fine man
135	Allas, that I schulde see this sight	
	Of my sone so semely to see.†	
	Allas, that this blossome so bright	
	†Untrewly is tugged to this tree.	
	Allas!	
140	My lorde, my leyffe,*	beloved
	With full grete greffe,*	suffering
	Hyngis* as a theffe,	hangs
	Allas, he did never trespasse.	

	JESUS: Thou woman, do way of* thy wepyng,	stop
145	For me may thou no thyng amende.*	assuage
	My fadirs wille to be wirkyng,*	carrying out

---

120 *ragged and rent* covered with rags and lacerated
130 For I must buy your salvation very painfully
131ff. [Mary's lament is an expansion – modelled, like Christ's, on the devotional lyric – of the silent role she plays in the Gospel accounts of the crucifixion]
132 Who is put to death agonisingly like this
136 *semely to see* handsome to look at
138 Is treacherously nailed to this tree

        For mankynde my body I bende.
        MARY: Allas, that thou likes noght to lende,†
        Howe schulde I but wepe for thy woo?
150   †To care nowe my comforte is kende,
        Allas, why schulde we twynne* thus in twoo   separate
             For evere?
        JESUS: Womanne, in stede of me,
        †Loo, John thi sone schall bee.
155   John, see to thi modir free,*   noble
             For my sake do thou thi devere.*   duty

        MARY: Allas, sone, sorowe and site,*   grief
        †That me were closed in clay;
        A swerde of sorowe me smyte,
160   †To dede I were done this day.
        JOHN: A, modir, so schall ye noght saie.
        I pray youe, be pees* in this presse,*   keep quiet   throng
        For with all the myght* that I maye,   strength
        Youre comforte I caste to encresse†
165   In dede.
        Youre sone am I,
        Loo, here redy –
        And nowe forthy*   therefore
             I praye yowe hense for to speede.*   hasten

170   MARY: †My steven for to stede or to steere,
        †Howe schulde I, such sorowe to see,
        My sone that is dereworthy* and dere,   precious
        Thus doulfull a dede* for to dye?   death

---

148   *thou likes noght to lende*   you do not want to stay
150   Now my comfort has been led into sorrow
154–5   [John 25.26–7. John is the disciple 'whom Jesus loved']
158   If only I were shut up in the earth
160   [so that] I might be put to death today
164   *caste to encresse*   plan to increase
170–1   How should I stop or restrain my noise

JOHN: A, dere modir, blynne of this blee,†
175 Youre mournyng it may not amende.
MARY CLEOPHAS: A, Marie, take triste unto the,†
For socoure to the will he sende
    This tyde.*   On this occasion, today
JOHN: Fayre modir, faste
180 Hense latte us caste.*   go
MARY: To he be paste,*   Until he is dead
 Wille I buske* here baynly* to bide.   make ready willingly

JESUS: †With bittirfull bale have I bought,
Thus, man, all thi misse for te mende,
185 On me for to looke lette* thou noght,   leave off
Howe baynly my body I bende.
No wighte* in this worlde wolde have wende,*   person believed
What sorowe I suffre for thy sake;
Manne, kaste the* thy kyndynesse be kende,*   endeavour known
190 Trewe tente unto me that thou take,
    And treste.*   faith
†For foxis ther dennys* have thei,   dens
Birdis hase ther nestis to paye,*   for their comfort
But the sone of man this daye,
195 †Hase noght on his heed for to reste.

THIEF ON LEFT: If thou be Goddis sone so free,*   noble
Why hyng thou thus on this hille?
To saffe* nowe thi selffe late us see,   save
And us now, that spedis for to spille.†

---

174 *blynne of this blee* cease this grief
176 *take triste unto the* have faith
183–4 With very painful suffering I have paid the penalty in this way, man, in order to alleviate all your wrongdoing
192–5 [Matthew 8.20 and Luke 9.58]
195 Has nothing on which to lay his head
199 *spedis for to spille* are on the point of death

200	THIEF ON RIGHT: Manne, stynte of thy steven* and be stille,*	noise quiet
	†For douteles thy God dredis thou noght;	
	†Full wele are we worthy ther till:	
	†Unwisely wrange have we wrought,	
	Iwisse.*	indeed
205	Noon ille* did hee,	no evil
	Thus for to dye;	
	†Lord, have mynde of* me	remember
	What* thou art come to thi blisse.	when

	JESUS: For sothe, sonne, to the schall I saie,	
210	†Sen thou fro thy foly will falle,	
	With me schall dwelle nowe this daye,	
	In paradise, place principall.	
	*Heloy, heloy!**	Eli, eli [Hebrew: my God, my God]
	My God, my God, full free,	
215	†*Lamazabatanye,*	
	Whar to* forsoke thou me	why
	In care?*	to sorrow
	And I did nevere ille	
	This dede* for to go tille,*	death to
220	†But be it at thi wille.	
	A, me thristis sare.†	

	BOY: A drinke schalle I dresse* the, in dede,	prepare for
	A draughte that is full dayntely dight.†	
	Full faste schall I springe for to spede,†	
225	I hope* I schall holde* that I have hight.*	believe keep to promised

---

201 For obviously you do not fear your God
202 We have fully deserved this
203 Foolishly, we have done wrong
207–8 [Luke 23.42]
210 Since you desire to turn away from your sinfulness
215 Lama sabachthani (Hebrew: why have you forsaken me?) [Matthew, 27.46]
220 But let it be according to your will
221 *me thristis sare*   I have a grievous thirst [John 19.28]
223 *dayntely dight*   elegantly set forth
224 *springe for to spede*   leap to make haste

CAIAPHAS: Sir Pilate, that moste is of myght,†
Harke! '*Heely*'† how harde I hym crye.
He wenys* that that worthely wight* — believes   good man
Him hastes* for to helpe hym in hye* — hastens   quickly
230   In his nede.
PILATE: If he do soo
He schall have woo.
ANNAS: He wer oure foo
If he dresse hym* to do us that dede. — plans

235 BOY: That dede for to dresse* yf he doo, — arrange
In sertis* he schall rewe* it full sore; — for sure   regret
Nevere the less, if he like it noght, loo,
Full sone may he covere that care.†
Nowe, swete sir, youre wille yf it ware,†
240 A draughte here of drinke have I dreste;* — prepared
†To spede for no spence that ye spare,
But baldely* ye bib* it for the beste. — straight way   drink
For why* — because
†Aysell* and galle — vinegar
245 Is menged with alle.†
Drynke it ye schalle –
Youre lippis, I halde* thame full drye. — believe

JESUS: Thi drinke it schalle do me no deere,* — harm
†Wete thou wele, ther of will I none.
250 Nowe, fadir, that formed alle in fere,* — alike, together
To thy moste* myght make I my mone.* — greatest   complaint
Thi wille have I wrought* in this wone,* — performed   city
Thus ragged and rente on this roode,

---

226 *that moste is of myght*   who is greatest in power
227 [Caiaphas thinks Jesus is calling for help from Elijah, the Old Testament prophet (I Kings 17ff.)]
238 *covere that care*   be relieved of that anguish
239 *youre wille yf it ware*   if you want it
241 May you not hold back [from drinking it] quickly because of the expense
244–5 [Matthew 27.34]
245 *menged with alle*   mixed in as well
248 Understand this, I do not want any of it

Thus doulffully to dede* have thei done. — death
255 †Forgiffe thame, be grace that is goode;
  Thai ne wote noght† what it was.
My fadir, here* my bone,* — hear prayer
For nowe all thyng is done.
My spirite to thee right sone
260   Comende I, *in manus tuas*.† [*Jesus dies*]

MARY: Now dere sone, Jesus so jente,* — noble
Sen* my harte is hevy as leede, — since
O* worde wolde I witte* or* thou wente. — one know before
Allas, nowe my dere sone is dede,
265 Full rewfully refte† is my rede.* — support
Allas, for my darlyng so dere.
JOHN: A, modir, ye halde uppe youre heede,
And sigh noght with sorowes so seere,* — many
  I praye.
270 MARY CLEOPHAS: It dose hir pyne* — It causes her pain
To see hym tyne.* — die
Lede we her heyne,* — hence
  This mornyng* helpe hir ne maye. — grief
[*John and the two Maries go off*]

CAIAPHAS: Sir Pilate, parceyve,* I you praye, — understand
275 Oure costemes* to kepe wele ye canne. — customs
†Tomorne is* oure dere sabott* daye, — tomorrow sabbath [Saturday]
†Of mirthe muste us meve ilke a mane.

255–6 [Luke 23.34]
256 *ne wote noght* do not know at all
260 *in manus tuas* into your hands [Luke 23.46]
265 *rewfully refte* sadly snatched away
276 [John 19.31: 'And the Jews therefore, because . . . the bodies should not remain on the cross for the sabbath day, (for that sabbath day was a high day), besought Pilate that . . . they might be taken away']
277 Each one of us must celebrate

        Yone warlous† nowe waxis* full wane*   grow pale
        And nedis muste thei beried be.
280 Delyver ther dede,† sir, and thane
        Shall we sewe* to oure saide solempnite†   proceed
            In dede.
        PILATE: It schalle be done
        In wordis fone;*   few
285 Sir knyghtis, go sone,
           To yone harlottis* you hendely take heede,†   scoundrels

        Tho caytiffis† thou kille with thi knyffe,
        †Delyvere, have done thei were dede.
        SOLDIER: Mi lorde, I schall lenghe so ther liffe,†
290 That tho brothelles* schall nevere bite brede.   rascals
        PILATE: Ser* Longeus,† steppe forthe in this steede,* Sir place
        This spere, loo, have halde* in thy hande,   grasp
        To Jesu thou rake fourthe,† I rede,*   advise
        And sted nought,† but stiffely* thou stande   firm
295   A stounde.*   for a moment
        In Jesu side
        Schoffe* it this tyde.*   shove time
        No lenger bide*   wait
           But grathely* thou go to the grounde.†   quickly
                [*Longeus pierces Jesus' side*]

300 LONGEUS: O maker unmade, full of myght,
        O Jesu, so jentill and jente,*   noble

---

278 *warlous*   warlocks, devils
280 *Delyver ther dede*   finish them off
281 *saide solempnite*   solemn feast
286 *hendely take heede*   take good care
287 *Tho caytiffis*   those wretches
288 Hurry, finish them off
289 *lenghe so ther liffe*   prolong their lives in such a way
291 [The man who pierced Jesus' side is simply 'one of the soldiers' in John 19.34. He is called Longeus or Longinus in the apocryphal *Gospel of Nicodemus* (*c*. AD 400); in the thirteenth century *Golden Legend* he becomes, as here, a blind man whose sight is miraculously restored when Christ's blood falls on his eyes]
293 *rake fourthe*   step forward
294 *sted nought*   do not pause
299 *grounde*   foot of the cross

That sodenly has sente me my sight,
Lorde, lovyng to the be it lente.†
On rode arte thou ragged and rente,
305 Mankynde for to mende of* his mys;* — turn aside from   sin
Full spitously* spilte is and spente* — cruelly   poured out
Thi bloode, lorde, to bringe us to blis
    Full free.* — noble
A, mercy, my socoure,* — succour
310 Mercy, my treasoure,
Mercy, my savioure,
    Thi mercy be markid* in me. — shown

CENTURION: †O wondirfull werkar,* iwis,* — creator   indeed
†This weedir is waxen full wan –
315 Trewe token I trowe* that it is — believe
That mercy is mente* unto mane. — intended
Full clerly consayve* thus I cane — conceive, understand
†No cause in this corse couthe thei knowe,
Yitt, doulfull,* thei demyd* hym thane — miserable   judged
320 To lose thus his liffe be ther lawe,
    No righte.* — wrongfully
Trewly I saie,
Goddis sone verraye* — true
Was he this daye
325   That doulfully to dede thus is dight.* — put
[*Enter Joseph of Arimathea*]

JOSEPH: That lorde lele,* ay lastyng* in lande, — just   everlasting
Sir Pilate, full preste* in this presse,* — promptly   crowd
†He save the be see and be sande,
†And all that is derworth on deesse.

---

303 *lovyng to the be it lente*   praise be offered unto you
313–25   [This stanza expands Luke 23.44–6 and Mark 15.39]
314   This weather has grown very dark
318   No ground for complaint could they show in this man
328   May he save you throughout the whole world
329   And all those worthy people in positions of power

330	PILATE: Joseph† this is, lely* no lesse,*	certainly in truth
	To me arte thou welcome, iwisse;	
	Do saie me the soth* or* thou sesse,*	truth before cease
	Thy worthyly* wille, what it is	worthy
	Anone.*	directly
335	JOSEPH: To the I praye,	
	Giffe me in hye*	quickly
	Jesu bodye,	
	In gree* it for to grave* al alone.	fittingly bury

	PILATE: Joseph sir, I graunte the that geste;*	guest
340	I grucche* noght to grath* hym in grave.	grudge array
	†Delyver, have done he were dreste,	
	†And sewe, sir, oure sabott to saffe.	
	JOSEPH: With handis and harte that I have,	
	I thanke the, in faith, for my frende.	
345	†God kepe the thi comforte to crave,	
	For wightely* my way will I wende*	promptly take
	In hye.	
	To do that dede	
	†He be my speede,	
350	†That armys gun sprede,	
	Manne kynde be* his bloode for to bye.*	by redeem

[Enter Nichodemus.]†

	NICHODEMUS: †Weill mette, sir. In mynde gune I meffe	
	For Jesu, that juged was unjente.*	ignobly
	Ye laboured for license* and leve*	permission leave
355	To berye his body on bente.*	in the ground

---

330 [*Joseph this is*   this greeting identifies Joseph of Arimathea to the audience]
341 Be quick, finish laying him out
342 And proceed, sir, to preserve our sabbath
345 May God preserve you to seek your comfort
349–50 May he whose arms stretched out be my protector
351 [Nichodemus' role in the entombment derives from John 19.39. To him was attached the apocryphal *Gospel of Nicodemus* (c. AD 400), deeply influential on later narratives of the Passion]
352 Well met, sir. I became concerned

	JOSEPH: Full myldely that matere I mente,*	spoke of
	And that for to do will I dresse.*	prepare
	NICHODEMUS: †Both same I wolde that we wente,	
	†And lette not for more ne for lesse.	
360	For why*	because
	Oure frende was he,	
	Faithfull and free.	
	JOSEPH: Therfore go we	
	To berie that body in hye.*	quickly

[*They go to the cross*]

365	All mankynde may marke* in his mynde	attend
	To see here this sorowfull sight;	
	No falsnesse in hym couthe* thei fynde,	could
	That doulfully to dede thus is dight.	
	NICHODEMUS: He was a full worthy wight,	
370	Nowe blemysght* and bolned* with bloode.	blemished swollen
	JOSEPH: Ya, for that* he maistered* his myght,	because reined in
	Full falsely thei fellid* that foode,*	slew young warrior
	I wyne* –	believe
	Bothe bakke and side,	
375	His woundes wide.	
	Forthi this tyde*	occasion
	Take we hym doune us betwene.	
	NICHODEMUS: Betwene us take we hym doune	
	And laie hym on lenthe on this lande.*	flat place
380	JOSEPH: †This reverent and riche of rennoune,	
	Late us halde* hyme and halse* hym with hande.	hold embrace
	†A grave have I garte here be ordande	
	†That nevere was in noote,* it is newe.	in use

---

358 I should like us to go together
359 And not to delay on anyone's account
380 This honoured and richly famous man
382 I have had a grave prepared here
382–3 [John 19.41: 'and in the garden [was] a new sepulchre, wherein was never man yet laid']

NICHODEMUS: To this corse* it is comely accordande,†   body
385   To dresse hym with dedis full dewe†
        This stounde.*   at this time
JOSEPH: A sudarye,*   shroud
    Loo, here have I.
    Wynde hym forthy,*   therefore
390   And sone schalle we grave* hym in grounde.   bury

NICHODEMUS: In grounde late us grave hym and goo;
    Do liffely,* latte us laie hym allone.   act quickly
    Nowe, saviour, of* me and of moo   as for   others
    †Thou kepe us in clennesse ilkone.
395 JOSEPH: To thy mercy nowe make I my moone,
    As saviour be see and be sande:†
    Thou gyde me, that my griffe* be al gone,   grief
    With lele liffe† to lenge* in this lande,   remain
       And esse.*   ease
400 NICHODEMUS: Seere oynementis† here have I
    Brought for this faire body;
    †I anoynte the, forthy,
       With myrre* and aloes.   myrrh

JOSEPH: This dede it is done ilke a dele,†
405 And wroughte is this werke wele,* iwis.   well
    To the, kyng, on knes here I knele,
    That baynly* thou belde* me in blisse.   willingly   shelter

---

384 *comely accordande*   sweetly fitting
385 *dedis ful dewe*   appropriate rites
394 May you keep each one of us pure
396 *be see and be sande*   throughout the whole world
398 *With lele liffe*   in holy living
400 *Seere oynementis*   various ointments
402–3 [John 19.39]
404 *ilk a dele*   completely

NICHODEMUS: He highte* me full hendely* to be his,   called graciously
A nyght* whan I neghed* hym full nere;   one night approached
410   Have mynde, lorde, and mende me of mys,†
    For done is oure dedis full dere
          This tyde.
  JOSEPH: This lorde so goode
    That schedde his bloode,
415   †He mende youre moode
      †And buske on this blis for to bide.
[*They all go off*].

---

410   *mende me of mys*   absolve me of my sins
415   May he lead you to repentance
416   And prepare you to remain in this bliss

Sir Thomas Malory
c. 1416–71

Le Morte Darthur is one of the earliest, and certainly the finest, works of imaginative English prose written in the middle ages. Its author tells us that he is Sir Thomas Malory, that he is in prison, and that he finished writing his book in 1469 or 1470. Of the various fifteenth-century Thomas Malorys we know of, the one most likely to have been the author is Sir Thomas Malory of Newbold Revel in Warwickshire. A country gentleman's son, probably born round 1416, he was for a time an MP and justice of the peace. In the 1440s he fell foul of the law for the first time and thereafter was charged with a series of violent crimes for which he spent most of the 1450s in jail. He was free by 1462, but by 1468 had become involved in a plot against Edward IV and was imprisoned then or soon after. During this imprisonment he finished Le Morte Darthur, which covers the life of the legendary King Arthur, from his conception to his death, in eight separate but related books.

Malory was probably released from prison within months of finishing Le Morte Darthur and died in 1471. William Caxton printed an edited text in 1485; in 1935 a manuscript version dating from the 1470s came to light in the library of Winchester College. The text below is taken from that manuscript.

In writing Le Morte Darthur Malory drew heavily on a number of earlier works, including the thirteenth-century French Arthurian prose romances known as the Vulgate cycle, and on the French prose Tristan. He also knew the alliterative Morte Arthure, which he rendered into prose. 'The Maid of Ascolat' (formerly erroneously read as 'Astolat') provides a good example of Malory's method of working. He had two versions of the story to hand: one in the French Vulgate La Mort le Roi Artu and the other a fifteenth-century English version of the end of that work known as the stanzaic Le Morte Arthur. He borrowed aspects of both, recasting them, however, so as to give the story a fresh emphasis; where the French maid is knowing and sophisticated, Malory's Elaine le Blanke is caught up in a train of events too adult and too complicated for her to understand. Malory's style is direct and unbookish; his handling of dialogue, with its undertow of unstated implication, is masterly.

'The Maid of Ascolat' comes from the seventh book of *Le Morte Darthur*. Lancelot, the greatest knight of King Arthur's Round Table, has returned from the Quest of the Holy Grail, which he has failed to achieve because of his long-standing love affair with Queen Guinevere. This relationship, which Arthur for the time being ignores, provokes hatred among Lancelot's enemies and sorrow among his friends. It is to be the death of the Maid of Ascolat. Malory's version should be compared with Tennyson's very different interpretation of the story in 'The Lady of Shalott'.

From LE MORTE DARTHUR
[The Fair Maid of Ascolat]

Thus hit passed untyll Oure Lady day of the Assumpcion.† Within a fiftene days* of that feste the kynge lete crye† a grete justyse* and a turnement that sholde be at that day at Camelott, otherwyse callyd Wynchester;† and the kyng lete cry that he and the Kynge of Scottes wolde juste ayenst all the worlde. And whan thys cry was made, thydir cam many good knyghtes, that ys to sey the Kynge of North Galis,* and Kynge Angwysh of Irelonde, and the Kynge with the Hondred Knyghtes, and Syr Galahalte the Haute† Prynce, and the Kynge of Northumbirlonde, and many other noble deukes and erlis of other dyverse† contreyes. So kynge Arthure made hym redy to departe to hys justis, and wolde have had the quene† with hym; but at that tyme she wolde nat, she seyde, for she was syke* and myght nat ryde.

fortnight
jousts

Wales

sick

[*Oure Lady day of the Assumpcion* 15 August, feast of the Assumption of the Blessed Virgin]
lete cry ordered to be proclaimed
[*Camelott, otherwyse callyd Wynchester* Camelot, long associated with Arthur, is probably identified by Malory with Winchester (which figures in other Arthurian narratives) because the city was known to have been a centre of power in Roman and Anglo-Saxon times. (Cf. *King Orfeo*, line 49, where 'Traciens' is identified with Winchester.)]
Haute high [Galahalte is not the same person as Galahad; see below]
other dyverse various other
[*the quene* Guinevere, who loves Sir Launcelot (see note below). Their adultery later leads to open conflict among Arthur's followers, and the breakup of the Round Table]

'That me repentith,'* seyde the kynge, 'for thys seven yere ye saw nat such a noble felyship togydirs excepte the Whytsontyde† whan Sir Galahad† departed frome the courte.' [I regret]

'Truly,' seyde the quene, 'ye muste holde me excused. I may nat be there.'

And many demed* the quene wolde nat be there because of Sir Launcelot,† for he wolde nat ryde with the kynge, for he seyde he was nat hole* of the play* of Sir Madore.† Wherefore the kynge was hevy and passynge wroth,† and so he departed towarde Wynchestir with hys felyship. And so by the way the kynge lodged at a towne that was called Ascolot, that ys in Englysh Gylforde,† and there the kynge lay* in the castell. [believed] [healed wound] [stayed]

So whan the kynge was departed the quene called Sir Launcelot unto her and seyde thus:

'Sir, ye ar gretly to blame thus to holde you behynde* my lorde. What woll youre enemyes and myne sey and deme? "Se how Sir Launcelot holdith hym ever* behynde the kynge, and so the quene doth also, for that they wolde have their plesure togydirs." And thus woll they sey,' seyde the quene. [stay behind] [always]

'Have ye no doute, madame,' seyde Sir Launcelot. 'I alow youre witte. Hit ys of late com syn† ye were woxen* so wyse! And therefore, madam, at thys nyght I woll take my reste, and to-morow betyme* I woll take my way towarde Wynchestir. But wytte you well,'† seyde Sir Launcelot unto the quene, 'at that justys I woll be ayenste the kynge and ayenst all hys felyship.' [grown] [early]

'Sir, ye may thee do as ye lyste,'* seyde the quene, 'but be my counceyle ye shall nat be ayenst youre kynge [please]

[*Whitsontyde* Whitsun, the feast of Pentecost, fifty days after Easter]
[*Sir Galahad* Launcelot's son, who led the Quest for the Holy Grail. The departure of the knights on the Quest was marked by a great tournament]
[*Sir Launcelot* Launcelot du Lac, son of King Ban of Benwick (in France), Arthur's chief knight and Guinevere's lover]
[*Sir Madore* in the previous story, Launcelot had been wounded in single combat against Sir Mador de la Porte, who had falsely accused Guinevere of murder]
passynge wroth exceedingly angry
Gylforde Guildford, in Surrey
alow . . . syn command your intelligence. It is only recently that
wytte you well know well, understand

and your felyshyp, for there bene full many hardé* knyghtes of youre bloode.'†   *brave*

'Madame,' seyde Sir Launcelot, 'I shall take the adventure that God woll gyff me.'

And so uppon the morne erly he harde* masse and dyned, and so he toke hys leve of the quene and departed.   *heard*

And than he rode so muche* unto* the tyme he com to Ascolott, and there hit happynd hym that in the evenyngtyde* he cam to an olde barownes† place that hyght* Sir Barnarde of Ascolot. And as Sir Launcelot entird into hys lodgynge, Kynge Arthure aspyed hym as he dud walke* in a gardeyne besyde the castell: he knew hym welle inow.*   *far   until   time   called   walked   enough*

'Well, sirs,' seyde Kynge Arthure unto hys knyghtes that were by hym besyde the castell, 'I have now aspyed one knyght,' he seyde, 'that woll play hys play* at the justys, I undirtake.'   *play his part*

'Who ys that?' seyde the knyghtes.

'At thys tyme ye shall nate wyte for† me!' seyde the kynge and smyled, and wente to hys lodgynge.

So whan Sir Launcelot was in hys lodgyng and unarmed in hys chambir, the olde barown, Sir Barnarde, com to hym and wellcomed hym in the beste maner. But he knew nat Sir Launcelot.

'Fayre sir,' seyde Sir Launcelot tylle* hys oste, 'I wolde pray you to lende me a shylde† that were nat opynly knowyn, for myne ys well knowyn.'   *to*

'Sir,' seyde hys oste, 'ye shall have youre desire, for mesemyth† ye bene one of the lyklyest* knyghtes that ever I sawe, and therefore, sir, I shall shew you freynship.' And seyde, 'Sir, wyte you well I have two sunnes that were but late† made knyghtes. And the eldist hyght* Sir Tirry, and he was hurte that same day he was made knyght, and he may nat ryde; and hys shylde ye shalle have, for that ys nat knowyn, I dare sey, but here and in no place else.' And hys yonger sonne hyght Sir Lavayne. 'And if hit please you, he shall ryde with you   *finest looking   is called*

---

bloode   kinship [The Round Table is made up of various family groups. One of the most important is that formed by Launcelot and his close relatives Bors, Ector, Lionel and their followers (see note below). Guinevere warns Launcelot that he may find himself – as he does – fighting his own kin]
barownes   baron's [A baron was the lowest rank of the nobility]
wyte for me   learn (it) from me
shylde   shield [Knights in armour were identified by the heraldic devices on their shields]
mesemyth   it seems to me
but late   only lately

unto that justis, for he ys of* hys ayge stronge and ·for
wyght.* For much my herte gyvith unto you, that ye ·vigorous
sholde be a noble knyght.† And therefore I praye you
to telle me youre name,' seyde Sir Barnarde.

90 'As for that,' seyd Sir Launcelot, 'ye must holde me
excused as at thys tyme. And if God gyff me grace to
spede* well at the justis I shall com agayne and telle ·succeed
you my name. But I pray you in ony wyse* lete me have ·in any case
your sonne, Sir Lavayne, with me, and that I may have
95 hys brothers shylde.'

'Sir, all thys shall be done,' seyde Sir Barnarde.

So thys olde barown had a doughtir that was called
that tyme the Fayre Maydyn of Ascolot, and ever she
behylde† Sir Launcelot wondirfully.* And, as the booke ·in admiration
100 sayth, she keste such a love unto† Sir Launcelot that she
cowde never withdraw hir loove, wherefore she dyed;
and her name was Elayne le Blanke.† So thus as she cam
to and fro, she was so hote in love that she besought* ·begged
Sir Launcelot to were uppon hym at the justis a tokyn†
105 of hers.

'Damesell,' seyde Sir Launcelot, 'and if I graunte you
that, ye may sey that I do more for youre love than ever
I ded for lady or jantillwoman.'

Than he remembird hymself* that he wolde* go to the ·recalled ·wanted to
110 justis disgysed, and because he had never aforne* borne ·before
no maner of tokyn of no damesell,† he bethought hym* ·decided
to bere a tokyn of hers, that none of hys bloode thereby
myght know hym. And than he seyde, 'Fayre maydyn, I
woll graunte you to were a tokyn of youres uppon myne
115 helmet. And therefore what ys hit? Shewe ye hit me.'

'Sir,' she seyde, 'hit ys a rede sleve of myne, of scarlet,†
well embrowdred with grete perelles.'* ·pearls

And so she brought hit hym. So Sir Launcelot resseyved
hit and seyde, 'Never dud I erste* so much for no ·before
120 damesell.'

---

my herte gyvith . . . noble knyght I am warmly disposed towards you, [because I think] that you must be a noble knight
behylde looked at
keste such a love unto fell so much in love with
le Blanke the fair (French) [It should be 'la Blanche'; Malory's French is often inaccurate (as in *Le Morte Darthur*, which should be 'La')]
tokyn token [A knight wore a lady's token – some item such as brooch or a sleeve (as here) – to show that he was fighting at a tournament in her honour]
damesell young lady
scarlet a rich cloth (not a colour)

Than Sir Launcelot betoke the fayre mayden hys shylde in kepynge,† and prayde her to kepe hit untill tyme that he com agayne. And so that nyght he had myrry reste and grete chere,* for thys damesell Elayne was ever aboute Sir Launcelot all the whyle she myght be suffirde.*

So uppon a day, on the morne, Kynge Arthure and all hys knyghtis departed, for there the kyng had tarryed three dayes to abyde* his noble knyghtes. And so whan the kynge was rydden, Sir Launcelot and Sir Lavayne made them redy to ryde, and aythir* of them had whyght shyldis, and the rede sleve Sir Launcelot lete cary† with hym. And so they toke their leve at* Sir Barnarde, the olde barowne, and at hys doughtir, the Fayre Mayden, and than they rode so longe tylle that they cam to Camelot, that tyme called Wynchester, and there was grete pres* of kyngis, deukes, erlis, and barownes, and many noble knyghtes. But there Sir Launcelot was lodged pryvaly* by meanys of Sir Lavayne with a ryche burgeyse,† that no man in that towne was ware* what they were. And so they reposed them there tyll Oure Lady day of the Assumpcion that* the grete justes sholde be.

So whan trumpettis blew unto the fylde and Kynge Arthur was sette on hyght* uppon a chafflet* to beholde who ded beste (but, as the Freynshe booke seyth,† the kynge wold nat suffir* Sir Gawayne† to go frome hym, for never had Sir Gawayne the bettir and* Sir Launcelot were in the fylde, and many tymes was Sir Gawayne rebuked* so whan Sir Launcelot was in the fylde in ony justis dysgysed), than som of the kyngis, as Kynge Angwysh of Irelonde and the Kynge of Scottis, were that tyme turned to be uppon the syde of Kynge Arthur. And than the othir party† was the Kynge of North Galis, and the Kynge with the Hondred Knyghtis, and the kynge of Northhumbirlonde, and Sir Galahalte the Halte Prynce.

---

betoke . . . in kepynge committed his shield to the fair maiden's care
lete cary ordered to be carried
burgeyse burgess, freeman of a town
[*as the Freynshe book seyth* one of Malory's sources for this story is the thirteenth-century French *La Mort le Roi Artu*, which he uses very freely]
[*Sir Gawayne* Gawain, Arthur's nephew, is one of his leading knights. He and his brothers, Gareth, Gaheris, Aggravayne and Mordred, form another powerful kin group]
party side [The jousts are not a series of individual combats but a melée between two large groups of knights, like teams in a football match]

But thes three kyngis and thys duke was passynge
wayke* to holde ayenste Arthurs party, for with hym *weak*
were the nobelyst knyghtes of the worlde. So than they
160 withdrew them,* aythir party frome othir, and every *themselves*
man made hym redy in his beste maner to do what he
myght. Than Sir Launcelot made hym redy and put the
rede slyeve uppon hys helmette and fastened hit faste.

And so Sir Launcelot and Sir Lavayne departed oute
165 of Wynchestir pryvayly and rode untyll a litill leved* *leafy*
woode behynde the party that hylde ayenste Kynge
Arthure party. And there they hylde hem stylle† tylle the
partyes smote togydirs.* And than cam in the Kynge off *clashed*
Scottis and the kynge of Irelonde on Kynge Arthurs
170 party, and ayenste them cam in the Kynge of Northumbirlonde and the Kynge with the Hondred Knyghtes.
And there began a grete medlé,† and there the kynge of
Scottis smote downe* the Kynge of Northumbirlonde, *unhorsed*
and the Kynge with the Hondred Knyghtes smote downe
175 Kynge Angwysh of Irelonde. Than Sir Palamydes, that
was one Arthurs party, he encountird with Sir Galahalte,
and ayther of hem smote downe other, and aythir party
halpe* their lordys on horseback agayne. So there began *helped*
a stronge assayle* on bothe partyes. And than come in *assault*
180 Sir Braundyles, Sir Sagramoure le Desyrous, Sir Dodynas
le Saveayge, Sir Kay la Senesciall, Sir Gryffelet le Fyze
de Dieu, Sir Lucan de Butlere, Sir Bedwere, Sir Aggravayne, Sir Gaherys, Sir Mordred, Sir Melyot de Logrys,
Sir Ozanna le Cure Hardy, Sir Saphyr, Sir Epynogrys,
185 Sir Gallerowne of Galeway, all thes fiftene knyghtes,
that were knyghtes of the Rounde Table. So thes with
mo other† cam in togydir and bete abacke the kynge of
Northumbirlonde and the kynge of North Walys.

Whan Sir Launcelot saw thys, as he hoved* in the *waited*
190 lytyll leved wood, than he seyde unto Sir Lavayne, 'Se
yondir ys a company of good knyghtes, and they holde
them togydirs as borys* that were chaced with doggis.' *boars*

'That ys trouth,' seyde Sir Lavayne.

'Now,' seyde Sir Launcelot, 'and* ye woll helpe a *if*
195 lityll, ye shall se the yonder felyship that chacith now

---

hylde hem stylle remained without moving
medlé melée [see note above]
mo other others in addition

thes men on oure syde, that they shall go as faste
backwarde as they wente forewarde.'

'Sir, spare ye* nat for my parte,' seyde Sir Lavayne,   hold back
'for I shall do what I may.'

200   Than Sir Launcelot and Sir Lavayne cam in at the
thyckyst of the prees,* and there Sir Launcelot smote   press, throng
downe Sir Brandeles, Sir Sagramour, Sir Dodynas, Sir
Kay, Sir Gryfflet, and all thys he ded with one speare,
and Sir Lavayne smote downe Sir Lucan de Butlere and
205 Sir Bedwere. And than Sir Launcelot gate another grete
speare, and there he smote downe Sir Aggravayne and
Sir Gaherys, Sir Mordred, Sir Melyot de Logrys, and Sir
Lavayne smote downe Sir Ozanna le Cure Hardy. And
than Sir Launcelot drew hys swerde, and there he smote
210 on the ryght honde and on the lyft honde, and by grete
forse he unhorsed Sir Safir, Sir Epynogrys and Sir
Galleron. And than the knyghtes of the Table Rounde
withdrew them abacke aftir they had gotyn* their horsys   retrieved
as well as they myght.

215   'A, mercy Jesu!' seyde Sir Gawayne. 'What knyght ys
yondir that doth so mervaylous dedys in that fylde?'

'I wote* what he ys,' seyde the kyng, 'but as at thys   know
tyme I woll nat name hym.'

'Sir,' seyde Sir Gawayne, 'I wolde sey hit were Sir
220 Launcelot by hys rydynge and hys buffettis* that I se   blows
hym deale. But ever mesemyth† hit sholde nat be he, for
that* he beryth the rede slyve uppon hys helmet; for I   because
wyst* hym never beare tokyn at no justys of lady ne   knew
jantillwoman.'

225   'Lat hym be,' seyde Kynge Arthure, 'for he woll be
bettir knowyn and do more or ever* he departe.'   before

Than the party that was ayenst Kynge Arthur were
well comforted, and than they hylde hem togydirs† that
befornhande were sore rebuked.* Than Sir Bors, Sir   sorely beaten
230 Ector de Marys and Sir Lyonell,† they called unto them
the knyghtes of their blood, as Sir Blamour de Ganys,
Sir Bleoberys, Sir Alyduke, Sir Galyhud, Sir Galyhodyn,
Sir Bellyngere le Bewse. So thes nine knyghtes of Sir
Launcelottis kynne threst in† myghtyly, for they were

---

ever mesemyth   I keep on thinking
hylde hem togydirs   kept together
[*Sir Bors, Sir Ector de Marys and Sir Lyonell*   Ector is Launcelot's brother; Bors and Lionel are his cousins]
threst in   pressed forward

all noble knyghtes, and they of* grete hate and despite* / out of malice
thought to rebuke Sir Launcelot and Sir Lavayne, for
they knew hem* nat. And so they cam hurlyng togydirs / them
and smote downe many knyghtes of North Walys and
of Northumbirlonde. And whan Sir Launcelot saw them
fare* so, he gate* a grete speare in hys honde, and there / attack got
encountird with hym all at onys, Sir Bors, Sir Ector, and
Sir Lyonell. And they three smote hym at onys with
their spearys, and with fors of themselff† they smote Sir
Launcelottis horse revers* to the erthe. And by / backwards
myssefortune Sir Bors smote Sir Launcelot thorow the
shylde into the syde, and the speare brake and the hede
leffte* stylle in the syde. / was left

Whan Sir Lavayne saw hys mayster lye on the grounde
he ran to the Kynge of Scottis and smote hym to the
erthe; and by grete forse he toke hys horse and brought
hym to Sir Launcelot and, magré* them all, he made / in spite of
hym to mownte uppon that horse. And than Sir Launcelot gate a speare in hys honde, and there he smote Sir
Bors, horse and man, to the erthe and in the same wyse
he served Sir Ector and Sir Lyonell; and Sir Lavayne
smote downe Sir Blamour de Gaynys. And than Sir
Launcelot drew hys swerde, for he felte hymself so sore
hurte that he wente there to have had hys deth.† And
than he smote Sir Bleoberis such a buffet on the helmet
that he felle downe to the erthe in a sowne,* and in the / faint
same wyse he served Sir Alyduke and Sir Galyhud. And
Sir Lavayne smote downe Sir Bellyngere that was sone
to Alysaunder le Orphelyn.* / the Orphan

And by† thys was done, was Sir Bors horsed agayne
and in cam with Sir Ector and Sir Lyonell, and all they
three smote with their swerdis uppon Sir Launcelottis
helmet. And whan he felte their buffettis, and with that* / thereupon
hys wounde greved hym grevously, than he thought to
do what he myght whyle he cowde endure. And than
he gaf Sir Bors such a buffette that he made hym
bowghe* hys hede passynge lowe; and therewithall he / bow
raced of* hys helme and myght have slayne him, but / snatched off
whan he saw his vysayge so pulde hym downe.* And in / unhorsed him
the same wyse he served Sir Ector and Sir Lyonell; for,

---

with fors of themselff   with the weight of their bodies
wente there . . . deth   believed he had received his death-wound there
by   by the time that

as the booke seyth, he myght have slayne them, but whan he saw their visages hys herte myght nat serve hym thereto,† but leffte hem there.

And than afterward he hurled into the thyckest prees of them alle, and dyd there the merveyloust† dedes of armes that ever man sawe, and ever Sir Lavayne with hym. And there Sir Launcelot with hys swerde smote downe and pulled downe, as the Freynsh booke seyth, mo* than thirty knyghtes, and the moste party were of the Table Rounde. And there Sir Lavayne dud full well that day, for he smote downe ten knyghtes of the Table Rounde.

'Mercy Jesu,' seyde Sir Gawayne unto Kynge Arthur, 'I mervayle what knyght that he ys with the rede sleve.'

'Sir,' seyde Kyng Arthure, 'he woll be knowyn or ever* he departe.'

And than the kynge blew unto lodgynge,† and the pryce* was gyvyn by herowdis unto the knyght with the whyght shylde that bare the rede slyve. Than cam the Kynge of North Galys, and the Kynge of Northhumbirlonde, and the Kynge with the Hondred Knyghtes, and Sir Galahalte the Haute Prince, and seyde unto Sir Launcelot: 'Fayre knyght, God you blysse, for muche have ye done for us thys day. And therefore we pray you that ye woll com with us, that ye may resceyve the honour and the pryce as ye have worshypfully* deserved hit.'

'Fayre lordys,' seyde Sir Launcelot, 'wete you well, gyff* I have deserved thanke I have sore bought hit, and that me repentith hit, for I am never lyke* to ascape with the* lyff. Therefore, my fayre lordys, I pray you that ye woll suffir† me to departe where me lykith,* for I am sore hurte, and I take no forse† of none honoure, for I had levir* repose me than to be lorde of all the worlde.'

And therewithall he groned pyteuously* and rode a grete walop* awaywarde* from them untyll he cam undir a woodys evyse.* And whan he saw that he was frome the fylde nyghe a myle, that he was sure he myght

---

hys herte ... thereto he did not have the heart
merveyloust most marvellous
blew unto lodgynge signalled the end of the day's jousting
suffir allow
take no forse set no store by

nat be seyne, than he seyde with an hyghe* voyce and — loud
315 with a grete grone, 'A, jantill* knyght, Sir Lavayne! — noble
Helpe me that thys truncheone* were oute of my syde, — spear-shaft
for hit stykith† so sore that hit nyghe sleyth* me.' — is killing

'A, myne owne lorde,' seyde Sir Lavayne, 'I wolde
fayne† do that myght please you, but I drede me sore,* — greatly fear
320 and* I pulle oute the truncheoune, that ye shall be in — if
perelle of dethe.'

'I charge you,' seyde Sir Launcelot, 'as ye love me,
draw hit oute!' And therewithall* he descended frome — thereupon
hys horse, and ryght so ded Sir Lavayne; and forthwithall
325 he* drew the truncheoune oute of hys† syde, and gaff a — Lavayne
grete shryche and a gresly grone,† that the blood braste* — burst
oute, nyghe a pynte at onys, that at the laste he sanke
downe uppon hys arse and so sowned* downe, pale and — fainted
dedly.* — deathly

330 'Alas,' seyde Sir Lavayne, 'what shall I do?' And than
he turned Sir Launcelot into the wynde, and so he lay
there nyghe half an owre as* he had bene dede. And so — as if
at the laste Sir Launcelot caste up hys yghen* and seyde, — eyes
'A, Sir Lavayne, helpe me that I were on my horse! For
335 here ys faste* by, within thys two myle, a jantill ermyte† — close
that somtyme was a full noble knyght and a grete lorde
of possessyons, and for grete goodnes he hath takyn
hym to wyllfull* poverté and forsakyn myghty londys. — voluntary
And hys name ys Sir Bawdwyn of Bretayne,† and he ys
340 a full noble surgeon and a good leche.* Now lat se* — doctor see
and helpe me up that I were there,† for ever my
harte gyvith me† that I shall never dye of my cousyne
jermaynes† hondys.'

And than with grete payne Sir Lavayne holpe* hym — helped
345 uppon hys horse, and than they rode a gret walop
togydirs, and ever Sir Launclot bled, that hit ran downe
to the erthe. And so by fortune they cam to an ermytayge
whiche was undir a woode, and a grete clyff on the othir

---

stykith is embedded
wolde fayne want very much to
hys Launcelot's
gaff a grete . . . grone [Launcelot] gave a great shriek and a terrible groan
ermyte hermit [Hermits withdrew from society for religious reasons, to escape the temptations of the world. See the headnote on Richard Rolle]
[*Bretayne* probably Brittany]
that I were there so that I might be there
my harte gyvith me I am inclined to believe
cousyne jermaynes first cousin's [see n. to line 230]

syde, and a fayre watir rennynge under hit. And than
Sir Lavayne bete on the gate with the but of hys speare
and cryed faste, 'Lat in, for Jesus sake!' And anone there
cam a fayre chylde to hem and asked them what they
wolde.*   *wanted*

'Fayre sonne,' seyde Sir Lavayne, 'go and pray thy
lorde the ermyte for Goddys sake to late* in here a   *let*
knyght that ys full sore wounded. And thys day, telle
thy lorde, I saw hym do more dedys of armys than ever
I herde sey that ony man ded.' So the chylde wente in
lyghtly* and than he broght the ermyte, whych was a   *promptly*
passynge lycly* man. Whan Sir Lavayne saw hym he   *fine-looking*
prayde hym for Goddys sake of succour. 'What knyght
ys he?' seyde the ermyte. 'Ys he of the house of Kynge
Arthure or nat?'

'I wote* nat,' seyde Sir Lavayne, 'what he ys, nother*   *know   nor*
what ys hys name, but well I wote I saw hym do
mervaylously thys day as of dedys of armys.'

'On whos party was he?' seyde the ermyte.

'Sir,' seyde Sir Lavayne, 'he was thys day ayenste
Kynge Arthure, and there he wanne the pryce of all the
knyghtis of the Rounde Table.'

'I have seyne the day', seyde the ermyte, 'I wolde have
loved hym the worse bycause he was ayenste my lorde
Kynge Arthure, for sometyme I was one of the felyship,
but now I thanke God I am othirwyse disposed. But
where ys he? Lat me se hym.'

Than Sir Lavayne broght the ermyte to hym. And
whan the ermyte behylde hym as he sate leenynge uppon
hys sadyll-bowe, ever bledynge spiteuously,* and ever   *grievously*
the knyght ermyte thought that he sholde know hym;
but he coude nat brynge hym to knowlech* bycause he   *mind*
was so pale for bledyng. 'What knyght ar ye?' seyde the
ermyte, 'and where were ye borne?'

'My fayre lorde,' seyde Sir Launcelot, 'I am a straun-
gere and a knyght aventures* that laboureth† thorow-   *knight errant*
oute many realmys for to wynne worship.'* Than the   *honour*
ermyte avysed* hym bettir, and saw by a wounde on   *examined*
hys chyeke that he was Sir Launcelot.

'Alas,' seyde the ermyte, 'myne owne lorde! Why
layne* you youre name from me? Perdeus,* I ought to   *conceal   by God*
know you of ryght,* for ye ar the moste nobelyst knyght   *justifiably*

---

† *laboureth*   journeys painfully

of the worlde. For well I know you for Sir Launcelot.'

'Sir,' seyde he, 'syth* ye know me, helpe me, and* ye may, for Goddys sake! For I wolde be oute of thys payne at onys, othir to deth othir† to lyff.'   *since if*

395 'Have ye no doute,'* seyde the ermyte, 'for ye shall lyve, and fare* ryght well.' And so the ermyte called to hym two of hys servauntes, and so they bare* hym into the ermytayge, and lyghtly* unarmed hym and leyde him in hys bedde. And than anone* the ermyte staunched
400 hys bloode and made hym to drynke good wyne, that he was well refygowred† and knew hymself.† For in thos dayes hit was nat the gyse* as ys nowadayes, for there were none ermytis in tho dayes but that they had bene men of worship and of prouesse,* and tho* ermytes
405 hylde grete householdis and refreysshed* people that were in distresse.   *fear not / get on / bore / quickly / straight away / fashion / valour those / succoured*

Now turne we unto Kynge Arthure and leve we Sir Launcelot in the ermytayge. So whan the kyngis were togydirs on both partyes, and the grete feste* sholde be
410 holdyn,* Kynge Arthure asked the kynge of North Galis and their felyshyp where was that knyght that bare the rede slyve. 'Lat brynge hym† before me, that he may have hys lawde* and honoure and the pryce, as hit ys ryght.'   *feast / held / praise*

415 Than spake Sir Galahalte the Haute Prynce and the Kynge with the Hondred Knyghtes, and seyde, 'We suppose that knyght ys myscheved* so that he ys never lyke to se you nother none* of us all. And that ys the grettyst pyté that ever we wyste* of ony knyght.'   *hurt / nor any / knew*

420 'Alas,' seyde Kynge Arthure, 'how may thys be? Ys he so sore hurte? But what ys hys name?' seyde Kynge Arthure.

'Truly,' seyde they all, 'we know nat hys name, nother frome whens he cam, nother whother he wolde.'†

425 'Alas,' seyde the kynge, 'thys ys the warste tydyngis that cam to me thys seven yere! For I wolde nat for all the londys I welde* to knowe and wyte† hit were so that that noble knyght were slayne.'   *rule*

'Sir, knowe ye ought* of hym?' seyde they all.   *anything*

---

othir ... othir either ... or
refygowred restored to vigour
knew himself regained consciousness
Lat brynge hym let him be brought
whother he wolde where he was going to
wyte understand

430 'As for that,' seyde Kynge Arthure, 'whether I know hym other none,* ye shall nat know for* me what man he ys. But Allmyghty Jesu sende me good tydyngis of hym.' And so seyde they all.

no from

'Be my hede,'* seyde Sir Gawayne, 'gyff* hit so be
435 that the good knyght be so sore hurte, hit ys grete damage† and pité to all thys londe, for he ys one of the nobelyst knyghtes that ever I saw in a fylde handyll speare or swerde. And iff he may be founde I shall fynde hym, for I am sure he ys nat farre frome thys contrey.'

upon my life if

440 'Sir, ye beare you well,' seyde Kynge Arthure, 'and ye shall fynde hym, onles* that he be in such a plyte that he may nat welde* hymselff.'

*unless
control*

'Jesu defende!'* seyde Sir Gawayne. 'But wyte well, I shall know what he ys and* I may fynde hym.'

*forbid
if*

445 Ryght so Sir Gawayne toke a sqyre with hym uppon hakeneyes* and rode all aboute Camelot within six or seven myle, but sone he com agayne* and cowde here no worde of hym. Than within two dayes Kynge Arthure and all the felyshyp returned unto London agayne. And
450 so as they rode by the way† hyt happened Sir Gawayne at Ascolot to lodge with Sir Barnarde, thereas* was Sir Launcelot lodged. And so as Sir Gawayne was in hys chamber to repose hym, Sir Barnarde, the olde barowne, cam in to hym, and hys doughtir Elayne, to chere* hym
455 and to ask hym what tydyngis, and who ded beste at the turnemente of Wynchester.

*riding horses
came back*

where

welcome

'So God me helpe,' seyde Sir Gawayne, 'there were two knyghtes that bare two whyght shyldys, but one of them bare a rede sleve uppon hys hede, and sertaynly
460 he was the beste knyght that ever I saw juste in fylde. For I dare sey,' seyde Sir Gawayne, 'that one knygyht with the rede slyve smote downe fourty knyghtes of the Rounde Table, and his felow ded ryght well and worshipfully.'

465 'Now blyssed be God,' seyde thys Fayre Maydyn of Ascolate, 'that that knyght sped* se welle! For he ys the man in the worlde that I firste loved, and truly he shall be the laste that ever I shall love.'

succeeded

'Now, fayre maydyn,' seyde Sir Gawayne, 'ys that
470 good knyght your love?'

---

damage source of grief
by the way on their way

'Sertaynly, sir,' she seyde, 'he ys my love.'
'Than know ye hys name?' seyde Sir Gawayne.
'Nay, truly, sir,' seyde the damesell, 'I know nat hys name nothir frome whens he com,* but to sey that I love hym, I promyse God and you I love hym.'   *came*
'How had ye knowlecch of hym firste?' seyde Sir Gawayne.
Than she tolde hym, as ye have harde before, and how hir fadir betoke* hym her brother to do hym servyse, and how hir fadir lente hym her brothirs, Sir Tyrryes, shylde: 'and here with me he leffte hys owne shylde.'   *gave*
'For what cause ded he so?' seyde Sir Gawayne.
'For thys cause,' seyde the damesell, 'for* hys shylde was full well knowyn amonge many noble knyghtes.'   *because*
'A, fayre damesell,' seyde Sir Gawayne, 'please hit you to lette me have a syght of that shylde.'
'Sir,' she seyde, 'hit ys in my chambir, coverde wyth a case,* and if ye woll com with me ye shall se hit.'   *cover*
'Nat so,' seyde Sir Barnarde to hys doughter, 'but sende ye for that shylde.'
So whan the shylde was come Sir Gawayne toke of* the case, and whan he behylde that shylde and knew hyt anone* that hit was Sir Launcelottis shylde and hys owne armys,* 'A, Jesu mercy!' seyde Sir Gawayne, 'now ys my herte more hevyar than ever hit was tofore.'*   *off / immediately / coat-of-arms / before*
'Why?' seyde thys mayde Elayne.
'For I have a grete cause,' seyde Sir Gawayne. 'Ys that knyght that owyth* thys shylde youre love?'   *owns*
'Yee truly,' she sayde, 'my love ys he. God wolde* that I were hys love!'   *would God*
'So God me spede,'* seyde Sir Gawayne, 'fayre damesell, ye have ryght† for and* he be youre love, ye love the moste honorabelyst knyght of the worlde and the man of moste worship.'   *God help me / if*
'So methought* ever,' seyde the damesell, 'for never ar* that tyme no knyght that ever I saw loved I never none arste.'†   *I believed / before*
'God graunte,' seyde Sir Gawayne, 'that aythir of you may rejoyse othir,† but that ys in a grete aventure.† But

ye have ryght   you are justified
no knyght ... none arste   I have never previously loved any knight that I have ever seen
aythir of you ... othir   you may make one another happy
in a grete aventure   very uncertain

truly,' sayde Sir Gawayne unto the damesell, 'ye may sey ye have a fayre grace,† for why* I have knowyn that noble knyght thys four-and-twenty yere, and never or that day I nor none othir knyght, I dare make good,* saw never nother* herde say that ever he bare tokyn or sygne of no lady, jantillwoman, nor maydyn at no justis nother turnemente. And therefore, fayre maydyn, ye ar much beholdyn to hym† to gyff hym thanke. But I drede me,'* seyde Sir Gawayne, 'that ye shall never se hym in thys worlde, and that ys as grete pité as ever was of ony erthely man.'

because
assert
nor

fear

'Alas,' seyde she, 'how may thys be? Ys he slayne?'

'I say nat so,' seyde Sir Gawayne, 'but wete* you well he ys grevously wounded, by all maner of sygnys, and by meanys of syght† more lycklyer* to be dede than to be on lyve. And wyte* you well he ys the noble knyght Sir Launcelot, for by thys shylde I know hym.'

know
likely
know

'Alas!' seyde thys Fayre Maydyn of Ascolat, 'how may thys be? And what was hys hurte?'

'Truly,' seyde Sir Gawayne, 'the man in the worlde that loved beste hym hurte hym. And I dare sey,' seyde Sir Gawayne, 'and* that knyght that hurte hym knew the verry sertaynté that he had hurte Sir Launcelot, hit were the moste* sorow that ever cam to hys herte.'

if
greatest

'Now, fayre fadir,' seyde than Elayne, 'I requyre you gyff me leve to ryde and seke hym, othir ellis I wote well I shall go oute of my mynde. For I shall never stynte* tyll that I fynde hym and my brothir, Sir Lavayne.'

cease

'Do ye as hit lykith you,'† seyde hir fadir, 'for sore me repentis of† the hurte of that noble knyght.'

Ryght so the Mayde made hyr redy and departed before Sir Gawayne, makynge grete dole.* Than on the morne Sir Gawayne com to Kynge Arthure and tolde hym all how he had founde Sir Launcelottis shylde in the kepynge of the Fayre Mayden of Ascolat.

lamentation

'All that knew I aforehande,' seyde Kynge Arthure, 'and that caused me I wolde nat suffir you to have ado† at the grete justis, for I aspyed hym whan he cam untyll

---

fayre grace   good fortune
much beholdyn to hym   under a great obligation to him
by meanys of syght   as far as one can see
as hit lykith you   as you please
sore me repentis of   I greatly regret
caused me . . . have ado   was the reason I did not want to allow you to fight

hys lodgyng, full late in the evenyng, into Ascolat. But
grete mervayle have I,' seyde Kynge Arthure, 'that ever
he wolde beare ony sygne of ony damesell, for ar* now
I never herde sey nor knew that ever he bare ony tokyn
of none erthely woman.'

'Be my hede, sir,' seyde Sir Gawayne, 'the Fayre
Maydyn of Ascolat lovith hym mervaylously well – what
hit meanyth, I cannat sey. And she ys ryddyn aftir to
seke hym.'

So the kynge and all com to London, and there
Gawayne all opynly* disclosed hit to all the courte that
hit was Sir Launcelot that justed beste. And whan Sir
Bors harde* that, wyte you well he was an hevy* man,
and so were all hys kynnysmen. But whan the quyene
wyst* that hit was Sir Launcelot that bare the rede slyve
of the Fayre Maydyn of Ascolat, she was nygh* ought*
of her mynde for wratthe. And than she sente for Sir
Bors de Ganys in all haste that myght be.† So whan Sir
Bors was come before the quyene she seyde, 'A, Sir Bors!
Have ye nat herde sey how falsely Sir Launcelot hath
betrayed me?'

'Alas, madame,' seyde Sir Bors, 'I am aferde he hath
betrayed hymselff and us all.'†

'No forse,'* seyde the quene, 'though he be distroyed,
for he ys a false, traytoure knyght.'

'Madame,' seyde Sir Bors, 'I pray you sey ye no more
so, for wyte you well I may nat here no such langayge
of* hym.'

'Why so, Sir Bors?' seyde she. 'Shold I nat calle hym
traytoure whan he bare the rede slyve uppon hys hede
at Wynchester at the grete justis?'

'Madame,' seyde Sir Bors, 'that slyeve-berynge re-
pentes me,* but I dare say he dud beare hit to none
evyll entent,† but for thys cause he bare the rede slyve,
that none of hys blood shold know hym. For or than*
we nother none of us all† never knew that ever he
bare tokyn or sygne of maydyn, lady, nothir jantillwoman.'

before

publicly

heard   sad

knew
nearly   out

no matter

talk about

I regret

before then

---

all haste that myght be all possible haste
[*he hath betrayed . . . us all* Bors changes the sense of Guinevere's insult; he says that Launcelot
has delivered himself to the enemy – death – and taken his followers with him, since they rely
completely on his leadership]
to none evyll entent without any evil purpose
we nother none of us all neither you nor I nor any of us

'Fy on hym!' seyde the quene. 'Yet for all hys pryde and bobbaunce,* there ye proved youreselff better man than he.'

'Nay, madam, sey ye nevermore so, for he bete me and my felowys, and myght* have slayne us and he had wolde.'†

'Fy on hym!' seyde the quene. 'For I harde Sir Gawayne say before my lorde Arthure that hit were mervayle to telle the grete love that ys betwene the Fayre Maydyn of Ascolat and hym.'

'Madam,' seyde Sir Bors, 'I may nat warne Sir Gawayne to sey† what hit pleasith hym, but I dare sey, as for my lorde Sir Launcelot, that he lovith no lady, jantillwoman, nother mayden, but as he lovith all inlyke muche.† And therefore, madam,' seyde Sir Bors, 'ye may sey what ye wyll, but wyte you well I woll hast me to syke* hym and fynde hym wheresumever* he be, and God sende me good tydyngis of hym!'

And so leve we them there, and speke we of Sir Launcelot, that lay in grete perell. And so as thys fayre madyn Elayne cam to Wynchester she sought there all aboute, and by fortune Sir Lavayne, hir brothir, was ryddyn to sporte hym† to enchaff* hys horse. And anone as* thys maydyn Elayne saw hym she knew hym, and than she cryed on-lowde* tylle* hym. And whan he herde her he com to her, and anone with that* she asked hir brother, 'How dothe my lorde, Sir Launcelot?'

'Who tolde you, syster, that my lordys name was Sir Launcelot?' Than she tolde hym how Sir Gawayne by hys shylde knew hym.

So they rode togydirs tyll that they cam to the ermytayge, and anone she alyght.* So Sir Lavayne brought her in to Sir Launcelot, and whan she saw hym ly so syke and pale in hys bed she myght nat speke, but suddeynly she felle downe to the erthe in a sowghe,* and there she lay a grete whyle. And when she was releved* she shryked and seyde, 'My lord, Sir Launcelot! Alas, whyghe* lye ye in thys plyte?' And than she sowned* agayne. And than Sir Launcelot prayde Sir Lavayne to take hir up, 'and brynge hir hydir to me'.

---

and he had wolde   had he wanted to
warne . . . to sey   prevent Sir Gawain from saying
inlyke muche   equally deeply
sporte hym   enjoy himself

And whan she cam to herself Sir Launcelot kyste her
and seyde, 'Fayre maydyn, why fare* ye thus? For ye
put me to more payne. Wherefore make ye no such
chere,† for and* ye be com to comforte me, ye be ryght
wellcom; and of thys lytyll hurte that I have I shall be
ryght hastely hole,* by the grace of God. But I mervayle',
seyde Sir Launcelot, 'who tolde you my name.'
    And so thys maydyn tolde hym all how Sir Gawayne
was lodged with hir fader, 'and there by youre shylde
he dyscoverde youre name.'
    'Alas!' seyde Sir Launcelot, 'that repentith me* that
my name ys knowyn, for I am sure hit woll turne untyll*
angir.' And than Sir Launcelot compaste* in hys mynde
that Sir Gawayne wolde telle Quene Gwenyvere how he
bare the rede slyve and for whom, that he wyst well
wolde turne unto grete angur.
    So thys maydyn Elayne never wente frome Sir Launce-
lot, but wacched* hym day and nyght and dud such
attendaunce to hym† that the Freynshe booke seyth there
was never woman dyd never more kyndlyer for man.
Than Sir Launcelot prayde Sir Lavayne to make aspyes*
in Wynchester for Sir Bors if he cam there, and tolde
hym by what tokyns he sholde know hym: by a wounde
in hys forehede. 'For I am sure,' seyde Sir Launcelot,
'that Sir Bors woll seke me, for he ys the same good
knyght that hurte me.'
    Now turne we unto Sir Bors de Ganys, that cam untyll
Wynchestir to seke aftir hys cosyne Sir Launcelot. And
whan he cam to Wynchester Sir Lavayne leyde wacche*
for Sir Bors. And anone he had warnyng of hym, and
so he founde hym, and anone he salewed* hym and
tolde hym frome whens he com.
    'Now, fayre knyght,' seyde Sir Bors, 'ye be wellcom,†
and I requyre you that ye woll brynge me to my lorde
Sir Launcelot.'
    'Sir,' seyde Sir Lavayne, 'take youre horse, and within
thys owre ye shall se hym.'
    So they departed and com to the ermytayge. And
whan Sir Bors saw Sir Launcelot lye in hys bedde,
dede* pale and discoloured, anone Sir Bors loste hys

Wherefore ... chere   and so don't be in such [poor] spirits
dud such attendaunce to hym   gave him such service
ye be wellcom   I am glad to see you

countenaunce,† and for kyndenes and pité he myght nat speke but wepte tendirly a grete whyle. But whan he myght speke he seyde thus: 'A, my lorde Sir Launcelot, God you blysse* and sende you hasty recoveryng! For full hevy am I of* my mysfortune and of myne unhappynesse. For now I may calle myself unhappy,* and I drede me that God ys gretely displeasyd with me, that He wolde suffir* me to have such a shame for* to hurte you that ar all oure ledar† and all oure worship;† and therefore I calle myselff unhappy. Alas, that ever such a caytyff* knyght as I am sholde have power by unhappines* to hurte the most noblyst knyght of the worlde! Where I so shamefully sette uppon you and overcharged† you, and where ye myght have slayne me, ye saved me; and so ded nat I, for I and all oure bloode ded to you their utteraunce.* I mervayle,' seyde Sir Bors, 'that my herte or my bloode wolde serve* me. Wherefore, my lorde Sir Launcelot, I aske you mercy.'

'Fayre cousyn,' seyde Sir Launcelot, 'ye be ryght wellcom. And wyte you* well, overmuche* ye sey for the plesure of me whych pleasith me nothynge† for why* I have the same isought.* For I wolde with pryde have overcom you all, and there in my pryde I was nere* slayne, and that was in myne owne defaughte;* for I myght have gyffyn you warnynge of my beynge there, and than had I had no hurte. For hit ys an olde-seyde sawe:† there ys harde batayle thereas* kynne and frendys doth batayle ayther ayenst other,† for there may be no mercy, but mortall warre. Therefore, fayre cousyn,' seyde Sir Launcelot, 'lat thys langage overpasse,† and all shall be wellcom that God sendith. And latte us leve of* thys mater and speke of some rejoysynge, for thys that ys done may nat be undone; and lat us fynde a remedy how sone that I may be hole.'*

Than Sir Bors lenyd* uppon hys beddys syde and tolde Sir Launcelot how the quene was passynge wrothe†

---

loste his countenance   was discomposed
all oure ledar   leader of us all
all oure worship   source of honour of us all
overcharged   pressed hard against
pleasith me nothynge   does not please me at all
olde-seyde sawe   long-repeated saying
ayther ayenst other   one against the other
lat thys langage overpasse   let this talk be forgotten
passynge wrothe   extremely angry

with hym, 'because ye ware* the rede slyve at the grete   wore
705 justes'. And there Sir Bors tolde hym all how Sir
Gawayne discoverde hit 'by youre shylde' that he leffte
with the Fayre Madyn of Ascolat.
'Than ys the quene wrothe?' seyde Sir Launcelot.
'Therefore am I ryght hevy, but I deserved no wrath,
710 for all that I ded was bycause I wolde nat† be knowyn.'
'Sir, ryght* so excused I you,' seyde Sir Bors, 'but all   just
was in vayne, for she seyde more largelyer† to me than
I to you sey now. But, sir, ys thys she,' seyde Sir Bors,
'that ys so busy aboute you, that men calle the Fayre
715 Maydyn of Ascolat?'
'Forsothe,* she hit ys,'* seyde Sir Launcelot, 'that by   indeed   it is she
no meanys I cannat put her fro me.'
'Why sholde ye put her frome you?' seyde Sir Bors.
'For she ys a passyng fayre damesell, and well besayne*   good-looking
720 and well taught.† And God wolde,* fayre cousyn,' seyde   would God
Sir Bors, 'that ye cowde love her, but as to that I may
nat nother dare nat counceyle you.† But I se well,' seyde
Sir Bors, 'by her dyligence aboute you that she lovith
you intyerly.'*   entirely
725 'That me repentis,'* seyde Sir Launcelot.   I regret
'Well,' seyde Sir Bors, 'she ys nat the firste that hath
loste hir payne† uppon you, and that ys the more pyté.'
And so they talked of many mo* thynges.   more
And so within three or four dayes Sir Launcelot
730 wexed† bygge* and lyght.* Than Sir Bors tolde Sir   strong active
Launcelot how there was sworne a grete turnement
betwyxt Kyng Arthure and the Kynge of North Galis,
that sholde be uppon Allhalowmasse day, besydes
Wynchestir. 'Is that trouth?' seyde Sir Launcelot. 'Than
735 shall ye abyde* with me stylle a lityll whyle untyll that   wait
I be hole, for I fele myself resonabely bygge and stronge.'
'Blessed be God!' seyde Sir Bors.
Than they were there nyghe a moneth togydirs, and
ever* thys maydyn Elayne ded ever hir dyligence and   always
740 labour† both nyght and day unto Sir Launcelot, that

---

wolde nat did not want to be
more largelyer more intemperately
taught brought up
I may not . . . conceyle you I can not, nor do I dare, advise you
loste hir payne wasted her efforts
wexed grew
ded ever . . . labour kept on applying herself and working

there was never chylde nother wyff more mekar* tyll*   meeker to
fadir and husbande than was thys Fayre Maydyn of
Ascolat; wherefore Sir Bors was gretly pleased with her.
    So uppon a day,* by the assente of Sir Lavayne, Sir   one day
745 Bors, and Sir Launcelot, they made the ermyte to seke
in woodys for diverse* erbys, and so Sir Launcelot made   various
fayre Elayne to gadir erbys for hym to make hym a
bayne.* So in the meanewhyle Sir Launcelot made Sir   bath
Lavayne to arme hym at all pecis,† and there he thought
750 to assay hymselff† upon horsebacke with a speare,
whether he myght welde† hys armour and hys speare
for hys hurte† or nat. And so whan he was uppon hys
horse he steyrred hym† freyshly,* and the horse was   vigorously
passyng lusty† and frycke* because he was nat laboured*   eager exercised
755 of a moneth before. And than Sir Launcelot bade Sir
Lavayne gyff hym that grete speare, and so Sir Launcelot
cowchyd that speare in the reeste.† The courser* lepte   war-horse
myghtyly whan he felte the spurres, and he that was
uppon hym, whiche was the nobelyst horseman of the
760 worlde, strayned hym* myghtyly and stabely,* and kepte   himself firmly
stylle the speare† in the reeste. And therewith Sir Launce-
lot strayned hymselff so straytly,* with so grete fors, to   severely
gete the courser forewarde that the bottom of hys
wounde braste* both within and withoute,† and there-   burst
765 withall† the bloode cam oute so fyersely that he felte
hymselff so feble that he myght nat sitte uppon hys
horse. And than Sir Launcelot cryed unto Sir Bors, 'A,
Sir Bors and Sir Lavayne, helpe! For I am com unto
myne ende!'
770   And therewith he felle downe on the one syde to the
erth lyke a dede coorse.* And than Sir Bors and Sir   body
Lavayne cam unto hym with sorow-makynge oute of
mesure,† and so by fortune thys mayden, Elayne, harde*   heard

---

at all pecis   completely
assay hymselff   test himself
welde   move with ease
for his hurte   because of his injury
steyrred him   urged him on
lusty   active
cowchyd that ... reeste   lowered that lance into the rest [a bracket attached to the side of the breastplate which bore the weight of the lance]
kepte stylle the speare   held the lance steady
within and withoute   inside and out
therewithall   at the same time
oute of mesure   immeasurable

their mournynge. And than she cam, and whan she
founde Sir Launcelot there armed in that place she cryed
and wepte as she had bene wood.† And than she kyssed
hym and ded what she myght to awake hym, and than
she rebuked her brothir and Sir Bors, and called hem
false traytours, and seyd,
    'Why wolde ye take hym oute of hys bed? For and
he dye, I woll appele* you of hys deth!'   accuse
    And so with that cam the ermyte, Sir Bawdewyn of
Bretayne, and whan he founde Sir Launcelot in that
plyte he seyde but lityll, but wyte you well he was wroth.
But he seyde, 'Lette us have hym in', and anone they
bare hym into the ermytage and unarmed hym, and
leyde hym in hys bedde. And evermore hys wounde bled
spiteuously,* but he stirred no lymme off hym.† Than   grievously
the knyght-armyte* put a thynge in hys nose and a litill   hermit
dele* of watir in hys mowthe, and than Sir Launcelot   amount
waked of hys swowghe.* And than the ermyte staunched   faint
hys bledyng, and whan Sir Launcelot myght speke he
asked why he put hys lyff so in jouperté.*   jeopardy
    'Sir,' seyde Sir Launcelot, 'because I wente* I had be believed
stronge inowghe,* and also Sir Bors tolde me there   enough
sholde be at Halowmasse† a grete justis betwyxte Kynge
Arthure and the Kynge of Northe Galys. And therefore
I thought to assay myselff, whether I myght be there or
not.'
    'A, Sir Launcelot,' seyde the ermyte, 'youre harte and
youre currayge woll never be done untyll youre laste day!
But ye shall do now be* my counceyle: lat Sir Bors   according to
departe frome you, and lat hym do at that turnemente
what he may. And, by the grace of God,' seyde the
knyght ermyte, 'be that† the turnemente be done* and   finished
he comyn hydir* agayne, sir, ye shall be hole,* so† that here healed
ye woll be governed by me.'
    Than Sir Bors made hym redy to departe frome
hym, and Sir Launcelot seyde, 'Fayre cousyn, Sir Bors,
recommaunde me unto all tho* ye owght recommaunde   those
me unto, and I pray you enforce youreselff† at that justis

---

as she had bene wood as if she had been mad
he stirred . . . off hym he did not move any of his limbs
Halowmasse 1 November, All Saints' Day
be that by the time that
so provided that
enforce youreselff exert yourself

that ye may be beste, for my love. And here shall I abyde
you, at the mercy of God, tyll youre agayne-commynge.'*   return

And so Sir Bors departed and cam to the courte of
Kynge Arthure, and tolde hem in what place he leffte
Sir Launcelot.

'That me repentis!' seyde the kynge. 'But syn* he shall   since
have hys lyff, we all may thanke God.'

And than Sir Bors tolde the quene what jouperté Sir
Launcelot was in whan he wolde a asayde† hys horse:
'And all that he ded* was for the love of you, because   did
he wolde a bene at thys turnemente.'

'Fy on hym, recreayde* knyght!' seyde the quene. 'For   coward
wyte you well I am ryght sory and* he shall have hys   if
lyff.'

'Madam, hys lyff shall he have,' seyde Sir Bors, 'and
who that wolde* otherwyse, excepte you, madame, we   would like
that ben* of hys blood wolde helpe to shortyn their   are
lyves. But, madame,' seyde Sir Bors, 'ye have ben
oftyntymes displeased with my lorde Sir Launcelot, but
at all tymys at the ende ye founde hym a trew knyght.'
And so he departed.

And than every knyght of the Rounde Table that were
there that tyme presente made them redy to that justes
at Allhalowmasse.† And thidir drew many knyghtes of
diverse contreyes. And as Halowmasse drew nere, thydir
cam the Kynge of North Galis, and the Kynge with the
Hondred Knyghtes, and Sir Galahalt the Haute Prynce
of Surluse. And thider cam Kynge Angwysh of Irelonde,
and the Kynge of Northumbirlonde, and the Kynge of
Scottis. So thes three kynges com to Kynge Arthurs
party.

And so that day Sir Gawayne ded grete dedys of
armys and began first, and the herowdis† nombirde*   counted
that Sir Gawayne smote downe twenty knyghtes. Than
Sir Bors de Ganys cam in the same tyme, and he was
numbirde that he smote downe twenty knyghtes; and
therefore the pryse was gyvyn betwyxt* them bothe, for   between
they began firste and lengist* endured. Also Sir Gareth,†   longest
as the boke seyth, ded that day grete dedis of armys, for

---

a asayde have tried out
Allhalowmasse All Saints' Day [see note above]
herowdis heralds [who acted as referees at tournaments]
[*Sir Gareth* Gawain's youngest brother, singled out here in preparation for a subsequent story in which he is accidentally killed by Launcelot, with disastrous consequences]

he smote downe and pulled downe thirty knyghtes; but
whan he had done that dedis he taryed* nat, but so   *delayed*
departed, and therefore he loste hys pryse. And Sir
Palamydes† ded grete dedis of armys that day, for
855 he smote downe twenty knyghtes; but he departed
suddeynly, and men demed* that he and Sir Gareth rode   *believed*
togydirs to som maner* adventures.   *some kind of*
    So whan thys turnement was done Sir Bors departed,
and rode tylle he cam to Sir Launcelot, hys cousyne.
860 And than he founde hym walkyng on hys feete, and
there aythir made grete joy of other, and so he tolde Sir
Launcelot of all the justys, lyke as ye have herde.
    'I mervayle', seyde Sir Launcelot, 'that Sir Gareth,
whan he had done such dedis of armys, that he wolde
865 not tarry.'
    'Sir, thereof we mervayled all,' seyde Sir Bors, 'for but
if hit were* you, other* the noble knyght Sir Trystram,   *except for you*   *or*
other the good knyght Sir Lamorake de Galis,† I saw
never knyght bere so many knyghtes and smyte downe
870 in so litill a whyle as ded Sir Gareth. And anone as* he   *as soon as*
was gone we all wyst nat where he becom.'†
    'Be my hede,'† seyde Sir Launcelot, 'he ys a noble
knyght and a myghty man and well-brethed;† and yf he
were well assayed,'† seyd Sir Launcelot, 'I wolde deme*   *judge*
875 he were good inow* for ony knyght that beryth the   *enough*
lyff.† And he ys jantill,† curteyse* and ryght   *courteous*
bownteuous,* meke and mylde, and in hym ys no maner   *open-handed*
of male engynne,† but playne,* faythfull an trew.'   *straightforward*
    So than they made hem redy to departe frome the
880 ermytayge. And so uppon a morne they toke their horsis,
and this Elayne le Blanke with hem. And whan they
cam to Ascolat there were they well lodged and had
grete chere* of Sir Barnarde, the olde baron, and of Sir   *hospitality*
Tirré, hys sonne.
885 And so uppon the morne, whan Sir Launcelot sholde

[*Sir Palamydes*   a converted Saracen, who figures in an earlier story]
[*Sir Trystram . . . Sir Lamorake de Galis*   Tristram, lover of Isolde, is the hero of an earlier book of the *Morte Darthur*, in which Lamorak also figures until he is killed by Gawain's brothers. These three – Launcelot, Tristram and Lamorak – are touchstones of secular knighthood]
we all . . . becom   none of us knew what became of him
Be my hede   upon my life
well-brethed   sound in wind
assayed   put to the test
bereth the lyff   living
jantill   well-bred
male engynne   guile

departe, fayre Elayne brought hir fadir with her, and Sir Lavayne, and Sir Tyrré, and than thus she sayde: 'My lorde, Sir Launcelot, now I se ye woll departe frome me. Now, fayre knyght and curtayse knyght,' seyde she, 'have mercy uppon me, and suffir me nat to dye for youre love.'

'Why, what wolde you that I dud?'† seyde Sir Launcelot.

'Sir, I wolde have you to my husbande,' seyde Elayne.

'Fayre damesell, I thanke you hartely,' seyde Sir Launcelot, 'but truly,' seyde he, 'I caste me† never to be wedded man.'

'Than, fayre knyght,' seyde she, 'woll ye be my paramour?'*   *lover*

'Jesu defende me!'† seyde Sir Launcelot. 'For than I rewarded youre fadir and youre brothir full evyll for their grete goodnesse.'

'Alas, than', seyde she, 'I muste dye for youre love.'

'Ye shall nat do so,' seyde Sir Launcelot, 'for wyte you well, fayre mayden, I myght have bene maryed and I had wolde,† but I never applyed me* yett to be maryed.   *tried* But bycause, fayre damesell, that ye love me as ye sey ye do, I woll for youre good wylle and kyndnes shew to you som goodnesse. That ys thys: that wheresomever ye woll besette* youre herte uppon som good knyght that   *set* woll wedde you, I shall gyff you togydirs* a thousand   *jointly* pounde† yerly, to you and to youre ayris.* This muche   *heirs* woll I gyff you, fayre mayden, for youre kyndnesse, and allweyes whyle I lyve to be youre owne knyght.'

'Sir, of all thys', seyde the maydyn, 'I woll none,† for but yff* ye woll wedde me, other to be my paramour at   *unless* the leste,† wyte you well, Sir Launcelot, my good dayes are done.'

'Fayre damesell,' seyde Sir Launcelot, 'of thes two thynges ye must pardon me.'

Than she shryked shirly* and felle downe in a sowghe.   *shrilly* And than women bare hir into her chambir, and there

---

wolde you that I dud do you want me to do
caste me have resolved
Jesu defende me God forbid
and I had wolde if I had wanted to
[*a thousande pounde* a thousand pounds a year was a huge sum. Malory's own annual income was about twenty pounds]
I woll none I do not want any
at the leste at least

she made overmuche sorowe.† And than Sir Launcelot wolde* departe, and there he asked Sir Lavayne what he wolde do.

wanted to

'Sir, what sholde I do,' seyde Sir Lavayne, 'but folow you, but if* ye dryve me frome you or commaunde me to go frome you.' Than cam Sir Barnarde to Sir Launcelot and seyde to hym,

unless

'I cannat se but that my doughtir woll dye for youre sake.'

'Sir, I may nat do withall,'† seyde Sir Launcelot, 'for that me sore repentith, for I reporte me to youreselff† that my profir* ys fayre. And me repentith,' seyde Sir Launcelot, 'that she lovith me as she dothe, for I was never the causer of hit; for I reporte me unto youre sonne, I never erly nother late profirde her bownté* nother fayre behestes.* And as for me,' seyde Sir Launcelot, 'I dare do that a knyght sholde do, and sey tht she ys a clene mayden for me,† bothe for dede and wylle. For I am ryght hevy of hir distresse, for she ys a full fayre maydyn, goode and jentill, and well itaught.'*

offer

favour
promises

brought up

'Fadir,' seyde Sir Lavayne, 'I dare make good† she ys a clene maydyn as for my lorde Sir Launcelot; but she doth as I do, for sythen* I saw first my lorde Sir Launcelot I cowde never departe frome hym, nother noght I woll,† and I may folow hym.'

since

Than Sir Launcelot toke hys leve, and so they departed and cam to Wynchestir. And whan Kynge Arthur wyst that Sir Launcelot was come hole and sownde, the kynge made grete joy of hym, and so ded Sir Gawayne and all the knyghtes of the Rounde Table excepte Sir Aggravayne and Sir Mordred.† Also Quene Gwenyver was woode wrothe† with Sir Launcelot, and wolde by no meanys speke with hym, but enstraunged herselff frome hym. And Sir Launcelot made all the meanys that he

---

she made . . . sorowe she wept excessively
I may . . . withall I can do nothing at all
reporte . . . youreselff ask you to confirm
a clene . . . me a virgin as far as I am concerned
dare make good guarantee
nother . . . I woll nor do I want to
[*Sir Aggravayne and Sir Mordred* Gawain's treacherous brothers, enemies of Launcelot. Mordred, who is Arthur's son by his sister, Gawain's mother, later seizes Arthur's throne]
woode wrothe insanely angry

myght for to speke with the quene, but hit wolde nat be.

Now speke we of the Fayre Maydyn of Ascolat that made such sorow day and nyght that she never slepte, ete, nother dranke, and ever she made hir complaynte unto Sir Launcelot. So whan she had thus endured a ten dayes, that she fyebled† so that she muste nedis passe oute of thys worlde, than she shrove her clene† and resseyved hir Creature,† and ever she complayned stylle uppon Sir Launcelot. Than hir gostly fadir† bade hir leve such thoughtes. Than she seyde, 'Why sholde I leve such thoughtes? Am I nat an erthely woman? And all the whyle the brethe ys in my body I may complayne me, for my belyve* ys that I do none offence, though I love an erthely man, unto God, for He fourmed* me thereto,* and all maner of good love comyth of God. And other than good love loved I never Sir Launcelot du Lake. And I take God to recorde,* I loved never none but hym, nor never shall, of erthely creature; and a clene maydyn I am for hym and for all othir. And sitthyn* hit ys the sufferaunce* of God that I shall dye for so noble a knyght, I beseche the, Hyghe Fadir of Hevyn, have mercy uppon me and my soule, and uppon myne unnumerable paynys that I suffir may be alygeaunce* of parte of my synnes. For, swete Lorde Jesu,' seyde the fayre maydyn, 'I take God to recorde I was never to the† grete offenser* nother ayenste† thy lawis but* that I loved thys noble knyght, Sir Launcelot, oute of mesure.† And of myselff, good Lorde, I had no myght* to withstonde the fervent love, wherefore I have my deth!'

And than she called hir fadir, Sir Bernarde, and hir brothir, Sir Tirry, and hartely she prayd hir fadir that hir brothir myght wryght a lettir lyke as she ded endite,† and so hir fadir graunted her. And whan the lettir was wryten, worde by worde lyke as she devised* hit, than she prayde hir fadir that she myght be wacched* untylle

belief
created   for that

as witness

since
will

remission

offender   except

power

dictated
watched over

---

fyebled grew weak
shrove her clene made her confession
Creature Creator [in the eucharist]
gostly fadir spiritual father, confessor
the thee
nother ayenste nor [was I] against
oute of mesure immeasurably, excessively
lyke as she ded endite as she composed (it) [Like Margery Brews (see p. 540), the Fair Maid cannot write]

she were dede. 'And whyle my body ys hote* lat thys *warm*
lettir be put in my ryght honde, and my honde bounde
995 faste to the letter untyll that I be colde. And lette me be
put in a fayre bed with all the rychyste clothys* that I *cloths*
have aboute me, and so lat my bed and all my rychyst
clothis be ledde† with me in a charyat* unto the nexte* *hearse nearest*
place where the Temmys† ys. And there lette me be put
1000 within a barget,* and but one man with me, such as ye *barge*
truste, to stirre* me thidir;† and that my barget be *row*
coverde with blacke samyte† over and over.† And thus,
fadir, I beseche you, lat hit be done.'
    So hir fadir graunte her faythfully all thynge sholde
1005 be done lyke as she had devised. Than hir fadir and hir
brothir made grete dole* for her. And whan thys was *lamentation*
done, anone* she dyed. *shortly*
    And whan she was dede the corse* and the bedde all *body*
was lad* the nexte way unto the Temmys, and there a *carried*
1010 man and the corse, and all thynge as she had devised,
was put into the Temmys. And so the man stirred the
bargett unto Westmynster, and there hit rubbed† and
rolled too and fro a grete whyle or* ony man aspyed *before*
hit.
1015 So by fortune Kynge Arthure and Quene Gwenyver
were talkynge togydirs at a wyndow, and so as they
loked into the Temmys they aspyed that blacke barget
and had mervayle what hit mente. Than the kynge called
Sir Kay and shewed hit hym.
1020 'Sir,' seyde Sir Kay, 'wete you well, there ys som new
tydynges.'
    'Therefore go ye thidir,' seyde the kynge to Sir Kay,
'and take with you Sir Braundiles and Sir Aggravayne,
and brynge me redy* worde what ys there.' *prompt*
1025 Than these three knyghtes departed and cam to the
barget and wente in. And there they founde the fayryst
corse lyyng in a ryche bed that ever they saw, and a
poore man syttynge in the bargettis ende, and no worde
wolde he speke. So thes three knyghtes returned unto
1030 the kynge agayne and tolde hym what they founde.

---

ledde   carried
[*Temmys*   the river Thames, which flows to London and Westminster, where Arthur's court is. The nearest point on the Thames to Guildford (Ascolat) is at a distance of thirteen miles]
thider   thither
samyte   a rich cloth
over and over   all around
[*rubbed*   the barge scrapes against the quay at Westminster]

'That fayre corse woll I se,' seyde the kynge.

And so the kynge toke the quene by the honde and wente thydir. Than the kynge made the barget to be holde faste, and than the kynge and the quene wente in with sertayne knightes with them. And there he saw the fayryst woman ly in a ryche bed, coverde unto her myddyll with many rych clothys, and all was cloth of golde, and she lay as she had smyled.† Than the quene aspyed the lettir in hir right hande and tolde the kynge. Than the kynge toke hit and seyde, 'Now am I sure thys lettir woll telle us what she was, and why she ys com hyddir.'

So than the king and the quene wente out of the bargette and so commaunded a sertayne* to wayte uppon† the barget. And so whan the kynge was com to hys chambir he called many knyghtes aboute hym and seyde that he wolde wat opynly† what was wryten within that lettir. Than the kynge brake hit† and made a clerke* to rede hit, and thys was the entente* of the lettir:

'Most noble knyght, my lorde Sir Launcelot, now hath dethe made us two at debate† for your love. And I was your lover, that men callid the Fayre Maydyn of Ascolate. Therefore unto all ladyes I make my mone† that for my soule ye pray and bury me at the leste, and offir ye my masse-peny:† thys ys my laste requeste. And a clene maydyn I dyed, I take God to wytnesse. And pray for my soule, Sir Launcelot, as thou art pereles.'*

Thys was all the substaunce in the lettir. And whan hit was rad* the kynge, the quene and all the knyghtes wepte for pité of the dolefull* complayntes. Than was Sir Launcelot sente for, and whan he was com Kynge Arthure made the lettir to be rad to hym. And whan Sir Launcelot harde* hit worde by worde, he seyde, 'My lorde Arthur, wyte you well I am ryght hevy* of the deth of thys fayre lady. And God knowyth I was never causar of her deth be my wyllynge,† and that woll I

someone
uppon

secretary
import

incomparable

read
sorrowful

heard
very sad

---

as she had smyled   as if she were smiling
wayte uppon   look after
wat opynly   know publicly
brake hit   broke [the seal on] it
at debate   at variance
make my mone   complain, lament
[*masse-peny*   offering of money made at a mass; here, by mourners at the Maid's requiem mass]
be my wyllynge   intentionally

reporte me unto her owne brothir† that here ys, Sir
Lavayne. I woll nat say nay,'* seyde Sir Launcelot, 'but   deny
that she was both fayre and good, and much I was
1070 beholdyn* unto her, but she loved me oute of mesure.'   obliged
'Sir,' seyde the quene, 'ye myght have shewed hir som
bownté* and jantilnes* whych myght have preserved   favour   courtesy
hir lyff.'
'Madame,' seyde Sir Launcelot, 'she wolde none other
1075 wayes† be answerde but that she wolde be my wyff
othir* ellis my paramour,* and of thes two I wolde not   or   mistress
graunte her. But I proffird her, for her good love that
she shewed me, a thousand pound yerely to her and to
her ayres, and to wedde ony maner of knyght that she
1080 coude fynde beste to love in her harte. For, madame,'
seyde Sir Launcelot, 'I love nat to be constrayned to
love, for love muste only aryse of the harte selff,* and   itself
nat by none* constraynte.'   any
'That ys trouth, sir,' seyde the kynge, 'and with many
1085 knyghtes love ys fre in hymselffe,† and never woll be
bonde;† for where he* ys bonden he lowsith* hymselff.'   it   unlooses
Than seyde the kynge unto Sir Launcelot, 'Sir, hit
woll be youre worshyp* that ye oversé* that she be   honour   see to it
entered worshypfully.'†
1090 'Sir,' seyde Sir Launcelot, 'that shall be done as I can
beste devise.'†
And so many knyghtes yode* thyder to beholde that   went
fayre dede mayden, and so uppon the morn she was
entered rychely. And Sir Launcelot offird her masse-
1095 peny;† and all tho* knyghtes of the Table Rounde that   those
were there at that tyme offerde with Sir Launcelot. And
than the poure man wente agayne* wyth the barget.   returned
Than the quene sent for Sir Launcelot and prayde
hym of mercy for why that† she had ben wrothe with
1100 hym causeles.
'Thys ys nat the firste tyme,' seyde Sir Launcelot, 'that
ye have ben displese with me causeles. But, madame,

---

reporte me . . . brothir ask her own brother to confirm
none other wayes no other way
in hymselffe in itself
bonde bound
entered worshypfully buried honourably
devise contrive, manage
[*masse-peny* by offering her mass-penny, Launcelot acts as chief mourner]
of mercy for why that forgiveness because

ever I muste suffir* you, but what sorow that I endure,   endure
ye take no forse.'†
So thys passed on all that wynter, with all maner of
huntynge and hawkynge; and justis and turneyes were
many betwyxte* many grete lordis. And ever in all placis   among
Sir Lavayn gate* grete worshyp, that he was nobely   acquired
defamed* amonge many knyghtis of the Table Rounde.   renowned
Thus hit past on tylle Crystemasse, and than every day
there was justis made for a dyamonde: who that justed
best shulde have a dyamounde. But Sir Launcelot wolde
nat juste but if† hit were a grete justes cryed;* but Sir   proclaimed
Lavayne justed there all the Crystemasse passyngly*   exceedingly
well, and was beste praysed, for there were but feaw
that ded so well. Wherefore all maner of knyghtes
demed* that Sir Lavayn sholde be made knyght of the   considered
Table Rounde at the next feste of Pentecoste.

---

take no forse   pay no regard
but if   unless

Robert Henryson
c. 1420–before 1505–6

Robert Henryson was possibly born in the early 1420s. In 1462 a Robertus Henrysone, who may be the poet, was incorporated into the university of Glasgow as a graduate with degrees from elsewhere in arts and canon law. This Henryson was described as *venerabilis* ('venerable'), and so was presumably at least forty. A Robert Henryson, notary public, is mentioned in the late 1470s in records from Dunfermline, Fife, and early printed editions of his works identify the poet as a Dunfermline schoolmaster. Henryson's fellow Scot, William Dunbar, laments his death in 'I that in Heill was and Gladness' (see p. 545), which can be dated 1505–6.

Henryson's major works are *The Fables*, a collection of Aesopic and Reynardian animal tales, each with a moral interpretation, from which *The Preaching of the Swallow* is taken; *The Testament of Cresseid*, an expansion of Book V of Chaucer's *Troilus and Criseyde*, in which Cresseid is punished with leprosy; and *Orpheus and Eurydice*, a moralised version of the classical myth. All of these are written largely in rhyme royal, the stanza which Chaucer introduced into English in *The Parliament of Fowls*. Henryson, like other fifteenth-century Scots writers, read Chaucer and Lydgate, but he was evidently also deeply familiar with alliterative styles. *The Preaching of the Swallow* is probably based on a very brief Latin fable in an Aesopic collection made around 1175 by Gualterus Anglicus (Walter the Englishman). This collection was widely used in schools in the later middle ages, and Henryson the schoolmaster may have read it with his pupils. His expansion of the Latin is partly a matter of the closely-observed presentation of everyday life, but this is placed in the wider intellectual context which is characteristic of his work. As with many of the other *Fables*, the story of the foolish birds who cannot transcend the cycle of the seasons of which they are a part is more open and more compassionate than the morality that concludes it.

The text is taken from the 1571 Bassandyne print, occasionally corrected from National Library of Scotland, Advocates' MS 1.1.6 (Bannatyne MS).

From THE FABLES
The Preaching of the Swallow

The hie prudence,* and wirking* mervelous,   *lofty wisdom works*
The profound wit* of God omnipotent,   *wisdom*
Is sa perfyte,* and sa ingenious,   *so perfect*
Excellent* far all mannis jugement,   *excelling*
5   For quhy* to him all thing is ay* present   *because always*
Rycht as it is or ony tyme sall be,
Befoir the sicht* of his divinitie.   *sight*

Thairfoir our saull with sensualitie
So fetterit* is in presoun* corporall   *fettered prison*
10   We may not cleirlie understand nor se
God as he is, nor thingis celestiall.
†Our mirk and deidlie corps materiale
Blindis the spirituall operatioun,
Lyke as† ane man wer bundin* in presoun.   *bound*

15   In *Metaphisik*† Aristotell sayis
That mannis saull* is lyke ane bakkis ee†   *soul*
Quhilk* lurkis* still als lang as licht* of day is   *which hides light*
And in the gloming cummis furth to fle;*   *fly*
Hir ene* ar waik,* the sone* scho* may not se: *eyes weak sun she*
20   Sa is our saull with fantasie* opprest*   *delusion weighed down*
To knaw the thingis in nature manifest.

For God is in his power infinite
And mannis saull is febill and over* small,   *too*
Of understanding waik and unperfite*   *imperfect*
25   To comprehend him that contenis* all.   *contains*
Nane* suld presume, be ressoun* naturall,   *none reason*
To seirche* the secreitis of the Trinitie,   *explore*
Bot trow* fermelie and lat all ressoun* be.   *believe arguments*

---

12   Our blind and mortal physical body
14   *Lyke as* in the same way as if
15   [*Metaphysik* the comparison of the weakness of man's understanding with the blindness of the bat comes from the *Metaphysics* of the Greek philosopher Aristotle (385–322 BC), often quoted from the thirteenth century on]
16   *bakkis ee* bat's eye

	Yit nevertheles we may haif knawlegeing†	
30	Of God almychtie be* his creatouris,	by means of
	That he is gude, fair, wyis* and bening.*	wise benign
	Exempill tak be thir† jolie flouris,	
	Rycht sweit of smell and plesant of colouris,	
	Sum grene, sum blew, sum purpour,* quhyte and reid,	purple
35	Thus distribute* be gift of his godheid.	distributed
	The firmament† payntit with sternis* cleir	stars
	From eist to west rolland* in cirkill round,	rolling
	†And everilk planet in his proper spheir	
	In moving makand harmonie and sound,	
40	The fyre, the air, the watter and the ground –	
	Till* understand it is aneuch,* iwis,*	to enough for sure
	That God in all his werkis wittie* is.	wise
	Luke weill* the fische that swimmis in the se;	consider well
	Luke weill in eirth all kynd of bestyall;*	animals
45	The foulis fair, sa forcelie* thay fle,	strongly
	Scheddand* the air with pennis* grit* and small;	parting wings great
	Syne* luke to man, that he maid last of all,	afterwards
	Lyke to his image and his similitude:	
	Be thir* we knaw that God is fair and gude.	these
50	All creature he maid for the behufe*	benefit
	Of man and to his supportatioun,*	support
	In to* this eirth, baith under* and abufe,*	in below above
	In number, wecht,* and dew* proportioun,	weight fitting
	The difference of tyme and ilk* seasoun,	each
55	†Concorddand till our opurtunitie,	
	As daylie by experience we may se.	

---

29 *haif knawlegeing* have information
32 *Exampill tak be thir* take the example of these
36 [*firmament* the outermost sphere of the fixed stars, whose westward motion is dictated by the *primum mobile* (first mover) beyond it]
38–9 [The seven planets travel round the earth in their concentric spheres, each creating a different musical note with its motion]
55 In accordance with our need

The somer with his jolie mantill grene,
With flouris fair furrit* on everilk fent,*   (fur-)trimmed opening
Quhilk Flora† goddes, of the flouris quene,
60 Hes to that Lord as for his seasoun lent,
And Phebus† with his goldin bemis gent*   beautiful
Hes purfellit* and payntit plesandly,   adorned
With heit and moysture stilland* from the sky.   distilling

Syne harvest hait,* quhen Ceres† that goddes   hot autumn
65 Hir barnis* benit* hes with abundance,   barns filled
And Bachus, god of wyne, renewit hes
The tume* pyipis* in Italie and France   empty casks
With wynis wicht* and liquour of plesance,*   strong pleasing
And *copia temporis*† to fill hir horne,*   cornucopia
70 That never wes full of quheit* nor uther corne.   wheat

Syne wynter wan,* quhen austerne* Eolus,†   gloomy severe
God of the wynd, with blastis boreall,*   northern
The grene garment of somer glorious
Hes all to-rent* and revin* in pecis small;   torn apart split
75 Than flouris fair faidit with froist man* fall,   must
And birdis blyith changeis thair noitis sweit
In styll murning,† neir slane* with snaw and sleit.   nearly slain

Thir dalis* deip with dubbis* drounit is,   valleys pools
Baith hill and holt* heillit* with frostis hair,*   woodland covered hoar
80 †And bewis bene are bethit, bair of blis,
Be wickit windis of the winter wair.*   ?worse
All wyld beistis than from the bentis bair*   bare fields
Drawis* for dreid unto thair dennis deip,   move
†Coucheand for cauld in coifis thame to keip.

---

59 [*Flora* Roman goddess of flowers and spring]
61 [*Phebus* the sun]
64 [*Ceres* Roman goddess of the fruits of the earth]
69 *copia temporis* the season's plenty
71 [*Eolus* Aeolus, god of the winds in classical myth]
77 *In styll murning* in silent mourning
80 And boughs fine are withered, stripped of delight
84 Lying down in caves to protect themselves against the cold

85	Syne cummis ver* quhen winter is away,	spring
	†The secretar of somer with his sell,	
	Quhen columbie* up keikis* throw the clay	columbine peeps
	Quhilk fleit† wes befoir with froistes fell.*	many
	The mavis* and the merle* beginnis to mell,*	thrush blackbird sing
90	The lark on loft,* with uther birdis smale*	on high small
	Than drawis furth fra derne,* over doun and daill.	hiding
	That samin* seasoun, in to ane soft morning,	same
	Rycht blyth* that bitter blastis wer ago,*	happy gone
	Unto the wod,* to se the flouris spring	wood
95	And heir the mavis sing and birdis mo,*	other
	I passit furth,* syne* lukit* to and fro	forth then looked
	To se the soill that wes richt sessonabill,†	
	Sappie,* and to resave* all seidis abill.	moist receive
	Moving thusgait,* grit* myrth I tuke in mynd	in this way great
100	Of lauboraris* to se the besines,*	labourers activity
	†Sum makand dyke, and sum the pleuch can wynd,	
	Sum sawand* seidis fast frome place to place,	sowing
	The harrowis hoppand* in the saweris trace.†	hopping
	It was grit joy to him that luifit* corne	loved
105	To se thame laubour, baith* at evin and morne.	both
	And as I baid* under ane bank full bene,*	paused comfortable
	In hart gritlie rejosit* of that sicht,	gladdened
	Unto ane hedge, under ane hawthorne grene,	
	Of small birdis thair come ane ferlie flicht†	
110	And doun belyif* can on the leifis licht†	at once
	On everilk* syde about me quhair I stude,	every
	Rycht mervellous, ane mekill* multitude.	great

---

86 [*secretar . . . sell* spring is seen as summer's secretary, authorised to use the latter's seal or imprint]
88 *fleit* put to flight
97 *richt sessonabill* very seasonable
101 Some making a wall, and some drove the plough
103 *saweris trace* sower's track
109 *ferlie flicht* marvellous flock
110 *can . . . licht* alighted

	Amang the quhilks* ane swallow loud couth cry,*	which cried
	On that hawthorne hie in the croip* sittand:	treetop
115	'O ye birdis on bewis* heir me by,	boughs
	Ye sall weill knaw and wyislie understand:	
	Quhair danger is or perrell appeirand,*	likely
	It is grit wisedome to provyde befoir*	in advance
	It to devoyd,* for dreid* it hurt yow moir.'	remove fear
120	'Schir swallow,' quod the lark agane* and leuch,*	in reply laughed
	'Quhat have ye sene that causis yow to dreid?'	
	'Se ye yone churll,'† quod scho, 'beyond yone pleuch,	
	Fast sawand hemp – lo, see! – and linget† seid?	
	Yone lint will grow in lytill tyme in deid,	
125	And thairof will yone churll his nettis mak,*	make
	Under the quhilk he thinkis us to tak.*	catch
	'Thairfoir I reid* we pas* quhen he is gone	advise go
	At evin,* and with our naillis scharp and small	evening
	Out of the eirth scraip we yone seid anone*	directly
130	And eit it up; for gif* it growis we sall*	if shall
	Have cause to weip heirefter ane* and all.	one
	†So we remeid thairfoir furthwith *instante*,	
	†*Nam levius lædit quicquid prævidimus ante.*	
	'For clerkis* sayis it is nocht sufficient	scholars
135	To considder that is befoir thyne ee;*	eye
	Bot prudence is ane inwart argument	
	That garris* ane man provyde befoir* and se	makes in advance
	Quhat gude, quhat evill is liklie for to be,	
	Of everilk thingis at the fynall end,*	very end
140	And swa fra perrell the better him defend.'	

---

122   *yone churll*   that peasant over there
123   [*hemp . . . linget*   hemp fibres were used in making ropes, while flax (*linget*: lint) fibres were used for linen yarn and cloth. At ll. 204–10 Henryson shows a detailed knowledge of the processes and vocabulary of linen yarn-making]
132   Therefore let us ensure that we remedy it straight away instantly
133   For what we provide against beforehand does us less harm

The lark, lauchand,* the swallow thus couth scorne,* *laughing mocked*
And said scho fischit lang befoir the net:
†"The barne is eith to busk that is unborne;
All growis nocht† that in the ground is set;
145 The nek to stoup* quhen it the straik* sall get *bend blow*
Is sone aneuch;* deith on the fayest† fall.' *enough*
Thus scornit thay the swallow ane and all.

Despysing thus hir helthsum* document,* *salutary teaching*
The foulis ferlie* tuke thair flicht anone. *suddenly*
150 Sum with ane bir† thay braidit* over the bent,* *passed field*
And sum agane ar to the grene wod* gone. *wood*
Upon the land† quhair I wes left allone,
I tuke my club and hamewart couth I carie,†
Swa ferliand* as I had sene ane farie. *marvelling*

155 Thus passit furth quhill* June, that jolie tyde,* *until time*
And seidis that wer sawin of beforne
Wer growin hie, that* hairis* mycht thame* hyde *so that hares themselves*
And als* the quailye* craikand* in the corne. *also corncrake croaking*
I movit furth, betwix midday and morne,
160 Unto the hedge under the hawthorne grene
Quhair I befoir the said birdis had sene.

And as I stude, be aventure and cace,†
The samin* birdis as I haif said yow air† *same*
I hoip* because it wes their hanting place,† *suppose*
165 Mair of succour† or yit mair solitair* – *isolated*
Thay lychtit doun;† and, quhen thay lychtit wair* *were*
The swallow swyth* put furth ane pietuous pyme,† *quickly*
Said: 'Wo is him can not bewar in tyme.

---

143 The child that is not yet born is easy to clothe
144 *All growis nocht* not everything grows
146 *fayest* those most fated to die
150 *bir* whirring noise
152 *Upon the land* on the ground
153 *couth I carie* I went
162 *be aventur and cace* by accident and chance
163 *said yow air* told you of before
164 *hanting place* customary haunt
165 *Mair of succour* more sheltered
166 *lychtit doun* came to land
167 *pietuous pyme* pitiable lament

'O, blind birdis, and full of negligence,
170 Unmyndfull of your awin prosperitie,
Lift up your sicht and tak gude advertence;* *heed*
Luke to the lint* that growis on yone le.* *flax meadow*
Yone is the thing I bad* forsuith* that we, *asked indeed*
Quhill it wes seid, suld rute furth of† the eird;
175 Now is it lint, now is it hie on breird.†

'Go yit quhill it is tender, young and small,
And pull it up; let it na mair* incres. *no greater*
My flesche growis,* my bodie quaikis all; *shudders*
Thinkand on it I may not sleip in peis.'
180 Thay cryit all and bad the swallow ceis* *cease*
And said: 'Yone lint heirefter will do gude,
For linget* is to lytill birdis fude.* *flax-seed food*

'We think, quhen that yone lint bollis* ar ryip,* *seed-pods ripe*
To mak us feist† and fill us of the seid,
185 Magré* yone churll, and on it sing and pyip.'* *despite pipe*
'Weill,' quod the swallow, 'freindes,* hardilie beid.† *friends*
Do as ye will, bot certane, sair* I dreid *sorely*
Heirefter ye sall find als sour as sweit,
Quhen ye ar speldit† on yone carlis speit.* *spit*

190 'The awner* of yone lint ane fouler is, *owner*
Richt cautelous* and full of subteltie. *cunning*
His pray full sendill tymis† will he mis
Bot gif* we birdis all the warrer† be. *unless*
Full mony* of our kin he hes gart de† *many*
195 And thocht it bot ane sport to spill thair blude;
†God keip me fra him, and the halie rude.'

---

174 *rute furth of* root out of
175 *hie on breird* sprouting high
184 *To mak us feist* to feast ourselves
186 *hardilie beid* so be it
189 *speldit* split open
192 *sendill tymis* seldom
193 *warrer* more alert
194 *gart de* put to death
196 May God and the holy rood protect me from him

	Their small birdis haveand* bot lytill thocht	having
	Of perrell that micht fall be aventure,*	by chance
	The counsell of the swallow set at nocht,	
200	Bot tuke thair flicht and furth togidder* fure;*	together went
	Sum to the wode, sum markit* to the mure.*	proceeded moor
	I tuke my staff, quhen this wes said and done,	
	And walkit hame,* for it drew neir the none.	home

	The lint ryipit,* the carll pullit the lyne,†	ripened
205	†Rippillit the bollis and in beitis set,	
	It steipit* in the burne* and dryit syne,*	soaked stream afterwards
	And with ane bittill* knokkit it and bet,*	mallet beat
	Syne swingillit* it weill and hekkillit* in the flet;†	scraped combed
	His wyfe it span and twynit* it in to threid,	twisted
210	Of quhilk the fowlar nettis maid in deid.	

	The wynter come,* the wickit wind can blaw,*	came blew
	The woddis grene were wallowit* with the weit;*	withered wet
	†Baith firth and fell with froistys were maid faw,	
	†Slonkis and slaik maid slidderie with the sleit;	
215	†The foulis fair for falt thay fell of feit;	
	On bewis* bair it wes na bute* to byde,*	boughs remedy stay
	Bot hyit* unto housis thame* to hyde.	hastened themselves

	Sum in the barn, sum in the stak of corne	
	Thair lugeing* tuke* and maid thair residence.	shelter took
220	†The fowlar saw and grit aithis hes sworne,	
	†Thay suld be tane trewlie for thair expence.	
	His nettis hes he set with diligence,	
	And in the snaw he schulit* hes ane plane*	dug open space
	And heillit* it all over with calf* agane.	covered chaff

---

204 *pullit the lyne* gathered the flax
205 combed the seed-pods and placed [the flax] in bundles
208 *in the flet* inside the house
213 Both wood and hill were dappled by the frosts
214 Hollows and valleys made slippery by the sleet
215 The fair birds could not stand for lack of food
220 The bird-catcher saw, and has sworn great oaths
221 [that] they should certainly be caught because of what they cost

225	Thir small birdis seand* the calf was glaid;*	seeing glad
	Trowand* it had bene corne, thay lychtit doun,†	believing
	Bot of the nettis na presume* thay had,	anticipation
	Nor of the fowlaris fals intentioun;	
	To scraip and seik thair meit* thay maid thame boun.†	food
230	The swallow on ane lytill branche neir by,	
	Dreiddand for gyle,† thus loud on thame couth cry:*	cried
	'In to that calf scraip quhill* your naillis bleid;	until
	Thar is na corne, ye laubour all in vane.	
	Trow ye yone churll for pietie* will yow feid?	pity
235	Na, na, he hes it heir layit* for ane trane.*	laid trap
	Remove, I reid,* or ellis ye will be slane.	advise
	His nettis he hes set full prively,*	secretly
	Reddie to draw; in tyme be war† for thy.'*	therefore
	Grit fule is he that puttis in dangeir	
240	His lyfe, his honour, for ane thing of nocht.*	valueless
	Grit fule is he that will not glaidlie heir	
	Counsall in tyme, quhill* it availl him nocht.	until
	Grit fule is he that hes na thing in thocht	
	Bot thing present, and efter* quhat may fall	afterwards
245	Nor of the end hes na memoriall.†	
	Thir* small birdis for hunger famischit* neir,	these famished
	Full besie scraipand for to seik thair fude,	
	The counsall of the swallow wald not heir,	
	Suppois* thair laubour did thame lytill gude.	although
250	Quhen scho* thair fulische* hartis understude,	she foolish
	Sa indurate,* up in ane tre scho flew.	obdurate
	With that* this churll over thame his nettis drew.	whereupon
	Allace, it wes grit hart sair† for to se	
	That bludie bowcheour* beit thay* birdis doun,	butcher those
255	And for till* heir, quhen thay wist weill to de,†	to

226 *lychtit doun* landed
229 *maid thame boun* set to work
231 *Dreiddand for gyle* fearful of a trick
238 *be war* be on the watch
245 *na memoriall* no recollection
253 *hart sair* grief at heart
255 *wist weill to de* fully understood they were going to die

	Thair cairfull* sang* and lamentatioun.	sad song
	Sum with ane staf he straik* to eirth on swoun,*	struck stunned
	Of sum the heid he straik, of sum he brak the crag;†	
	Sum half on lyfe* he stoppit* in his bag.	alive stuffed
260	And quhen the swallow saw that thay wer deid,	
	'Lo,' quod scho, 'thus it happinnis mony syis*	times
	On thame that will not tak counsall nor reid*	advice
	Of prudent men or clerkis* that ar wyis.	scholars
	This grit perrell I tauld thame mair than thryis;†	
265	Now ar thay deid, and wo is me† thairfoir!'	
	Scho tuke hir flicht, bot I hir saw no moir.	

MORALITAS

	Lo, worthie folk, Esope,† that nobill clerk,	
	Ane poet worthie to be lawreate,†	
	Quhen that he waikit* from mair autentik† werk,	was released
270	With uther ma,* this foirsaid fabill wrate*	besides wrote
	Quhilk at this tyme may weill be applicate*	applied
	To gude morall edificatioun,	
	Haifand* ane sentence* according to ressoun.*	possessing meaning reason

	†This carll and bond, of gentrice spoliate,	
275	Sawand* this calf* thir small birdis to sla,*	sowing chaff slay
	It is the feind* quhilk* fra the angelike state	devil which
	Exylit is as fals apostata,*	apostate
	Quhilk day and nycht weryis not† for to ga,*	go
	Sawand poysoun and mony wickit thocht	
280	In mannis saull quhilk Christ full deir hes bocht.	

---

258 *brak the crag* broke the neck
265 *wo is me* I am deeply grieved
267 [*Esope* Aesop, the Greek author to whom a series of animal fables are attributed, supposedly lived in the mid-sixth century BC. Latin Aesopic fables were widely used in schools in the middle ages]
268 *lawreate* crowned with laurel   [The title of laureate, with the ceremonial crowning with bay, was conferred by medieval universities on distinguished poets writing in Latin. John Skelton was so honoured by the universities of Oxford, Cambridge and Louvain]
269 *mair autentik* more authoritative
274 This peasant and bondman deprived of higher feeling
278 *weryis not* does not tire

And quhen the saull, as seid in to the eird,*   *earth*
Gevis consent unto delectatioun,*   *pleasure*
The wickit thocht beginnis for to breird*   *sprout*
In deidlie sin, quhilk is dampnatioun.
285   Ressoun is blindit with affectioun
And carnall lust growis* full grene and gay,   *grows*
Throw consuetude* hantit* from day to day.   *habit practised*

Proceding furth be use and consuetude,
The sin ryipis and schame is set on syde;
290   The feynd plettis* his nettis scharp and rude,*   *plaits rough*
And under plesance* previlie* dois hyde.   *pleasure secretly*
Syne on the feild he sawis calf full wyde*   *far*
Quhik is bot tume* and verray vanitie†   *empty*
Of fleschlie lust and vaine prosperitie.

295   Thir hungrie birdis wretchis we may call,
As scraipand* in this warldis vane plesance,†   *scraping*
Greddie to gadder gudis temporall†
Quhilk as* the calf ar tume without substance,   *which like*
Lytill of availl* and full of variance,*   *profit changeability*
300   Lyke to the mow* befoir the face of wind   *dust*
Quhiskis* away and makis wretchis blind.   *whisks*

This swallow quhilk eschaipit is* the snair,   *has escaped*
The halie preichour weill may signifie,
Exhortand folk to walk* and ay be wair*   *watch be alert*
305   Fra nettis of our wickit enemie
Quha sleipis not, bot ever is reddie,
Quhen wretchis in this warldis calf dois scraip,
To draw his net, that they may not eschaip.

Allace, quhat cair, quhat weiping is* and wo,   *there is*
310   Quhen saull and bodie departit ar in twane!*   *two*
The bodie to the wormis keitching* go,   *kitchen*

---

293   *verray vanitie*   true worthlessness
296   *vane plesance*   empty delight
297   *gudis temporall*   worldly goods

	The saull to fyre, to everlestand* pane.	everlasting
	Quhat helpis than this calf, thir gudis vane,†	
	Quhen thow art put in Luceferis† bag	
315	And brocht to hell, and hangit be the crag?*	neck
	Thir hid* nettis for to persave* and se,	hidden perceive
	This sarie* calf wyislie* to understand,	vile wisely
	Best is bewar in maist* prosperitie,	greatest
	For in this warld thair is na thing lestand.*	lasting
320	Is* na man wait* how lang his stait* will stand,	there is [who] knows prosperity
	His lyfe will lest, nor how that he sall end	
	Efter his deith, nor quhidder* he sall wend.	whither
	Pray we thairfoir quhill* we are in this lyfe	while
	For four thingis: the first, fra sin remufe;*	remove
325	The second is to seis* all weir* and stryfe;	cease war
	The thrid* is perfite* cheritie and lufe;*	third perfect love
	The feird* thing is, and maist for oure behufe,†	fourth
	That is, in blis with angellis to be fallow.*	fellow
	And thus endis the preiching of the swallow.	

---

313 *thir gudis vane* these trifling goods
314 *Luceferis* Lucifer's [the devil's]
327 *maist for oure behufe* of greatest benefit for us

William Caxton
1422–1491/2

William Caxton was England's first printer. A mercer by trade, he learned the new art of printing in Cologne and Bruges, where he lived as a member of the community of English merchants (and latterly as its leader) for around thirty years. In 1476 he returned to England and set up his press near Westminster Abbey. One of the first books he printed was Chaucer's *Canterbury Tales* (1477), and he later printed Sir Thomas Malory's *Le Morte Darthur* (1485). As well as promoting English authors – he also printed Gower and Lydgate – Caxton made his own translations from French into English of works which were fashionable in courtly circles in Burgundy, to which he had had access at Bruges through the patronage of the Princess Margaret, English wife of the duke of Burgundy. One of the works he translated is Ramon Llull's *The Book of the Order of Chivalry*, a handbook of knightly conduct, Caxton's epilogue to which is given below. Many of Caxton's publications contain long prologues and epilogues written by the printer himself, which are, like modern publisher's 'blurbs', designed to increase the book's sales. Thus his dedication of *The Book of the Order of Chivalry* to Richard III (who, despite Caxton's prayers, was killed at Bosworth Field only a year or so later) and his assurance that the book is not for common people but for 'noble gentylmen', is an appeal to his readers' snobbery at a time of social fluidity. When he advises them to read *Perceforest* and Froissart's *Chronicles*, neither of which was available in English, he is assuming they can read French. But if that is the case, why translate *The Book of the Order of Chivalry* for them? The implication is, perhaps, that by mentioning these and other names Caxton hopes to associate his book with the glamorous, upper-class world of European chivalry and, contrary to his avowed intentions, make that chivalry accessible to a wider readership.

The text is from *The Prologues and Epilogues of William Caxton*, ed. W. J. B. Crotch, EETS, OS 176 (1929).

From THE BOOK OF THE ORDER OF CHIVALRY
Epilogue

Here endeth *The Book of th'Ordre of Chyvalry*, whiche book is translated oute of Frensshe into Englysshe at a requeste of a gentyl† and noble esquyer† by me, William Caxton, dwellynge in Westmynstre besyde London in the most best wyse† that God hath suffred† me, and
5 accordynge to the copye which the sayd squyer delyverd to me. Whiche book is not requysyte† to every comyn man to have, but to noble gentylmen that by their vertu entende to come and entre into the noble ordre of chyvalry, the whiche in these late dayes hath ben used† accordyng to this booke heretofore† wreton, but forgeton, and th'exersy-
10 tees† of chyvalry not used, honoured ne exercysed† as hit hath ben in ancyent tyme, at whiche tyme the noble actes of the knyghtes of Englond that used chyvalry were renomed† thurgh the unyversal world. As for to speke tofore† th'yncarnacion of Jhesu Cryste: where were there ever ony lyke to Brenius and Belynus,† that from the grete Brytayne,
15 now called Englond, unto Rome and ferre beyonde conquered many royammes† and londes, whos noble actes remayne in th'old hystoryes of the Romayns? And syth† the Incarnation of Oure Lord, byhold that noble kyng of Brytayne, kyng Arthur, with al the noble knyghtes of the Round Table, whos noble actes and noble chyvalry of his knyghtes
20 occupye soo many large volumes, that is a world or as thyng incredyble to byleve. O, ye knyghtes of Englond, where is the custome and usage of noble chyvalry that was used in tho† dayes? What do ye now, but go to the baynes† and playe atte† dyse? And some, not wel advysed, use not honest† and good rule, ageyn† alle ordre of knyghthode. Leve

gentyl well-bred
esquyer esquire, one rank below that of knight
wyse manner
suffred allowed
requysyte needful
used practised
heretofore previously
exersytees activities
exercysed performed
renomed renowned
tofore before
[*Brenius and Belynus* mythical figures in British pseudo-history, believed to have conquered Rome]
royammes kingdoms
syth since
tho those
baynes baths
atte at the
honest honourable
ageyn against

25 this. Leve it, and rede the noble volumes of Saynt Graal,† of Lancelot,†
of Galaad, of Trystram, of Perseforest, of Percyval, of Gawayn† and
many mo. Ther shall ye see manhode, curtosye and gentylnesse!† And
loke in latter dayes of the noble actes syth the Conquest, as in Kyng
Rychard dayes Cuer de Lyon,† Edward the Fyrste, and the Thyrd, and
30 his noble sons, Syre Robert Knolles,† Syr Johan Hawkwode,† Syr Johan
Chaundos,† and Syre Gaultier Mauny.† Rede Froissart.† And also behold
that vyctoryous and noble kynge, Harry the Fyfthe,† and the captayns
under hym: his noble bretheren,† th'erle of Salysbury, Montagu,† and
many other whoos names shyne gloryously by their vertuous noblesse
35 and actes that they did in th'honour of th'ordre of chyvalry. Allas, what
doo ye, but slepe and take ease, and ar al disordred fro† chyvalry? I
wold demaunde a question – yf I shold not displease – how many
knyghtes ben ther now in Englond that have th'use and th'exercyse† of
a knyghte, that is to wete,† that he knoweth his hors and his hors hym?
40 That is to say, he beynge redy at a poynt† to have al thyng† that longeth†
to a knyght: an hors that is accordyng† and broken after his hand;† his
armures and harnoys† mete† and syttyng,† and so forth, et cetera. I
suppose and† a due serche shold be made ther shold be many founden
that lacke,† the more pyté is. I wold it pleasyd oure soverayne lord that

---

[*Saynt Graal*   the Holy Grail, the object of a quest undertaken by Arthur's knights]
[*Lancelot . . . Gawayn*   heroes of widely-read romances current in English and French (though there is no English version of *Perceforest*)]
gentylnesse   nobility
[*Kyng Rychard dayes Cuer de Lyon*   the days of King Richard the Lionheart (Richard I, 1189–99)]
[*Syre Robert Knolles* and *Syr Johan Chaundos* were successful captains who fought the French in the 1350s and 1360s
Syr Johan Hawkwode   an English mercenary captain of the late fourteenth century]
[*Syre Gaultier Mauny*   a Hainault knight who fought the French for Edward III in the 1340s]
[*Froissart*   all these knights figure in the chivalric *Chronicles* of the Frenchman Jean Froissart (?1325–*c.* 1400)]
[*Harry the Fyfthe*   King Henry V of England (1413–22), victor of the battle of Agincourt]
[*his noble bretheren*   the dukes of Clarence (d.1421), Bedford (d.1435) and Gloucester (d.1447)]
[*Salysbury, Montagu*   Richard Neville, earl of Salisbury (d.1460) and his father-in-law Thomas Montague, Henry V's lieutenant]
disordred fro   excluded from the order of
th'use and th'exercyse   the experience and the training
that is to wete   namely
at a poynt   in one place
al thyng   everything
longeth   belongs
accordyng   suitable
broken after his hand   schooled to his authority
harnoys   harness
mete   appropriate
syttyng   fitting
and   if
lacke   are wanting

THE BOOK OF THE ORDER OF CHIVALRY

45 twyes or thryes in a yere – or at the lest ones – he wold do crye justes of pees,† to th'ende that every knyght shold have hors and harneys, and also the use and craft of a knyght, and also to tornoye† one ageynste one, or two ageynst two, and the best to have a prys, a dyamond or jewel, suche as shold please the prynce. This shold cause gentylmen to
50 resorte to th'auncyent customes of chyvalry, to grete fame and renomee,† and also to be alwey redy to serve theyr prynce whan he shalle calle them or have nede. Thanne late† every man that is come of noble blood and entendeth to come to the noble ordre of chyvalry rede this lytyl book, and doo therafter in kepyng the lore and commaundements therin
55 comprysed. And thenne I doubte not he shall atteyne to th'ordre of chyvalry, et cetera. And thus thys lytyl book I presente to my redoubted naturel and most dradde† soverayne lord, Kyng Rychard, kyng of Englond and of Fraunce,† to th'ende that he commaunde this book to be had and redde unto other yong lordes, knyghtes and gentylmen
60 within this royame, that the noble ordre of chyvalry be herafter better used and honoured than it hath ben in late dayes passed. And herin he shall do a noble and vertuouse dede. And I shalle pray almyghty God for his long lyf and prosperous welfare, and that he may have vyctory of all his enemyes, and after this short and transitory lyf to have
65 everlastyng lyf in heven, where as is joye and blysse, world without ende.
Amen.

---

do crye justes of pees   order jousts of peace [with bated weapons] to be announced
tornoye   joust
renomee   renown
late   let
dradde   feared
[*Kyng Richard . . . of Fraunce*   Richard III (1483–5). Despite the loss of all their former French territories apart from Calais, the English still claimed the throne of France]

Paston Letters
15th century

Several collections of family letters survive from the late middle ages, of which the largest is the correspondence of the Pastons of Norfolk written over three generations in the fifteenth century. The Paston letters deal with private as well as family and business matters, and provide an incomparable record of the way in which people talked and felt in one part of England at the end of the middle ages. The letters that follow were written to members of the third generation of Pastons, children of the formidable widow Margaret and her husband John I who died in 1466.

Richard Calle to Margery Paston

Richard Calle was a Suffolk man who was head bailiff to the Paston family. In the late 1460s he and Margery Paston, sister of Sir John Paston II who was then head of the family, fell in love, to the chagrin of Margery's mother, Margaret, and her brothers who had hoped for a much more advantageous marriage for her. Nevertheless the couple revealed that they were betrothed, and the church regarded a solemn plighting of troth – even without witnesses – as a legal marriage. Margery was questioned by the bishop of Norwich – as was Richard Calle – but despite her family's threats would not forswear her promise to Calle. In the end her mother and brothers had to acknowledge that the couple were married, but Margery was forbidden her mother's house thereafter and cut out of her will (though the Calle children were remembered). Richard Calle was too valuable a servant to dismiss and he remained in the Pastons' employ for several years. His personal integrity is manifest in this letter, which he wrote to Margery at a time in 1469 when the lovers had been forcibly separated and Margery seemed to be wavering in the face of her family's opposition. He urges her to reveal their secret betrothal, and bring matters to a head. Possibly it was the terms in which this letter is written that gave her the courage to comply.

Richard Calle writes to Margery Paston

Myn owne lady and mastres,* and befor God very trewe — mistress
wyff, I wyth herte full sorowefull recomaunde me† unto
you as he that can not be mery nor nought schal be tyll
it be otherwice wyth us thenne* it is yet; for thys lyff — than
5 that we lede nough* is nowther* plesur† to Godde — now neither
nor to the worlde, concederyng the gret bonde of
matrymonye that is made betwix* us, and also the greete — between
love that hath be,* and as I truste yet is, betwix us, and — has been
as on my parte never gretter. Wherfor I beseche Almyghty
10 Godde comfort us as sone* as it plesyth hym, for we — quickly
that ought of very ryght† to be moost together ar moost
asondre;* me semyth† it is a thousand yere agoo son* — apart since
that I speke wyth you. I had lever† thenne all the goode* — money
in the worlde I myght be wyth you. Alas, alas, goode
15 lady, full litell remembre they what they do that kepe
us thus asonder; four tymes in the yere ar they acursid
that lette* matrymonye.† It causith many men to deme — prevent
in hem they have large consyence in other maters as
wele as herin.† But what, lady, suffre as ye have do† and
20 make you as mery as ye can, for iwys,* lady, at the — certainly
longe wey† Godde woll of hys ryghtwysnes* helpe hys — righteousness
servauntys that meane truly and wolde leve* accordyng — live
to hes lawys, &c.†

I undrestonde, lady, ye have hadde as moche sorwe* — sorrow
25 for me as any gentelwoman hath hadde in the worlde;
as wolde Godd† all that sorwe that ye have hadde had
rested upon me so that ye hadde be discharged† of it,
for iwis, lady, it is to me a deethe to her* that ye be — hear
entreted otherwice thenne† ye ought to be. This is a

---

recomaunde me commend myself
plesur pleasing
of very ryght rightfully
me semyth it seems to me
had lever would rather
[*four tymes in the yere . . . matrymonye* a list of offences entailing excommunication was read out in churches at Christmas, Easter, Whitsun and All Saints' Day; among these was the prevention of lawful matrimony]
It causeth . . . as wele as herin it makes many people believe that they are unscrupulous in other matters as well as this one
what, lady, suffre as ye have do however, lady, put up with it as you have done
at the longe wey in the long run
&c. et cetera (and so on)
as wolde Godde I would to God
be discharged been relieved
be entreted otherwice thenne are treated differently from [the way in which]

30 peyneful lyfe that we lede; I con not leve thus wythoute
it be† a gret displesure to Godde.

Also like you† to wete* that I had sent you a letter   know
be* my ladde* from London, and he tolde me he myght   by servant
not speeke wyth you, ther was made so gret awayte
35 upon hym and upon you boothe.† He tolde me John
Threscher come* to hym in your name and seide that   came
ye sent hym to my ladde for a letter or a token weche*   which
I schulde have sent you; but he truste* hym not, he   trusted
wold not delyver hym noon.† After that he brought hym
40 a rynge, seyng that ye sent it hym, comaundyng hym
that he schulde delyver the letter or token to hym, weche
I conceyve sethen be my ladde it was not be your
sendyng, it was be my mastres and Ser Jamys avys.†
Alas, what meane they? I suppose they deeme* we be   think
45 not ensuryd together;† and if they so doo I mervell, for
thenne they are not wele aviced,* remembryng the   advised
pleynes that I breke to my mastres at the begynnyng,
and I suppose be you bothe, and ye dede as ye ought to
do of very ryght.† And if ye have do* the contraré, as I   done
50 have be enformed ye have do, ye dede nouther con-
cyensly† nor to the plesure of Godde, wythoute* ye dede   unless
it for feere and for the tyme to pleace suche as were at
that tyme aboute you; and if ye so dede it for this cauce
it was a resonable cauce, concederyng the grete and
55 importable* callyng upon† that ye hadde, and many an   unbearable
ontrewe* tale was made to you of me, weche God   untrue
knowyth I was never gylty of.

My ladde tolde me that my mastres your modre*   mother
axyd* hym if he hadde brought any letter to you, and   asked
60 many other thyngys sche bare hym an hande,† and

I con not leve thus wythoute it be I do not know how to live in this way without its being
like you may it please you
ther was made ... upon you boothe so close a watch was kept on both him and you
delyver hym noon hand over anything to him
weche I conceyve ... Ser Jamys avys which I assume – since according to my boy it was not sent from you – was at the instigation of my mistress and Father James
[*my mastres and Ser Jamys* Margery's mother, Margaret Paston, and Father James Gloys, the family chaplain]
ensuryd together betrothed to each other
the pleynes that I breke ... of very ryght the plain truth [about their relationship] that I revealed to my mistress at the beginning, and I believe [it was revealed] by you as well, if you did as you ought rightly to do
concyensly in good conscience
callyng upon accusations
bare hym an hande accused him of

amonge all other at the last sche seide to hym that I
wolde not make her prevy† to the begynnyng but sche
supposyd I wolde at the endyng. And as to that, God
knowyth sche knewe it furst of me* and non other.† I   from me
65 wott not what her mastreschip meneth,† for be my
trowthe† ther is no gentylwoman on lyve* that my herte   alive
tendreth† more then it dothe her, nor is lother† to
displese, savyng only your person, weche of very ryght
I ought to tender and love beste, for I am bounde therto
70 be* the lawe of Godde, and so wol do whyle that I leve,   by
what som ever falle of it.†

    I supose and ye telle hem sadly† the trouthe they wole
not dampne ther soules for us. Though I telle hem the
trouthe they woll not beleve me as weele* as they woll   well
75 do you. And therfor, goode lady, at the reverence of†
Godde be pleyne* to hem and telle the trouthe, and if   plain, open
they woll in no wice* agree thereto, betwix God, the   way
Deelfe,* and them be it; and that perell† that we schulde   devil
be in I beseche Godde it may lye upon them and not
80 upon us. I am hevy* and sory to remembre ther   depressed
disposicion. God sende them grace to gyde all thyngys
weele, as wele I wolde they dede.† Godde be ther gide
and sende them peas and reste, &c.

    I mervell moche that they schulde take this mater so
85 heedely* as I undrestonde they doo, remembryng it is   rashly
in suche case* as it can not be remedyed, and my desert,†   situation
upon every behalfe† it is for to be thought ther schulde
be non* obstacle ayenst* it. And also, the worchipful†   no   against
that is in them is not in your mariage, it is in ther owne
90 mariage†, weche* I beseche Godde sende hem suche as   which

---

make her prevy   confide in her
non other   no-one else
I wott not . . . meneth   I do not know what her ladyship has in mind
be my trowthe   upon my oath
tendreth   has regard for
lother   more unwilling
what som ever falle of it   whatsoever comes of it
I supose . . . sadly   I believe that if you tell them firmly
at the reverence of   out of reverence for
perell   peril (to the soul)
as wele I wolde they dede   as well as I wish they did
and my desert   and [remembering] what I deserve
upon every behalfe   in every respect
worchipful   honour
[*the worchipful that is . . . ther owne mariage*   Margery's brothers were all unmarried at this date; for John Paston III's businesslike approach to marriage as a means of advancing his own and his family's interests, see the following letters]

may be to ther worschip and plesur to Godde and to
ther hertys eace, for ell* were it gret pety.   else

    Mastres, I am aferde* to write to you, for I undrestond   afraid
ye have shewyd my letters that I have sent you befor
95 this tyme; but I prey you lete no creatur se this letter.
As sone as ye have redde it lete it be brent,† for I wolde
no man schulde se it in no wice.† Ye had no wrytyng
from me this two yere, nor I wolle not sende you no
mor; therfor I remytte* all this matre to your wysdom.   hand over
100 Almyghty Jesu precerve, kepe, and geve you your
hertys desire, weche I wotte* weele schulde be to Goodys   know
plesur, &c. This letter was wreten wyth as greete peyne
as ever wrote I thynge* in my lyfe, for in goode feyth I   anything
have be ryght seke* and yet am not veryly weele at eace,   sick
105 God amend it, &c.

Margery Brews to John Paston III

The following two letters were written around St Valentine's day, 14 February 1477, by Margery Brews to John Paston III whom she hoped to marry. (John was the brother of Margery Paston [see previous letter] and of Sir John, the head of the family.) The marriage negotiations had run into difficulties over the size of the settlement offered by Margery's father, Sir Thomas Brews. John Paston hoped for a larger amount and had the support of Margery's mother, but she was unable to convince her husband (who had other marriageable daughters to provide for as well). Margery's two letters were written during this uncertain period. She could not write herself, but dictated them to Sir Thomas's secretary; the clumsy verses in her first letter show, however, that although she was not literate she was not entirely cut off from the world of literature. The story has a happy outcome; the couple were married later in the year and had at least two sons.

---

lete it be brent   have it burnt
in no wice   at all

Margery Brews writes to John Paston III

1477, February

Ryght reverent and wurschypfull* and my ryght wele- *honourable*
beloved Voluntyne, I recommande me† unto yowe full
hertely,* desyring to here* of yowr welefare, whech I *warmly   hear*
beseche Almyghty God long for to preserve unto hys
5 plesure and yowr hertys desyre. And yf it please yowe
to here of my welefare, I am not in good heele* of body *health*
ner* of herte, nor schall be tyll I here from yowe; *nor*

    For ther wottys* no creature what peyn that I endure, *knows*
    And for to be deede† I dare it not dyscure.* *reveal*

10 And my lady my moder hath labored* the mater† to my *canvassed*
fadure full delygently, but sche can no more gete then
ye knowe of, for the whech† God knowyth I am full
sory.
    But yf that ye loffe* me, as I tryste verely† that ye do, *love*
15 ye will not leffe* me therfor; for if that ye hade not *forsake*
halfe the lyvelode* that ye hafe, for to do the grettyst *income*
labure† that any woman on lyve* mygth, I wold not *living*
forsake yowe.

    And yf ye commande me to kepe me true wherever I
20   go
    Iwyse* I will do all my mygth yowe to love and never *indeed*
       no mo.†
    And yf my freendys say that I do amys,* thei schal *amiss, wrong*
       not me let* so for to do, *prevent*
25   Myn herte me byddys† ever more to love yowe
    Truly over* all erthely thing. *above*
    And yf thei be never so wroth,† I tryst it schall be
       bettur in tyme commyng.

---

recommande me commend myself
for to be deede to prevent my dying
the mater the question of the marriage settlement
for the whech for which
tryste verely truly believe
do the grettyst labure make the greatest effort
no mo anyone else
me byddys commands me
yf thei be never so wroth however angry they be

No more to yowe at this tyme, but the Holy Trinité
have yowe in kepyng. And I beseech yowe that this bill*   letter
be not seyn of* non erthely creature safe* only yourselfe,   seen by   save
&c. And thys lettur was indyte* at Topcroft† wyth full   composed
hevy herte, &c.
                         Be* your own M. B.   by

                       1477, February

Ryght wurschypffull and welebelovyd Volentyne, in my
moste umble* wyse I recommande me unto yowe, &c.   humble
And hertely I thanke yowe for the letture whech that ye
sende* me be* John Bekurton, wherby I undyrstonde   sent by
and knowe that ye be purposyd* to com to Topcroft in   intend
schorte tyme, and wythowte any erand or mater but
only to hafe a conclusyon of† the mater betwyx* my   between
fadur and yowe. I wolde be most glad of any creature
on lyve* so that† the mater myght growe to effect.† And   living
ther as* ye say, and* ye com and fynde the mater no   where if
more toward then† ye dyd afortyme* ye wold no more   previously
put my fadur and my lady my moder to no cost ner
besenesse for that cause a good wyle afture, weche†
causyth myn herte to be full hevy;* and yf that ye com   sad
and the mater take to non effecte,† then schuld I be
meche* more sory and full of hevynesse.*   much sadness
    And as for myselfe, I hafe don and undyrstond* in   understood
the mater that* I can or may, as Good knowyth. And I   what
lete yowe pleynly undyrstond that my fader wyll no
more money parte wythall in that behalfe† but an
hundred pounds and fifti marke, whech is ryght far fro*   from
the acomplyshment of yowr desyre. Wherfor, yf that ye
cowde be content wyth that good* and my por persone,   money
I wold be the meryest mayden on grounde.† And yf ye
thynke not yowrselfe so satysfyed, or that ye myght hafe

Topcroft   south of Norwich; the home of Sir Thomas Brews and his family
hafe a conclusyon of   bring to an end
so that   provided that
growe to effect   reach a conclusion
more toward then   further forward than
ye wold no more ... a good wyle afture, weche   you would not want to put my father and my
lady my mother to any expense or trouble for that reason for a good while afterwards, which
take to non effecte   does not come to a conclusion
in that behalfe   on that account
on grounde   on earth

mech more good, as I hafe undrystonde be yowe afor,†
good, trewe, and lovyng Volentyne, that ye take no such
labure uppon yowe as to com more for that mater;† but
let it passe, and never more to be spokyn of, as I may
30 be yowr trewe lover and bedewoman† duryng my lyfe.
　　No more unto yowe at thys tyme, but Almyghty Jesus
preserve yowe bothe body and sowle, &c.
　　　　　　　　　Be your Voluntyne MERGERY BREWS

---

be yowe afor　from you previously (John has possibly suggested that if he looked elsewhere for a bride he could get a larger dowry)
that ye take no such ... for that mater　do not go to all the trouble of coming again about that matter
bedewoman　well-wisher (literally, woman who prays for one)

William Dunbar
?1460–?1513

The Scottish poet William Dunbar was possibly born around 1460. He is known to have been a graduate, and a man of that name took a bachelor's degree from St Andrews in 1477 and a master's in 1479. Dunbar received a pension from King James IV of Scotland (1488–1513) between 1500 and 1513, after which his name is not recorded and he may have died then or soon after. What his role at court was is not clear, though by 1504 he had become a priest and is later described as a chaplain. In a number of poems – including 'Lucina Shining in Silence of the Night' and 'Into these Dark and Drublie Days' – he refers to his financial insecurity, and although we should be wary of deducing a biography from the verse, nevertheless poems such as these do express the uncertain predicament of those dependent on royal benevolence.

Dunbar wrote a large number of poems, many of them to do with court life, and with specific people and occasions. He is a strikingly versatile writer: his longest works, *The Golden Targe* and *The Treatise of the Two Married Women and the Widow*, are, respectively, a courtly allegory in elegant rhyme royal and a bawdy poem in unrhymed alliterative long lines in which three women discuss the sexual performances of their husbands. In some poems he exploits a colloquial vein whose meanings can now only be guessed at; in others he writes in a high style of glittering virtuosity; on many occasions he moves from one kind of language to another within the same poem. He uses many different forms and metres, and in this is much more experimental than Robert Henryson, the leading Scottish poet of the previous generation, though Dunbar does not have Henryson's gift for narrative. Something of his range of subject matter and styles – public and private, comic and serious, courtly and moral, sacred and secular – can be seen in the selection of poems below.

I THAT IN HEILL WAS AND GLADNESS

(Text from Rouen print, c. ?1508)

I that in heill* wes and gladnes	health
Am trublit now with greit seiknes	
And feblit* with infermite:	weakened
†Timor mortis conturbat me.	

5 Our plesance* heir is all vane glory;   *enjoyment*
    This fals world is but transitory.
    The flesch is brukle,* the fend* is sle:*   *frail devil cunning*
    Timor mortis conturbat me.

    The stait of man dois change and vary;
10 Now sound, now seik,* now blith, now sary,*   *sick sorry*
    Now dansand* mery, now like* to dee:*   *dancing likely die*
    Timor mortis conturbat me.

    No stait in erd* heir standis sickir.*   *earth sure*
    As with the wynd wavis the wickir*   *willow*
15 Wavis this warldis vanite:
    Timor mortis conturbat me.

    Onto the ded* gois all estatis: *death*
    Princis, prelotis and potestatis,*   *potentates*
    Baith rich and pur, of al degre:
20 Timor mortis conturbat me.

    He takis the knythis* in to* feild,   *knights in*
    Anarmyt* under helme and scheild.   *armed*
    Victour he is at all mellé:*   *combat*
    Timor mortis conturbat me.

25 That strang unmercifull tyrand
    Takis, on the moderis breist sowkand,*   *sucking*
    The bab,* full of benignite: *baby*
    Timor mortis conturbat me.

---

4 The fear of death distresses me [from one of the responses in the Office of the Dead]

He takis the campion* in the stour,*   champion   battle
30 The capitane closit in the tour,
The lady in bour full of bewte:
Timor mortis conturbat me.

He sparis no lord for his piscence,*   power
Na clerk* for his intelligence;   scholar
35 His awfull strak* may no man fle: stroke
Timor mortis conturbat me.

Art-magicianis* and astrologgis,*   magicians   astrologers
Rethoris,* logicianis and theologgis* –   rhetoricians   theologians
†Thame helpis no conclusionis sle:
40 *Timor mortis conturbat me.*

In medicyne the most* practicianis,   greatest
Lechis,* surrigianis* and phisicianis,   doctors   surgeons
Thame self fra ded may not supple:*   deliver
Timor mortis conturbat me.

45 I se that makaris* amang the laif*   poets   rest
Playis heir ther pageant, syne* gois to graif.   then
Sparit is nought ther faculte:*   profession
Timor mortis conturbat me.

He has done petuously* devour   pitiably
50 The noble Chaucer,† of makaris flour,
The monk of Bery† and Gower,† all thre:
Timor mortis conturbat me.

The gud syr Hew of Eglintoun,†
And eik* Heryot† and Wyntoun†   also
55 He has tane* out of this cuntré: taken
Timor mortis conturbat me.

---

39 No subtle conclusions come to their aid
50 [*Chaucer* Geoffrey Chaucer (*c*. 1343–1400)]
51 [*The monk of Bery* John Lydgate (1370–1449) of Bury St Edmunds   *Gower* John Gower (*c*. 1330–1408)]
53 [*syr Hew of Eglintoun* ?Sir Hugh Eglinton of that Ilk (died 1377); no surviving works]
54 [*Heryot* unknown   *Wyntoun* Andrew Wyntoun, author of the *Oryginale Chronykil of Scotland* (*c*. 1420)]

>   That scorpion fell* has done infek†   cruel
>   Maister Johne Clerk† and James Afflek†
>   Fro balat-making† and trigide:*   tragedy
> 60 Timor mortis conturbat me.
>
>   Holland† and Barbour† he has berevit.*   snatched away
>   Allace, that he nought with us levit*   left
>   †Schir Mungo Lokert of the Le:
>   Timor mortis conturbat me.
>
> 65 Clerk of Tranent† eik he has tane
>   That maid the anteris* of Gawane;†   adventures
>   Schir Gilbert Hay† endit has he:
>   Timor mortis conturbat me.
>
>   He has Blind Hary† and Sandy Traill†
> 70 Slaine with his schour of mortall haill,
>   Quhilk* Patrik Johnestoun† myght nought fle: which
>   Timor mortis conturbat me.
>
>   †He hes reft Merseir his endite,
>   That did in luf so lifly* write,   freshly
> 75 So schort, so quyk, of sentence hie:†
>   Timor mortis conturbat me.

---

57 *done infek* poisoned
58 [*Maister Johne Clerk* possibly author of poems in the Bannatyne MS attributed to 'Clerk'. 'Maister' here and at ll. 82 and 89 denotes a university graduate   *James Afflek* unknown]
59 *balat-making* composing poetry
61 [*Holland* Richard Holland, author of *The Buke of the Howlat* (?1448)   *Barbour* John Barbour (c. 1320–1395), author of *The Bruce*]
63 [*Schir Mungo Lokert of the Le* Lockhart of the Lea d.1489; no surviving works]
65 [*Clerk of Tranent* unknown]
66 [*anteris of Gawane* Sir Gawain, nephew of King Arthur, is the hero of several poems. This one is unidentified]
67 [*Schir Gilbert Hay* author of *The Buik of Alexander the Conquerour* (?1460) and translator of French chivalric prose writings]
69 [*Blind Hary* author of *The Actis and Deidis of . . . Schir William Wallace* (c. 1475)   *Sandy Traill* unknown]
71 [*Patrik Johnestoun* recorded as a producer of court entertainments in the 1470s and 1480s]
73 He has taken Merseir's writing away   [*Merseir* possibly author of poems in the Bannatyne MS attributed to 'Mersar']
75 *sentence hie* lofty matter

He has tane Roull of Aberdene†
And gentill* Roull of Corstorphin;†   noble
Two bettir fallowis did no man se:
80 Timor mortis conturbat me.

In Dunfermlyne† he has done roune*   whispered
With Maister Robert Henrisoun.†
Schir Johne the Ros† enbrast* has he: embraced
Timor mortis conturbat me.

85 And he has now tane, last of aw,*   all
Gud gentill Stobo† and Quintyne Schaw,†
Of quham all wichtis* has pete:*   everyone pity
Timor mortis conturbat me.

Gud Maister Walter Kennedy†
90 †In poynt of dede lyis veraly;
Gret reuth* it wer that so suld be: pity
Timor mortis conturbat me.

Sen* he has all my brether tane,   since
He will naught lat me lif alane.†
95 On forse* I man his nixt pray be: inevitably
Timor mortis conturbat me.

Sen for the deid remeid* is none,   remedy
Best is that we for dede dispone,*   prepare for
†Eftir our dede that lif may we:
100 Timor mortis conturbat me.

---

77 [*Roull of Aberdene* unknown]
78 [*Roull of Corstorphine* unknown. One of these may be the author of *The Cursing of Sir Johine Rowlis* in the Bannatyne MS]
81 [*Dunfermlyne* Dunfermline, in Fife, where Henryson is known to have lived]
82 [*Maister Robert Henrisoun* Robert Henryson (fl. 1450–c. 1505)]
83 [*Schir Johne the Ros* possibly Sir John the Ross of Mountgrenan (d.1494) or Sir John Ross of Halkhead (dead before 1502); neither is known as a poet and no works survive]
86 [*Stobo* familiar name of John Reid, secretary to James IV (d.1505). No surviving works. Since Stobo is apparently only recently dead, 'I that in Heill was' is generally dated 1505–6   *Quintyne Schaw* author of a poem in the Maitland Folio MS; alive in 1504]
89 [*Maister Walter Kennedy* (?1460–1508), author of *The Passioun of Christ* and other poems in the Asloan, Bannatyne and Maitland Folio MSS; Dunbar's opponent in *The Flyting of Dunbar and Kennedy*]
90 Truly lies at the point of death
94 *me lif alane* only me live
99 So that we may live after our death

DONE IS A BATTLE ON THE DRAGON BLACK

(Text from National Library of Scotland, Advocates' MS 1.1.6 [Bannatyne MS])

Done is a battell on the dragon† blak;
Our campioun* Chryst confoundit hes† his force;*   champion   power
The yettis* of hell ar brokin with a crak;   gates
†The signe triumphall rasit is of the croce.
5   The divillis trymmillis* with hiddous voce;*   tremble   voice
†The saulis ar borrowit* and to the bliss can go;   redeemed
Chryst with his blud our ransonis dois indoce:†
†<i>Surrexit Dominus de sepulchro.</i></p>

Dungin* is the deidly dragon Lucifer,   beaten
10   The crewall serpent with the mortall stang,*   sting
The auld kene tegir* with the teith on char*   tiger   bared
Quhilk in a wait† hes lyne* for us so lang,*   lain   long
Thinking to grip us in his clows strang.†
The mercifull lord wald nocht† that it wer so;
15   He maid him for to felye of† that fang:*   prey
Surrexit Dominus de sepulchro.

---

1   [*the dragon*   the devil, Lucifer (l. 9), presented as a dragon guarding a treasure (ll. 1 and 39), a serpent (l. 10), a tiger (l. 11), and a jailer (l. 34), against whom Jesus has fought on behalf of mankind]
2   *confoundit hes*   has confounded
4   The victorious symbol of the cross is raised
6   [Alludes, as does the whole stanza, to Christ's 'harrowing of hell' in the period between the crucifixion and the resurrection when, according to medieval tradition, he descended into hell and released the souls of the righteous who had died before his coming. See *Piers Plowman*, Passus 18 for another treatment of this theme]
7   *ransonis dois indoce*   endorses our ransoms
8   The Lord has risen from the tomb   [From the mass for Easter Day]
12   *in a wait*   in ambush
13   *clows strang*   strong claws
14   *wald nocht*   did not wish
15   *felye of*   fail to achieve

	He, for our saik that sufferit* to be slane	allowed [himself]
	And lyk a lamb† in sacrifice wes dicht,*	was offered
	Is lyk a lyone rissin* up agane	risen
20	†And as gyane raxit him on hicht;	
	Sprungin* is Aurora† radius* and bricht;	risen radiant
	On loft* is gone the glorius Appollo,†	on high
	The blisfull day departit* fro the nycht:	[is] separated
	Surrexit Dominus de sepulchro.	
25	The grit* victour agane is rissin on hicht	great
	That for our querrell to the deth wes woundit;	
	The sone* that wox* all paill† now schynis bricht,	sun grew
	And dirknes clerit,† our fayth is now refoundit.*	re-established
	The knell of mercy fra the hevin is soundit;	
30	The Cristin* ar deliverit of* thair wo;	Christians from
	The Jowis* and their errour ar confoundit:	Jews
	Surrexit Dominus de sepulchro.	
	The fo is chasit, the battell is done ceis;*	finished
	†The presone brokin, the jevellouris fleit and flemit;	
35	The weir* is gon, confermit is the peis,*	war peace
	The fetteris lowsit* and the dungeoun temit;*	undone emptied
	The ransoun maid, the presoneris redemit,*	redeemed
	The feild is win,* ourcumin* is the fo,	won overcome
	†Dispulit of the tresur that he yemit:	
40	*Surrexit Dominus de sepulchro.*	

---

18 [*lyk a lamb* the images used for Christ of the lamb, the lion (l. 19), and the giant (l. 20) are all biblical in origin]
20 And like a giant stretched himself on high
21 [*Aurora* Roman goddess of the dawn; here used of Christ]
22 [*Appollo* Apollo, Roman god of the sun; here used of Christ]
27 [*The sone ... paill* alludes both to Christ as Apollo and to the darkening of the sun at the hour of his death on the cross (Luke 23.45)]
28 *dirknes clerit* darkness cleared
34 The prison broken, the jailers scared away and put to flight
39 Despoiled of the treasure that he guarded

MY HEAD DID ACHE YESTER NIGHT

(Text from Cambridge University Library, MS Moore LL.v.10 [Reidpeth MS])

    My heid did yak* yester nicht†   ache
    †This day to mak that I na micht.
       †So sair the magryme dois me menyie,
       Perseing* my brow as ony ganyie,*   piercing arrow
5   That scant† I luik* may on the licht.*   look light

    And now, schir, laitlie† eftir mes,*   mass
    †To dyt thocht I begowthe to dres,
       The sentence* lay full evill* till find,   drift hard
       †Unsleipit, in my heid behind,
10 Dullit* in dulnes* and distres.   dulled sluggishness

    Full oft at morrow* I upryse   in the morning
    Quhen that my curage† sleipeing lyis;
       For† mirth, for menstrallie* and play,*   music-making amusement
       For din nor danceing nor deray,*   revelry
15 It will not walkin* me no wise.†   awaken

---

1 *yester nicht* last night
2 So that today I have been unable to write poetry
3 The migraine afflicts me so grievously
5 *scant* hardly at all
6 *laitlie* a short while ago
7 Though I began getting ready to write
9 Lacking in sleep, at the back of my head
12 *curage* creative energy
13 *For* for the sake of
15 *no wise* in any way

SWEET ROSE OF VIRTUE AND OF GENTLENESS

(Text from Magdalene College, Cambridge, MS 2553 [Maitland Folio MS])

Sweit rois of vertew[†] and of gentilnes,* — nobility
Delytsum* lyllie of everie lustynes,* — delightful pleasure
   Richest in bontie* and in bewtie cleir* — goodness fair
   And everie vertew that is deir,[†]
5 Except onlie that ye ar mercyles.

   In to your garthe[†] this day I did persew;* — enter
   Thair saw I flowris that fresche were of hew.* — hue
      [†]Baithe quhyte and rid moist lusty wer to seyne
      And halsum* herbis upone stalkis grene, — health-giving
10 Yit leif nor flour fynd could I nane* of rew.[†] — none

   I dout* that Merche with his caild* blastis keyne* — fear cold fierce
   Hes slane this gentill* herbe that I of mene,[†] — noble
      Quhois petewous* deithe dois* to my hart sic* — pitiable causes such
      pane
      [†]That I wald mak to plant his rute agane,
15 So confortand* his levis unto me bene.* — comforting are

---

1 *vertew* moral excellence
4 [*that is deir* editors often emend this line to 'that is held most deir' in order to regularise the rhythm, but Dunbar's metrical intentions are not clear]
6 *garthe* enclosed garden
8 Both white and red, were most beautiful to see
10 *rew* the herb, rue; pity
12 *of mene* speak of
14 That I would like to have its root planted again

IN TO THESE DARK AND DRUBLIE DAYS

(Text from Maitland Folio MS)

[†]In to thir dirk and drublie dayis
  Quhone* sabill* all the hevin arrayis   when black
    With mystie vapouris, cluddis* and skyis,   clouds
    Nature all curage* me denyis   energy
5   Of sangis,* ballattis* and of playis.   for songs poems

  Quhone that the nycht dois lenth* in houris   lengthen
  With wind, with haill and havy schouris,[†]
    [†]My dulé spreit dois lurk for schoir;
    My hairt for langour* dois forloir[†]   wretchedness
10 For laik of symmer* with his flouris.   summer

  I walk,* I turne, sleip may I nocht;*   wake not
  I vexit am with havie* thocht.*   burdensome thought
    This warld all ovir I cast* about,   think
    And ay* the mair* I am in dout*   always more apprehension
15 The mair that I remeid* have socht.*   remedy sought

  I am assayit* on everie syde.   assailed
  Despair sayis ay:* 'In tyme provyde   always
    And get sum thing quhairon* to leif,*   whereon live
    Or with grit* trouble and mischeif*   great harm
20 [†]Thow sall in to this court abyd.'

  Than Patience sayis, 'Be not agast;*   afraid
  Hald* Hoip* and Treuthe within the fast   hold hope
    And lat Fortoun wirk furthe* hir rage   work out
    Quhone* that no rasoun* may assuage,   when reason
25 Quhill* that hir glas be run and past.'   until

---

1 In these dark and gloomy days
7 *havy schouris* heavy showers
8 My doleful spirit shrinks at the menacing prospect
9 *forloir* become desolate
20 You shall remain in this court

And Prudence in my eir sayis ay,
†'Quhy wald thow hald that will away,
   Or craif* that* thow may have no space,†   *crave what*
   †Thow tending to ane uther place,
30 A journay going everie day?'

And than sayis Age, 'My freind, cum neir
And be not strange,* I the requeir.*   *aloof ask you*
   Cum, brodir,* by the hand me tak.*   *brother take*
   Remember thow hes compt† to mak*   *make*
35 Of all thi tyme thow spendit* heir.'   *spent*

†Syne Deid castis upe his yettis wyd,
†Saying, 'Thir oppin sall the abyd.
   Albeid* that thow wer never sa stout,*   *even if bold*
   Undir this lyntall* sall thow lowt:†   *lintel*
40 Thair is nane uther way besyde.'*   *at hand*

For feir of this all day I drowp.*   *am dispirited*
No gold in kist* nor wyne in cowp,*   *chest cup*
No ladeis bewtie nor luiffis* blys   *love's*
   †May lat me to remember this,
45 †How glaid that ever I dyne or sowp.

Yit quhone the nycht begynnis to schort*   *shorten*
   †It dois my spreit sum pairt confort
      †Of thocht oppressit with the schowris.
   Cum, lustie symmer, with thi flowris
50 That I may leif* in sum disport.   *live*

---

27 Why do you want to keep what is bound to depart
28 *no space* for no length of time
29 You [who are] moving towards another place
34 *hes compt* have an account
36 Then Death throws open his wide gates
37 Saying: These, open, shall await you
39 *lowt* bend your head
44 Can stop me remembering this
45 However cheerfully I dine or sup
47 It consoles my spirits in part
48 Weighed down by showers of thought

LUCINA SHINING IN SILENCE OF THE NIGHT

(Text from Bannatyne MS)

	Lucina* schynnyng* in silence of the nicht,	the moon shining
	The hevin being all full of sternis* bricht,	stars
	To bed I went bot thair I tuke no rest.	
	With havy* thocht I wes so soir* opprest	sad sorely
5	That sair I langit† eftir dayis licht.	
	Of Fortoun† I complenit* hevely*	complained sadly
	That scho* to me stude so contrariowsly,†	she
	And at the last, quhen I had turnyt oft,	
	For weirines on me ane slummer* soft	a slumber
10	Come* with ane dremyng and a fantesy.*	came vision
	†Me thocht Deme Fortoun with ane fremmit cheir	
	Stude me beforne* and said on* this maneir:*	before in manner
	†'Thow suffer me to wirk gif thow do weill,	
	†And preis the nocht to stryfe aganis my quheill	
15	Quhilk* every warldly thing dois turne and steir.*	which guide
	'Full mony ane man I turne unto the hicht*	height
	And makis als* mony full law* to doun licht.†	as low
	Up on my staigis* or* that thow ascend,	steps before
	Trest* weill thy truble neir* is at ane end,	believe nearly
20	Seing thir taikinis;† quhairfoir thow mark* thame rycht:	interpret

---

5 *sair I langit* I longed bitterly
6 [*Fortoun* Fortune was frequently personified as a female figure (derived from the late Roman goddess Fortuna) with a wheel which symbolised the changeability of events under her control]
7 *stude so contrariowsly* stood in such opposition
11 It seemed to me that Dame Fortune with a strange appearance
13 You allow me to act if you do well
14 And do not exert yourself to contend against my wheel
17 *doun licht* be brought down
20 *thir taikinis* these signs

†Thy trublit gaist sall neir moir be degest
Nor thow in to no benifice† beis possest,†
†Quhill that ane abbot† him cleith in ernis pennis
And fle* up in the air amangis the crennis*   fly   cranes
25   And as ane falcone fair* fro eist to west.   make his way

'He sall ascend as ane horreble grephoun;*   griffin
Him meit sall in the air ane scho dragoun.*   she-dragon
Thir* terrible monsteris sall togidder thrist*   these   copulate
And in the cludis* gett* the Antechrist†   clouds   beget
30   Quhill* all the air infeck* of thair pusoun.*   while   is infected   poison

'Undir Saturnus fyrie regioun†
Symone Magus† sall meit him, and Mahoun,†
And Merlyne† at the mone* sall him be bydand,*   moon   waiting for
And Jonet† the weido* on ane bussome* rydand*   widow   broomstick   riding
35   Of wichis with ane windir* garesoun.*   marvellous   troop

'And syne* thay sall discend with reik* and fyre   then   smoke
And preiche in erth the Antechrystis impyre:*   empire
Be than it salbe* neir this warldis end.'   shall be
With that this lady sone fra* me did wend;*   from   go
40   Sleipand and walkand* wes frustrat* my desyre.   waking   frustrated

---

21   Your troubled spirit shall never more be at rest
22   [*benifice* an ecclesiastical office from which the holder derived an income. See 'Into these Dark and Drublie Days', l. 18, where Dunbar seems to draw attention again to his lack of preferment]   *beis possest* be in possession
23   Until an abbot dress himself in eagle's feathers
[*ane abbot* alludes to the exploits of John Damian, abbot of Tongland, in Kirkcudbrightshire, whose pseudo-scientific experiments were encouraged by James IV of Scotland (1488–1513). It is reported that Damian attached feathers to himself and attempted to fly from the walls of Stirling Castle, breaking a thigh in the process]
29   [*Antechrist* the chief antagonist of Christ ('that denieth the Father and the Son' [I John 2.22]), whose coming is a sign of the end of the world; often seen as the beast which is given power by the dragon in Revelation 1–4. The whole poem satirises the apocalyptic terrors of the age, which were expressed in popular prophecies of the imminent end of the world]
31   [*Saturnus fyrie regioun* the outermost of the planetary spheres]
32   [*Symone Magus* a magician mentioned in the Acts of the Apostles who, according to later legend, tried to impress the emperor Nero with his demonic powers of flight   *Mahoun* a pagan god, or the devil (from Mahomet)]
[*Merlyne* a wizard and prophet associated particularly with Arthurian legend, son of a princess and an incubus]
34   [*Jonet the weido* Janet, typical name for a witch]

Quhen I awoik, my dreme it wes so nyce,*   extraordinary
Fra every wicht* I hid it as a vyce   person
†Quhill I hard tell be mony suthfast wy
Fle wald† ane abbot up in to the sky
45 †And all his fethreme maid wes at devyce.

Within my hairt confort I tuke full sone.
'Adew,' quod* I, 'my drery dayis ar done.'   said
Full weill I wist* to me wald* nevir cum thrift*   knew would prosperity
Quhill that twa* monis* wer sene up in the lift*   two moons heaven
50 Or quhill ane abbot flew aboif* the mone.   above

---

43 Until I heard it said by many a truthful person
44 *fle wald* wanted to fly
45 And all his plumage was perfectly made

John Skelton
?1460–1529

John Skelton was born around 1460, probably in the north of England. He seems to have studied at Oxford and Cambridge, and both universities, as well as Louvain in the Low Countries, later conferred on him the title *laureatus* (laureate) for his expertise in Latin rhetoric. During the late 1490s he became tutor to Prince Henry (who came to the throne in 1509 as Henry VIII).

In 1498 Skelton took holy orders, and from 1504 at the latest was rector of Diss in Norfolk, where he lived for several years. By 1513 he had become *orator regius* (royal orator) to his former pupil, Henry VIII. He fell out with Cardinal Wolsey, whom he attacked in a series of satires written in the early 1520s before the two were reconciled. He died in 1529.

Skelton's English poems include a number of longer works: *The Bowge of Court* (?1498, though possibly much earlier); *Philip Sparrow* (?1505), prompted by the death of a sparrow owned by Jane Scrope; a morality play, *Magnificence* (?1515–16, though possibly earlier or later); *Eleanor Rumming* (printed ?1521), depicting a grotesque alehouse keeper and her customers; the anti-Wolsey satires, *Speak Parrot*, *Colin Clout* and *Why Come Ye Not to Court?*; and *The Garland of Laurel*, which was probably written over many years and celebrates Skelton's own laureation.

'Merry Margaret' is taken from this last work. The other short poems included below are quite different in tone: some of them are semi-dramatic, and all of them use a range of language in which puns, colloquialisms and insults jostle with more elevated or literary kinds of discourse. 'Merry Margaret' and 'Gup, Scot' are written in 'Skeltonics', short lines with irregular rhythm.

The texts are all from John Scattergood's 1983 edition of Skelton's English poems. The notes are indebted to his commentary.

WOMANHOOD, WANTON, YE WANT!

    Womanhod, wanton, ye want!*   *lack*
    Youre medelyng, mastres,* is manerles;*   *mistress unmannerly*
    Plente of yll, of goodnes skant,
    †Ye rayll at ryot, recheles.
5   To prayse your porte* it is nedeles;   *conduct*
    †For all your 'Draffe'* yet and your 'Dreggys',*   *leavings dregs*
    †As well borne as ye full oft tyme beggys.

    Why so koy* and full of skorne?   *disdainful*
    †'Myne horse is sold, I wene',* you say;   *believe*
10 †'My new furryd gowne, when it is worne –
    †Put up* your purs, ye shall non pay!'   *put away*
    By Crede,* I trust to se the day,   *the creed*
    As proud a pohen* as ye sprede,†   *peahen*
    Of me and other ye may have nede.

15 Though angelyk* be youre smylyng,   *like an angel*
    Yet is youre tong an adders tayle,
    Full lyke a scorpyon styngyng
    All those by whom ye have avayle.†
    Good mastres Anne, there ye do shayle!†
20 †What prate ye, praty pyggys-ny?
    I truste to quyte* you or* I dy!   *pay back before*

    Youre key† is mete* for every lok,   *fit*
    Youre key is commen and hangyth owte;
    Youre key is redy, we nede not knok
25 Nor stand long wrestyng* there aboute;   *struggling*
    Of youre doregate* ye have no doute.*   *entrance fear*
    But one thyng is: that ye be lewde!*   *ignorant*
    Holde youre tong, now, all beshrewde!†

---

4 You complain about dissipation, ill-advisedly
6 [*Draffe ... Dreggys* these slighting terms have presumably been used by Mistress Anne to describe those (including himself) whom the poet is defending]
7 People as well born as you are very often beggars
9–11 [A specimen of Mistress Anne's boastful and patronising conversation]
13 *sprede* display your plumage
18 *have avayle* derive advantage
19 *shayle* make a mistake
20 What nonsense are you talking, pretty poppet?
[*pyggys-ny* literally, pig's-eye; possibly the name of a flower; an inelegant term of endearment]
22 [*key* there is clearly a sexual innuendo here, as well as an allusion to the Key inn (see l. 30), of which Mistress Anne may be the hostess]
28 *all beshrewde* utterly cursed

To mastres Anne, that farly* swete,* — wondrous sweet one
30   That wonnes* at the Key in Temmys Strete. — dwells

THE ANCIENT ACQUAINTANCE, MADAM

The auncient acquaintance, madam, betwen us twayn,* — two
The famylyaryté, the formar dalyaunce,* — intimacy
Causyth me that I can not myself refrayne,* — restrain
But that I must wryte for my plesaunt pastaunce* — recreation
5   Remembryng your passyng goodly countenaunce,
Your goodly port,* your bewteous visage, — demeanour
Ye may be countyd comfort of all corage.* — desire

Of all your feturs* favorable to make tru discripcion, — features
I am insuffycyent to make such enterpryse;
10   For thus dare I say, without tradiccyon,* — deception
That Dame Menolope† was never half so wyse;
Yet so it is that a rumer* begynnyth for to ryse — rumour
How in good horsmen† ye set your hole delyght,
And have forgoten your old, trew, lovyng knyght.

15   Wyth bound and rebound, bounsyngly† take up
†Hys jentyll curtoyl, and set nowght by small naggys!
Spur up at the hynder* gyrth† with, 'Gup,* — rear gee up
   morell,* gup!' — bay horse
With, 'Jayst ye,* Jenet of Spayne,† for your tayll waggys,' — ?whoa
Ye cast* all your corage uppon such courtly haggys!† — throw away
20   †'Have in sergeaunt ferrour, myne horse behynde is bare.'
He rydyth well the horse, but he rydyth better the mare.

---

11 [*Dame Menolope* apparently Hippolyta, queen of the Amazons, a warlike race of women who used men as servants]
13 [*good horsmen* this phrase initiates a series of double-entendres, between horse-riding and sexual activity, that extends through the next two stanzas. Skelton's colloquial and punning language is often difficult to interpret exactly]
15 [*bound ... rebound ... bounsyngly* these movements seem to refer both to horse-riding and sexual activity, as well as to the idea of the woman returning to her husband. 'Bounce' means 'thump' as well as 'bound like a ball']   *bounsyngly* with vigorous movement
16 His noble horse with a docked tail [or tunic] and pay no heed to small horses [or testicles]
17 *gyrth* strap round a horse's belly
18 [*Jenet of Spayne* a 'jenet' was a Spanish horse; a 'Janet (or Jenot)-of-the-stews' was a prostitute]
19 *haggys* disgusting old men
20 Bring the officer in charge of horses, my horse has lost its hind shoes

THE ANCIENT ACQUAINTANCE, MADAM 561

    †Ware,* ware, the mare wynsyth* wyth her wanton hele!   *watch out   kicks up*
    †She kykyth with her kalkyns and keylyth with a clench;
    She goyth wyde behynde† and hewyth never a dele:†
25 Ware gallyng* in the widders,* ware of that wrenche!*   *chafing   withers*
                                                                                          trick
    It is perlous* for a horseman to dyg in the trenche.   *dangerous*
    Thys grevyth your husband, that ryght jentyll knyght,
    And so with your servantys he fersly doth fyght.

    So fersly he fytyth, hys mynde is so fell,*   *angry*
30 That he dryvyth them doune with dyntys* on ther day-wach.†   *blows*
    He bresyth* theyr braynpannys* and makyth them to swell,   *breaks   skulls*
    Theyre browys all to-brokyn,* such clappys* they cach;*   *broken   blows*
                                                                                          receive
    Whose jalawsy* malycyous makyth them to lepe the hach!†   *jealousy*
    By theyr conusaunce* knowing how they serve a wily py:*   *emblem*
                                                                                           magpie
35 Ask all your neybours whether that I ly.

    It can be no counsell* that is cryed at the cros.†   *secret*
    For your jentyll husband sorowfull am I;
    Howbeit, he is not furst hath had a los.
    Advertysyng* you, madame, to warke more secretly,   *warning*
40 Let not all the world make an owtcry;
    Play fayre-play, madame, and loke ye play clene,
    Or ells with gret shame your game wylbe sene.

22–8 [There is possibly an implication in this stanza that the woman has a sexual disease, which is why she is dangerous. See also l. 41: 'loke ye play clene'; (but note that 'clappys' in l. 32 does not mean 'gonorrhoea' at this date)]
23 She kicks with her horseshoes and kills with a rivet
24 [*She goyth wide behynde* may mean 'she (as horse) walks with her back legs apart', but 'wide' may also refer to the dispersal of her favours. 'heweth' possibly means 'utters a shout' (as a huntsman to dogs); that is, she does not give warning of the 'gallyng in the widders' (l. 25) that men will receive from her]
24 *hewyth never a dele* gives no warning shout at all
30 *day-wach* daytime stint of service
33 *lepe the hach* jump over the hatch   [A hatch is the bottom half of a split door; 'to lepe the hach' means to make a quick getaway]
36 *cryed at the cross* shouted at the street corner

MERRY MARGARET

    Mirry Margaret,†
    As mydsomer flowre,
    Jentill* as fawcoun*   nobly-born   falcon
    Or hawke of the towre;

5   With solace and gladnes,
    Moche mirthe and no madnes,

    All good and no badnes,
    So joyously,
    So maydenly,
10 So womanly
    Her demenyng*   bearing
    In every thynge,
    Far, far passynge
    That I can endyght,*   describe
15 Or suffice to wryght
    Of mirry Margarete,
    As mydsomer flowre,
    Jentyll as fawcoun
    Or hawke of the towre,

20 As pacient and as styll,*   quiet
    And as full of good wyll,
    As fayre Isaphill;†
    Colyaunder,*   coriander
    Swete pomaunder,*   pomander
25 Good Cassaunder;†
    Stedfast of thought,
    Wele made, wele wrought;
    Far may be sought
    Erst* that ye can fynde   before
30 So corteise,* so kynde   well-bred
    As mirry Margarete,
    This midsomer flowre,
    Jentyll as fawcoun
    Or hawke of the towre.

---

1 [*Margaret* wife of John Hussey; born Margaret Blount of Mangotsfield, died 1492]
22 [*Isaphill* Hypsipile saved the life of her father, was forsaken by her lover Jason, and separated from her children]
25 [*Cassaunder* Cassandra, daughter of Priam, King of Troy, unshakeably predicted the destruction of the city]

MY DARLING DEAR, MY DAISY FLOWER

†With 'Lullay, lullay', lyke a chylde,
Thou slepyst to long, thou art begylde!* .... deceived

'My darlyng dere, my daysy floure,
Let me,' quod he, 'ly* in your lap.' .... lie
'Ly styll,' quod she, 'my paramoure,* .... lover
Ly styll hardely,* and take a nap.' .... boldly
5 Hys hed was hevy, such was his hap,* .... luck
All drowsy, dremyng, dround in slepe,
That of hys love he toke no kepe,†
   With hey, lullay, etc.

With 'Ba,* ba ba,' and 'bas,* bas, bas', ... kiss ?kiss, ?low
She cheryshed* hym both cheke and chyn .... petted
10 That* he wyst* never where he was; .... so that knew
He had forgoten all dedely syn.
He wantyd wyt† her love to wyn:
He trusted her payment and lost all hys pray.* .... prey
She left hym slepyng and stale away,
   With hey, lullay, etc.

15 The ryvers rowth,* the waters wan;* .... rough dark
†She sparyd not to wete her fete.
She wadyd over, she found a man
That halsyd* her hartely* and kyst her swete. .... embraced warmly
Thus after her cold she cought a hete.†
20 'My lefe',* she sayd, 'rowtyth* in hys bed; .... love snores
I wys* he hath an hevy hed,' .... indeed
   With hey, lullay, etc.

Refrain [*With lullay, lullay, lyke a chylde* there are several medieval lyrics which use this lullaby burden. Here it is applied to a drunken soldier who is abandoned by a woman while in a stupor]
  7 *toke no kepe* paid no heed
12 *wanted wyt* lacked the sense
16 She did not hold back from wetting her feet
19 *cought a hete* got warm

What dremyst thou, drunchard, drousy pate?*   sleepy head
Thy lust* and lykyng* is from the gone;   desire pleasure
Thou blynkerd blowboll,* thou wakyst to* late;   drunkard too
25   Behold, thou lyeste, luggard,* alone!   sluggard
Well may thou sygh, well may thou grone,
To dele wyth her so cowardly;
I wys, powle hachet,† she bleryd thyne I!*   eye

GUP, SCOT

Gup,* Scot,†   gee up
Ye blot:†
†*Laudate*
†'*Caudate*',
5   Set in better
Thy pentameter.
This Dundas,
This Scottishe as*   ass
He rymes and railes
10   That Englishmen have tailes.
    †*Skeltonus laureatus,*
Anglicus natus,
Provocat Musas
Contra Dundas
15   *Spurcissimum Scotum,*
Undiquae notum,
Rustice fotum,
Vapide potum.†

---

28   *powle hachet*   soldier with a pole-axe
1   [*Scot*   the Scottish author (possibly George Dundas, knight of Rhodes) of a Latin epigram on the old canard that Englishmen have tails: *Anglicus a tergo caudam gerit; est canis ergo/Anglice caudate, cape caudam ne cadat a te/Ex causa caude manet Anglica gens sine laude.* (The Englishman has a tail behind; therefore he is a dog. Tailed Englishman, hold your tail in case it drops off. Because of its tail(s) the English nation is without praise.)]
2   *blot*   make a mess of writing
3–4   [*Laudate 'Caudate'*   'Praise "Caudate"'; Skelton seems to be pointing out an error in Dundas's scansion, by ironically inviting people to admire it. The last syllable of 'caudate' in the second hexameter line of Dundas's epigram, is short, but Dundas treats it as long. This reading explains ll. 2 and 5–6, which mock Dundas as a writer]
4   You tailed one [see note]
11–18   Skelton the laureate, born an Englishman, summons the Muses against Dundas, foulest Scot, notorious everywhere, raised in the sticks, filthy drunk

	Skelton laureat†	
20	After this rate*	style
	Defendeth with his pen	
	All Englysh men	
	Agayn* Dundas,	against
	That Scottishe asse.	
25	Shake thy tayle, Scot, lyke a cur,	
	For thou beggest at every mannes dur.*	door
	Tut, Scot, I sey,	
	Go shake the, dog, hey!	
	Dundas of Galaway†	
30	With thy versyfyeng rayles	
	How they have tayles.	
	By Jesu Christ,	
	Fals Scot, thou lyest:	
	But behynd in our hose*	stockings
35	We bere there a rose†	
	For thy Scottyshe nose,	
	†A spectacle case	
	To cover thy face,	
	†With, *tray deux ase*.*	three, two, ace
40	A tolman* to blot,	?penman
	†A rough foted* Scot!	rough-footed
	Dundas, sir knave,	
	Why doste thow deprave*	disparage
	This royall reame,*	realm
45	Whose radiant beame	
	And relucent* light	shining
	Thou hast in despite,†	
	Thou donghyll knyght?	
	But thou lakest might,*	lack power
50	Dundas, dronken and drowsy,	
	Skabed,* scurvy and lowsy,	scabbed
	Of unhappy generacion*	birth
	And most ungracious nacion.	

19 [*laureat* Skelton held the title of *laureatus* from the universities of Oxford, Cambridge and Louvain]
29 [*Galaway* Galloway, in south-west Scotland, which had a reputation for wildness]
35 [*a rose* an emblem of the English royal house of Tudor]
37–8 [Possibly the image suggests that the English buttocks might grip the Scottish nose in the way that spectacles do]
39 [*tray, deux, ase* a throw at dice but perhaps also a pun: French *tres doux* 'very sweet', and English *as* 'ass' or possibly 'arse']
41 [Scottish soldiers were notorious for wearing rough rawhide brogues. See Lawrence Minot's 'Scots Out of Berwick', l. 19]
47 *hast in despite* hold in contempt

>   Dundas,
> 55   That dronke asse,
>   That ratis* and rankis*   nags   rages
>   That prates* and prankes*   talks idly   struts about
>   †On Huntley bankes,
>   Take this our thankes;
> 60   †Dunde, Dunbar,
>   Walke, Scot,
>   Walke, sot,
>   Rayle not so far.

---

58 [*Huntley bankes* in Roxburghshire; the scene of Thomas's meeting with the fairy queen in the fourteenth-century ballad romance *Thomas of Ercildoune*. Skelton apparently uses it here as an appropriate locale for Scottish nonsense]
60 [Dundee and Dunbar were both sea-ports on the east coast of Scotland that were periodically attacked by the English. The precise date of this poem is unknown, but its general context seems to be the hostilities between the two nations that culminated in the battle of Flodden (1513) and its aftermath. Flodden was an English victory]

Gavin Douglas
1476–1522

Gavin Douglas was born in 1476, the third son of Archibald Douglas, fifth earl of Angus in Scotland. Like many other younger sons of noble families, he was trained for the church. He took an MA at the university of St Andrews in 1494 and possibly went on to study at Paris before becoming provost of St Giles', Edinburgh. In 1501 he wrote an allegorical dream poem, *The Palace of Honour*, but the work for which he is best known is his translation into Scots of the *Aeneid* of Virgil (70–19 BC). He undertook this in 1512–13 at the instance of Henry, Lord Sinclair, completing it shortly before the battle of Flodden (1513) in which Sinclair and King James IV of Scotland were killed. James's death had momentous consequences for Douglas, since the king's widow, Margaret Tudor, sister of Henry VIII of England, quickly married the poet's nephew. Douglas owed his advancement to the bishopric of Dunkeld in 1515 to her efforts on his behalf, but he subsequently suffered – as did his whole family – when Margaret and her husband became estranged. He died, probably of the plague, in London in 1522.

Douglas's is the first translation of the *Aeneid* into any form of English. The Latin text he used was that made around 1500 by the Dutch humanist Jocus Badius Ascensius, with a lengthy prose commentary. Douglas included an additional thirteenth book, in which Aeneas marries Lavinia and is later deified, which was written in 1428 by the Italian humanist Maphaeus Vegius and which was commonly incorporated into Virgil's poem. Douglas also wrote original prologues to each of the thirteen books in a variety of styles and metres.

The first extract is taken from Book 6, in which Aeneas visits the underworld where he encounters the shade of Dido who has killed herself for love of him. The second extract forms the opening of the prologue to the thirteenth book, in which the poet walks forth on a summer's evening, falls asleep in a garden and is visited in his dream by Maphaeus Vegius who urges him to get on with his task of translating. This, and two others of his prologues, are among the first poems in English devoted largely to the description of landscape.

From ENEADOS
Book 6, chapter 7, lines 55–108
[Aeneas meets Dido in the Underworld]

    Amang otheris the Phenyssyane* Dido[†]   Phoenician
    Within the gret wod* walkis to and fro,   wood
    The greyn* wound gapand in hir breist all new,   fresh
    Quhom as the Trojane[†] barroun* nerrer* drew,   lord nearer
5   And throw the dyrk* schaddowis first dyd knaw* –   dark recognise
    Sikwys[†] as quha* throw clowdy skyis saw,   one who
    Or, at the leist, wenys* he heth do se,[†]   believes
    The new moyn* quhen first upwalxis* sche –   moon rises
    The terys leyt* he fall, and tendyrly   let
10 [†]With hartly lufe begrat hir thus in hy:
    [†]'O fey Dido, sen I persave the heyr,
    A sovir* warnyng, now I knaw ful cleir,   true
    Was schawin me, at* thou with swerd was slaw,*   that slain
    [†]Byreft thi self the lyfe, and brocht of daw.
15 Allace, I was the causar of thy ded!*   death
    By al the starnys* schynys* abone* our hed,   stars [that] shine above
    And be the goddis abone, to the I swer,*   swear
    And be the faith and lawté,* gif* ony* heir   fidelity if any
    Trewth may be fund* deip undir erd,'* quod* he,   found earth said
20 'Malgré* my wyl, Pryncës, sa mot I the,[†]   despite
    [†]From thy costis depart I was constrenyt.
    Bot* the commandment of the goddis onfenyt,*   only unfeigned
    [†]Quhais gret mychtis hes me hyddir dryve,
    To pas* throwout thir dirk* schaddowis belyve,*   pass dark at once
25 [†]By gowsty placis, welch savorit, must and hair,
    Quhar profund nycht perpetual doith repar,*   resorts

---

1 [*Phenyssyane Dido* Dido was born in the Phoenician city of Tyre and became queen of Carthage in north Africa. She killed herself after her lover Aeneas left her at the gods' command]
4 [*the Trojane barroun* Aeneas, hero of the *Aeneid*; member of the Trojan royal house who fled the city after its fall, travelling to Carthage and thence to Italy]
6 *Sikwys*   in such a way
7 *heth do se*   has seen
10 With heartfelt love wept for her thus quickly
11 O doomed Dido, since I perceive you here
14 [you] robbed yourself of life and put to death
20 *sa mot I the*   as I may prosper
21 I was forced to depart from your coasts
23 Whose great power has driven me here
25 By dreary places, foul smelling, musty and freezing

	Compellit me from the forto dissevir;†	
	Nor in my mynde ymagyn mycht I nevir,	
	For my departing or absens, iwys,*	indeed
30	Thou suldist kaucht† sa gret dyseys* as this.	misery
	†Do stynt thy pays! Abide, thou gentil wight,	
	Withdraw the not sa* sone furth of* my sight!	so beyond
	Quham* fleist thou? This is the lattir* day,	whom last
	By werdis schape,† that with the speke I may.'	
35	With sik* wordis Eneas, full of wo,	such
	†Set him to meys the sprete of Queyn Dido,	
	Quhilk,* all inflambit,* full of wreth and ire,	which inflamed
	†With acquart luke glowand hait as fyre,	
	Maid him to weip and sched furth teris* wak.*	tears watery
40	All fremmytly* frawart* hym, as he spak,	hostilely away from
	Hir eyn* fixit apon the grond held sche,	eyes
	Moving na mair* hir curage,* face nor bre,*	more expression brow
	Than scho* had bene a statu of marbil stane,*	[if] she stone
	Or a ferm rolk* of Mont Marpesyane.†	rock
45	Bot finaly, full swyft scho wiskis* away,	darts
	Aggrevit* fled in the darn* woddis* gray,	resentful secret woods
	Quhar as Sycheus,† hir first spows, ful suyr*	sure
	Corespondis to† hir desyre and cuyr,*	care
	Rendring in lufe amouris equivalent.†	
50	And, netheles,* fast eftir hir furth sprent*	nevertheless hastened
	Ene,* perplexit of* hir sory cace,*	Aeneas by predicament
	And weping gan hir follow a weil lang space,†	
	Regratand* in his mynd, and had piete*	regretting pity
	Of the distres that movit* hir so to fle.	compelled

27 *forto dissever* to separate
30 *suldist kaucht* should have experienced
31 Stand still! Wait, noble creature
34 *werdis schape* fate's decree
36 Set himself to appease the ghost of Queen Dido
38 With averted gaze glowing hot as fire
44 [*Mont Marpesyane* Mount Marpesus on the island of Paros was famous for its marble]
47 [*Sycheus* Dido's husband Sychaeus of Tyre, dead before her meeting with Aeneas. Douglas calls him her 'first spouse', though she did not marry Aeneas]
48 *Corespondis to* is in harmony with
49 *amouris equivalent* affection equal [to hers]
52 *weil lang space* very long distance

Prologue 13

[A Summer Evening]

	Towart the evyn, amyd the symmyris* heit,	summer's
	Quhen in the Crab† Appollo* held hys sete,	the sun
	Duryng the joyus moneth tyme* of June,	month
	As gone neir* was the day and supper doyn,*	nearly finished
5	I walkyt furth abowt the feildis tyte,*	quickly
	†Quhilkis tho replenyst stud full of delyte,	
	With herbys, cornys, catal,* and frute treis,	cattle
	Plente of stoir,* byrdis and byssy beys,*	livestock bees
	In amerant* medis* fleand* est and west,	emerald meadows flying
10	Eftir laubour to tak the nychtis* rest.	night's
	And as I lukit on the lift* me by,	heavens
	All byrnand* red gan walxin† the evyn sky:	burning
	The son enfyrit† haill,* as to my sight,	entirely
	Quhirlit* about* hys ball with bemys brycht,	whirled around
15	Declynand* fast towart the north† in deid,	descending
	And fyry Phegon,† his dun nychtis steid,	
	Dowkit* hys hed sa* deip in fludis* gray	ducked so streams
	That Phebus* rollis doun undir hell away;	the sun
	And Esperus† in the west with bemys brycht	
20	Upspryngis, as forrydar* of the nycht.	forerunner
	Amyd the hawchis,† and every lusty* vaill,*	flat lands pleasant valley
	The recent* dew begynnys doun to scaill,*	fresh fall
	To meys† the byrnyng quhar* the son had schyne,*	where shone
	†Quhilk tho was to the neddir warld declyne:	
25	At every pilis* poynt and cornys croppis*	grass-blade's tops
	The techrys† stude, as lemand* beryall* droppis,	gleaming crystal
	And on the hailsum* herbis, cleyn but* wedis,	beneficent entirely without
	Lyke cristal knoppis* or smal silver bedis.	buds

---

2 [*the Crab* the sun (Apollo) is in the zodiacal sign of Cancer: mid-June to mid-July]
6 Which then stood replenished, full of delight
12 *gan walxin* began to grow
13 *enfyrit* set on fire
15 [*towart the north* in Scotland the sun sets in the north-west in June]
16 [*Phegon* Phlegon, traditionally the dark colour of nightfall, is one of the four horses which, in classical myth, pull the sun's chariot]
19 *Esperus* Hesperus, the evening star
21 *hawchis* flat lands
23 *meys* assuage
24 Which by then had descended to the lower world
26 *techrys* water-drops

	The lyght begouth* to quynchyng owt† and faill,	began
30	The day to dyrkyn,* declyne and devaill;*	darken fail
	The gummys* rysis, doun fallis the donk* rym,*	mists damp haze
	Baith* heir and thar scuggis* and schaddois† dym.	both shades
	Upgois the bak* with hir pelit* ledderyn flycht,†	bat hairless
	The lark discendis from the skyis hycht,*	height
35	Syngand hir complyng sang,† efter hir gys,*	manner
	To tak hir rest, at matyn hour† to rys.*	rise
	Owt our* the swyre* swymmys the soppis† of myst,	over valley
	The nycht furthspred† hir cloke with sabill* lyst,*	black hem
	That* all the bewté* of the fructuus* feld	so that beauty fruitful
40	Was with the erthis umbrage* cleyn ourheld;*	shade covered
	Baith man and beste, fyrth,* flude and woddis* wild	forest woods
	Involvyt* in tha* schaddois warryn syld.†	wrapped those
	Still war the fowlis fleis† in the air,	
	All stoir* and catall seysit* in thar lair,	flocks settled
45	And every thing, quharso thame lykis best,†	
	Bownys* to tak the hailsum nychtis rest	prepares
	Eftir the days laubour and the heyt.*	heat
	Clos* warryn* all and at thar soft quyet,	shut in were
	But* sterage* or removing, he or sche,	without motion
50	Owder* best, byrd, fysch, fowle, by land or sey.	either
	And schortlie, every thing that doith repar	
	In† firth or feild, flude, forest, erth or ayr,	
	Or in the scroggis,* or the buskis ronk,†	brushwood
	†Lakis, marrasis, or thir pulys donk,	
55	Astabillit* lyggis* still to slepe, and restis;	settled lies
	Be the smaill byrdis syttand on thar nestis,	
	The litill mygeis,* and the unrusum* fleys,*	midges restless flies
	Laboryus emmotis,* and the bissy beys;	ants

---

29 *quynchyng out* be extinguished
32 *schaddois* shadows
33 *ledderyn flycht* leathern wings
35 *complyng sang* song for compline [Like monks, the lark sings the canonical hours; compline is the evening service]
36 *matyn hour* time for matins [The same metaphor as in the previous line: matins is the morning service]
37 *soppis* little clouds
38 *furthspred* spread forth
42 *warryn syld* were concealed
43 *fowlis fleis* birds [that] fly
45 *qhuarso thame likis best* wherever pleases them most
51–2 *doith repar/In* frequents
53 *buskis ronk* dense bushes
54 Lakes, marshes or these damp pools

†Als weill the wild as the taym bestiall,
60 And every othir thingis gret and small,
    Owtak* the mery nychtgaill,* Philomeyn,†   except nightingale
    That on the thorn sat syngand fra* the spleyn;*   from spleen
    †Quhais myrthfull notis langyng fortil heir,
    Ontill* a garth† undir a greyn lawrer*   into laurel
65 I walk* onon, and in a sege* down sat,   walked seat
    Now musyng apon this and now on that.
    I se the poill,* and eik* the Ursis* brycht,   pole star also Great Bear
    And hornyt Lucyn† castand bot dym lycht,
    Becaus the symmyr skyis schayn* sa cleir;   shone
70 †Goldyn Venus, the mastres* of the yeir,   mistress
    And gentill Jove with hir participate,*   in conjunction
    Thar bewtuus* bemys sched in blyth estait:*   beauteous state
    That* schortly, thar as* I was lenyt doun,†   so that where
    For* nychtis* silens, and this byrdis soun,*   because of night's sound
75 On sleip I slaid.*   I fell asleep

---

59 The wild animals as well as the tame
61 [*Philomeyn* according to classical legend, the nightingale was once a woman called Philomela who was raped by her brother-in-law; hence she sings from the spleen]
63 Longing to hear the joyful notes of which
64 *garth* enclosed garden
68 *hornyt Lucyn* horned Lucina [the new moon]
70–1 [*Venus . . . Jove* the planets Venus and Jupiter]
73 *lenyt doun* reclined

Thomas More
1478/9–1535

Thomas More was born in 1478 or 1479, the son of a London barrister. As a boy he was placed in the household of Cardinal Morton, Henry VII's chancellor, who, aware of More's precocious intelligence, advised that he be sent to Oxford in 1492 or 3 where he learned Latin and Greek. From Oxford he went to Lincoln's Inn where he trained for the law; in the early years of the sixteenth century he lived in the London Charterhouse (Carthusian monastery) and seems to have seriously considered becoming a monk. Instead he married and embarked on a public career in the city of London. He was a friend of the great Dutch humanist, Desiderius Erasmus (1466–1536), who spent several years in England and dedicated to More his *Encomium Moriae* (*Praise of Folly*, with a pun on More's name).

Around 1513 More wrote his first major work, *The History of King Richard III*, in both Latin and English. He did not finish either version and the book was not printed in his lifetime. In 1517 he published his satire *Utopia*, which was written in Latin, and which confronts the question of whether the humanist can enter royal service without compromising himself. Clearly this was an urgent issue for More: in 1517 he entered royal service himself as a member of the privy council. In 1529 he succeeded Cardinal Wolsey as Henry VIII's Chancellor, after Wolsey had failed to get the king's marriage to Katherine of Aragon annulled by the pope. During the 1520s Lutheranism had spread to England and More became increasingly involved in anti-Protestant polemic. Nevertheless the momentous pressure of events could not be reversed. In 1533 Henry VIII renounced the authority of the pope, divorced his wife and married Anne Boleyn. All men of influence were required to swear an oath in support of the 1534 Act of Succession, the preamble to which declared Henry's first marriage invalid. More refused to swear this oath; he was imprisoned and beheaded in 1535 on a false charge of having denied Henry VIII's supremacy of the Church of England.

Richard III is a study in the tyranny which More hated all his life and which in the end killed him. His account of Richard's usurpation of the throne, based on reminiscences and hearsay some thirty years after events, is not always reliable as a factual record but, taken up by Shakespeare in his *Richard III*, has become part of national legend. Despite the murder of his nephews which, though not provable against him, he probably perpetrated, the real Richard seems to have been more ordinary than the demonic and tormented figure that More creates. This is humanist historiography shaped by Latin models and, with its densely ironic prose, a new voice in English.

The text is from the 1557 edition of *The Workes of Sir Thomas More.*

From THE HISTORY OF RICHARD III
[The Character of Richard III]

Richarde, the third sonne,† of whom we now entreate,* — treat
was in witte and courage egall* with either of them,† in — equal
bodye and prowesse farre under them bothe: little of
stature, ill-fetured of limmes, croke-backed, his left
5 shoulder much higher then his right, hard favoured† of
visage, and suche as is in states† called warlye,* in other — martial
menne otherwise; he was malicious, wrathfull, envious,
and from afore his birth, ever frowarde.* It is for trouth — perverse
reported that the Duches his mother† had so muche a
10 doe* in her travaile† that shee coulde not bee delivered — difficulty
of hym uncutte,† and that hee came into the worlde with
the feete forwarde, as menne bee borne outwarde,† and
(as the fame* runneth) also not untothed,† whither* — report whether
menne of hatred reporte above the trouthe, or elles that
15 nature chaunged her course in hys beginninge, whiche†
in the course of his lyfe many thinges unnaturallye
committed. None* evill captaine was hee in the warre, — no
as to whiche his disposicion was more metely* then for — fitted
peace. Sundrye* victories hadde hee, and sommetime — various

[*third sonne* Richard Neville, duke of Gloucester (1452–85), was the third son of Richard, duke of York]
[*either of them* his elder brothers, Edward IV (1461–83) and George Neville, duke of Clarence (died 1478)]
hard favoured ugly
states persons of rank
[*the Duches his mother* Cecily, duchess of York (died 1495)]
travaile labour
uncutte without surgery
as menne bee borne outwarde as men are carried out [of the world; i.e. in their coffins]
untothed lacking teeth
whiche who (Richard)

20 overthrowes,* but never in defaulte as for† his owne   *defeats*
parsone,* either of hardinesse* or polytike order. Free   *person courage*
was hee called of dyspence,* and sommewhat above hys   *expenditure*
power liberall; with large* giftes hee get him unstedfaste   *generous*
frendeshippe, for whiche hee was fain* to pil* and   *willing steal*
25 spoyle in other places, and get him stedfast hatred. Hee
was close* and secrete, a deepe dissimuler,† lowlye† of   *secretive*
counteynaunce, arrogant of heart, outwardly
coumpinable* where he inwardely hated, not letting†   *friendly*
to kisse whome hee thoughte to kyll: dispitious* and   *pitiless*
30 cruell, not for evill will alway, but ofter† for ambicion,
and either for the suretie* or encrease of his estate.   *conservation*
Frende and foo was muche what indifferent;† where his
advauntage grew, he spared no mans deathe whose life
withstoode his purpose. He slewe with his owne handes
35 King Henry the Sixt,† being prisoner in the Tower, as
menne constantly saye, and that without commaunde-
mente or knoweledge of the King,† whiche woulde
undoubtedly, yf he had entended that thinge, have
appointed that boocherly* office to some other then his   *butcherly*
40 owne borne brother. Somme wise menne also weene*   *believe*
that his drifte,* covertly convayde, lacked not in helping   *plotting*
furth* his brother of Clarence† to his death, whiche hee   *forward*
resisted openly, howbeit* somwhat (as menne demed)*   *though judged*
more faintly then he that wer hartely minded to his
45 welth.† And they that thus deme, think that he, long
time in King Edwardes life, forethought* to be king in   *planned*
case† that the king his brother (whose life hee looked
that evil dyete shoulde shorten) shoulde happen to
decease (as in dede he did) while his children were yonge.

---

in defaulte as for due to failure of
dissimuler dissembler
lowlye humble
letting neglecting
ofter more often
was muche what indifferent were treated in much the same way
[*King Henry the Sixt* Henry VI (1422–61) was dethroned by Edward IV in 1461; he was restored temporarily in 1470–1 but the crown was regained by Edward and Henry was put to death in May 1471 on Edward's orders]
the King Edward IV
[*his brother of Clarence* George Neville, duke of Clarence, was attainted for treason in 1477 and sentenced to death while a prisoner in the Tower. His brother, Edward IV, could not bring himself to give the command for the execution, which was finally carried out in 1478 on the orders of the Speaker of the House of Commons]
then that he wer hartely minded to his welth than one who was sincerely concerned with his [Clarence's] welfare
in case in the event

And thei deme that for thys intente he was gladde of his
brothers death, the Duke of Clarence,† whose life must
nedes* have hindered hym so entendynge, whither†   necessarily
the same Duke of Clarence hadde kepte him true to his
nephew† the yonge King, or enterprised* to be Kyng   undertaken
himselfe. But of al this pointe is there no certaintie, and
whoso divineth* uppon conjectures maye as wel shote*   guesses shoot
to farre as to short. How beit,* this have I by credible   nevertheless
informacion learned, that the selfe* nighte in whiche   same
Kynge Edwarde died, one Mystlebrooke,† longe ere* mor-   before
nynge, came in greate haste to the house of one Pottyer†
dwellyng in Reddecrosse Strete without Crepulgate;†
and when he was with hastye rappyng quickly letten*   let
in, hee shewed* unto Pottyer that Kynge Edwarde was   revealed
departed. 'By my trouthe,† manne,' quod* Pottier, 'then   said
wyll my mayster, the Duke of Gloucester, bee kynge.'
What cause hee hadde soo to thynke harde it is to saye:
whyther hee, being toward* him, anye thynge knewe   close to
that hee suche thynge purposed, or otherwyse had anye
inkelynge thereof, for hee was not likelye to speake it
of noughte.† But nowe to returne to the course of this
hystorye, were it that the Duke of Gloucester hadde of
olde foreminded* this conclusion, or was nowe at erste†   intended
thereunto moved and putte in hope by the occasion of
the tender age of the younge Princes, his nephues (as
opportunitye and lykelyhoode of spede* putteth a manne   success
in courage of that* hee never entended), certayn is it   that which
that hee contrived theyr destruccion, with the usurpacion
of the regal* dignitye uppon hymselfe. And for as muche   royal
as hee well wiste* and holpe* to mayntayn a long   knew helped
continued grudge and hearte brennynge† betwene the
Quenes kinred† and the Kinges blood,† eyther partye*   side

---

his brothers death, the Duke of Clarence the death of his brother, the Duke of Clarence
whither whether
[*his nephew* Edward IV's son, prince Edward (1470–?83), never crowned as Edward V, who was heir to the throne]
[*Mystlebrooke* possibly Edward IV's servant William Mistlebrook (died 1513)]
[*Pottyer* possibly Richard's servant, Richard Potter]
without Crepulgate outside Cripplegate [one of the gates of the City of London]
By my trouthe upon my word
of noughte for no reason
at erste for the first time
hearte brennynge heart-burning, resentment
[*the Quenes kinred* the Woodvilles, the family of Edward IV's wife Elizabeth]
the Kinges blood the relatives of Edward IV

envying others authoritye, he nowe thought that their
devision shoulde bee (as it was in dede) a fortherlye* — favourable
begynnynge to the pursuite of his intente and a sure
85 ground for the foundacion of al his building, yf he might
firste under the pretext of revengynge of olde displeasure
abuse the anger and ygnoraunce of the tone* partie, to — one
the destruccion of the tother, and then wynne to his
purpose as manye as he coulde; and those that coulde
90 not bee wonne, myght be loste ere they looked
therefore.* For of one thynge was hee certayne, that if — for it
his entente were perceived, he shold soone have made
peace beetwene the bothe parties with his owne bloude.†

[The Murder of the Princes in the Tower]

King Richarde, after his coronacion† takyng his way to
Gloucester to visit in his newe honor the towne of which
he bare the name of his old,† devised* as he roode to — planned
fulfil that thing which he before had intended. And
5 forasmuch as his minde gave him† that, his nephewes
living, men woulde not recken that hee could have right
to the realm, he thought therfore without delay to rid* — get rid of
them, as though the killing of his kinsmen could amend* — improve
his cause, and make him a kindly* King. Whereuppon — lawful
10 he sent one John Grene whom he specially trusted unto
Sir Robert Brakenbery,† Constable of the Tower, with
a letter and credence* also, that the same Sir Robert — recommendation
shoulde in any wise* put the two children to death. This — manner
John Grene did his errande unto Brakenbery, kneling
15 before Our Lady† in the Tower, who plainely answered
that he would never putte them to death to dye therfore,†
with which answer John Grene, returning, recounted
the same to Kynge Richarde at Warwick yet in his way.†
Wherwith he toke such displeasure and thought that the

[with his owne bloude   that is, he would have been killed]
[after his coronacion   Richard III was crowned on 6 July 1483]
[he bare the name of his old   before seizing the throne ('his newe honor'), Richard had been duke of Gloucester]
forasmuch as his minde gave him   insofar as he realised
[Sir Robert Brackenbery   Brackenbury was appointed constable by Richard]
Our Lady   a statue of the Blessed Virgin
to dye therfore   even if he were to die for refusing
yet in his way   still on his journey

20   same night he said unto a secrete* page of his: 'Ah,   confidential
     whome shall a man trust? Those that I have broughte
     up my selfe, those that I had went* would most surely   believed
     serve me, even those fayle me, and at my commaunde-
     mente wyll do nothyng for me.' 'Sir,' quod his page,
25   'there lyeth one on your paylet† without* that I dare   outside
     well say, to do your grace pleasure, the thyng were right
     harde that he wold refuse,'† meaning this by† Sir James
     Tyrell,† which was a man of right goodlye parsonage,*   appearance
     and for natures gyftes woorthy to have served a muche
30   better Prince, if he had well served God and by grace
     obtayned as muche trouthe and good wil as he had
     strength and witte.* The man had an high† heart, and   intelligence
     sore longed upwarde,† not rising yet so fast as he had
     hoped, being hindered and kept under by the meanes of
35   Sir Richarde Ratclife† and Sir William Catesby,† which
     longing for† no moo partners of the Princes favour,
     and namely* not for hym whose pride thei wist† would   especially
     beare no pere,† kept him by secrete driftes* oute of all plots
     secrete trust. Whiche thyng this page wel had marked
40   and knowen; wherefore, thys occasion offered, of very
     speciall frendship he toke his time to put him* forward   Tyrell
     and by such wise doe him good, that al the enemies he
     had except the devil could never have done him so
     muche hurte. For upon this pages wordes King Richard
45   arose (for this communication* had he sitting at the   conversation
     draught,* a convenient carpet for such a counsaile) and   privy
     came out in to the pailet chamber,† on which he found
     in bed Sir James and Sir Thomas Tyrels,† of parson like†
     and brethren* of blood, but nothing of kin in   brothers

---

on your paylet in your bedchamber
that I dare well say to ... he wold refuse of whom I dare well say that the thing that he would refuse [to do] in order to perform a service for your grace would be very difficult
meaning this by referring to
[*Sir James Tyrell* Sir James Tyrell (1445–1502), a confidant of Richard, who had served with him against the Scots in 1482]
high proud
sore longed upward strongly desired to rise
[*Sir Richard Ratcliffe* knight of the body and sheriff of Westmorland; killed in 1485 at Bosworth]
[*Sir William Catesby* Speaker of the House of Commons in 1484 and esquire of the body. Both Ratcliffe and Catesby were members of Richard's council and inspired popular hatred]
longing for desiring
wist knew
beare no pere suffer no equal
pailet chamber sleeping-quarters
[*Sir Thomas Tyrels* James's younger brother (1450–1510)]
of parson like of similar appearance

50	condicions.† Then said the King merely* to them, 'What, sirs, be ye in bed so soone?' and, calling up Syr James, brake to him secretely his mind† in this mischievous* matter, in whiche he founde him nothing strange.* Wherfore on the morow† he sente him to Brakenbury	simply evil reluctant
55	with a letter by which he was commaunded to deliver Sir James all the kayes* of the Tower for one nyght, to the ende he might there accomplish the Kinges pleasure in such thing as he had geven him commaundement. After which letter delivered and the kayes received, Sir	keys
60	James appointed the night nexte ensuing to destroy them, devysing before† and preparing the meanes. The Prince, as soone as the Protector† left that name and toke himself as King, had it shewed unto him that he should not reigne, but his uncle should have the crowne.	
65	At which worde the Prince, sore abashed, began to sigh and said: 'Alas, I woulde my uncle woulde lette me have my lyfe yet, though I lese* my kingdome.' Then he that tolde him the tale used him with good wordes,† and put him in the best comfort he could. But forthwith was the	lose
70	Prince and his brother bothe shet* up and all other removed from them, onely one called Black Wil or William Slaughter except,* set to serve them and see them sure.* After whiche time the Prince never tyed his pointes,† nor ought rought* of hymselfe, but with	shut excepted secure took care
75	that young babe hys brother† lingered in thought and heavines† til this tratorous death delivered them of* that wretchednes. For Sir James Tirel devised that thei shold be murthered in their beddes, to the execucion wherof he appointed Miles Forest, one of the foure that	from
80	kept them, a felowe fleshed in† murther before time. To him he joyned one John Dighton, his own horsekeper, a big, brode, square, strong knave. Then al the other beeing removed from them, thys Miles Forest and John	

---

nothing of kin in condicions not related at all in character
brake to him secretely his mind told him in confidence what he planned
on the morow next day
devysing before planning in advance
[*Protector* Richard had been made Protector of the realm on the death of Edward IV in April 1483; his usurpation of the crown in July 1483 made it clear that Edward's son, the rightful heir, would not be allowed to inherit]
used him with good wordes spoke to him kindly
pointes laces on a doublet
[*that young babe his brother* Richard, duke of York (1473–?83)]
heavines despondency
fleshed in inured to

Dighton about midnight (the sely* children lying in their   poor
  85   beddes) came into the chamber and sodainly lapped*   bound
         them up among the clothes, so bewrapped* them and   wrapped up
         entangled them, keping down by force the fetherbed and
         pillowes hard unto their mouthes, that, within a while
         smored* and stifled, theyr breath failing, thei gave up   smothered
  90   to God their innocent soules into the joyes of heaven,
         leaving to the tormentors their bodyes dead in the bed.
         Whiche* after that the wretches parceived, first by the   who
         strugling with the paines of death, and after long lying
         styll, to be throughly dead, they laide their bodies naked
  95   out uppon the bed and fetched Sir James to see them.
         Which upon the sight of them caused those murtherers
         to burye them at the stayre foote, metely† depe in the
         grounde under a great heape of stones. Than rode Sir
         James in great hast to King Richarde and shewed him
 100   al the maner of the murther, who gave hym gret thanks
         and, as som say, there made him knight. But he allowed
         not, as I have heard, the burying in so vile a corner,
         saying that he woulde have them buried in a better place
         because thei wer a Kinges sonnes. Loe, the honourable
 105   corage* of a Kynge! Wherupon thei say that a prieste   disposition
         of Syr Robert Brakenbury toke up the bodyes again and
         secretely entered* them in such place as, by the occasion   buried
         of his deathe whiche onely† knew it, could never synce
         come to light. Very trouthe is it and well knowen that
 110   at such time as Syr James Tirell was in the Tower, for
         treason† committed agaynste the most famous prince
         King Henry the Seventh†, bothe Dighton and he were
         examined and confessed the murther in maner above
         writen, but whither the bodies were removed thei could
 115   nothing tel. And thus, as I have learned of them that
         much knew and litle cause had to lye, were these two
         noble princes, these innocent tender children, borne of
         moste royall bloode, brought up in great wealth, likely
         long to live to reigne and rule in the realme, by traytorous
 120   tiranny taken, depryved of their estate,* shortly shitte*   rank   shut
         up in prison, and privily* slaine and murthered, theyr   secretly

---

metely fittingly [given the crime]
whiche onely who alone
[*treason* Sir James Tyrell was executed in 1502 for his part in a treasonable conspiracy]
[*King Henry the Seventh* Henry VII (1485–1509), Richard's successor, who married the princes'
sister Elizabeth. The story of Tyrell's confession is now discounted by historians]

bodies cast God wote* where by the cruel ambicion of their unnaturall uncle and his dispiteous* tormentors. Which things on every part wel pondered, God never gave this world a more notable example, neither in what unsuretie* standeth this wordly wel,† or what mischief worketh the prowde enterprise of an hyghe heart, or finally what wretched end ensueth such dispiteous crueltie. For first to beginne with the ministers: Miles Forest at Sainct Martens† pecemele† rotted away; Dighton in dede yet walketh on a live† in good possibilitie to bee hanged ere* he dye, but Sir James Tirel dyed at Tower hill, beheaded for treason. King Richarde himselfe, as ye shal herafter here, slain in the fielde,† hacked and hewed of his enemies handes, haryed on horsebacke dead, his here* in despite† torn and togged* lyke a cur dogge; and the mischief* that he tooke,* within lesse then thre yeares of the mischiefe that he dyd; and yet all the meane time spente in much pain and trouble outward, much feare, anguish, and sorow within. For I have heard by credible report of such as wer secrete* with his chamberers† that, after this abhominable deede done, he never hadde quiet in his minde, hee never thought himself sure. Where he went abrode, his eyen* whirled about, his body privily fenced,* his hand ever on his dager, his countenance and maner like one alway ready to strike againe;* he toke ill rest a nightes, lay long wakyng and musing, sore weried with care and watch, rather slumbred then slept, troubled wyth feareful dreames, sodainly sommetyme sterte* up, leape out of his bed and runne about the chamber; so was his restles herte continually tossed and tumbled with the tedious impression and stormy remembrance of his abominable dede.

knows
pitiless

insecurity

before

hair pulled
harm received

intimate

eyes
protected

back

started

---

wel prosperity
[*Sainct Martens* in sanctuary at St Martin's, Westminster]
pecemele bit by bit
yet walketh on a live still remains alive
[*in the fielde* Richard was killed at the battle of Bosworth Field on 22 August 1485]
despite contempt
chamberers gentlemen of his chamber

Bibliography

HISTORY, SOCIETY, CULTURE, RELIGION, ART

Anglo-Saxons, The, ed. J. Campbell (Oxford: Phaidon, 1982).
Blair, P. H., *An Introduction to Anglo-Saxon England* (Cambridge: Cambridge University Press, 1955).
Bolgar, R. R., *The Classical Heritage and its Beneficiaries* (Cambridge: Cambridge University Press, 1954).
Chaytor, H. J., *From Script to Print* (Cambridge: Cambridge University Press, 1945).
Clanchy, M. T., *From Memory to Written Record: England 1066–1307* (London: Edward Arnold, 1979).
Cobban, A. B., *The Medieval Universities, their Development and Organization* (London: Methuen, 1975).
Finberg, H. P., *The Formation of England 550–1042* (New York and London: Norton, 1974).
Huizinga, J., *The Waning of the Middle Ages* (London: Edward Arnold, 1924).
Keen, M., *England in the Later Middle Ages* (London: Methuen, 1973).
Knowles, D., *The Religious Orders in England* (Cambridge: Cambridge University Press, 1940; 2nd edn, 1963).
Mathew, G., *The Court of Richard II* (London: Murray, 1968).
McKisack, M., *The Fourteenth Century 1307–99* (Oxford: Clarendon Press, 1959).
Morris, C., *The Discovery of the Individual 1050–1200* (London: SPCK; New York: Harper & Row, 1972).
Murray, A., *Reason and Society in the Middle Ages* (Oxford: Clarendon Press, 1978).
Nicholson, R., *Scotland in the Later Middle Ages* (Edinburgh: Oliver and Boyd, 1974).
Orme, N., *English Schools in the Middle Ages* (London: Methuen, 1973).
Pantin, W. A., *The English Church in the Fourteenth Century* (Cambridge: Cambridge University Press, 1955).
Poole, A. L., *From Domesday Book to Magna Carta* (Oxford: Clarendon Press, 1951).
Rickert, M., *Painting in Britain in the Middle Ages* (Harmondsworth: Penguin, 1954).
Shahar, S., *The Fourth Estate: A History of Women in the Middle Ages* (London: Methuen, 1983).

Smalley, B., *The Study of the Bible in the Middle Ages* (Oxford: Blackwell, 1941; Notre Dame, Ind: University of Notre Dame Press, 1964; 3rd edn, 1983).
Southern, R. W., *Western Society and the Church in the Middle Ages* (Harmondsworth: Penguin, 1970).
Southern, R. W., *The Making of the Middle Ages* (London: Hutchinson, 1953).
Stenton, Sir F., *Anglo-Saxon England* (Oxford: Clarendon Press, 1946; 3rd edn, 1971).
Stone, L., *Sculpture in Britain in the Middle Ages* (Harmondsworth: Penguin, 1955).
Thrupp, S., *The Merchant Class of Medieval London* (Chicago: University of Chicago Press, 1948).
Tuck, A., *Crown and Nobility 1272–1461* (London: Fontana, 1985).
Women in Medieval Society, ed. S. M. Stuard (Pittsburgh: Pittsburgh University Press, 1976).

GENERAL LITERARY STUDIES

Alexander, M., *Old English Literature* (London: Macmillan, 1983).
Arthurian Literature in the Middle Ages, ed. R. S. Loomis (Oxford: Clarendon Press, 1969).
Auerbach, E., *Mimesis* (Berne, 1946; trans. W. Trask, Princeton, NJ: Princeton University Press, 1953).
Barron, W. R. J., *English Medieval Romance* (London: Methuen, 1987).
Bennett, H. S., *Chaucer and the Fifteenth Century* (Oxford: Clarendon Press, 1947).
Bennett, J. A. W., *Middle English Literature*, ed. D. Gray (Oxford: Clarendon Press, 1986).
Bennett, J. A. W., *The Poetry of the Passion* (Oxford: Clarendon Press, 1982).
Blake, N., *The English Language in Medieval Literature* (London: Dent; Totowa, NH: Rowman & Littlefield, 1979).
Brewer, D. S., *English Gothic Literature* (London: Macmillan, 1983).
Burrow, J. A., *Medieval Writers and their Work* (Oxford: Clarendon Press, 1982).
Burrow, J. A., *Ricardian Poetry* (London: Routledge & Kegan Paul, 1971).
Chambers, E. K., *English Literature at the Close of the Middle Ages* (Oxford: Clarendon Press, 1945).
Coleman, J., *English Literature in History 1350–1400: Medieval Readers and Writers* (London: Hutchinson, 1981).
Colledge, E., *The Medieval Mystics of England* (London: John Murray, 1962).
Curtius, E. R., *European Literature and the Latin Middle Ages* (Berne: A. C. Frank AG Verlag, 1948; trans. W. Trask, London: Routledge & Kegan Paul, 1953).
Dronke, P., *The Medieval Lyric* (London: Hutchinson, 1968).

English Court Culture in the Later Middle Ages, ed. V. J. Scattergood and J. W. Sherborne (London: Duckworth, 1983).
Everett, D., *Essays on Middle English Literature*, ed. P. Kean (Oxford: Clarendon Press, 1955).
Gradon, P., *Form and Style in Early English Literature* (London: Methuen, 1971).
Gray, D., *Themes and Images in the Medieval English Religious Lyric* (London: Routledge & Kegan Paul, 1972).
Green, R. F., *Poets and Princepleasers: Literature and the Court in the Late Middle Ages* (Toronto: Toronto University Press, 1980).
Greenfield, Stanley B. and Calder, Daniel G., *A New Critical History of Old English Literature* (New York: New York University Press; London, University of London Press, 1986).
Kane, G., *Middle English Literature* (London: Methuen, 1951).
Kennedy, Charles W., *Early English Christian Poetry* (London: Hollis & Carter, 1952).
Ker, W. P., *The Dark Ages* (London: Macmillan, 1904; Connecticut: Hyperion, 1957).
Ker, W. P., *English Literature, Medieval* (London: Macmillan, 1912).
Ker, W. P., *Epic and Romance* (London: Macmillan, 1896; New York: Dover, 1957).
Later Middle Ages, The, ed. S. Medcalf (London: Methuen, 1981).
Lewis, C. S., *The Allegory of Love* (Oxford: Clarendon Press, 1936).
Lewis, C. S., *The Discarded Image* (Cambridge: Cambridge University Press, 1964).
Literature and Western Civilisation, vol. 2, *The Mediaeval World*, ed. D. Daiches and A. Thorlby (London: Aldus Books, 1973).
Mehl, D., *The Middle English Romances of the Thirteenth and Fourteenth Centuries* (London: Routledge & Kegan Paul, 1968).
Middle English Alliterative Poetry and its Literary Background, ed. D. Lawton (Cambridge: D. S. Brewer, 1982).
Murphy, J. J., *Rhetoric in the Middle Ages* (Berkeley, Los Angeles and London: University of California Press, 1974).
Muscatine, C., *Poetry and Crisis in the Age of Chaucer* (Notre Dame and London: University of Notre Dame Press, 1974).
Owst, G. R., *Literature and Pulpit in Medieval England* (Cambridge: Cambridge University Press, 1933).
Pearsall, D., *Old English and Middle English Poetry* (London: Routledge & Kegan Paul, 1977).
Raw, B., *The Art and Background of Old English Poetry* (London: Edward Arnold, 1978).
Salter, E., *Fourteenth-Century English Poetry: Contexts and Readings* (Oxford: Clarendon Press, 1983).
Shippey, T. A., *Old English Verse* (London: Hutchinson, 1972).
Spearing, A. C., *Medieval Dream-Poetry* (Cambridge: Cambridge University Press, 1976).
Stevens, J., *Medieval Romance* (London: Hutchinson, 1973).
Swanton, M., *English Literature Before Chaucer* (London: Methuen, 1987).

Turville-Petre, T., *The Alliterative Revival* (Cambridge: D. S. Brewer, 1977).
Wickham, G., *The Medieval Theatre* (London: Weidenfeld & Nicolson, 1974).
Wilson, R. M., *Early Middle English Literature* (London: Methuen, 1939).
Woolf, R., *The English Religious Lyric in the Middle Ages* (Oxford: Clarendon Press, 1968).
Woolf, R., *The English Mystery Plays* (Oxford: Clarendon Press, 1972).
Wrenn, C. L., *A Study of Old English Literature* (London: Harrap, 1967).

INDIVIDUAL AUTHORS AND TEXTS
Old English

Allen, J. B. and Calder, Daniel, G., *Sources and Analogues of Old English Poetry: The Major Latin Texts in Translation* (Cambridge: D. S. Brewer; Totowa, NJ: Rowman & Littlefield, 1976).
Anglo-Saxon Poetic Records, The, ed. G. P. Krapp and E. V. K. Dobbie, 6 vols (New York: Columbia University Press; London: Routledge & Kegan Paul, 1931–54).
Anglo-Saxon Chronicle, The, trans. and ed. G. N. Garmonsway (London: Dent; New York: Dutton, 1953).
Anglo-Saxon Prose, ed. and trans. M. Swanton (London: Dent; Totowa, NJ: Rowman & Littlefield, 1975).
Battle of Maldon, The, ed. E. V. Gordon, with supp. by D. G. Scragg (Manchester: Manchester University Press, 1976).
Bede, *A History of the English Church and People*, trans. and ed. L. Sherley-Price, rev. R. E. Latham (Harmondsworth: Penguin, 1968).
Beowulf, trans. and ed. M. Alexander (Harmondsworth: Penguin, 1973).
Beowulf and its Analogues, ed. and trans. G. N. Garmonsway and J. Simpson (London: Dent; New York: Dutton, 1968).
Beowulf, ed. C. L. Wrenn, 3rd edn, rev. W. F. Bolton (London: Harrap, 1973).
Bradley, S. A. J., *Anglo-Saxon Poetry* (rev. edn, London: Dent; New York, Dutton, 1983).
Dream of the Rood, The, trans. and ed. M. Swanton (Manchester: Manchester University Press, 1970).
Earliest English Poems, The, trans. and ed. M. Alexander (Harmondsworth: Penguin, 1977).
Old English Riddles from the Exeter Book, trans. and ed. M. Alexander (London: Anvil Press Poetry, 1983).
Seafarer, The, ed. I. L. Gordon (London: Methuen, 1966).
Seven Old English Poems, ed. John C. Pope (New York and London: Norton, 2nd edn, 1981).
Shippey, T. A., *Beowulf* (London: Edward Arnold, 1972).
Wanderer, The, ed. T. P. Dunning and A. J. Bliss (London: Methuen, 1969).

Twelfth and thirteenth centuries

Ancrene Wisse, Parts 6–7, ed. G. Shepherd (London and Edinburgh: Nelson, 1959).
English Lyrics of the Thirteenth Century, ed. C. Brown (Oxford: Clarendon Press, 1932).
Dobson, E. J., *The Origins of Ancrene Wisse* (Oxford: Clarendon Press, 1976).
Harley Lyrics, The, ed. G. L. Brook (Manchester: Manchester University Press, 1948, 3rd edn, 1964).
Hume, K., *The Owl and the Nightingale: the Poem and its Critics* (Toronto and Buffalo: University of Toronto Press, 1975).
Owl and the Nightingale, The, ed. E. G. Stanley (London and Edinburgh: Nelson, 1960).
Peterborough Chronicle 1070–1154, The, ed. C. Clark (Oxford: Clarendon Press, 1958).
Ringbom, H., *Studies in the Narrative Technique of Beowulf and Lawman's Brut* (Abo: Acta Academica Aboensis Humaniore A 36, 1968).

Fourteenth century

Allen, D., 'Orpheus and Orfeo: the Dead and the Taken', *Medium AEvum*, 33 (1964), 102–11.
Barbour, John, *Barbour's Bruce*, ed. M. P. McDiarmid and J. A. C. Stevenson (Edinburgh: Scottish Text Society, 4th ser., 12, 1980–3).
Bennett, J. A. W., *The Parlement of Foules: an Interpretation* (Oxford: Clarendon Press, 1957).
Benson, L. D., *Art and Tradition in Sir Gawain and the Green Knight* (New Brunswick, NJ: Rutgers University Press, 1965).
Bloomfield, M., *Piers Plowman as a Fourteenth-Century Apocalypse* (New Brunswick, NJ: Rutgers University Press, 1962).
Burrow, J. A., *A Reading of Sir Gawain and the Green Knight* (London: Routledge & Kegan Paul, 1965).
Burrow, J. A., 'The Audience of *Piers Plowman*', *Anglia*, 75 (1957), 373–84.
Cambridge Chaucer Companion, The, ed. P. Boitani and J. Mann (Cambridge: Cambridge University Press, 1986).
Chaucer, Geoffrey, *The Parlement of Foulys*, ed. D. S. Brewer (London and Edinburgh: Nelson, 1960).
Chaucer and the Italian Trecento, ed. P. Boitani (Cambridge: Cambridge University Press, 1983).
Chaucer: Sources and Backgrounds, ed. R. P. Miller (New York: Oxford University Press, 1977).
Fisher, J. H., *Gower, Moral Philosopher and Friend of Chaucer* (New York: New York University Press; London: Methuen, 1964).
Frank, R. W., *Piers Plowman and the Scheme of Salvation* (New Haven, Conn: Yale University Press, 1957).

Friedman, J. B., *Orpheus in the Middle Ages* (Cambridge, Mass: Harvard University Press, 1970).
Kane, G., *Chaucer* (Oxford: Oxford University Press, 1984).
Letts, M., *Sir John Mandeville, the Man and his Book* (London: Batchworth Press, 1949).
Mann, J., *Chaucer and Medieval Estates Satire* (Cambridge: Cambridge University Press, 1973).
Minnis, A. J., *Gower's Confessio Amantis: Responses and Reassessments* (Cambridge: D. S. Brewer, 1983).
Molinari, P., *Julian of Norwich* (London: Longmans, Green, 1958).
Muscatine, C., *Chaucer and the French Tradition* (Berkeley and Los Angeles: University of California Press, 1957).
Norton-Smith, J., *William Langland* (Leiden: E. J. Brill, 1983).
Pearsall, D., *The Canterbury Tales* (London and Boston: Allen & Unwin, 1985).
Robertson, D. W., Jr, *A Preface to Chaucer: Studies in Medieval Perspectives* (Princeton, NJ: Princeton University Press, 1962).
Rolle, Richard, *English Writings*, ed. H. E. Allan (Oxford: Clarendon Press, 1931).
Spearing, A. C., *The Gawain-Poet* (Cambridge: Cambridge University Press, 1970).
Stokes, M., *Justice and Mercy in Piers Plowman* (London, 1984).
Wilson, E., *The Gawain-Poet* (Leiden: E. J. Brill, 1976).

Fifteenth and early sixteenth centuries

Atkinson, C. W., *Mystic and Pilgrim: the Book and the World of Margery Kempe* (Cornell: Cornell University Press, 1983).
Bawcutt, P., *Dunbar the Makar* (Oxford: Clarendon Press, forthcoming).
Bawcutt, P., *Gavin Douglas* (Edinburgh: Edinburgh University Press, 1976).
Benson, L. D., *Malory's Morte Darthur* (Cambridge, Mass: Yale University Press, 1976).
Blake, N. F., *Caxton and his World* (London: Andre Deutsch, 1969).
Field, P. J. C., *Chronicle and Romance: A Study of Malory's Prose Style* (London, 1970).
Fish, S. E., *John Skelton's Poetry* (New Haven and London: Yale University Press, 1965).
Fox, A. L., *Thomas More: History and Providence* (Oxford: Clarendon Press, 1983).
Gray, D., *Robert Henryson* (Leiden: E. J. Brill, 1979).
Heiserman, A. R., *Skelton and Satire* (Chicago: University of Chicago Press, 1961).
Kolve, V. A., *The Play Called Corpus Christi* (Stanford, Ca: University of California Press; London: Edward Arnold, 1966).
Lambert, M., *Style and Vision in Le Morte Darthur* (New Haven, Conn: Yale University Press, 1975).
MacQueen, J., *Robert Henryson* (Oxford: Clarendon Press, 1967).

Malory, Sir Thomas, *The Works of Sir Thomas Malory*, ed. E. Vinaver (Oxford: Clarendon Press, 1947; 2nd edn, 1967).
Marius, R., *Thomas More* (New York: Knopf; London: Dent, 1982).
Painter, G. D., *William Caxton* (London: Chatto & Windus, 1977).
Paston Letters and Papers of the Fifteenth Centuries, ed. N. Davis, 2 vols (Oxford: Clarendon Press, 1971–6).
Pearsall, D., *John Lydgate* (London: Routledge & Kegan Paul, 1970).
Riddy, F., *Sir Thomas Malory* (Leiden: E. J. Brill, 1987).
Ross, I. S., *William Dunbar* (Leiden: E. J. Brill, 1981).
Skelton, John, *The Complete English Poems*, ed. J. Scattergood (Harmondsworth: Penguin, 1983).
'The King's Good Servant': Sir Thomas More 1477/8–1535, ed. J. B. Trapp and H. Schulte (Ipswich: Boydell; Totowa NJ: Rowman & Littlefield, 1977).
Wakefield Pageants in the Towneley Cycle, The, ed. A. C. Cawley (Manchester: Manchester University Press, 1958).
York Plays, The, ed. R. Beadle (London: Edward Arnold, 1982).

ANTHOLOGIES AND READERS

A Guide to Old English, ed. B. Mitchell and F. C. Robinson (Toronto and Buffalo: University of Toronto Press; Oxford: Blackwell, 1982, 2nd edn, 1985).
Early Middle English Verse and Prose, ed. J. A. W. Bennett and G. V. Smithers (Oxford: Clarendon Press, 1966, 2nd edn, 1968).
English Verse, 1300–1500, ed. J. Burrow (London: Methuen, 1971).
Fourteenth-Century Verse and Prose ed. K. Sisam (Oxford: Clarendon Press, 1921).
Longer Scottish Poems 1375–1650, ed. P. Bawcutt and F. Riddy (Edinburgh: Scottish Academic Press, 1987).
Old English Verse and Prose, ed. R. Fowler (London: Routledge & Kegan Paul, 1966).
Sweet's Anglo-Saxon Primer, ed. N. Davis (Oxford: Clarendon Press, 1953).
Sweet's Anglo-Saxon Reader, ed. D. Whitelock (Oxford: Clarendon Press, 1970).
The Oxford Book of Late Medieval Verse, ed. D. Gray (Oxford: Clarendon Press, 1985).

DICTIONARIES

A Chaucer Glossary, ed. N. Davis, D. Gray, P. Ingham and A. Wallace-Handrill (Oxford: Clarendon Press, 1979).

A Dictionary of the Older Scottish Tongue, ed. W. A. Craigie and A. J. Aitken (Chicago and London: University of Chicago Press; Aberdeen: Aberdeen University Press, 1937–).

An Anglo-Saxon Dictionary, ed. J. Bosworth and T. Toller (Oxford: Oxford University Press, 1898; supplement, 1921).

Middle English Dictionary, ed. H. Kurath and S. M. Kuhn (Ann Arbor, Mich: University of Michigan Press, 1952–).

Index of First Lines

Alas, how shold I synge?   151
Amang otheris the Phenyssyane Dido   568
A marchant whilom dwelled at Seint Denys   369
And Arthur Winchestre tha burh bilai wel faste   123
And quhen the gud king gan thaim se   188
An forthi, thegh the Nightingale   133
A poor widwe, somdel stape in age   383
Athelstan the King, captain of men   88
Attend! We have heard of the thriving of the throne of Denmark   22

Bytwene Mersh ant Averil   152

Done is a battell on the dragon blak   549

For certes, fader Genius   251
Fore thaem neidfaerae naenig uuirthit   8

Gup, Scot   564

He ordered then that each young warrior   92
Hi ne may cume to mi lef   148
Hwaet! A dream came to me at deep midnight   14

I am fire-fretted, and I flirt with Wind   11
I am the scalp of myself, skinned by my foeman   10
Icham of Irlaunde   151
I have wrought these words together out of a wryed existence   71
I'm the world's wonder, for I make women happy   10
In a somer seson, whan softe was the sonne   197
In a tabernakil of a towre   422
In a valey of this restles mynde   417
In to thir dirk and drublie dayis   553
I sing my own true story, tell my travails   79
'I suddenly am   102
I that in heill wes and gladnes   545

I was by the sand at the sea-wall once   12

Jhesu, God sonn, Lord of magesté   183

Lat no man booste of konnyng nor vertu   427
Lord, what these weders ar cold and I am yll happyd   439
'Lordynges,' quod he, 'in chirches whan I preche   350
Lucina schynnyng in silence of the nicht   555

May hell's door be closed   101
Men are fond of me. I am found everywhere   11
Mercy es maste in my mynde, for mercy es that I mast prayse.   185
Mirie it is while sumer ilast   148
Mirry Margaret   562
My heid did yak yester nicht   551

Nou shrinketh rose ant lylie flour   155
Now shall I unseal myself to yourself alone   73
Nu we sculan herian heofonrices Weard   6

'Often the solitary man enjoys   76

Pacience is a poynt, thagh hit displese ofte.   287
Princes proude that beth in pres   232

Quanne hic se on rode   149

Sees, seniours, and see what I saie   470
Skottes out of Berwik and of Abirdene   177
Sweit rois of vertew and of gentilnes   552

Than grymly Sir Gawayne gryppis hys wapyn   405
The auncient acquaintance, madam, betwen us twayn   560
The groves are hung   103
The hie prudence, and wirking mervelous   520
The lyf so short, the craft so long to lerne   324
The men of my tribe would treat him as game   75
This hanselle has Arthur of aventurus on fyrst   271
Towart the evyn, amyd the symmyris heit   570

Wayland knew the wanderer's fate   19
Well-wrought this wall: Weirds broke it.   69
Were beth they biforen us weren   149
We redyn ofte and fynde ywryte   159
When it is earth I tread, make tracks upon water   9
When the nyhtegale singes the wodes waxen grene   154
With 'Lullay, lullay,' lyke a chylde   563
Wolleward and weteshoed went I forth after   209
Womanhod, wanton, ye want!   559
Wynter wakeneth al my care   157

Index of Authors

Aelfric 104
Alfred, King 83

Barbour, John 187
Bede 3

Caedmon 6
Caxton, William 532
Chaucer, Geoffrey 322
Cynewulf 100

Douglas, Gavin 567
Dunbar, William 545

Gower, John 250

Henryson, Robert 519

Julian of Norwich 262

Kempe, Margery 432

Langland, William 194
Layamon 121
Lydgate, John 426

Malory, Sir Thomas 487
Mandeville, Sir John 246
Minot, Laurence 177
More, Thomas 573

Rolle, Richard 179

Skelton, John 559

Wulfstan 108